370/360
Assembler
Language
Programming

John Wiley and Sons

New York
Chichester
Brisbane
Toronto

370/360 Assembler Language Programming

Nancy Stern
Hofstra University

Alden Sager
Nassau Community College

Robert A. Stern
Nassau Community College

Library of Congress Cataloging in Publication Data:

Stern, Nancy
   370/360 assembler language programming.
   Includes indexes.
    1. IBM 370 (Computer)—Programming. 2. IBM 360
(Computer)—Programming. 3. Assembler language (Computer
program language). I. Sager, Alden, joint author.
II. Stern, Robert A., joint author. III. Title.
QA. 76.8.I123S73   001.6'42   78-10504
ISBN 0-471-03429-0

Printed in the United States of America

10 9 8 7 6 5 4 3 2

To
Flora Dusing
Joseph Perlman
Lori Anne Stern
Melanie Mara Stern

Preface

Objectives

Assembler language programming is a relatively complex programming language that necessitates the learning of machine architecture and structure. For that reason it is somewhat more difficult to teach than the higher level languages.

Because of the complexities of the language and the need to learn about machine configuration, the textbooks in this field are generally inadequate. Many computer language books suffer from a reference manual approach, which concentrates on rules rather than applications. This approach is particularly distressing in assembler textbooks, since this subject requires far more explanation and illustration than do other languages.

This textbook is intended to be both readable and pedagogically sound. It uses numerous examples for illustrative purposes; it enables students to write simple programs very early and, in general, simplifies a difficult subject. Hence, we have abandoned the reference manual approach for a simple step-by-step introduction that includes numerous examples, self-tests, and questions designed to introduce students to the kind of approach they will need in programming realistic problems in this language.

We have provided numerous programs along with dumps to illustrate not only the mechanics of the language but also the actual operation of the computer. Similarly, we have integrated many problems that emphasize programming logic rather than rules in an effort to teach the techniques of efficient programming as well as the basics of the language.

Organization

This is neither a reference manual nor a programmed instruction type of textbook. Instead, it integrates the advantages of both. The result is a combined textbook–workbook. Complementing the explanations of each topic are numerous questions and answers. In addition, each chapter reinforces previously learned material with computer-run illustrations and self-evaluating problem programs.

The student will benefit from this book's organization. The fragmented approach of many texts makes it extremely difficult for the student to understand how to organize a program effectively. He or she may understand each individual instruction, but the relationship of each program step may remain difficult to conceptualize. The text enables the reader to write complete assembler language programs, however simple, after the first few lessons, in an effort to provide insight into the relationships among individual instructions. Not only are segments of programs provided in each chapter, but at all points previous learning is reinforced and interrelationships among segments are emphasized by illustrating programs in their entirety.

Student Market

This book has been written for the junior-college or four-year college student. It is anticipated that the reader will have had some previous exposure to computer concepts. While it is not essential that the reader be familiar with programming concepts, an understanding of the fundamental operations of a computer system is necessary. The material covered in an introductory computer course would normally be adequate for this purpose.

This textbook has been written primarily for IBM 370/360[1] DOS and OS users, as well as Amdahl 470 users. In addition, UNIVAC 9000 users will find most of this book applicable to their systems. Any instructions that are not the same for these systems are so noted.

Unique Features of this Text

1. Pedagogic Approach   We have *not* attempted to be complete. Instead, we present material that can be effectively covered in a one- or two-semester college course on assembler language. Moreover, we present the instructions that are most frequently used by programmers. There are approximately 45 instructions emphasized throughout the book.

After completing the text, the student should be able to code simple and intermediate level programs. In short, assembler language is introduced in much the same way as higher-level programming languages such as COBOL, BASIC, and FORTRAN.

For students who have had some previous exposure to programming, this text provides an understanding of the fundamental differences between high-level and low-level programming.

The book is divided into units each of which represents a cohesive entity. Each chapter in a unit not only presents new data but reinforces previous concepts. There are numerous self-evaluating quizzes throughout each chapter and one comprehensive quiz at the end of each chapter. These will assist the students in testing their understanding of concepts; hence, solutions are supplied.

There is also a complete, tested program provided at the end of each chapter to illustrate all the concepts presented in that chapter. One illustrative set of specifications is defined and described (with corresponding input and output data) in Chapter 4. These same specifications become the source of the sample program in all the succeeding chapters. Hence, each chapter contains a complete program that reinforces the topic of the chapter as well as the topics presented in previous chapters.

At the end of each chapter is a list of key terms used in that chapter. In addition, all key terms used throughout the book have been compiled in the glossary in Appendix A. Also at the end of each chapter is a series of review questions and practice problems to be coded. These may be assigned by the instructor as homework.

---

[1] We refer to 370/360 systems, rather than 360/370, since the 360 is no longer in production.

2. Business Orientation   From the very beginning, this book emphasizes simplified business applications. It is organized so that the instructions most typically used for business applications appear early in the text. The Move statement, Arithmetic statements, and Logical statements provide the framework for an entire unit in which business problems are emphasized. Once students have mastered these basic concepts, we introduce the more complex instruction formats.

3. Housekeeping   The manner in which most books cover the typical housekeeping and I/O routines is somewhat cumbersome. Generally, these concepts are left to the end of the book. The major disadvantage of this approach is that students will not be able to run full programs in their entirety until the book has been almost completed. We have introduced a method that we believe is most effective in handling these routines. They are presented, at the very beginning, as a program *shell*. All of the concepts are briefly explained and references provided to indicate where further explanations may be found. This shell becomes the foundation for all illustrative programs in the text. The student can then use this shell to write programs in their entirety from the very beginning.

4. Two Levels of Debugging   Debugging in assembler language is a somewhat complex task. Some authors explain debugging techniques in a separate manual. We present debugging on two levels. In Unit III it is first presented on a simplified level. This has the dual purpose of reinforcing the material presented in Unit II and introducing the student, in an elementary way, to debugging techniques. Then in Unit V we present the more sophisticated steps involved in debugging programs.

5. Attention to Structured Programming   Structured programming, an exceedingly important programming technique, has been included in an effort to enhance the efficiency and organization of students' programs.

Notes to Instructors

1. Some chapters have "HELPFUL HINTS" after specified sections. These provide students with techniques that can be used to apply in more advanced ways the concepts presented. These HINTS are not intended for all students, just for those who like a challenge.

2. The section on Job Control Language (JCL) was placed in Appendix B so that instructors can assign it with the first problem program to be run on the computer. Since each teacher decides when that point is reached, we decided to separate the topic from the main body of the text. It should be noted that the appendix simply provides an introduction to the topic. The actual JCL required for any particular installation may vary, depending upon how the system was generated.

3. If the course is being taught in one semester, a recommended syllabus would include Chapters 1 to 7, selected topics from Chapters 8 to 10, and Chapters 11, 12, and 15. For a two-semester course, the student can get into more advanced topics included in Chapters 13, 14, and 16 to 18.

We would like to thank Harice Seeds for her invaluable review of the manuscript and Wanda Mocarski for typing the manuscript. We would also like to express special appreciation to Gene Davenport, our editor at Wiley, for his assistance and support in bringing this project to fruition. Finally, we would like to thank Lori and Melanie Stern for their assistance in preparing the index.

Nancy Stern
Alden Sager
Robert A. Stern

Contents

UNIT VI: **Advanced Concepts**

APPENDIX

UNIT I

Computer Concepts

Chapter 1

Introduction to Assembler Language Programming

A. Computer Programming

What Is a Program? No matter how complex a computer system may be, its actions are directed by individual computer instructions designed and tested by a computer programmer. The *program* consists of a set of instructions that will operate on input data and convert it to output. A computer, then, can function only as efficiently and effectively as it is programmed.

Machine Language All instructions that operate on data must be in *machine language*. For the programmer to actually write instructions using this machine code is difficult and cumbersome. One must keep track of actual storage locations and complex computer codes.

Symbolic Languages Since programming in machine language is so difficult, symbolic programming languages have been devised that are easier to code and debug. It is important to remember that programs written in a symbolic programming language are *not* executable; they must be *translated* into machine language before they can be run. The computer itself performs this translation process under the control of a special program called a *translator*.

Programmers, then, rarely write instructions in the machine's own language because of the complexity involved. Rather, they write a set of instructions called a *source program* in one of many symbolic programming languages. This source program cannot be executed directly or operated upon by the computer until it has been translated into machine language. The translation process uses the source program itself as input and produces a machine language equivalent called an *object program* that is then executable (Figure 1-1).

Programming Errors While the computer is performing this translation process, any errors detected by the translator program will be listed. That is, any violation of a programming rule will be designated as an error. For example, if the instruction to add two numbers in storage should be coded as **AP** in a symbolic language and instead was erroneously coded as **A**, then the computer will print an error message called a *diagnostic*. If the errors that result are of considerable magnitude, the translation process will be terminated.

Note that errors detected during the translation process are simply rule violations. *Logic errors*, those in which the sequences of programming steps have not been coded properly, cannot be detected during this process. During translation, the machine has no way of judging the logic in a program. This can be tested only by executing or running the program in a trial run.

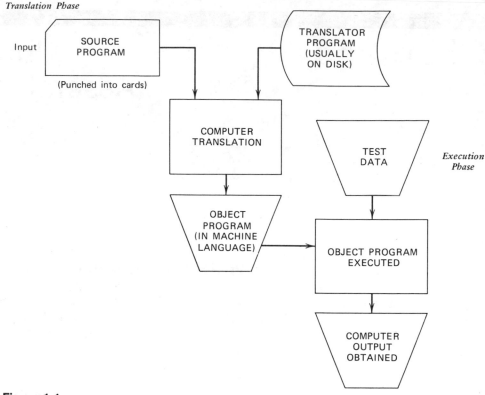

Figure 1-1

If there are no rule violations in the source program, the translation process will convert all symbolic instructions to their machine language equivalent. The object program can then be executed or tested, or it may be stored on tape, disk, or even cards for future processing.

B. Assembler Language Programming

There are numerous programming languages, but they may be categorized in the following two ways:

Types of Programming Languages

Type	Examples	Features
1. High-level	COBOL FORTRAN BASIC PL/1	a. Easy to code b. Least like the machine's own language c. Less efficient for the machine
2. Low-level	Assembler language	a. More difficult to code b. Most like the machine's own language c. More efficient for the machine

High-Level Languages High-level languages such as COBOL, FORTRAN, BASIC, and PL/1 are designed to simplify the programmer's task by using instructions that are either English-like or that contain common mathematical expressions. These languages require complex translation processes since they use codes that are very different from the machine's own codes. This complex translation process is called a *compilation*. The special program that takes a source program written in a high-level language and converts it to an object program in machine language is called a *compiler.*

A compiler program performs a translation or compilation by taking each symbolic instruction and generating from it numerous machine language instructions. The single COBOL instruction COMPUTE A = B + C − D, for example, will translate into several machine language instructions. Since each symbolic instruction is equivalent to many machine language instructions, we call the compilation a *1-to-many* process:

> One high-level instruction = many machine language instructions

The complexity of this compilation results in a translation process that usually takes a good deal of computer time to complete.

Low-Level Languages   An assembler or low-level language is more difficult for the programmer to code because it is very similar to the machine's own language. The translation process required for low-level languages is called an *assembly* and the program that performs this translation is called an *assembler.*

In general, for each assembler language instruction, only one machine language instruction is generated. Hence, the assembler language is referred to as a 1-to-1 language:

> One assembler language instruction translates into one
> machine language instruction.

Later on, you will find that there are several high-level instructions called *macros* that can be coded in the assembler language and that generate numerous machine language instructions. The bulk of the instructions coded in this language, however, produce only one object statement for each source statement.

Since the assembly process is not nearly as complex a translation as the compilation, the time required for this translation is minimal.

Machine Language   Note that each computer system has its own unique machine language. Hence, a Honeywell computer will have a different machine language from an IBM computer. Since each computer's machine language is unique and since assembler languages are very similar to machine language, assembler language formats vary depending upon the computer used.

Whereas high-level languages have become standardized so that they can be run on a wide variety of computer systems, assembler languages are much more machine-dependent.

The assembler language that will be described in this text is applicable to *four* computer systems all of which have very similar machine language codes:

> **Applicability of assembler language considered in this textbook**
>
> AMDAHL 470 Series[1]
> IBM S/360 Series
> IBM S/370 Series
> UNIVAC 9000 Series

Any assembler instruction that is *not* the same for all of these systems will be noted.

The following chart provides a more comprehensive understanding of computer languages:

Types of Programming Languages

Type	Examples	Translator	Features
High-level	COBOL FORTRAN BASIC PL/1	Compiler	a. Easy to code b. 1-to-many conversion c. Requires long, complex translation process d. Standardized or computer-independent
Low-level	Assembler Language	Assembler	a. More difficult to code b. 1-to-1 conversion c. Requires short, simplified translation process d. Computer-dependent

SELF-EVALUATING QUIZ

Each question in the exercises will be followed by five asterisks which signal that the solution will follow. Use a sheet of paper to cover the solutions when testing yourself.

1. The set of instructions that operates on input data and converts it to output is called a _____ .
   *****
   program

2. The programmer writes a program in a _____ language.
   *****
   symbolic

3. In order to be executed or run, each program must be in _____ language.
   *****
   machine

4. Programs are rarely written in machine language because _____ .
   *****
   the codes and addresses that must be remembered are complex and cumbersome

5. The process used to convert a symbolic program to machine language is called a _____ .
   *****
   translation (assembly or compilation)

[1] It should be noted that the Amdahl 470 series of computers is designed for the same operating environment as the IBM System/360 and System/370. Amdahl assemblers use the same set of instructions as the IBM assemblers.

6. The program written in a symbolic language by the programmer is called the _____ .
    *****
    source program

7. The program translated into machine language is called the _____ .
    *****
    object program

8. State the names of the *two* processes required to obtain output from a program.
    *****
    Translation
    Execution

9. What types of languages make programming easier but require more computer time for translation?
    *****
    High-level or compiler languages

10. What types of languages help one understand how the computer actually operates and result in more efficient translation processes?
    *****
    Low-level or assembler languages

Why Study Assembler Language?

For students who have knowledge of high-level programming languages such as COBOL, FORTRAN, BASIC and PL/1 (and even for students who have not), assembler language programming will be a truly unique experience. Unlike high-level coding, assembler language programming provides you with an understanding of how the machine itself actually operates on data. This understanding will enable you to program with the utmost efficiency and the highest level of interaction with the computer itself.

Many of the mysteries of computer processing will be unveiled when studying assembler language. Those who have programmed in a high-level language may have experienced (1) the frustration of encountering a processing error that you were unable to understand because you were unfamiliar with the machine's actual method of operation and (2) the desire to learn more about how the computer actually operates on data.

An Analogy

Students who are interested in learning about computer processing are most frequently taught high-level languages. This is not unlike the situation in which an English-speaking person who wants to learn foreign language X (machine operations) is taught instead language Y (high-level symbolic operations) because it is easier than X. If Y, the easier, intermediate, high-level language can be automatically translated into X, the language of actual importance, then communication is fostered.

While such a learning procedure, either in a linguistic or programming sense, is initially highly desirable since it facilitates understanding, eventually the interested student realizes that some meaning is lost in a complex double-faceted translation. This is why foreign languages are learned directly even if they are exceedingly complex and that is why programmers ought to understand assembler language since it is so similar to machine language.

Purpose of the Text

It is the objective of this text to teach assembler language in an effort to (1) reduce the symbolism inherent in other programming languages and (2) to emphasize, instead, how the computer actually operates. Such an objective will add a dimension to the student's understanding of computer processing that is simply not possible when studying high-level languages.

Note that this introduction is not meant to diminish the value of high-level programming. High-level languages are extremely useful and important methods of communicating with computers. Accomplishing sophisticated and complex tasks are often not feasible without the use of such languages. These languages, however, sacrifice (1) efficiency and (2) a clear understanding of how the computer actually operates on data. By studying assembler language we will emphasize these two elements.

C. Features of a Computer System

Since assembler language is so similar to the machine's own method of processing, several features of a computer system that you may not have learned in an introductory course are important to understand.

1. Computer System (Figure 1-2)   A computer system consists of a series of devices that interact to read input data, process it, and produce output. The units that comprise this system are:

a. Input devices

b. Output devices

c. Console typewriter for communicating with the system

d. Central processing unit (CPU)

Figure 1-2   IBM SYSTEM/370 (Courtesy IBM).

2. Central Processing Unit   The CPU is the "brain" of the computer system, controlling all the operations to be performed.

The CPU consists of, typically, hundreds of thousands of storage positions. The following are stored in these positions:

a. Data that has been read—located in an input area.
b. Work areas—used for processing data.
c. Actual instructions.
d. Processed data that will serve as output—in an output area.

A position of storage is referred to as a *byte*, where each byte is generally used to store one *character* of data. A character may be a letter, digit, or special symbol such as a $ or *.

Some computers utilize the concept of virtual storage, which is a technique of treating the CPU as if it had more storage capacity than it actually has. Thus, for example, a computer with a CPU of 250,000 bytes can be made to function as if it has, instead, several million bytes.[2]

Each byte, or storage position, in the CPU has its own *address*. The illustration in Figure 1-3 shows a CPU with a storage capacity, or *memory size*, of 256,000 bytes. Notice that the address of the first byte is usually designated as 0, the second byte as 1, and so forth.

Each byte is analogous to a cell or slot that stores a character of data. The actual method of representing characters within storage will be discussed in Chapters 2 and 3.

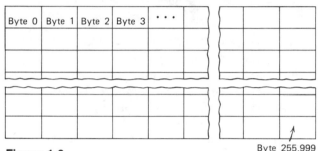

Figure 1-3   Byte 255,999

3. General Registers   *Registers* are specific areas of the CPU that may be used for particular purposes. For example, registers may be used as high-speed accumulators in arithmetic operations.

The CPU contains *16* general purpose registers numbered 0 to 15, each *four* bytes long. Only registers 2–12 are available for normal assembler language processing, the others being used for special purposes.

Throughout this text, but particularly in Units IV–VI, we will explore the ways in which registers may be used for processing data.

4. The Supervisor   The operations of the computer system are under the control of a monitor or control program commonly called a *supervisor*. The supervisor, which is usually supplied by the manufacturer as part of the operating system, controls the actual operations performed by the system. It must be loaded into the CPU before any programs can be processed.

When an assembler language program is entered as input for translation, for example, the supervisor:

a. Calls for the assembler program to produce an object program.
b. Transfers control to the object program for execution.

Note that the supervisor, as well as the input to be processed and the programs to be executed, is stored in the central processing unit (CPU) in actual storage locations called *addresses*. Computer systems are said to utilize the *stored program concept*, which means that instructions, like data, are stored in these actual locations.

[2] See Appendix H for a more detailed discussion of how a virtual storage system operates.

The computer system can thus be pictured in general terms as shown in Figure 1-4.

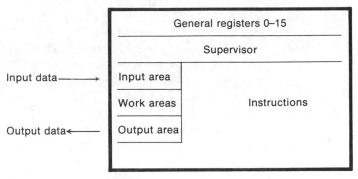

Figure 1-4 Schematic of CPU.

5. Types of Computer Operations

a. Instructions That Operate on Data in Storage: Decimal Operations

Decimal instructions operate on data in main storage. These instructions are discussed in Unit 2 of this text. They include, for example, data transfer and decimal arithmetic operations.

b. Instructions That Use Registers: Binary Operations

Binary instructions operate on data contained in registers. These can be instructions utilizing registers only or utilizing both registers and main storage.

Binary operations are performed on data in registers. Since the computer actually operates on data in binary form and since registers that serve as accumulators are an efficient method of processing data, binary operations are faster than decimal operations.

In Units IV and V we consider this type of instruction.

Floating point instructions also use registers. Since they are complex to code and not necessary for simple or intermediate-level programs, they will not be discussed in this text.

SELF-EVALUATING QUIZ

1. Each storage position in a computer is referred to as a _____.
   *****
   byte

2. Associated with each byte of storage is a(n) _____ by which we can locate that position.
   *****
   address

3. Computer operations are under the control of a monitor program called a _____.
   *****
   supervisor

4. In addition to locations in main storage there are 16 _____ numbered _____ to _____ that may be used for processing data.
   *****
   general registers
   0–15

5. (True or False) Binary operations utilize registers.
   *****
   True

6. (True or False) The supervisor is part of the operating system.
    *****
    True
7. (True or False) The supervisor must be loaded into the CPU before process-
    ing can occur.
    *****
    True
8. (True or False) A computer system consists of only one unit called a CPU.
    *****
    False. There are input and output units and a console typewriter as well.
9. (True or False) Registers must be used for arithmetic operations in as-
    sembler language programs.
    *****
    False. They *may* be used, but they are not always necessary.
10. (True or False) A program, along with input data, is loaded into actual
    storage locations.
    *****
    True

D. Coding Assembler Language Programs

Assembler language programs are generally written on *coding* or *program sheets*
as shown in Figure 1-5. The coding sheet has space for 80 columns of information. Each *line* of a coding sheet will be keypunched into one punched card.[3]
The entire deck of cards keypunched from the coding sheets is called the *source
program* or *source deck*.

Let us examine the coding sheet more closely. The main body of the form
is subdivided into columns 1–72 that will be keypunched into card columns
1–72 respectively.

**Identification
Sequence: 73–80**
There is also provision for an optional program identification number called
"Identification Sequence" that references positions 73–80. This field is used to
identify a program and to indicate the sequence of cards as well. Its use makes
it easier for the programmer to keep track of the sequence of instructions in
the deck in case cards are lost or dropped and resequencing is necessary.

Here is a typical entry in columns 73–80.

STERNØ1Ø
STERNØ2Ø
STERNØ3Ø
.
.
.

Slashing Zeros
Before discussing the entry itself, notice that the zeros contain slashes through
them. Since it is very common for programmers and keypunch operators to
mistakenly punch a zero for the letter O and vice versa, a convention is
generally established at a computer center where either zeros or letter O's are
slashed. For illustrations in this text, we have adopted the convention of slashing
zeros to distinguish them from the letter O.

---

[3] Assembler language programs are sometimes keyed into a terminal rather than
punched onto cards.

UNIVAC

PROGRAM

ASSEMBLER CODING FORM

UNIVAC 9000 SERIES

PROGRAMMER_____ DATE_____ PAGE____ OF____ PAGES

LABEL	b OPERATION b	OPERAND	b	COMMENTS		

UD1-1548   ◆ SPERRY RAND

Figure 1-5 Courtesy of Sperry Univac, a division of Sperry Rand Corp.

Coding the Identification

"STERN" identifies the deck and the numbers are used for sequencing. The first card generally has number Ø1Ø, the second Ø2Ø, etc. They are numbered by tens so that insertions may be made easily. If an entry is inadvertently omitted and must be inserted between numbers Ø3Ø and Ø4Ø, it may be sequenced as Ø31. Note that this Identification-Sequence is used to prevent errors and to assist the programmer in organizing the deck. It is *not* utilized by the computer.

Continuation: CC 72 If an instruction requires more than one line of coding, it may be continued on the next line. In such cases, a nonblank character is coded in column 72 of the line *to be continued.* That is, if two lines are required for an instruction, only the first one will contain a character in column 72. For all instructions that are coded on a single line, column 72 must remain blank.

Body of Form: CC 1–71 Columns 1–71 are used for the actual coding of each statement. By examining the coding sheet in Figure 1–5, we can see that each statement can consist of from one to four entries:

NAME or LABEL
OPERATION
OPERAND
COMMENTS

The coding sheet is designed so that these entries for each instruction are *always* placed in the same columns in a uniform manner. This facilitates the keypunching and reading of the program.[4]

A brief description of each entry will provide insight into the nature of assembler language instructions.

1. NAME (Columns 1–8)

This entry, which is optional, is used to identify a statement. It may consist of a label or symbolic address so that another instruction can branch to it:

Example

LABEL	OPERATION	OPERAND	COMMENTS
STEP1	AR	3,4	THIS IS A TYPE OF ADD INSTRUCTION
	.		ADT'L
	.		INSTRUCTIONS FOLLOW
	.		
	B	STEP1	THIS IS A BRANCH-RETURNS CONTROL TO STEP1

The NAME field is also used to define a storage area:

Example

LABEL	OPERATION	
HOLD	DS	CL5

HOLD, which is coded in the NAME field, becomes the symbolic address by which the field is referenced.

Since both instructions and data are placed in actual storage locations, they can both be referenced by a symbolic address called a NAME.

Rules for Forming NAMES or LABELS
1. Use 1 to 8 characters.
2. Must start in column 1.
3. The first character must be alphabetic.
4. No blanks or special characters other than @, #, $ allowed within the name.

---

2. OPERATION Entry (Columns 10–14)

This entry is used to specify the actual operation to be performed, such as adding and moving. This is called an operation or *op code*. The term *mnemonic* refers to the symbolic operation that is coded in assembler language. Beginning in Unit II, we will discuss many of the op codes that may be used in this language.

3. OPERAND Entry (beginning in column 16)

This field identifies and describes the data fields to be operated on. Depending upon the instruction format, there may be one or two operands associated

---

[4] The programmer can, if desired, write instructions free-form without using the suggested columns for each entry. If the free-form style is used, all that is required is that each entry be separated by a blank.

with each instruction. Most instructions utilize two operands, separated by a comma (no space after the comma).

Examples

(1)   Add AMT to TOTAL is coded as follows:

LABEL	OPERATION	OPERAND
	10	16
	AP	TOTAL,AMT

(2)   Add register 3 to register 7 is coded as follows:

LABEL	OPERATION	
	10	16
	AR	7,3

Rules for Forming Operand Names
1.   Use 1 to 8 characters.
2.   The first character must be alphabetic.
3.   No blanks or special characters except $, @, #.

Each symbolic operand specified in the OPERAND field normally will be defined elsewhere in the program in the NAME field. Hence the rules for forming such names are the same.

Example

LABEL	OPERATION	OPERAND
	10	16
	AP	TOTAL,AMT
	.	
	.	
	.	
TOTAL	DS	PL5
AMT	DS	PL3

4. COMMENT Entry

Used to supply explanatory or descriptive information about a particular instruction. The COMMENT appears in the OPERAND section of the coding sheet and is separated from the last operand by at least one space.

Examples

	LABEL	OPERATION	OPERAND	COMMENTS
		10	16	
(1)		AP	TOTAL,AMT	TOTAL = SUM OF ALL AMTS
(2)		AR	7,3	REGISTER3 = QTY, REGISTER7 = SUM

Note that the COMMENT entry is strictly optional and does not affect the execution of the program in any way. It may, however, be enormously helpful to the programmer by providing brief reminders of the purpose of specific instructions.

The comment included along with an instruction may not go beyond column 71 of any line. If more comprehensive comments are desired, whole lines may be reserved for comments only. By coding an * in column 1, the entire line, from columns 1–71, is treated as a comment:

Example

LABEL	OPERATION	OPERAND
1	10 16	
* THIS	PROGRAM	WILL READ SALARY CARDS AND
* PROVIDE EACH	EMPLOYEE WITH A 20% BONUS
BEGIN	GET	
	•	
	•	
	•	

SELF-EVALUATING QUIZ

1. Assembler language programs are written on _____ sheets.
   *****
   coding or program

2. Each line of a coding sheet corresponds to one _____ in the program deck.
   *****
   card

3. The deck of cards keypunched from the coding sheets is called the _____ .
   *****
   source deck

4. Optional entries on the coding sheet include _____ , _____ , and _____ .
   *****
   Name or label
   comment
   Identification sequence (columns 73–80)

5. The rules for forming operand names are _____ .
   *****
   1 to 8 characters
   no blanks or special characters except $, @, #
   the first character must be alphabetic

6. Indicate the two ways in which comments may be specified.
   *****
   leave a blank after the last operand and continue until column 71
   code * in column 1 of any line—this makes the entire line a comment

7. Column 72 is called a _____ column and is used to _____ .
   *****
   continuation
   indicate that the instruction is too long for a given line and will be continued on the next line

Indicate what, if anything, is wrong with the following labels:

8. NO GO
   *****
   No embedded blanks permitted

9. DISCT%
   *****
   % not permitted

10. SALESAMOUNT
    *****
    too long

11. 1A
    *****
    must begin with an alphabetic character
12. SAM
    *****
    OK

KEY TERMS
Address
Assembler language
Assembly (assembler)

Binary operations
Bytes

Central processing unit (CPU)
Compilation (compiler)
Computer system

Diagnostics

Execution

High-level programming language

Input area

Logic errors
Low-level programming language

Machine language
Memory size
Mnemonic

Object program
Operand
Operation code
Output area

Program
Program sheets

Registers

Source program
Supervisor
Symbolic address
Symbolic programming language

Translator

Virtual storage

Review Questions   1. Programs in machine language are called
    a. Source programs
    b. Symbolic programs
    c. Object programs
    d. Both a and b

2. Which of the following statements is false?
    a. The object program must be tested to determine if it is correct.

b. A program written in a symbolic language is not directly executable on a computer.

c. The assembly process checks for rule violations in the source program.

d. The assembly program checks for logic errors in the source program.

3. Which of the following names are valid?
   a. $AMT
   b. X9Y
   c. GROSS PAY
   d. DEPENDENTS

4. Which of the following statements is false?
   a. Symbolic names used as operands must be defined elsewhere in the program.
   b. Operands in a single instruction must be separated by commas.
   c. An operand describes the data or storage area to be operated on by the instruction.
   d. Machine instructions do not require operands.

5. (True or False) The entries on a coding sheet may be separated by one or more blanks.

6. Comments are coded in assembler language by coding
   a. C in column 1
   b. An * in column 4
   c. An * in column 1
   d. A blank in column 1
   e. None of the above

7. (True or False) The supervisor program is another name for an assembler program.

8. (True or False) When a machine language program is being executed, the supervisor must be in main storage.

Chapter 2

Data Representation and Numbering Systems

Introduction

Data is entered into a computer in normal alphanumeric form as letters, digits, and special characters. Similarly, information is produced as output from the computer in the same readable, alphanumeric form. Internally, however, data is represented by a *computer code*. While this computer code varies from computer to computer, certain features are standard and thus independent of the specific system. It is the purpose of this chapter to discuss just how data is represented and manipulated by computer systems in general.

All computer codes use the *binary numbering system* in some form or another. We shall discuss this system in detail in the following section. Note, however, that the binary numbering system uses two digits, 0 and 1, to represent every possible number. This system is ideally suited to computers for one important reason. The 0's are represented internally in the computer as an off-state and the 1's as an on-state. Hence computer circuits are on or off depending upon the binary representation of numbers. Where magnetic cores are used to denote data, the '1' state is represented by a core that is magnetized, the '0' state is represented by a core that is demagnetized.

In this chapter, we will consider the following:

- The representation of numbers in binary form.

- Procedures to be used in converting binary numbers to decimal form and decimal numbers to binary form.

- Ways in which binary numbers are added and subtracted internally by the computer.

- The actual computer code on the S/360 and S/370 that makes use of binary numbers: the hexadecimal system.

- The internal computer code which represents numbers, letters, and special characters using some form of the binary numbering system: EBCDIC.

A. Review of Decimal Numbers

Let us begin by reviewing some features of our own decimal numbering system that apply also to the binary numbering system.

The decimal system, like the binary system, is a *positional* numbering system. This implies that each digit has a different significance or value depending upon its position in a sequence of numbers.

The decimal system utilizes ten distinct digits 0–9. We sometimes refer to it as a *base 10* system. Each position can contain one of ten digits and, in addition, each position can be expressed as a factor of 10. The following is a schematic of the positional values in the decimal or base 10 system.

Value of Each Position Expressed as Integers	1000	100	10	1
Value of Each Position Expressed as a Power of 10	10^3	10^2	10^1	10^0

Using this schematic, we can see that the fifth position in the base 10 system indicates the number of 10000's or 10^4, and so on.

Explanation of Powers of 10 Hence, the first position has unit or 10^0 value. (Any number with exponent [1] of zero is equal to 1.) The second position has value 10, or 10 raised to the first power. The third position has value 100, or 10 raised to the second power or 10×10. The fourth position has value 1000 or 10 raised to the third power or $10 \times 10 \times 10$.

Thus the number 384 may be expressed as

10^2	10^1	10^0	Exponential value of position
100	10	1	Integer value of position
3	8	4	Decimal number

$$4 \times 1 = \quad 4$$
$$8 \times 10 = \quad 80$$
$$3 \times 100 = \underline{\;300}$$
$$384$$

To obtain the value three hundred and eighty and four from the three digits 384, we multiply each digit by its positional value. This method of multiplying any digit by its positional value to determine the value of the entire number is the exact method we will be using to determine the decimal equivalent of binary numbers

The decimal numbering system, as indicated, has 10 unique digits, 0 to 9. To represent the numbers 0 to 9 we merely use the digits 0 to 9. To represent the next number, however, we cannot use an additional digit, since no additional digit exists. Instead, we proceed with the next position (10's position) by putting a 1 there and initializing the units position at zero. Thus we have:

0
1
2
⋮
9 → Initialize units position; add 1 to tens position.
10
11
⋮
19

[1] The term exponent is used to denote a number raised to a specified power. That is, an exponent of 2 indicates a number raised to the second power, or a number multiplied by itself twice. Thus $5^2 = 5 \times 5 = 25$, and $4^3 = 4 \times 4 \times 4 = 64$.

With 1 more than 19, we initialize the units position at zero again and add 1 to the tens position. Thus we have:

19 → Initialize units position; add 1 to tens position.
20
.
.
.

29 → Initialize units position; add 1 to tens position.
30
.
.
.

99 → Initialize units position; initialize tens position; add 1 to hundreds
100   position.

When we have utilized all digits in the units and tens positions (99), we proceed to the next position, the hundreds, and begin again by initializing units and tens at zero: 100.

While this entire introduction may seem trite and obvious, we shall see that the basic elements are similar in all positional numbering systems.

B. Binary Numbers

The binary numbering system is a *base 2* system where only the digits 0 and 1 are used. This is ideally suited to computer processing, where 0 is used to represent an off-state and 1 is used to represent an on-state.

Using the binary numbering system, all numbers are represented by a series of 0's and 1's. Let us consider first the logical manner in which numbers are incremented using this system and then we will proceed to the positional representation of binary numbers.

1. Numeric Representation   With only 2 digits, we can only represent the numbers 0 and 1 using a single digit. To represent a 2 we must use the next position and initialize the units position at 0. Thus 10 in binary, or base 2, is a 2 in decimal. A 3 would be 11; to represent a 4 we must initialize these two first positions and place a 1 in the third position. Thus 100 in binary is a 4 in decimal. A 5 would be 101. Notice that the sequence is 0, 1, then proceed to the next position and initialize (10, 11, 100, and so on).

Binary	Decimal
0	0
1	1
10	2
11	3
100	4
101	5
110	6
111	7
1000	8
.	.
.	.

Notice that any decimal number can be represented by a sequence of 0's and 1's in the binary system, but that it generally takes far more digits in the binary system to represent a number than in the decimal system.

Let us now consider the *positional* attribute of binary numbers. You will recall that the decimal or base 10 system has these positional values:

...	10^3	10^2	10^1	10^0	Exponential value of position
...	1000	100	10	1	Integer value of position

That is, a 1 in the second position and a 0 in the units position (10) is the number after 9. When the largest single digit has been reached, we proceed to the next position, initializing the first position with zero.

Since this system has a base 10, each position has a value that is a factor of 10. The first position is 10^0 or 1, the second is 10^1 or 10, . . . , the seventh position would be 10^6 or 1,000,000.

The binary numbering system has a base of 2. Thus each position has a value that is a factor of 2. We have then:

...	2^4	2^3	2^2	2^1	2^0	Exponential value of position
...	16	8	4	2	1	Integer value of position

You will recall that any number raised to the zero power is 1; 2^1 is 2; 2^2 is 2×2 or 4; 2^3 is $2 \times 2 \times 2$ or 8, and so on. The two binary digits are 0 and 1. To represent the number 2, we must use the next position. Thus 10 in binary is 2 in decimal. That is:

```
2 | 1      ← Integer value of position

1 | 0      ← Binary number

        → 0 × 1 = 0
        → 1 × 2 = 2
              2  Decimal equivalent
```

We say, then, $10_2 = 2_{10}$ (10 in base 2 = 2 in base 10).

2. Determing the Decimal Equivalent of a Binary Number

Thus all positional numbering systems are similar. To obtain the decimal equivalent of a number in any base, multiply the digits by their positional values and add the results.

Example 1 $1001_2 = (?)_{10}$

Find the decimal equivalent of 1001 in binary (represented as 1001_2, where the subscript denotes the base).

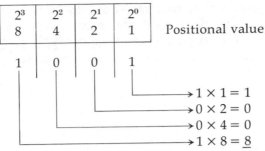

2^3	2^2	2^1	2^0
8	4	2	1

Positional value

| 1 | 0 | 0 | 1 |

$1 \times 1 = 1$
$0 \times 2 = 0$
$0 \times 4 = 0$
$1 \times 8 = \underline{8}$
9   Decimal equivalent

Thus $1001_2 = 9_{10}$. We can simplify this calculation by eliminating all multiplications where 0 is a factor. Thus we have

2^3	2^2	2^1	2^0
8	4	2	1

| 1 | 0 | 0 | 1 |

$1 \times 1 = 1$
$1 \times 8 = \underline{8}$
9

In short, the binary digit 8 and the binary digit 1 are "on," the others are "off." That is, the 8-bit and the 1-bit are on, where bit is an abbreviation for *b*inary dig*it*.

Example 2 $1110_2 = (?)_{10}$

8	4	2	1
1	1	1	0

$1 \times 2 = 2$
$1 \times 4 = 4$
$1 \times 8 = \underline{8}$
14

Solution: $(14)_{10}$

Example 3 $11101_2 = (?)_{10}$

2^4	2^3	2^2	2^1	2^0
16	8	4	2	1

| 1 | 1 | 1 | 0 | 1 |

$1 \times 1 = 1$
$1 \times 4 = 4$
$1 \times 8 = 8$
$1 \times 16 = \underline{16}$
29

Solution: $(29)_{10}$

Thus, given any binary number we can find its decimal equivalent by the following technique.

> **Given Binary Number—Find Its Decimal Equivalent**
> 1. Determine positional value of each digit.
> 2. Add the positional values for all positions that contain a 1.

1. The decimal system has a base of ___(number)___ while the binary system has a base of ___(number)___ .
   *****
   10; 2

2. Since numbers are frequently represented within the computer as a series of on-off switches, the _____ numbering system is exceedingly well suited to computer processing.
   *****
   binary or base 2

3. (True or False) All numbers must be fed into the computer in binary form.
   *****
   False. Decimal numbers as well as binary numbers can be entered as input.

4. (True or False) There are numbers that can be expressed in base 2 that cannot be expressed in base 10.
   *****
   False

5. (True or False) In general, more binary digits are necessary to represent a number than is necessary in the decimal numbering system.
   *****
   True

6. $2^2 = $ _____ .
   *****
   $2^2 = 2 \times 2 = 4$

7. $2^5 = $ _____ .
   *****
   $2^5 = 2 \times 2 \times 2 \times 2 \times 2 = 32$

8. $2^0 = $ _____ .
   *****
   1. Any number raised to the zero power is 1.

9. $10^0 = $ _____ .
   *****
   1

10. Find the decimal equivalent for each of the following
    a. 11011_2
    b. 1101_2
    c. 1111_2
    d. 11001_2
    e. 11111_2
    *****

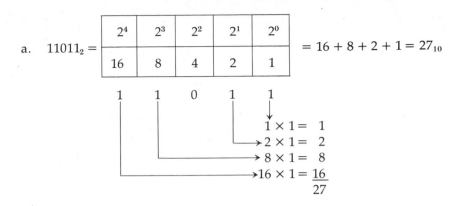

a. $11011_2 =$

2^4	2^3	2^2	2^1	2^0
16	8	4	2	1

$= 16 + 8 + 2 + 1 = 27_{10}$

1 1 0 1 1

$1 \times 1 = 1$
$2 \times 1 = 2$
$8 \times 1 = 8$
$16 \times 1 = \underline{16}$
27

b. $1101_2 =$

8	4	2	1
1	1	0	1

$= 1 + 4 + 8 = 13_{10}$

c. $1111_2 =$

8	4	2	1
1	1	1	1

$= 8 + 4 + 2 + 1 = 15_{10}$

d. $11001_2 =$

16	8	4	2	1
1	1	0	0	1

$= 16 + 8 + 1 = 25_{10}$

e. $11111_2 =$

16	8	4	2	1
1	1	1	1	1

$= 16 + 8 + 4 + 2 + 1 = 31_{10}$

3. Determining the Binary Equivalent of a Decimal Number

Computers generally represent numeric data in binary form or a variation of this form where digits are indicated by a series of on-off switches, circuits, or magnetized spots. Keep in mind that numeric data is entered, as input, in standard decimal form and then converted by the computer itself to a binary representation. Before the data is produced as output it is again converted to decimal form.

Thus far, we have some idea of the way in which binary numbers are converted into decimal numbers. In this section, we will learn the manner in which the binary equivalent of a decimal number may be determined.

This conversion process is a relatively simple task when small numbers are used. That is, we merely employ the positional values of binary numbers to find the right combination of digits.

Example 1 $10_{10} = (?)_2$

This example concerns itself with determining what combination of 1, 2, 4, 8, 16, 32, . . . will equal 10.

It is clear that we do not need to use more than four binary digits to represent 10_{10}, since the fifth positional value is 16 which is greater than 10_{10}. Hence, we must determine what combination of 8, 4, 2, 1, will equal 10.

There is only one such combination. The numbers $8 + 2 = 10$. Thus our binary equivalent is

8	4	2	1	Integer value of position
1	0	1	0	Binary number

In order to represent the decimal number 10 in binary form, the 8-bit (or *b*inary dig*it*) and the 2-bit are on while the others are off.

Thus $10_{10} = 1010_2$.

Example 2 $(14)_{10} = (?)_2$

Here, again, we use four binary digits since the next position has a value of 16, which exceeds the required quantity. Again, we must determine what combination of 8, 4, 2, 1 will produce 14.

There is only one such combination: 8, 4, 2 bits are on $(8 + 4 + 2 = 14)$, while the 1-bit is off.

Thus $(14)_{10} = (1110)_2$.

Example 3 $(23)_{10} = (?)_2$

Here, we must use a combination of the numbers 16, 8, 4, 2, 1 which will produce 23. We must determine which bits are "on." The 16-bit must be on, since 8, 4, 2, 1 bits can produce a maximum decimal number of 15. Thus the 16-bit must be on to obtain a number larger than 15. The 8-bit is off since 16-8 produces 24, which exceeds the required number. Thus the 16-4-2-1 bits are on and only the 8-bit is off. We have, then,

$$(23)_{10} = (10111)_2$$

This method of determining the combination of positional values that produces the required number is useful only with small numbers. Consider the task of finding the combination of binary numbers for the decimal number 1087, for example. In short, the above method is too cumbersome for larger decimal numbers.

There is a technique called the *remainder method* which may be used to convert a decimal number to any other numbering system. The technique is as follows:

Remainder Method for Converting Decimal Numbers into any Other Base
1. Divide the decimal number by the base (for a binary equivalent, we divide by 2).
2. Indicate the remainder, which will be either 0 or 1 in the case of binary division.
3. Continue dividing into each quotient (result of previous division) until the divide operation produces a zero quotient or result.
4. The equivalent number in the base desired is the numeric *remainders* reading from the last division to the first.

Several examples will clarify this procedure.

Example 4 $(38)_{10} = (?)_2$

Remainder

Begin by dividing numbers
by the base 2.

Divide previous
result, 19, by base.

Indicates
the end ——→

$$
\begin{array}{r}
19 \\
2\,\overline{)\,38} \\
9 \\
2\,\overline{)\,19} \\
4 \\
2\,\overline{)\,9} \\
2 \\
2\,\overline{)\,4} \\
1 \\
2\,\overline{)\,2} \\
0 \\
2\,\overline{)\,1}
\end{array}
$$

0	Indicate the remainder
1	Indicate the remainder.
1	.
0	.
0	
1	

—Resultant binary number
reads from bottom
to top (100110)

When the divide operation produces a quotient or result of zero, then the process is terminated. The binary equivalent, reading from the last division to the first is:

$$(38)_{10} = (100110)_2$$

We should check our result to insure its accuracy:

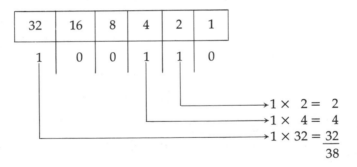

32	16	8	4	2	1
1	0	0	1	1	0

$$
\begin{aligned}
1 \times 2 &= 2 \\
1 \times 4 &= 4 \\
1 \times 32 &= \underline{32} \\
&\;38
\end{aligned}
$$

Using the remainder method for converting from decimal to binary, it is a more efficient procedure to perform the first divide operation at the bottom of the work sheet and work up.

The following is exactly equivalent to Example 4 above:

Remainder

$$
\begin{array}{r}
0 \\
2\,\overline{)\,1} \\
2\,\overline{)\,2} \\
2\,\overline{)\,4} \\
2\,\overline{)\,9} \\
2\,\overline{)\,19} \\
2\,\overline{)\,38}
\end{array}
\qquad
\begin{array}{l}
1 \\
0 \\
0 \\
1 \\
1 \\
0
\end{array}
$$

In this way, the result is read from top to bottom: $(100110)_2$.

Example 5

$(67)_{10} = (?)_2$

To find the binary equivalent by determining the combination of positional values can be a long and arduous procedure where the numbers are large. Instead we may use the remainder method:

```
                    Remainder

        0
      2⌐1              1
      2⌐2              0
      2⌐4              0
      2⌐8              0
      2⌐16             0
      2⌐33             1
      2⌐67             1
```

Thus the result, reading from top to bottom is: $(1000011)_2 = (67)_{10}$. All operations should be checked for accuracy. Let us make certain that $(1000011)_2$ is indeed equivalent to $(67)_{10}$.

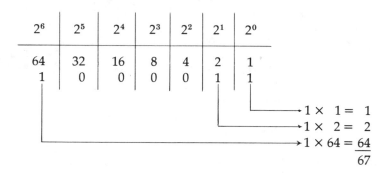

2^6	2^5	2^4	2^3	2^2	2^1	2^0
64	32	16	8	4	2	1
1	0	0	0	0	1	1

$$1 \times 1 = 1$$
$$1 \times 2 = 2$$
$$1 \times 64 = \underline{64}$$
$$67$$

**SELF-
EVALUATING
QUIZ**

1. The binary numbering system uses ___(number)___ digits.
2. The digits used in the binary numbering system are _____ and _____ .
3. The binary numbering system is ideally suited to computer processing because the digit _____ represents the _____-state and the digit _____ represents the _____-state.
4. The term bit is an abbreviation for _____ _____ .
5. The decimal and binary numbering systems are called _____ numbering systems since the location or position of each digit is significant.
6. The binary numbering system has a base of _____ .
7. The binary number 1011 is equivalent to the decimal number _____ .
8. The binary number 110110 is equivalent to the decimal number _____ .
9. The binary number 11101 is equivalent to the decimal number _____ .
10. The largest decimal number that can be represented by 4 binary digits is _____ .
11. The binary equivalent of the decimal number 86 is _____ .
12. The binary equivalent of the decimal number 101 is _____ .
13. The method used to convert a decimal number to a number in another system is called the _____ _____ .

Solutions

1. Two
2. 0; 1
3. 0; "off"
   1; "on"
4. *Binary digit*
5. Positional
6. 2

7. 11:

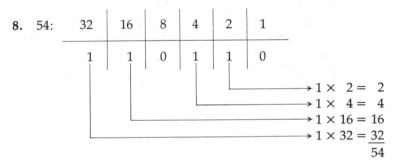

$$1 \times 1 = 1$$
$$1 \times 2 = 2$$
$$1 \times 8 = \underline{8}$$
$$11$$

8. 54:

32	16	8	4	2	1
1	1	0	1	1	0

$$1 \times 2 = 2$$
$$1 \times 4 = 4$$
$$1 \times 16 = 16$$
$$1 \times 32 = \underline{32}$$
$$54$$

9. 29:

16	8	4	2	1
1	1	1	0	1

$$16 + 8 + 4 + 1 = 29$$

10. 15

11. $(1010110)_2$ *Remainder*

```
        0
    2 | 1          1
    2 | 2          0
    2 | 5          1
    2 | 10         0
    2 | 21         1
    2 | 43         1
    2 | 86         0
```

12. $(1100101)_2$ *Remainder*

```
        0
    2 | 1          1
    2 | 3          1
    2 | 6          0
    2 | 12         0
    2 | 25         1
    2 | 50         0
    2 | 101        1
```

13. Remainder method

4. Addition and Subtraction of Binary Numbers

Thus far, we have seen that binary numbers are ideally suited to computer processing since they can be used to represent the on-off state of circuits. An "on" condition in storage can be indicated by a 1; an "off" condition by a 0.

We have learned how to convert numbers from binary to decimal by utilizing the positional values and how to convert from decimal to binary by using the remainder method.

This section will consider the addition and subtraction of binary numbers as they are handled by the computer.

The addition of binary numbers follows a simple schematic:

Addition of Binary Numbers
For Each Position:
1. $1 + 0 = 1$
2. $0 + 1 = 1$
3. $0 + 0 = 0$
4. $1 + 1 = 0$ with a carry of 1 to the next position.

Example 1

$10_2 + 11_2 = (?)_2$

Binary	Decimal
10	2
+ 11	+3
101	5

Units position: $0 + 1 = 1$
Two's position: $1 + 1 = 0$ with carry of 1
Four's position: carry of $1 +$ zero (nothing) $= 1$

Thus, we have 101 as the sum.

Example 2

$1101_2 + 1010_2 = (?)_2$

Binary	Decimal
1101	13
+1010	+10
10111	23

Notice that in each example, we checked our solution by converting the binary numbers to decimal and then determining if the decimal sum was equal to the binary total. If not, then an error was made in the binary addition.

The process of binary subtraction is somewhat more complicated than addition. Note that a computer does not perform simple subtraction in the manner that we customarily perform it. It performs subtraction by a series of negative additions. In this way, the same addition mechanisms can be used for subtraction as well.

Subtraction of Binary Numbers (General Rule)
1. *Complement* the subtrahend (number to be subtracted) by converting all 1's to 0's and all 0's to 1's.
2. Proceed as in addition.
3. Cross off the high-order or leftmost digit (a 1 when the number is positive) and add a 1 to the total (called end-around-carry).

Example 3

$$1101_2 - 1000_2 = (?)_2$$

Binary	Decimal	
1101	13	Minuend
−1000	− 8 −	Subtrahend
	5	Difference

1. Complement the subtrahend or number to be subtracted:
    Complement of 1000 = 0111 converting all zeros to ones and all ones to zeros.

2. Proceed as in addition using complemented value as factor to be added.

    ```
      1101
    +0111
    10100
    ```

3. Cross off high-order 1 and add it to result:

    ```
    1̷0100
    +└──→1
     0101
    ```

    Answer is 0101_2 or 101_2 since leftmost zero has no value.
    Since $101_2 = 5_{10}$, the binary subtraction solution is correct.

Example 4

$$11101_2 - 11000_2 = (?)_2$$

Binary	Decimal	
11101	29	Minuend
−11000	−24 −	Subtrahend
	5	Difference

1. Complement the subtrahend:
    Complement of 11000 = 00111

2. Proceed as in addition:

    ```
      11101
    +00111
    100100
    ```

3. End-Around-Carry:

    ```
    1̷00100
    +└──→1
      101
    ```

This procedure for subtraction, which is the method used by the computer, is called *complementation and end-around carry*.

In the above examples, notice that the subtrahend, or number to be subtracted, was always smaller than the number to be subtracted from. If, however, the subtrahend is larger than the minuend, or number being subtracted from, we must modify Step 3 in the rules for subtraction.

**Subtraction of Binary Numbers
(If Subtrahend Is Larger Than Minuend)**
1. Complement the subtrahend (number to be subtracted) by converting all 1's to 0's and all 0's to 1's.
2. Proceed as in addition.
3. Complement the result and place a negative sign in front of the answer.

Example 5

Binary	Decimal	
11000	24	Minuend
−11101	−29 −	Subtrahend
	−5	Difference

1. Complement the subtrahend:
   Complement of 11101 = 00010
2. Proceed as in addition:
   11000
   +00010
   11010

3. Complement the result and add negative sign to it:
   Complement of 11010 = 00101
   Answer = −00101 or −5$_{10}$

Example 6

Binary	Decimal	
1101	13	Minuend
−11001	−25 −	Subtrahend
	−12	Difference

1. Complement the subtrahend:
   Complement of 11001 = 00110

2. Proceed as in addition:
   1101
   +00110
   10011

3. Complement the result and add negative sign:
   Complement of 10011 = 01100
   Answer = −1100$_2$ or −12$_{10}$

5. Representing Negative Numbers in Binary Form

The following steps illustrate how a negative number can be represented in binary form.

Steps for Finding Binary Equivalent of a Negative Number
1. Represent the number as a positive value in binary form.
2. Replace all 0's by 1's and all 1's by 0's. This is known as *complementation*.
3. Add 1 to the result.

Example 1

Represent −5 in binary using 16 bits.

1. Represent the number as a positive value in binary form.
   0000000000000101

2. Complement the number.
   1111111111111010

3. Add 1 to the result.
   (1111111111111011)$_2$ = (−5)$_{10}$

   It should be noted that a negative number in binary always has a 1 in the high-order (leftmost) bit of the field. A zero means the number is *positive*.

1111111111111011   0000000000000101

↑   ↑

Designates number   Designates number
as negative   as positive

Example 2
Represent −10 in binary using 16 bits.

1. Represent the number as a positive value in binary form.
    0000000000001010

2. Complement the number.
    1111111111110101

3. Add 1 to the result.
    $(1111111111110110)_2 = (-10)_{10}$

SELF-EVALUATING QUIZ

1. The addition of $1 + 0$ or $0 + 1$, in binary, results in _____.
2. The addition of $1 + 1$, in binary, results in _____.
2. The method used by the computer for subtraction of binary numbers is called _____.

4.
    11011
    +10011

5.
    11111
    +11011

6.
    111
    +101
    110

7.
    11011
    −10011

8.
    111011
    −110001

9.
    010110
    −110001

10. $(-8)_{10} = (?)_2$ (Use 16 bits.)
11. $(-14)_{10} = (?)_2$ (Use 16 bits.)

Solutions

1. 1
2. 0 with a carry of 1
3. Complementation and end-around-carry
4. 101110   (27 + 19 = 46)
5. 111010   (31 + 27 = 58)
6. 10010   (7 + 5 + 6 = 18)
7.
    11011
    +01100   27 − 19 = 8
    100111
    ↳→1
    1000

$$8 \qquad 111011$$
$$+001110 \qquad 59 - 49 = 10$$
$$\overline{\cancel{1}001001}$$
$$\underline{\quad\quad\rightarrow 1}$$
$$1010$$

9. 010110
     $+001110$

      $100100;$ complement $= 011011;$

    Answer $= -11011;$ $(22 - 49 = -27)$

10. 1111111111111000

11. 1111111111110010

C. Hexadecimal Numbers

1. Representing Numeric Data with Hexadecimal Numbers

We have seen that a computer uses binary numbers rather than decimal numbers to perform arithmetic operations. This is because the two binary numbers 1 and 0 can be made to correspond to the on-off state of computer circuits.

Note however that it is not feasible for the computer to utilize an entire storage position to represent one binary digit. Binary numbers utilize many positions to represent relatively small numbers. While the decimal number 23 would use two storage positions, one for the 2 and one for the 3, its binary equivalent 10111 would utilize 5 storage positions. Thus to have the computer store a single binary digit in one storage position would make inefficient use of large storage capability.

In this section, we will see that 4 binary digits can be grouped together to produce a digit in the base 16 or *hexadecimal* numbering system. In computers that represent data in base 16, such as the S/360 and S/370, each storage position can be used to store two hexadecimal digits, with each such digit corresponding to four binary digits.

In base 10, there are ten unique digits 0 to 9. In base 2, there are two unique digits, 0 and 1. In base 16, as you might expect, there are sixteen unique digits. Since we are familar only with ten individual digits, the remaining six are represented as letters A to F:

Hexadecimal	Decimal
0	0
⋮	⋮
9	9
A	10
B	11
C	12
D	13
E	14
F	15

2. Determining the Decimal Equivalent of a Hexadecimal Number

Note that while the decimal numbering system has only *10* digits 0 to 9, the hexadecimal numbering system requires 6 more individual characters to represent numbers 10 to 15. Arbitrarily, the letters A to F were selected to represent these numbers.

To determine the next number after F in the hexadecimal system (or 15 in decimal) we must utilize the next position. That is, $(10)_{16} = (16)_{10}$. Since the hexadecimal numbering system has a base of 16, each positional value can be expressed as a factor of 16:

$\cdots$	16^3	16^2	16^1	16^0
$\cdots$	4096	256	16	1

To determine, then, $(10)_{16}$ in base 10 we have:

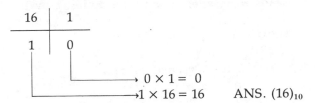

$$0 \times 1 = 0$$
$$1 \times 16 = 16 \quad \text{ANS. } (16)_{10}$$

We use the same method as previously discussed to convert from any numbering system to the decimal system: multiply each digit by its positional value and then obtain the sum or total. Do not become confused by the use of hexadecimal digits A to F. When performing any arithmetic operation, merely convert them to their decimal counterpart (10 to 15, respectively.)

Example 1

$(AF)_{16} = (?)_{10}$

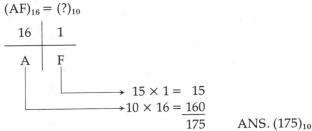

$$15 \times 1 = 15$$
$$10 \times 16 = \underline{160}$$
$$175 \quad \text{ANS. } (175)_{10}$$

Example 2

$(B6A)_{16} = (?)_{10}$

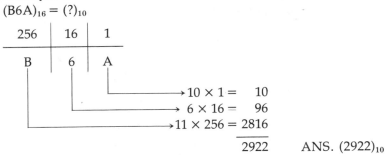

$$10 \times 1 = 10$$
$$6 \times 16 = 96$$
$$11 \times 256 = 2816$$
$$\overline{2922} \quad \text{ANS. } (2922)_{10}$$

Find the decimal equivalent of the following hexadecimal numbers:

1. $(2E)_{16} = (?)_{10}$

*****

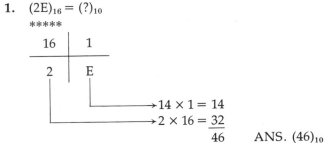

$$14 \times 1 = 14$$
$$2 \times 16 = \underline{32}$$
$$46 \quad \text{ANS. } (46)_{10}$$

2. $(A23)_{16} = (?)_{10}$

*****

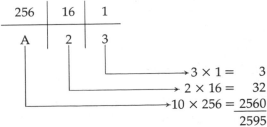

$$3 \times 1 = 3$$
$$2 \times 16 = 32$$
$$10 \times 256 = \underline{2560}$$
$$2595 \quad \text{ANS. } (2595)_{10}$$

3. Determining the Hexadecimal Equivalent of a Decimal Number

To convert from the hexadecimal numbering system to the decimal system we use the remainder method, by dividing by 16.

Example 1

$$(382)_{10} = (?)_{16}$$

Remainder in Hex.

```
          0          1
   16 ⌐ 1          7
   16 ⌐ 23         E
   16 ⌐ 382
```

———————— Reading from top to bottom

ANS. $(17E)_{16}$

Example 2

$$(1583)_{10} = (?)_{16}$$

Remainder in Hex.

```
          0          6
   16 ⌐ 6          2
   16 ⌐ 98         F
   16 ⌐ 1583
```

ANS. $(62F)_{16}$

SELF-EVALUATING QUIZ

Find the hexadecimal equivalent of the following decimal numbers.

1. $(132)_{10} = (?)_{16}$

*****

```
          0        8
   16 ⌐ 8        4
   16 ⌐ 132
```

ANS. $(84)_{16}$

2. $(214)_{10} = (?)_{16}$

```
          0      D
   16 ⌐ 13     6
   16 ⌐ 214
```

ANS. $(D6)_{16}$

Use of a Conversion Table

To simplify the conversion of decimal numbers to their hexadecimal equivalents, and hexadecimal numbers to their decimal equivalents, we can use the following conversion table.

Decimal Value

Hex Digit	Position 6	Position 5	Position 4	Position 3	Position 2	Position 1
0	0	0	0	0	0	0
1	1,048,576	65,536	4,096	256	16	1
2	2,097,152	131,072	8,192	512	32	2
3	3,145,728	196,608	12,288	768	48	3
4	4,194,304	262,144	16,384	1024	64	4
5	5,242,880	327,680	20,480	1280	80	5
6	6,291,456	393,216	24,576	1536	96	6
7	7,340,032	458,752	28,672	1792	112	7
8	8,388,608	524,288	32,768	2048	128	8
9	9,437,184	589,824	36,864	2304	144	9
A	10,485,760	655,360	40,960	2560	160	10
B	11,534,336	720,896	45,056	2816	176	11
C	12,582,912	786,432	49,152	3072	192	12
D	13,631,488	851,968	53,248	3328	208	13
E	14,680,064	917,504	57,344	3584	224	14
F	15,728,640	983,040	61,440	3840	240	15

Converting a Hexadecimal Number to Its Decimal Equivalent Each hex digit is converted, one at a time, into its decimal equivalent. This is accomplished by locating the value of that digit in the column of the table which corresponds to that digit's place in the number. The sum of all the converted digits is the decimal equivalent of the hexadecimal number. The following example illustrates these steps.

Example 1

$$(5AC)_{16} = (?)_{10}$$

1. Locate the digit C in the *first* (rightmost) column, since it is the rightmost digit in the number. Its value is 12.

2. Locate the digit A in the *second* column. Its value is 160.

3. Locate the digit 5 in the *third* column. Its value is 1280.

4. Add the values together.
    12 + 160 + 1280 = 1452

Thus, $(5AC)_{16} = (1452)_{10}$

Converting a Decimal Number to Its Hexadecimal Equivalent To convert a decimal number into its hexadecimal equivalent, we use the following procedure.

1. Find an entry in the table that is *closest* to the decimal number being converted *without exceeding* it. The hex digit to be used for that position in the hexadecimal number is found at the left of the table.

2. To find the *next* digit in the hexadecimal number, subtract the closest value previously found from the number that was being converted. Take this *remainder* and repeat step 1.

The following example will clarify this procedure.

Example 2

$$(1627)_{10} = (?)_{16}$$

1. The closest number to 1627 in the table is 1536 in the *third* column from the right. The hexadecimal equivalent therefore has 3 digits in it. The

leftmost digit will be a 6, which is the hex digit that corresponds to the number 1536.

2. The remainder at this point is 91 (1627 − 1536).

3. The closest number to 91 is 80. Therefore, the next hex digit will be a 5.

4. The remainder at this point is 11 (91 − 80). This is a B in hex, which is found by looking at the left of the table.

Since there is no remainder at this point, all the conversions have been made. We therefore have this result:

$$(1627)_{10} = (65B)_{16}$$

4. Addition and Subtraction of Hexadecimal numbers

Arithmetic operations in hexadecimal are similar to those in other numbering systems. Perform the operation on each column decimally, convert the decimal number to hexadecimal, and proceed.

Example 1

$(BAD)_{16} + (431)_{16} = (?)_{16}$

```
      B  A  D
      4  3  1
      F  D  E
```

$11 + 4 = 15 = F$ $10 + 3 = 13 = D$ $13 + 1 = 14 = E$

ANS. $(FDE)_{16}$

Example 2

$(CBA)_{16} + (627)_{16} = (?)_{16}$

```
      C  B  A
   +  6  2  7
   1  2  E  1
```

$12 + 6 = 18_{10} = 12_{16}$ $11 + 2 + 1 \text{ (carry)} = 14_{10} = E_{16}$ $10 + 7 = 17_{10} = 11_{16} \text{ (carry 1)}$

ANS. $(12E1)_{16}$

Keep in mind that the carrying of hexadecimal numbers to the next postion is performed in exactly the same manner as in the decimal numbering system. A sum of 16 results in a carry of 1 ($10_{16} = 16_{10}$).

Example 3

$(83E)_{16} + (F6F)_{16} = (?)_{16}$

```
      8  3  E
      F  6  F
   1  7  A  D
```

$14 + 15 = (29)_{10} = (1D)_{16} \text{ (carry 1)}$

ANS. $(17AD)_{16}$

We can subtract hexadecimal numbers by again converting each digit to decimal for each position and then converting the difference obtained back to hexadecimal. Note that the system of borrowing from or exchanging with the next position results in an exchange of 16 rather than 10.

Example 4

$(26)_{16} - (7)_{16} = (?)_{16}$

$$
\begin{array}{cccl}
26 & 1 & (16+6) & \text{(16 borrowed from 2nd position)}\\
\underline{-7} = - & & \underline{7} & \\
& 1 & F &
\end{array}
$$

ANS. $(1F)_{16}$

On some computers, specifically the IBM line, computer printouts *of storage locations* and their contents are specified in hexadecimal. While the normal program output is printed decimally, any program specifications are indicated in hexadecimal. Thus programmers are required to understand positional numbering theory to assist in computer processing.

When errors or "bugs" exist in a program or when programmers wish to pinpoint the contents of specific storage locations for testing purposes, they must be able to perform hexadecimal arithmetic. This is because *core dumps*, or displays of storage contents, are given in hexadecimal. Thus a programmer may be advised that a program began at hexadecimal location 28E6 and that an error occurred at location 3EF2. The program listing has the address of each instruction, but only in relative terms, that is, from address 0000 on with no relation to where the program began. Thus to obtain the absolute error point and to find the corresponding instruction, the starting point, 28E6, must be subtracted from 3EF2 to obtain the absolute error point.

In order to extract items from storage, then, the average programmer must understand hexadecimal arithmetic:

$$
\begin{array}{l}
3EF2\\
\underline{-28E6}\\
160C \qquad \text{Absolute error point}
\end{array}
$$

5. Converting from Hexadecimal to Binary and from Binary to Hexadecimal

At the start of this section, we indicated that hexadecimal numbers are used by some computers because they effectively reduce 4 binary digits to a single digit in base 16. That is, we can represent any 4 binary digits by a single hexadecimal digit.

Given any binary number, regardless of its size, we can convert it to a hexadecimal number by dividing it into groups of four digits and representing each group with a single hexadecimal digit.

Example 1

$(1101001101110111)_2 = (?)_{16}$

8421	8421	8421	8421
1101	0011	0111	0111
D	3	7	7

ANS. $(D377)_{16}$

Example 2

$(101101111)_2 = (?)_{16}$

0001	0110	1111
1	6	F

ANS. $(16F)_{16}$

Note that when the binary number does not consist of a multiple of four digits, it can be enlarged by using high-order or insignificant zeros. That is, 11 is the same as 0011, which has 4 digits. Because of the simple relation between binary and hexadecimal digits, the computer can represent data in hexadecimal, by still maintaining the binary (on-off state) configuration.

Notice also that it is sometimes easier to determine the *decimal* equivalent of a *binary* number by first finding its hexadecimal equivalent. A large binary number requires numerous calculations to determine the positional values, and then to convert to decimal. The conversion process is simplified from hexadecimal to decimal and since we can easily represent binary numbers as hexadecimal numbers, the double conversion often simplifies the operations.

Let us consider the binary number in Example 2 directly above.

$(101101111)_2$

Suppose we wish to find its decimal equivalent. We can use the standard method by determining each positional value and then adding all "on" positions. Or we can convert the number to hexadecimal and obtain 16F as in the example. Then we can convert:

$$
\begin{array}{c|c|c}
256 & 16 & 1 \\
1 & 6 & F
\end{array}
$$

$$
\begin{aligned}
15 \times 1 &= 15 \\
6 \times 16 &= 96 \\
1 \times 256 &= \underline{256} \\
& \quad 367
\end{aligned}
$$

ANS. $(367)_{10}$

Often we find that the time it takes to convert large binary numbers to the decimal numbering system is significantly reduced by performing the intermediate conversion to hexadecimal.

SELF-
EVALUTING
QUIZ

1. $(8E6)_{16} = (?)_{10}$
2. $(9FC)_{16} = (?)_{10}$
3. $(1387)_{10} = (?)_{16}$
4. $(8365)_{10} = (?)_{16}$
5.   8EC
   $\underline{+DE2}$

6.   9CC
   $\underline{+DEE}$

7.   9CE
   $\underline{-8DF}$

8.   AEC
   $\underline{-932}$

9. $(11011111110111)_2 = (?)_{16}$
10. $(111111101111)_2 = (?)_{16}$

Solutions   **1.** $(8E6)_{16} = (?)_{10}$

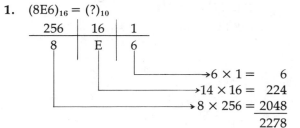

ANS. 2278

2. $(9FC)_{16} = (?)_{10}$

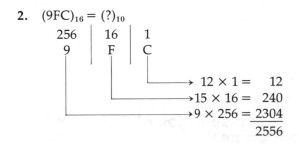

ANS. 2556

3. $(1387)_{10} = (?)_{16}$

Remainder in Hex.

```
             0            5
   16 ⌐ 5                 6
   16 ⌐ 86                B
   16 ⌐ 1387
   ANS. 56B
```

4. $(8365)_{10} = (?)_{16}$

Remainder in Hex.

```
             0            2
   16 ⌐ 2                 0
   16 ⌐ 32                A
   16 ⌐ 522               D
   16 ⌐ 8365
```

ANS. 20AD

5.   8EC
   DE2
   ―――
   16CE

6.   9CC
   DEE
   ―――
   17BA

7.   9CE
   −8DF
   ―――
    EF

8.   AEC
   −932
   ―――
   1BA

9. $(11011111110111)_2$

0011	0111	1111	0111
3	7	F	7

ANS. $(37F7)_{16}$

10. $(111111101111)_2$

1111	1110	1111
F	E	F

ANS. $(FEF)_{16}$

D. Representation of Characters in Storage

1. The EBCDIC Code

We have seen that through a combination of on-off bits, or binary digits, it is possible to represent any number. Many computers group binary numbers in sets of four in an effort to conserve storage so that data may be represented internally in the hexadecimal numbering system.

Most computer systems use some variation of the binary representation to store all characters including letters and special symbols. We will now discuss in detail the internal computer code used on the S/360 and S/370. This code is called **EBCDIC** (pronounced eb-ce-dick), which means *Extended Binary Coded Decimal Interchange Code*. Using **EBCDIC**, it is possible to represent 256 characters. The characters that can be represented in **EBCDIC** include numbers, letters (lowercase as well as uppercase or capital letters), special symbols, and control characters.

Using the **EBCDIC** code, each storage position consists of 8 bits. On many machines, including the IBM 360/370 systems, a single storage position consisting of 8 bits is called a *byte*.

Each byte is divided into a zone portion consisting of 4 bits and a digit portion consisting of 4 bits, producing what is referred to as the *zoned-decimal format*.

Zone	Digit

Byte

The zone portion of the byte is represented in exactly the same manner as the digit portion. Each portion consists of 4 *binary* circuits, with the following positional values:

Byte

Zone				Digit			
8	4	2	1	8	4	2	1

The *digit* portion of the byte consists of 4 bits with positional values of 8-4-2-1 or 2^3-2^2-2^1-2^0. Each decimal digit 0–9 can be represented by some combination of 8-4-2-1 "on" bits. The decimal number 9, for example, can be represented as 1001, where 1 means an "on" state and 0 means an "off" state.

The *zone* portion of the byte uses 4 bits with positional values 8-4-2-1 to represent the Hollerith zones 12, 11, and 0. You will recall that the Hollerith zones are used as follows:

12 + digit = A–I
11 + digit = J–R
 0 + digit = S–Z

For the zone portion, the Hollerith zones are represented as follows:

Hollerith Zone	EBCDIC Equivalent
12	1100
11	1101
0	1110

Note that the 11 and 0-zones do *not* have EBCDIC codes of 11 and 0.

Thus the letter A in Hollerith, a 12-zone and a 1 punch, is:

Zone   Digit

| 8 | 4 | 2 | 1 | 8 | 4 | 2 | 1 | Positional value |
| 1 | 1 | 0 | 0 | 0 | 0 | 0 | 1 | Bits |

Byte

The 12-zone corresponds to 1100, a 12 in binary, and the 1 is 0001. A hexadecimal printout of this byte would be C1 (8 + 4 in the hexadecimal system is a C). That is, the zone and digit portions are treated independently for printout purposes.

The letter T corresponding to 0–3 punches in Hollerith is represented as:

Zone   Digit

Hex Printout
E3

| 8 | 4 | 2 | 1 | 8 | 4 | 2 | 1 |
| 1 | 1 | 1 | 0 | 0 | 0 | 1 | 1 |

Character
T

0-Zone   3-Digit

In a hexadecimal printout, the T would be represented as E3. Numeric characters are also represented in this form. For *unsigned* numbers, all zone bits are on. Thus we have 1111 as the zone portion of all unsigned numbers. The number 8 then is represented in a byte as:

	Zone				Digit			
	8	4	2	1	8	4	2	1
	1	1	1	1	1	0	0	0

Actual value   +   8
Hexadecimal representation F   8

The 1111 in the zone portion of a byte is used to denote an unsigned number that is assumed to be positive. The number 1111 was selected because it would make unsigned numbers the highest in the collating or sorting sequence. Note that an unsigned 5 in a hexadecimal printout of storage would read as F5.

A definitive positive sign is denoted by 1100 (hex C) and a minus sign by 1101 (hex D).

The following chart summarizes the representation of the zone portion of characters in EBCDIC and hexadecimal.

Summary of Zone Representation

Hollerith	EBCDIC	Hexadecimal
12	1100	C
11	1101	D
0	1110	E
No zone (unsigned numbers)	1111	F

Note that, as indicated in the previous section, each group of 4 bits or binary digits can be used to represent a single hexadecimal digit. Thus a shorthand method for representing characters in EBCDIC is to represent them as 2 hexadecimal digits. Since each hexadecimal digit is used to represent 4 binary digits, 2 hexadecimal digits are needed to represent 1 byte or 8 bits.

E6 in hexadecimal represents the EBCDIC code for W:

	Zone				Digit			
	1	1	1	0	0	1	1	0

                E   6

This is equivalent to 0–6 in Hollerith or the letter W.

F5 in hexadecimal represents the zoned decimal format in EBCDIC for a positive 5:

Zone	Digit
F	5
1111	0101

All unsigned numbers in zoned decimal format are represented hexadecimally with an F followed by a digit.

The following chart shows the EBCDIC, Hollerith, and hexadecimal codes for the letters and numbers.

Character	EBCDIC Zone	EBCDIC Digit	Hollerith	Hexadecimal
A	1100	0001	12-1	C1
B	1100	0010	12-2	C2
C	1100	0011	12-3	C3
D	1100	0100	12-4	C4
E	1100	0101	12-5	C5
F	1100	0110	12-6	C6
G	1100	0111	12-7	C7
H	1100	1000	12-8	C8
I	1100	1001	12-9	C9
J	1101	0001	11-1	D1
K	1101	0010	11-2	D2
L	1101	0011	11-3	D3
M	1101	0100	11-4	D4
N	1101	0101	11-5	D5
O	1101	0110	11-6	D6
P	1101	0111	11-7	D7
Q	1101	1000	11-8	D8
R	1101	1001	11-9	D9
S	1110	0010	0-2	E2
T	1110	0011	0-3	E3
U	1110	0100	0-4	E4
V	1110	0101	0-5	E5
W	1110	0110	0-6	E6
X	1110	0111	0-7	E7
Y	1110	1000	0-8	E8
Z	1110	1001	0-9	E9
0	1111	0000	0	F0
1	1111	0001	1	F1
2	1111	0010	2	F2
3	1111	0011	3	F3
4	1111	0100	4	F4
5	1111	0101	5	F5
6	1111	0110	6	F6
7	1111	0111	7	F7
8	1111	1000	8	F8
9	1111	1001	9	F9

2. Packed Format   Thus far, we have seen how data may be represented in zoned decimal format using one byte of storage for each character.

For numeric items, we have seen how a byte can store one digit, where the zone portion is equivalent to all bits on, a hexadecimal F, and the digit portion is the binary equivalent of decimal numbers 0 to 9.

Consider the number 68254. Using zoned-decimal format, it would take 5 bytes to represent this number in storage, one for each digit. The zone portion of each byte would indicate all bits on, as shown below.

It really is unnecessary to represent a zone for each digit within the number. That is, one zone for the entire field to indicate that the number is in fact positive would suffice. There is a method that can be employed so that the computer eliminates or strips the zone of all digits except one to indicate the sign. Thus the zone portion of each byte can be employed to represent *another digit.* In this way, *two* digits can be represented by a single byte. This technique is called *packing* and is a main advantage of using the EBCDIC configuration.

It operates as follows:

1. The zone and digit portions of the *low-order* or rightmost digit are switched.
2. All other zones are stripped and 2 digits are *packed* into 1 byte.

Example 1

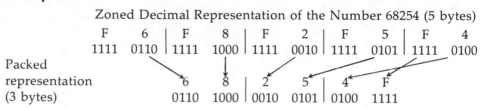

Zoned Decimal Representation of the Number 68254 (5 bytes)

F	6	F	8	F	2	F	5	F	4
1111	0110	1111	1000	1111	0010	1111	0101	1111	0100

Packed
representation
(3 bytes)

6	8	2	5	4	F
0110	1000	0010	0101	0100	1111

Example 2

Representation of 835674 in Zoned Decimal Format (6 Bytes)

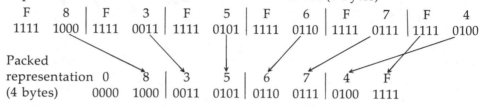

F	8	F	3	F	5	F	6	F	7	F	4
1111	1000	1111	0011	1111	0101	1111	0110	1111	0111	1111	0100

Packed
representation
(4 bytes)

0	8	3	5	6	7	4	F
0000	1000	0011	0101	0110	0111	0100	1111

Thus all 1's or a hexadecimal F in the low-order 4 bits of a byte indicates that the byte contains a packed number. (All 1's could not be used to represent any single digit.)

Note in Example 1 that the number in zoned-decimal format utilizes 5 bytes while in packed format it utilizes only 3 bytes. A major advantage of packing numbers is to conserve storage.

In Example 2, in order to complete or "fill up" the high-order byte, we add 4 zero bits at the beginning of the field.

Thus, for numeric fields, we can save considerable storage space by using the packed format. In addition the computer *requires* numeric fields to be packed in order to perform arithmetic operations. To print out or display numeric fields, however, they must be in zoned-decimal format.

SELF-EVALUATING QUIZ

1. In the hexadecimal numbering system,   (number)   binary digits are grouped to represent a single hexadecimal digit.
2. A single storage position consisting of   (number)   bits is called a _____ .
3. Each byte is divided into a _____ portion and a _____ portion, each of which consists of   (number)   bits.
4. The letter C is represented in a byte as _____ .
5. The letter M is represented in a byte as _____ .
6. The *unsigned* number 8 is represented in a byte as _____ .
7. The *signed* number +8 is represented in a byte as _____ .
8. Four 1's in the zone portion of a byte are used to denote _____ .
9. How would the letter D appear in a hexadecimal printout?
10. How would the unsigned number 7 (in one byte) appear in a hexadecimal printout?
11. Using zoned-decimal format, how many bytes are required to store the unsigned number 118753?

12. In packed format, the above number would require __(number)__ bytes.
13. (True or False) Numeric fields must be packed in order to perform arithmetic operations.

Solutions

1. 4
2. 8
   Byte
3. Zone
   Digit
   4
4. 1100   0011   or   C3   in hex
   zone   digit
5. 1101   0100   or   D4   in hex
   zone   digit
6. 1111   1000   or   F8   in hex
   zone   digit
7. 1100   1000   or   C8   in hex
   zone   digit
8. An unsigned number that is assumed to be positive
9. Binary   1100   0100
   Hexadecimal   C   4
10. Binary   1111   0111
    Hexadecimal   F   7
11. 6 (One for each digit)
12. 4 (01 18 75 3F)
13. True

Review Questions

1. Determine the decimal equivalents of the following binary numbers:
   a. 10011111
   b. 11100
   c. 110011
2. Determine the binary equivalents of the following decimal numbers:
   a. 234
   b. 435
   c. 333
3. Add the following binary numbers and indicate the sum in binary form. Check your work by converting each number back into decimal form:
   a. 11101111 + 1111101111
   b. 111111011101 + 1111011
   c. 1110111 + 111111
4. Determine the decimal equivalents of the following hexadecimal numbers:
   a. 6FFE
   b. 70FD
   c. 67EE
5. Determine the hexadecimal equivalents of the following decimal numbers:
   a. 10678
   b. 16745
   c. 2345
6. How are the following decimal numbers represented in binary form in 16 bits?
   a. −18
   b. +20
   c. 35

7. Indicate how the following characters would appear in a hexadecimal print-out.
   a. E
   b. 5
   c. —7

KEY TERMS
Binary number
Bit
Byte

Complementation
Complementation and end-around-carry

Extended Binary Coded Decimal Interchange Code (EBCDIC)

Hexadecimal numbering system
High-order

Packed format
Positional numbering system

Remainder method

Zoned-decimal format

Chapter 3

Defining Storage Areas and Constants

I. The Define Storage (DS) Statement

How Storage Is Used All data processed by the computer, like all instructions read into the computer, is placed in main storage in addressable locations called *bytes*. Machine language instructions reference these storage locations by their actual numeric address. Assembler language instructions may reference them by *symbolic addresses* called NAMES or LABELS. Hence, if a TOTAL field is to contain the sum of all input amount fields, it may, for example, occupy storage positions 1000–1003 when assembled. The programmer, however, need not keep track of such actual addresses but can reference a field by its symbolic name. The add instruction:

LABEL	OPERATION 10	16	OPERAND
	AP		TOTAL,AMT

for example, which adds AMT to TOTAL, references two symbolic storage areas called **AMT** and **TOTAL** that must be converted to actual machine addresses during the assembly process.

> **Summary**
> 1. All data processed by the computer, as well as all instructions, is placed in addressable storage locations called bytes.
> 2. The assembler language programmer may refer to these locations by symbolic names, but the computer assigns actual byte locations to them during the assembly process.

A. Types of Storage Areas All data processed by the computer may be categorized as either variable or constant data.

1. Variable Data
Variable data is data that changes within the program. For most programs, storage must be reserved for the following three types of variable data areas.

a. Input Areas When an input record is read, the data is automatically transmitted to main storage. The programmer must define and describe an input area that will receive this data. Since the contents of data fields within the input area change each time a record is read, such fields are said to contain *variable* data.

b. Output Areas   After data has been processed, it is used to create output information. An area in storage must be reserved for data to be produced as output. Since output data also changes during execution of a program, the fields defined in this area are referred to as variable.

c. Work Areas   During processing, intermediate fields, not part of input and not part of output, are nonetheless frequently necessary for processing. Such fields may be used, for example, to store some intermediate result of an arithmetic operation, or to hold some code for comparison purposes.

In summary, these types of areas are used to store variable data, data that does not remain constant but that changes during the execution of the program.

2. Constant Data

Constant data is data that remains the same during the execution of the program.

Suppose, for example, that we wish to multiply each input amount field by 0.05, the tax rate. This tax rate is *not* a value that is entered as input but is nevertheless required for processing. We call 0.05 a *constant*, since it is a form of data required for processing that is *not* dependent upon the input to the system.

Similarly, suppose we wish to edit input cards and print the message 'INVALID RECORD' for any erroneous card. The message 'INVALID RECORD' will be part of output, but it is not entered as input to the system. Rather, it is a constant field, defined within the program and required for processing.

B. Establishing Storage Areas and Constants   Both variable data and constants must be established or defined by the programmer in an area of the program reserved for such entries. The following statements may be used:

Establishing Storage Areas and Constants
DS   reserves storage for variable data (for a field or record)
DC   defines a constant within storage

Note that all input areas, work areas, and output areas are defined with a DS statement. All constants to be used within the program are defined and described by DC statements. All DS and DC statements will be coded at the *end* of each program after the end-of-job routines.

C. DS Statement   All variable data that is entered or produced as output must be defined with a DS statement. This includes record descriptions and field descriptions within each record.

1. The Record Description

A *record* is a unit of information of a specific nature. A debit record, for example, is a group of related items that together form a unit of information. A print record or header record defines the format for a printed line. Input and output areas are usually defined by one or more DS statements that describe each record layout.

2. Field Descriptions Within Records

A group of consecutive positions that together represent a specific kind of data is called a field. Fields within records and fields used by the program as work areas must be defined with a DS statement.

Format of DS **Statement**

Field or record name	Define storage	Item description
Name	DS	Operand

Note, again, that the DS statement does not cause any actual data to be generated. Rather, it simply reserves storage and assigns a name to that storage area.

Examples

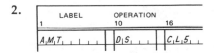

Character or
zoned-decimal format   Length

1.   80 character field or record

        CARDIN   DS   CL80

This statement defines an 80-position zoned decimal area called CARDIN.

2.

LABEL	OPERATION	
1	10	16
A M T	D S	C L 5

This statement defines a 5-position storage area called AMT that will contain data in zoned-decimal form.

D. Specifications of
DS Statements

Name Field

The field or record name conforms to the rules for forming operands:

> **Rules for Forming Names or Labels-Review**
> 1. Use 1 to 8 characters.
> 2. Letters, digits, $, #, @ may be used.
> 3. No blanks or other special characters.
> 4. Must begin in column 1 of the coding sheet.

Operand or Item Description

NAME   DS   *OPERAND*

               dtLn

               d = duplication factor
                      number of fields to be defined by this entry

               t = type of data
                     C = character or zoned-decimal format
                     X = hexadecimal format
                     P = packed format
                     B = binary format

               L = length
                     it is coded on the form as L

               n = number of bytes in the field

Example

LABEL	OPERATION	
1	10	16
INAREA	DS	5CL8Ø

Numeric zeros are slashed to distinguish them from the letter O.

This entry defines five 80-position fields that will be filled with zoned-decimal data.

NOTE: If the operand field or item description does not begin with a duplication factor, the number of fields is assumed to be one (that is, one field is defined).

Example

LABEL	OPERATION	
1	10	16
HEXNUM	DS	XL15

defines *one* 15-position hexadecimal field.

NOTE: A zero as duplication factor is used when a field or record is to be subdivided.

Example

LABEL	OPERATION	
1	10	16
CARDIN	DS	ØCL8Ø
AMT1	DS	CL5
AMT2	DS	CL5
REST	DS	CL7Ø

CARDIN is subdivided into three fields.

It should be noted that CARDIN and AMT1 are labels that refer to the same address, as shown below.

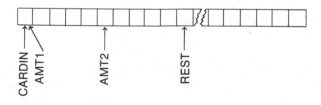

NOTE: If a DS entry contains no name, then storage will be reserved but the item will not be accessed by name by the program.

Example

Card input is to be used as follows:

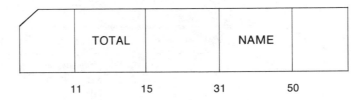

| TOTAL | | NAME | |

11   15   31   50

Only the TOTAL and NAME fields are to be accessed by the program. To define these two fields, with no entries between them, would cause the computer to assume that they are consecutive fields, which they are not. Hence the following could be coded:

LABEL	OPERATION	
1	10	16
CARDIN	DS	ØCL8Ø
	DS	CL1Ø
TOTAL	DS	CL5
	DS	CL15
NAME	DS	CL2Ø
	DS	CL3Ø

This indicates the proper alignment and makes available for processing both the TOTAL and NAME fields. Output print areas are frequently defined in this manner since they usually contain blank areas between data fields for ease of reading.

> NOTE: When using a duplication factor of 0, which indicates that a field or record is to be subdivided, all bytes must be accounted for.

VALID:

LABEL	OPERATION	
1	10	16
CARDIN	DS	ØCL8Ø
AMT	DS	CL5
DESCRIPT	DS	CL25
	DS	CL5Ø

INCORRECT: Entire card has not been defined.

LABEL	OPERATION	
1	10	16
CARDIN	DS	ØCL8Ø
AMT	DS	CL5
DESCRIPT	DS	CL25

E. How the Computer Defines Storage Areas

Fields defined by DS statements are assigned storage locations in the precise order in which they are coded. A *location counter* assigns an address to each storage area defined by a DS as each DS is encountered. The address references the *high-order* or *leftmost* position of each field or record.

Example

Assume the location counter is ready to begin assembling storage areas at hexadecimal location 1000.

Location Counter	Name	Operation	Operand
1000	READIN	DS	0CL80
1000	MANNO	DS	CL4
1004	HRSWKD	DS	CL6
100A	DATE	DS	CL6
1010	GROSS	DS	CL6
1016	FEDTAX	DS	CL6
101C		DS	CL52

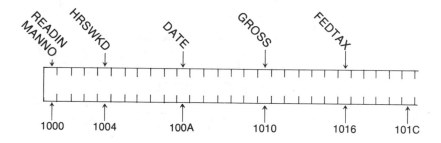

READIN refers to storage position 1000, but it references the full 80-position area as well.

MANNO, then, is a 4-byte field beginning in storage position 1000, HRSWKD is a 6-byte field beginning in storage position 1004, and so on.

Any storage area, as well as any record, can be subdivided by using a duplication factor of zero (0).

In the above, we could substitute the following for DATE:

LABEL	OPERATION	
1	10	16
DATE	DS	0CL6
MONTH	DS	CL2
DAY	DS	CL2
YEAR	DS	CL2

In this way we can access the full six-position date as needed or any subfield within it as well:

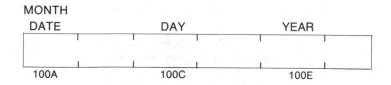

F. Additional Formats for DS Statements

Certain instructions in assembler language require that the data be operated on be a specific length and that it be defined on specific boundaries. For example, binary operations sometimes require a data field to consist of 4 bytes and to be placed in a storage address which itself is divisible by four. Four bytes of storage are called a *fullword* and an instruction that requires a data field to be placed in an address divisible by four is said to require a *fullword boundary*.

Binary operations operate on the following types of data fields.

Formats for Fields Used in Binary Operations

Type	Number of Bytes	Boundary Requirements
Halfword	2	Storage address must be divisible by 2.
Fullword	4	Storage address must be divisible by 4.
Doubleword	8	Storage address must be divisible by 8.

In addition to defining data fields as containing zoned-decimal (character), hexadecimal or packed data, it is also possible to use a DS statement to define halfword, fullword or doubleword fields by using a type of H, F or D, respectively. The use of H, F, or D locates data at addresses divisible by 2, 4, or 8 respectively. Because halfword, fullword, and doubleword fields are used in binary operations, data entered in such fields must be entered in binary form.

Examples

1.

LABEL	OPERATION	
TOTAL	DS	F

establishes five 2-byte or halfword storage locations, each on a halfword divisible by 4).

2.

LABEL	OPERATION	
AMT	DS	5H

establishes five 2-byte or halfword storage locations, each on a halfword boundary (address divisible by 2).

3.

LABEL	OPERATION	
RESULT	DS	0D

This statement reserves storage for a field to be subdivided and begins the location counter on a doubleword boundary (address divisible by 8).

It is assumed that RESULT will be further subdivided as follows.

LABEL	OPERATION	
RESULT	DS	0D
QUOTIENT	DS	BL4
REMAINDR	DS	BL4

Full Format for DS

NAME	DS	Operand
1–8 Characters: Letters, digits, $, @, # No blanks or other special characters		dtLn where: d = duplication factor t = type C = character X = hexadecimal P = packed B = binary F = fullword H = halfword D = doubleword Not used with F, H or D { L = length n = number of bytes reserved

Storage areas are printed on a source listing in hexadecimal form. To determine whether a field has been placed in an address divisible by 2, 4, or 8, it is necessary to convert the rightmost or *low-order* hexadecimal digit in the address to binary.

To determine the boundary alignment:

1. A low-order or rightmost binary zero insures halfword alignment.

2. Two low-order or rightmost binary zeros insure fullword alignment.

3. Three low-order or rightmost binary zeros insure doubleword alignment.

Example
1. LOCATION

    68A$\boxed{2}$ This digit is used to determine boundary.
    It converts to 001$\boxed{0}$in binary.
    There is only one low-order zero.
    Thus the address is on the halfword boundary.

2. LOCATION

    68A$\boxed{C}$ This digit is used to determine boundary.
    It converts to 1100 in binary.
    There are two low-order zeros.
    Thus the address is on the fullword boundary.

3. LOCATION

    68A$\boxed{0}$ This digit is used to determine boundary.
    It converts to 0000 in binary.
    There are three low-order zeros.
    This address is on the doubleword boundary.

SELF-EVALUATING QUIZ

1. (True or False) A DS causes data to be stored at a symbolic address.
  Indicate what, if anything, is wrong with the following DS statements: (2–5)
2. DS   C3
3. DS   CLX'80'
4. DS   PL4
5. DS   FP
6. (True or False) A DS statement must have a label or name associated with it.
7. The symbolic name refers to the *(high-order/low-order)* byte of a field.
8. (True or False) In the statement:
    DS   ØCL5
    the Ø means that the field will be further subdivided.
9. The statement:
    DS   F
    actually achieves two results. Name them.
10. A fullword consists of __(number)__ bytes.
11. Each byte consists of __(number)__ bits.
12. Each byte can be expressed as __(number)__ hexadecimal digits.
13. Indicate the location counter for each of the following:

Location Counter	Name	Operation	Operand
2ØØØ	OUTAREA	DS	ØCL132
		DS	CL2Ø
	NAME	DS	CL2Ø
		DS	CL2Ø
	ADDRESS	DS	CL4Ø
		DS	CL1Ø
		DS	CL22
	*		
	TOTAL	DS	D
	DATE	DS	ØCL4
	MONTH	DS	CL2
	YEAR	DS	CL2

14. Indicate what is wrong with the following.

    1. AOK   DS   CL4
    2. NO GO   DS   CL10
    3.   COLUMN1 DS   CL5
    4. 7UP   DS   CL7
    5. SPL*CHAR   DS   CL1
    6. SOVRYLONG DS   CL10
    7. WRONGOP   SD   CL15
    8. NOTYPE   DS   L15

Solutions

1. False. DS statements simply reserve storage; they do not place data in the fields.
2. DS C*L*3
3. X or C but not both; 80 is coded without quotes.
4. Okay
5. F not consistent with P; fullword will contain binary data.
6. False
7. High-order
8. True
9. Four bytes of storage is reserved; the address of the field is divisible by four.
10. Four
11. Eight
12. Two
13. Note that the location counter is specified in hex in the problem:

Location Counter	Name	Operation	Operand
Hex			
2000	OUTAREA	DS	ØCL132
2000		DS	CL2Ø
2014	NAME	DS	CL2Ø
2028		DS	CL2Ø
203C	ADDRESS	DS	CL4Ø
2064		DS	CL1Ø
206E		DS	CL22
2083	*		
2088	TOTAL	DS	D
2090	DATE	DS	ØCL4

2090	MONTH	DS	CL2
2092	YEAR	DS	CL2

NOTE: **OUTAREA** occupies hex positions 2000–2083; **TOTAL** cannot begin in the next storage position, however, since its address must be divisible by 8 and 2084 is not. The next address divisible by 8 is 2088.

14.   1.   Okay

See listing in Figure 3-1 for remaining entries.

```
*          INVALID DEFINE STORAGE INSTRUCTIONS
*
NO GO     DS    CL10           BLANKS NOT PERMITTED
 COLUMN1  DS    CL5            MUST BEGIN IN COLUMN 1, NOT 2
7UP       DS    CL7            BEGINS WITH A NUMBER
SPL*CHAR  DS    CL1            CONTAINS SPECIAL CHARACTER *
SOVRYLONG DS    CL10           TOO LONG
WRONGOP   SD    CL15           INVALID OPERATION FIELD
NOTYPE    DS    L15            INVALID TYPE SPECIFICATION
          END
```

Figure 3-1

II. Defining Constants

A. Format

Whereas the DS statement is specifically used for reserving storage where variable data is to be entered, a DC statement not only specifies the size and type of field but the *actual contents* of the field as well.

DC statements contain the same specifications as DS statements but can also indicate actual data:

Format

NAME   DC   dtLn 'c'
                                  ↓ Actual contents
                          Optional

The actual contents to be placed in the field are specified with single quote marks.

Examples

	LABEL	OPERATION	OPERAND
	1	10	16
1.	MESSAGE	DC	CL10 'TAPE ERROR'
2.	PTOT	DC	PL3,'12345'
3.	TOTAL	DC	F'1046'

(Data defined by H, F or D types will be converted to binary by the computer.)

B. Object Codes Generated by DC Statements

1. Zoned-Decimal Format

For each DC statement specified in your program, an area of storage is defined (as with DS). In addition, actual contents are placed in the field according to the specifications provided.

To ensure the proper value in your DC's make certain that the length specification conforms to the actual contents placed in the field.

If the specification for a field is *not* the same as the contents assigned, then the computer will make certain adjustments, but not necessarily the ones intended by the programmer.

Example: The Field Contains More Positions Than Are Defined by the Constant.

LABEL	OPERATION	
1	10	16
NAME	DC	CL4'AB'

A 4-position field is defined and only 2 characters are entered. In such a case low-order or rightmost positions are filled with spaces.

A	B	⌀	⌀

↑
NAME

⌀ = blank

In EBCDIC this would appear as:

C 1	C 2	4 0	4 0	Hexadecimal representation
A	B	⌀	⌀	Character representation

> **RULE:** Zoned-decimal data is placed in the field from left to right, low-order (rightmost) unfilled positions are filled with spaces.

Example 2: Constant Defined Is Larger Than the Length of the Field.

LABEL	OPERATION		OPERAND
1	10	16	
CODE	DC		CL3'ABCD'

Since the machine will establish a three-position area in storage, only three characters of data will actually be stored. Since zoned-decimal data is moved from left to right, the 'D' will be *truncated* or lost:

A	B	C	Character representation
C 1	C 2	C 3	Hexadecimal representation

↑
CODE

To ensure the proper values in your DC statements, make certain that the length of the field assigned is exactly the same as the number of characters in your constant. This applies to all formats.

2. Hexadecimal Format

If X is specified as the type of the DC, the constant must be specified in hexadecimal form. To specify hexadecimal constants for the above two entries, we would have:

a.

LABEL	OPERATION		OPERAND
1	10	16	
NAME	DC		XL4'C1C24040'

b.

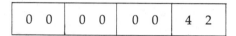

	LABEL	OPERATION 10	OPERAND 16
1	C,O,D,E	D,C	X,L,4,' ,C,1,C,2,C,3,C,4,'

> RULE: Hexadecimal data is placed in the field from right to left. High-order (leftmost) unfilled positions are filled with zeros.

When numeric data is entered in hexadecimal form, it is assumed to be packed.

	LABEL	OPERATION 10	16
1	A,M,T	D,C	X,L,4,' ,4,2,'

generates:

0 0	0 0	0 0	4 2

The specification XL4'123456C' results in

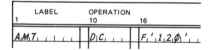

01	23	45	6C

3. H, F, or D
The constant is defined in decimal and automatically converted by the computer to binary form.

Example

	LABEL	OPERATION 10	16
1	A,M,T	D,C	F,' ,1,2,0,'

Review of Truncation and Padding
The programmer must make certain that the number of bytes assigned to a field is large enough to accommodate the result. If not, truncation will occur. The type of truncation depends upon the field specification:

Type	Truncation
C	Right
X	Left
P	Left
B	Left
F	Left
H	Left
D	Left

High-order digits will be truncated from all fields that are too short to accommodate the entire results *except* where character specification is indicated.

Example 1:   Truncation of High-Order Digits in P Field

LABEL	OPERATION 10	16	OPERAND
A,M,T,1	D,C		P,L,3,'+1,2,3,4,5,6'

will result in

2	3	4	5	6	C

AMT1

The high-order 1 was truncated. The plus sign is denoted by hex C.

All fields except C-type function as above.

Example 2:   Truncation of Low-Order Characters in C Field

LABEL	OPERATION 10	16	OPERAND
C,O,D,E	D,C		C,L,4,'A,B,C,D,E'

will result in:

A	B	C	D

CODE

low order 'E' was truncated

Similarly, if a field is larger than the number of characters specified, high-order bytes will be zero-filled in all cases except for character fields. In character fields, data is placed beginning in the leftmost bytes, and rightmost bytes are filled with blanks.

Example 1:   Padding of Zeros in P Field

LABEL	OPERATION 10	16
A,M,T,2	D,C		P,L,3,'1,2'

will result in:

0	0	0	1	2	C

C = +

AMT2

High-order zeros pad the field.

NOTE: All fields are aligned as in this example. That is, the symbolic name addresses the high-order (leftmost) byte.

Example 2

LABEL	OPERATION 10	16	OPERAND
C,O,D,E,2	D,C		C,L,6,'A,B,C,D,E'

will result in

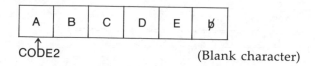

CODE2 (Blank character)

C. Additional considerations

1. Relationship between DS's and DC's

Note that if you inadvertently use a DS instead of a DC to define a constant in storage, *no* error messages will be generated. Instead, the appropriate storage area will be reserved but the value specified will be ignored.

Common Error

LABEL	OPERATION	OPERAND
1	10 16	
C O D E	D S	C L 4 ' A B C D '

coded instead of

LABEL	OPERATION	OPERAND
1	10 16	
C O D E	D C	C L 4 ' A B C D '

In the former, a 4-position area will be reserved for CODE, but the value 'ABCD' will *not* be entered. DS statements simply reserve storage. You may, however, use a DC to define a storage area without specifying a value. The following is a valid statement:

LABEL	OPERATION	
1	10 16	
C T R	D C	X L 4

Although a DC may be used in this way, it is a good idea to develop the technique of using DS for storage definitions and DC for constants. Later on, this will make debugging easier.

2. Length of a Constant

A DC can define a constant that contains as many as 120 characters. Defining a constant of this size would require *two* coding lines:

> **Rules for Extending a DC to Two Lines**
> 1. Name, operation, and operand of first line are exactly the same as in previous examples.
>   Since the constant has not been completely defined by the end of the line, no end quote is specified.
> 2. A C (or any other character) is placed in column 72 of the first line.
> 3. The constant continues in column 16 of the next line and ends with a quote mark.

Example

LABEL	OPERATION	OPERAND	COMMENTS	
1	10 16			72
V E R Y L O N G	D C	C ' T H I S I S A C O N S T A N T W H I C H I S		C
		V E R Y L O N G '		

1. What would be the result of the following:

    SAM   DC   CL2'THINK'

2. The F, H or D-type DC contains a constant that is specified in _____ format but that is converted by the computer to _____ format.

3. Indicate the contents in hexadecimal and character form of the resulting fields:

    a.   DC   F'0'

    b.   DC   XL3'C1C3C5'

    c.   DC   CL6'ABC'

    Indicate the actual number of bytes required for the following constants:

4. C'12345'

5. X'123456'

6. X'1234567890'

7. F'23'

8. H'14' .

9. The number +2 stored in a word of memory using a packed decimal format would be represented in hexadecimal as:

    a.   F2F0F0F0

    b.   00000002

    c.   0000002C

    d.   F0F0F0C2

    e.   None of the above

10. Which of the following represents the instruction necessary to reserve a doubleword of memory labeled TEST, which will begin on a doubleword boundary:

    a.   TEST   DS   CL8

    b.   TEST   DC   CL8

    c.   TEST   DS   F

    d.   TEST   DS   D

    e.   a and b above

    Show how each of the following items of data is stored within the computer's memory. If any of the data will not fit in the size locations provided, indicate the *type* of error. Give your answers in hexadecimal, being sure to indicate what is in every byte.

11. 98: in zoned-decimal format in 2 bytes of memory.

12. +98: in packed-decimal format in a doubleword of memory.

13. −30: in packed-decimal format in a word of memory

14. 3,000,000,000: in a word, packed-decimal format

15. SNAP: in EBCDIC in 4 bytes of memory

16. 205: in EBCDIC in 3 bytes of memory

17. 205: in packed decimal in a word of memory

Solutions

1. TH (INK would be truncated because of the length specification)

2. Decimal
    Binary

3. a.

00	00	00	00

    Hexadecimal representation

   b.

C 1	C 3	C 5

    Hexadecimal representation

A	C	E

    Character representation

c.

C 1	C 2	C 3	4 0	4 0	4 0	Hexadecimal representation
A	B	C	ø	ø	ø	Character representation

4. 5 bytes
5. 3 bytes; no sign generated | 12 | 34 | 56 |
6. 5 bytes | 12 | 34 | 56 | 78 | 90 |
7. 4 bytes; F defines a fullword.
8. 2 bytes
9. c
10. d
11. | F 9 | F 8 |
12. | 0 0 | 0 0 | 0 0 | 0 0 | 0 0 | 0 0 | 0 9 | 8 C |
13. | 0 0 | 0 0 | 0 3 | 0 D |
14. Constant is too long; truncation will occur; all zeros are placed in field.
15. | E 2 | D 5 | C 1 | D 7 |
16. | F 2 | F 0 | F 5 |
17. | 00 | 00 | 20 | 5F |

KEY TERMS

Binary representation
Byte

Constant

Doubleword

Field
Fullword

Halfword
Hexadecimal (hex) format

Packed form

Variable data

Zoned-decimal form

Review Questions

1. Show the bit pattern generated for the following constants:

ITEM1	DC	F'432'
ITEM2	DC	P'23'
ITEM3	DC	X'F3'
ITEM4	DC	CL4'12AB'

2. Write DC statements for
   a. 5 fullwords containing zeros.
   b. a halfword whose binary representation is 1111000100011110.
   c. a 5-byte field with value 'NANCY'.
   d. a three-byte field with each byte containing F3.
   e. a packed decimal field containing −123.

3. Provide a pictorial representation of storage areas and locations generated by the following:

1002	DC	CL4'ABC'
	DC	3PL3'−12'
	DC	XL6'F3F2F5F0F3F1'

```
DC      3F'0'
DC      2F
DC      H
DC      D
```

4. The DS instruction:
   a. generates blanks in a field.
   b. generates zeros in a field.
   c. reserves storage.
   d. reserves storage and places whatever is specified in the operand in the field.

5. Labels or names of data fields are coded:
   a. in any column.
   b. in any column after column 8.
   c. in column one only.
   d. following an asterisk.
   e. none of the above.

6. The instruction
   BLANK   DS   CL1' '
   a. stores a space in the printout area.
   b. stores a hex 40 in the location called BLANK.
   c. reserves one byte of storage.
   d. will usually cause a problem at execution time.
   e. c and d.

7. The letter C is represented in storage
   a. by Hollerith code.
   b. in hex by C1.
   c. by a decimal 194.
   d. all of the above.
   e. none of the above.

8. If a word is stored in the computer's memory, the byte addressed is:
   a. the high-order.
   b. the low-order.
   c. rightmost.
   d. least significant.
   e. none of these.

9. A word consists of _____ hex digits.
   a. 2
   b. 4
   c. 8
   d. 16
   e. 32

10. Alphanumeric data is stored in the computer's memory in a code called

    _____ .
    a. BCD
    b. Hollerith
    c. EBCDIC
    d. ANSI
    e. None of the above

UNIT II

Programming Business Problems in Assembler Language

Chapter 4   Program Shell

Thus far we have discussed the basic concepts necessary to understand assembler language programming. In this chapter, we will learn to:

1. Perform necessary "housekeeping" routines.
2. Access input and output files or data sets.
3. Read and write information.
4. Perform necessary end-of-job operations.

We will explain some fundamental instructions that are necessary in almost all assembler language programs. Once you understand them, you can simply incorporate them, line by line, in all your programs. We will provide coding sheets at the end of this chapter as well as at the end of the book that already contain these instructions. It will thus be a simple matter to use them as a standard *shell* of instructions for all of your programs. Your job will be to supply the specific logic that is needed for each program, using the standard shell as a base.

Sample Programs   We begin by considering a sample program that will illustrate the structure of assembler language. The objective of this program is simply to read in cards with the format shown in Figure 4-1 and list them out on the printer as shown in the same figure.

Card Format

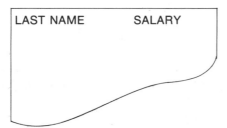

Printed Report

Figure 4-1

A Note on Operating Systems

You will recall that assembler language programs are typically run either under OS (*Operating System*) or DOS (*Disk Operating System*), depending on the particular computer being used. It should be noted that most instructions in assembler language programs are identical, regardless of which system (OS or DOS) is being used. However, since there are some differences, we will illustrate the above program under both OS and DOS to demonstrate that with little difficulty, a program written for one system can be modified easily to run on another. Even if you will be running under DOS, it is recommended that you examine the following OS program to familiarize yourself with the basic concepts and the distinctions.

A. OS Sample Program

Figure 4-2 illustrates an OS program that will read in data cards and print them out. For your convenience, explanatory comments have been added to key instructions to explain their purpose. However, only that part of the program within the box must be supplied as instructions to the computer.

We will now examine the program in detail. Do not be confused by the seeming complexity. As noted, most of the instructions will be included line by line in *all* OS programs you will write to read in cards and print out information.

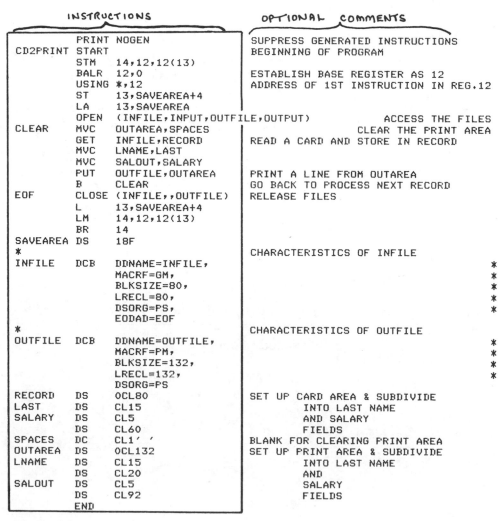

```
              INSTRUCTIONS                          OPTIONAL COMMENTS

          PRINT  NOGEN                  SUPPRESS GENERATED INSTRUCTIONS
CD2PRINT  START                         BEGINNING OF PROGRAM
          STM    14,12,12(13)
          BALR   12,0                   ESTABLISH BASE REGISTER AS 12
          USING  *,12                   ADDRESS OF 1ST INSTRUCTION IN REG.12
          ST     13,SAVEAREA+4
          LA     13,SAVEAREA
          OPEN   (INFILE,INPUT,OUTFILE,OUTPUT)        ACCESS THE FILES
CLEAR     MVC    OUTAREA,SPACES                    CLEAR THE PRINT AREA
          GET    INFILE,RECORD          READ A CARD AND STORE IN RECORD
          MVC    LNAME,LAST
          MVC    SALOUT,SALARY
          PUT    OUTFILE,OUTAREA        PRINT A LINE FROM OUTAREA
          B      CLEAR                  GO BACK TO PROCESS NEXT RECORD
EOF       CLOSE  (INFILE,,OUTFILE)      RELEASE FILES
          L      13,SAVEAREA+4
          LM     14,12,12(13)
          BR     14
SAVEAREA  DS     18F
*                                       CHARACTERISTICS OF INFILE
INFILE    DCB    DDNAME=INFILE,                                           *
                 MACRF=GM,                                               *
                 BLKSIZE=80,                                             *
                 LRECL=80,                                               *
                 DSORG=PS,                                               *
                 EODAD=EOF
*                                       CHARACTERISTICS OF OUTFILE
OUTFILE   DCB    DDNAME=OUTFILE,                                         *
                 MACRF=PM,                                              *
                 BLKSIZE=132,                                           *
                 LRECL=132,                                             *
                 DSORG=PS
RECORD    DS     OCL80                  SET UP CARD AREA & SUBDIVIDE
LAST      DS     CL15                        INTO LAST NAME
SALARY    DS     CL5                         AND SALARY
          DS     CL60                        FIELDS
SPACES    DC     CL1' '                 BLANK FOR CLEARING PRINT AREA
OUTAREA   DS     OCL132                 SET UP PRINT AREA & SUBDIVIDE
LNAME     DS     CL15                        INTO LAST NAME
          DS     CL20                        AND
SALOUT    DS     CL5                         SALARY
          DS     CL92                        FIELDS
          END
```

Figure 4-2

Analysis of the Instructions

> NOTE: These instructions will be considered standard for our pro-
> grams throughout the text. Most of them are required for
> proper assembly and execution. Because of their seeming com-
> plexity, they will be treated as *precoded* entries. The following
> explanation has been included for reference only.

I. Housekeeping Instructions

The instructions shown in the boxed areas in Figure 4-3 are *standard* for every
OS program. They are necessary for efficient assembly and execution. We will
refer to these instructions as "housekeeping" instructions since, although they
are not part of the program logic, they still must be routinely included in each
program.

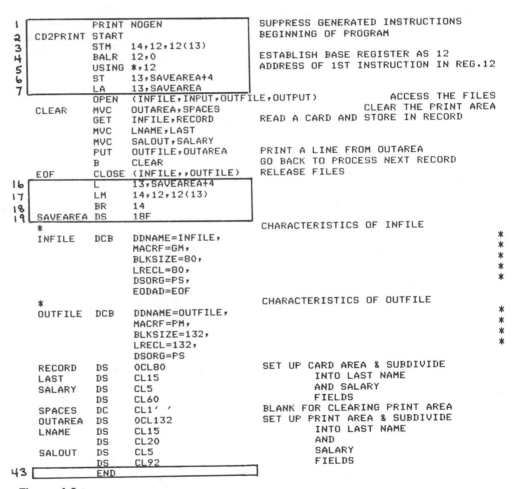

```
 1              PRINT  NOGEN                              SUPPRESS GENERATED INSTRUCTIONS
 2    CD2PRINT  START                                    BEGINNING OF PROGRAM
 3              STM    14,12,12(13)
 4              BALR   12,0                               ESTABLISH BASE REGISTER AS 12
 5              USING  *,12                               ADDRESS OF 1ST INSTRUCTION IN REG.12
 6              ST     13,SAVEAREA+4
 7              LA     13,SAVEAREA
              OPEN   (INFILE,INPUT,OUTFILE,OUTPUT)              ACCESS THE FILES
      CLEAR   MVC    OUTAREA,SPACES                             CLEAR THE PRINT AREA
              GET    INFILE,RECORD               READ A CARD AND STORE IN RECORD
              MVC    LNAME,LAST
              MVC    SALOUT,SALARY
              PUT    OUTFILE,OUTAREA             PRINT A LINE FROM OUTAREA
              B      CLEAR                       GO BACK TO PROCESS NEXT RECORD
      EOF     CLOSE  (INFILE,,OUTFILE)           RELEASE FILES
16            L      13,SAVEAREA+4
17            LM     14,12,12(13)
18            BR     14
19    SAVEAREA DS    18F
      *                                          CHARACTERISTICS OF INFILE
      INFILE  DCB    DDNAME=INFILE,                                              *
                     MACRF=GM,                                                   *
                     BLKSIZE=80,                                                 *
                     LRECL=80,                                                   *
                     DSORG=PS,                                                   *
                     EODAD=EOF
      *                                          CHARACTERISTICS OF OUTFILE
      OUTFILE DCB    DDNAME=OUTFILE,                                             *
                     MACRF=PM,                                                   *
                     BLKSIZE=132,                                                *
                     LRECL=132,                                                  *
                     DSORG=PS
      RECORD  DS     0CL80                       SET UP CARD AREA & SUBDIVIDE
      LAST    DS     CL15                                INTO LAST NAME
      SALARY  DS     CL5                                 AND SALARY
              DS     CL60                                FIELDS
      SPACES  DC     CL1' '                      BLANK FOR CLEARING PRINT AREA
      OUTAREA DS     0CL132                      SET UP PRINT AREA & SUBDIVIDE
      LNAME   DS     CL15                                INTO LAST NAME
              DS     CL20                                AND
      SALOUT  DS     CL5                                 SALARY
              DS     CL92                                FIELDS
43            END
```

Figure 4-3

Line	Instruction	Explanation
1	PRINT NOGEN	INSTRUCTION MEANING: Suppresses the printing of all in-structions generated for each macro. This simplifies the appearance of the listing and the debugging process. REFERENCE: See Chapter 10.

Line	Instruction	Explanation
2	CD2PRINT START	TERMS: CD2PRINT—Name of program. INSTRUCTION MEANING: Tells computer where program called CD2PRINT starts. REFERENCE: See Chapter 18.
3, 6, 7, 19	STM 14,12,12(13) • • ST 13,SAVEAREA+4 LA 13,SAVEAREA • • • SAVEAREA DS 18F	TERMS: STM—Store Multiple ST—Store LA—Load Address DS—Define Storage INSTRUCTION MEANING: These four instructions save addresses stored in registers so that processing can continue after a system interrupt occurs. REFERENCE: See Appendix D.
4, 5	BALR 12,0 USING *,12	TERMS: BALR—Branch and Link Register INSTRUCTION MEANING: The BALR instruction establishes register 12 as the *base register*. The USING instruction tells the computer that the address of the first instruction in the program will be found in register 12. REFERENCE: See Chapter 18 and Appendix F.
16, 17, 18	L 13,SAVEAREA+4 LM 14,12,12(13) BR 14	TERMS: L—Load LM—Load Multiple BR—Branch to register INSTRUCTION MEANING: These three instructions are necessary to return control to the operating system after the program has been run. This is similar to a STOP RUN instruction. REFERENCE: See Chapters 11, 12, 18, and Appendix D.
43	END	INSTRUCTION MEANING: This must be the last instruction in the program. It terminates the assembly process. (It tells the assembler where the end of the program is located.)[1] REFERENCE: See Chapter 10.

[1] By examining Figure 4-3, you can see that we have adopted the convention of placing file descriptions (DCB's) as well as record and field descriptions (DS's) at the *end* of the program. If we were to locate these entries at the beginning of the program, we would have to add an operand to the END statement. This operand would consist of the label of the first *executable* instruction. In Figure 4.3, that instruction would be the STM.

II. The Access and I/O Macros

The instructions shown in the boxed areas in Figure 4-4 are typical access and I/O macros to provide input and output operations. Here, again, you will need to include them, as illustrated, in your programs. The explanation that follows is for your information only.

```
          PRINT NOGEN              SUPPRESS GENERATED INSTRUCTIONS
CD2PRINT START                     BEGINNING OF PROGRAM
          STM   14,12,12(13)
          BALR  12,0               ESTABLISH BASE REGISTER AS 12
          USING *,12               ADDRESS OF 1ST INSTRUCTION IN REG.12
```

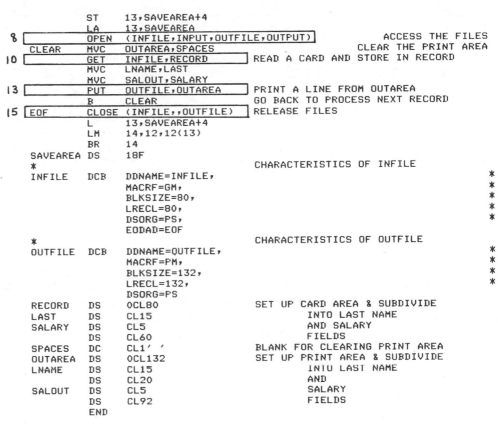

```
                  ST     13,SAVEAREA+4
                  LA     13,SAVEAREA
     8            OPEN   (INFILE,INPUT,OUTFILE,OUTPUT)        ACCESS THE FILES
          CLEAR   MVC    OUTAREA,SPACES              CLEAR THE PRINT AREA
    10            GET    INFILE,RECORD        READ A CARD AND STORE IN RECORD
                  MVC    LNAME,LAST
                  MVC    SALOUT,SALARY
    13            PUT    OUTFILE,OUTAREA      PRINT A LINE FROM OUTAREA
                  B      CLEAR                GO BACK TO PROCESS NEXT RECORD
    15   EOF      CLOSE  (INFILE,,OUTFILE)    RELEASE FILES
                  L      13,SAVEAREA+4
                  LM     14,12,12(13)
                  BR     14
          SAVEAREA DS    18F
          *                          CHARACTERISTICS OF INFILE
          INFILE  DCB    DDNAME=INFILE,                                    *
                         MACRF=GM,                                         *
                         BLKSIZE=80,                                       *
                         LRECL=80,                                         *
                         DSORG=PS,                                         *
                         EODAD=EOF
          *                          CHARACTERISTICS OF OUTFILE
          OUTFILE DCB    DDNAME=OUTFILE,                                   *
                         MACRF=PM,                                         *
                         BLKSIZE=132,                                      *
                         LRECL=132,                                        *
                         DSORG=PS
          RECORD  DS     0CL80               SET UP CARD AREA & SUBDIVIDE
          LAST    DS     CL15                     INTO LAST NAME
          SALARY  DS     CL5                      AND SALARY
                  DS     CL60                     FIELDS
          SPACES  DC     CL1' '        BLANK FOR CLEARING PRINT AREA
          OUTAREA DS     0CL132        SET UP PRINT AREA & SUBDIVIDE
          LNAME   DS     CL15                   INTO LAST NAME
                  DS     CL20                   AND
          SALOUT  DS     CL5                    SALARY
                  DS     CL92                   FIELDS
                  END
```

Figure 4-4

Line	Instruction	Explanation
8	OPEN (INFILE,INPUT,OUTFILE,OUTPUT)	TERMS: INFILE—Name assigned by programmer to the card file. INPUT—Designates INFILE as an input file. OUTFILE—Name assigned by programmer to the print file. OUTPUT—Designates OUTFILE as an output file. INSTRUCTION MEANING: Accesses the I/O devices associated with the files named. When a computer accesses a device, it determines if the I/O unit is ready to be used. If not, execution is suspended. In addition, certain checking functions regarding header labels are performed when a tape or disk device is accessed.
10	GET INFILE,RECORD	TERMS: INFILE—name assigned to the card file. RECORD—area in storage where card data is temporarily stored. INSTRUCTION MEANING: This macro instructs the computer to read in or GET one physical record from INFILE and store it in the storage area called RECORD.
13	PUT OUTFILE,OUTAREA	TERMS: OUTFILE—Name assigned to the print file. OUTAREA—Area in storage from which a line will be printed. INSTRUCTION MEANING: This macro instructs the computer to transmit the information from the storage area OUTAREA to the output device associated with OUTFILE, in this case, the printer. Thus, one line will be printed.

Line	Instruction	Explanation
15	EOF CLOSE (INFILE,,OUTFILE)	TERMS: EOF—Label of instruction (abbreviation for end of file). INFILE—Name of the card file. OUTFILE—Name of the print file. INSTRUCTION MEANING: When the end-of-data condition is reached for the input file INFILE, the computer automatically branches to this instruction, as discussed below. The CLOSE macro closes or releases the files named.

III. File, Record, and Field Descriptions

The computer must be supplied with detailed descriptions as to the characteristics of each file being used and the layouts of the I/O records. These details are essential so that when the access and I/O macros discussed above (OPEN, GET, PUT, CLOSE) are executed, the computer knows the devices to be used and the precise format of the data being read in or printed out. The instructions shown in the boxed areas in Figure 4-5 illustrate the file, record, and field definitions used in this program.

```
               PRINT NOGEN               SUPPRESS GENERATED INSTRUCTIONS
      CD2PRINT START
               STM   14,12,12(13)
               BALR  12,0                ESTABLISH BASE REGISTER AS 12
               USING *,12                ADDRESS OF 1ST INSTRUCTION IN REG.12
               ST    13,SAVEAREA+4
               LA    13,SAVEAREA
               OPEN  (INFILE,INPUT,OUTFILE,OUTPUT)         ACCESS THE FILES
      CLEAR    MVC   OUTAREA,SPACES                 CLEAR THE PRINT AREA
               GET   INFILE,RECORD       READ A CARD AND STORE IN RECORD
               MVC   LNAME,LAST
               MVC   SALOUT,SALARY
               PUT   OUTFILE,OUTAREA     PRINT A LINE FROM OUTAREA
               B     CLEAR               GO BACK TO PROCESS NEXT RECORD
      EOF      CLOSE (INFILE,,OUTFILE)   RELEASE FILES
               L     13,SAVEAREA+4
               LM    14,12,12(13)
               BR    14
      SAVEAREA DS    18F
               *                         CHARACTERISTICS OF INFILE
   21 INFILE   DCB   DDNAME=INFILE,                                         *
   22                MACRF=GM,                                             *
   23                BLKSIZE=80,                                           *
   24                LRECL=80,                                             *
   25                DSORG=PS,                                             *
   26                EODAD=EOF
               *                         CHARACTERISTICS OF OUTFILE
   28 OUTFILE  DCB   DDNAME=OUTFILE,                                        *
   29                MACRF=PM,                                             *
   30                BLKSIZE=132,                                          *
   31                LRECL=132,                                            *
   32                DSORG=PS
   33 RECORD   DS    0CL80               SET UP CARD AREA & SUBDIVIDE
   34 LAST     DS    CL15                        INTO LAST NAME
   35 SALARY   DS    CL5                         AND SALARY
   36          DS    CL60                        FIELDS
   37 SPACES   DC    CL1' '              BLANK FOR CLEARING PRINT AREA
   38 OUTAREA  DS    0CL132              SET UP PRINT AREA & SUBDIVIDE
   39 LNAME    DS    CL15                        INTO LAST NAME
   40          DS    CL20                        AND
   41 SALOUT   DS    CL5                         SALARY
   42          DS    CL92                        FIELDS
               END
```

Figure 4-5

Line	Instruction	Explanation

21–26	`INFILE   DCB   DDNAME=INFILE,`
	`MACRF=GM,`
	`BLKSIZE=80,`
	`LRECL=80,`
	`DSORG=PS,`
	`EODAD=EOF`
		TERMS: DCB = Data Control Block
		DDNAME = Data Definition Name
		MACRF = Macro Form
		BLKSIZE = Block Size
		LRECL = Logical Record Length
		DSORG = Data Set Organization
		EODAD = End-of-Data Address
		(These entries may appear in any order.)
		INSTRUCTION MEANING: The DCB macro describes the characteristcs of the file INFILE as follows:
		
		1. The DDNAME specifies the symbolic names that will be used in a JCL (*Job Control Language*) statement to assign an actual I/O device to the file named INFILE.
		2. The MACRF operand indicates that a GET (G) macro will be used to read in records from the file. The "M" indicates that the data is to be moved (M) to the area specified in the GET macro, which in this program is RECORD.
		3. The BLKSIZE operand tells the computer that each *physical* record contains 80 bytes.
		4. LRECL operand specifies that each *logical* record contains 80 bytes.
		5. The DSORG operand indicates that the records are in physical sequential (PS) order, since we are dealing with a card file.
		6. The EODAD operand instructs the computer to branch to the instruction labeled EOF when there is no more input data so that the end-of-job routine can be performed.
		
		These entries may be coded as individual items on separate lines (with a character in column 72) or in paragraph form, across the page.

28–32	`OUTFILE  DCB   DDNAME=OUTFILE,`
	`MACRF=PM,`
	`BLKSIZE=132,`
	`LRECL=132,`
	`DSORG=PS`
		TERMS: DDNAME—Data Definition Name
		MACRF—Macro Form
		BLKSIZE—Block Size
		LRECL—Logical Record Length
		DSORG—Data Set Organization
		(These entries may appear in any sequence.)
		INSTRUCTION MEANING: This DCB macro describes the characteristics of the file OUTFILE. The operands have the same meaning as those discussed above for the INFILE DCB. Notice the following, however:
		1. The MACRF operand indicates that a PUT (P) macro will be used to write out or transmit information from storage to the output device associated with OUTFILE. The "M" indicates that the data is to be moved (M) from the area specified in the PUT macro. In this program, that area is called OUTAREA.
		2. We are using a printer with 132 print positions per line, as indicated by the BLKSIZE and LRECL operands.
		3. The DSORG operand specifies that the output will be physical sequential (PS), since we are dealing with a printer.
		4. Notice that there is no EODAD entry, since we only test for the end-of-data condition on an *input* file.
		
		These entries may be coded as individual items on separate lines (with a character in column 72) or in paragraph form across the page.

Line	Instruction	Explanation
33–36	RECORD DS OCL80 LAST DS CL15 SALARY DS CL5 DS CL60	TERMS: DS—Define Storage CL—Character Length RECORD—name of input area The DS's and DC's are coded after the end of job routines. INSTRUCTION MEANING: The first DS instruction defines the storage area RECORD that will be used to store one input record. The first zero in OCL80 specifies that the area, which will hold 80 bytes of data or 80 characters, will be subdivided into the fields defined by the following DS instructions. Thus, RECORD is subdivided into three fields: LAST (for last name), consisting of 15 bytes; SALARY, consisting of 5 bytes; and, an unlabeled area of 60 bytes to complete the description of an 80-byte card. REFERENCE: See Chapter 3.
38–42	OUTAREA DS OCL132 LNAME DS CL15 DS CL20 SALOUT DS CL5 DS CL92	TERMS: DS—Define Storage CL—Character Length OUTAREA—name of output area INSTRUCTION MEANING: The first DS instruction defines the storage area OUTAREA that will be used to accumulate the information to be printed on each line. The zero in front of CL132 indicates that this area will be subdivided into the fields specified by the following DS instructions. Thus, for example, the first field in OUTAREA will be the field LNAME (for last name), consisting of 15 bytes. The next field has no name but is defined as 20 bytes long. This area will provide for spacing between the first field printed out, LNAME, and the next field SALOUT (for salary out). Notice that the last DS (unlabeled) is 92 bytes long so that all the fields will add up to the 132 positions in OUTAREA. REFERENCE: See Chapter 3.
37	SPACES DC CL1' '	TERMS: DC—Define Constant C—Character L1—Length of 1 byte SPACES—name of constant INSTRUCTION MEANING: This constant, consisting of a one-position blank, is located *immediately before* the output area OUTAREA, and will be used to clear that area, as discussed below. REFERENCE: See Chapter 3.

IV. Logic Instructions

Thus far, we have discussed housekeeping instructions, access and I/O macros, and file, record, and field descriptions. Although record and field descriptions will vary from one program to another, the other items are basically standard. Note that the illustrated program prints information from input cards. To utilize different I/O media, only slight modifications would be required.[2]

We will now discuss the logic instructions in this program that are shown in the boxed area in Figure 4-6. This is the key part of the program. It includes instructions that will vary, depending on the specific program logic.

[2] This text concentrates on programs that use card input and printed output. Consult the reference manual for your computer system for the minor changes required for other I/O media.

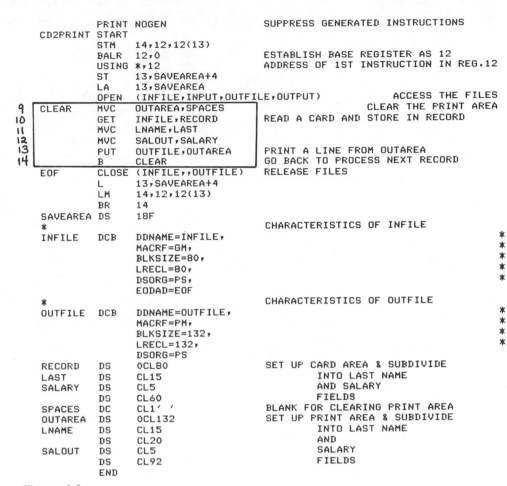

```
                    PRINT  NOGEN                      SUPPRESS GENERATED INSTRUCTIONS
            CD2PRINT START
                    STM   14,12,12(13)
                    BALR  12,0                        ESTABLISH BASE REGISTER AS 12
                    USING *,12                        ADDRESS OF 1ST INSTRUCTION IN REG.12
                    ST    13,SAVEAREA+4
                    LA    13,SAVEAREA
                    OPEN  (INFILE,INPUT,OUTFILE,OUTPUT)          ACCESS THE FILES
      9     CLEAR   MVC   OUTAREA,SPACES                         CLEAR THE PRINT AREA
     10             GET   INFILE,RECORD               READ A CARD AND STORE IN RECORD
     11             MVC   LNAME,LAST
     12             MVC   SALOUT,SALARY
     13             PUT   OUTFILE,OUTAREA             PRINT A LINE FROM OUTAREA
     14             B     CLEAR                       GO BACK TO PROCESS NEXT RECORD
            EOF     CLOSE (INFILE,,OUTFILE)           RELEASE FILES
                    L     13,SAVEAREA+4
                    LM    14,12,12(13)
                    BR    14
            SAVEAREA DS   18F
            *                                         CHARACTERISTICS OF INFILE
            INFILE  DCB   DDNAME=INFILE,                                              *
                          MACRF=GM,                                                  *
                          BLKSIZE=80,                                                *
                          LRECL=80,                                                  *
                          DSORG=PS,                                                  *
                          EODAD=EOF
            *                                         CHARACTERISTICS OF OUTFILE
            OUTFILE DCB   DDNAME=OUTFILE,                                            *
                          MACRF=PM,                                                  *
                          BLKSIZE=132,                                               *
                          LRECL=132,                                                 *
                          DSORG=PS
            RECORD  DS    0CL80                       SET UP CARD AREA & SUBDIVIDE
            LAST    DS    CL15                              INTO LAST NAME
            SALARY  DS    CL5                               AND SALARY
                    DS    CL60                              FIELDS
            SPACES  DC    CL1' '                      BLANK FOR CLEARING PRINT AREA
            OUTAREA DS    0CL132                      SET UP PRINT AREA & SUBDIVIDE
            LNAME   DS    CL15                              INTO LAST NAME
                    DS    CL20                              AND
            SALOUT  DS    CL5                               SALARY
                    DS    CL92                              FIELDS
                    END
```

Figure 4-6

Line	Instruction	Explanation
9	CLEAR MVC OUTAREA,SPACES	TERMS: CLEAR—label of instruction MVC—Move Character OUTAREA—name of output area SPACES—constant INSTRUCTION MEANING: Move the constant SPACES to OUTAREA. This will clear the area by putting blanks in all the bytes. REFERENCE: See Chapter 5.
11, 12	MVC LNAME,LAST MVC SALOUT,SALARY	TERMS: MVC—Move Character LAST—input field SALARY—input field LNAME—output field SALOUT—output field INSTRUCTION MEANING: These instructions move the input fields LAST and SALARY from the input area (RECORD) to the output fields LNAME and SALOUT in the output area (OUTAREA). REFERENCE: See Chapter 5.

Line	Instruction	Explanation
14	B CLEAR	TERMS: B—Branch CLEAR—label of instruction to branch to INSTRUCTION MEANING: Go to the instruction labeled CLEAR. In this manner, we will repeat the sequence of reading in a card and processing it. However, before we get the next card (if there is one) we want to clear the output area so that it will be ready to accumulate a new line of information to be printed out. REFERENCE: See Chapter 6.

By examining the above program, you should note that most OS programs involving card input and printed output will simply require this shell in addition to whatever logic is required between the GET and PUT macros. This shell of instructions will remain basically the same. Because of this fact, we have provided a partially completed coding sheet in Figure 4-7. It contains those instructions that will appear in *every* OS program you write that uses card input and produces printed output. We have inserted comment cards, designated by an asterisk (*) in column 1, to remind you of what needs to be inserted at specific points in the program.

LABEL	OPERATION	OPERAND	COMMENTS
	PRINT	NOGEN	
	START	[PLACE NAME OF PROGRAM IN COLS 1-8]	
	STM	14,12,12(13)	
	BALR	12,0	
	USING	*,12	
	ST	13,SAVEAREA+4	
	LA	13,SAVEAREA	
	OPEN	(INFILE,INPUT,OUTFILE,OUTPUT)	
CLEAR	MVC	OUTAREA,SPACES	
	GET	INFILE,RECORD	
** LOGIC	GOES	HERE	
**	:		
	PUT	OUTFILE,OUTAREA	
	B	CLEAR	
** INCLUDE	END	-OF-JOB ROUTINES HERE, THEN CLOSE; IF NO EOJ ROUTINE, INCL:	
EOF	CLOSE	(INFILE,OUTFILE)	
	L	13,SAVEAREA+4	
	LM	14,12,12(13)	
	BR	14	
SAVEAREA	DS	18F	
RECORD	DS	0CL80	
** PLACE	DS'S	FOR FIELDS IN INPUT RECORD HERE	
SPACES	DC	CL1' '	
OUTAREA	DS	0CL132	
** PLACE	DS'S	FOR FIELDS IN OUTPUT RECORD HERE - INCLUDING BLANK AREAS	
INFILE	DCB	DDNAME=INFILE,MACRF=GM,BLKSIZE=80,LRECL=80,DSORG=PS,	*
		EODAD=EOF	
OUTFILE	DCB	DDNAME=OUTFILE,MACRF=PM,BLKSIZE=132,LRECL=132,DSORG=PS	
	END		

Figure 4-7

B. DOS Sample Program

Now that we have examined an OS program, we will look at a sample DOS program. You will see that the instructions are very similar to those used under OS. While the housekeeping instructions and file descriptions will require some modification, the I/O macros, logic instructions, and record and field descriptions will be *identical*. The access macros will simply require a different format. Thus, if you have followed the discussion of a sample OS program, you should have little difficulty in understanding the sample DOS program in Figure 4-8. For the sake of comparison, this program accomplishes the same tasks as the OS program discussed earlier in this chapter.

```
          PRINT NOGEN                      SUPPRESS GENERATED INSTRUCTIONS
CD2PRINT  START                            BEGINNING OF PROGRAM
          BALR  12,0                       ESTABLISH REG 12 AS BASE REGISTER
          USING *,12                       ADDRESS OF 1ST INSTRUCTION IN REG 12
          OPEN  INFILE,OUTFILE             ACCESS THE FILES
CLEAR     MVC   OUTAREA,SPACES             CLEAR THE PRINT AREA
          GET   INFILE,RECORD              READ A CARD AND STORE IN RECORD
          MVC   LNAME,LAST
          MVC   SALOUT,SALARY
          PUT   OUTFILE,OUTAREA            PRINT A LINE FROM OUTAREA
          B     CLEAR                      GO BACK TO PROCESS NEXT RECORD
EOF       CLOSE INFILE,OUTFILE             RELEASE FILES
          EOJ                              STOP THE PROGRAM
*                                          CHARACTERISTICS OF INFILE
INFILE    DTFCD DEVADDR=SYSIPT,                                             *
                BLKSIZE=80,                                                 *
                IOAREA1=BUFFRIN,                                           *
                WORKA=YES,                                                 *
                DEVICE=2540,                                               *
                TYPEFLE=INPUT,                                             *
                EOFADDR=EOF
*                                          CHARACTERISTICS OF OUTFILE
OUTFILE   DTFPR DEVADDR=SYSLST,                                            *
                BLKSIZE=132,                                               *
                IOAREA1=BUFFROUT,                                          *
                WORKA=YES,                                                 *
                DEVICE=1403
BUFFRIN   DS    CL80
BUFFROUT  DS    CL132
RECORD    DS    0CL80                      SET UP CARD AREA & SUBDIVIDE
LAST      DS    CL15                       INTO LAST NAME
SALARY    DS    CL5                        AND SALARY
          DS    CL60
SPACES    DC    CL1' '                     BLANK FOR CLEARING PRINT AREA
OUTAREA   DS    0CL132                     SET UP PRINT AREA & SUBDIVIDE
LNAME     DS    CL15                       INTO LAST NAME
          DS    CL20
SALOUT    DS    CL5                        SALARY FIELD
          DS    CL92
          END
```

Figure 4-8

I. Housekeeping Instructions

The housekeeping instructions, or those instructions that will appear in every DOS program for proper assembly and execution, are shown in the boxed areas in Figure 4-9.

You will notice that all of these housekeeping instructions were used in the sample OS program except for the EOJ macro. The purpose of the EOJ macro is simply to indicate to the computer that the program has been executed and that control can be returned to the operating system.

```
              PRINT  NOGEN              SUPPRESS GENERATED INSTRUCTIONS
CD2PRINT  START                         BEGINNING OF PROGRAM
              BALR   12,0               ESTABLISH REG 12 AS BASE REGISTER
              USING  *,12               ADDRESS OF 1ST INSTRUCTION IN REG 12
              OPEN   INFILE,OUTFILE     ACCESS THE FILES
CLEAR         MVC    OUTAREA,SPACES     CLEAR THE PRINT AREA
              GET    INFILE,RECORD      READ A CARD AND STORE IN RECORD
              MVC    LNAME,LAST
              MVC    SALOUT,SALARY
              PUT    OUTFILE,OUTAREA    PRINT A LINE FROM OUTAREA
              B      CLEAR              GO BACK TO PROCESS NEXT RECORD
EOF           CLOSE  INFILE,OUTFILE     RELEASE FILES
              EOJ                       STOP THE PROGRAM
*                                       CHARACTERISTICS OF INFILE
INFILE    DTFCD  DEVADDR=SYSIPT,
                 BLKSIZE=80,                                              *
                 IOAREA1=BUFFRIN,                                        *
                 WORKA=YES,                                              *
                 DEVICE=2540,                                            *
                 TYPEFLE=INPUT,                                          *
                 EOFADDR=EOF                                             *
*                                       CHARACTERISTICS OF OUTFILE
OUTFILE   DTFPR  DEVADDR=SYSLST,
                 BLKSIZE=132,                                            *
                 IOAREA1=BUFFROUT,                                       *
                 WORKA=YES,                                              *
                 DEVICE=1403                                            *
BUFFRIN   DS     CL80
BUFFROUT  DS     CL132
RECORD    DS     0CL80               SET UP CARD AREA & SUBDIVIDE
LAST      DS     CL15                INTO LAST NAME
SALARY    DS     CL5                 AND SALARY
          DS     CL60
SPACES    DC     CL1' '              BLANK FOR CLEARING PRINT AREA
OUTAREA   DS     0CL132              SET UP PRINT AREA & SUBDIVIDE
LNAME     DS     CL15                INTO LAST NAME
          DS     CL20
SALOUT    DS     CL5                 SALARY FIELD
          DS     CL92
          END
```

Figure 4-9

II. Access and I/O Macros

The access and I/O macros for this program are shown in the boxed areas in Figure 4-10.

Notice that the I/O macros (GET and PUT) are identical to those used in the OS program. Notice, also, that while the OPEN and CLOSE macros serve the same purpose as under OS, their formats are slightly different under DOS. In DOS, the names of the files to be opened or closed are simply listed, *without* the use of parentheses. In addition, the OPEN macro does *not* include a designation as to whether a particular file is input or output. We will see below how this problem is handled in the file description.

III. File, Record, and Field Descriptions

The instructions that define the characteristics of the files, records, and fields are shown in the boxed areas in Figure 4-11.[3]

Notice that the descriptions of the input and output areas, RECORD and OUTAREA, are identical to those used in the OS program.

[3] Some computer systems do not have available in their relocatable libraries certain IOCS (Input/Output Control System) routines. If you receive an error message when executing your program that indicates an *unresolved external reference,* see Appendix E for the required additions to your program.

```
            PRINT NOGEN                        SUPPRESS GENERATED INSTRUCTIONS
CD2PRINT START                                 BEGINNING OF PROGRAM
            BALR  12,0                         ESTABLISH REG 12 AS BASE REGISTER
            USING *,12                         ADDRESS OF 1ST ,INSTRUCTION IN REG 12
            OPEN  INFILE,OUTFILE               ACCESS THE FILES
CLEAR       MVC   OUTAREA,SPACES               CLEAR THE PRINT AREA
            GET   INFILE,RECORD                READ A CARD AND STORE IN RECORD
            MVC   LNAME,LAST
            MVC   SALOUT,SALARY
            PUT   OUTFILE,OUTAREA              PRINT A LINE FROM OUTAREA
            B     CLEAR                        GO BACK TO PROCESS NEXT RECORD
EOF         CLOSE INFILE,OUTFILE              RELEASE FILES
            EOJ                                STOP THE PROGRAM
*                                              CHARACTERISTICS OF INFILE
INFILE   DTFCD DEVADDR=SYSIPT,                                              *
            BLKSIZE=80,                                                     *
            IOAREA1=BUFFRIN,                                                *
            WORKA=YES,                                                      *
            DEVICE=2540,  ·                                                 *
            TYPEFLE=INPUT,                                                  *
            EOFADDR=EOF
*                                              CHARACTERISTICS OF OUTFILE
OUTFILE  DTFPR DEVADDR=SYSLST,                                             *
            BLKSIZE=132,                                                    *
            IOAREA1=BUFFROUT,                                               *
            WORKA=YES,                                                      *
            DEVICE=1403
BUFFRIN  DS    CL80
BUFFROUT DS    CL132
RECORD   DS    OCL80                           SET UP CARD AREA & SUBDIVIDE
LAST     DS    CL15                            INTO LAST NAME
SALARY   DS    CL5                             AND SALARY
         DS    CL60
SPACES   DC    CL1' '                          BLANK FOR CLEARING PRINT AREA
OUTAREA  DS    OCL132                          SET UP PRINT AREA & SUBDIVIDE
LNAME    DS    CL15                            INTO LAST NAME
         DS    CL20
SALOUT   DS    CL5                             SALARY FIELD
         DS    CL92
         END
```

Figure 4-10

```
            PRINT NOGEN                        SUPPRESS GENERATED INSTRUCTIONS
CD2PRINT START                                 BEGINNING OF PROGRAM
            BALR  12,0                         ESTABLISH REG 12 AS BASE REGISTER
            USING *,12                         ADDRESS OF 1ST INSTRUCTION IN REG 12
            OPEN  INFILE,OUTFILE               ACCESS THE FILES
CLEAR       MVC   OUTAREA,SPACES               CLEAR THE PRINT AREA
            GET   INFILE,RECORD                READ A CARD AND STORE IN RECORD
            MVC   LNAME,LAST
            MVC   SALOUT,SALARY
            PUT   OUTFILE,OUTAREA              PRINT A LINE FROM OUTAREA
            B     CLEAR                        GO BACK TO PROCESS NEXT RECORD
EOF         CLOSE INFILE,OUTFILE              RELEASE FILES
            EOJ                                STOP THE PROGRAM
*                                              CHARACTERISTICS OF INFILE
15  INFILE   DTFCD DEVADDR=SYSIPT,                                          *
16             BLKSIZE=80,                                                  *
17             IOAREA1=BUFFRIN,                                             *
18             WORKA=YES,                                                   *
19             DEVICE=2540,                                                 *
20             TYPEFLE=INPUT,                                               *
21             EOFADDR=EOF
    *                                          CHARACTERISTICS OF OUTFILE
23  OUTFILE  DTFPR DEVADDR=SYSLST,                                          *
24             BLKSIZE=132,                                                 *
25             IOAREA1=BUFFROUT,                                            *
26             WORKA=YES,                                                   *
27             DEVICE=1403
28  BUFFRIN  DS    CL80
29  BUFFROUT DS    CL132
30  RECORD   DS    OCL80                       SET UP CARD AREA & SUBDIVIDE
    LAST     DS    CL15                         INTO LAST NAME
    SALARY   DS    CL5                          AND SALARY
             DS    CL60
    SPACES   DC    CL1' '                       BLANK FOR CLEARING PRINT AREA
    OUTAREA  DS    OCL132                       SET UP PRINT AREA & SUBDIVIDE
    LNAME    DS    CL15                         INTO LAST NAME
             DS    CL20
    SALOUT   DS    CL5                          SALARY FIELD
             DS    CL92
         END
```

Figure 4-11

Line	Instruction	Explanation
15–21	INFILE DTFCD DEVADDR=SYSIPT, BLKSIZE=80, IOAREA1=BUFFRIN, WORKA=YES, DEVICE=2540, TYPEFLE=INPUT, EOFADDR=EOF	TERMS: INFILE—name of card file DTFCD—Define the File on Card Reader/Punch DEVADDR—Device Address BLKSIZE—Block Size IOAREA1—name of input buffer WORKA—Work Area TYPEFLE—Type of File EOFADDR—End-of-File Address (These entries can appear in any order.) INSTRUCTION MEANING: This DTF macro describes the characteristics of the input file called INFILE: 1. The symbolic unit name of the input device to be used is SYSIPT, which is short for *system input* and which is the name for the card reader for most systems. 2. The operand BLKSIZE specifies that each input record will contain 80 bytes. 3. The IOAREA1 operand specifies that we want one *buffer* (or I/O area) to be used with this file. We have arbitrarily called the buffer BUFFRIN (for buffer in), which must be defined by a DS instruction as 80 bytes long. 4. The WORKA operand indicates that we want a work area in storage. This will increase the efficiency of handling input records. 5. The file will be on the IBM 2540 card reader, as specified by the DEVICE operand. 6. The TYPEFLE operand designates this card file as an input one. We could also have a card file as output, which occurs when the computer produces punched cards. 7. The EOFADDR operand indicates the instruction to be branched to when the end-of-file condition is reached. EOF, then, is the label of the end-of-file routine. These entries may appear as individual items on separate lines (with a character in column 72) or in paragraph form across the page.
23–27	OUTFILE DTFPR DEVADDR=SYSLST, BLKSIZE=132, IOAREA1=BUFFROUT, WORKA=YES, DEVICE=1403	TERMS: OUTFILE—name of the print file DTFPR—Define the File on the Printer DEVADDR—Device Address BLKSIZE—Block Size IOAREA1—name of the output buffer WORKA—Work Area (These entries may appear in any sequence.) INSTRUCTION MEANING: This DTF macro describes the characteristics of the output file OUTFILE as follows: 1. The symbolic unit name of the output device to be used is SYSLST, which is short for *system list*. This is a symbolic name for the "printer" on most systems. 2. The operand BLKSIZE specifies that each output record will contain 132 bytes, since we are using a printer with 132 print positions per line. 3. The IOAREA1 operand specifies that we want one buffer (or I/O area) to be used with this file. We have arbitrarily called the buffer BUFFROUT (for buffer out), which must be defined by a DS instruction as 132 bytes long. 4. The WORKA operand indicates that we want a work area in storage to increase the efficiency of handling output records. 5. The DEVICE associated with this file is the IBM 1403 printer. These entries may appear as individual items on separate lines (with a character in column 72) or they may appear in paragraph form across the page.

Line	Instruction	Explanation
28	BUFFRIN DS CL80	TERMS: DS—Define Storage C—Character L80—Length 80 INSTRUCTION MEANING: This instruction sets up an area in storage 80 bytes long that will serve as the *input* buffer. REFERENCE: See Chapter 3.
29	BUFFROUT DS CL132	TERMS: DS—Define Storage C—Character L132—Length 132 INSTRUCTION MEANING: This instruction sets up an area in storage 132 bytes long that will serve as the *output* buffer. REFERENCE: See Chapter 3.

IV. Logic Instructions

You will notice in Figure 4-11 that the logic instructions from the OPEN macro through the CLOSE macro are *identical* to those used in the OS program.

We have thus seen that a program written to be run under OS contains virtually the same instructions used under DOS. Essentially, it is the housekeeping instructions and file descriptions (DTF's or DCB's) that will vary slightly. For your convenience, Figure 4-12 shows a coding sheet with the "shell" or basic instructions that will be included in every DOS program you will write. It will then be an easy matter for you simply to copy these instructions every time you write a program and then add the specific logic that is necessary.

LABEL	OPERATION	OPERAND / COMMENTS
	PRINT	NOGEN
	START	[PLACE NAME OF PROGRAM IN COLS. 1-8.]
	BALR	12,0
	USING	*,12
	OPEN	INFILE,OUTFILE
CLEAR	MVC	OUTAREA,SPACES
	GET	INFILE,RECORD
** LOGIC	GOES	HERE
**	:	
	PUT	OUTFILE,OUTAREA
	B	CLEAR
** INCLUDE END	OF JOB ROUTINES HERE, THEN CLOSE—IF NO EOJ ROUTINE INCL:	
EOF	CLOSE	INFILE,OUTFILE
	EOJ	
INFILE	DTFCD	DEVADDR=SYSIPT,BLKSIZE=80,IOAREA1=BUFFRIN,WORKA=YES,
		DEVICE=2540,TYPEFLE=INPUT,EOFADDR=EOF
OUTFILE	DTFPR	DEVADDR=SYSLST,BLKSIZE=132,IOAREA1=BUFFROUT,WORKA=YES,
		DEVICE=1403
BUFFRIN	DS	CL80
BUFFROUT	DS	CL132
RECORD	DS	0CL80
** PLACE	DS'S	FOR FIELDS IN INPUT RECORD HERE
SPACES	DC	CL' '
OUTAREA	DS	0CL132
** PLACE	DS'S	FOR FIELDS IN OUTPUT RECORD HERE—INCLUDING BLANK AREAS
** ALL OTHER	DS'S	AND DC'S NECESSARY FOR PROCESSING GO HERE
	END	

Figure 4-12 Shell for DOS program.

KEY TERMS
Block Size (BLKSIZE)
Branch
Buffer

Constant

Disk Operating System (DOS)

Field
File

Housekeeping instructions

I/O Macro

Job Control Language (JCL)

Label
Logical record

Macro

Operating System (OS)

Physical record

Record

SELF EVALUATING QUIZ

1. The instructions coded in this chapter are (*standard, nonstandard*).
2. A housekeeping routine is one which _____.
3. (True or False) I/O macros are different depending upon whether a program is being assembled on a DOS or OS system.
4. Indicate the meaning of the first zero (0) in the following:
   CARDIN   DS   0CL80
5. BLKSIZE for card input will always be _____ and BLKSIZE for printed output will usually be _____.
6. An EOF condition is reached when _____.
7. A PRINT NOGEN instruction will suppress the printing of the _____.
8. An assembler language instruction that generates several machine language instructions is called a _____.
9. An example of the above is any (*type*) instruction.
10. Labels are used in programs to provide _____.
11. The last instruction in every assembler language program must be _____.
12. The main purpose of the OPEN macro is to _____.
13. A _____ macro instructs the computer to read in one physical record from the file indicated and store it in a designated storage area.
14. A _____ macro instructs the computer to transmit information from a designated storage area to the appropriate output device.
15. The purpose of a DCB macro (OS) or DTF macro (DOS) is to _____.
16. (True or False) The print area typically includes unlabeled areas such as DS CL10.
17. The purpose of the instruction in Question 16 is to _____.
18. One way of clearing an output area is to _____.
19. A comment card is designated by a(n) _____ in column 1.
20. A buffer is a(n) _____.
21. Indicate what errors, if any, exist in the program in Figure 4-13.

```
*                                                                    *
*                       HOUSEKEEPING INSTRUCTIONS GO HERE            *
*                                                                    *
             OPEN    (INFILE,INPUT,OUTFILE,OUTPUT)
READ         MVC     OUTAREA,SPACES
             GET     CARDFILE,RECORD
             MVC     LNAME,LAST
             MVC     FNAME,FIRST
             MVC     SALOUT,SALARY
             PUT     OUTFILE,OUTAREA
             B       READRTN
EOF          CLOSE   (INFILE,OUTFILE)
*
RECORD       DS      0CL80
SPACES       DC      CL1' '
OUTAREA      DS      0CL132
             DS      CL5
LNAME        DS      CL15
             DS      CL20
FNAME        DS      CL10
             DS      CL20
SALOUT       DS      CL5
BLANK        DS      CL50
SAVEAREA     DS      18F
INFILE       DCB     DDNAME=INFILE,MACRF=GM,BLKSIZE=80,
                     LRECL=80,DSORG=PS,EODAD=EOF
PRTFILE      DCB     DDNAME=OUTFILE,MACRF=PM,BLKSIZE=132,LRECL=132,DSORG=PS
             END
```

Figure 4-13

Solutions
1. Standard
2. Is required for efficient assembly and execution of all programs.
3. False
4. The record will be further subdivided.
5. 80; 132
6. An end-of-file is sensed—there are no more input records.
7. Machine language equivalents of a macro.
8. Macro
9. I/O
10. Branch points
11. END
12. Determine if the required I/O units are ready to be used.
13. GET
14. PUT
15. Describe the characteristics of a particular file.
16. True
17. Provide spacing between output fields
18. Move (MVC) a constant consisting of a blank to the output area. The constant, defined as a one-position blank, must be located immediately before the output area.
19. * (asterisk)
20. I/O area
21. See Figure 4-14.

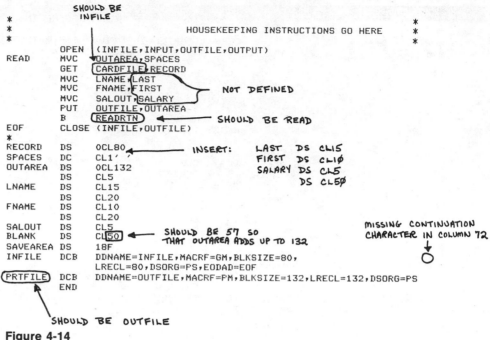

```
*                    SHOULD BE
                     INFILE
*                                      HOUSEKEEPING INSTRUCTIONS GO HERE        *
*                                                                              *
          OPEN    (INFILE,INPUT,OUTFILE,OUTPUT)
READ      MVC     OUTAREA,SPACES
          GET     CARDFILE,RECORD
          MVC     LNAME,LAST
          MVC     FNAME,FIRST              NOT DEFINED
          MVC     SALOUT,SALARY
          PUT     OUTFILE,OUTAREA
          B       READRTN           ←——  SHOULD BE READ
EOF       CLOSE   (INFILE,OUTFILE)
*
RECORD    DS      0CL80          ←——  INSERT:   LAST  DS  CL15
SPACES    DC      CL1' '                        FIRST DS  CL10
OUTAREA   DS      0CL132                        SALARY DS CL5
          DS      CL5                                  DS  CL50
LNAME     DS      CL15
          DS      CL20
FNAME     DS      CL10
          DS      CL20
SALOUT    DS      CL5
BLANK     DS      CL50    ←——  SHOULD BE 57 SO      MISSING CONTINUATION
SAVEAREA  DS      18F          THAT OUTAREA ADDS UP TO 132   CHARACTER IN COLUMN 72
INFILE    DCB     DDNAME=INFILE,MACRF=GM,BLKSIZE=80,
                  LRECL=80,DSORG=PS,EODAD=EOF
PRTFILE   DCB     DDNAME=OUTFILE,MACRF=PM,BLKSIZE=132,LRECL=132,DSORG=PS
          END
```

SHOULD BE OUTFILE

Figure 4-14

Chapter 5

Move Statements

A. Storage-to-Storage Move Instruction: MVC

1. Description   In writing programs it is frequently necessary to move data from one storage location to another. Sometimes only a single character is moved, but, most often, groups of characters called *fields*, are moved. Since the data movement occurs entirely within main storage, the instruction is classified as a *Storage-to-Storage* instruction. The move character instruction may appear as follows:

Operation 10	Operand 16
MVC	FIELD1, FIELD2

Instruction:	MVC
Meaning:	Move Characters
Operand 1:	The receiving field (FIELD1 above) refers to a storage location or address.
Operand 2:	The sending field (FIELD2 above) refers to a storage location or address.
Result:	The contents of the second operand (sending field) is duplicated at the first operand: the sending field remains unchanged.

Example 1

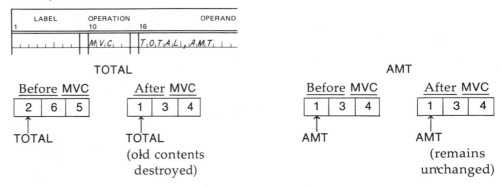

Note that although the MVC is referred to as a move instruction, this is really a misnomer. As the above example demonstrates, the operation really involves a duplication. After the instruction is executed, the contents of the sending field are the same as before the execution.

2. Applications

The MVC or move character instruction is generally used by the programmer to transmit data from an input area to an output area. It is used most often to move data in character or EBCDIC form, as opposed to data in packed or binary form. Since input and output areas usually contain data in EBCDIC form, the MVC instruction is ideally suited for data transfers of I/O fields.

The MVC instruction can also be used to move data from an input area to a work area established by a DS, where it will be processed (used in calculations, edited, and so on) and later moved to the output area.

Another common use of the move character instruction is to provide the programmer with the capability of moving page and column headings from one area of storage to the output area. After moving all the data to be printed to the output area, a PUT (output) command normally will be issued to transfer the output data to the printing device. Headings, descriptive information and end-of-job messages usually are produced in this manner.

A most important use of the move character instruction is the clearing of the output area, by filling it with spaces or blanks. This is necessary to ensure that a new line of printed data is produced on a cleared or clean line, thereby removing or erasing the characters printed in the preceding print operation. You will recall that data remains in a storage location until other data replaces it. The clearing of the output may take place at any time, but this action is usually performed immediately before each GET command by the programmer.

The following chart briefly reviews the uses of the MVC instruction.

Applications of the MVC (Move Character) Instruction

Purpose	Move data, usually in EBCDIC, between locations in storage
Use	1. Move data between I/O areas. 2. Move data to and from work areas. 3. Move headings and titles to the output area. 4. Clear the output area.

3. Rules for Storage-to-Storage Move Instructions

Consider the following example:

Example 1

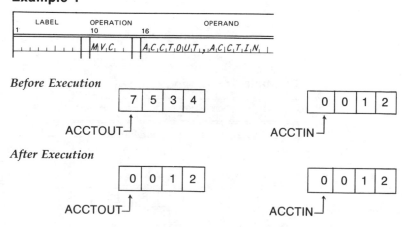

Before Execution

After Execution

The symbolic names ACCTOUT and ACCTIN, refer to the *high-order position*, or the first (leftmost) byte of the named locations. The second operand is the sending field and the first operand is the receiving field. The data in the second operand replaces the previous contents of the first operand. After execution of the instruction, the first operand contains an exact copy of the second operand. The second operand remains unchanged. Movement of the data is from left to right, from high order to low order, within each operand. Each byte of data is moved until the receiving field is filled. The Central Processing Unit (CPU) requires four steps to move the four bytes as illustrated, since one byte is moved at each step.

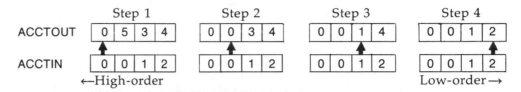

The number of bytes moved depends upon the length of the fields, which may vary from 1 to 256 bytes. The data is always moved one byte at a time from left to right. Movement continues until the number of bytes specified in the *first* operand, the receiving field, have all been filled. The CPU will assume that the second operand is the same length.

Example 2

	LABEL	OPERATION 10	16	OPERAND
1		MVC		NAMEOUT,NAMEIN

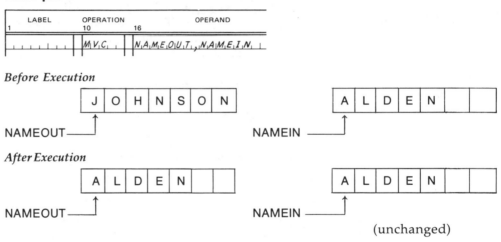

In this example, both the sending and receiving fields are seven bytes in length and, therefore, the CPU will require seven steps, one per byte, to complete the move. Note that the blanks in the two low-order positions of the sending field are treated as characters; that is, they overlay characters in the receiving field in the ordinary way.

Thus far, in the examples given, the entire sending field was transmitted to the receiving field. Hence, the MVC produced the same results at the receiving field as appeared at the sending field.

MVC on Fields of Unequal Length
Let us now consider a different case.

Example 3
Operand 1 has fewer bytes than operand 2.

	LABEL	OPERATION 10	16	OPERAND
1		MVC		NAMEOUT,NAMEIN

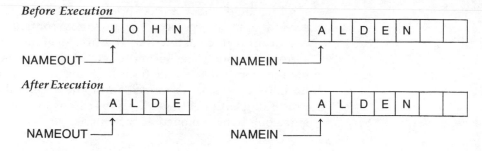

When fields of data are not the same size, the length of the move is strictly determined by the *length* of the first operand, unless otherwise specified.[1]

In the above case, the four-position NAMEOUT field caused a four-position move. Low-order characters of data in the sending field were not moved. Clearly, the programmer must make certain that the receiving field in an MVC operation is large enough to accommodate the results.

> RULE 1: Unless otherwise specified, the number of characters moved by an MVC instruction is determined by the length of the receiving field.

The following examples will serve as a review:

Example 4

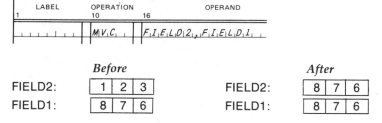

When fields are the same length, the MVC results in the duplication of the contents of Operand 2 at Operand 1.

Example 5

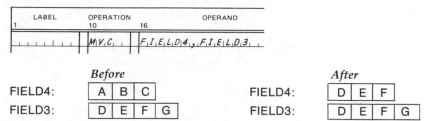

[1] We will see later in this chapter how we can explicitly indicate the number of bytes to be moved.

Example 6

	LABEL	OPERATION 10	16	OPERAND
1		MVC		FIELD6,FIELD5

Before

FIELD6: | 6 | 7 | A | B |

FIELD5: | 1 | 2 | 3 | 5 | 6 |

After

FIELD6: | 1 | 2 | 3 | 5 |

FIELD5: | 1 | 2 | 3 | 5 | 6 |

MVC Where Operand 2 Has Fewer Bytes Than Operand 1

If the receiving field is longer than the sending field, movement proceeds past the contents of the sending field, moving consecutive positions from adjacent fields. Consider the following example.

Example 7

Suppose we establish three storage fields:

	LABEL	OPERATION 10	16	OPERAND
1	AMT1	DC		CL3'123'
	AMT2	DC		CL2'45'
	AMT3	DC		CL2'67'

These fields will appear in storage consecutively since they are assembled in the same order as they are coded:

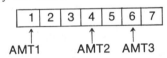

| 1 | 2 | 3 | 4 | 5 | 6 | 7 |

AMT1   AMT2 AMT3

The instruction MVC AMT1, AMT2 will result in a *three*-position move because AMT1, the receiving field, is three positions long. Since AMT2 contains only *two* positions with contents 45, the move will continue transmitting data from the *next* position of the adjacent field. Hence, the result would be:

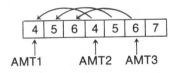

| 4 | 5 | 6 | 4 | 5 | 6 | 7 |

AMT1   AMT2 AMT3

If the intent of that instruction was to transmit one field to another, as it usually is, the MVC resulted in the movement of too many characters. One method to alleviate the problem is to define AMT2 as a three-position field.

	LABEL	OPERATION 10	16	OPERAND
1	AMT1	DC		CL3'123'
	AMT2	DC		CL3'45 ' ONE BLANK BYTE EXTRA
	AMT3	DC		CL2'67'

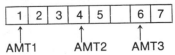

| 1 | 2 | 3 | 4 | 5 | | 6 | 7 |

AMT1   AMT2 AMT3

The instruction MVC AMT1, AMT2 would then produce:

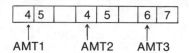

Review—MVC
RULE: Number of characters moved is determined by receiving field.
1. When the sending and receiving fields are the same size, the receiving field will duplicate the sending field.
2. When the receiving field is shorter than the sending field, truncation will occur.
3. When the receiving field is longer than the sending field, additional characters from positions adjacent to the sending field will be moved to the receiving field.

Figure 5-1 illustrates a program that prints one line for each *two* cards read in. Figure 5-2 shows a sample report produced by this program.

```
*                                          *
*                       HOUSEKEEPING INSTRUCTIONS GO HERE   *
*                                          *
CLEAR    MVC    OUTAREA,SPACES
         GET    INFILE,CARD1
         MVC    LNAME,LAST
         MVC    FNAME,FIRST
         GET    INFILE,CARD2
         MVC    STRTOUT,STREET
         MVC    CITYOUT,CITY
         MVC    STATEOUT,STATE
         PUT    OUTFILE,OUTAREA
         B      CLEAR
*                                          *
*                       HOUSEKEEPING INSTRUCTIONS GO HERE   *
*                       ALONG WITH DCB OR DTF MACROS        *
*                                          *
CARD1    DS     0CL80       CARD NO. 1
SOCSEC   DS     CL9            *
LAST     DS     CL15           *
FIRST    DS     CL10           *
         DS     CL46           *
CARD2    DS     0CL80       CARD NO. 2
SSNO     DS     CL9            *
STREET   DS     CL20           *
CITY     DS     CL10           *
STATE    DS     CL2            *
         DS     CL39           *
SPACES   DC     CL1' '
OUTAREA  DS     0CL132
         DS     CL10
LNAME    DS     CL15
         DS     CL5
FNAME    DS     CL10
         DS     CL5
STRTOUT  DS     CL20
         DS     CL5
CITYOUT  DS     CL10
         DS     CL1
STATEOUT DS     CL2
         DS     CL49
         END
```

Figure 5-1

```
BROWN               LEROY          1 MAIN ST.              BROOKLYN    NY
NEWMAN              PAUL           35 E. 83 ST.            NEW YORK    NY
DEAN                JAMES          2 LAKE DR.              SETAUKET    NJ
```

Figure 5-2

In Figure 5-3, we have a program that prints *three* lines for each card read in. Sample output is shown in Figure 5-4.

```
*                                            HOUSEKEEPING INSTRUCTIONS GO HERE   **
*                                                                                **
*
CLEAR       MVC     LINE1,SPACES1
            MVC     LINE2,SPACES2
            MVC     LINE3,SPACES3
            GET     INFILE,RECORD
            MVC     LNAME,LAST
            MVC     FNAME,FIRST
            PUT     OUTFILE,LINE1
            MVC     STRTOUT,STREET
            PUT     OUTFILE,LINE2
            MVC     CITYOUT,CITY
            MVC     STATEOUT,STATE
            PUT     OUTFILE,LINE3
            MVC     LINE1,SPACES1
            PUT     OUTFILE,LINE1
            B       CLEAR
*                                                                                **
*                                            HOUSEKEEPING INSTRUCTIONS GO HERE   **
*                                            ALONG WITH DCB OR DTF MACROS        **
*                                                                                **
RECORD      DS      0CL80
LAST        DS      CL15
FIRST       DS      CL10
            DS      CL11
STREET      DS      CL20
CITY        DS      CL10
STATE       DS      CL2
            DS      CL12
SPACES1     DC      CL1' '
LINE1       DS      0CL132      NAME LINE
            DS      CL10            *
LNAME       DS      CL15            *
            DS      CL5             *
FNAME       DS      CL10            *
            DS      CL92            *
SPACES2     DC      CL1' '
LINE2       DS      0CL132      ADDRESS LINE
            DS      CL10            *
STRTOUT     DS      CL20            *
            DS      CL102           *
SPACES3     DC      CL1' '
LINE3       DS      0CL132      CITY & STATE LINE
            DS      CL10            *
CITYOUT     DS      CL10            *
            DS      CL1             *
STATEOUT    DS      CL2             *
            DS      CL109           *
            END
```

Figure 5-3

```
BROWN               LEROY
1 MAIN ST.
BROOKLYN    NY


DERNBY              JOYCE
57 WAYNE DR.
SETAUKET    NY


WATSON              RICHARD
129 ROCHESTER LA.
QUEENS      NY
```

Figure 5-4

1. The operation code of a move character instruction is _____ .
2. In an MVC instruction, the first operand is called the _____ field and the second operand is called the _____ field.
3. Movement of data in an MVC instruction is from (*left/right*) to (*left/right*).
4. The field name specified for any operand refers to the (*high/low*)-order position.
5. (True or False) If the sending field is larger than the receiving field, the MVC will result in the truncation of sending field characters.
6. (True or False) If the receiving field is larger than the sending field, the MVC will fill the receiving field with blanks.
7. Fill in the missing blanks:

MVC   CODE1, CODE2

CODE1   CODE2

	Before	After		Before	After
a.	1 2 4			4 6 3	
b.	4 9 2 0			7 3 2 6 8	
c.	1 2 7			1 3	

8. Assume the following DC coding:

```
FLD1      DC      CL3'42A'
FLD2      DC      CL2'61'
FLD3      DC      CL3'411'
```

The fields will appear in storage as follows:

4	2	A	6	1	4	1	1

↑F L D 1   ↑F L D 2   ↑F L D 3

Indicate the results of the following instructions. Treat each instruction independently using the above data.

```
a.  MVC     FLD1,FLD2
b.  MVC     FLD2,FLD3
```

Solutions
1. MVC
2. Receiving
   Sending
3. Left
   Right
4. High or leftmost
5. True
6. False. Movement will continue with adjacent positions in storage until the receiving field is filled

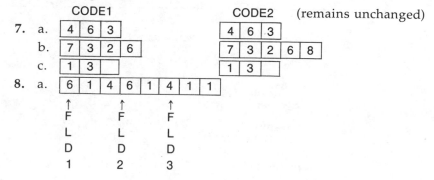

CODE1   CODE2   (remains unchanged)

7. a. | 4 | 6 | 3 | | 4 | 6 | 3 |
   b. | 7 | 3 | 2 | 6 | | 7 | 3 | 2 | 6 | 8 |
   c. | 1 | 3 | | 1 | 3 |

8. a. | 6 | 1 | 4 | 6 | 1 | 4 | 1 | 1 |

↑F L D 1   ↑F L D 2   ↑F L D 3

b.

4	2	A	4	1	4	1	1

```
   ↑           ↑       ↑
   F           F       F
   L           L       L
   D           D       D
   1           2       3
```

4. Types of Move Operations

The move character instruction may be of two types: *implicit* and *explicit*. Implicit moves are those we discussed in the previous section where the length of the move is strictly determined by the length of the first operand.

An explicit move instruction contains a length specifier that allows the programmer to indicate the precise number of bytes to be moved:

Examples

LABEL	OPERATION 10	OPERAND 16
	MVC	ACCTOUT(4),ACCTIN
	MVC	NAMEOUT(10),NAMEIN

In Example 1, the number of characters moved will be *four* regardless of the size of the operands; similarly, Example 2 specifies a ten-byte move.

Explicit moves result in fewer programming errors since the programmer can more easily determine the number of characters moved.

It is strongly recommended that the implied MVC be avoided since programming errors may occur if the receiving and sending fields are not the same size. However, when the programmer clearly understands the MVC operation, or when the receiving and sending fields are the same length, the use of the explicit MVC is unnecessary.

Comparing Implicit and Explicit Moves
Example 3

For the following example, OUTAREA is defined as having a length of ten bytes and initially contains spaces or blanks while ACCTIN is defined as an input area of four bytes and contains the number 0012. The consecutive positions following ACCTIN are identified in order to explain the result of the operation.

LABEL	OPERATION 10	OPERAND 16
	MVC	OUTAREA,ACCTIN

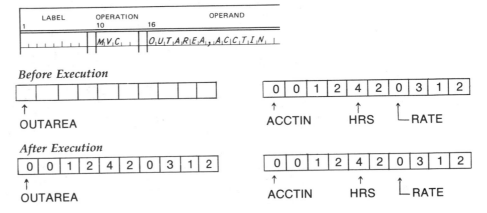

The first operand or receiving field is ten bytes in length and therefore ten bytes will be moved since the explicit length was not specified. The consecutive positions following ACCTIN will be moved even if this was *not* the programmer's intent. We identified these areas as HRS and RATE in order to illustrate that the CPU will continue to move the data, one byte at a time until the number of bytes implied by the first operand has been moved. If, however, only the contents of ACCTIN is to be duplicated at OUTAREA, the following explicit move can be used instead:

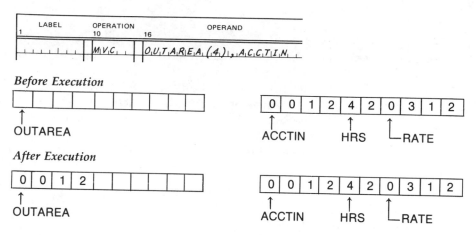

LABEL	OPERATION 10	OPERAND 16
	M V C	O U T A R E A (4) , A C C T I N

Before Execution

OUTAREA

0	0	1	2	4	2	0	3	1	2

ACCTIN   HRS   └RATE

After Execution

0	0	1	2						

OUTAREA

0	0	1	2	4	2	0	3	1	2

ACCTIN   HRS   └RATE

To test your understanding of the move character instruction carefully examine the examples below. Where an explicit length is not given, the length of the first operand is equal to the number of characters shown in the illustration.

Examples

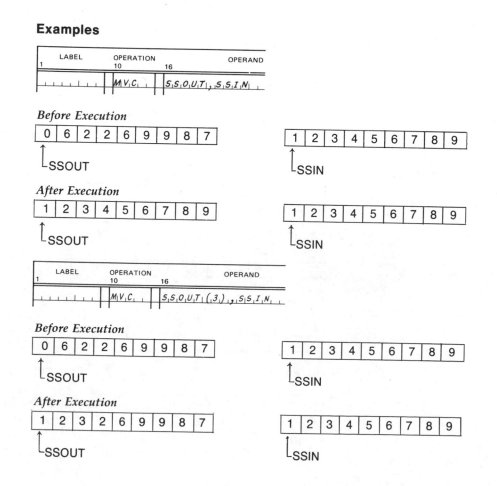

LABEL	OPERATION 10	OPERAND 16
	M V C	S S O U T , S S I N

Before Execution

0	6	2	2	6	9	9	8	7

└SSOUT

1	2	3	4	5	6	7	8	9

└SSIN

After Execution

1	2	3	4	5	6	7	8	9

└SSOUT

1	2	3	4	5	6	7	8	9

└SSIN

LABEL	OPERATION 10	OPERAND 16
	M V C	S S O U T (3) , S S I N

Before Execution

0	6	2	2	6	9	9	8	7

└SSOUT

1	2	3	4	5	6	7	8	9

└SSIN

After Execution

1	2	3	2	6	9	9	8	7

└SSOUT

1	2	3	4	5	6	7	8	9

└SSIN

We will now summarize the rules of the move character instruction.

Rule Summary

Move Character Instruction (MVC)

1. First Operand—Receiving field, contents change.
2. Second Operand—Sending field, contents remain the same.[2]
3. Data moved one byte at a time from left to right.
4. From 1 to 256 bytes may be moved with a single MVC instruction.
5. Contents of the first operand are replaced by the contents of the second.
6. The number of bytes moved depends on whether an explicit or implicit MVC is used.
   (a) Explicit—length in digits specified in first operand.
   (b) Implicit—length of first operand determines number of characters moved.

SELF-EVALUATING QUIZ

1. In the 360/370 System, the move character (MVC) instruction is classified as a (*storage-to-storage/register*) type instruction.
2. An instruction that may be used to clear the output area or set up headings is called _____ .
3. In clearing the output areas the programmer moves _____ to the area defined as output.
4. There are two operands used with the MVC instruction. The first operand is the _____ field while the second is the _____ field.
5. A symbolic name can be used as an operand only if it is defined as a _____ or a _____ .
6. A single MVC instruction allows from _____ to _____ characters to be moved.
7. Indicate the results of the following instruction:

   MVC   EMPNO,INDATA

   Before

   | 1 | 2 | 3 | 4 | 5 | | 7 | 8 | 9 | 0 | 1 |

   EMPNO   INDATA

8. How many steps would be required to complete the move character instruction given in Question 7?
9. The MVC instruction moves _____ byte(s) at a time, starting with the (*high/low*)-order position.
10. When the number of bytes to be moved is not explicitly stated, then the move is said to be _____ , meaning that the number of bytes moved depends on the length of the _____ operand.
11. As a precaution, it is advised that all move character instructions be of the _____ type.
12. The instruction MVC NAME(10),TITLE is of the _____ type and would move _____ bytes of data.
13. Let us assume that areas in storage have the following length specifications:

    DESC (7)   TOTAL (4)   PRICE (4)   PART (12)

---

[2] When the sending and receiving fields overlap, the second operand may change. This topic is discussed later in the chapter.

These storage areas appear as shown below. Indicate the results in storage after each of the following operations is performed. Treat each problem independently; that is, assume the original contents for each problem:

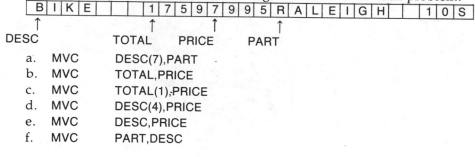

| B | I | K | E | | | | 1 | 7 | 5 | 9 | 7 | 9 | 9 | 5 | R | A | L | E | I | G | H | | | 1 | 0 | S |

DESC   TOTAL   PRICE   PART

a.	MVC	DESC(7),PART
b.	MVC	TOTAL,PRICE
c.	MVC	TOTAL(1),PRICE
d.	MVC	DESC(4),PRICE
e.	MVC	DESC,PRICE
f.	MVC	PART,DESC

Solutions

1. Storage-to-storage
2. Move character (MVC)
3. Spaces or blanks
4. Receiving
   Sending
5. DS (define storage)
   DC (define constant)
6. 1
   256

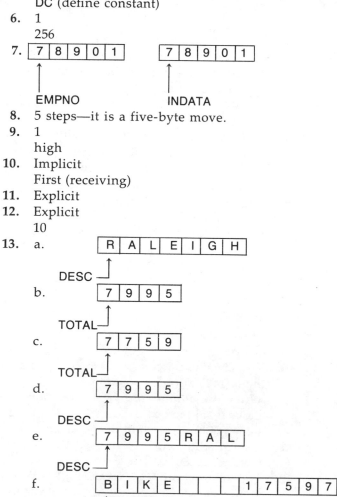

7. | 7 | 8 | 9 | 0 | 1 | | 7 | 8 | 9 | 0 | 1 |

   EMPNO   INDATA

8. 5 steps—it is a five-byte move.
9. 1
   high
10. Implicit
    First (receiving)
11. Explicit
12. Explicit
    10
13. a. | R | A | L | E | I | G | H |

    DESC ⌐

    b. | 7 | 9 | 9 | 5 |

    TOTAL ⌐

    c. | 7 | 7 | 5 | 9 |

    TOTAL ⌐

    d. | 7 | 9 | 9 | 5 |

    DESC ⌐

    e. | 7 | 9 | 9 | 5 | R | A | L |

    DESC ⌐

    f. | B | I | K | E | | | | 1 | 7 | 5 | 9 | 7 |

    PART

5. Self-Defining Operands in MVC Instructions   It is possible in assembler language to define a constant as the second operand in an MVC or any storage-to-storage instruction. In such a case, the sending field is called a *self-defining operand*. For example, a message such as

'END OF JOB' could be included in the sending field of a move instruction, thereby eliminating the usual DC (define constant) used to define the characters in storage. The instruction

LABEL	OPERATION 10	OPERAND 16
	MVC	LINEOUT(10),=C'END OF JOB'

would create a character string containing the message 'END OF JOB', and would then move this ten-byte message to the storage area called LINEOUT.

In order for the assembler to identify the self-defining operand, it is necessary to begin the operand with an equal sign, followed by the constant as shown above. The rules for establishing self-defining operands are essentially the same as for specifying constants (DCs). Again, the length specifier should be used in the first operand if the correct results are to be achieved. Examples of self-defining operands are illustrated below:

LABEL	OPERATION 10	OPERAND 16	COMMENTS
	MVC	MSSG(5),=C'ERROR'	
	MVC	MSSG(5),=X'C5D9D9D6D9'	THIS IS EBCDIC FOR 'ERROR'
	MVC	MSSG(4),=C'7 UP'	
	MVC	MSSG(4),=X'F740E4D7'	THIS IS EBCDIC FOR '7 UP'

Self-defining constants can be established in character, hexadecimal or binary form. The = sign as the first position of the second operand signals the computer that a constant is to be defined.

The following box summarizes self-defining operands.

Self-Defining Operands
1. A self-defining operand must begin with an equal sign.
2. The next character must be a valid descriptor such as C (character), X (hexadecimal), B (binary), P (packed).
3. The data is defined in the same manner as a define constant.
4. Self-defining data may appear only in the second operand, the sending field, of a storage-to-storage instruction.

With regard to programming efficiency, it is advisable to use self-defining operands for one-of-a-kind messages. Frequently referenced messages or texts are more efficiently programmed using the conventional define constants.

Length of Moves

The self-defining operand to be transmitted should be the same length as:

1. the length specified in an explicit move; or

2. the length of the receiving field in an implicit move.

If the self-defining operand is longer than the first operand, then truncation will occur. If the self-defining operand is shorter, then the first operand will continue receiving data from additional storage positions. Since, at this point, we have no way of knowing where the self-defining operand was stored, the additional contents of the receiving field cannot be predicted. (The self-defining constants are placed in a 'literal pool' at the end of the program.)

The following examples will illustrate the point.

Examples

Objective

To observe how data is moved when the self-defining operand is a different length than the receiving field.

LABEL	OPERATION	OPERAND
	MVC	FORT,=C'1250'

We will assume that FORT has been defined as DS CL3 for the first example and as DS CL5 for the second.

Before MVC

1. FORT—3 bytes | 4 | 5 | 6 |
2. FORT—5 bytes | 9 | 2 | 5 | 3 | 6 |

After MVC

| 1 | 2 | 5 | Unpredictable

| 1 | 2 | 5 | 0 | | ←

SELF EVALUATING QUIZ

1. Code a statement to move the constant 'OUT OF LUCK' to an 11-byte storage area called HASH.
2. Code a statement to move the constant 'ERR102' to a 10-byte storage area called MESH.
3. Code a statement to move the constant 'MEA CULPA' to a 6-byte storage area called CHECKIT.
4. In each of the above cases, the second operand in the MVC instruction is called a _____ .
5. (True or False) A constant may be set up as a DC or may appear as a self-defining operand in a storage-to-storage instruction.
6. The MVC instruction
   a. moves one character at a time.
   b. moves the entire field as a block.
   c. pads blanks at the right.
   d. a and c.
   e. none of these.

Solutions

1. MVC   HASH,=C'OUT OF LUCK' (NOTE: Either implicit or explicit move may be used.)
2. MVC   MESH(6),=C'ERR102' (NOTE: You must use an explicit move since MESH is longer than the constant.)
3. The constant will be truncated unless CHECKIT is made longer:
   MVC   CHECKIT,=C'MEA CULPA'
4. Self-defining operand
5. True
6. a

B. Move Immediate Instruction: MVI

Purpose   Often, there is a need to move *one byte* of data into a particular storage area where that data has not been defined in the program. The programmer may elect to: (a) assign a symbolic name to a defined constant (DC) and code an MVC instruction; (b) use a self-defining operand; or (c) simply use the Move Immediate (MVI) instruction. With the MVI instruction, the programmer accomplishes two tasks in one step:

1. Defines 1 byte of data in the sending field (second operand).

2. Moves that data to the receiving field, a location in storage (first operand).

Typical applications of this instruction include moving dollar signs ($) or other special characters to the output in order to improve the readability of a report.

MVI Format We previously learned that the MVC instruction moves data from one location in storage to another; hence the MVC is classified as a Storage-to-Storage instruction. In contrast, the Move Immediate instruction is of the Storage Immediate (SI) type.[3] The data to be moved is *defined* in the second operand and therefore is referred to as immediate data. *One* byte, and *only* one byte, of data is moved from the second operand to the high-order byte of the first operand. All of the following examples produce the identical results, the only difference is the format used to define the immediate data. In all three instructions, a dollar sign is defined and moved to the storage location called AMT:

LABEL	OPERATION	OPERAND
	MVI	AMT,C'$' CHARACTER DATA
	MVI	AMT,X'5B' HEXADECIMAL DATA
	MVI	AMT,B'01011011' BINARY DATA

Character Representation

Before

| 0 | 2 | 3 |

AMT

After

| $ | 2 | 3 |

AMT

Hexadecimal Representation

Before

| F0 | F2 | F3 |

AMT

After

| 5B | F2 | F3 |

AMT

Binary Representation

Before

| 11110000 | 11110010 | 11110011 |

AMT

After

| 01011011 | 11110010 | 11110011 |

AMT

If the MVI instruction had not been used, the following two instructions could have been substituted:

LABEL	OPERATION	OPERAND
	MVC	AMT(1),DOLLAR
	.	
	.	
	.	
DOLLAR	DC	C'$'

---

[3] The instruction type is an extremely important concept which is specifically used for debugging purposes. See Chapter 14.

or a self-defining operand could have been used:

LABEL	OPERATION	OPERAND
	MVC	AMT(1),=C'$'

Note that we use an equal sign when coding a self-defining operand, but that no equal sign is used for an immediate operand.

As shown, the programmer can code the one byte of data using any of the three formats illustrated. For example, if it is necessary to move the EBCDIC representation of the number one to an area called NUMB, any one of the following immediate instructions can be used:

LABEL	OPERATION	OPERAND
	MVI	NUMB,C'1'
*		
	MVI	NUMB,X'F1' EBCDIC FOR NO. 1
*		
	MVI	NUMB,B'11110001' BINARY FOR NO. 1

The final choice is usually a simple matter of preference. However, there are limitations:

Review

Character data   One character must be specified and enclosed in single quotes ' '.

Hexadecimal data   Two hexadecimal digits must be specified and enclosed in single quotes.

Binary data   Eight binary digits must be specified and enclosed in single quotes.

Remember that the storage immediate instruction does not have a length specifier and that the implied length is one byte of data only. The following examples will serve as a further review:

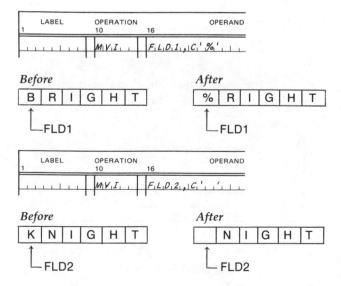

LABEL	OPERATION	OPERAND
	MVI	FLD1,C'%'

Before

B	R	I	G	H	T

└─FLD1

After

%	R	I	G	H	T

└─FLD1

LABEL	OPERATION	OPERAND
	MVI	FLD2,C' '

Before

K	N	I	G	H	T

└─FLD2

After

	N	I	G	H	T

└─FLD2

1. The MVI instruction is of the _____ type.
2. How many bytes are moved with a single MVI instruction? How many hex digits? Bits?
3. An immediate operand is the (*sending/receiving*) field or the (*first/second*) operand.
4. When using the hexadecimal immediate format, how many digits must be specified?
5. The immediate operand does not begin with an equal sign but is followed by the letter _____ when specifying character data.
6. Blanks (*may/may not*) be embedded between the quote marks when using the MVI instruction.
7. Which of the following self-defining operands are not valid in an MVI instruction:

   a. X'40'   d. XF1   g. C'THE'   j. C'
   b. C'FØ'   e. C'4'   h. B'12001111'   k. X'00'
   c. B'1111'   f. J'3'   i. X'G3'

8. The difference between a self-defining operand in an MVC instruction and an MVI instruction is _____ .
9. Examine the program excerpt in Figure 5-5. Indicate what errors, if any exist in the instructions shown.

```
NEXT-10   MVC    OUTAREA,SPACES
          GET    INFILE,RECORD
          MVC    LNAME,LAST
          MVC    FNAME,FIRST
          MVC    SALOUT, SALARY
          MVI    DOLLAR,X'$'
          PUT    OUTFILE,OUTAREA
          B      NEXT-10
          .
          .
RECORD    DS     OCL80              CARD FORMAT
LAST      DS     CL15                   *
FIRST     DS     CL10                   *
SALARY    DC     CL5                    *
          DS     CL50                   *
SPACES    DC     CL1' '
OUTAREA   DS     OCL132             PRINT FORMAT
          DS     CL5                    *
LNAME     DS     CL15                   *
          DS     CL20                   *
FNAME     DS     CL10                   *
          DS     CL19                   *
DOLLAR    DS     CL1                    *
SALOUT    DS     CL5                    *
BLANK     DS     CL57                   *
```

Figure 5-5

1. Storage Immediate (SI)
2. 1
   2
   8
3. Sending
   Second
4. 2; that is, X'5B', for example
5. C
6. May not; only *one* character is permitted.
7. b. 1 character permitted
   c. 8 bits must be specified
   d. Missing quote marks.
   f. J is not a valid type.
   g. Too many characters.

h.   2 is not a binary digit.

i.   G is not a hex number.

j.   Only 1 quote mark.

k.   Not a standard character.

8.   MVI—only one character; MVC—any number of characters; also equal sign used in self-defining operand and not used in immediate operand.

9.   See Figure 5-6.

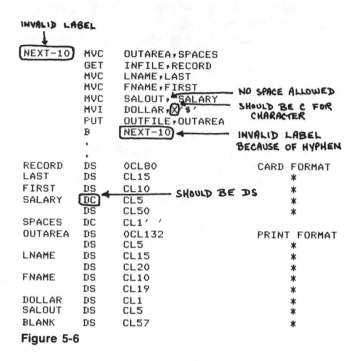

Figure 5-6

C. Relative Addressing and the MVC Instruction

A typical problem facing the programmer is referencing data within a record or area that does not contain a symbolic name. For example, assume the data shown below:

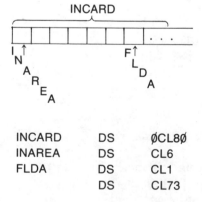

```
INCARD      DS      ØCL8Ø
INAREA      DS      CL6
FLDA        DS      CL1
            DS      CL73
```

The data resides in storage and the programmer is required to reference the sixth position of INAREA. This data can only be referenced using relative addressing or by assigning a symbolic name to the area. With relative addressing, we use a symbolic name near the data and count from there the number of bytes needed to reach the desired storage location. Therefore, the sixth position of INCARD can be referenced by INAREA+5 or by FLDA-1. When using relative addressing note that the operand contains three parts in the following sequence:

1. A symbolic address near the required data is referenced.

2.ˑ A + or − sign.

3. An integer representing the displacement from the symbolic address.

Note that embedded blanks are *not* permitted in the operand. Consider the example below:

LABEL	OPERATION 10	16 OPERAND
	MVC	GENDER(1),INAREA+5
*		
*	OR	
*		
	MVC	GENDER(1),FLDA-1

Before

| F |
↑
GENDER

| 0 | 1 | 2 | 3 | | M | 6 |
↑   ↑
INAREA   FLDA

After

| M |
↑
GENDER

| 0 | 1 | 2 | 3 | | M | 6 |
↑   ↑
INAREA   FLDA

This illustrates how data can be moved to a storage location called GENDER, by either of the MVC instructions shown which use relative addressing. Examining the instructions, we find:

1. The receiving field is GENDER.

2. The sending field is INAREA+5 or FLDA-1.

3. The length is explicitly specified as one byte *by the first operand*.

For the next example, assume the programmer desires to move the digits 175, from the storage area illustrated below to an area named WT.

Before

| 2 | 2 | 5 | | 6 | 7 | 1 | 7 | 5 | 2 | 7 |
WT   HEIGHT   AGE

HEIGHT + 2 ↑↑ ⌐—AGE − 3

LABEL	OPERATION		OPERAND
1	10	16	
	MVC		WT(3),HEIGHT+2
*			
*	OR		
*			
	MVC		WT(3),AGE-3

After

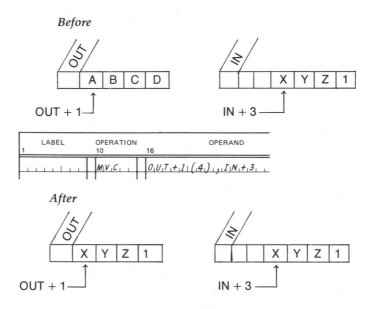

The instructions demonstrate how relative addressing can be used. Notice that the length specifier is critical in controlling the number of bytes to be moved.

Relative addressing may also be used to reference data in *both* operands of a move instruction. This is illustrated below where 4 bytes of data are to be moved from the fourth position of IN to the second position of OUT:

Before

OUT | | A | B | C | D | |

OUT + 1

IN | | | | X | Y | Z | 1 |

IN + 3

LABEL	OPERATION		OPERAND
1	10	16	
	MVC		OUT+1(4),IN+3

After

OUT | | X | Y | Z | 1 | |

OUT + 1

IN | | | | X | Y | Z | 1 |

IN + 3

We observe that:

1. The receiving field begins in OUT+1.

2. The sending field begins in IN+3.

3. The length specifier is 4 bytes in the first operand.

Note that if the length specifier had been omitted, the number of bytes contained in the DS statement for OUT would have been implied. Relative addressing is very important when referencing overlapped fields or data locations, as we will see below.

Figure 5-7 illustrates a program that produces the type of report shown in Figure 5-8. Figure 5-9 illustrates the same program using relative addressing.

```
*                                                                              *
*                                        HOUSEKEEPING INSTRUCTIONS GO HERE     *
*                                                                              *
            MVC     OUTAREA,SPACES
            MVC     CNAMEOUT(4),=C'NAME'
            MVC     AMTOUT(3),=C'AMT'
            MVC     DATE(4),=C'DATE'
            PUT     OUTFILE,OUTAREA
CLEAR       MVC     OUTAREA,SPACES          CLEAR THE PRINT AREA
            GET     INFILE,RECORD           READ A CARD AND STORE IN RECORD
            MVI     AMTOUT-1,C'$'
            MVC     CNAMEOUT(20),CNAME
            MVC     AMTOUT(5),AMT
            MVC     DATE(8),=C'12-11-80'
            PUT     OUTFILE,OUTAREA              PRINT A LINE FROM OUTAREA
            B       CLEAR                   GO BACK TO PROCESS NEXT RECORD
*                                                                              *
*                                        HOUSEKEEPING INSTRUCTIONS GO HERE     *
*                                        ALONG WITH DCB OR DTF MACROS          *
*                                                                              *
RECORD      DS      OCL80
CNAME       DS      CL20
AMT         DS      CL5
            DS      CL55
SPACES      DC      CL1' '
OUTAREA     DS      OCL132
            DS      CL10
CNAMEOUT    DS      CL20
            DS      CL10
AMTOUT      DS      CL5
            DS      CL5
DATE        DS      CL8
            DS      CL74
            END
```

Figure 5-7

```
NAME                          AMT        DATE
PAUL NEWMAN                   $97321      12-11-80
JOHN WAYNE                    $32170      12-11-80
ROBERT REDFORD               $41625      12-11-80
MICKEY MOUSE                 $21387      12-11-80
```

Figure 5-8

```
*                                                                              *
*                                        HOUSEKEEPING INSTRUCTIONS GO HERE     *
*                                                                              *
            MVC     OUTAREA,SPACES
            MVC     OUTAREA+10(4),=C'NAME'
            MVC     OUTAREA+40(3),=C'AMT'
            MVC     OUTAREA+50(4),=C'DATE'
            PUT     OUTFILE,OUTAREA
CLEAR       MVC     OUTAREA,SPACES          CLEAR THE PRINT AREA
            GET     INFILE,RECORD           READ A CARD AND STORE IN RECORD
            MVI     OUTAREA+39,C'$'
            MVC     OUTAREA+10(20),RECORD
            MVC     OUTAREA+40(5),RECORD+20
            MVC     OUTAREA+50(8),=C'12-11-80'
            PUT     OUTFILE,OUTAREA         PRINT A LINE FROM OUTAREA
            B       CLEAR                   GO BACK TO PROCESS NEXT RECORD
*                                                                              *
*                                        HOUSEKEEPING INSTRUCTIONS GO HERE     *
*                                        ALONG WITH DCB OR DTF MACROS          *
*                                                                              *
RECORD      DS      CL80
SPACES      DC      CL1' '
OUTAREA     DS      CL132
            END
```

Figure 5-9

D. Overlapped Fields and the MVC Instruction

As already noted, the arrangement of data fields in storage is established by the order of the define constant (**DC**) and/or define storage (**DS**) instructions. Since the storage areas are assigned sequentially, the following shows how a block of data would be set up by the instructions given:

Name	Operation	Operand
FLDA	DS	CL1
FLDB	DS	CL2
FLDC	DS	CL3

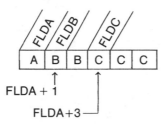

In this example, FLDB can be considered the second position in FLDA; that is, it can be accessed as FLDA+1 as well as FLDB. Similarly, FLDC is the fourth position in FLDA and can be specified as FLDA+3. It can also be specified as the third position in FLDB, or as FLDB+2. This is the manner in which fields are said to *overlap*. The significance of overlapped fields is especially important when moving data.

When the sending field is shorter than the receiving field, the data next to the shorter sending field will be included in the move. For example, using the data above, consider the following:

Instruction

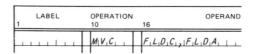

Results

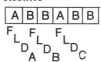

The instruction would generate the characters **ABB** in **FLDC** since a length of three bytes was implied by the move instruction.

We will now analyze the effects of overlapped fields with the instruction shown below:

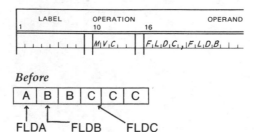

Before

FLDC is 3 bytes; hence a 3-byte move follows.

				Byte Moved	
	FLDB	FLDC		From	To
1.	A B B Ȼ B C C			FLDB	FLDC
2.	A B B B Ȼ B C			FLDB+1	FLDC+1
3.	A B B B B Ȼ B			FLDB+2 (FLDC)	FLDC+2

After

FLDA   FLDB   FLDC

A B B B B

The byte-by-byte movement does not produce what you may have expected. Note that the 3 bytes starting at **FLDB** initially contained the characters **BBC** but, as a result of the move instruction, both the sending field **FLDB**, and the receiving field, **FLDC**, were filled with B's. The filling of a field with a particular character from an adjoining area is referred to as *propagation*. The next example further illustrates this concept:

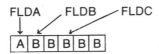

LABEL	OPERATION 10	OPERAND 16
	MVC	FLDB(5),FLDA

			Byte Moved	
	FLDA FLDB FLDC		From	To
	A A̸B B C C C		FLDA	FLDB
	A A A̸B C C C		FLDA+1	FLDB+1
	A A A Ȼ C C		FLDA+2	FLDB+2
	A A A A Ȼ C		FLDA+3	FLDB+3
	A A A A A Ȼ		FLDA+4	FLDB+4

FLDA FLDB FLDC

A B B C C C
Before

FLDA FLDB FLDC

A A A A A A
After

The instruction will propagate the letter A throughout the entire data area. The key to this concept is realizing that the character to be propagated (A) is located immediately before the receiving field. *It is only when this condition prevails that propagation will take place.*

Clearing the Output Area   The programmer cannot automatically assume that an output print area is cleared when execution begins. Rather, one of the first programming requirements is to clear this area to insure that data from a previous program does not affect the next output record. This is best accomplished by an **MVC** operation that propagates spaces or blanks throughout the output area. For propagation, remember to define the desired character (space) *immediately before* the field to receive the propagated characters. Therefore, the following instructions would be coded.

LABEL	OPERATION	OPERAND
	MVC	LINEOUT(132),SPACES
	.	
	.	
	.	
SPACES	DC	CL1' '
LINEOUT	DS	CL132
	.	
	.	

Spaces are propagated throughout the area called LINEOUT, thereby clearing that area in preparation for the construction of the next line of print.

Another method of clearing the output area can be used in which the storage area named **SPACES** need not be defined. The concept is essentially the same as the previous example, except that we initially place a space in the first position of LINEOUT and then propagate the space throughout the area. The instruction to accomplish this would be coded as shown below.

LABEL	OPERATION	OPERAND
	MVI	LINEOUT,X'40'
	MVC	LINEOUT+1(131),LINEOUT

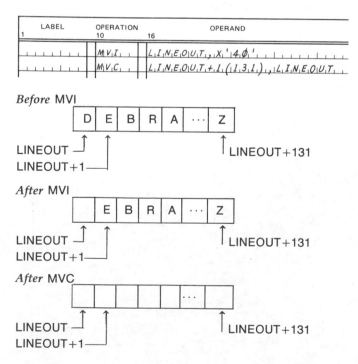

Before MVI

After MVI

After MVC

Note that the move immediate (MVI) instruction places a space in the first byte of **LINEOUT**, and the MVC instruction is then used to propagate spaces throughout the output area LINEOUT. Also note that the length of the MVC is 131 bytes and not 132, since the move (MVC) begins in LINEOUT+1.

1. The method used to reference data that has not been assigned a symbolic name is called _____ .

2. (True or False) The following is a valid instruction using relative addressing:

   MVC   AGEOUT,PDATA+5(2)

3. (True or False) The displacement must be positive (+) when using relative addressing.

4. (True or False) Blanks are not permitted before or after the displacement sign in an operand.

5. If the card input area is called IN, how could the programmer reference card column 80?

6. Identify the invalid relative addresses:

a.	LINE+7	e.	OUT+3.
b.	IN+K	f.	6+TEMP
c.	OFF*2	g.	OUTAREA+100
d.	INDY−5	h.	DATA+0

7. Code the instruction to move the digits 78 in the example below to an area called QTY.

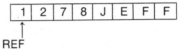

REF

8. Write the two move instructions necessary to fill a six-byte field called CREDIT with asterisks (*).

9. To clear the output area with the given instruction, what must the relationship be between the defined constant (SPACE) and the output area (OUTAREA).

10. Code the instruction to move the message THE END to the fifth position of LINEOUT. Use a self-defining operand.

For each of the following instructions, specify whether its *format* is valid or invalid:

	LABEL	OPERATION	OPERAND
11.		MVC	FLDA+80,FLDB−3
12.		MVC	FLDC(10),FLDA(7)
13.		MVC	FLDA+10,C='ERROR'
14.		MVI	FLDA,FLDB
15.		MVC	=C'ERROR',FLDA
16.		MVI	FLDA,=C'*'
17.		MVC	FLDB−10(13),=C'ERROR IN DATA'
18.		MVI	FLDA+25,X'FL'
19.		MVC	FLDB,FLDA−7

20. If FLDA = 12345 (5 bytes) and FLDB = 173 (3 bytes), what is the result of the following:

```
                    MVC       FLDA,FLDB
```
a. 00173
b. 173bb (b means a blank)
c. 12173
d. 123
e. None of these
NOTE: Explain your answer.

21. Examine the program in Figure 5-10 and indicate what errors, if any, exist.

```
*
*               HOUSEKEEPING INSTRUCTIONS GO HERE
*
READ     GET    INFILE,CARDIN
         MVC    LINEOUT,SPACES
         MVC    LINEOUT,CARDIN
         PUT    OUTFILE,LINEOUT
         B      READ
*
*               HOUSEKEEPING INSTRUCTIONS GO HERE
*               ALONG WITH DTF OR DCB MACROS
CARDIN   DS     CL80
SPACES   DC     CL1' '
LINEOUT  DS     CL132
         END
```

Figure 5-10

Solutions

1. Relative addressing
2. False. The length specifier is used with the *first* operand:
    ```
              MVC       AGEOUT(2),PDATA+5.
    ```
3. False. Negative displacements are also permissible.
4. True
5. IN+79
6. b. K is not a decimal number
    c. * is not permitted
    e. . is not permitted
    f. Incorrect order
    NOTE: *h. Is valid* but is the same as DATA
7. MVC   QTY(2),REF+2
8. MVI   CREDIT,C'*' (or MVC   CREDIT(1),=C'*')
    MVC   CREDIT+1(5),CREDIT
    Be sure *never* to use the = sign with the MVI instruction.
9. The space must precede OUTAREA:
    ```
                        SPACE     DC      C' '
                        OUTAREA   DS      CL132
    ```
10. MVC   LINEOUT+4(7),=C'THE END'
11. Valid
12. Invalid. Only one operand may have an explicit length.
13. Invalid. Should read:
    ```
                        MVC     FLDA+10,=C'ERROR'
    ```
    (Second operand invalid in the question.)
14. Invalid. When using the MVI instruction, the second operand must be a one-byte immediate operand.
15. Invalid. The first operand is the receiving field and may not be a self-defining operand.
16. Invalid. The second operand in an MVI instruction is not a self-defining operand but an immediate operand: no = in the second operand:
    ```
                        MVI     FLDA,C'*'
    ```
17. Valid
18. Valid
19. Valid

20. e. The results of the operation cannot be determined with the information given. Since the receiving field determines the length of the move, 5 bytes of data will be transferred. The first three bytes of FLDA will be replaced with '173' of FLDB; the low-order two bytes of FLDA will be replaced with whatever data appears in the two positions following FLDB, that is, FLDB+3 and FLDB+4.

21. The second MVC should have an explicit length specified. An implicit length of 132 is indicated. Since CARDIN is only 80 bytes long, the MVC will cause 52 characters of unwanted data to be moved to LINEOUT. The instruction should be written as:

       MVC   LINEOUT(80),CARDIN

KEY TERMS

Explicit operation (MVC)

Field

High-Order position

Immediate instruction (MVI)
Implicit operation (MVC)

Low-Order position

Overlapped fields

Propagation

Receiving field
Relative addressing

Self-defining operand
Sending field
Storage-to-storage (SS) instruction

Truncation

Review Questions   Consider the following for Questions 1–4.

    FIELDA   DC   CL4'ABCD'
    FIELDB   DC   CL3'EFG'
    FIELDC   DC   CL4'HIJK'

1. Indicate how these fields would appear in storage.
2. What character is contained in the position represented by:
    a. FIELDA+2
    b. FIELDB−3
    c. FIELDC+1
3. Indicate the result of the following
    a. MVC   FIELDC,FIELDA
    b. MVC   FIELDB,FIELDC
    c. MVC   FIELDA,FIELDB
4. Alter the above instructions so that precisely three characters are moved each time.
5. Using a self-defining operand as the sending field,
    a. Move two zeros to a field called SUM.
    b. Move 'A-OK' to a field called MESSAGE.
    c. Move '123' to a field called CODE.

6. Will the following series of instructions properly clear the print area? Explain your answer.

                       MVC   PRINT, BLANKS
                        .
                        .
                        .

        PRINT   DS   ØCL132
        BLANKS   DC   CL1' '
                        .
                        .
                        .

7. Indicate the result of the following instructions, assuming AX to be a three-position field, with contents ABC.
   a. MVI   AX,C'3'
   b. MVI   AX+2,C'4'

8. Indicate the results of the following operations, assuming TIME is a four-position field.
   a. MVC   TIME,=C'1123'
   b. MVC   TIME,=C'123'
   c. MVC   TIME,=C'12345'
   d. MVC   TIME,=C'12'
   e. MVC   TIME,=C'1'

9. (True or False) An explicit move with a length specifier always produces the same results as an implied move.

10. Indicate what, if anything, is wrong with the following statements:
    a. MVI   OUT,C'43'
    b. MVC   OUT,C'233'
    c. MVC   IN,OUT(2)
    d. MVC   IN(4),OUT(3)
    e. MVC   IN(280),OUT
    f. MVC   IN+7,OUT−3

Problems

1. Write a program to print data from cards. The input is as follows:

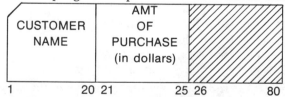

Output should appear as follows:

NAME	AMT	DATE
(customer name)	(amt of purchase)	(date of run-entered as a constant)

There will be one line of data for each card read.

Print positions: customer name   11–30
                    amt of purchase   41–45
                    date (xx-xx-xx)   51–58

With every amount, print a $ in print position 40.

2. Consider the following card input:

NAME	STREET	CITY AND STATE	ZIP	
1 20	21 40	41 60	61 65	80

For each card, print three lines of data as follows:

Print positions 31–50   NAME
Print positions 31–50   STREET
Print positions 31–55   CITY, STATE and ZIP

3. Write a program to create one printed line for every group of two input cards. The input consists of two types of card records:

Credit Record		*Debit Record*	
1–20	Customer name	1–20	Customer Name
21–25	Amt of Credit ($)	21–40	Address
26–80	Not Used	41–45	Amt of Debit
		46–80	Not Used

Chapter 6

Compare Instructions, With Data in Character Form

Programming Logic

Program statements are executed in the order in which they appear unless the computer is instructed to do otherwise. Frequently, it is necessary to alter the normal flow of execution. This is accomplished by instructing the computer to change the sequence of instructions to be executed, and to proceed to another point in the program. This process is called *branching*. Branching may be of two types, conditional and unconditional. As the term implies, an unconditional branch will *always* cause a branch to a particular instruction regardless of existing conditions, while a conditional branch requires that certain conditions be met within the program in order for the branch to take place. In high-level languages, these branches appear as GO TO and IF–THEN instructions.

Unconditional Branching

An unconditional branch will always alter the path of a program regardless of existing conditions. Unconditional branching is the method used to instruct the computer to return to the beginning of a program and start processing over again. This repeated execution of a series of instructions is referred to as *looping*. Examine the flowchart excerpt in Figure 6-1. An unconditional branch

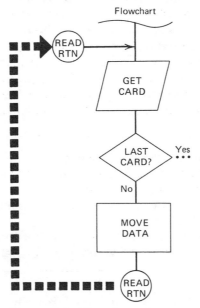

Figure 6-1 Flowchart of an unconditional branch operation.

to the read instruction is required to process the next set of data. The instruction for this branch could be written as:

Operation		Operand
10 14		16
B		READRTN

where B is the operation code for **BRANCH**. **READRTN** is a label that identifies the **GET** instruction. It appears in the *NAME* field of the **GET** statement.

Hence, an excerpt of the program coded from the flowchart would appear as follows:

LABEL	OPERATION	OPERAND
1	10	16
READRTN	GET	INFILE,RECORD
	MVC	OUTAREA(80),RECORD
	.	
	.	
	.	
	B	READRTN

Unlike other instructions, the unconditional branch has only one operand. A symbolic name used as an operand in a branch instruction *must* appear in the name field of some instruction in the program. Since these names are used to identify a statement, they are frequently referred to as *labels*. The branch instruction transfers control to the instruction with the label or name indicated. At some point in the program, there must be a statement with the specified NAME field or LABEL, as shown in Figure 6-1. Hence, **B READRTN** is valid only if there is a statement called **READRTN** in the program. A label is assigned to an instruction by placing the name in the NAME field of the coding sheet (columns 1 through 8), as illustrated. *Labels are not assigned to each instruction,* only to instructions that will serve as branch points. When branching to some *routine* or sequence of instructions, the first instruction of that routine must have a label. The label should also be descriptive and meaningful so that it can serve to document the program. The label **READRTN**, for example, is more descriptive than R, although the latter is an equally valid label.

Rules for Forming Labels (Review)
1. Begins in column one: 1–8 characters long.
2. First character must be a letter.
3. Remaining characters may be any combination of letters (A–Z), numbers (0–9) or @, #, or $.
4. No spaces or special characters other than @, #, $ are permitted.
5. There are *no* reserved words with special meaning.

The following examples illustrate those labels that are valid and those that are not. If the label is not valid, then the reason for the error is noted.

Label	Valid	Invalid	Reason for Error
XRAY	X		
7UP		X	Label must start with a letter.
EMP-NO		X	Hyphen is a special character.
B147UP	X		
HAMILTON	X		
CHK RTN		X	No spaces in a label
OUTPUTRTN		X	Too long
U.S.A.		X	Periods are special characters.

SELF-EVALUATING QUIZ

1. (True or False) Every instruction should be assigned a label.
2. The two types of branches are _____ and _____ .
3. Program statements are usually executed in _____ .
4. In order to alter the normal program flow, a(n) _____ instruction must be used.
5. A series of instructions executed over and over again is called a _____ .
6. The operation code for an unconditional branch is written as _____ .
7. The operand for an unconditional branch must identify the first instruction of a routine and would also therefore appear in the _____ field of the coding form.
8. What, if anything, is wrong with the following labels?

	LABEL	OPE 10
a.	STEP 5	
b.	1STCLASS	
c.	TOTAL12	
d.	NAME-IN	
e.	SUM%	
f.	CHECKIT 12	

Solutions

1. False. Only those branched to
2. Conditional
   unconditional
3. Sequence
4. Branch
5. Loop
6. B
7. Name or label

8. a.   Embedded blank not permitted
    b.   Label must begin with alphabetic character
    c.   Okay
    d.   No hyphens in a label
    e.   No % in label
    f.   Too long

Conditional Branches

We will define a conditional statement as any statement that tests for the existence of some condition and causes a branch to be made if that condition is found.

A *simple conditional* tests for a specific relation or condition:

Examples of Simple Conditional Tests
Is one field equal to another field (=)?
Is one field less than another field (<)?
Is one field greater than another field (>)?

If the condition is met, a *conditional branch* occurs. If not, the program proceeds to the next sequential step.

A few examples will illustrate simple conditional tests and branches. See Figure 6-2.

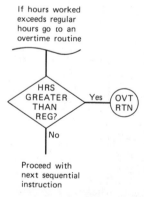

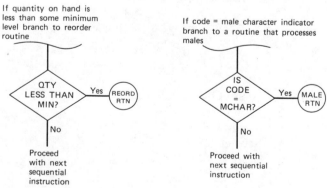

Figure 6-2   Examples of conditional branches.

To be an effective programmer, it is not enough simply to learn the rules of a programming language. We must be able to apply these rules in order to solve logic problems. The conditional statement, as illustrated, is of prime importance in solving these logic problems and is, therefore, an integral part of all programming languages.

In high-level languages, the conditional is generally coded by a single IF . . . THEN statement. In assembler language, however, this task requires two instructions:

The Conditional Branch
1. *Compare* two fields.
   The result of the comparison sets a condition code.
2. *Branch* depending upon the condition code.

The Compare Instruction and the Condition Code

The purpose of the compare instruction is to compare two operands. This instruction automatically sets an internal *condition code* that can then be tested. A branch is then executed depending upon the status of the code. Note, however, that compare instructions do not alter the contents of either operand.

Compare Logical Character (CLC) Instruction

The Compare Logical Character (CLC) instruction is classified as a storage-to-storage instruction and is used to set the condition code when comparing two quantities in main storage. While two operands being tested may be in any format, the CLC instruction is most commonly used with EBCDIC data. We will see that the field having the *higher binary value* will be considered the greater field.

Format

Operation		Operand
10 14		16
CLC		OP1,OP2

Instruction:	CLC
Meaning:	Compare logical character: Storage-to-storage. (Both operands are storage areas.)
Result:	Condition code is set to high, low, equal depending upon the compare: high—Operand 1 is greater than Operand 2. low—Operand 1 is less than Operand 2. equal—Operand 1 = Operand 2.
Operands:	May be in any format—most commonly EBCDIC May be explicit or implicit Operand 2 may be a self-defining operand.
Length:	Maximum—256 byte comparison Length of comparison is determined by specification of first operand
Limitation:	The CLC is best used for alphanumeric comparisons and comparisons of *unsigned* numbers.

The number of bytes to be compared may vary from 1 to 256. As a result of the comparison, the condition code will be set to equal, low or high depending upon the contents compared. Review the collating sequence or the relative weights of each character within the 360/370 system since this is the basis for all CLC comparisons. See Figure 6-3.

Just as with the MVC instruction, the CLC instruction may be of two types, explicit or implicit. An explicit compare includes a length specifier. In an implicit compare, the length of the first operand determines the length of the comparison. An example of both types follows:

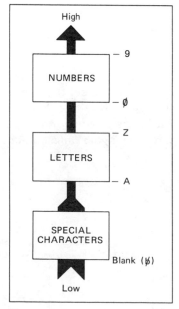

Figure 6-3 Collating sequence.

Examples

	LABEL	OPERATION 10	16	OPERAND
1.		C L C	H R S (2) , T I M E	E X P L I C I T C O M P A R E
2.		C L C	H R S , T I M E	I M P L I C I T C O M P A R E

CLC is the operation code.
HRS is the first operand and a symbolic address or location in storage.
TIME is the second operand and a symbolic address or location in storage.

In Example 1, the (2) is the explicit length specifier. A two-position compare will result regardless of the length of the fields. In Example 2, the length of HRS will determine the number of positions compared.

In a CLC instruction, the *first* operand is compared to the *second* operand. The comparison begins in the high-order position and thereafter proceeds from left to right, one character at a time. As we will see below, this left-to-right comparison makes the CLC particularly useful for comparing alphanumeric, as opposed to numeric, data.

The comparison is terminated in one of two ways:
1. An unequal condition occurs. At this point:
   a. if the character in operand 1 is less than the character in operand 2, a *low condition* occurs.
   b. if the character in operand 1 is greater than the character in operand 2, a *high condition* occurs.
2. The end of the first operand is reached by either:
   a. the implicit length of the first operand, or
   b. the length specifier indicated in the first operand.

In the following examples, assume that the length of the first operand implies the length of the comparison, and that the data is in EBCDIC form.

Operand 1	Operand 2	Number of Characters Compared	Result
712	699	1	High (operand 1 greater than operand 2)
72	72	2	Equal
1446	1447	4	Low (operand 1 less than operand 2)
− 007	+ 007	3	High

The last example clearly illustrates that the CLC instruction does not compare characters on an *algebraic* basis, but instead performs a *binary* comparison of the EBCDIC characters (F0 F0 D7 > F0 F0 C7). There are instructions to compare packed data *algebraically*, but they will be treated in the next chapter.

When using the CLC instruction for comparing numeric fields, you must therefore be careful, since the results of comparisons are not always what one might ordinarily expect. Signed fields and fields that contain blanks or high-order zeros have binary representations that can result in illogical comparisons. The following table is a list of values in descending sequence.

Values in Descending Sequence

Number	Hex Representation	Binary Representation					
		F	1	F	2		
12	F1F2	1111	0001	1111	0010		
		F	1	D	2		
−12	F1D2	1111	0001	1101	0010		
		F	1	C	2		
+12	F1C2	1111	0001	1100	0010		
		F	0	F	1	F	2
012	F0F1F2	1111	0000	1111	0001	1111	0010
		4	0	F	1	F	2
⌀12	40F1F2	0100	0000	1111	0001	1111	0010

Note that the bits are compared, one by one until an inequality occurs or until the first operand is terminated. When 12 is compared to −12, for example, we have

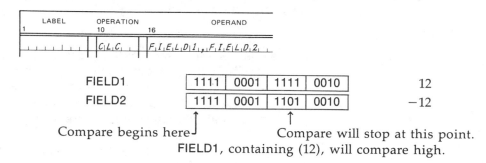

FIELD1 | 1111 | 0001 | 1111 | 0010 | 12
FIELD2 | 1111 | 0001 | 1101 | 0010 | −12

Compare begins here⌐   Compare will stop at this point.
        FIELD1, containing (12), will compare high.

To compare −12 to +12, we have:

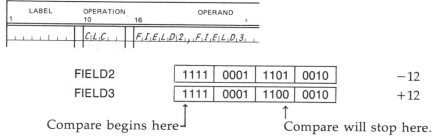

FIELD2 | 1111 | 0001 | 1101 | 0010 | −12
FIELD3 | 1111 | 0001 | 1100 | 0010 | +12

Compare begins here⌐   Compare will stop here.
        FIELD2 (−12) will compare high. Despite the fact that −12 is, in reality, less than +12, the binary representation is deceptive. To compare signed numbers, then, you should use the compare as noted in the next chapter.

Using the CLC,

    12 is greater than −12

    −12 is greater than +12

    +12 is greater than 012

    012 is greater than ⌀12

When comparing alphanumeric fields, the normal collating sequence is followed. For example.

    ABCD is less than BBCD

    BBCD is less than ZBCD

    ZBCD is less than 1BCD

    ABCD is less than ACCD

    ⌀BDC is less than ABCD

    ABCD is less than ABCE

Note that the CLC instruction is best used for normal alphanumeric comparisons and comparisons of *unsigned* numbers.

Now that the basis for comparison has been explained, we will examine the CLC instruction through a few examples. For the sake of simplicity, the data is shown in character or EBCDIC form rather than in hex form.

Example 1

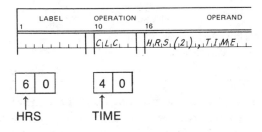

Results

Number of bytes actually compared   1
Condition   high
(Operand 1 is greater than operand 2.)

Example 2

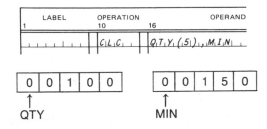

Results

Number of bytes actually compared   4
(inequality reached)
Condition   low

Example 3

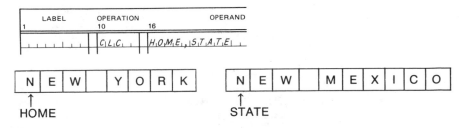

Results

Number of bytes actually compared   5
(inequality reached)
Condition   high

Example 4

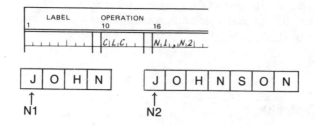

Results

Number of bytes actually compared   4
(end of first operand reached)
Condition   equal

Rules for the Compare Logical Character
1. The data contained in the operands may be in any format; however, the EBCDIC form is most common.
2. The first operand is compared to the second.
3. The binary comparison is from left to right, one character at a time, until an inequality occurs or until the end of the first operand is reached.
4. The length of the comparison depends upon whether an explicit or implicit compare is used.

SELF EVALUATING QUIZ   Given the following data in storage, determine the number of bytes compared and the setting of the condition code for each instruction executed.

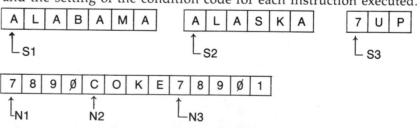

Instruction	Resulting Condition	Number of Bytes Compared	Explanation of Result
1. CLC S1,S2			
2. CLC S3,S1			
3. CLC S2(3),S1			
4. CLC S3(3),N1			
5. CLC N2,S2			
6. CLC N1,N3			
7. CLC N3,N1			
8. CLC S3(1),N3			

*****

Solutions

	Instruction	Resulting Condition	Number of Bytes Compared	Explanation of Result
1.	CLC S1,S2	Low	4	Letter B is less than the letter S.
2.	CLC S3,S1	High	1	The number 7 is greater than the letter [...]
3.	CLC S2(3),S1	Equal	3	
4.	CLC S3(3),N1	Low	2	The letter U is less than the number 8.
5.	CLC N2,S2	High	1	C is greater than A
6.	CLC N1,N3	Equal	4	N1 contains 4 bytes-7890 equals 7890.
7.	CLC N3,N1	High	5	N3 contains 5 bytes-78901 compares high to 7890C.
8.	CLC S3(1),N3	Equal	1	Explicit one byte comparison.

Branch on Condition

Once the condition code has been set by a compare instruction, a conditional branch statement can be used to alter the flow of logic, depending upon an existing condition.

As with unconditional branch instructions, the operand field contains the name or label of an instruction. To code the unconditional branch B STEP5 means that STEP5 is the name of a statement within the program:

LABEL	OPERATION	OPERAND
1	10 16	
S,T,E,P,5	M,V,C,	L,I,N,E,O,U,T,,M,S,S,G,

The conditional branch instructions use operation codes as follows:

Summary: Branch on Condition

Operation	Meaning	Operand Condition	Numeric Setting of Internal Condition Code
BH	Branch on high	First greater than second ($>$)	2
BL	Branch on low	First less than second ($<$)	1
BE	Branch on equal	First = second	0
BNE	Branch not equal	First not equal second ($\neq$)	1 or 2
BNH	Branch not high	First less than or equal to second ($\leq$)	0 or 1
BNL	Branch not low	First greater than or equal to second ($\geq$)	0 or 2

Condition Code

The compare instruction automatically sets the condition code to 0, 1, 2 depending upon whether the first operand is equal to, less than, or greater than the second operand. In coding the branch instruction, the programmer need not use these codes. To cause a branch to STEP6 if the first operand equals the second operand, for example, we code:

    BE   STEP6

The BE instruction causes the computer to test for a condition code of 0. Condition codes are included here for reference purposes only, since the programmer need not know the corresponding numeric values except for debugging purposes.

Examples

1. The conditional branch instructions can be coded as follows:

If condition code High (A > B), then branch to RTN1.

2.

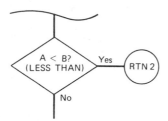

3.

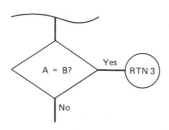

4.

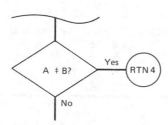

Note that for any given condition there are several ways to flowchart and code the conditional branch. For example, the following two illustrations result in the same logic:

Method 1

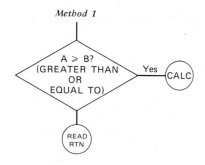

	LABEL	OPERATION		
1		10	16	
		$C L C$	A , B	
		$B N L$	$C A L C$	
		B	$R E A D R T N$	

Method 2

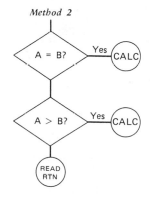

	LABEL	OPERATION		
1		10	16	
		$C L C$	A , B	
		$B E$	$C A L C$	
		$B H$	$C A L C$	
		B	$R E A D R T N$	

A third method of coding follows:

	LABEL	OPERATION		
1		10	16	
		$C L C$	A , B	
		$B L$	$R E A D R T N$	
		B	$C A L C$	

The efficient programmer can write a program with a minimum number of steps. Therefore, method 1 and method 3 above would be preferable.

SELF EVALUATING QUIZ

Convert the following flowchart symbols to Assembler Language Coding:

1.

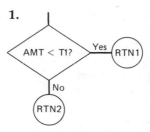

2.

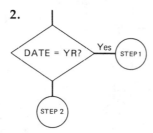

3.

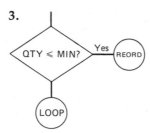

4.

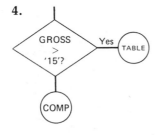

5. For each of the program excerpts (a) to (g) that follow, indicate which branch will occur for the conditions specified below:

a.	CLC	X,Y		b.	CLC	X,Y
	BE	ERROR			BNE	BEGIN
	B	BEGIN			B	ERROR
c.	CLC	Y,X		d.	CLC	X,Y
	BH	BEGIN			B	ERROR
	B	ERROR			BNE	BEGIN
e.	CLC	Y,X		f.	CLC	Y,X
	BL	ERROR			BNL	BEGIN
	B	BEGIN			B	ERROR
			g.	CLC	X,Y	
				BNH	BEGIN	
				B	ERROR	

Condition	a	b	c	d	e	f	g
X < Y							
X = Y							
X > Y							

One of the series of instructions above contains a logic error. Can you find it?

6. For each of the following program excerpts listed below indicate:
   (1) The condition code setting.
   (2) The number of bytes compared.
   (3) Whether or not a branch occurs (say yes or no).

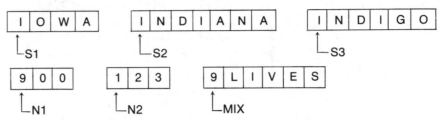

	Coding		Condition	Number of Bytes Compared	Does Branch Occur?
a.	CLC	S1,S2			
	BL	RTN1			
b.	CLC	S3,S2			
	BH	RTN2			
c.	CLC	S2(4),S3			
	BE	RTN3			
d.	CLC	S1,S3			
	BNL	RTN4			
e.	CLC	N1,N2			
	BNE	RTN5			
f.	CLC	N1,MIX			
	BL	RTN6			

Solutions 1.

LABEL	OPERATION	OPERAND
	CLC	AMT1,T1
	BL	RTN1
	B	RTN2
*		
*	ALTERNATE METHOD	
*		
	CLC	AMT1,T1
	BNL	RTN2
	B	RTN1

2.

LABEL	OPERATION	OPERAND
	CLC	DATE,YR
	BE	STEP1
	B	STEP2
*		
*	ALTERNATE METHOD	
*		
	CLC	DATE,YR
	BNE	STEP2
	B	STEP1

3.

```
LABEL     OPERATION     OPERAND
          CLC           QTY,MIN
          BNH           REORD
          B             LOOP
*
*         ALTERNATE METHOD
*
          CLC           QTY,MIN
          BH            LOOP
          B             REORD
```

4.

```
LABEL     OPERATION     OPERAND
          CLC           GROSS,=C'15'
          BH            TABLE
          B             COMP
*
*         ALTERNATE METHOD
*
          CLC           GROSS,=C'15'
          BNH           COMP
          B             TABLE
```

5.

Condition	a	b	c	d	e	f	g
X < Y	BEGIN	BEGIN	BEGIN	ERROR	BEGIN	BEGIN	BEGIN
X = Y	ERROR	ERROR	ERROR	ERROR	BEGIN	BEGIN	BEGIN
X > Y	BEGIN	BEGIN	ERROR	ERROR	ERROR	ERROR	ERROR

d. The unconditional branch to ERROR precedes the conditional branch; hence, the unconditional branch always occurs, regardless of the condition. The BNE instruction is never executed.

6.

	Coding		Condition	Number of bytes compared	Does branch occur?
a.	CLC	S1,S2			
	BL	RTN1	High	2	No
b.	CLC	S3,S2			
	BH	RTN2	High	5	Yes
c.	CLC	S2(4),S3			
	BE	RTN3	Equal	4	Yes
d.	CLC	S1,S3			
	BNL	RTN4	High	2	Yes
e.	CLC	N1,N2			
	BNE	RTN5	High	1	Yes
f.	CLC	N1,MIX			
	BL	RTN6	High	2	No

Inclusive and Exclusive Comparisons

Testing whether the contents of a field is between two endpoints is sometimes confusing to programmers. For example, suppose we wish to branch to PRINTRTN if FIELDA is between 4 and 9. Are we to branch to PRINTRTN if

FIELDA equals 4 or only if PRINTRTN is greater than 4? Similarly, are we to branch to PRINTRTN if FIELDA equals 9 or only if it is less than 9? To phrase these questions a different way, should the comparison be *inclusive* or *exclusive* of endpoints?

Example 1

Branch to PRINTRTN if FIELDA is between 4 and 9, inclusive of the endpoints. Otherwise, branch to BEGIN.

    If FIELDA:

    (a) = 4;

or

    (b) is greater than 4 and less than 9
       (FIELDA > 4 and FIELDA < 9);

or

    (c) = 9;

then a branch to PRINTRTN should occur.

    This can be simply stated as:

    Branch to PRINTRTN if $4 \leqslant$ FIELDA $\leqslant 9$

This can be programmed as:

LABEL	OPERATION	OPERAND
	CLC	FIELDA,=C'4'
	BL	BEGIN
	CLC	FIELDA,=C'9'
	BH	BEGIN
	B	PRINTRTN

The above causes a branch to BEGIN if FIELDA is less than 4 or more than 9. Thus, a branch to PRINTRTN will occur if FIELDA is between 4 and 9 inclusive. Note that there are several correct methods that may be used to code this problem. The following is also correct.

LABEL	OPERATION	OPERAND	COMMENTS
*		ALTERNATE METHOD FOR BRANCHING TO PRINTRTN	
*		IF FIELDA IS BETWEEN 4 AND 9 INCLUSIVE	
*			
	CLC	FIELDA,=C'4'	
	BNL	NEXTTEST	
	B	BEGIN	
NEXTTEST	CLC	FIELDA,=C'9'	
	BNH	PRINTRTN	
	B	BEGIN	

Example 2

Branch to PRINTRTN if FIELDA is between 4 and 9, *exclusive* of the endpoints. Otherwise, branch to BEGIN.

    If FIELDA:

    (a) is greater than 4 (FIELDA > 4)

and

    (b) is less than 9 (FIELDA < 9)

branch to PRINTRTN.

This can be simply stated as

Branch to **PRINTRTN** if 4 < FIELDA < 9

One method of programming this is:

LABEL	OPERATION 10	OPERAND 16	COMMENTS
	CLC	FIELDA,=C'4'	
	BNH	BEGIN	BRANCH ON = OR LESS THAN 4
	CLC	FIELDA,=C'9'	
	BNL	BEGIN	BRANCH ON = OR GREATER THAN 9
	B	PRINTRTN	

The above causes a branch to **BEGIN** if FIELDA is less than or equal to 4. A branch to **BEGIN** also occurs if FIELDA is greater than or equal to 9. Hence, a branch to **PRINTRTN** will occur if FIELDA is greater than 4 and less than 9. An alternate method of coding this is:

LABEL	OPERATION 10	OPERAND 16
	CLC	FIELDA,=C'4'
	BH	NEXTTEST
	B	BEGIN
NEXTTEST	CLC	FIELDA,=C'9'
	BL	PRINTRTN
	B	BEGIN

Unless otherwise noted, the use of the term "between" in this text will mean *inclusive* of the endpoints. Hence to branch to **STEP1** if X is between 10 and 100 can be represented as:

If 10 ≤ X ≤ 100 branch to **STEP1**.

SELF EVALUATING QUIZ

Indicate, in each of the following, the condition(s) that cause a branch to ERROR:

```
1.  CLC     IN,=C'1234'
    BNH     ERROR
    B       STEP1
2.  CLC     OUT,=C'222'
    BL      STEP5
    B       ERROR
3.  CLC     FLDA,=C'236'
    BL      STEP2
    CLC     FLDA,=C'923'
    BH      STEP6
    B       ERROR
4.  CLC     FLDB,=C'ABC'
    B       STEP2
    BH      ERROR
```

Solutions

1. A branch to **ERROR** occurs when **IN** is less than or equal to 1234 (≤1234).
2. A branch to **ERROR** occurs when **OUT** is greater than or equal to 222 (≥222).
3. A branch to **ERROR** occurs when FLDA is between 236 and 923, inclusive (236 ≤ FLDA ≤ 923).

4. A branch to ERROR *never* occurs. The unconditional branch to STEP2 *precedes* the branch on condition and, hence, the computer automatically transfers control to STEP2, regardless of the comparison. Such programming is normally invalid.

Compare Logical Immediate (CLI)

Instruction:	CLI
Meaning:	Compare logical immediate
Operand 1:	Storage area
Operand 2:	One byte constant expressed in zoned-decimal, hexadecimal, or binary form
	NOTE: *No* = sign precedes the constant.
Result:	Condition codes are set depending upon how Operand 1 compares to Operand 2.
Limitations:	Only *one* byte comparison can be made.

Branches coded immediately after a CLI instruction will be executed as follows:

Types of Branches that can be Executed Following CLI		
Op Code	Instruction	Meaning
BE	Branch equal	Branch if Operand 1 of CLI Instruction = Operand 2
BH	Branch high	Operand 1 > Operand 2
BL	Branch low	Operand 1 < Operand 2
BNE	Branch not equal	Operand 1 ≠ Operand 2
BNH	Branch not high	Operand 1 = Operand 2 or Operand 1 < Operand 2
BNL	Branch not low	Operand 1 = Operand 2 or Operand 1 > Operand 2

Examples

1.

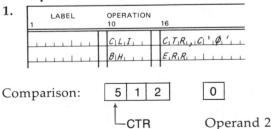

LABEL	OPERATION	
	CLI	CTR,C'0'
	BH	ERR

Comparison:

| 5 | 1 | 2 | | 0 |

⌐CTR   Operand 2

Only the high-order byte is compared. A branch to ERR will occur since 5 > 0.

2.

LABEL	OPERATION	OPERAND
	CLI	CARDIN+79,C'Z'
	BE	NEXT

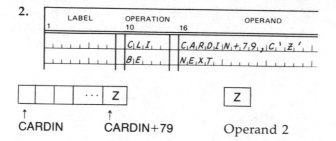

CARDIN   CARDIN+79   Operand 2

Only one byte is compared. A branch to **NEXT** will occur.

3.

LABEL	OPERATION	OPERAND
	CLI	CTR,B'11000001'
	BE	STEP1

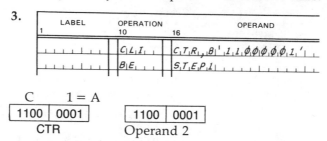

Result of comparison: = (branch to **STEP1** *will* occur)

Figure 6-4 illustrates a program that reads in cards and prints out only the names of the females. A female has a 1 in column 26; a male has a code of 2.

```
*
*
*                                    HOUSEKEEPING INSTRUCTIONS GO HERE     *
*                                                                         *
         MVC     OUTAREA,SPACES
         MVC     OUTAREA+20(15),=C'LIST OF FEMALES'
         PUT     OUTFILE,OUTAREA
         MVC     OUTAREA,SPACES
         MVC     FNAME(10),=C'FIRST NAME'
         MVC     LNAME(9),=C'LAST NAME'
         PUT     OUTFILE,OUTAREA
READ     MVC     OUTAREA,SPACES
         GET     INFILE,RECORD
         CLI     CODE,C'2'
         BE      READ
         MVC     LNAME,LAST
         MVC     FNAME,FIRST
         PUT     OUTFILE,OUTAREA
         B       READ
*                                                                         *
*                                    HOUSEKEEPING INSTRUCTIONS GO HERE     *
*                                    ALONG WITH DCB OR DTF MACROS          *
*                                                                         *
RECORD   DS      0CL80
LAST     DS      CL15
FIRST    DS      CL10
CODE     DS      CL1
         DS      CL54
SPACES   DC      CL1' '
OUTAREA  DS      0CL132
         DS      CL5
FNAME    DS      CL10
         DS      CL20
LNAME    DS      CL15
         DS      CL82
         END
```

Figure 6-4

Figure 6-5 illustrates a program that reads in cards with the following format. A report with headings is produced which lists the names and salaries of those people who earn over $15,000.

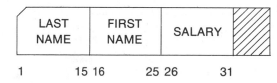

LAST NAME	FIRST NAME	SALARY	
1	15 16	25 26	31

```
*                                                                      *
*                                    HOUSEKEEPING INSTRUCTIONS GO HERE  *
*                                                                      *
         MVC    OUTAREA,SPACES
         MVC    OUTAREA+23(31),=C'EMPLOYEES WHO EARN OVER $15,000'
         PUT    OUTFILE,OUTAREA
         MVC    OUTAREA,SPACES
         PUT    OUTFILE,OUTAREA          PRINT BLANK LINE
         MVC    LNAME(9),=C'LAST NAME'
         MVC    FNAME(10),=C'FIRST NAME'
         MVC    SALOUT(6),=C'SALARY'
         PUT    OUTFILE,OUTAREA
         MVC    OUTAREA,SPACES
         PUT    OUTFILE,OUTAREA          PRINT BLANK LINE
READ     MVC    OUTAREA,SPACES
         GET    INFILE,RECORD
         CLC    SALARY,=C'15000'
         BNH    READ
         MVC    LNAME,LAST
         MVC    FNAME,FIRST
         MVC    SALOUT,SALARY
         MVI    SALOUT-1,C'$'
         PUT    OUTFILE,OUTAREA
         B      READ
*                                                                      *
*                                    HOUSEKEEPING INSTRUCTIONS GO HERE  *
*                                    ALONG WITH DCB OR DTF MACROS       *
*                                                                      *
RECORD   DS     0CL80                    CARD FORMAT
LAST     DS     CL15                       *
FIRST    DS     CL10                       *
SALARY   DS     CL5                        *
         DS     CL50                       *
SPACES   DC     CL1' '
OUTAREA  DS     0CL132                   PRINT FORMAT
         DS     CL5                        *
LNAME    DS     CL15                       *
         DS     CL20                       *
FNAME    DS     CL10                       *
         DS     CL20                       *
SALOUT   DS     CL5                        *
         DS     CL57                       *
         END
```

Figure 6-5

SELF EVALUATING QUIZ

1. A compare instruction automatically sets a(n) _____ .
2. (True or False) The **CLC** instruction is most commonly used with EBCDIC data.
3. If **FLDA** contains −9 and **FLDB** contains +9, the instruction **CLC FLDA,FLDB** will result in the condition code being set to (*high/low/equal*).
4. (True or False) The **CLC** instruction is best used for alphanumeric comparisons and comparisons of signed numbers.

5. (True or False) The following two sets of instructions are equivalent:

    a. CLC   FLDA,FLDB
       BNH   RTN1
       B   RTN2

    b. CLC   FLDA,FLDB
       BL   RTN1
       B   RTN2

6. The **CLI** instruction can be used to compare up to (<u>number</u>) bytes of data.

7. Determine the values of AMT1, AMT2 and AMT3 after execution of the following instructions. The three fields have the following values before execution.

F0	F1	F0

AMT1

F1	F2	F3

AMT2

F0	F1	F0

AMT3

```
        CLC     AMT1,AMT3
        BNE     STEP5
        MVC     AMT3,AMT2
        CLC     AMT3,AMT1
        BL      READRTN
STEP5   MVI     AMT1+2,C'1'
```

8. Code a routine to branch to **PRINT** if a field called **WEIGHT** is between 110 and 125 pounds. Otherwise, branch to **READRTN**. Assume **WEIGHT** is defined as follows:

    WEIGHT   DS   CL3

9. Code a routine to branch to **PRINT** for input cards that contain data on blue-eyed, blonde females. Otherwise, branch to **READRTN**. Cards appear as follows:

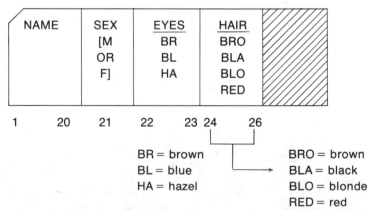

10. Code a routine to branch to **TOTALRTN** for insurance cards representing male, New York state residents, between 18 and 25 years old. Otherwise, branch to **READRTN**.

NAME	SEX (M OR F)	STATE (NY NJ MA . . ·)	AGE (IN YRS)	

1   20   21   22   23 24   25 26   80

Solutions

1. Condition code
2. True
3. High (D9 > C9)
4. False. (*un*signed numbers and alphanumeric data)
5. False. For (a), a branch to RTN2 occurs if FLDA is greater than FLDB, whereas in (b), a branch to RTN2 occurs if FLDA is greater than *or equal* to FLDB.
6. one
7.

F0	F1	F1

AMT1

F1	F2	F3

AMT2

F1	F2	F3

AMT3

8.

LABEL	OPERATION	OPERAND	COMMENTS
	CLC	WEIGHT,=C'110'	
	BNL	NEXTTEST	
	B	READRTN	
NEXTTEST	CLC	WEIGHT,=C'125'	
	BNH	PRINT	
	B	READRTN	
*	NOTE:	WE ASSUMED THAT 'BETWEEN' MEANT INCLUSIVE	

9.

LABEL	OPERATION	OPERAND
READRTN	GET	INAREA,RECORD
	CLC	SEX,=C'F'
	BNE	READRTN
	CLC	EYES,=C'BL'
	BNE	READRTN
	CLC	HAIR,=C'BLO'
	BNE	READRTN
	B	PRINT
*		
RECORD	DS	0CL80
NAME	DS	CL20
SEX	DS	CL1
EYES	DS	CL2
HAIR	DS	CL3
	DS	CL54

The following is a "short—cut" method.

LABEL	OPERATION	OPERAND	COMMENTS
READRTN	GET	INAREA,RECORD	
	CLC	TESTAREA,=C'FBLBLO'	COMPARE SEX, EYES, HAIR AS A GROUP
	BNE	READRTN	
	B	PRINT	
*			
RECORD	DS	0CL80	
NAME	DS	CL20	
TESTAREA	DS	CL6	
	DS	CL54	

10.

LABEL	OPERATION 10	OPERAND 16
READRTN	GET	INAREA,RECORD
	CLC	SEX,=C'M'
	BNE	READRTN
	CLC	STATE,=C'NY'
	BNE	READRTN
	CLC	AGE,=C'18'
	BL	READRTN
	CLC	AGE,=C'25'
	BH	READRTN
	B	TOTALRTN
*		
RECORD	DS	ØCL8Ø
NAME	DS	CL2Ø
SEX	DS	CL1
STATE	DS	CL2
AGE	DS	CL2
	DS	CL55

KEY TERMS
Branching
Condition code
Conditional branch
Exclusive comparison
Explicit comparison
Implicit comparison
Inclusive comparison
Label
Loop
Routine
Simple conditional
Unconditional branch

Review Questions State whether FIELDA is equal to, less than or greater than FIELDB:

	FIELDA	FIELDB
1.	012	12
2.	120	12
3.	−89	+89
4.	ABC	ABCØ
5.	43	+43

NOTE: the comparison which is performed is as follows:
```
CLC     FIELDA,FIELDB
```

Convert each of the above to EBCDIC form in order to determine the answer.

6. Write a routine to branch to NOTEMP if C is between 98 and 100, inclusive.

7. Write a routine to branch to NOTEMP if C is between 98 and 100, exclusive.

8. For each of the following, indicate:
   a. The condition code setting.
   b. Number of bytes actually compared.
   c. Whether or not the branch actually occurs.
   The contents of each data field is specified below:

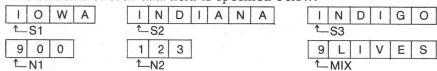

	Coding		Condition	Number of Bytes Compared	Does Branch Occur?
a.	CLC	MIX(1),N1			
	BNH	RTNA			
b.	CLC	N1,MIX			
	BNH	RTN7			
c.	CLC	S1,N1			
	BNE	RTN8			
d.	CLC	S2,N2			
	BNE	RTNB			
e.	CLC	S3,N1			
	BNH	RTNC			

Practice Programs

1. Consider the following card format:

LAST NAME	FIRST NAME	CODE 1=FEMALE 2=MALE	SALARY (integers)	WEIGHT (in pounds)	HEIGHT (in inches)	

1   15 16   25 26   27   31 32   34 35   36

   Print the names of all
   (a) males taller than 6 feet (72 inches) and weighing more than 200 pounds with the message 'RUGGED'.
   (b) females weighing between 105 and 125 pounds and between 60 inches and 67 inches with the message 'JUST RIGHT'.

2. Write a program to read in cards as shown and print the smallest of the three numbers on each card.

NO1	NO2	NO3	

1   3 4   6 7   9

3. Write a program to print out patient name and diagnosis for each of the following input medical cards:

   1–20 Patient name
      21 Lung infection   1—if found
                              0—if not found
      22 Temperature   1—high
                              0—normal

23 Sniffles   1—present
                            0—absent
24 Sore throat   1—present
                            0—absent
25–80 Not used

NOTES:
(a) Output is a printed report with heading: **DIAGNOSIS REPORT.**
(b) If the patient has lung infection and temperature, diagnosis is **PNEUMONIA.**
(c) If the patient has a combination of two or more symptoms (except the combination of lung infection and temperature), the diagnosis is **COLD.**
(d) If the patient has any single symptom, the diagnosis is **PHONY.**
(e) If the patient has no symptoms, the diagnosis is **HEALTHY.**

Chapter 7

Introduction to Decimal Arithmetic Operations

Up to this point, our processing has been limited to simply moving data from one location in storage to another and comparing fields in character form. In this chapter we will consider simple arithmetic operations.

Input data, as we already know, is in **EBCDIC** or zoned-decimal format, and as such cannot be used for calculations. In order to carry out storage to storage arithmetic, numeric data must be in a form called *packed decimal.* You will recall that packed-decimal data uses less storage than the conventional zoned-decimal format. Input data fields must be converted to the packed-decimal format by a **PACK** instruction before we can perform an arithmetic operation. Numeric fields to be packed are usually entered in the zoned-decimal format. Note that they should *not* contain blanks. Blank characters are invalid in numeric data fields. When blanks are packed and later used in arithmetic operations, a data exception or other error may occur.

Review of Packed-Data Format

We will now briefly review the packed-data format. A five-digit number is stored in the general configuration as shown below,

```
        Byte    Byte    Byte
       ┌───┬───┬───┬───┬───┬───┐
       │ D │ D │ D │ D │ D │ S │
       └───┴───┴───┴───┴───┴───┘
         ↑
SNAME ───┘
```

where

　　D denotes a decimal digit 0–9
　　S indicates the sign of the field, positive (hex 'F' or 'C') or negative (hex 'D')
　　SNAME is the symbolic name assigned to the field

You will recall that two decimal digits are packed into each byte, except for the low-order byte that contains the sign and one digit. In order to convert **EBCDIC** input data to this packed-decimal format, a **PACK** instruction is used. For example, if card data was read into an area named **CARDIN**, and the first five card columns contained the number 12345, the data would be read into the computer and stored in zoned-decimal format as follows:

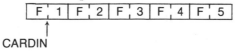

```
       ┌───┬───┬───┬───┬───┬───┬───┬───┬───┬───┐
       │ F │ 1 │ F │ 2 │ F │ 3 │ F │ 4 │ F │ 5 │
       └───┴───┴───┴───┴───┴───┴───┴───┴───┴───┘
         ↑
CARDIN ──┘
```

In order for this data to be used in decimal arithmetic calculations, it must be packed. It would then be represented as follows:

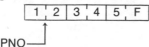

PNO

We will now examine the PACK instruction.

Operation 10	Operand 16
PACK	OP1,OP2

Instruction: PACK

Meaning: Before an arithmetic operation can be performed, fields must be in packed format.

Operands: Second operand packed into first operand.

Result: In first operand.

Length: Determined by first operand, which can be implicit or explicit.
Maximum length—16 bytes.

Limitation: 1.   When constants are used in arithmetic operations, they must be in packed-decimal format.
2.   Zoned-Decimal data that is to be packed should *not* contain any blanks, or other nonnumeric data.

The PACK Instruction

Before *any* arithmetic operation can be performed in assembler language, the numeric fields must be packed. All system 360/370 instructions reference the leftmost or high-order position of each operand. The actual execution of the PACK instruction, however, proceeds from *right* to *left* within the operands.

The PACK instruction converts EBCDIC or zoned-decimal data from the second operand, the sending field, into packed data in the first operand, the receiving field. It is a storage-to-storage instruction, which means that both operands are storage addresses; that is, neither indicates a general register.

Example 1

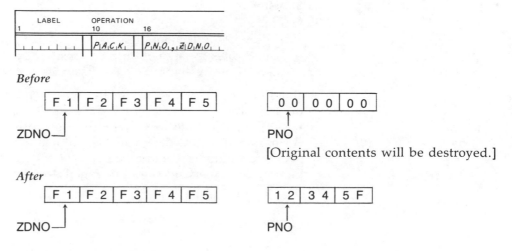

ZDNO would be defined as a character or zoned-decimal field:

LABEL	OPERATION	OPERAND	COMMENTS
1	10 16		
ZDNO	DS	CL5 THE VALUE '12345' IS ENTERED BY SOME INSTRUCTION	
*			
*	ZDNO	COULD ALSO BE DEFINED AS FOLLOWS:	
*			
ZDNO	DC	CL5'12345'	

PNO would be defined as a packed field:

LABEL	OPERATION	OPERAND	COMMENTS
1	10 16		
PNO	DS	PL3 THE VALUE '000' IS ENTERED BY SOME INSTRUCTION	

PNO could also be defined as follows:

LABEL	OPERATION	
1	10 16	
PNO	DC	PL3'000'

The zoned-decimal data in the second operand is packed into the first operand by proceeding one byte at a time from right to left in the step sequence indicated:

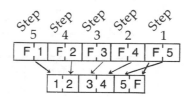

The sign and digits are moved from the second operand (sending field) to the first operand (receiving field) and are *not* checked for validity. This is why the packing of blanks or spaces (hex 40) can result in an invalid sign digit. Here is an illustration of this problem.

Invalid Operand

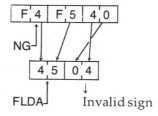

If **FLDA** were to be used later for decimal arithmetic, a data exception would occur since the sign (4) is invalid. The sign of a packed field must be an **F** or **C** for + or **D** for −.

Implicit Pack   The maximum length for either operand is 16 bytes. When no length is explicitly specified, the length of the first operand determines the length of the pack operation. Example 1 above illustrates an implicit pack where the receiving field determines the length of the pack.

Explicit Pack   The length may be *explicitly* stated as

1	LABEL	OPERATION 10	16	OPERAND
		PACK	PNO(3),ZDNO	

and the results would be identical to those shown in Example 1.

We now proceed to analyze the results when the receiving field in a PACK instruction is either larger than necessary or too small.

Example: Receiving Field Larger Than Necessary for Packing Sending Field

1	LABEL	OPERATION 10	16	OPERAND
		PACK	SAME,NO	

After Execution

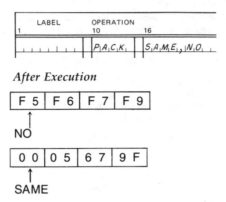

When packing a 4-byte field into a 4-byte area, the high-order positions of the receiving field are filled with zeros. The following example again illustrates a PACK instruction where the receiving field, operand 1, is larger than necessary:

1	LABEL	OPERATION 10	16	OPERAND
		PACK	TOTAL,AMT	
		.		
		.		
		.		
TOTAL		DS	PL4	
AMT		DC	CL3'123'	

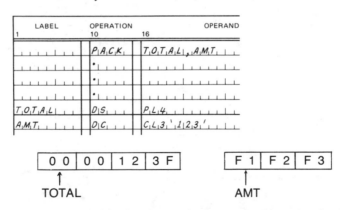

Note that a field may be packed into itself, as in the following:

1	LABEL	OPERATION 10	16	
		PACK	NO,NO	

Before Execution

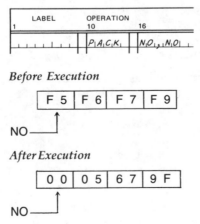

By packing a field into itself, the programmer need not establish an additional storage area for the packed results. If, however, the original EBCDIC format of the data is necessary for printing, it should be moved to the output area *before* it is packed.

NOTE: Packed data, if inadvertently printed, will not be in a readable form.

Receiving Field Too Small to Accommodate Packed Results

If the receiving field is too small to contain the packed data, the high-order positions are truncated.

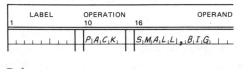

Before

In order to accommodate the entire result, the length of a packed field may be calculated as follows:

$$\text{Packed length} = \frac{\text{length in zoned decimal}}{2} + 1$$

For the illustration above, **SMALL** must be at least three bytes long:

$$\frac{4}{2} + 1 = 3$$

When the zoned-decimal field contains an odd number of digits, the packed length based on the formula will not be a whole number. For example,

$$\text{Length in zoned decimal} = 3$$
$$\text{Packed length} = \frac{3}{2} + 1 = 2.5$$

In such cases, the packed length is computed as the whole number, *without* the fractional part. In the above case the packed length would be 2.

Packed Constants

Data may be established in storage in packed format for use in arithmetic operations. The following illustrate the packed format.

Constants Defined with Implicit Length

LABEL	OPERATION	OPERAND		Field		
AMT1	DC	P'025'		0 2	5 C	
AMT2	DC	P'-246'		2 4	6 D	

Constants Defined with
Explicit Lengths

LABEL	OPERATION	OPERAND		Field
AMT3	DC	PL2'025'		0 2 / 5 C
AMT4	DC	PL3'025' RESULT:HIGH-ORDER Ø'S		0 0 / 0 2 / 5 C
AMT5	DC	PL3'4732687' RESULT: TRUNCATION		3 2 / 6 8 / 7 C

Summary of PACK Instruction

1. The second operand contains zoned-decimal numbers to be packed and stored in the first operand.
2. Each operand is referenced by the symbolic name assigned to its high-order position.
3. The operands are processed one byte at a time, from right to left.
4. The maximum size of either operand is 16 bytes.
5. The number of digits packed depends on the first operand that may be explicitly or implicitly defined.
6. If the first operand is too long, high-order zeros will be inserted.
7. If the first operand is too short, high-order digits in the second operand will be truncated.
8. Fields are not checked for valid sign or digit representation during the pack operation.
9. A field may be packed into itself.

SELF-EVALUATING QUIZ

1. In order to perform decimal arithmetic, the data must be in ___(number)___ form.
2. Only _____ are permitted in fields that are going to be packed.
3. The sign in a packed-data field is located in the rightmost position of the (*low/high*)-order byte.
4. A zoned-decimal field of 7 bytes could be stored in an area of ___(number)___ bytes in length when packed.
5. A pack instruction is of what type?
6. (True or False) Once a field is packed, it may again be packed to save storage.
7. The zoned-decimal data that is to be packed appears in the (*first/second*) operand.
8. The length of the pack operation is dependent upon the (*first/second*) operand.
9. (True or False) The length of the pack may be explicitly or implicitly defined.
10. (True or False) When an invalid sign is generated in the packed field, the programmer is notified via an error message and program interrupt.
11. If the first operand of a PACK instruction contained 2 bytes and the second operand contained the number 1234 in zoned-decimal format, the result produced would be _____ .
12. When the first operand is larger than the second, the high-order position(s) of the field is/are filled with (*spaces/zeros/nothing*).
13. (True or False) In executing a PACK instruction, the operation proceeds from left to right.

14. Indicate the results in each of the following:

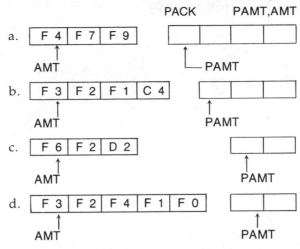

Solutions

1. Packed decimal
2. Digits 0–9, along with a sign (no blanks or special characters)
3. Low
4. 4
5. Storage-to-storage (SS)
6. False
7. Second
8. First
9. True
10. False. The sign is not checked. However, an arithmetic operation performed on a field with an invalid sign will cause a program interrupt.
11. 234F; truncation will occur.
12. Zeros
13. False: right to left.

14.

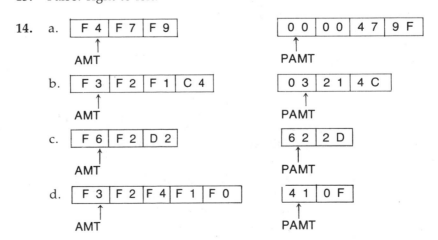

Decimal Addition: The Add Packed Instruction (AP)

Operation 10	Operand 16
AP	OP1,OP2

Add Packed

Instruction: AP
Meaning: Add Packed decimal numbers.
Operands: Second operand added to first; second operand can be literal of form: =P' '.
Result: In first operand; second operand unchanged (second operand may be self-defining).
Lengths: Both fields may be implicit or explicit; 16-byte limit.
Limitation: Make certain receiving field is large enough for answer.

The Add Packed instruction is a storage-to-storage instruction that adds *two packed-decimal fields*. The contents of the second operand are added to the contents of the first operand one byte at a time from right to left, that is, from low order to high order. The result of the addition is placed in the first operand. An example of the Add Packed (**AP**) instruction is:

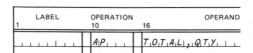

Before Execution

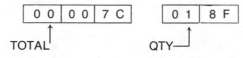

After Execution

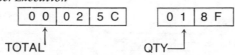

In this example, the first operand (**TOTAL**) is larger than the second (**QTY**) and the high-order positions (**TOTAL**) are filled with zeros. The first operand must always contain enough bytes to hold the largest result anticipated by the programmer.

The AP Instruction Follows the Normal Rules of Addition
1. If both operands are signed positive (C or F), or both are signed negative (D), addition is performed and the corresponding sign, C or D, is placed in the field. In the System 360/370, the sign of a positive field is changed from a *hex* F to a *hex* C whenever decimal arithmetic operations are performed. The sign of a negative field is represented by a hex D.
2. If one operand is signed positive (C or F) and the other is signed negative, (D), subtraction is performed and the sign of the larger (C or D) is placed in the field.

Examples

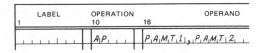

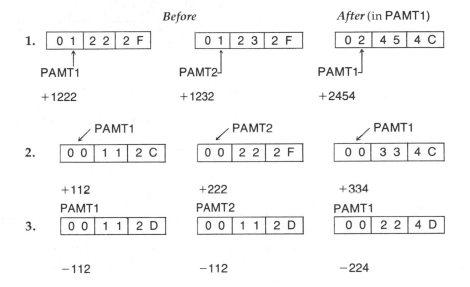

	Before		*After* (in PAMT1)
1.	0 1 2 2 2 F	0 1 2 3 2 F	0 2 4 5 4 C
	PAMT1	PAMT2	PAMT1
	+1222	+1232	+2454
2.	0 0 1 1 2 C (PAMT1)	0 0 2 2 2 F (PAMT2)	0 0 3 3 4 C (PAMT1)
	+112	+222	+334
3.	0 0 1 1 2 D PAMT1	0 0 1 1 2 D PAMT2	0 0 2 2 4 D PAMT1
	−112	−112	−224

RULE: Adding two negative numbers produces a negative result.

	PAMT1	PAMT2	PAMT1
4.	0 0 5 5 2 D	0 0 7 7 2 F	0 0 2 2 0 C
	−552	+772	+220

RULE: Adding one negative to one positive number: subtract smaller from larger and use sign of larger.

	PAMT1	PAMT2	PAMT1
5.	0 0 8 7 2 D	0 0 5 3 1 F	0 0 3 4 1 D
	−872	+531	−341

RULE: Same as (4) above.

With the **AP** instruction, length specifiers may be omitted as illustrated, or included in *both* the first and second operands. When omitted, the first operand determines the number of bytes to be added. The previous instruction may be written in explicit form as follows:

LABEL	OPERATION 10	OPERAND 16
	AP	PAMT1(3),PAMT2(3)

Explicit Add

In using the explicit form of the **AP** instruction, the length specifiers should be the same as those prescribed in the defined storage (DS) instructions. If this practice is not followed, an error may occur because of an invalid sign. For example, consider the following instruction that would result in an error:

I
N
V
A
L
I
D

LABEL	OPERATION 10	OPERAND 16
	AP	TOTAL(3),QTY(1)
	.	
	.	
	.	
QTY	DC	PL2'018'
TOTAL	DC	PL3'000'

Since **QTY** is defined as 2 bytes, this would create an error since the second operand, **QTY(1)**, references *only* the high-order byte that contains the digits 01. The field **QTY** appears in storage as follows:

0	1	8	C

Note no sign digit is present in **QTY(1)**. The second operand is therefore invalid. It is thus advisable for the programmer to recheck the defined lengths of the fields when using the explicit form of the **AP** instruction to ensure that the length indicated includes the sign bits. This checking practice will also serve to ensure that the receiving field is defined larger than the sending field.

A few examples of valid explicit **AP** instructions are:

LABEL	OPERATION 10	OPERAND 16	Contents of FLD1	Contents of FLD2	Results Stored in FLD1
	AP	FLD1(3),FLD2(2)	07134C	066C	07200C
	AP	FLD1(2),FLD2(1)	097C	5D	092C
	AP	FLD1(2),FLD2(2)	097C	098D	001D
	AP	FLD1(2),FLD2+1(1)	097C	013C	100C

Note in the last example that only 3 is added to 97.

Size of Receiving Field

The first operand or receiving field must be large enough to hold the result of the addition or else an error condition called an *arithmetic overflow* may result. Consider the following instruction.

Example of Arithmetic Overflow

LABEL	OPERATION	OPERAND
1	10 16	
** EXAMPLE OF		ARITHMETIC OVERFLOW
*		
	AP	SUM,TOOMUCH

Before Execution

9	9	9 C		1 C

↑SUM   ↑TOOMUCH

After Execution

0	0	0 C		1 C

↑SUM   ↑TOOMUCH

Overflow and loss of the digit 1 occur.

In the above, an overflow condition occurs that may result in an interrupt which terminates processing.

In all arithmetic operations, both operands must contain packed data with valid signs; otherwise another type of error, *a data exception,* may occur. Unlike the **PACK** instruction that packs results without checking for the validity of the sign, the **AP** instruction results in a "data exception" error if the sign of either operand is invalid.

The following instructions will produce a data exception because the signs are invalid. Invalid signs are circled for ease of identification.

Symbolic Instruction	Contents Operand 1	Contents Operand 2	Comment
AP TOTL(2),NG(2)	00 | 0C	45 | 0 | ④	A preceding PACK instruction packed a blank in NG, resulting in an invalid sign digit.
AP QTY,ZD	01 | 2C	F1 | F | ②	The second operand was not packed.
AP QTYP,PFIVE	01 | C | ②	5C	QTYP was packed twice.
AP SUM,P1	C1 | D2 | E | ⑤	1C	The first operand contains EBCDIC data.

Application of the AP Instruction: Performing Multiplication through Repeated Addition

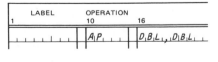

LABEL	OPERATION	
1	10 16	
	AP	DBL,DBL

Before   *After*

1	2	3 C		2	4	6 C

DBL⌐   DBL⌐

This instruction effectively doubles the contents of the location called DBL. If the instruction were repeated again, the final result would be the same as multiplying the field DBL by 4. In many instances, this method is not only simple, but also an efficient means of multiplication.

Summary of the Add Packed Instruction
1. The second operand is added to the first, one byte at a time, from low order to high order.
2. Both operands must contain packed-decimal data with valid signs, or else a data exception will occur.
3. The resulting sum is stored in the first operand in packed form; a positive result will contain a hex C in the sign position; a negative result will produce a hex D.
4. Length specifiers may be included in both operands or the length of the operation can be implied by the length of the first operand.
5. If the first operand is too small to contain all the significant digits of the addition, an overflow occurs and processing may terminate.
6. If the first operand is larger than the results produced, addition will take place normally.
7. A field may be added to itself, a process that doubles the contents of the field.

**SELF
EVALUATING
QUIZ**

1. In the Add Packed (AP) instruction, the sum replaces the (*first*/*second*) operand.
2. The positive integer '1' would occupy __(number)__ byte(s) in packed form and appear in storage as _____ .
3. A packed number representing −2000 would occupy __(number)__ bytes and appear in storage as _____ .
4. The AP instruction is classified as a _____ type of instruction.
5. Within each operand, addition takes place from _____ to _____ .
6. Determine the results of the following AP instructions. The length of each data field is as illustrated. Note if a data exception or overflow results.

0 1	2 3	4 F		1 0	0 D		3 C

FLDA ⌐   FLDB ⌐   FLDC ⌐

	Operation	Operand
a.	AP	FLDA,FLDB
b.	AP	FLDB,FLDC
c.	AP	FLDC,FLDA
d.	AP	FLDA(3),FLDC(1)
e.	AP	FLDA(2),FLDB(2)
f.	AP	FLDB(2),FLDB(2)
g.	AP	FLDC(1),FLDA+2(1)

Note in the last example that overlapping fields are permissible as long as a valid sign is involved. In other words, we simply added the 4F from FLDA to FLDC. Here is another example of this practice.

AP   FLDA(3),FLDA+2(1)

The result in FLDA would be | 0 1 | 2 3 | 8 C |

Solutions
1. First
2. 1
   1C
3. 3

02	00	0D

4. Storage-to-storage
5. Right (low-order)
   Left (high-order)
6. a. | 0 1 | 1 3 | 4 C | (in effect, subtraction occurs)

   b. | 0 9 | 7 D |

   c. Overflow

   d. | 0 1 | 2 3 | 7 C |

   e. Data exception (invalid sign for first operand)

   f. | 20 | 0D |

   g. | 7 C |

Unpack (UNPK) Instruction

You will recall from earlier in this chapter that zoned-decimal data was packed in order to perform decimal arithmetic. However, once the arithmetic operations are completed, the next step is to prepare the data for printing. It is therefore necessary to reverse the packing process and to convert the packed decimal data to its original zoned-decimal (EBCDIC) form so that it can be printed. The UNPK instruction is used for this purpose. Since the objective of unpacking is to prepare the data for printing, the defined output area is frequently used as the receiving field for the unpacked results.

The standard instructions to be performed for arithmetic operations thus include the following:

```
PACK
A
 R
  I
 S  T
  T  H
   A  M
    T  E
     E  T
      M  I
       E  C
        N
         T
          S
UNPK
```

Operation 10	Operand 16
UNPK	OP1,OP2

```
Instruction:    UNPK
Meaning:        Unpack a packed field so that it is converted to a zoned-
                decimal format.
Operand 1:      Receiving field should be described as zoned-decimal
                or "C" (character) field.
Operand 2:      Sending field must be in packed format.
Result:         The contents of the sending field is placed in the re-
                ceiving field in an unpacked format. The sending field
                remains unchanged.
Limitations:    Make certain that the number of positions specified for
                the receiving field is large enough to accommodate
                results, otherwise truncation will occur. Sixteen byte
                maximum for operands. Do not unpack a field into
                itself.
```

The following illustrates how the UNPK instruction operates:

Unpack (UNPK)
UNPK   OP1,OP2
Sending field [second operand]—packed decimal
receiving field [first operand]—zoned decimal
Schematic

LABEL	OPERATION 10	OPERAND 16
	UNPK	NUMBOUT,PNUMB
	.	
	.	
	.	
NUMBOUT	DS	CL3
PNUMB	DC	PL2'123'

Before Execution

NUMBOUT ⟶   ? ? ?   PNUMB ⟶   12 3C

(original contents of NUMBOUT does *not* affect UNPK)

PNUMB   12   3C

NUMBOUT   C3   *Step 1*

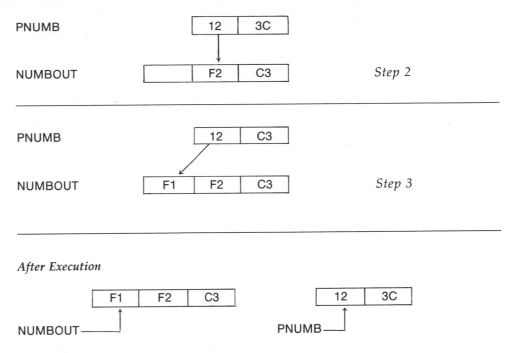

Step 2

Step 3

After Execution

It should be noted that both operands reference the high-order positions of data in storage and that the instruction is of the storage-to-storage type. Neither operand may exceed 16 bytes which, we have already learned, is a general rule for decimal instructions. Notice in the example that the fields are processed from *right* to *left*, that is, from low order to high order. The receiving field, the first operand, is usually considerably longer than the sending field. To establish the minimum number of bytes required in the first operand, the following formula can be used.

Calculating the Length of an Unpacked Field
Length (first operand) must be at least 2 × Length (second operand) − 1

Therefore, as our example illustrates, the minimum length of **NUMBOUT** is calculated as follows:

$$\text{Length (NUMBOUT)} = 2 \times \text{length (PNUMB)} - 1$$
$$= 2 \times 2 - 1$$
$$= 3$$

Usually, as a precaution, the receiving field is *defined longer* than necessary. When this occurs, the high-order position(s) are filled with zoned zeros, represented in hex as **F0**. Zoned zero characters will print as zeros and, hence, must be considered when planning the output layout.

The example below illustrates what happens if the receiving field is not large enough to accommodate the unpacked results.

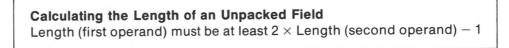

Before Execution
PAMT

After Execution
SMALL

| F3 | F4 | C5 |

NOTE: High-order **12** in **PAMT** is truncated.

When the length specifiers are omitted, the length of the first operand determines the number of bytes to be unpacked. However, one or both operands may contain explicit length specifiers. We might therefore write an **UNPK** instruction in explicit form as follows:

LABEL	OPERATION	OPERAND
	U N P K	H R S O U T (5) , P H R S (2)

Again, this method of explicitly controlling the lengths of both operands is recommended. Unpacking into the output area using implicit instead of explicit length specifiers often results in program errors. Consider the following:

LABEL	OPERATION	OPERAND
	U N P K	O U T A R E A , T O T A L
	.	
	.	
	.	
O U T A R E A	D S	C L 1 3 2

The first operand in this example *must* contain a length specifier or an attempt would be made to use the implied length of the defined storage area (132 bytes). Since both operands are limited to 16 bytes in an **UNPK** instruction, an error would be indicated by the assembler for this instruction.

A problem exists with all of the unpacked fields shown in the above examples. If these fields were to be printed immediately after unpacking, the last byte in every instance would print as a letter. This is because the sign generated by decimal arithmetic is either a hex 'C' (plus) or hex 'D' (minus). After unpacking, the sign combines with a digit to produce a letter in the low-order byte. For example, the unpacking of (positive) digits 1 through 9 would result in the hex configuration C1 through C9, which would print as the letters A through I. See Table 7.1 for a listing of how low-order bytes of packed fields might print if signs were not stripped. The method used for stripping this sign is treated as the next topic. Let us first be sure we understand the **UNPK** instructions by performing the following exercises.

1. The UNPK instruction is of the _____ type.
2. The first operand is the (*sending/receiving*) field while the second operand is the (*sending/receiving*) field.
3. Data in the second operand must be in _____ format.
4. The results of the UNPK instruction are found in the _____ operand in _____ form.
5. For unpacking a 4-byte packed-decimal field, the minimum length of the first operand must be _____ bytes.

Table 7.1. Possible Configurations in the
Low-Order Byte of an Unpacked Field.

Actual Meaning	Character Printed	Hex Representation	Binary Representation	
+0	&	C0	1100	0000
+1	A	C1	1100	0001
+2	B	C2	1100	0010
+3	C	C3	1100	0011
+4	D	C4	1100	0100
+5	E	C5	1100	0101
+6	F	C6	1100	0110
+7	G	C7	1100	0111
+8	H	C8	1100	1000
+9	I	C9	1100	1001
−0	—	D0	1101	0000
−1	J	D1	1101	0001
−2	K	D2	1101	0010
−3	L	D3	1101	0011
−4	M	D4	1101	0100
−5	N	D5	1101	0101
−6	O	D6	1101	0110
−7	P	D7	1101	0111
−8	Q	D8	1101	1000
−9	R	D9	1101	1001

6. The maximum length of either operand is ___(number)___ bytes.
7. The first operand is usually (*longer/shorter*) than the second.
8. The high-order digits may be lost when the (*first/second*) operand is too short.
9. When the first operand is longer than required, the high-order bytes are filled with (*zeros/zoned zeros/spaces*).
10. (True or False) The following is a valid set of instructions:

```
        UNPK              LINEOUT+10,PQTY
          .
          .
          .
PQTY    DS                PL5
          .
          .
          .
LINEOUT DS                CL132
```

11. Indicate the contents of FLDB for each of the following instructions. Note when truncation will occur.

FLDA is represented as: | 12 | 34 | 5D |
                                    ↑
                                  FLDA

```
a.  UNPK    FLDB(5),FLDA
b.  UNPK    FLDB(7),FLDA
c.  UNPK    FLDB(4),FLDA(3)
d.  UNPK    FLDB(1),FLDA+2(1)
e.  UNPK    FLDB(5),FLDA+1(2)
f.  UNPK    FLDB(3),FLDA(2)
```

12. Examine the program in Figure 7-1 and indicate the results that will print out. Use the data defined by the DC statements.

```
*
*                                       HOUSEKEEPING INSTRUCTIONS GO HERE    *
*                                                                           *
ADD1        MVC     OUTAREA,SPACES
            AP      PAMT1,PAMT2
            UNPK    OUTAMT,PAMT1
            PUT     OUTFILE,OUTAREA
*
ADD2        MVC     OUTAREA,SPACES
            AP      PAMT3,PAMT2
            UNPK    OUTAMT,PAMT3
            PUT     OUTFILE,OUTAREA
*
ADD3        MVC     OUTAREA,SPACES
            AP      PAMT5,PAMT5
            UNPK    OUTAMT,PAMT5
            PUT     OUTFILE,OUTAREA
*
ADD4        MVC     OUTAREA,SPACES
            AP      PAMT8,=P'223'
            UNPK    OUTAMT,PAMT8
            PUT     OUTFILE,OUTAREA
*
ADD5        MVC     OUTAREA,SPACES
            PACK    PAMT6,AMT6
            PACK    PAMT7,AMT7
            AP      PAMT6,PAMT7
            UNPK    OUTAMT,PAMT6
            PUT     OUTFILE,OUTAREA
*
*                                       HOUSEKEEPING INSTRUCTIONS GO HERE   *
*                                       ALONG W/DCB OR DTF MACRO FOR OUTFILE*
*                                                                          *
SPACES      DC      CL1' '
OUTAREA     DS      0CL132
OUTAMT      DS      CL6
            DS      CL126
PAMT1       DC      P'1234'
PAMT2       DC      P'-226'
PAMT3       DC      P'-438'
PAMT4       DC      P'2387'
PAMT5       DC      P'4218'
AMT6        DC      C'197'
AMT7        DC      CL3'18N'            18N IN CHARACTER FORM IS -185
PAMT6       DS      PL2
PAMT7       DS      PL2
PAMT8       DC      P'992'
            END
```

Figure 7-1

Solutions

1. Storage-to-storage
2. Receiving
   Sending
3. Packed decimal
4. First
   Zoned-decimal (EBCDIC)
5. 7
6. 16
7. Longer. (It is the receiving field.)
8. First
9. Zoned zeros
10. False. The implied length is 122 bytes: LINEOUT+10 to LINEOUT+131.
11. a. | F1 | F2 | F3 | F4 | D5 |
    b. | F0 | F0 | F1 | F2 | F3 | F4 | D5 |
    c. | F2 | F3 | F4 | D5 | (The high-order digit is dropped; truncation occurs.)
    d. | D5 |
    e. | F0 | F0 | F3 | F4 | D5 |
    f. | F1 | F2 | 43 | ; error condition, since 4 is not a valid sign.
12. See Figure 7.2.

```
00100H
00066M
00843F
00021E
00001B
```
Figure 7-2

Or Logical Immediate

As previously illustrated, the last byte of a field that has been unpacked will print as a letter, and not as a number, as desired. Decimal arithmetic instructions generate a sign that is either a hex C or D but not the hex F required of numbers in EBCDIC or zoned-decimal format. To correct this problem, the sign in the last byte of an unpacked field must be changed to a hex F. The *Or Logical Immediate* (OI) instruction, a storage-immediate (SI) type, can be used for this purpose. Consider the following:

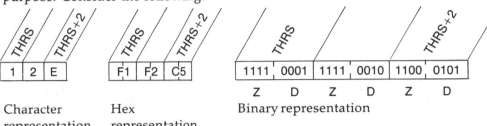

Character   Hex   Binary representation
representation representation

In order to properly print the digit 5 contained in THRS+2, the programmer must change the *binary digits* (bits) of the zone portion from 1100 (hex C), to 1111 (hex F). The bit pattern of the digit portion of the byte must remain unchanged. The OI instruction allows the programmer to set up a binary pattern or *mask* and perform "logical OR" operations between this pattern and the single byte to be modified, that is, THRS+2. The instruction may appear as follows:

LABEL	OPERATION 10	OPERAND 16
** METHOD	ONE	**
*		
	OI	THRS+2,X'F0'
*		
** METHOD	TWO	**
*		
	OI	THRS+2,B'11110000'

where the immediate operand X'F0' contains the binary pattern $\boxed{1111\,0000}$.

Before Execution   *After Execution*

| F1 | F2 | C5 | | F1 | F2 | F5 |

The mask operates as follows:

1 in mask.	Changes the corresponding bit in the receiving field to a 1.
0 in mask.	Leaves the corresponding bit in the receiving field unchanged.

To change the sign bits of an unpacked field to 1111, and to leave the digit portion unchanged, we therefore use the mask '1111 0000'.

All arithmetic operations will thus contain the following sequence of instructions where fields are to be printed:

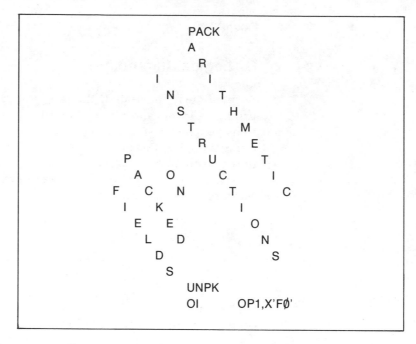

Figure 7-3 illustrates how the above sequence of instructions can be used to count the number of cards in a card file.

```
*                                                                    *
*                                      HOUSEKEEPING INSTRUCTIONS GO HERE   *
*                                                                    *
          MVC     OUTAREA,SPACES
READ      GET     INFILE,RECORD
          AP      TOTAL,=P'1'
          B       READ
EOF       MVC     MESSAGE,=C'TOTAL NO OF CARDS IS '
          UNPK    TOTOUT,TOTAL
          OI      TOTOUT+4,X'FO'      CHANGE SIGN FROM HEX C TO HEX F
          PUT     OUTFILE,OUTAREA
*                                                                    *
*                                      HOUSEKEEPING INSTRUCTIONS GO HERE   *
*                                      ALONG WITH DCB OR DTF MACROS        *
*                                                                    *
TOTAL     DC      PL5'00000'
RECORD    DS      CL80
SPACES    DC      CL1' '
OUTAREA   DS      OCL132
MESSAGE   DS      CL21
TOTOUT    DS      CL5
          DS      CL106
          END
```

Figure 7-3

**SELF-
EVALUATING
QUIZ**

1. The Or Logical Immediate (OI) is of the _____ type instruction.
2. When data is unpacked, the last byte will contain a hex _____ or hex _____, according to whether the data is positive or negative.
3. If a byte containing 1C were unpacked and printed, the letter _____ would appear in the output.
4. Each operand in the OI instruction is __(number)__ byte(s) in length.

5. The OI instruction sets up an immediate _____ against which the data in the first operand is processed.
6. When processing the mask, the result will only be 0 when the first operand contains a _____ and the second operand contains a _____.
7. In order for a zoned-decimal (EBCDIC) digit to print correctly, the zone must contain a hex _____ or binary _____.
8. Indicate the results of the following OI operations in both binary and hexadecimal.

	Data		Mask		Results
	First Operand		Second Operand		First Operand
	Binary	Hex	Binary	Hex	
a.	1100 1001	C9	1111 0000	F0	
b.	1101 0111	D7	1111 0000	F0	
c.	0100 0000	40 (blank)	1111 0000	F0	
d.	1101 0011	D3	1111 0000	F0	
e.	1100 0001	C1	1111 0000	F0	

9. When using the OI instruction to correct for the sign, the second operand will always be _____ (in hex form) or _____ (in binary form).

Solutions

1. Storage immediate
2. C
   D
3. A (hex C1)
4. 1
5. Mask or binary pattern
6. Zero
   Zero
7. F
   1111
8.

	Binary		Hex
a.	1111	1001	F9
b.	1111	0111	F7
c.	1111	0000	F0
d.	1111	0011	F3
e.	1111	0001	F1

9. X'F0'
   B'11110000'
   NOTE: An equal sign in the second operand of an OI instruction is invalid.

An Alternate Method for Replacing the Sign Portion of Unpacked Fields with Hex F: The Move Zone Instruction (MVZ)

The Move Zone (MVZ) instruction serves the same purpose as the Or Immediate (OI); that is, it replaces the sign portion of unpacked numeric fields with the hex value F. As we have already learned, in order for the System 360/370 to print unpacked numeric fields, the sign in the low-order byte must be changed to a hex F. Therefore, if a field contains a hex C or hex D resulting from decimal arithmetic, the sign must be changed to conform to the ordinary zoned-decimal format before it is printed. This method simply moves the zone from one of the high-order positions of the field that is an F to the low-order (sign) position. Let us consider that a field called (THRS) has just been unpacked, and an MVZ instruction is to be used to change the sign. The instruction and the unpacked area called THRS may appear as shown below:

Example 1

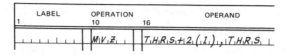

	LABEL	OPERATION		OPERAND
1		10	16	
		MVZ		THRS+2(1),THRS

Before

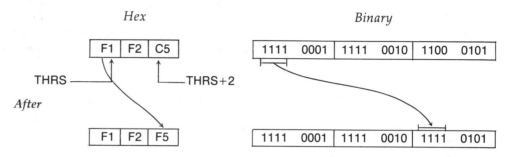

Hex   *Binary*

| F1 | F2 | C5 |

| 1111 | 0001 | 1111 | 0010 | 1100 | 0101 |

THRS ———   ———THRS+2

After

| F1 | F2 | F5 |

| 1111 | 0001 | 1111 | 0010 | 1111 | 0101 |

Example 2

MVZ   ZNUM+4(1),ZNUM+3
         ZNUM references a 5-byte field.
         Assume ZNUM is unpacked and is signed positive.

Before Execution

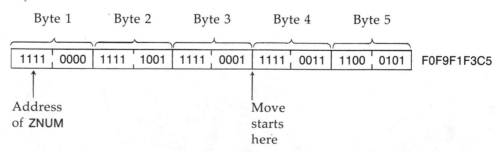

Byte 1   Byte 2   Byte 3   Byte 4   Byte 5

| 1111 | 0000 | 1111 | 1001 | 1111 | 0001 | 1111 | 0011 | 1100 | 0101 | F0F9F1F3C5 |

Address   Move
of ZNUM   starts
                 here

Result

Zone portion of byte 4 [ZNUM+3] is moved to zone portion of byte 5.

| 1111 | 0000 | 1111 | 1001 | 1111 | 0001 | 1111 | 0011 | 1111 | 0101 | F0F9F1F3F5 |

Note that the MVZ instruction moves *only* the zone portion (the 4 high-order bits) from one byte to another, while the numeric portion of the receiving field remains unchanged. The MVZ is another storage-to-storage instruction that is very similar in operation to the MVC. We will therefore briefly summarize its operation as follows.

Summary of MVZ
1. Meaning: move zone
2. First operand: Receiving field, contents of zone portion change.
3. Second operand: Sending field remains unchanged.
4. Zone portion is moved one byte at a time from left to right; digit portion remains unchanged.
5. To replace one zone *only*, we must use the explicit form specifying a (1) to denote a one-zone move.
6. From 1 to 256 bytes may be referenced with a single MVZ instruction.
7. One or more zones of the first operand are replaced by the zone(s) of the second operand.
8. The number of zones in the first operand that are replaced depends on either
   a. the explicit length specified in the first operand, or
   b. the implicit length of the first operand.

Since we are only concerned with moving the zone from a nearby byte, the previous example could also be written:

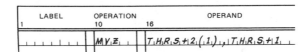

LABEL	OPERATION	OPERAND
	MVZ	THRS+2(1),THRS+1

and the results produced would be identical to those of the previous example.

The MVZ is not limited to changing the zone configuration of just one byte, as the following example illustrates:

LABEL	OPERATION	OPERAND
	MVZ	FLDA,FLDB

Before

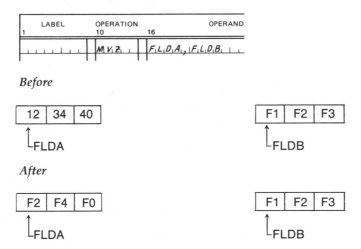

12	34	40

↑
└FLDA

F1	F2	F3

↑
└FLDB

After

F2	F4	F0

↑
└FLDA

F1	F2	F3

↑
└FLDB

SELF-EVALUATING QUIZ

1. The MVZ instruction moves the four (*high/low*)-order bits of each byte.
2. Once arithmetic operations are completed and a field is unpacked, the (*high/low*)-order byte will contain a hex C or hex D, depending upon the sign.
3. The number of bytes affected by an MVZ instruction depends upon the length of the (*first/second*) operand or a _____ .

4. From 1 to __(number)__ bytes may be referenced by a single MVZ statement.
5. Determine the results stored in FLDA for each of the following situations. Treat each situation independently.

   FLDA contains | 11 | 22 | 33 | 44 | 55 |
   FLBB contains | C6 | FF | D8 | F9 | 40 |

   a. MVZ   FLDA,FLDB
   b. MVZ   FLDA+1(4),FLDB
   c. MVZ   FLDA+4(1),FLDB+1
   d. MVZ   FLDA(1),FLDB
   e. MVZ   FLDA+2(3),FLDB+1

6. (True or False) The move zone instruction is in the SI format.
7. (True or False) Overlapping fields are not permitted with the MVZ instruction.
8. When using the MVZ instruction on overlapped fields, the field(s) usually contain (*packed/zoned-decimal*) data.

Solutions

1. High (zone portion or 4 leftmost bits)
2. Low (rightmost)
3. First
   length specifier in the first operand
4. 256
5. a. | C1 | F2 | D3 | F4 | 45 |
   b. | 11 | C2 | F3 | D4 | F5 |
   c. | 11 | 22 | 33 | 44 | F5 |
   d. | C1 | 22 | 33 | 44 | 55 |
   e. | 11 | 22 | F3 | D4 | F5 |
6. False. (Storage-to-storage)
7. False. (They are used to change the sign.)
8. Zoned-decimal

Decimal Subtraction: The Subtract Packed Instruction (SP)

Operation 10	Operand 16
SP	OP1,OP2

Instruction:	SP
Meaning:	Subtract Packed-Decimal Fields.
Operands:	Both must be packed data fields (Operand 2 can be a packed self-defining constant.)
	Both fields have a 16-byte limit.
	Both fields can use implicit or explicit length specifiers.
Result:	The second operand is subtracted from the first.
	The result is placed in operand 1.
	Operand 2 remains unchanged.
Limitations:	Make certain that receiving field is large enough to accommodate the answer or an overflow will occur.

The Subtract Packed (SP) instruction subtracts the contents of the second operand from the first operand. The arithmetic result is placed in the first operand. Once again, both operands must contain packed-decimal data and the rules for overflow, data exception, and field sizes are the same as presented under the Add Packed (AP) decimal instruction. Results of subtraction operations in general may need some review since subtracting signed numbers can sometimes be confusing. There is one basic rule to follow.

> *RULE:* Change the sign of the number to be subtracted, (the second operand), and proceed as in addition.

Examples

1. $(+151) - (+51) = 151 + (-51) = +100$

2. $(+200) - (+400) = 200 + (-400) = -200$

3. $(-151) - (-51) = -151 + (+51) = -100$

4. $(-200) - (-100) = (-200) + (+100) = -100$

The following examples illustrate the SP instruction:

	Operation	Operand	Contents of FLDB (in decimal)	Contents of FLDA (in decimal)	Results in FLDB (in decimal)
a.	SP	FLDB,FLDA	00 | 78 | 9C	00 | 08 | 9C	00 | 70 | 0C (+)
b.	SP	FLDB(3),FLDA(2)	00 | 00 | 7C	01 | 3D	00 | 02 | 0C (+)
c.	SP	FLDB(2),FLDA(2)	00 | 7C	01 | 3C	00 | 00 | 6D (−)
d.	SP	FLDB(2),FLDA(2)	00 | 7D	99 | 9C	Overflow
e.	SP	FLDB(3),FLDA(1)	56 | 78 | 9C	9F	56 | 78 | 0C (+)
f.	SP	FLDB(2),FLDA(1)	56 | 78 | 9C	F9	Data exception

Note that when the first operand is too small to contain the results, overflow occurs. If the first operand is of sufficient size, subtraction will take place normally, provided that both operands contain valid signs.

Figure 7-4 illustrates a program that reads in cards with the following format and produces the type of report shown. (The wavy lines indicate data filled in by the computer, based on the input records processed.)

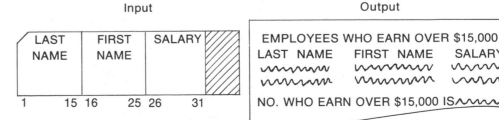

```
*                                                                      *
*                                      HOUSEKEEPING INSTRUCTIONS GO HERE *
*                                                                      *
        MVC     OUTAREA,SPACES
        MVC     OUTAREA+23(31),=C'EMPLOYEES WHO EARN OVER $15,000'
        PUT     OUTFILE,OUTAREA
        MVC     OUTAREA,SPACES
        PUT     OUTFILE,OUTAREA            PRINT BLANK LINE
        MVC     LNAME(9),=C'LAST NAME'
        MVC     FNAME(10),=C'FIRST NAME'
        MVC     SALOUT(6),=C'SALARY'
        PUT     OUTFILE,OUTAREA
        MVC     OUTAREA,SPACES
        PUT     OUTFILE,OUTAREA            PRINT BLANK LINE
READ    MVC     OUTAREA,SPACES
        GET     INFILE,RECORD
        CLC     SALARY,=C'15000'
        BNH     READ
        AP      COUNT,=P'1'
        MVC     LNAME,LAST
        MVC     FNAME,FIRST
        MVC     SALOUT,SALARY
        MVI     SALOUT-1,C'$'
        PUT     OUTFILE,OUTAREA
        B       READ
EOF     MVC     OUTAREA,SPACES
        PUT     OUTFILE,OUTAREA
        MVC     OUTAREA(29),=C'NO. WHO EARN OVER $15,000 IS '
        UNPK    OUTAREA+29(3),COUNT
        OI      OUTAREA+31,X'F0'
        PUT     OUTFILE,OUTAREA
*                                                                      *
*                                   HOUSEKEEPING INSTRUCTIONS GO HERE   *
*                                   ALONG WITH DCB OR DTF MACROS        *
*                                                                      *
COUNT   DC      PL2'0'
RECORD  DS      0CL80                     CARD FORMAT
LAST    DS      CL15                          *
FIRST   DS      CL10                          *
SALARY  DS      CL5                           *
        DS      CL50                          *
SPACES  DC      CL1' '
OUTAREA DS      0CL132                    PRINT FORMAT
        DS      CL5                           *
LNAME   DS      CL15                          *
        DS      CL20                          *
FNAME   DS      CL10                          *
        DS      CL20                          *
SALOUT  DS      CL5                           *
        DS      CL57                          *
        END
```

Figure 7-4

For Questions 1–6, what, if anything, is wrong with the sequence of instructions indicated:

```
1.          SP      OP1,OP2
            .
            .
            .
    OP1     DS      CL1Ø
    OP2     DS      CL5
```

```
2.          SP      OP3,OP4
            .
            .
            .
    OP3     DS      PL2Ø
    OP4     DS      PL15
```

3.		SP	OP5,OP6
			.
			.
			.
	OP5	DC	PL2'+826'
	OP6	DC	PL2'−335'

4.		SP	= P'1ØØ',OP7

5.		SP	OP8,=P'1ØØ'
			.
			.
			.
	OP8	DC	PL3'ØØØ'

6.		S	OP9,OP1Ø
			.
			.
			.
	OP9	DS	PL4
	OP10	DS	PL3

For Questions 7–10, indicate the results of each of the instructions, using the following constants:

	FLD1	DC	PL3'+105'
	FLD2	DC	PL3'+250'
7.	SP	FLD1,FLD2	
8.	SP	FLD1,FLD1	
9.	SP	FLD2,FLD1	
10.	SP	FLD2,FLD2	

Solutions

1. Character or zoned-decimal format for each DS is incorrect.
2. Operands cannot be more than 16 bytes.
3. Result would be
   $826 − (−335) = +1161$
   but OP5 is not large enough to accommodate this result.
4. The first operand of SP instruction is receiving field; it cannot be a self-defining operand.
5. Nothing wrong.
6. SP not S.
7. $−145$ (105 − 250)
8. $+0$
9. $+145$
10. $+0$

KEY TERMS

Binary pattern

Data exception

EBCDIC
Explicit length

Implicit length

Mask

Overflow

Packed-decimal format
Packing

Truncation

Unpacking

Zoned-decimal format

Review Questions   1.   What will be the resulting values in FLD1 and FLD2 after execution of the
following instructions:

```
SP      FLD2,FLD1
AP      FLD2(3),FLD2(3)
.
.
.
FLD1    DC      P'-06531'
FLD2    DC      P'+09265'
```

2.   Indicate the errors, if any, in the following program excerpt:

LABEL	OPERATION 10	OPERAND 16
	AP	SUM,=C'1'
	AP	TOTAL,FLDA
	UNPK	TOTAL,OUTAMT
	.	
	.	
	.	
FLDA	DC	PL2Ø'Ø1'
OUTAREA	DS	ØCL132
OUTAMT	DS	CL1Ø

3.   Using the arithmetic operations AP and SP, compute the following:
C = 4 × A − 2 × B

4.   FIELD1 contains 92 43 9C, FIELD2 contains 00 00 01 32 4C. Would the instruction AP   FIELD1,FIELD2 cause an overflow?

5.   Indicate the results in the following:

```
AP      TOTAL,TAX
SP      TOTAL,=P'100'
.
.
.
TOTAL   DC      PL6'123456'
TAX     DC      PL3'2345'
```

6.   Indicate the results in the following:

```
AP      FIELD1,FIELD2
AP      FIELD1,FIELD3
UNPK    AMT,FIELD1
MVZ     AMT+5(1),AMT+6
.
.
.
AMT     DS      CL7
FIELD1  DC      PL4'2231'
FIELD2  DC      PL4'-1230'
FIELD3  DC      PL4'+2235'
```

Practice Problems   1. Consider the following card input:

Card Columns	Field
1–20	NAME
21–25	AMT1
26–30	AMT2
80	CODE

    a. If CODE=1, print NAME and the sum of AMT1 and AMT2.

    b. If CODE=2, print NAME and the difference of AMT1 − AMT2.

    c. If CODE ≠ 1 or 2, print NAME and 'ERROR'.

2. Consider the following card input:

Card Columns	Field
1–20	NAME
21–25	SALESAMT
26–30	SALARY

    a. If SALESAMT is between $300 and $1000, print NAME and extended salary where

$$\text{Extended salary} = \text{SALARY} + 150$$

    b. If SALESAMT is between $1001 and $5000, print NAME and extended salary where

$$\text{Extended salary} = \text{SALARY} + 250$$

    c. If SALESAMT is greater than $5000, print NAME and extended salary where

$$\text{Extended salary} = \text{SALARY} + 500$$

    d. If SALESAMT is less than $300, print NAME and reduced salary where

$$\text{Reduced salary} = \text{SALARY} - 100.$$

3. Write a program to create a printed report from the following transaction records:

Card Columns	Field
1–5	Transaction number
6–20	Customer name
21–25	Amount 1
26–30	Amount 2
31–35	Amount of discount

The output format is as follows:

Print Positions	Field
1–15	Customer name
26–30	Transaction number
41–45	Total
56–60	Amount due
71–74	Date (month and year)
75–132	Not used

NOTES:

1. Total = Amount 1 + Amount 2
2. Amount due = Total − Amount of discount
3. Place today's date in the date field.

Chapter 8

Advanced Decimal Arithmetic Instructions

A. Zero and Add Packed (ZAP)

Operation 10	Operand 16
ZAP	OP1,OP2

Instruction:	ZAP
Meaning:	Zero and Add Packed Decimal
	1. Sets receiving field (first operand) to zero.
	2. Adds packed-decimal contents of sending field to 1st operand.
Results:	Packed contents of sending field transmitted to receiving field; high-order positions are zero-filled when the receiving field is longer than the sending field.
Operands:	Second operand must be in packed format or be a self-defining packed constant.
Length:	Determined by the first operand that may be implicit or explicit; maximum length—16 bytes.

Purpose The purpose of this instruction is to clear the receiving field and move the packed contents of the sending field to it. You will recall that fields to be used as totals must be cleared prior to any accumulation. ZAP is frequently used for that purpose.

Illustration

Compute

$$TOTAL = A + B - C$$

Assume all fields are in packed format.

Without knowing the initial contents of TOTAL, the following routine would produce unpredictable, and thus incorrect, results.

LABEL	OPERATION 10	16
	AP	TOTAL,A
	AP	TOTAL,B
	SP	TOTAL,C

The following routine, which uses the ZAP instruction, will produce the correct results *regardless* of the initial contents of TOTAL.

LABEL	OPERATION	
1	10	16
	ZAP	TOTAL,A
	AP	TOTAL,B
	SP	TOTAL,C

Examples

1. Both operands are of the same length.

LABEL	OPERATION		OPERAND
1	10	16	
	ZAP		TOTAL,TRAN

Before Execution

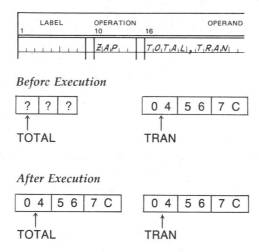

After Execution

2. First operand (receiving field) is longer than the second operand (sending field).
Result: High-order zeros fill the receiving field.

LABEL	OPERATION		OPERAND
1	10	16	
	ZAP		FLDA,TRAN

Before Execution

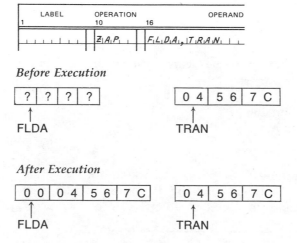

After Execution

3. First operand is too small to accommodate packed contents of second operand.

Result: a. Overflow condition occurs—condition code 3 is set.

b. Processing terminates (on some systems).

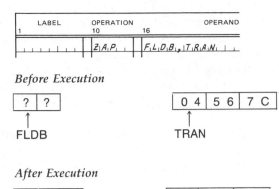

LABEL	OPERATION	OPERAND
	ZAP	FLDB,TRAN

Before Execution

?	?

↑
FLDB

0	4	5	6	7 C

↑
TRAN

After Execution

5	6	7 C	(overflow)

↑
FLDB

0	4	5	6	7 C

↑
TRAN

The same rules apply if the second operand is a self-defining packed operand such as =P'04567':

LABEL	OPERATION	OPERAND
*	EXAMPLE	S (1), (2) AND (3)
*		USING SELF-DEFINING OPERANDS
*		
	ZAP	TOTAL,=P'+04567'
*		
	ZAP	FLDA,=P'+04567'
*		
	ZAP	FLDB,=P'+04567'

Alternate to ZAP The following two excerpts produce the same results:

METHOD 1

LABEL	OPERATION	OPERAND
	ZAP	SUM,=P'0'
	.	
	.	
	.	
SUM	DS	PL5

METHOD 2

LABEL	OPERATION	OPERAND
	.	
	.	
	.	
	.	
SUM	DC	PL5'0'

When SUM is a field to be cleared only once, at the beginning, then the single DC entry on the right will suffice. When, however, SUM must be cleared for several different routines, the ZAP should be used.

While an MVC will also move the packed contents of one field to another, it produces the desired results only if the sending and receiving fields are exactly the same size. Otherwise, the MVC, which begins moving leftmost positions, will truncate differently or fail to fill with high-order zeros, depending upon the size of the receiving field. In short, it is recommended that MVC's be avoided in transmitting packed fields. The MVC instruction is intended for moving data in zoned-decimal format.

It should also be noted that the condition code is *not* set by the MVC instruction, while it is by the ZAP instruction.

Summary The ZAP instruction clears a field by setting it to zero and then performs an add operation according to the same rules as defined for the AP instruction in Chapter 7.

Zero and Add Packed (ZAP) Summary
1. The first operand is cleared to zero, and the contents of the second operand are added to the first, one byte at a time from *right* to *left.*
2. The *second operand* must contain valid packed-decimal data or a data exception will occur.
3. The result is stored in the first operand.
4. Length specifiers may be included in either or both operands.
5. If the first operand is too long, zeros will be filled in the high-order position(s).
6. If the first operand is too small to contain all of the significant digits of the first operand, overflow will result.
7. The second operand may be self-defining as long as the data is specified in the packed-decimal format.

SELF-EVALUATING QUIZ

For Questions 1–3, indicate the results of the following instruction:

LABEL	OPERATION 10	OPERAND 16
	ZAP	PAMT1,PAMT2

Note that the original contents of PAMT1 do not affect the results.

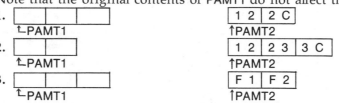

1. [| |]   [1 2 | 2 C]
   └PAMT1   ↑PAMT2

2. [|]   [1 2 | 2 3 | 3 C]
   └PAMT1   ↑PAMT2

3. [| |]   [F 1 | F 2]
   └PAMT1   ↑PAMT2

For Questions 4–6, indicate the results of the following:

LABEL	OPERATION 10	OPERAND 16
	ZAP	FLD1,=P'05'

4. [| |]
   FLD1———↑

5. [|]
   FLD1———↑

6. [ ]
   FLD1———↑

Solutions
1. [0 0 | 1 2 | 2 C]
2. [2 3 | 3 C]   Overflow occurs: condition code is set to 3.
3. Invalid. PAMT2 must be in packed form.
4. [0 0 | 0 0 | 5 C]
5. [0 0 | 5 C]
6. [5 C]   Overflow occurs: condition code is set to 3.

HELPFUL HINTS

Using ZAP to test for *signed values.*

The ZAP instruction automatically sets a condition code as follows:

Condition code	Meaning
0	Second operand is 0.
1	Second operand is negative.
2	Second operand is positive.
3	Second operand is larger than first—overflow.

Hence, you can ZAP a field into itself, which does not change any contents, and then test the condition code to determine if the value of the field is 0, negative or positive:

Conditions That Can Follow ZAP

Instruction	Meaning
BZ	Branch on Zero
BM	Branch on Minus
BP	Branch on Positive
BO	Branch on Overflow

Example

Branch to NEGRTN if SUM is negative:

LABEL	OPERATION 10	16
	ZAP	SUM,SUM
	BM	NEGRTN

B. Multiplying Packed Fields

Introduction   In this unit we will use the following example to demonstrate how multiplication is performed.

Example   A card is defined as follows:

LABEL	OPERATION 10	16
CARDIN	DS	0CL80
NAME	DS	CL20
PRICE	DS	CL3
QTY	DS	CL2
	DS	CL55

Operation to Be Performed	Terms	Sample Contents
PRICE	Multiplicand	999
× QTY	Multiplier	99
RESULT	Product	98901

Since all fields in the multiplication must contain packed data, we will establish the following storage areas.

LABEL	OPERATION	
1	10	16
PRICEPKD	DS	PL2
QTYPKD	DS	PL2

We will then be able to pack the input fields PRICE and QTY into these areas before multiplication is performed. Notice that PRICEPKD is established as a *two*-byte field because the input field PRICE contains 3 digits. You will recall that it requires 2 bytes to hold 3 digits and a sign in packed form. Similarly, QTYPKD is set up as a 2-byte field into which we can pack the field QTY. Two bytes are necessary to hold 2 digits plus a sign.

Multiplication Steps
1. Determine the size of the resultant field or product.
2. Move the multiplicand (number to be multiplied) to the first operand.
3. Multiply the multiplicand (first operand) by the multiplier (second operand), with the product replacing the first operand.

---

1. *Determining the Size of the Resultant Field or Product*
The number of bytes in the product field of a multiplication can be determined by adding the length of the bytes in the packed multiplicand (PRICE) to the length of the bytes in the packed multiplier (QTY):

Number of bytes in packed multiplicand	= 2
Number of bytes in packed multiplier	= 2
Number of bytes in the product	= 4

It is essential that the programmer establish a large enough field for the product of a multiplication. If the product field is too small to hold the results, an overflow condition will occur that may cause a program interrupt.

Length of product = Number of bytes in packed multiplier + number of
   (in bytes)   bytes in packed multiplicand

Example
Consider the following:

$$\text{UNITPR} \quad \text{DS} \quad \text{CL4}$$
$$\text{QTY} \quad \text{DS} \quad \text{CL3}$$

If these fields are to be multiplied, UNITPR will be packed into a 3-byte field:

$$\frac{4 \text{ digits} + 1}{2} = 2.5$$

$$= 3 \text{ bytes}$$

QTY will be packed into a 2-byte field: $\frac{3 \text{ digits} + 1}{2} = 2$ bytes

The product field will require 5 bytes: 3 + 2.

Using the example where PRICE and QTY are to be multiplied with PRICE as a 3-digit field and QTY as a 2-digit field, PRICE would be packed into a 2-byte area and QTY into a 2-byte area as well. Hence the field called RESULT that will contain the product must be defined as follows:

LABEL	OPERATION	
1	10	16
R,E,S,U,L,T	D,S	P,L,4

2. *The Multiplicand Must Be Packed and Moved to the First Operand*

Data is read into the computer in zoned-decimal format and must be packed prior to any arithmetic operations. Before performing a multiplication operation, the packed multiplicand must be *moved* to a field large enough to accommodate the product. The field to which it is moved will be used as the first operand in the multiply operation. Note that we do *not* use an MVC to move the multiplicand to the resultant field. Rather, we use a ZAP that clears the resultant field and then adds in the packed-decimal contents of the multiplicand.

Method 1

Before Execution

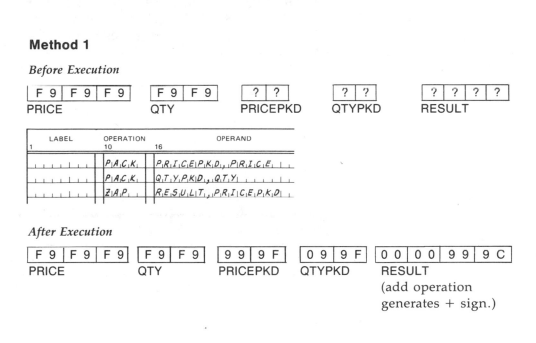

After Execution

Method 2: (No need to establish PRICEPKD)

LABEL	OPERATION	OPERAND
1	10	16
	P,A,C,K	Q,T,Y,P,K,D,,,Q,T,Y
	P,A,C,K	R,E,S,U,L,T,,,P,R,I,C,E

In both cases, the multiplicand, PRICE, and the multiplier, QTY, are packed and the packed multiplicand is placed in the RESULT field. It is important to note that a PACK or ZAP instruction is used to put the multiplicand in the RESULT field. This will ensure that there will be *zeros* in the high-order positions of the first operand *before* multiplication is performed. If this requirement is not met, an interrupt will occur.

3. *Multiply Packed*

Instruction:	MP
Meaning:	Multiply Packed Decimal
	1. First operand contains multiplicand in packed form.
	2. Second operand contains multiplier in packed form.
Results:	Product replaces multiplicand as first operand in packed form; second operand remains unchanged.
Operands:	Second operand may be packed field or self-defining packed constant.
Length:	a. Length of second operand (multiplier) must not exceed 8 bytes—that is, 15 digits and a sign.
	b. Length of multiplier must be less than length of first operand.
	c. Length of first operand must be large enough to hold the product.
Limitations:	Use ZAP or PACK to place multiplicand in first operand to ensure that zeros will be in the high-order positions of the first operand before multiplication.

The following examples assume that PRICEPKD, a 2-byte packed field, was moved into RESULT and that QTY is a packed field.

		Before		After	Comment
		RESULT	QTY	RESULT	
MP	RESULT,QTY	00 90 0C	01 2C	10 80 0C	Error: Three bytes insufficient even though in this particular case, the result would fit: 2 bytes + 2 bytes require 4 bytes.
MP	RESULT,QTY	00 00 90 0C	01 2C	00 10 80 0C	With four bytes, zeros are placed in high-order positions. RESULT *must* be four bytes or more.
MP	RESULT,QTY	90 0C	01 2C	80 0C	Error: With two bytes, overflow occurs: condition code set to 3.
MP	RESULT,QTY	00 00 08 89 0C	01 2C	00 01 06 68 0C	Okay. Five bytes in RESULT is fine.
MP	RESULT,QTY	00 00 99 9C	09 99 9C	99 89 00 1C	Assuming QTY is three bytes; four bytes is insufficient.

Examples

Consider the following input:

LABEL	OPERATION	
1	10	16
STUDENTS	DS	ØCL8Ø
NAME	DS	CL2Ø
CREDITS	DS	CL2
RATEPER	DS	CL3
	DS	CL55

The following program excerpt computes tuition where

TUITION = RATEPER × CREDITS:

	LABEL	OPERATION	OPERAND
		1	10	16
1.		PACK	PRATE,RATEPER
2.		PACK	PCREDITS,CREDITS
3.		ZAP	TUITION,PRATE
4.		MP	TUITION,PCREDITS
*			
*			
PRATE		DS	PL2
PCREDITS		DS	PL2
TUITION		DS	PL4 (2 + 2 BYTES)

Sample Data

Before Execution

F1	F2	F0

↑
RATEPER

F1	F5

↑
CREDITS

1. PACK   PRATE,RATEPER

After Execution

12	0F

↑
PRATE

PRATE = 2 bytes
$$\frac{3 \text{ digits (RATE)} + 1}{2}$$

2. PACK   PCREDITS,CREDITS

01	5F

↑
PCREDITS

PCREDITS = 2 bytes
$$\frac{2 \text{ digits (CREDITS)} + 1}{2}$$
Rounded

3. ZAP   TUITION,PRATE

00	00	12	0C

└─TUITION

TUITION = 4 bytes
2 bytes (PCREDITS)
+ 2 bytes (PRATE)

4.   MP   TUITION,PCREDITS | 00 | 01 | 80 | 0C |

⌐TUITION

(TUITION will need to be unpacked and edited
before it is printed.)

Consider the following input:

LABEL	OPERATION 10	16
CARDREC	DS	0CL80
NAME	DS	CL20
PRINC	DS	CL5
RATE	DS	CL3
	DS	CL52

The following program excerpt computes INTEREST where

INTEREST = PRINC × RATE

	LABEL	OPERATION 10	16 OPERAND
1.		PACK	PPRINC,PRINC
2.		PACK	PRATE,RATE
3.		ZAP	INTEREST,PPRINC
4.		MP	INTEREST,PRATE
	*		
	PPRINC	DS	PL3
	PRATE	DS	PL2
	INTEREST	DS	PL5

Sample Data

Before Execution

| F1 | F5 | F0 | F0 | F0 |

↑
PRINC

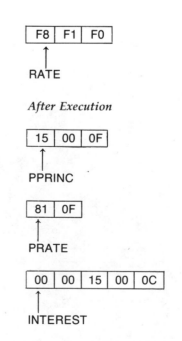

| F8 | F1 | F0 |

↑
RATE

After Execution

| 15 | 00 | 0F |

↑
PPRINC

| 81 | 0F |

↑
PRATE

| 00 | 00 | 15 | 00 | 0C |

↑
INTEREST

1.   PACK   PPRINC,PRINC

2.   PACK   PRATE,RATE

3.   ZAP   INTEREST,PPRINC

4.   MP   INTEREST,PRATE

01	21	50	00	0C

↑
INTEREST

NOTE: This problem is actually being used to multiply a principal of $15000 by an interest rate that in reality is 8.10% or 0.0810. Hence the answer indicated, 12150000, will print, when edited, as $1215.00. Edit procedures are considered in the next chapter.

Summary
Multiply Packed (MP)

1. Determine the size of the product field, the first operand, using the formula provided: Number of bytes in packed multiplier + number of bytes in packed multiplicand.
2. Place the multiplicand in the first operand (the number to be multiplied).
3. Both the multiplicand and multiplier must be in packed format. The product is in packed format.
4. The second operand (multiplier) may not exceed 15 digits and a sign (or 8 bytes), or a specification error will result.
5. The product (first operand after execution) is in packed format and is limited to 31 digits and the sign, or 16 bytes.
6. If the product field is incorrectly defined too small, an overflow condition will result.
7. When the product field is larger than necessary, normal multiplication will take place.

**SELF-
EVALUATING
QUIZ**

1. A product is produced by multiplying the _____ by the _____.
2. When a 5-digit number is multiplied by a 3-digit number, the product field should be __(number)__ bytes long.
3. Before we multiply, the _____ must be placed in the first operand.
4. The multiplier is referenced by the (*first/second*) operand.
5. After execution, the product is found in the (*first/second*) operand in the _____ format.
6. If both operands are not packed a(n) _____ will occur.
7. (True or False) Neither operand may exceed 8 bytes.
8. (True or False) If the product field is too small, the low-order (rightmost) digits will be truncated.
9. Write a routine to multiply A by B and place the answer in C where A and B are defined as follows:

A	DS	CL3
B	DS	CL3

10. Write a routine to multiply D by 154 and place the answer in E where D is defined as follows:

D	DS	CL5

Solutions

1. Multiplicand (number to be multiplied)
   Multiplier
2. 5 [3 packed bytes + 2 packed bytes]
       (5 digits)   (3 digits)

3. Multiplicand—larger field
4. Second
5. First
   packed
6. Data exception
7. False. The first operand may be 16 bytes in length.
8. False. The high-order digits are lost, and an overflow condition occurs.
9.

LABEL	OPERATION	
	PACK	PACKA,A
	PACK	PACKB,B
	ZAP	C,PACKA
	MP	C,PACKB
*		
PACKA	DS	PL2
PACKB	DS	PL2
C	DS	PL4

10.

LABEL	OPERATION	OPERAND	COMMENTS
	PACK	PACKD,D	
	ZAP	E,PACKD	
	MP	E,=P'154'	
*			
PACKD	DS	PL3	
E	DS	PL5 THE CONSTANT P'154' WOULD	
*		REQUIRE 2 BYTES: 2 + 3 = 5	

C. Dividing Packed Fields

The divide procedure is directly analogous to the multiply procedure. Let us use the following example:

Example

A card is defined as follows.

LABEL	OPERATION	
CARDIN	DS	0CL80
COURSE	DS	CL20
TGRADES	DS	CL4
PUPILS	DS	CL3
	DS	CL53

Example

Operation To Be Performed	Terms	Sample

ANSWER ←

PUPILS⟌TGRADES ←
— Quotient + remainder
— dividend
— divisor

0075—quotient
110⟌8355
770
655
550
105—remainder

NOTE: We will not illustrate solutions with decimal or fractional components until the next section.

The three facets to the divide operations are analogous to the multiply:

Divide
1. Determine the size of the field that will contain the result—*both* the quotient *and* remainder.
2. Move the packed dividend to the first operand—the result field.
3. Divide the packed dividend (first operand) by the packed divisor (second operand). The answer appears in the first operand.

---

1. *Determine the Size of the Field That Will Contain the Result.*
The result includes both a quotient and a remainder.

Determine Length of Result
1. The length of the result equals the length of the quotient plus the length of the remainder.
2. The length of the *quotient* will be equal to the length in bytes of the packed *dividend*. (Four digits in the example = 3 bytes.)
3. The length of the *remainder* will be equal to the length in bytes of the packed *divisor*. (Three digits in the example = 2 bytes.)

The final answer, the quotient and remainder, are stored in *one* field, with the quotient in the high-order (leftmost) positions and the remainder in the low-order (rightmost) positions. The quotient and the remainder each have their own signs. The length of the field is determined as follows:

a. Calculate the packed length of the quotient and the remainder. Remember, these are the same lengths as the dividend and divisor.
The quotient will be 4 digits; hence 3 bytes are required.
The remainder will be 3 digits; hence 2 bytes are required.

b. Number of bytes of first operand = number of bytes of quotient + number of bytes of remainder
$$= 3 + 2$$
$$= 5$$

2. *Move the Packed Dividend to the First Operand—the Result Field.*
As with multiplication, all fields must be packed. Either of the two alternatives given below may be used.

Method 1

LABEL	OPERATION	OPERAND
	PACK	PGRADES,TGRADES
	PACK	PPUPILS,PUPILS
	ZAP	ANSWER,PGRADES
*		
PGRADES	DS	PL3
PPUPILS	DS	PL2
ANSWER	DS	PL5

Method 2

LABEL	OPERATION	OPERAND
	PACK	PUPILS,PUPILS
	PACK	ANSWER,TGRADES
*		
PPUPILS	DS	PL2
ANSWER	DS	PL5

The calculations indicate that a minimum of 5 bytes are necessary to contain the entire answer in our illustration. The first three bytes will store the quotient and the last two bytes will contain the remainder. It is recommended that the programmer code the Define Storage instruction for this area as follows:

LABEL	OPERATION	OPERAND
ANSWER	DS	ØPL5
QUOTNT	DS	PL3
RMDR	DS	PL2

When division is completed, using the above designations the programmer can directly reference both the quotient (QUOTNT) and remainder (RMDR) for unpacking purposes. The answer produced might appear in the form:

Relative Addressing   Direct Addressing

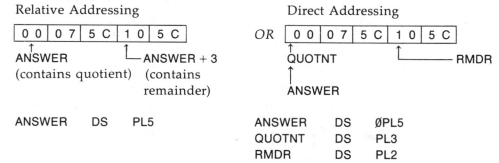

Relative Addressing	Direct Addressing
ANSWER — (contains quotient) ANSWER + 3 (contains remainder)	QUOTNT ANSWER RMDR
ANSWER DS PL5	ANSWER DS ØPL5
	QUOTNT DS PL3
	RMDR DS PL2

Relative addressing length specifiers must be used if the area (ANSWER) is not subdivided. This initial planning is essential to use the Divide Packed (DP) instruction effectively.

3. *Divide Packed*

Instruction:	DP
Meaning:	Divide Packed decimal
	1. First operand contains dividend in packed form.
	2. Second operand contains divisor in packed form.
Results:	Second operand unchanged.
	First operand:
	1. High-order bytes (same number as dividend) contain quotient with sign
	2. Low-order bytes (same number as divisor) contain remainder with sign.
Operands:	Second operand may be packed field or self-defining packed constant.
Length:	First operand may not exceed 16 bytes.
	Second operand may not exceed 8 bytes.
Limitations:	An effort to divide by zero (zero divisor) will cause an error.

The following illustrates how the Divide Packed (DP) instruction operates:

LABEL	OPERATION	OPERAND
	10	16
1.	PACK	PGRADES,TGRADES
2.	PACK	PPUPILS,PUPILS
3.	ZAP	ANSWER,PGRADES
4.	DP	ANSWER,PPUPILS
*		
PGRADES	DS	PL3
PPUPILS	DS	PL2
ANSWER	DS	ØPL5
QUOTNT	DS	PL3
RMDR	DS	PL2

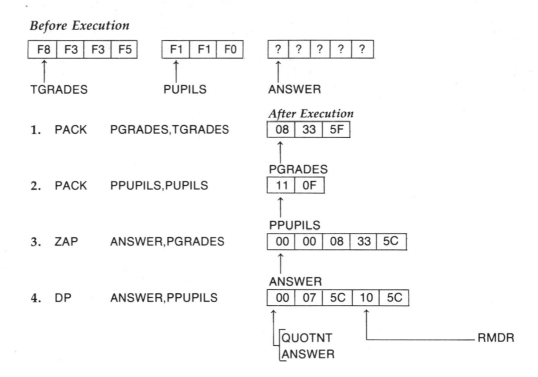

Before Execution

| F8 | F3 | F3 | F5 | | F1 | F1 | F0 | | ? | ? | ? | ? | ? |

↑ TGRADES   ↑ PUPILS   ↑ ANSWER

After Execution

1. PACK   PGRADES,TGRADES
| 08 | 33 | 5F |
↑ PGRADES

2. PACK   PPUPILS,PUPILS
| 11 | 0F |
↑ PPUPILS

3. ZAP   ANSWER,PGRADES
| 00 | 00 | 08 | 33 | 5C |
↑ ANSWER

4. DP   ANSWER,PPUPILS
| 00 | 07 | 5C | 10 | 5C |
↑ QUOTNT / ANSWER   RMDR

Notice that the dividend (PGRADES) was moved to the first operand (ANSWER) by a **ZAP** instruction. After the division is performed, the first operand (ANSWER) contains a quotient (QUOTNT) of 00075, and a remainder (RMDR) of 105. *Both* the quotient and the remainder have signs included. Note that the remainder in this example will never exceed 3 digits. Similarly, had we divided by 1, we would produce the largest possible quotient (08335), which is the same number of bytes as the dividend.

In the next example, we will divide a 6-digit dividend (TSALES) by a 2-digit divisor (QTY). Our calculations indicate the following:

a. Quotient = 4 bytes
Remainder = 2 bytes
b. Bytes in 1st operand = bytes in quotient + bytes in remainder = 4 + 2 = 6

The Define Storage instructions for the first operand would therefore be set up as follows:

LABEL	OPERATION	
1	10	16
ANSWER	DS	ØPL6
AVGSALE	DS	PL4
RMDR	DS	PL2

The following illustrates how **TSALES** is packed and moved to the first operand (**ANSWER**) and then divided by QTY:

	LABEL	OPERATION		OPERAND
	1	10	16	
1.		PACK	PSALES,TSALES	
2.		PACK	PQTY,QTY	
3.		ZAP	ANSWER,PSALES	
4.		DP	ANSWER,PQTY	
*				
CARDREC	DS	ØCL8Ø	
TSALES	DS	CL6	
QTY	DS	CL2	
	DS	CL7,2	
*			
PSALES	DS	PL4	
PQTY	DS	PL2	
ANSWER	DS	ØPL6	
AVGSALE	DS	PL4	
RMDR	DS	PL2	

Before Execution

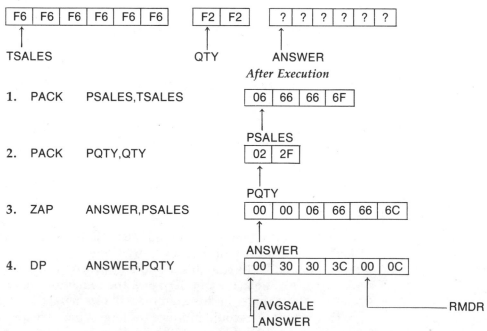

The quotient (**AVGSALE**) is equal to 30303 with a remainder of 0. These results could be unpacked and printed by referring to the storage areas named **AVGSALE** and **RMDR**.

The sample Divide Pack instruction can also be written using a self-defining operand:

LABEL	OPERATION		OPERAND
1	10	16	
	DP	ANSWER,=P'22'	

The results produced would be identical to those previously illustrated.

Errors Caused by Zero Divisors

Another important fact to consider is that the divisor must never be equal to zero. If it is, a *decimal divide exception* will occur. This problem can again be avoided by using the ZAP instruction to set the condition code, and branching on a zero condition to an error routine called ZERODIV. The instructions necessary for this test are:

LABEL	OPERATION 10	16	OPERAND	COMMENTS
	ZAP		DIVSOR,DIVSOR	(DOES NOT CHANGE VALUE -
*				JUST SETS CONDITION CODE)
	BZ		ZERODIV	

The DP procedure will now be summarized. Note that many of its characteristics are similar to the MP (Multiply Pack) instruction.

Summary of DP Instruction
1. Determine the size of the quotient and remainder in bytes, in order to set up the first operand.
2. Place the dividend in the first operand.
3. Both the dividend and divisor must be in packed format.
4. The resulting quotient and remainder are in packed format.
5. The second operand may not exceed 8 bytes.
6. The first operand may not exceed 16 bytes.
7. The second operand may be self-defining.
8. A decimal divide exception will occur if:
   a. Second operand equals zero.
   b. First operand is too small to contain the quotient and the remainder (overflow).

HELPFUL HINTS

1. Obtaining a percentage

Suppose we wish to obtain the percentage of students in a school who have taken an introductory data processing course. We discover that fifty (50) students of 500 have taken the course. How do we compute the percentage? The mathematical formula is as follows:

$$\frac{50}{500} = 500\overline{)50.0}^{\;0.10} = 10\%$$

To use the divide instruction as described would produce the following

$$500\overline{)50}^{\;0}\;\nearrow\text{Quotient}$$
$$\underline{0}$$
$$50 \longleftarrow \text{Remainder}$$

The division does *not* produce any decimal or fractional results. Since we wish to obtain a percentage, we can do the following:

$$\% = 100 \times \text{decimal value}$$

[Example: $10\% = 100 \times .10$]

$$\frac{\text{Dividend}}{\text{Divisor}} \times 100 = \%$$

Example: $\dfrac{50}{500} \times 100 = \%$

$$\frac{5000}{500} = \%$$

$$500\overline{)5000}^{\,10} = 10\%$$

Hence in order to obtain a percentage when we divide, we must multiply the dividend by 100 *prior to* the division. The result will be integers that refer to the actual percentage.

2.   P format in DS

Note that DS areas in storage, even those used in arithmetic operations, can be established in P or even C format. Since DS simply reserves space for a storage area, coding ANSWER, for example,

```
ANSWER    DS    CL5
```

or

```
ANSWER    DS    PL5
```

is really of no consequence. The P or the C is merely for documentation purposes. To use the field ANSWER in an arithmetic operation, however, it must contain *packed data only*.

Figure 8-1 illustrates a program to read in cards with the following format and produce the report shown. (The wavy lines indicate data that will be filled in by the computer, depending upon the input processed.) Figure 8-2 shows the logic used.

Notice that in the EOF routine, the UNPK instruction is:

```
UNPK    OUTAREA+27(3),HOLD+2(2)
```

HOLD is a 6-byte packed field that, after the DP instruction, will appear as follows:

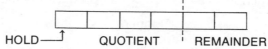

HOLD⟶   QUOTIENT   REMAINDER

Since we are finding a percentage, we know that the *maximum* amount in HOLD will be 100%. This would be represented as follows:

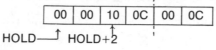

HOLD⟶ HOLD+2

```
*                                                                        *
*                                 HOUSEKEEPING INSTRUCTIONS GO HERE  *
*                                                                        *
*
           MVC     OUTAREA,SPACES
           MVC     OUTAREA+23(31),=C'EMPLOYEES WHO EARN OVER $15,000'
           PUT     OUTFILE,OUTAREA
           MVC     OUTAREA,SPACES
           PUT     OUTFILE,OUTAREA          PRINT BLANK LINE
           MVC     LNAME(9),=C'LAST NAME'
           MVC     FNAME(10),=C'FIRST NAME'
           MVC     SALOUT(6),=C'SALARY'
           PUT     OUTFILE,OUTAREA
           MVC     OUTAREA,SPACES
           PUT     OUTFILE,OUTAREA          PRINT BLANK LINE
READ       MVC     OUTAREA,SPACES
           GET     INFILE,RECORD
           AP      TOTEMP,=P'1'
           CLC     SALARY,=C'15000'
           BNH     READ
           AP      COUNT,=P'1'
           MVC     LNAME,LAST
           MVC     FNAME,FIRST
           MVC     SALOUT,SALARY
           MVI     SALOUT-1,C'$'
           PUT     OUTFILE,OUTAREA
           B       READ
EOF        MVC     OUTAREA,SPACES
           PUT     OUTFILE,OUTAREA
           MVC     OUTAREA(27),=C'% WHO EARN OVER $15,000 IS '
           ZAP     NUM,COUNT
           MP      NUM,=P'100'
           ZAP     HOLD,NUM
           DP      HOLD,TOTEMP
           UNPK    OUTAREA+27(3),HOLD+2(2)
           OI      OUTAREA+29,X'F0'
           PUT     OUTFILE,OUTAREA
*                                                                        *
*                                 HOUSEKEEPING INSTRUCTIONS GO HERE  *
*                                 ALONG WITH DCB OR DTF MACROS       *
*                                                                        *
*
COUNT      DC      PL2'0'
HOLD       DS      PL6
TOTEMP     DC      PL2'0'
NUM        DS      PL4
RECORD     DS      OCL80                    CARD FORMAT
LAST       DS      CL15                     *
FIRST      DS      CL10                     *
SALARY     DS      CL5                      *
           DS      CL50                     *
SPACES     DC      CL1' '
OUTAREA    DS      OCL132                   PRINT FORMAT
           DS      CL5                      *
LNAME      DS      CL15                     *
           DS      CL20                     *
FNAME      DS      CL10                     *
           DS      CL20                     *
SALOUT     DS      CL5                      *
           DS      CL57                     *
           END
```

Figure 8-1

You will recall that after division, the quotient and the remainder each have their own sign—in this case, C for positive. Notice that the two high-order bytes of HOLD are zero-filled. Consequently, when we unpack the quotient, we can refer to HOLD+2(2) without losing any of the result.

SELF-EVALUATING QUIZ

1. A quotient is the _____ of a divide operation.
2. Quotients are obtained by dividing a _____ by a _____.
3. The length of the resultant field in a divide operation must be equal to the sum of the _____ and _____.

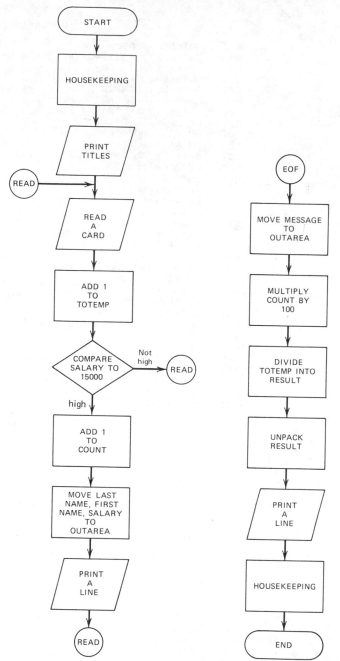

Figure 8-2

4. The high-order bytes of the resultant field in a divide operation are the
    _____ and the lower-order bytes are the _____.
5. An effort to divide by _____ will cause an error.
6. In a divide operation, the second operand may be a _____ or a
    _____.
7. Prior to the **DP** operation, the _____ is placed in the result field.
8. The quotient will be the same size as the _____ field and the re-
    mainder will be the same size as the _____ field.
What if anything is wrong with the routines in Questions 9 and 10?
9. A = B ÷ C

        3 bytes   2 bytes
    NOTE: B and C are already packed.

LABEL	OPERATION	
1	10	16
	ZAP	A,C
	DP	A,B
*		
A	DS	PL5

10. $D = \dfrac{E}{F}$ E = 4 bytes
F = 3 bytes
E and F are packed.

LABEL	OPERATION	
1	10	16
	ZAP	D,E
	DP	D,F
*		
D	DS	PL6

11.   Consider the following input areas:

LABEL	OPERATION	
1	10	16
SALESREC	DS	0CL80
TOTALPR	DS	CL5
QTY	DS	CL2
	DS	CL73

Write a routine to divide **TOTALPR** by **QTY** to obtain **UNITPR**.

12.   Consider the following input areas:

LABEL	OPERATION	
1	10	16
STUDENTS	DS	0CL80
NAME	DS	CL20
TUITION	DS	CL4
RATE	DS	CL3
	DS	CL53

Write a routine to divide **TUITION** by **RATE** to obtain **NOCREDS**.

Solutions   1.   Result
2.   Dividend
Divisor
3.   Packed dividend in bytes
Packed divisor in bytes
4.   Quotient
Remainder
5.   Zero
6.   Packed-decimal field
Self-defining packed operand
7.   Dividend
8.   Dividend
Divisor
9.   Result obtained is A = C ÷ B not B ÷ C
10.   D is not large enough to accommodate the results. It should be 7 bytes long (4 for quotient and 3 for remainder).

11.

LABEL	OPERATION	OPERAND	COMMENTS
	PACK	PACK1,TOTALPR	
	PACK	PACK2,QTY	
	ZAP	UNITPR,PACK1	
	DP	UNITPR,PACK2	
*			
PACK1	DS	PL3	
PACK2	DS	PL2	
UNITPR	DS	PL5	(ANSWER WILL BE IN 3 HIGH-ORDER BYTES)

12.

LABEL	OPERATION	OPERAND
	PACK	PTUITION,TUITION
	PACK	PRATE,RATE
	ZAP	NOCREDS,PTUITION
	DP	NOCREDS,PRATE
*		
PTUITION	DS	PL3
PRATE	DS	PL2
NOCREDS	DS	PL5

D. Comparing Packed Fields

Operation 10	Operand 16
CP	OP1,OP2

Instruction:	CP
Meaning:	Compare Packed Decimal.
	Sets condition code depending upon results of an algebraic comparison.
	First operand is compared to second operand.
Results:	Both operands are unchanged.
	Condition Code is set so that a branch on Low, Equal, or High can be performed.
Operands:	First operand must contain packed-decimal data.
	Second operand must also contain packed-decimal data or be a self-defining packed constant.

Purpose The CP instruction is used to compare two packed-decimal fields. The comparison is *algebraic*, meaning that the sign is included in the test, with the result that negative quantities have a lesser value than positive quantities. The Compare Packed (CP) instruction is similar in many respects to the CLC instruction previously studied. A major difference, however, is that the two operands are compared algebraically. That is, negative numbers are considered to have less value than positive numbers. The condition code is set depending upon the relative value of the first operand as compared to the second operand, and neither operand is changed. The following instructions could be used to determine if an **HRS** field is greater than 40 and to branch to an overtime routine (**OVERTIME**) if it is. Both operands must be in packed-decimal format.

LABEL	OPERATION 10	OPERAND 16
	CP	HRS,FORTY
	BH	OVRTIME
	.	
	.	
	.	
FORTY	DC	P'40'

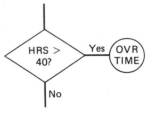

Let us review the condition code settings:

Relationship	Condition Code	Condition	Condition Met
First operand equals second operand.	0	Equal	BNH BNL BE
First operand is less than (<) second operand.	1	Low	BL BNH BNE
First operand is greater than (>) second operand.	2	High	BNL BH BNE

Examples

LABEL	OPERATION 10	16
	CP	P1,P2

	Contents of P1	Contents of P2	Result
1.	123C	00123C	Equal (+123 = +00123)
2.	0C	123C	Low (0 < 123)
3.	456C	456D	High (+456 > −456)
4.	017C	018C	Low (17 < 18)
5.	022F	022C	Equal (022 = +022)
6.	1D	5D	High (−1 > −5)
7.	0C	0D	Equal (negative and positive zeros are considered equal.)
8.	1F2F3F	01234C	Data exception (P1 is not a valid packed field.)

The **CP** instructions could also be written using a self-defining operand as shown below. Remember, however, that both operands must contain packed data.

```
     LABEL      OPERATION            OPERAND
 1              10        16
 |  |  |  |  |   C P  |  |  |  H R S , = P ' 4 0 '  |  |  |
 |  |  |  |  |   B H  |  |  |  O V R T I M E  |  |  |  |  |
```

The CP instruction is summarized as follows:

Summary
1. The CP instruction is an algebraic compare; negative operands have a lesser value than positive operands.
2. Both operands are in the packed format, or a data exception will occur.
3. The first operand is compared to the second operand.
4. When unequal fields are compared, the shorter field is extended with high-order zeros.
5. Plus zero (0C or 0F) and minus zero (0D) are considered equal.

Figure 8-3 shows a program that totals all the odd numbers from 1–99.

SELF-EVALUATING QUIZ

1. (True or False) The CP instruction may be used to compare alphanumeric data.
2. (True or False) When executed, the CP instruction sets a condition code depending on the relationship of the first operand to the second.
3. The contents of (*first/second/both/neither*) operand(s) is (are) changed when the CP instruction is carried out.
4. (True or False) The data referenced by both operands must be in the zoned-decimal format.
5. (True or False) A positive zero has a greater value than a negative zero.
6. (True or False) The second operand of a CP statement can contain a self-defining operand.

```
*                                                                      *
*                                    HOUSEKEEPING INSTRUCTIONS GO HERE  *
*                                                                      *
ODDRTN    AP      SUM,ODD
          AP      ODD,=P'2'
          CP      ODD,=P'101'
          BE      PRINT
          B       ODDRTN
PRINT     MVC     OUTAREA,SPACES
          MVC     MESSAGE,=C'TOTAL OF ODD NOS.1-99 IS '
          UNPK    SUMOUT,SUM
          OI      SUMOUT+4,X'F0'       CHANGE SIGN FROM HEX C TO HEX F
          PUT     OUTFILE,OUTAREA
*                                                                      *
*                                    HOUSEKEEPING INSTRUCTIONS GO HERE  *
*                                    ALONG W/DCB OR DTF MACRO FOR OUTFILE*
*                                                                      *
SPACES    DC      CL1' '
OUTAREA   DS      OCL132
MESSAGE   DS      CL25
SUMOUT    DS      CL5
          DS      CL102
SUM       DC      PL5'00000'
ODD       DC      PL2'01'
          END
```

Figure 8-3

7. Determine the values of AMT1, AMT2, and AMT3 after execution of the instructions indicated below. The three fields have the following initial values:

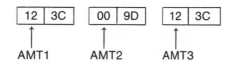

LABEL	OPERATION	OPERAND
	AP	AMT1,AMT3
	CP	AMT1,=P'+123'
	BL	READRTN
	AP	AMT1,AMT2
	CP	AMT1,=P'+126'
	BNH	READRTN
	AP	AMT1,=P'+111'

8. Compute 5 × A using the arithmetic operation AP only. Note that 5 × A = A + A + A + A + A. Use a loop for this routine. Assume A is in packed form.

9. Compute A × B using the arithmetic operation AP only. Note that A × B = A + A + ... + A. Assume A and B are both packed.
   └─B times─┘

10. Compute N! where N is a two-digit packed field.

$$N! = N \text{ factorial} = N \times (N-1) \times (N-2) \times \ldots \ldots 1$$

11. Examine the program in Figure 8-4 that is supposed to determine the percentage of employees who earn under $9000. Indicate any errors that exist. Indicate if the following instructions are valid or invalid using the data shown. The overflow condition is considered invalid.

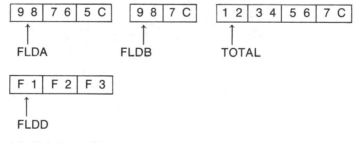

(a) Valid   (b) Invalid
12. PACK   FLDD,FLDD
13. AP   TOTAL,FLDB
14. CLC   FLDD,=C'ØØØ'
15. AP   FLDA(3),FLDB(2)
16. ZAP   TOTAL,FLDB(2)
17. AP   TOTAL,TOTAL
18. AP   FLDA,FLDD
19. SP   FLDA,FLDB(1)
20. PACK   TOTAL,FLDA
21. AP   FLDA,FLDD(1)
22. AP   FLDB,=P'1'
23. UNPACK TOTAL,FLDA
24. AP   FLDA,TOTAL
25. UNPK   TOTAL,FLDB
26. SP   FLDB,FLDB
27. ZAP   FLDA,FLDD

```
*
*                                        HOUSEKEEPING INSTRUCTIONS GO HERE  *
*                                                                           *
READ      GET    INFILE,RECORD
          A      TOTNUM,=P'1
          CLC    SALARY,=C'9000'
          BNH    READ
          AP     TOTAL,=P'1'
          B      READ
EOF       MVC    OUTAREA(27),=C'% WHO EARN UNDER $9,000 IS '
          ZAP    CNT,TOTAL
          MP     CNT,=P'100'
          ZAP    RSLT,CNT
          DP     RSLT,TOTNUM
          UNPK   OUTAREA+27(4),RSLT
          OI     OUTAREA+29,X'F0'
          PUT    OUTFILE,OUTAREA
*                                                                           *
*                                        HOUSEKEEPING INSTRUCTIONS GO HERE  *
*                                        ALONG WITH DCB OR DTF MACROS       *
*                                                                           *
TOTAL     DC     PL2'0'
RSLT      DS     PL6
TOTNUM    DC     PL2'0'
CNT       DS     PL4
RECORD    DS     0CL80                   CARD FORMAT
LAST      DS     CL15                         *
FIRST     DS     CL10                         *
SALARY    DS     CL5                          *
          DS     CL50                         *
SPACES    DC     CL1' '
OUTAREA   DS     CL132
          END
```

Figure 8-4

Solutions

1. False (only packed-decimal data)
2. True
3. Neither
4. False (packed decimal only)
5. False (both are equal)
6. True

7.

34	8C		00	9D		12	3C

    AMT1   AMT2   AMT3

8.

LABEL	OPERATION	OPERAND
	ZAP	TOTAL,A
LOOP	AP	CTR,=P'1'
	CP	CTR,=P'5'
	BE	FINISH
	AP	TOTAL,A
	B	LOOP
*		
TOTAL	DS	PL5
CTR	DC	P'0'

9.

LABEL	OPERATION	OPERAND
	ZAP	TOTAL,A
LOOP	AP	CTR,=P'1'
	CP	CTR,B
	BE	FINISH
	AP	TOTAL,A
	B	LOOP
*		
TOTAL	DS	PL5
CTR	DC	PL2'0'

10.

LABEL	OPERATION	OPERAND
	ZAP	ANSWER,N
LOOP	SP	N,=P'1'
	CP	N,=P'0'
	BE	PRINT
	MP	ANSWER,N
	B	LOOP

11. See Figure 8-5.

12. Valid

13. Valid

14. Valid

15. Valid

16. Valid

17. Valid

18. Invalid; FLDD is not in packed form.

19. Invalid. FLDB(1) contains no sign.

20. Invalid; FLDA is already packed.

21. Invalid; FLDD is not in packed form.

22. Valid

23. Mnemonic Operation Code is invalid; it should be 'UNPK'.

24. Invalid; overflow results.

25. Invalid; a length specifier is required.

26. Valid

27. Invalid; FLDD is not in packed form.

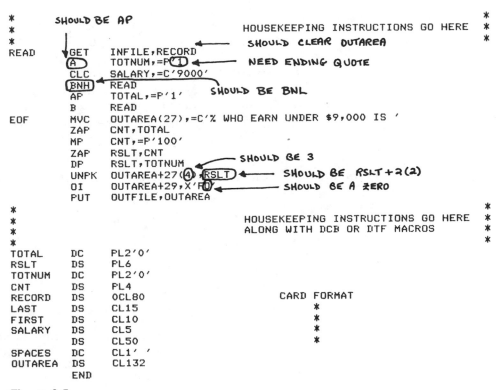

```
*              SHOULD BE AP                                                    *
*                                            HOUSEKEEPING INSTRUCTIONS GO HERE *
*                                            SHOULD CLEAR OUTAREA             *
READ     GET    INFILE,RECORD   ←
         A      TOTNUM,=P'1     ←        NEED ENDING QUOTE
         CLC    SALARY,=C'9000'
         BNH    READ                     SHOULD BE BNL
         AP     TOTAL,=P'1'
         B      READ
EOF      MVC    OUTAREA(27),=C'% WHO EARN UNDER $9,000 IS '
         ZAP    CNT,TOTAL
         MP     CNT,=P'100'
         ZAP    RSLT,CNT
         DP     RSLT,TOTNUM             SHOULD BE 3
         UNPK   OUTAREA+27(4),RSLT  ←   SHOULD BE RSLT+2(2)
         OI     OUTAREA+29,X'F0'    ←   SHOULD BE A ZERO
         PUT    OUTFILE,OUTAREA
*                                                                             *
*                                            HOUSEKEEPING INSTRUCTIONS GO HERE *
*                                            ALONG WITH DCB OR DTF MACROS     *
*                                                                             *
TOTAL    DC     PL2'0'
RSLT     DS     PL6
TOTNUM   DC     PL2'0'
CNT      DS     PL4
RECORD   DS     0CL80                    CARD FORMAT
LAST     DS     CL15                        *
FIRST    DS     CL10                        *
SALARY   DS     CL5                         *
         DS     CL50                        *
SPACES   DC     CL1' '
OUTAREA  DS     CL132
         END
```

Figure 8-5

KEY TERMS

Algebraic comparison

Dividend
Divisor

Multiplicand
Multiplier

Product

Quotient

Remainder

Review Questions   For questions 1 to 3, assume the following card format as input:

LABEL	OPERATION 10	16
CARDIN	DS	ØCL8Ø
A	DS	CL3
B	DS	CL4
C	DS	CL5
D	DS	CL3
	DS	CL65

Compute the following, creating as many DS's as you need:
1. $X = A + B \times C$
2. $Y = D^2$ ($D^2 = D \times D$)
3. $Z = D \times A - B$
4. Compute **FICA** (social security tax) where **FICA** = 5.85% of the first $17,500 earned. Assume **SALARY** is a zoned-decimal field. HINT: 5.85% = 585 when multiplied by 1000.
5. Compute Celsius temperature when Fahrenheit (**F**) is read in, in zoned-decimal format:

$$C = \frac{5}{9} \ (F - 32)$$

6. Write a routine to print the total of the amount fields for each group of 20 input cards. Assume that the input cards are entered in multiples of 20.
7. Compute **TUITION** from a field (zoned-decimal) called **CREDITS**:
   a. Tuition is $30/credit if the student is taking 12 credits or less.
   b. Tuition is $360 for students taking more than 12 credits.

Problems   1. Write a program to create a report from the following card records:

   1–20 Employee name
   21–22 Hours worked
   23–25 Rate
   26–80 Not used

   Output report:

   1–20 Employee name
   41–45 Gross pay

   Gross pay = reg hours × rate + overtime hours × rate × 1.5
   Overtime hours are those hours exceeding 40.

2. Write a program to summarize accident records to obtain the following information:

a. Percentage of drivers under 25.
b. Percentage of drivers who are female.
c. Percentage of drivers from New York.

There is one card record for each driver involved in an accident in the past year:

1–4 Driver number
5   State code (1 for New York)
6–9 Birth date (Month and Year)
10   Sex (M for male, F for female)
11–80 Not used

Results should be printed with constants:

% OF DRIVERS UNDER 25
% OF DRIVERS FEMALE
% OF DRIVERS FROM NY

HINT: Multiply the numerator of each fraction by 100 to obtain the corresponding percentage.

3. Write a program to read detail Bank Transaction Cards with the following format:

1–19 Name of depositor
  20 Type 1-Previous balance, 2-Deposit, 3-Withdrawal
21–25 Account number
26–30 Amount xxxxx
31–80 Not used

The cards are in sequence by account number. Type 1 records exist for each account number followed by Types 2 and 3, if they exist. Types 2 and 3 may be present for a given account number and may appear in any sequence.

Print out the name of the depositor and his current balance (Previous Balance + Deposits − Withdrawals). Also print the heading **BANK REPORT**.

Chapter 9 Print Options

Introduction

The printed report is the primary form of computer output. The purpose of the printed document is to provide management with clear, concise reports that are easy to read and interpret.

For these reasons, four features not applicable to other forms of output must be considered when preparing reports.

1. Printing of Headers

Header information includes report name, date, page number, and field designations. Headers, or headings, are essential for clear presentation when printing output. *Each* page of a report should contain heading information that identifies the report, just in case the page is misplaced or in case individual pages are sent to different users.

2. Editing of Printed Data

A punched card, for example, may have two amount fields with the following data:

00450, 3872658

Although these fields are acceptable on cards or other forms of output, the printed report must contain this information in *edited form* to make it more readable. Hence, $450.00 and $38,726.58, for example, are clearer methods of presenting the same data.

Editing is defined as the manipulation of fields of data to make them clearer and neater for their specific purpose. The editing of data is of prime consideration when printing information.

3. Spacing of Forms

Forms, unlike other types of output, must be properly spaced for ease of reading. Certain entries must be single spaced, others double spaced, still others triple spaced, and so on. Printed output must have adequate margins at both the top and bottom of the form. This requires the computer to be programmed to sense the end of a form and then to transmit the next line of information to a new page.

4. Alignment of Data

Reports do not have fields of information adjacent to one another as is the practice with other forms of output. Rather, printed reports usually contain data that is spaced neatly and evenly across the page. Normally, 132 characters can be printed on a single line. Many of them, however, are left blank for ease of reading. Some printers limit the user to 100 or 120 characters per line.

All of the items specified above require special programming. For that reason, we will study the preparation of a printed report as a separate chapter.

Before we get into the actual programming of printed reports, we will first examine:

1. The Printer Spacing Chart used to plan the format of the report.

2. The nature of continuous forms that must be considered when printing reports.

3. The use of the carriage control tape for sensing the end of a page and for skipping lines.

Printer Spacing Chart: A Tool Used in Preparing Reports

A *Printer Spacing Chart,* sometimes called a Print Layout Sheet, is commonly used to assist the programmer in the preparation of reports. See Figure 9-1. This chart is used for aligning data in a report so that (1) headers appear properly margined in the middle of the page and so that (2) data fields are properly aligned under column headings and evenly spaced across the page. You will note from Figure 9-1a that the Printer Spacing Chart is used to designate the precise print positions in which data will be placed.

The steps necessary to code the printing of the headings are illustrated in Figure 9-2. Note that the coding is simplified since we are using a printer spacing chart, combined with the programming techniques of relative addressing. In order to place the M of MY-T-FINE MOTOR, INC. in print position 51, we simply refer to LINEOUT+50. It becomes a simple matter of determining what positions are to be used for headings once the printer spacing chart is completed.

Continuous Forms

Computer-generated reports are printed on *continuous forms.* A continuous form is a unit of perforated paper with each perforation indicating the end of an individual page. (After all continuous forms in a report have been generated, the individual pages must be burst, or separated, into single sheets.)

Unless the computer is instructed to do otherwise, it will treat the entire continuous form as one long sheet rather than as individual pages. That is, it will write each line and advance the paper, printing from one form to another and ignoring the fact that each is an individual page. At times, it may even print over the perforations, making the report very difficult to read.

Thus, even though printing is done from one continuous form to another, the computer must be instructed to observe page delineations. Printing, then, requires the following considerations:

---

1. Each page should begin with a heading.
2. Lines containing data, commonly called *detail lines*, generally follow.
3. A test for the end of the form is performed. If the end of an individual form is reached, we need to skip to a new page and write the heading again.

Carriage Control Tape

The computer can sense the end of a page or any other specific line of a form with the use of a *carriage control tape.* See Figure 9-3. This tape is attached to the printer and is used for (1) testing for a specific line or (2) skipping to a specific line.

The tape has horizontal lines that correspond to each line of the continuous form. A hole punched in one of the vertical rows on a given line can be used to test for a specific line or to skip to a specific line.

Figure 9-1

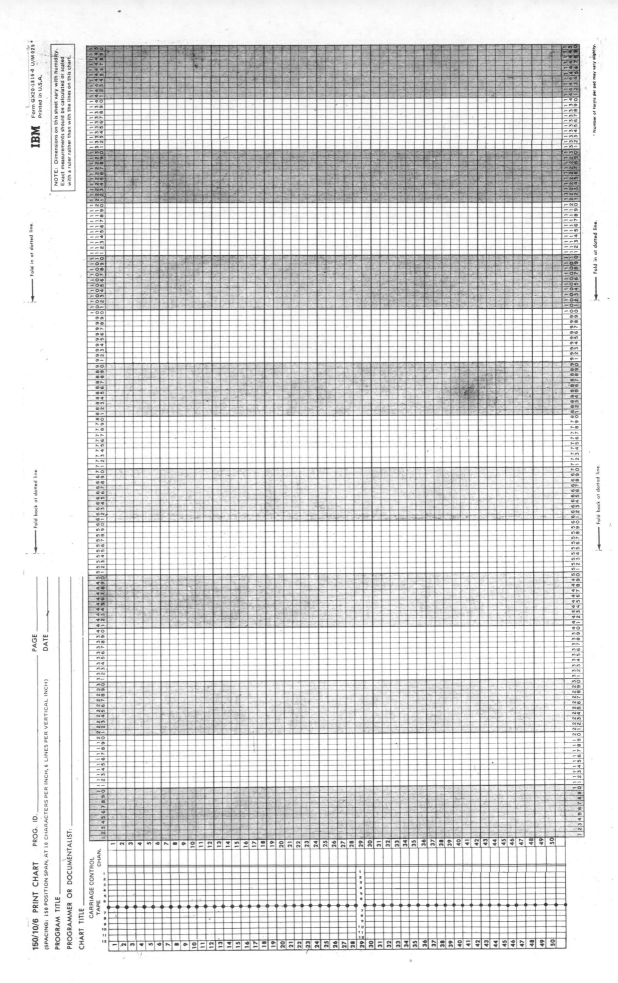

150/10/6 PRINT CHART   PROG. ID. _____   PAGE _____

(SPACING: 150 POSITION SPAN, AT 10 CHARACTERS PER INCH, 6 LINES PER VERTICAL INCH)   DATE _____

PROGRAM TITLE _____

PROGRAMMER OR DOCUMENTALIST: _____

CHART TITLE _____

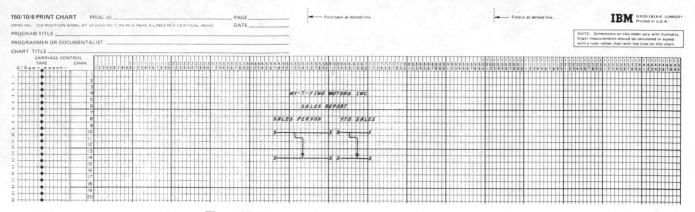

Figure 9-1a

We wish to (1) begin printing on line 6 and to (2) specify line 39 as our last print line of each page.

With a hole punched into channel 1 of line 6, we can instruct the computer to begin printing on a new page. By programming the computer to skip to the line with a hole in channel 1, we can position the tape and the printed form on line 6 of a new page. Note that we do not begin printing on lines 1–5 of a new page because that is too near the top and would not allow for an adequate margin.

Similarly, *each time* a line is printed, we can instruct the computer to test for a punch in channel 12. When such a punch is sensed, it means that the continuous form is on line 39, which is near the bottom. Hence, when the punch in channel 12 is sensed, we instruct the computer to skip to channel 1 (line 6) and to print a header on a new page.

Carriage control tapes, then, are used for:
1. Testing for a designated line number by punching a hole in a channel of a specified line and testing in our program for a hole in that channel.
2. Skipping to a specified line number by punching a hole in a channel of a specified line and programming the computer to skip to the line with a hole in that channel.

```
*                                                                     *
*                HEADING ROUTINE USING ASA CTLCHR                     *
*                                                                     *
HEADING   MVC    LINEOUT,SPACES
          MVC    LINEOUT+50(21),=C'MY-T-FINE MOTORS INC'
          MVI    LINEOUT,C'1'              ADVANCE TO TOP OF PAGE
          PUT    OUTFILE,LINEOUT
          MVC    LINEOUT,SPACES
          MVC    LINEOUT+53(12),=C'SALES REPORT'
          MVI    LINEOUT,C'0'              DOUBLE SPACE
          PUT    OUTFILE,LINEOUT
          MVC    LINEOUT,SPACES
          MVC    LINEOUT+46(21),=C'SALES PERSON'
          MVC    LINEOUT+63(9),=C'YTD SALES'
          MVI    LINEOUT,C'-'              TRIPLE SPACE
          PUT    OUTFILE,LINEOUT
          MVC    LINEOUT,SPACES
          MVI    LINEOUT,C'0'              DOUBLE SPACE
          PUT    OUTFILE,LINEOUT
```

Figure 9-2

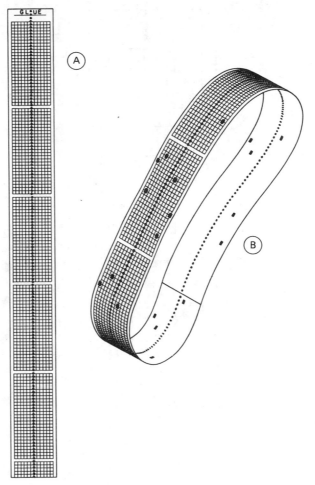

(A) Sample carriage control tape.

(B) Carriage control tape punched in the appropriate positions, ends taped, and ready to be used.

Figure 9-3   Carriage control tape.

We may use any of the 12 channels of the carriage control tapes. Channel 1 is generally designated for the first line of printing and Channel 12 for the last line of printing. In most computer centers, then, it is possible to write programs using these channels without having to punch holes in a new carriage control tape. Any other requirements in addition to the first and last line of printing would, however, mean that a new tape must be created. If, for example, all sub-totals were to print on line 30 of each page, an additional punch in a carriage control tape would need to be made.

Control (CNTRL) Macro

Two methods can be used to cause the printer to space the paper. Both can be designated with a CNTRL macro.

1. Space option (SP)

Unless otherwise indicated, a PUT statement will result in single spacing. With the use of the CNTRL Macro and a Space or SP option, we can also obtain double or triple spacing.

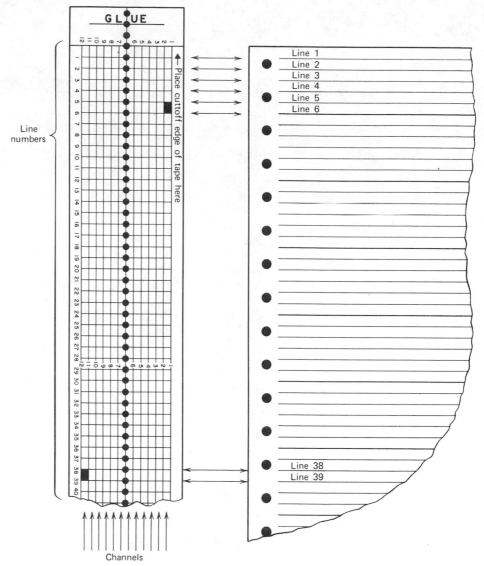

Figure 9-4

2. Skip option (SK)

The skip option is used to skip to a particular line. To do this a hole must be punched in a specified channel of the carriage control tape corresponding to that line. Hence, when channel 1 is specified, it means we want to advance to the top of a new page or the first line of print.

In short, an SK, or skip, option is used to advance the paper to a designated line. It makes use of the carriage control tape. An SP, or space, option is used to advance the paper 1, 2, or 3 lines. It *does not* make use of the carriage control tape.

The general format for the CNTRL macro is as follows:

Operation 10	Operand 16
CNTRL	*File name, Option, n, m*

where

File name is the name assigned to the DTFPR or the DCB for the print file
Option   SP for spacing, SK for skipping
n   denotes *immediate* carriage control—that is, *before* printing occurs
m   denotes *delayed* spacing or skipping—that is, *after* printing occurs

The *n* and *m* parameters allow advancing before and after the print (PUT) statements. For the SP option, *n* and *m* must range in value from 1 to 3 corresponding to single, double, or triple spacing. For the SK option, *n* and *m* indicate the channel to be skipped to.

Advancing to Top of Page

LABEL	OPERATION	OPERAND
1	10	16
	CNTRL	OUTFILE,SK,1
	PUT	OUTFILE,LINEOUT

The CNTRL macro orders an *immediate* skip to the line with a hole punched in channel 1, thereby advancing to the top of the form before the PUT is executed. At this location, a print command (PUT) is issued to print the heading created in the output area defined as LINEOUT.

Immediate Spacing

LABEL	OPERATION	OPERAND
1	10	16
	CNTRL	OUTFILE,SP,1
	PUT	OUTFILE,LINEOUT

The CNTRL macro causes the printer to advance immediately to the next line. The PUT statement then causes the printer to advance *another* line and print out the results. The net effect is that the printer has advanced two lines. The information printed out will thus be *double spaced*. See Figure 9-5.
Replacing the 1 with a 2 in the CNTRL macro, for example, will have a net effect of triple spacing.

Delayed Spacing

LABEL	OPERATION	OPERAND
1	10	16
	CNTRL	OUTFILE,SP,,2
	PUT	OUTFILE,LINEOUT

This option permits spacing after the print command (PUT) has been issued. Note that the CNTRL will cause the computer to space only *after* the PUT has been executed. The two commas indicate that *no* immediate spacing is required.

LABEL	OPERATION	OPERAND	
1	10	16	
	CNTRL	OUTFILE,SP,1	→ Single spacing
	PUT	OUTFILE,LINEOUT	→ Single spacing and printing

```
BROWN                         LEROY                    $22,234

MOSS                          SAM                      $21,212

GREENSPAN                     ANDY                     $23,888

DEAN                          JAMES                    $22,877

WHITE                         FORREST                  $22,555
```

Figure 9-5 How double spacing is achieved using CNTRL macro.

Note that the fourth parameter is coded by inserting an additional comma. *When delayed spacing is specified, the standard single spacing associated with the print instruction is eliminated.* The above example would therefore cause two lines to be spaced *after* the PUT instruction has been issued, which will result in double spacing, as shown in Figure 9-6.

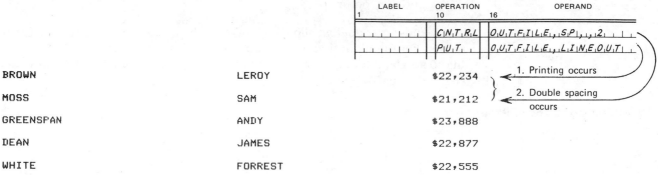

Figure 9-6   How delayed spacing is achieved using CNTRL macro.

Spacing Before and After Printing

The CNTRL macro allows us to space a form *both* before and after printing.

LABEL	OPERATION 10	16	OPERAND
	CNTRL		OUTFILE,SP,2,3
	PUT		OUTFILE,LINEOUT

Causes

1. Triple spacing before printing (2 lines + standard single spacing).

2. A line to be printed.

3. Triple spacing after printing (the after-print option suppresses the standard single spacing).

Note that we can also use the CNTRL macro to skip to a specified line *both* before and after printing.

DOS Considerations When Using CNTRL Macro

The entry   CONTROL = YES   *must* be included in the DTFPR file description.

The entry   CONTROL = YES   *may* also be included in PRMOD macro, if PRMOD is included.[1]

OS Considerations When Using CNTRL Macro

The entry   MACRF = PMC   must be included in the DCB for the print file.

---

[1] See Appendix E.

Summary of CNTRL Macro

1. The CNTRL macro is used to control spacing or skipping to a line. Skipping requires a hole punched in a specified channel on the carriage control tape.
2. The file name referenced must be the *same* symbolic name assigned in the DCB or DTF for the printer device.
3. The skip (SK) or space (SP) option must be specified with the CNTRL macro.
4. The third parameter (n) is to identify either the channel to be used for skipping purposes or the number of lines to be spaced before printing. When used with the space option, this spacing is in addition to the standard single spacing that occurs when a print operation is performed. Therefore, when 1 is specified, double spacing will occur. Channels 1–12 may be specified for the SK option and the digits 1–3 are permissible for the SP option.
5. The fourth parameter (m) is used to space lines *after* the printing operation. Any number of lines from 1 to 3 may be spaced. *Standard single spacing is eliminated when this option is used* and, therefore, a 2 specified as the fourth parameter will cause double spacing.
6. The entries $\boxed{CONTROL = YES}$ must be included in the DTF's and may be included in the PRMOD statements when using the CNTRL macro with DOS. With OS, the entry $\boxed{MACRF = PMC}$ must be included in the DCB.

SELF-EVALUATING QUIZ

1. Consider the Printer Spacing Chart in Figure 9-7. Write the series of statements that will print the header in the appropriate print positions.
2. Consider the following statement:

LABEL	OPERATION	OPERAND
1	10 16	
	CNTRL	OUTSIDE,SK,1

OUTSIDE is the _____ that is specified in the _____. The CNTRL macro is used, in general, for _____. SK in the above causes _____. The effect of the operation is to _____.

150/10/6 PRINT CHART   PROG. ID _____   PAGE _____

(SPACING: 150 POSITION SPAN, AT 10 CHARACTERS PER INCH, 6 LINES PER VERTICAL INCH)   DATE _____

PROGRAM TITLE _____

PROGRAMMER OR DOCUMENTALIST: _____

CHART TITLE _____

MONTHLY TRANSACTIONS

Figure 9-7

3. What is the major difference between spacing and skipping?
4. Consider the following instructions:

LABEL	OPERATION 10	16 OPERAND
	CNTRL	PRINTOUT,SP,3
	PUT	PRINTOUT,LINEOUT

PRINTOUT is assigned with a _____ or _____. LINEOUT
is defined with a _____. Printing occurs (*before/after*) spacing.
The paper is spaced __(number)__ lines.
5. Write an instruction to advance the paper two lines before printing.
6. Write an instruction to advance the paper to the line with a hole
punched in channel 1 after printing.

Solutions 1.

LABEL	OPERATION 10	16 OPERAND	COMMENTS
HEADING	MVC	LINEOUT,SPACES	
	MVC	LINEOUT+58,=C'MONTHLY TRANSACTIONS'	
	PUT	OUTFILE,LINEOUT	

2. File name
   DTFPR or DCB
   Spacing and skipping
   Skipping to a line with a hole in a specified channel (1)
   Advance the paper to a new page *before* printing
3. Skipping causes the paper to skip to a specified line, depending upon
   the punches in the carriage control tape. Spacing means advancing the
   paper one, two, or three lines. Spacing is independent of the carriage
   control tape.
4. DTFPR or DCB
   DS
   After
   3
5. CNTRL OUTFILE,SP,2
6. CNTRL OUTFILE,SK,,1

Using ASA Control Characters: An Alternative Method of Advancing Without Using the CNTRL Macro

IBM systems contain either 120 or 132 print positions per line, and in this text
we will assume that the printer contains 132 characters. When ASA (American
Standards Association) control characters are used, the output area will be defined as 133 bytes (*one more than necessary*) since the *first* print position is set
aside for carriage control:

LABEL	OPERATION 10	16
LINEOUT	DS	CL133

This means that the first position of the output area will *not* print. It is used
for controlling skipping and spacing operations. Any of the following American
Standards Association (ASA) carriage control characters can be placed in this
first position of the print area for carriage control purposes:

ASA Control Character		Hex Representation	Carriage Control Operation
Blank	(space)	40	Normal single spacing
0	(zero)	F0	Double spacing
–	(minus)	60	Triple spacing
1	(one)	F1	Skip to top of new page
+	(plus)	4F	Suppress advancing

An MVI (Move Immediate) instruction that moves one byte of data may be used to place the desired carriage control character in the first or high-order position of the output. This would be performed *prior* to the print or PUT command.

This method, then, is a substitute for the CNTRL macro for advancing the paper *prior to* printing. It may *not* be used, however, for automatically advancing the paper *after* printing, an option that is available only with the CNTRL macro.

Example 1

Print a line after double spacing:

LABEL	OPERATION 10	OPERAND 16
	MVI	LINEOUT,C'∅'
	PUT	OUTFILE,LINEOUT

or

LABEL	OPERATION 10	OPERAND 16
	MVI	LINEOUT,X'F∅'
	PUT	OUTFILE,LINEOUT

Example 2

Print a line at the top of a new page:

LABEL	OPERATION 10	OPERAND 16
	MVI	LINEOUT,C'1'
	PUT	OUTFILE,LINEOUT

or

LABEL	OPERATION 10	OPERAND 16
	MVI	LINEOUT,X'F1'
	PUT	OUTFILE,LINEOUT

Comparing CNTRL with MVI and ASA Characters

Figure 9-8 illustrates an entire procedure for printing headings that relies on the MVI instruction and the ASA characters being placed in the first print position. It performs the same spacing options as in Figure 9-9, which uses the CNTRL option.

Note that when using the ASA characters, the print line must be established as *133* characters, rather than 132, and that the first, or high-order position is used for carriage control and is *not* printed.

```
*                                                                    *
*                    HEADING ROUTINE USING ASA CTLCHR                *
*                                                                    *
HEADING  MVC    LINEOUT,SPACES
         MVC    LINEOUT+50(21),=C'MY-T-FINE MOTORS INC'
         MVI    LINEOUT,C'1'              ADVANCE TO TOP OF PAGE
         PUT    OUTFILE,LINEOUT
         MVC    LINEOUT,SPACES
         MVC    LINEOUT+53(12),=C'SALES REPORT'
         MVI    LINEOUT,C'0'             DOUBLE SPACE
         PUT    OUTFILE,LINEOUT
         MVC    LINEOUT,SPACES
         MVC    LINEOUT+46(21),=C'SALES PERSON'
         MVC    LINEOUT+63(9),=C'YTD SALES'
         MVI    LINEOUT,C'-'             TRIPLE SPACE
         PUT    OUTFILE,LINEOUT
         MVC    LINEOUT,SPACES
         MVI    LINEOUT,C'0'             DOUBLE SPACE
         PUT    OUTFILE,LINEOUT
```

Figure 9-8

DOS Considerations for the Use of ASA Characters

The DTF macro describing the print file must contain the following entry:

CTLCHR = ASA

Blocksize (BLKSIZE) is also increased to 133 to allow for the carriage control position. The DTF would now appear as follows:

LABEL	OPERATION	OPERAND	COMMENTS
OUTFILE	DTFPR	BLKSIZE=133,CTLCHR=ASA,DEVADDR=SYSLST,IOAREA1=BUFFROUT,	*
		WORKA=YES	

OS Considerations for Use of ASA Characters

The DCB macro describing printed output is changed as follows: The blocksize and logical record length operands are each increased to 133 to allow for carriage control. The DCB would now appear as follows:

LABEL	OPERATION	OPERAND	COMMENTS
OUTFILE	DCB	DDNAME=OUTFILE,MACRF=PM,BLKSIZE=133,LRECL=133,DSORG=PS	

```
*                                                                    *
*                    PRINT ROUTINE USING CNTRL MACRO                 *
*                                                                    *
HEADING  CNTRL  OUTFILE,SK,1             ADVANCE TO TOP OF PAGE
         MVC    LINTEOUT,SPACES
         MVC    LINEOUT+50(21),=C'MY-T-FINE MOTORS INC'
         PUT    OUTFILE,LINEOUT
         CNTRL  OUTFILE,SP,1             DOUBLE SPACE
         MVC    LINEOUT,SPACES
         MVC    LINEOUT+53(12),=C'SALES REPORT'
         CNTRL  OUTFILE,SP,,3            TRIPLE SPACE AFTER PRINT
         PUT    OUTFILE,LINEOUT
         MVC    LINEOUT,SPACES
         MVC    LINEOUT+46(21),=C'SALES PERSON'
         MVC    LINEOUT+63(9),=C'YTD SALES'
         CNTRL  OUTFILE,SP,,3            TRIPLE SPACE AFTER PRINT
         PUT    OUTFILE,LINEOUT
```

Figure 9-9

Review of I/O Changes Required for Carriage Control

Method	Format	Use	DOS Changes Required for		OS Changes Required for DCB
			DTFPR	PRMOD	
CNTRL Macro	CNTRL File name, Option, *n, m* Option—SP or SK *n*—immediate carriage control *m*—after print carriage control	Can be used for spacing or skipping before *and* after printing.	CONTROL = YES	CONTROL = YES	MACRF = PMC
ASA character placed in *high-order* byte of 133 character print area using MVI.	MVI PRINTOUT, C' ' ᵬ—single spacing 0—double spacing −—triple spacing 1—skip to top of page +—no advancing	Can be used for spacing or skipping *before* printing.	BLKSIZE = 133, CTLCHR = ASA		BLKSIZE = 133, LRECL = 133

☐ = entries to be coded as part of program.

The Print Overflow (PRTOV) Macro: For Use with On-Line Printers

As noted, a computer will print lines of data without paying any attention to perforations from one continuous form to another unless otherwise instructed. When the printing of data may require more than a single page of information, it is necessary to test for a *form overflow condition*. Usually a punch in channel 9 or 12 of the carriage control tape denotes that an end-of-page condition has been reached. Since a punch in channel 9 or 12 is made in the last line containing printed data, a form overflow condition, indicated by the PRTOV macro, tests for a punch in the corresponding channel.

> When a form overflow condition is reached, we usually instruct the computer to:
> 1. Advance the form to the top of the next page (channel 1 on the control tape)
>   or
> 2. Branch to a routine that produces a top-of-page heading, page numbers, date, and so on.

The format of the **PRTOV** instruction is:

Operation 10	Operand 16
PRTOV	*File name, n, Routine-name*

where

> *File name* is the name assigned to the DTF or the DCB for the print file.
>
> *n* is the channel number used to indicate the end of the page (channel 9 or channel 12, depending upon the standard used at the particular installation).
>
> *Routine-name* is an optional entry if a branch to a heading routine is desired. If this entry is omitted, **PRTOV** will cause the printer to skip to a new page automatically.

Example 1

After writing a detail line, test to see if there is a punch in channel 12. If there is, simply skip to a new page:

LABEL	OPERATION 10	16	OPERAND
	PUT	OUTFILE, LINEOUT	
	PRTOV	OUTFILE, 12	

In the instruction above, a form overflow condition is denoted by a punch in channel 12 of the carriage control tape. When such a punch is sensed, the input/output control system (IOCS) restores the carriage by advancing to the top of the next page (skip to channel 1). Whether or not an overflow condition has been sensed, the computer will continue executing with the next sequential instruction.

Example 2

Branch to a heading routine when an end-of-page has been sensed.

In this example, when the end-of-page condition is sensed (punch in channel 12), the control system should *not* automatically provide advancement to the top of the next page. Instead, a branch to the routine called **HEADING** should take place.

LABEL	OPERATION 10	16	OPERAND
	PUT	OUTFILE, LINEOUT	
	PRTOV	OUTFILE, 12, HEADING	

Hence, in the program excerpt above, the program will proceed to the next sequential instruction *unless* an overflow has occurred; when an overflow occurs, a branch to **HEADING** is performed.

To use print overflow in the earlier programming example (**MY-T-FINE MOTOR INC**), Figure 9-1*a*, we simply test for print overflow prior to branching to the read instruction. When overflow is detected, a branch to the routine called **HEADING** will cause the headings to be repeated on succeeding pages. See Figure 9-2 for the **HEADING** routine that has been previously illustrated.

DOS Considerations
The entry | PRINTOV = YES | *must* appear in the DTFPR file description.
The entry | PRINTOV = YES | *may* also be included in the PRMOD macro, discussed in Appendix E.

OS Considerations
Same as for CNTRL macro; that is, include the entry | MACRF = PMC |.

Summary of PRTOV Macro
1. The PRTOV macro is used to detect the end-of-page condition.
2. The file name referenced must be the same symbolic name assigned in the DCB or DTF for the printer device.
3. The second operand (*n*) identifies the channel to be tested for form overflow (usually channel 9 or 12).
4. When the third operand is omitted and the overflow condition is detected, the form automatically advances to the top of the next page.
5. When a routine name is given as the third operand and the overflow condition is detected, a branch to that routine takes place.
6. The routine name specified as the third operand must appear in the NAME field of the program (starting in column 1).
7. The entry | PRINTOV=YES | must appear in the DTF's and PRMOD statements when using the | PRTOV | macro with DOS. With OS, the entry | MACRF=PCM | must be included in the DCB.

Alternative Method for Testing for End-of-Page: Counting Lines[2]

An alternative method can be used for testing for form overflow, one not dependent upon carriage control. The major advantage of this second method is that it does not rely on carriage control tapes and is completely independent of the computer system (OS or DOS).

A counter is established and initialized. The counter is incremented each time a line is printed. In this way, the counter serves as a total of the number of lines actually printed. The programmer then determines exactly how many print lines are desired per page. When the counter is equal to that desired number, the program branches to a HEADING routine where headings are printed at the top of the next page.

In this way, the programmer can build into the program a routine that prints exactly 25 double-spaced lines per page or 50 single-spaced lines per page or whatever variation is desired.

[2] This method *must* be used for systems in which print operations are performed offline, usually with large-scale computers.

Example

Print 25 double-spaced detail lines per page:

LABEL	OPERATION	OPERAND
	CNTRL	OUTFILE,SP,1
	PUT	OUTFILE,,LINEOUT
	AP	CTR,=P'1'
	CP	CTR,=PL2'25'
	BE	HEADING
	B	READ
	.	
	.	
	.	
CTR	DC	PL2'00'
	.	

NOTE: If one or more of the options discussed in this section is not available with your **DOS** system, see Appendix E, "Generating IOCS Modules for **DOS** systems." (IOCS is an abbreviation for input-output control system.) Appendix E includes a discussion of **PRMOD** and **CDMOD** and how the options considered above may be incorporated in your programs.

SELF-EVALUATING QUIZ

1. An end-of-page condition is usually indicated by a punch in _____ of the _____.
2. Another name for an end-of-page condition is _____.
3. PRTOV can cause the computer to either _____ or _____.
4. (True or False) The alternative to the PRTOV (line counting) for testing for end of page requires more programming.
5. Indicate the advantage of the alternative to the PRTOV option.
6. Using the PRTOV option, write a statement to skip to a new page when a punch in channel 9 is sensed.
7. Using the line counting method, write a routine to print 20 triple-spaced lines per page.

Solutions

1. Channel 9 or channel 12
   Carriage control tape
2. Form overflow
3. Automatically skip to a new page (channel 1)
   Branch to a special routine (usually for the purpose of printing headings)
4. True
5. It is independent of the system and the punches in the carriage control tape. It must be used when the printer is offline.

6.

LABEL	OPERATION	OPERAND
	PUT	OUTFILE,,LINEOUT
	PRTOV	OUTFILE,9

7.

LABEL	OPERATION	OPERAND
	CNTRL	OUTFILE,SP,2
	PUT	OUTFILE,,LINEOUT
	AP	CTR,=PL1'1'
	CP	CTR,=PL2'20'
	BE	HEADING
	.	
	.	
CTR	DS	PL2'0'

Editing Printed Data

Data on input media is usually in concise or condensed form. The printed output, however, must contain additional specifications, such as $, ., +, or − signs, to make the fields more intelligible.

Editing is considered the manipulation of data fields to make them clearer and neater for their specific purpose. The following are considered editing functions:

---

1. Suppressing high-order or leading zeros.
2. Printing decimal points where decimal alignment is implied.
3. Printing dollar signs and commas.
4. Printing a plus or minus sign to reflect the value of a field.

The Edit command will *unpack* a field *and edit* according to the specifications indicated. There is *no* need to unpack or to replace zones with an OI or MVZ instruction. The UNPK, OI, and MVZ are only used when *no* editing is required.

Figure 9-10 illustrates an unedited report. Figure 9-11 illustrates the same data presented in edited form. Without editing, this report is somewhat cumbersome to read. Note the suppression of leading zeros in the dependents field and the dollar sign, commas, and decimal points in the YTD (Year-to-Date) field greatly increase the readability of the form.

The process of editing requires the following three steps.

Steps in Editing Data
1. An *edit pattern* is established that specifies the punctuation that will take place. The edit pattern is established as a Defined Constant (DC) or in a self-defining operand.
2. The edit pattern is moved (using MVC) either to a work area or to the output area.
3. The data is edited by using the edit (ED) instruction.

DEPT	EMPLOYEE	DEPENDENTS	YTD GROSS
00050	BODAS MICHAEL	003	000870400
00100	BRINDLE CALVIN	004	000940800
00150	CARTER JOHN	007	000630400
00150	DUNCAN LEONARD	002	000313600
00200	ELLIS FORREST	004	000473600
00200	FINE ROBERT	006	001267200
00250	HUNTER PHILIP	007	000256000

Figure 9-10

DEPT	EMPLOYEE	DEPENDENTS	YTD GROSS
50	BODAS MICHAEL	3	$ 8,704.00
100	BRINDLE CALVIN	4	$ 9,408.00
150	CARTER JOHN	7	$ 6,304.00
150	DUNCAN LEONARD	2	$ 3,136.00
200	ELLIS FORREST	4	$ 4,736.00
200	FINE ROBERT	6	$12,672.00
250	HUNTER PHILIP	7	$ 2,560.00

Figure 9-11

Note that the edit pattern field is moved or copied into the output area by an MVC instruction *prior* to the editing operation. This is because the edit pattern field is *destroyed* by each edit operation.

The data to be edited must be in *packed-decimal* form and is referenced as the second or sending operand in an ED instruction. The first operand always references a field containing a "pattern" of characters that controls the editing. After execution, the first operand contains the edited result in zoned-decimal format, while the second operand remains unchanged. For example, the instructions usually would be written in the following sequence:

LABEL	OPERATION 10	OPERAND 16
	MVC	LINEOUT (6),PATTERN
	ED	LINEOUT (6),PDATA
	:	
PATTERN	DC	

pattern characters
to be discussed

where

> **PATTERN** represents a 6-byte data pattern with special characters to be discussed
>
> **PDATA** is a 3-byte field containing 5 digits in packed form
>
> **LINEOUT** represents the output area

The pattern field consists of special characters, each with a specific purpose to achieve an editing function. Unfortunately, many of these characters are not printable symbols, and must be set up using a hexadecimal code, as in the following illustration:

LABEL	OPERATION 10	OPERAND 16
	MVC	LINEOUT (6),PATTERN
	ED	LINEOUT (6),PDATA
	:	
PATTERN	DC	XL6'402020202020'

or

LABEL	OPERATION 10	OPERAND 16
	MVC	LINEOUT (6),=X'402020202020'
	ED	LINEOUT (6),PDATA

In our examples, reference characters will be used to simplify the pattern set up, which are illustrated below. During editing, the leftmost (high-order) byte of the pattern must contain a *fill character*. The pattern, therefore, is always *1 byte longer* than the prescribed editing requires. The following table will serve as a reference.

Character	Hex Code	Reference to Be Used in Illustrations	Meaning
Digit Select	20	D for digit	Pattern is allowing for a digit.
Blank Fill	40	B for blank	A blank is placed in pattern.

Interpreting Edit Characters   **Suppression of Leading Zeros**

Nonsignificant or leading zeros are zeros appearing in the leftmost positions of a field and having no significant value. For example 00387 has two leading zeros that should be suppressed, or omitted, when printing. Note that the number 10000 has *no* leading zeros. All zeros have numeric significance, and none appear in the leftmost positions of the field.

To suppress leading zeros, we begin the edit pattern with a *fill character* that indicates the specific symbol or character that should replace high-order zeros. For example, if leading zeros are to be replaced by blanks, the fill character is a blank, or hex '40'.

If no other editing is to be performed, the edit pattern will contain the fill character and a hex '20' or digit select symbol for each character to be inserted from the sending field.

Using the previous illustration, we have

LABEL	OPERATION	OPERAND
	MVC	LINEOUT(6),=X'402020202020'
	ED	LINEOUT(6),PDATA

This will perform suppression on 5 decimal digits that are transmitted in packed format (3 bytes). In the following, D stands for digit select (digit to be entered on ED command) and B for blank.

Field	Hex Representation	Reference
PDATA	0 0 | 1 0 | 9 C	0 0 | 1 0 | 9 C
Edit Pattern	4 0 | 2 0 | 2 0 | 2 0 | 2 0 | 2 0	B | D | D | D | D | D
LINEOUT (after execution of ED)	4 0 | 4 0 | 4 0 | F 1 | F 0 | F 9	B | B | B | 1 | 0 | 9

NOTE: The zone of a packed-decimal field is converted to 'F' by the ED instruction.

Other examples using the BDDDDD edit pattern are shown below.

PDATA (Packed Decimal)	LINEOUT (Hex)	LINEOUT (Ref.)
1 2 | 3 4 | 5 C	40 | F1 | F2 | F3 | F4 | F5	B12345
0 1 | 2 3 | 4 C	40 | 40 | F1 | F2 | F3 | F4	BB1234
0 0 | 5 6 | 7 C	40 | 40 | 40 | F5 | F6 | F7	BBB567
0 0 | 0 9 | 0 C	40 | 40 | 40 | 40 | F9 | F0	BBBB90
0 0 | 0 0 | 8 C	40 | 40 | 40 | 40 | 40 | F8	BBBBB8
0 0 | 0 0 | 0 C	40 | 40 | 40 | 40 | 40 | 40	BBBBBB

B = blank

The fill character, then, is used in a pattern to replace high-order or leading zeros. When the fill character is a hex **40**, then leading zeros are replaced with blanks. In fact, any character may be used as the fill character, but the blank is the most common.

For the editing thus far described, the number of characters in the edit pattern is *one more* than the field to be edited.

How Editing Is
Actually Performed

Editing proceeds from *left* to *right*. All high-order zeros in the sending field are replaced with the fill character. Once a nonzero digit is received by the pattern, any zeros appearing to the right *will be printed*. In effect, an indicator within the CPU is turned on by a *nonzero digit* from the sending field. When the indicator is on, all remaining edit characters such as commas and zeros will appear in the output. This will be considered in detail shortly.

The fill character in an edit pattern may also be an *. In such case, 00025 will print as ***25. The asterisk is called a *check protection symbol*. Since blanks in an amount field of a check can be altered by dishonest people, asterisks are frequently substituted because they reduce the feasibility of tampering with data. For example, an amount printed as

| 547 |

can easily be changed to

| 99547 |

whereas

| **547 |

could be altered less easily.

Format for * as Fill Character

Character	Representation	Hex Code Used in Pattern
Asterisk	*	5C

Using hex 5C in place of 40 as a fill character will result in leading zeros being replaced with *'s.

The instruction for editing will be

LABEL	OPERATION 10	OPERAND 16
	MVC	LINEOUT(6),=X'5C2020202020'
	ED	LINEOUT,PDATA

Reference

| 0 0 | 1 0 | 9 C |

PDATA
(Sending field)

Hex Representation

| 0 0 | 1 0 | 9 C |

| * | D | D | D | D | D |

Edit Pattern

| 5 C | 2 0 | 2 0 | 2 0 | 2 0 | 2 0 |

| * | * | * | 1 | 0 | 9 |

LINEOUT (after execution)

| 5 C | 5 C | 5 C | F 1 | F 0 | F 9 |

Other examples are shown below.

PDATA (Packed Decimal)			LINEOUT (hex)(after ED)						LINEOUT Actual Results
12	34	5C	5C	F1	F2	F3	F4	F5	*12345
01	23	4C	5C	5C	F1	F2	F3	F4	**1234
00	56	7C	5C	5C	5C	F5	F6	F7	***567
00	09	0C	5C	5C	5C	5C	F9	F0	****90
00	00	8C	5C	5C	5C	5C	5C	F8	*****8
00	00	0C	5C	5C	5C	5C	5C	5C	******

1. The two instructions necessary to perform editing are _____ and _____.
2. In the MVC instruction, the second operand is called the _____.
3. In the MVC and the ED instructions, the first operand refers to _____.
4. The data to be edited appears in the _____ operand of the _____ instruction.
5. The data to be edited must be in _____ format.
6. Write a routine to print a 3-digit packed-decimal field called UNITS with zero suppression.
7. Write a routine to print a 4-byte packed-decimal field called TOTAL with asterisks used as the zero suppression symbol.

Solutions

1. MVC
   ED
2. Edit pattern field (established either as a constant or as a self-defining operand).
3. The receiving field, usually located in the print area.
4. Second
   ED
5. Packed decimal
6.

LABEL	OPERATION	OPERAND
	MVC	LINEOUT(4),=X'40202020'
	ED	LINEOUT(4),UNITS
	:	
UNITS	DS	PL2

7. Recall that a 4-byte packed field contains 7 digits plus a sign.

LABEL	OPERATION	OPERAND
	MVC	LINEOUT(8),=X'5C20202020202020'
	ED	LINEOUT(8),TOTAL
	:	
TOTAL	DS	PL4

Inserting Commas

Character Representation	Hex Code Used in Pattern
Comma	6B

To insert a comma in an edit pattern we simply place it in the position desired. To print 123456 as 123,456, for example, the edit pattern would appear as:

Edit Pattern	40	20	20	20	6B	20	20	20
Interpretation	B	D	D	D	,	D	D	D
	blank	digit	digit	digit	comma	digit	digit	digit

Note that a fill character in the edit pattern will not only cause suppression of leading zeros but suppression of leading commas as well. Hence, if a field with value 000245 were edited using the above edit pattern, it would print as 245 *without* a comma. The leftmost *five* positions are filled with blanks. Note that the field length specifier in the above is 8 bytes, which is the length of the pattern.

In the following examples, we will perform zero suppression and insert commas for clarity. The pattern necessary to accomplish this task will appear as:

B	D	D	,	D	D	D

The instructions to perform the editing are:

LABEL	OPERATION 10	16	OPERAND
	MVC		LINEOUT (7),=X'40202068202020'
	ED		LINEOUT (7),PDATA

Note that in this case the field length specifier is 7.

Example

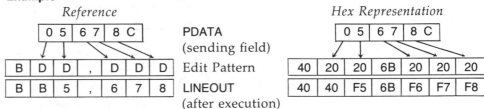

Reference

0 5	6 7	8 C

PDATA (sending field)

B	D	D	,	D	D	D

Edit Pattern

B	B	5	,	6	7	8

LINEOUT (after execution)

Hex Representation

0 5	6 7	8 C

40	20	20	6B	20	20	20

40	40	F5	6B	F6	F7	F8

Note that the nonzero indicator which controls the printing or suppression of the comma is on because a nonzero digit precedes the comma. Therefore, all remaining edit characters will transmit.

Other examples using the BDD,DDD edit pattern are shown below.

	PDATA			LINEOUT (Hex)						Reference
1.	12	34	5C	40	F1	F2	6B	F3	F4	F5	B12,345
2.	01	23	4C	40	40	F1	6B	F2	F3	F4	BB1,234
3.	00	56	7C	40	40	40	40	F5	F6	F7	BBBB567
4.	00	09	0C	40	40	40	40	40	F9	F0	BBBBB90
5.	00	00	8C	40	40	40	40	40	40	F8	BBBBBB8
6.	00	00	0C	40	40	40	40	40	40	40	BBBBBBB

Note that a nonzero digit was *not* found before the comma (6B), in 3–6. Therefore, the nonzero indicator is off and the comma does *not* appear in the final result.

Inserting Decimal Points

Character	Representation	Hex Code
Decimal point	.	4B

The decimal point is commonly used in business data processing reports. When the program is designed, field sizes and implied decimal points are established. Therefore the programmer understands exactly where decimal points are to be inserted even though they are not in the fields themselves. In the following examples, we will assume that the desired results represent dollars and cents. The pattern to be used will be established so that a decimal point will print.

Pattern reference	B	D	D	D	.	D	D
Pattern (hex)	40	20	20	20	4B	20	20

Here are the instructions for editing.

LABEL	OPERATION	OPERAND
	MVC	LINEOUT (7),=X'40202020 4B2020'
	ED	LINEOUT (7),PDATA

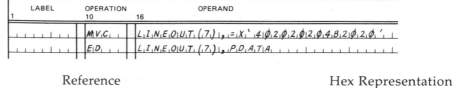

Reference   Hex Representation

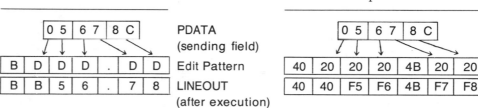

Other examples using the BDDD.DD pattern include:

	PDATA			LINEOUT (Hex)							Reference						
1.	12	34	5C	40	F1	F2	F3	4B	F4	F5	B	1	2	.	4	5
2.	01	23	4C	40	40	F1	F2	4B	F3	F4	B	B	1	2	.	3	4
3.	00	56	7C	40	40	40	F5	4B	F6	F7	B	B	B	5	.	6	7
4.	00	09	0C	40	40	40	40	40	F9	F0	B	B	B	B	B	9	0
5.	00	00	8C	40	40	40	40	40	40	F8	B	B	B	B	B	B	8
6.	00	00	00	40	40	40	40	40	40	40	B	B	B	B	B	B	B

The above results present some obvious problems. Whenever a field contains all zeros, the fill character is the only item that prints, as in (6) above. Moreover, when the first significant or nonzero character *follows* the decimal point, as in (4) and (5) above, the decimal point does *not* print. To cause edit characters to print even if no significant digit has been sensed, we use the *significant start character*.

Significant Start Character

Character	Representation	Hex
Significant start character	S	21

The significant start character functions like the digit select character in that it is replaced by:

a. A digit in the sending field when the nonzero indicator is on; that is, when a significant character has already been sensed.

or

b. A fill character when the indicator is off

However, the CPU indicator is *immediately turned on* when the significant start character has been reached. Therefore, all punctuation and digits to the *right* of the significant start character will be transmitted to the pattern. In the examples on p. 225, the best place to set up the significant start character is *directly before* the cents portion of the field. This is done to make certain that a decimal point prints even if there is no nonzero digit preceding it. The following, then, is used in place of the above:

Pattern Reference	B	D	D	S	.	D	D
Pattern (hex)	40	20	20	21	4B	20	20

The editing instructions would be:

```
     LABEL        OPERATION           OPERAND
1                 10        16
              MVC      LINEOUT(7),=X'40202021 4B2020'
              ED       LINEOUT(7),PDATA
```

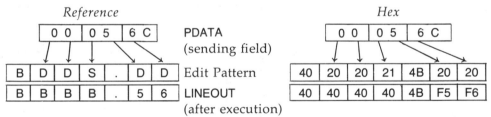

Reference

| | 0 0 | 0 5 | 6 C | PDATA (sending field) |

| B | D | D | S | . | D | D | Edit Pattern |
| B | B | B | B | . | 5 | 6 | LINEOUT (after execution) |

Hex

| | 0 0 | 0 5 | 6 C |

| 40 | 20 | 20 | 21 | 4B | 20 | 20 |
| 40 | 40 | 40 | 40 | 4B | F5 | F6 |

Note that the decimal point will print since the indicator was turned on by the significant start character that, like 20 (D), is replaced by a digit or fill character.

Here are other examples using the **BDDS.DD** pattern.

PDATA			LINEOUT (Hex)							Reference						
12	34	5C	40	F1	F2	F3	4B	F4	F5	B	1	2	3	.	4	5
01	23	4C	40	40	F1	F2	4B	F3	F4	B	B	1	2	.	3	4
00	56	7C	40	40	40	F5	4B	F6	F7	B	B	B	5	.	6	7
00	09	0C	40	40	40	40	4B	F9	F0	B	B	B	B	.	9	0
00	00	8C	40	40	40	40	4B	F0	F8	B	B	B	B	.	0	8
00	00	0C	40	40	40	40	4B	F0	F0	B	B	B	B	.	0	0

Inserting a Dollar Sign

Character	Representation	Hex
Dollar sign	$	5B

To insert the dollar sign we use the MVI instruction. Since each pattern field is at least one byte longer than the sending field, we simply move the dollar sign to the high-order position of the field. With this method, all the dollar signs in a particular column would align. For example, the instruction could be written in either of these two ways:

	LABEL	OPERATION 10	16	OPERAND	
1		MVI		LINEOUT,X'5B'	

	LABEL	OPERATION 10	16	OPERAND	
1		MVI		LINEOUT,C'$'	

Using the preceding examples, the output when printed would appear as:

```
$ 1 2 3 . 4 5
$   1 2 . 3 4
$      5 . 6 7
$        . 9 0
$        . 0 8
$        . 0 0
```

The dollar signs will align so that they all appear in the same print position.

Combining Characters   In the following examples, the comma, decimal point, and dollar sign all can be used. The pattern BDD,DDS.DD will be used to unpack and edit a 4-byte packed-decimal field that represents dollars and cents. At this point, you should be sufficiently familiar with the editing process so that only the sending and result fields need be illustrated.

	LABEL	OPERATION 10	16	OPERAND	COMMENTS
1		MVC		LINEOUT(10),=X'402020 6B2020214B2020'	
		ED		LINEOUT(10),PDATA	
		MVI		LINEOUT,C'$'	

PDATA	LINEOUT (Hex)	Reference
12 34 56 7C	5B F1 F2 6B F3 F4 F5 4B F6 F7	$ 1 2 , 3 4 5 . 6 7
04 56 78 9C	5B 40 F4 6B F5 F6 F7 4B F8 F9	$ B 4 , 5 6 7 . 8 9
00 23 45 6C	5B 40 40 40 F2 F3 F4 4B F5 F6	$ B B B 2 3 4 . 5 6
00 00 12 3C	5B 40 40 40 40 40 F1 4B F2 F3	$ B B B B B 1 . 2 3
00 00 02 6C	5B 40 40 40 40 40 40 4B F2 F6	$ B B B B B B . 2 6

Sign Control The editing specified thus far will print all fields as if they were positive. The low-order zone is ignored. Hence, the OI (Or Immediate) or MVZ (Move Zone) instruction is not needed to replace zones when the ED is used.

To print a minus sign for negative data fields, however, the rightmost position of the edit mask must contain a minus sign:

EDIT Mask

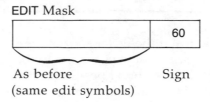

As before   Sign
(same edit symbols)

If the sending field is signed positive or unsigned, this rightmost position will be replaced with the fill character. If the sending field is signed negative, this rightmost postion will print as a minus sign.

The following examples illustrate how an edit pattern with sign control operates.

Pattern Reference	B	D	D	D	Sign Control
Pattern (hex)	40	20	20	20	60

The editing instructions appear as:

LABEL	OPERATION 10	16	OPERAND
	MVC		LINEOUT (5),=X'40202020 60'
	ED		LINEOUT (5),PDATA

PDATA	LINEOUT (Hex) (after Execution)	Reference
1 2 3 D	40 F1 F2 F3 60	B 1 2 3 −
1 2 3 F	40 F1 F2 F3 40	B 1 2 3 B
1 2 3 C	40 F1 F2 F3 40	B 1 2 3 B

The following table contains a review of the symbols that can be used in edit patterns.

Hex Code Used in Mask	Meaning
20	Digit select: Used for each digit to be transmitted from packed sending field.
40	Blank fill: To replace leading zeros with blanks.
5C	Asterisk (*) fill: To replace leading zeros with *.
6B	Comma: To insert commas.
4B	Decimal point: To insert period.

21	Significant start character: To digit select *and* to turn on indicator so that a decimal point will print even if no significant digit has been sensed.
60	Sign control: To print minus sign for negative amounts.
5B (Not part of Mask. Inserted after ED.)	Dollar sign: Inserted in high-order position with MVI instruction.

Figure 9-12 illustrates a program that incorporates the CNTRL macro and editing to print the names and salaries of employees who earn over $15,000. The percentage of employees in this category is printed at the end.

SELF-EVALUATING QUIZ

1. Write the edit pattern necessary to obtain the desired results:

Sending Field	*Receiving Field*
a. 002354	2,354
b. 00267859	2,678.59
c. 0087546	**87,546

2. Consider the following edit pattern:

   40 20 20 6B 20 20 20

   If 00235 is to be edited, will 235 or ,235 print?

3. Write the statement necessary to have a $ print in problem 1b, assuming that the receiving field is located at LINEOUT+49.

4. Indicate the number of digits to be transmitted for each type of editing illustrated below.

   a. 40 20 6B 20 20 20 4B 20 20
   b. 40 20 20 6B 20 20 20 4B 20 20 60
   c. 40 20 20 21 4B 20 20

5. Suppose the data to be edited in Question 4 is the following. Indicate the results.

   a. 002654
   b. 0038726
   c. 00046

What, if anything, is wrong with the following program excerpts:

6.
```
       MVC   LINEOUT(6),=X'4Ø2Ø2Ø2Ø2Ø4B2Ø2Ø'
       ED    LINEOUT(6),PDATA
         .
         .
PDATA  DS    PL4
```

7.
```
       MVC   LINEOUT(4),X'4Ø2Ø2Ø2Ø'
       ED    LINEOUT(4),PDATA
         .
         .
PDATA  DS    PL2
```

8.
```
       MVC   LINEOUT(5),=X'4Ø2Ø2Ø2Ø2Ø'
       ED    LINEOUT(5),PDATA
         .
         .
PDATA  DS    CL4
```

9.
```
       MVC   LINEOUT(9),=X'5C2Ø6B2Ø2Ø214B2Ø2Ø'
       ED    LINEOUT(9),PDATA
         .
         .
PDATA  DS    PL4
```

```
10.            MVC      LINEOUT(7),=X'5B20204B202020'
               ED       LINEOUT(7),PDATA
                .
                .
                .
       PDATA DS           PL3
11.            MVC      LINEOUT(7),PATT
               ED       LINEOUT(7),PDATA
                .
                .
                .
       PDATA DS           PL3
       PATT  DC           X'5C20214B202020'
```

```
*                                                                        *
*                                       HOUSEKEEPING INSTRUCTIONS GO HERE *
*                                                                        *
          CNTRL OUTFILE,SK,1          ADVANCE TO TOP OF PAGE
          MVC   OUTAREA,SPACES
          MVC   OUTAREA+23(31),=C'EMPLOYEES WHO EARN OVER $15,000'
          PUT   OUTFILE,OUTAREA
          MVC   OUTAREA,SPACES
          MVC   LNAME(9),=C'LAST NAME'
          MVC   FNAME(10),=C'FIRST NAME'
          MVC   SALOUT(6),=C'SALARY'
          CNTRL OUTFILE,SP,1,3 DBLE SPACE BEFORE & TRPLE SPACE AFTER PUT
          PUT   OUTFILE,OUTAREA
READ      MVC   OUTAREA,SPACES
          GET   INFILE,RECORD
          AP    TOTEMP,=P'1'
          CLC   SALARY,=C'15000'
          BNH   READ
          AP    COUNT,=P'1'
          MVC   LNAME,LAST
          MVC   FNAME,FIRST
          PACK  PKDSAL,SALARY
          MVC   SALOUT(6),=X'20206B202020'    EDIT WITH COMMA
          ED    SALOUT(6),PKDSAL
          MVI   SALOUT-1,C'$'
          PUT   OUTFILE,OUTAREA
          B     READ
EOF       MVC   OUTAREA,SPACES
          PUT   OUTFILE,OUTAREA
          MVC   OUTAREA(27),=C'% WHO EARN OVER $15,000 IS '
          ZAP   NUM,COUNT
          MP    NUM,=P'100'
          ZAP   HOLD,NUM
          DP    HOLD,TOTEMP
          MVC   OUTAREA+27(4),=X'40202020'
          ED    OUTAREA+27(4),HOLD+2
          PUT   OUTFILE,OUTAREA
*                                                                        *
*                                                                        *
*                                       HOUSEKEEPING INSTRUCTIONS GO HERE *
*                                       ALONG WITH DCB OR DTF MACROS      *
*                                                                        *
PKDSAL    DS    PL3
COUNT     DC    PL2'0'
HOLD      DS    PL6
TOTEMP    DC    PL2'0'
NUM       DS    PL4
RECORD    DS    0CL80                      CARD FORMAT
LAST      DS    CL15                         *
FIRST     DS    CL10                         *
SALARY    DS    CL5                          *
          DS    CL50                         *
SPACES    DC    CL1' '
OUTAREA   DS    0CL132                     PRINT FORMAT
          DS    CL5                          *
LNAME     DS    CL15                         *
          DS    CL20                         *
FNAME     DS    CL10                         *
          DS    CL20                         *
SALOUT    DS    CL5                          *
          DS    CL57                         *
          END
```

Figure 9-12

Solutions   1. a. X'402020206B202020'
b. X'402020206B2020204B2020'
c. X'5C2020206B202020'

2. 235
3. MVI   LINEOUT+49,X'5B'
4. a. 6 digits
b. 7 digits (4 bytes)
c. 5 digits; 21 also digit selects.
5. a. ƀƀƀƀ26.54
b. ƀƀƀƀ387.26ƀ
c. ƀƀƀƀ.46
6. Pattern is too large for 6-byte move.
7. Second operand in MVC is not a self-defining operand: it should be:
=X'40202020'
8. PDATA must be in packed-decimal format and have length of 3.
9. Self-defining operand must be as follows: =X'5C20206B2020214B2020' since
PDATA accommodates seven digits, not six.
10. 5B in a self-defining operand would generate $ as a zero suppression
character. This is normally not intended.
11. Okay.

KEY TERMS

Burst

Carriage control tape

Check protection symbol (*)

Continuous forms

Detail line

Editing

Form overflow condition

Header information

IOCS

Printer spacing chart

Skipping
Spacing

Review Questions   1. Explain the functions of the following HEADING routine in detail. Prepare a
Printer Spacing Chart that illustrates how the headings will print, includ-
ing spacing.

```
HEADING  MVC    LINEOUT,SPACES
         MVC    LINEOUT+50(21),=C'MY-T-FINE MOTORS INC'
         MVI    LINEOUT,C'1'
         PUT    OUTFILE,LINEOUT
         MVC    LINEOUT,SPACES
         MVC    LINEOUT+53(12),=C'SALES REPORT'
         MVI    LINEOUT,C'0'
         PUT    OUTFILE,LINEOUT
         MVC    LINEOUT,SPACES
         MVC    LINEOUT+46(21),=C'SALES PERSON'
         MVC    LINEOUT+63(9),=C'YTD SALES'
         MVI    LINEOUT,C' '
         PUT    OUTFILE,LINEOUT
         MVC    LINEOUT,SPACES
         MVI    LINEOUT,C'0'
         PUT    OUTFILE,LINEOUT
```

2. Indicate the purpose of the following routine. Explain an alternative method for achieving the same results.

```
          ZAP   LINES,=P'0'
READ      GET   INFILE,CARDIN
          MVC   LINEOUT,SPACES
          MVC   LINEOUT(80),CARDIN
          PUT   OUTFILE,LINEOUT
          AP    LINES,=P'1'
          CP    LINES,=P'10'
          BNL   HEADING
          B     READ
```

3. State the purpose of each entry in the following printout:

```
INFILE    DTFCD BLKSIZE=80,RECFORM=FIXUNB,DEVADDR=SYSIPT,      *
                WORKA=YES,IOAREAI=BUFFRIN,EOFADDR=EOF
```

```
OUTFILE   DTFPR BLKSIZE=133,DEVADDR=SYSLST,IOAREA1=BUFFROUT,   *
                CTLCHR=ASA,WORKA=YES
```

Answer True or False (4–6)

4. The sending field in the Edit instruction must be in packed format.

5. Both alphanumeric and numeric data may be edited with the use of the Edit instruction.

6. Using the Edit instruction, leading zeros are replaced by the fill character.

Consider the following instructions:

$$\text{MVC} \quad \text{OUTAREA,PATTERN}$$
$$\text{ED} \quad \text{OUTAREA,PDATA}$$

Indicate the results in **OUTAREA** in each of the following cases:

Before Execution

	Size of OUTAREA	PDATA	PATTERN
7.	7 bytes	00 58 7C	5C 20 20 6B 20 20 20
8.	9 bytes	00 67 8D	40 20 6B 20 20 20 4B 20 60
9.	9 bytes	00 67 8C	40 20 6B 20 20 20 4B 20 60
10.	10 bytes	00 00 00 7C	40 20 20 6B 20 20 20 4B 20 20
11.	10 bytes	00 00 00 7C	40 20 20 6B 20 20 21 4B 20 20
12.	5 bytes	00 00 5C	20 20 21 20 20

Practice Problems 1. Write a program to print an output report from the following card format:

1–5 Product number
6–8 Warehouse number
9–11 Quantity (may be negative in case of credit)
14–18 Unit price xxx.xx (to be interpreted as having $ and ¢ value)
19–38 Product description
39–41 Discount percent .xxx
42–46 Customer number
47–80 Not used

Output: Print line

3–7 Product number

10–29 Description	
32–38 Unit price	print decimal point; zero suppress; print dollar sign
40–43 Quantity	print minus sign, if present; zero suppress
48–58 Gross	print minus sign, if present; zero suppress; print decimal point; print $
60–71 Discount amount	print decimal point; zero suppress; print $
75–85 Net	zero suppress; decimal point; minus sign, if present; print $

Formulas

Gross = quantity × unit price
Discount amount = gross × discount percent
Net = gross − discount amount

Print heading PRODUCT LISTING on the top of the output page.

2. Write a program to print the total of the amount fields of groups of card records.

   Input:

   1–20 Name
   21–25 Amount xxx.xx
   26–80 Not used

   Output: Print

   11–30 Name
   41–50 Total (edited with dollar sign, comma, decimal point, and check protection)

   (NOTE: The name is the same for each group of records. The number of cards per group varies.)

3. Consider the following input card format.

1–20 Customer name (1-initial 1, 2-initial 2)	
21–25 Transaction amount for week 1	xxx.xx
26–30 Transaction amount for week 2	xxx.xx
31–35 Transaction amount for week 3	xxx.xx
36–40 Transaction amount for week 4	xxx.xx
41–46 Amount of credit	xxxx.xx
47–80 Not used	

Problem Definition

1. Print heading MONTHLY TRANSACTIONS

2. Print each data field edited

   a. Two spaces between initials of name.
   b. Print decimal point, dollar sign, − for negative transaction amount.
   c. Print decimal point, comma, dollar sign and * for credit amount.
   d. For each card record, print a balance due (transaction amounts − credit), dollar sign, operational sign, decimal point.

UNIT III

The Assembly and Interpreting the Contents of Storage

Chapter **10**

Understanding the Assembly Process

I. Introduction

Computer programs can be executed only if they are in absolute or actual machine language. An assembler language program must be translated, or assembled, into actual machine language before it can be executed or run.

The assembly process uses the programmer's assembler language program as input, the assembler or translator as the processor, and produces, as output, a machine language equivalent:

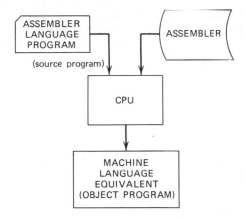

The Assembly Process The assembler program is generally provided by the computer manufacturer. It is called into the CPU, as needed, to translate source programs into object programs. Typically, the assembler is stored on a direct-access device such as a magnetic disk.

The three types of output of an assembler process generally consist of the following:

> 1. Object program.
>   A machine language equivalent of the source program.
>   This can be punched into cards or stored on tape or disk for future processing.
> 2. Source Program Listing with associated cross-referenced printouts.
> 3. Listing of diagnostics, or violations of rules.

Any rules that have been violated will cause the computer to print an error message. If an Add Packed instruction is coded as **A** instead of **AP**, for example, an error message will print. Any major error in the source program will result in an incomplete or erroneous object program that will not execute properly. In such cases the source program must be corrected and the translation process repeated. The object program created cannot be used, since it contains errors. Note that most programs must be translated several times before they are free from rule violations. Sample diagnostics will be discussed in Section II of this chapter.

Execution Phase—Testing the Program

After a translation phase has been successfully completed so that no diagnostics are generated, the program's ability to execute properly must be tested. Although the program contains no violation of rules, it may contain errors in logic that will cause inaccurate or incomplete processing. The Execution Phase is used to "debug" a program or to eliminate errors in it.

We run or execute a program with *test* or *sample* data. The programmer uses this sample data to test if the program executes properly. First, the expected results are computed manually by the programmer. Then the program is executed and the results obtained are compared against the manually produced results. If they match, then the program is executing properly. If they do not match, the cause of the error must be determined.

Test Data

Note that test data must be carefully prepared to incorporate all possible conditions. Every conceivable condition must be included so that all possibilities can be tested. Only in this way can one be assured that future scheduled runs of the program will be error-free.

Test data is usually prepared by programmers themselves. In a programming course, however, an instructor may provide it to insure its completeness. Figure 10-1 illustrates both the assembly and the execution phase.

Before we learn how to debug a program, there are some machine concepts that must be introduced.

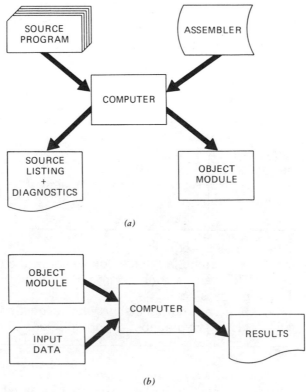

(a)

(b)

Figure 10-1(a)   Assembling a program.

Figure 10-1(b)   Executing a program.

Addressing

Defintion of Address

A computer's memory is subdivided into storage locations each of which is capable of storing a unit of information. Each storage location is called a *byte*. The byte consists of *8 bits* (*b*inary dig*its*) that can store a unit of information.

Communicating with the CPU so that both assembly and execution are achieved is a function of the Job Control Language. For students who have had no previous exposure to Job Control Language, see Appendix B "Communicating with the Operating System Using Job Control Language."

> **Subdivisions of Storage**
> Memory— storage capacity
> Byte— a single storage location
> Bit— one of 8 subdivisions of a Byte

The storage locations, or bytes, are said to be *addressable*. That is, storage locations can be accessed or referred to by a specific address. Every byte has a *unique* address, which means that no two storage addresses are the same. The concept is analogous to post office or safe deposit box numbers that are used to identify a single box. Such an address identifies a specific box number, *not* its contents.

How Addresses Are Specified

The address used to identify a storage location for most IBM computers consists of a 6-digit hexadecimal number. Thus storage locations can vary from 000000 to FFFFFF. This means that the maximum addressable byte is $16^6 = 2^{24} = 16,777,216_{10}$. Thus, a 6-digit hexadecimal number can represent storage addresses ranging, in decimal, from 0 to over 16 million. This latter number greatly exceeds the storage capacity of most computers, but a 6-digit representation was adopted by IBM as a standard to be uniformly used to identify storage locations of all its computers, regardless of size. Thus *all* IBM S/360 or S/370 computer systems, large and small, use storage locations from 000000–FFFFFF.

Using Addresses

Consider the following instruction:

AP   TOTAL,AMT

When the program using this instruction is assembled, **TOTAL** and **AMT** are placed in actual storage locations. In machine language, these fields are accessible only by their actual storage addresses. Hence, when reading a storage dump, as we will later, we must be able to identify the actual address of a specified field to determine what is in that field.

It is important to note that the *instruction itself* is also placed in storage. To debug a program, you must be able to find specific instructions, as well as fields, in storage. To do this, you must access them by their addresses.

Base and Displacement

Most computers are capable of operating on programs in a multiprogramming environment, that is, several programs can be in computer storage simultaneously. To accomplish this, each program that is read into the system must be *relocatable*. That is, programs are assembled with assigned addresses ranging from 0–4095 in decimal, or 000–FFF in hexadecimal. These programs are then *relocated* by the computer to wherever, in storage, there is room.

Programs, then, are referenced in actual machine language by an address that consists of several parts. For purposes of relocatability, the address consists of a displacement and the contents of the base register.

1. Displacement   A relative address, ranging from 000–FFF in hexadecimal (0–4095 in decimal), indicates how far from the starting point of the program a particular instruction is located. This distance, in bytes, is referred to as the displacement.

2. Base Register   This is a general register, from 2–12, assigned by the programmer to contain the actual starting point of the program. This actual starting point is loaded into the base register just prior to execution and will vary depending upon where in the computer there is room.

When the contents of the base register are added to the displacement, an effective or actual machine address is obtained.

> Effective address = contents of base register + displacement

Each register consists of 4 bytes, but not all 4 bytes are needed to determine the effective address. Only the *three low-order* bytes are used for this purpose. The high-order byte is ignored. Since storage locations are represented by a 6-digit hexadecimal number, only 3 bytes are necessary for specifying them. Let us amend the equation:

> Effective address = contents of base register + displacement
> (3 low-order bytes)   [dec 0–4095]
> [hex 000–FFF]

Since each section of a program is 4096 bytes in length, any program that is less than 4096 bytes can be written as one section.

Consider, however, a program that requires 12,000 bytes. By sectioning it into 4096-byte modules, we would have *three* sections of our program with a base address (and base register) for each.

Why Base and Displacement?

We have already indicated one major reason for the base and displacement concept—multiprogramming. There is an additional reason for utilizing this concept. Accessing an address in terms of a base register expressed as a single hex digit (0–F) and a three-position displacement (000–FFF) uses two less digits than the standard IBM 6-digit address. Since typical programs consist of hundreds of instructions with dozens of storage addresses that need to be accessed, this savings is substantial and significant.

Illustration of Advantage of   Consider the following:
Base-Displacement
Concept: Saving
of Storage

Op code	Address of operand 1	Address of operand 2

Without using base-displacement, each address would need to be specified in terms of a 6-digit or 3-byte field, that is,

Op CODE	. 01 2F 00	01 2F FF

If the op code were represented by a single byte, the above instruction might require 7 bytes of storage.

$$\frac{\text{Op code}}{1} + \frac{\text{Address of operand 1}}{3} + \frac{\text{Address of operand 2}}{3} = 7$$

(In actuality, instruction lengths will vary since additional elements must be considered.) Using the base-displacement concept however, we can reduce the length of such an instruction:

Op code	Address of operand 1	Address of operand 2

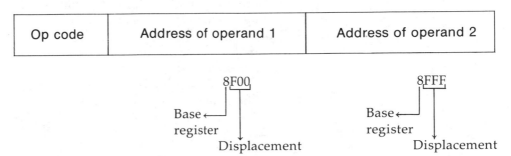

Using the base-displacement concept, we can reduce such an instruction by two bytes:

Op code   Operand 1   Operand 2
1 byte + 2 bytes + 2 bytes = 5

In this example the base register would be register 8 and would contain the base address 01 20 00 to match the problem above:

Operand 1			*Operand 2*		
01	20	00	Base		
	F	00	Displacement		
01	2F	00	Effective Address		

Operand 1
01 20 00 Base
    F 00 Displacement
01 2F 00 Effective Address

Operand 2
01 20 00 Base
    F FF Displacement
01 2F FF Effective Address

Summary
1. A program is a series of instructions stored in sequence. Each instruction is located a certain number of bytes from the starting point of the first instruction. This distance is referred to as displacement and allows access to any data within the section relative to the starting point.
2. When the program is ready to be loaded, the base register will point to a location in storage that will become the actual starting point of the program. This starting point is called the *program load address* or the *base address.*
3. Actual or effective storage addresses are obtained by adding a displacement value to the contents of a base register.
4. Each instruction contains the displacement in addition to the number of the general register that will be a base register.
5. Registers 2–12 may be used as a base register.
6. Only the 3 low-order bytes of the base register will contain the base address. The high-order byte is ignored.

1. Assuming that the base register contains 5144 (decimal), the displacement for the absolute (decimal) location 9170 is _____ .
2. Any actual machine language address can be located by adding its _____ to the contents of _____ .
3. Suppose that a program was relocated so that it started at location 9192 and consisted of three modules or sections.

Section 1	Section 2	Section 3

   The base register for section 1 would contain 9192. The base register for section 2 would contain _____ . The base register for section 3 would contain _____ .
4. Using the above example, do the displacements change for instructions in sections 2 and 3?
5. The displacement range for any base is __(number)__ to __(number)__ .
6. The base address is contained in the _____ .

Solutions

1. 4026_{10}
2. Displacement
   The base register
3. 13288 decimal (9192+4096)
   17384 decimal (+4096)
4. No. Displacement in all 3 sections is given in terms of a starting address, which is independent of the base address.
5. $\left.\begin{array}{l}0 \\ 4095\end{array}\right\}$ decimal or $\left.\begin{array}{l}0 \\ \text{FFF}\end{array}\right\}$ hexadecimal
6. Base register

Elements of an Assembly

The items that follow are aspects of the assembly process:

1. The program becomes a series of instructions occupying consecutive bytes in storage.
2. Each symbolic address assigned in the source program is converted to an actual machine language address.
3. Operation codes, or *mnemonics*, are translated into absolute machine language codes.
4. Areas of storage to be used as input, output, or work areas are assigned precise locations.
5. Constants are placed in actual storage locations.

The Location Counter

As we have already learned, a program is simply a series of instructions occupying consecutive bytes in storage. The purpose of the Location Counter is to keep track of the address or displacement of each instruction as it is being assembled. If each instruction were 1 byte in length, it would be a simple matter for the location counter to assign locations for each instruction in the program. As each instruction would be encountered by the assembler, a 1 would be added to the contents of the location counter. A program consisting of 100 instructions would therefore start at location 000 and end at location 064 hexadecimal or 100 decimal.

The length of an actual instruction is, however, *not* one byte but several bytes, depending upon the *format* of the instruction. Each instruction, given below, belongs to a particular format, and has a specific length.

Instruction Formats[1]

Description	Format	Length in Bytes
Register to Register	RR	2
Register to Indexed Storage	RX	4
Register to Storage	RS	4
Storage Immediate	SI	4
Storage to Storage	SS	6

Therefore, the location counter is incremented according to the length of the instruction. If the instruction is a storage to storage instruction, the location counter would be incremented by 6. After each instruction is assembled, the location counter changes according to *the length of the instruction*. The assembler knows the length of each instruction by examining the operation code. Different op codes require different instruction lengths. These can vary from 2, 4, or 6 bytes.

When the op code is a Define Constant (**DC**) or Define Storage (**DS**), the assembler must examine the operand to determine the *length* of the field. The values of the location counter in a typical program are illustrated in Figure 10-2. Note that ① LOC references the location counter which can vary from 000000–FFFFFF.

The Symbol Cross-Reference Table Every time a symbolic name is found in the name field of an instruction, the setting of the location counter (displacement) and the symbol are placed in the Symbol Table. The symbol table also provides the programmer with additional data that will facilitate debugging. Figure 10-3 will illustrate these points.

---

1. SYMBOL. Symbolic names defined within the program.
2. LEN. The length in bytes specified in *decimal.*
3. VALUE. The relative address (displacement) established by the location counter.
4. DEFN. The statement number of the source instruction at which this symbol was defined.
5. REFERENCES. The statement numbers of the source instructions that reference the symbol in their operands.

Assembly Process Summary
1. The assembler is a program provided by the manufacturer to translate source programs into object programs.
2. The input to the assembler is the source program and output is an object program and a source listing. The source listing may contain diagnostic messages if errors were detected in the program.
3. The location counter assigns storage locations to each instruction in the program.
4. The location counter is incremented 2, 4, or 6 bytes depending upon the type of instruction used.
5. Each name appearing in the name field of an instruction and its address are placed in the Symbol Table.

---

[1] This topic is discussed in Chapter 14.

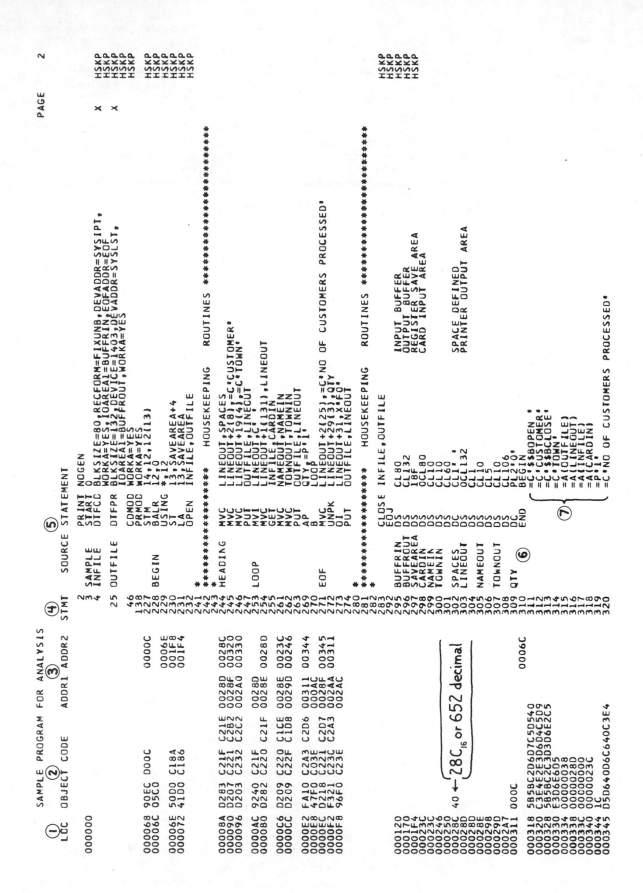

SAMPLE PROGRAM FOR ANALYSIS

```
 ①      ②          ③                    ④     ⑤
LOC    OBJECT CODE  ADDR1 ADDR2         STMT  SOURCE STATEMENT

000000                                    2   SAMPLE  PRINT NOGEN
                                          3   INFILE  START 0                                              X  HSKP
                                          4           DTFCD BLKSIZE=80,RECFORM=FIXUNB,DEVADDR=SYSIPT,         HSKP
                                                            WORKA=YES,IOAREA1=BUFFRIN,EOFADDR=EOF,            HSKP
                                         25   OUTFILE DTFPR BLKSIZE=132,DEVICE=1403,DEVADDR=SYSLST,        X  HSKP
                                                            IOAREA1=BUFFROUT,WORKA=YES                        HSKP
                                         46           CDMOD WORKA=YES                                         HSKP
000068 90EC D00C              0000C     138           PRMOD WORKA=YES                                         HSKP
                                        227           STM   14,12,12(13)                                     HSKP
000068 90EC D00C              0000C     228   BEGIN   BALR  12,0
00006C 05C0                             229           USING *,12
00006E 50D0 C18A              0006E     230           ST    13,SAVEAREA+4
000072 41D0 C186              001F8     231           LA    13,SAVEAREA
                              001F4     232           OPEN  INFILE,OUTFILE

                                        241   ********** HOUSEKEEPING ROUTINES **********
                                        242
00008A D283 C21F C21E 0028D 0028C       243   HEADING MVC   LINEOUT,SPACES
000090 D207 C221 C2B2 0028F 00320       244           MVC   LINEOUT+2(8),=C'CUSTOMER'
000096 D203 C232 C2C2 002A0 00330       245           MVC   LINEOUT+19(4),=C'TOWN'
                                        246           PUT   OUTFILE,LINEOUT
0000AC 9240 C21F      0028D             247           MVI   LINEOUT,C' '
0000B0 D282 C220 C21F 0028E 0028D       253   LOOP    MVC   LINEOUT+1(131),LINEOUT
0000C6 D209 C220 C1CE 0028E 0023C       254           GET   INFILE,CARDIN
0000CC D209 C22F C1D8 0029D 00246       255           MVC   NAMEOUT,NAMEIN
                                        261           MVC   TOWNOUT,TOWNIN
                                        262           PUT   OUTFILE,LINEOUT
0000E2 FA10 C2A3 C2D6 00311 00344       263           AP    QTY,=P'1'
0000E8 47F0 C03E      000AC             269           B     LOOP
0000EC D218 C22C C207 0028F 002AA       270   EOF     MVC   LINEOUT+2(25),=C'NO OF CUSTOMERS PROCESSED'
0000F2 F321 C23C C2A3 002AC 00311       271           UNPK  LINEOUT+29(3),QTY
0000F8 96F0 C23E      0002AC            272           OI    LINEOUT+31,X'F0'
                                        273           PUT   OUTFILE,LINEOUT
                                        274
                                        280   ********** HOUSEKEEPING ROUTINES **********
                                        281
                                        282           CLOSE INFILE,OUTFILE
                                        283           EOJ
000120                                  292   BUFFRIN DS    CL80         INPUT BUFFER
0001F4                                  295   BUFFROUT DS   CL132        OUTPUT BUFFER
00023C                                  296   SAVEAREA DS   18F          REGISTER SAVE AREA
00023C                                  297   CARDIN  DS    OCL80        CARD INPUT AREA
000246                                  298   NAMEIN  DS    CL10
000250        ← 28C₁₆ or 652 decimal    300   TOWNIN  DS    CL10
00028C 40                               301           DS    CL60
00028D                                  302   SPACES  DC    CL1' '       SPACE DEFINED
00028D                                  303   LINEOUT DS    OCL132       PRINTER OUTPUT AREA
00028E                                  304           DS    CL1
000298                                  305   NAMEOUT DS    CL5
000298                                  306           DS    CL5
0002A7                                  307   TOWNOUT DS    CL106
000311 000C                  0006C      308   QTY     DC    PL2'0'
000318 5B5BC2D6D7C5D540              309           BEGIN
000320 C3E4E2E3D6D4C5D9            310           END
000328 5B5BC2C3D3D6E2C5          311           =C'$$BOPEN '
000330 E3D6E6D5                  312           =C'CUSTOMER '
000334 00000038                  313           =C'$$BCLOSE'
000338 0000002D0                 314           =C'TOWN'
00033C 0000020C                  315           =A(OUTFILE)
000340 1C                        316           =A(LINEOUT)
000345 D5D640D6C640C3E4          317           =A(INFILE)
                                 318           =A(CARDIN)
                                 319           =P'1'
                                 320           =C'NO OF CUSTOMERS PROCESSED'
```

⑥ ⑦

Figure 10-2

CROSS-REFERENCE

① SYMBOL	② LEN	ID	③ VALUE	④ DEFN	⑤ REFERENCES						
BEGIN	00002	01	00006C	00228	0310	0021					
BUFFRIN	00080	01	000120	00295	0018	0044					
BUFFROUT	00132	01	000170	00296	0039						
CARDIN	00080	01	00023C	00298	0318						
EOF	00006	01	0000EC	00271	0020						
HEADING	00006	01	00008A	00244							
INFILE	00006	01	000000	00007	0238	0289	0317	0253	0254	0254	0271 0272 0273 0316
LINEOUT	00132	01	00028D	00303	0244	0245	0246				
LOOP	00004	01	0000AC	00253	0270						
NAMEIN	00010	01	00023C	00299	0261						
NAMEOUT	00010	01	00028E	00305							
OUTFILE	00006	01	000038	00028	0239	0290	0315				
QTY	00002	01	000311	00309	0269	0272					
SAMPLE	00001	01	000000	00003	0137	0226					
SAVEAREA	00004	01	0001F4	00297	0230	0231					
SPACES	00001	01	00028C	00302	0244						
TOWNIN	00010	01	000246	00307	0262						
TOWNOUT	00010	01	00029D	00307	0262						

Figure 10-3

Understanding the Assembler
Listing (See Figure 10-2)

1. LOC. This column contains the hex displacement value assigned to each instruction by the location counter. The first executable instruction contains START as the op code and is customarily assigned location zero. All other instructions are displaced relative to this starting point.

   a. Note that the next addressable LOC on the sample listing is 00 00 68. The area between is reserved for assembler-generated instructions or I/O control. The DTF's are macros that generate a series of instructions that, in this case, use 68 (hex) bytes of storage.

   ```
   LOC

   000000




   000068
   00006C

   00006E
   000072



   00008A
   000090
   .
   .
   .
   ```

   b. The STM instruction begins in position 068, the BALR in 6C. That is, STM is a 4-byte instruction occupying positions 068, 069, 06A, 06B. Using the LOC field, we can determine: (1) the actual storage locations of instructions and (2) the length of instructions.

2. OBJECT CODE. This field indicates the machine language equivalent of instructions, each being a maximum of 6 bytes long (SS). Since each byte is expressible as a 2-position hex number, the object code contains a maximum of 12 hex digits. Consider line 00 00 8A, which is the MVC instruction. It is a 6-byte instruction—12 hex digits. The minimum size for an instruction is 2 bytes (RR format). Hence the object code field can contain as few as 4 hex digits, 2 of them representing each byte. If the statement is a DC, then the object code contains the hex contents of each byte. Consider LOC 28C corresponding to the DC labeled SPACES. Note that it contains a hex 40, which is a blank.

   ```
   OBJECT CODE
   .
   .

   90EC D00C
   05C0

   50D0 C18A
   41D0 C186

   D283 C21F C21E
   D207 C221 C2B2
   .
   .
   ```

   Instructions will be analyzed in detail in a later chapter. All that is required at this point is that the student become aware of the different instruction formats and the different lengths associated with each. Also, the first 2 hex digits of all executable instructions contain the operation code.

For example, in the instruction identified as **BEGIN** the operation code of a **BALR** instruction is 05.

3. ADDR1 ADDR2. These columns refer to the addresses of the first and second operands. When storage to storage instructions are used, these addresses reference the actual locations assigned to the symbolic names. Note that these addresses reference locations where the symbolic names are defined in the program.

```
ADDR1  ADDR2
  *
  *
0028D  0028C
0028F  00320
002A0  00330

0028D
0028E  0028D
  *
  *
```

The **DC** or **DS** instruction establishes an actual area in storage that is assigned a storage address. Each time the named field is used in the program, the computer substitutes the actual address, instead, in the **ADDR** fields.

4. STMT. Each statement is assigned a STMT number by the computer. You will note that the numbers appear in ascending sequence. In some instances several numbers are skipped. This is because certain assembler language instructions coded by the programmer as *macro* instructions generate not one, but a series of actual machine language instructions. Only the instructions actually programmed are listed. Hence, **INFILE DTFCD** which is referred to as Statement 4, generated a series of instructions. We know this because the next sequential instruction is not number 5 but 25. The **DTF** macro then, actually generated 21 individual assembly language instructions.

```
STMT

   2
   3
   4

  25

  46
 138
 227
   *
   *
   *
```

The **PRINT NOGEN** statement is responsible for the suppression of macro-generated instructions. The use of this statement makes the program listing easier to read and decipher.

By removing the **PRINT NOGEN** statement, all macro-generated instructions will appear on the listing, and each will be identified by a plus (+) sign to the right of the statement number. In this case, all statement numbers would be consecutive.

5. SOURCE STATEMENT. These are the source instructions coded by the programmer. Again in the sample presented, macro instructions generated by the computer will be suppressed and will not appear on the listing because **PRINT NOGEN** was used.

```
        SOURCE STATEMENT

              PRINT NOGEN
SAMPLE    START 0
              .
              .
              .
```

6. **END BEGIN.** This statement indicates to the computer the first instruction to be *executed* once the assembly process has been completed. In the sample we are instructing the computer to begin execution at the BEGIN statement after the program has been assembled. All instructions prior to BEGIN are nonexecutable, that is, they are simply specifications to the computer. (An error would occur if we attempted to start executing at any instruction prior to the BEGIN statement.) A failure to include the proper operand in the END statement in our example will cause an error. If END is coded with *no* operand, the program will begin executing *at the first* instruction. If all DCB's (or DTF's), DC's, and DS's are defined at the end of the program, then an END without an operand would be fine.

```
END      BEGIN
```

7. Literal pool. The area following the END statement will usually contain the literals set up by the programmer. These are easily identified since they begin with an equal sign within the operand. The assembler places literal data in an area called the *literal pool* at the end of the program. The storing of data in the literal pool is very efficiently handled by the CPU, which ensures that the space used is minimized and that proper boundary alignment is maintained.

```
=C'$$BOPEN '
=C'CUSTOMER'
=C'$$BCLOSE'
=C'TOWN'
=A(OUTFILE)
=A(LINEOUT)
=A(INFILE)
=A(CARDIN)
=P'1'
=C'NO OF CUSTOMERS PROCESSED'
```

Linkage Editor Program   An object module is a program that has been assembled or compiled from a language such as Assembler, COBOL, or PL/1. An object module(s) is the input to the *linkage editor program*. With large complex programs the object module(s) may consist of a main program with several subprograms. These subprograms (subroutines) are independent CSECTs (control sections) frequently coded by different programmers working on a major project. The original source modules may have been coded in Assembler, COBOL, or FORTRAN, etc. The resulting object modules are, however, in machine language. These programs are interrelated in that data is passed back and forth between the main program and the subprograms, as well as interchanged between subprograms. This cross referencing of data is handled by the *linkage editor*. The main program and the subprograms may be assembled or compiled independently, but are linked together by the linkage editor. Similarly, if a program requires more than 4096 bytes, then two (or more) modules will be produced that need to be link-edited before execution.

The output of the linkage editor is a program phase. See Figure 10-4. This program phase can be executed immediately, or it can be catalogued in the core image library for later execution. A *link edit map* is also produced that lists all the control sections (CSECTs) that make up the program phase. (See Figure 10-5.) The link edit map provides the following information for the programmer's use.

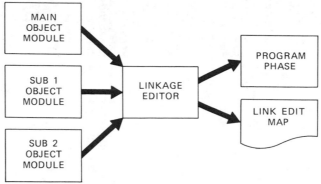

Figure 10-4

1. LABEL: Specifies the name of the program as declared in the START statement or a control section (CSECT) in the assembly. In this example, DEBUG is the name assigned.

2. LOADED: Indicates the hexadecimal starting position in storage where the program was loaded.

3. REL-FR: The relocation factor is used in reading core dumps. The value of the REL-FR must be added to the relative address (displacement) in order to find a desired location in primary storage. (Because of instructions performed prior to assigning a base register, the relocation factor may be a few bytes different from the base address.)

SELF-EVALUATING QUIZ

Consider the assembler listing in Figure 10-6.
1. What is the location of statement number 51?
2. How many bytes does statement number 51 actually contain?
3. (True or False) Statement numbers always appear in ascending sequence.
4. (True or False) Statement numbers are always consecutive.
5. (True or False) The programmer supplies the statement number that appears on the assembler listing.
6. Using statement number 48, find the storage locations of OUTAREA and SPACES.
7. LOC fields or displacements are always referenced as __(number)__ byte(s) or __(number)__ hexadecimal numbers.
8. (True or False) Omitting the PRINT NOGEN would cause an error.
9. (True or False) Omitting the label BEGIN in the END statement will cause an error.
10. (True or False) All literals are assembled at the end of the program.

Solutions
1. 00 00 7E
2. 4 bytes (7E, 7F, 80, 81)
3. True

PHASE	XFR-AD	LOCORE	HICORE	DSK-AD	ESD TYPE	① LABEL	② LOADED	③ REL-FR	
PHASE***	0640E0	064078	064501	001 02 01	CSECT	DEBUG	064078	064078	RELOCATABLE
					CSECT	IJCFZIW0	0643E0	0643E0	
					CSECT	IJDFCPZW	064458	064458	
					* ENTRY	IJDFZPZW	064458		
					* ENTRY	IJDFZZZW	064458		
					* ENTRY	IJDFCZZW	064458		

Figure 10-5

```
LOC      OBJECT CODE        ADDR1 ADDR2   STMT   SOURCE STATEMENT

                                            8   *                                                      SAM00080
                                            9   *                                                      SAM00090
                                           10   *            HOUSEKEEPING INSTRUCTIONS GO HERE          SAM00100
00000E                                     11         OPEN   (INFILE,INPUT,OUTFILE,OUTPUT)              SAM00110
00002A                                     25   READ  GET    INFILE,RECORD                             SAM00130
000038 F224 C108 C128   0010E 0012E        30         PACK   PKDSAL,SALARY                             SAM00140
000062 FA32 C10B C108   00111 0010E        46         AP     TOTAL,PKDSAL                              SAM00160
000068 47F0 C024        0002A              47         B      READ                                      SAM00170
00006C D283 C160 C15F   00166 00165        48   EOF   MVC    OUTAREA,SPACES                            SAM00180
000072 D218 C160 C2F2   00166 002F8        49         MVC    OUTAREA(25),=C'TOTAL ANNUAL SALARIES IS ' SAM00190
000078 F363 C179 C10B   0017F 00111        50         UNPK   OUTAREA+25(7),TOTAL                       SAM00200
00007E 96F0 C17F        00185              51         OI     OUTAREA+31,X'F0'                          SAM00210
000082                                     52         PUT    OUTFILE,OUTAREA                           SAM00220
000090                                     57         CLOSE  (INFILE,OUTFILE)                          SAM00230
                                          122   *                                                      SAM00270
                                          123   *            HOUSEKEEPING INSTRUCTIONS GO HERE          SAM00280
                                          124   *            ALONG WITH DCB MACROS                      SAM00290
                                          125   *                                                      SAM00300
                                                                                                       SAM00340
00010E                                    129   PKDSAL  DS   PL3                                        SAM00350
000111 0000000C                           130   TOTAL   DC   PL4'0'                                     SAM00360
000115                                    131   RECORD  DS   0CL80               CARD FORMAT           SAM00370
000115                                    132   LAST    DS   CL15                          *            SAM00380
000124                                    133   FIRST   DS   CL10                          *            SAM00390
00012E                                    134   SALARY  DS   CL5                           *            SAM00400
000133                                    135           DS   CL50                          *            SAM00410
000165 40                                 136   SPACES  DC   CL1' '                                     SAM00420
000166                                    137   OUTAREA DS   0CL132              PRINT FORMAT          SAM00430
000166                                    138           DS   CL5                           *            SAM00440
00016B                                    139   LNAME   DS   CL15                          *            SAM00450
00017A                                    140   FNAME   DS   CL20                          *            SAM00460
00018E                                    141           DS   CL10                          *            SAM00470
000198                                    142           DS   CL20                          *            SAM00480
0001AC                                    143   SALOUT  DS   CL5                           *            SAM00490
0001B1                                    144   BLANK   DS   CL57                                       SAM00540
                                          254           END
```

Figure 10-6

4. False. Actual machine language equivalents of macros need not be listed.
5. False. It is generated by the computer.
6. OUTAREA—166; SPACES—165.
7. 3
    6.
8. False. It would simply cause the generating of *all* machine language instructions including those derived from macros.
9. False
10. True

II. A Programmer's Guide to Debugging

Overview Preparation for debugging is of major importance in the debugging process. Just as flowcharting, prior to coding, facilitates the writing of the program, so, too, does *desk checking* facilitate the debugging process.

First, it is recommended that an 80–80 list of the source program be generated *before* assembling, in order to take a final look at the coding. An 80–80 list is 80 card columns printed into 80 print positions, one card per line. When the program is then viewed in its entirety, errors that may have gone unnoticed up to this point are frequently identifiable without utilizing valuable computer time. The programmer should then compare the flowchart with the coding to ensure that all of the flowchart symbols have been correctly translated into instructions. When this initial desk checking of the program has been completed, we are now ready to begin testing our program. We will discuss each of the three levels of errors that may occur in a program:

Levels of Errors

1. Syntax errors may occur producing diagnostic or error messages. These result when the rules of the language have been violated. The elimination of these errors is relatively straightforward and is the easiest problem to correct.

2. Errors may occur that are compensated for by the computer. That is, the computer automatically makes an adjustment called a *default*, which may or may not be what the programmer intended. Such defaults may be found during further desk checking, or they may be found during the test phase, if they resulted in unintended output.

3. Errors in logic may occur during execution of the program as described in the previous section. These errors require us to identify the instruction causing the problem or "bug" in our program.

We will now discuss each of these three areas in detail, applying them to packed-decimal instructions, and we will later utilize most of these concepts in debugging a sample program.

Assembler Diagnostics The assembler checks each instruction for the following.

> a. Valid symbolic names.
> b. Valid operation codes.
> c. Duplicate labels or symbolic names.
> d. Correct operands (type) for the op code specified.

After each invalid statement detected by the assembler, an error message will be printed. The error message may appear *after* the erroneous source statement as follows:

```
LOC    OBJECT CODE      ADDR1 ADDR2   STMT     SOURCE STATEMENT

00007E D283 C0CA C131  00134 0019B    269           MVC    LINEOUT,SPACES
000084 0000 0000                      270           MVI    LINEOUT,=C'*'
          *** ERROR ***
                                      271           MOVE   LINEOUT+1,LINEOUT
          *** ERROR ***
                                      272           PUT    OUTFILE,LINEOUT
                                      278 READ      GET    INFILE,CARDIN
0000A8 FA10 C1E2 C316  0024C 00380    284           AP     NOFLDS,=P'2'
0000AE F224 C132 C192  0019C 001FC    285           PACK   PFLDA,FLDA
0000B4 F224 C135 C1DD  0019F 00247    286           PACK   PFLDB,FLDB
```

The assembler may print the error message within the listing itself, as in the above, or the diagnostic messages may appear altogether at the end of the program or your system may provide both.

If the latter method of listing diagnostics or errors is provided, the statement number of the instruction and a message denoting the type of error are listed as below.

DIAGNOSTICS AND STATISTICS

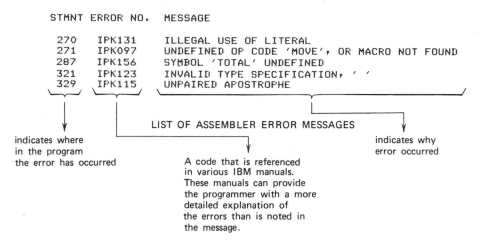

```
STMNT  ERROR NO.   MESSAGE

  270   IPK131     ILLEGAL USE OF LITERAL
  271   IPK097     UNDEFINED OP CODE 'MOVE', OR MACRO NOT FOUND
  287   IPK156     SYMBOL 'TOTAL' UNDEFINED
  321   IPK123     INVALID TYPE SPECIFICATION, ' '
  329   IPK115     UNPAIRED APOSTROPHE
```

LIST OF ASSEMBLER ERROR MESSAGES

indicates where
in the program
the error has occurred

A code that is referenced
in various IBM manuals.
These manuals can provide
the programmer with a more
detailed explanation of
the errors than is noted in
the message.

indicates why
error occurred

Thus, a more detailed explanation of the problem can be obtained from the appropriate programmer's guide that includes an expanded version of each error, by error number.

Errors Not Detected by the Assembler   This phase of debugging is learned and developed through experience. However, there are typical mistakes that are repeatedly made by the programmer; these can be avoided by carefully analyzing and desk checking the program. Five of these checks are listed below.

HINTS

1. Check all define constants (DC's) to ensure that the contents of the locations are as specified and intended. The contents of each DC is listed in hex under the **OBJECT CODE** heading of the source program. For example:

```
LOC    OBJECT CODE      ADDR1 ADDR2   STMT     SOURCE STATEMENT
00019C                                350           DS     C'END OF JOB'
```

No object code—DC should have been specified instead of DS.
DC would have generated some constant that would be specified
under OBJECT CODE.

2. Inspect all Define Storage (DS) specifications to ensure that each field is
of sufficient length to hold the largest result it is intended to contain.
For example, consider the following:

```
FLDA            DS          CL7
                 .
                 .
                 .

PFLDA           DS          PL3
```

PFLDA is too small to hold the packed representation of FLDA. Checking the program for such errors *before* it is executed may well save the
programmer hours of debugging later on.

3. When fields are subdivided, be sure that the total length of the
subdivisions equals the length of the whole. For example, consider
the following code:

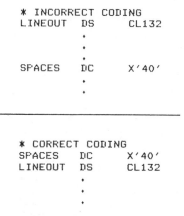

This coding would cause the total fields to be destroyed when the
first card was read. That is, 80 positions will be loaded into the area
beginning with NAME. Thus, because of incorrect coding, CC56 will
begin loading in TOTAL1, etc. The input data area *must* add up to
the 80 columns defined by the INDATA instruction.

4. Be sure to code the define constant (DC) for SPACES immediately
before the output area if the output area is to be properly cleared.

```
* INCORRECT CODING
LINEOUT   DS      CL132
              .
              .
              .
SPACES    DC      X'40'
              .
              .
```

```
* CORRECT CODING
SPACES    DC      X'40'
LINEOUT   DS      CL132
              .
              .
              .
```

If the coding is not correct, the instruction MVC LINEOUT(132),
SPACES will not propagate blanks in the correct way.

5. Remember to properly open and close all input and output files.

These are just a few of the precautionary measures that should be taken
during desk checking. In general, a careful review of your program after it has
been coded could save you hours of debugging and valuable computer time
later on.

Execution Errors   Execution errors fall into several categories, with the final result usually being an interrupt. In such a case, we say the program "bombs." When this happens, the instruction causing the problem must be identified so that corrective action can be taken. The *type of interrupt* specified by the system serves as the first clue in finding the source of the problem. The type of interrupts typically encountered with decimal instructions include:

1. Data exceptions

2. Decimal overflow and divide exceptions

3. Specification exceptions.[2]

The following problems are often associated with interrupts involving the decimal instruction set.

Data Exceptions

With packed-decimal arithmetic instructions, recall that the CPU checks each digit as well as the sign in the low-order byte for validity.

   When an invalid code is detected, a data exception occurs resulting in a program interrupt. The following problems may cause a data exception.

1. A numeric data field contains blanks or spaces in the low-order column. The PACK instruction will result in an invalid sign that will not itself cause the computer to "bomb." Rather, any packed-decimal operation such as AP, DP, CP, etc. performed on an invalid field will cause a data exception.

2. Failure to include the low-order byte when addressing a packed-decimal field. For example, consider the following:

FLDB

AP   TOTAL,FLDB(2) | 12 | 34 | 5C |

FLDB(2)

This results in a sending field that contains an invalid low-order byte, one with no sign. This error frequently occurs when incorrectly referencing overlapped fields.

3. A data field that contains EBCDIC or other data that fails to conform to the packed-decimal format. For example, when we add a field to TOTAL a data exception will occur.

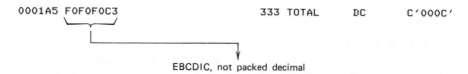

0001A5 F0F0F0C3   333 TOTAL   DC   C'000C'

EBCDIC, not packed decimal

4. In decimal multiplication, the first operand must contain as many *bytes* of high-order zeros as there are bytes in the multiplier (second operand) or a data exception will again result. Data exception error messages are listed on the last page of output in the following format.

```
OS03I PROGRAM CHECK INTERRUPTION - HEX LOCATION 1105EA - CONDITION CODE 2 - DATA EXCEPTION
OS00I JOB INST      CANCELED
```

Determining the instruction causing this problem is discussed in the sample programs appearing at the end of this chapter.

   [2] Chapter 14 contains a full discussion of interrupts.

Decimal Overflow and Decimal Divide Exceptions

Decimal overflow may occur when using the AP, SP, ZAP, and the SRP (Shift and Round Decimal)[3] instruction. Recall that when the receiving operand of a packed decimal instruction is too small to contain all of the significant digits resulting from an arithmetic operation, overflow will result.

A similar error is the decimal divide exception. A decimal divide exception always occurs when we inadvertently attempt to divide by zero. It will also occur if the first operand is too small to hold the quotient and remainder resulting from the divide operation. The interrupt may appear as follows:

```
OSO3I PROGRAM CHECK INTERRUPTION - HEX LOCATION 080634 - CONDITION CODE 2 - DECIMAL DIVIDE EXCEPTION
OSOOI JOB INST    CANCELED
```

Specification Exception

As discussed in the previous chapters, specification exceptions can occur in a variety of circumstances. Failure to adhere to one of the following rules will result in a specification exception:

1. In decimal multiplication, the length of the first operand must be greater than the length of the second operand.

2. In decimal multiplication, the multiplier may not exceed 8 bytes in length.

3. Similarly, in decimal division, the length of the first operand must be greater than the length of the second operand.

4. The divisor must not be greater than 8 bytes.

These examples are typical of those encountered in programming with decimal instructions. They provide a general review of problems that are frequently and repeatedly found in student programs.

A sample program will illustrate the techniques used in debugging. As we proceed, step by step in correcting the sample problem, the student will realize that the debugging procedure follows a systematic approach that can be improved with experience.

The Problem

A data card contains two fields, FLDA and FLDB in card columns 1–5 and 76–80 respectively. The program is to accumulate totals on both fields (TOTALA and TOTALB) and to also keep count of the number of fields (NOFLDA) processed. Once the last card has been read, the totals (TOTALA, TOTALB) will then be added together to produce a final sum (SUM). We want to print on the right of the form an average of the SUM field dividing it by the number of fields processed, with two decimal places. In order to print two decimal places, we must shift SUM left two positions (we will call the field SHIFT2LT). We do this by multiplying by 100. The average (AVERAGE) is calculated and finally the output is produced. The output is depicted below.

XXXXX	XXXXX	XXX.XX
TOTALA	TOTALB	AVERAGE

Run Number 1   Frequently the first assembly of the source program produces syntax errors that are detected by the assembler program. The first step is to identify and correct these errors. Each instruction will be analyzed one at a time in sequence within the program.

[3] See Chapter 17.

The first assembly of the program produced the results indicated in Figure 10-7. There are additional pages with various tables that accompany this listing but, for now, let us confine our consideration to just the listing itself. Note that this is a **DOS** listing. We will, however, assume I/O is correct so as not to trouble **OS** readers with **DOS** conventions. The rest of the program is independent of specific **DOS** or **OS** considerations.

Error 1

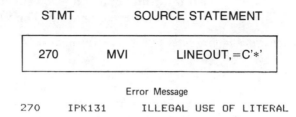

Error Message

270   IPK131   ILLEGAL USE OF LITERAL

The second operand of the MVI instruction must contain 1 byte of immediate data. The equal sign is not permitted.

Correction 1

Error 2

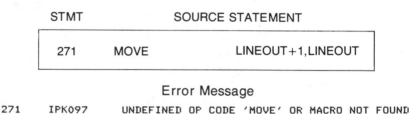

Error Message

271   IPK097   UNDEFINED OP CODE 'MOVE' OR MACRO NOT FOUND

The move character instruction was intended; however, an incorrect mnemonic (MOVE rather than MVC) was specified.

Correction 2

Note that the explicit form of the MVC has been incorporated in revising this instruction. If the explicit specification were omitted, an extra asterisk would be moved to the area immediately following LINEOUT. This would present problems if that field were to be used for packed decimal arithmetic operations.

Error 3

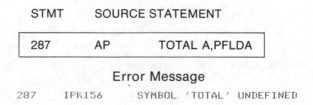

Error Message

287   IPK156   SYMBOL 'TOTAL' UNDEFINED

Examination of the instruction reveals that a space or blank was embedded in the operand. The assembler therefore assumed that everything after the space was a comment. Remember, the space is used to separate the fields in this free-form language.

Correction 3

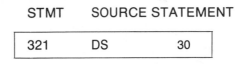

AP	TOTALA,PFLDA

Error 4

STMT	SOURCE STATEMENT
321	DS	30

Error Message

321   IPK123   INVALID TYPE SPECIFICATION, ' '

The type of define storage (X, C, P, F, H, etc.) was omitted in coding the instruction.

Correction 4

DS	CL30

Error 5

STMT	SOURCE STATEMENT		
328	PACK1	DC	PL1' '

Error Message

328   IPK115   UNPAIRED APOSTROPHE

When a field is defined as packed decimal, the assembler expects to find digits between the quotes. The space again signals the end of the operand; hence, the second apostrophe is ignored as indicated by the nature of the error message. Further inspection of the program logic reveals that this field is *not* referenced anywhere in the program, and its inclusion is unnecessary.

Correction 5

We will simply delete this instruction.

It is interesting to note that the description of the errors detected by the assembler for the most part are usually quite obvious, but in some instances they require further interpretation.

At this point, many student programmers would immediately resubmit their program believing that the "errors" have been corrected. However, it is important to stress the need for desk checking the program again. Several additional programming errors may be identified by the comments included in the instructions. Desk checking may uncover errors not detected by the assembler.

Errors Not Detected by the Assembler   As a general rule, recall that the programmer should check the hex contents of each define constant (DC). The following errors should therefore be identified and corrected.

```
LOC  OBJECT CODE  ADDR1 ADDR2   STMT  SOURCE STATEMENT            DOS/VS ASSEMBLER REL 34.0 17.21

000000                            1  DEBUG  PRINT NOGEN
                                  2  INFILE START 0
                                  3         DTFCD BLKSIZE=80,RECFORM=FIXUNB,DEVADDR=SYSIPT,             X   HSKP
                                                   WORKA=YES,IOAREA1=BUFFRIN,EOFADDR=EOF                    HSKP
                                 24  OUTFILE DTFPR BLKSIZE=132,DEVICE=1403,DEVADDR=SYSLST,IOAREA1=BUFFROUT,X  HSKP
                                                   CONTROL=YES,PRINTOV=YES,WORKA=YES                        HSKP
                                 45         CDMOD WORKA=YES,CONTROL=YES,PRINTOV=YES                         HSKP
                                137         PRMOD WORKA=YES,CONTROL=YES,PRINTOV=YES                         HSKP
000068 05C0                     257  BEGIN  BALR 12,0                                                       HSKP
       0006A                    258         USING *,12                                                     HSKP
                                259         OPEN INFILE,OUTFILE                                             HSKP
```

```
LOC  OBJECT CODE        ADDR1 ADDR2   STMT  SOURCE STATEMENT        DOS/VS ASSEMBLER REL 34.0 17.21

00007E D283 C0CE C133   00138 0019D   269        MVC   LINEOUT,SPACES
000084 0000 0300                      270        MVI   LINEOUT,=C'*'   EQUAL SIGN ILLEGAL
       *** ERROR ***
                                      271        MOVE  LINEOUT+1,LINEOUT   ILLEGAL OPERATION CODE
       *** ERROR ***
                                      272  READ  PUT   OUTFILE,LINEOUT
                                      278        GET   INFILE,CARDIN
0000A8 FA10 C1E4 C31E   0024E 00388   284        PACK  NOFLDS,=P'2'
0000AE F224 C134 C1DF   0019E 001FE   285        PACK  PFLDA,FLDA
0000B4 F224 C137 C1DF   001A1 00249   286        PACK  PFLDB,FLDB
0000BA 0000 0000 0000                 287        AP    TOTAL A,PFLDA   BLANKS ARE NOT PERMITTED IN OPERAND
       *** ERROR ***
0000C0 FA22 C13E C137   001A8 001A1   288        AP    TOTALB,PFLDB
0000C6 47F0 C02E        00098         289        B     READ
0000CA D283 C0CE C133   0019D         290  EOF   MVC   LINEOUT,SPACES
0000D0 FA23 C141 C13A   001AB 00138   291        AP    SUM,TOTALA
0000D6 D204 C0CE C1EE   0019D 00258   292        MVC   AOUT,PATTERN
0000DC DE04 C0CE C13A   0019D 00138   293        ED    AOUT,TOTALA
0000E2 FA23 C141 C13E   001AB 001A8   294        AP    SUM,TOTALB
0000E8 D204 C0DD C1EE   001A7 00258   295        MVC   BOUT,PATTERN
0000EE DE04 C0DD C13E   001A7 001A8   296        ED    BOUT,TOTALB
0000F4 F842 C1E9 C141   001E9 001AB   297        ZAP   SHIFT2LT,SUM
0000FA FC42 C1E9 C1E6   001E9 001E6   298        MP    SHIFT2LT,HUNDRED
000100 FD41 C1E9 C1EF   001E9 00250   299        DP    SHIFT2LT,NOFLDS
000106 D208 C31F        00389         300        MVC   AVERAGE,=X'402020202020202148B2020'
00010C DE08 C1E9        001E9         301        ED    OUTFILE,SHIFT2LT
00010C DE08 C1E9        001E9         302        PUT   OUTFILE,LINEOUT
                                      308        CLOSE INFILE,OUTFILE
```

```
000138                         317 LINEOUT EQJ     0CL132
                               320         DS      30
                *** ERROR ***  321

000138                         322 AOUT    DS      CL5
00013D                         323 BOUT    DS      CL10
000147                         324         DS      CL5
00014C                         325 AVERAGE DS      CL10
000156                         326         DS      CL9
00015F                         327         DC      CL62
                               328 PACK1   DC      PLI' '        ILLEGAL DEFINE CONSTANT
                *** ERROR ***

00019D 40                      329 SPACES  DC      CL1' '
0001A1                         330 PFLDA   DS      PL3
                               331 PFLDB   DS      PL3
0001A4 F0F0F0C3                332 TOTALA  DC      C'0000C'      SHOULD BE X TYPE SPECIFICATION, NOT C
0001A8 00000C                  333 TOTALB  DC      PL3'0'
0001AB                         334 SUM     DC      PL3'0'        USE DC FOR INITIALIZING, NOT DS
0001AE                         335 CARDIN  DS      CL80          ZERO MISSING FOR SUBDIVIDING
000203                         336 FLDA    DS      CL70
                               337 FLDB    DS      CL5
00024E 000C                    338 NOFLDS  DC      PL2'0'
000250 00100C                  340 HUNDRED DC      PL3'100'
                               341 SHIFT2LT DS     PL5
000258 40202020202020          342 PATTERN DC      X'40202020202020'

LOC    OBJECT CODE  ADDR1 ADDR2 SIMT  SOURCE STATEMENT          DOS/VS ASSEMBLER REL 34.0 17.21         PAGE  4

00025E                         344 BUFFRIN  DS     CL132
0002E2                         345 BUFFROUT DS     CL132
                   00068       346          BEGIN
                               347          END
000368 5B5BC2D6D7C5D540        348          =C'$$BOPEN '
000370 5B5BC2C3D3D6E2C5        349          =C'$$BCLOSE'
000378 00000038                350          =A(OUTFILE)
00037C 00000138                351          =A(LINEOUT)
000380 00000000                352          =A(INFILE)
000384 000001AE                353          =A(CARDIN)
000388 2C                      354          =P'2'
000389 40202020202021482020                 =X'40202020202021482020'
```

Figure 10-7

Statement 332

TOTALA	DC	C'000C'

This instruction does not initialize **TOTALA** to zero, but incorrectly sets up zoned-decimal data (**EBCDIC**) due to the C-type specification. Note that this did *not* result in an error message. Rather, the computer used the **C** or character format and the contents *defaulted* to that specification.

Correction 6

TOTALA	DC	X'00000C'

Statement 334

SUM	DS	PL3'0'

SUM is not initialized at zero since a **DS** was erroneously used, instead of a **DC**.

Correction 7

SUM	DC	PL3'0'

Statement 335

CARDIN	DS	CL80

FLDA and **FLDB** were to be defined within **CARDIN**; however a zero did not precede the **CL80** specification. References to **FLDA** or **FLDB**, then, as originally coded in the program would, in the end, result in an error when the program was executed.

Correction 8

CARDIN	DS	0CL80

While reviewing field subdivisions, we find the subdivisions of **LINEOUT** do not add up to 132 positions, but 131 instead. This correction requires us to change an instruction:

DS	CL62

must be changed to

Correction 9

DS	CL63

In the next run, we have incorporated all of the corrections mentioned thus far, with *one* exception. We failed to change the contents of **PACK1**. Hence, it still contains a blank. We did this to show you what will happen. The error is referenced as correction #10 in the revised program. We are now ready to proceed. Let us now consider the second computer run.

Computer Run Number 2   See Figure 10-8. (Cross reference tables have *not* been included for ease of presentation.) Note that *no* syntax errors have occurred. Thus, the execution phase may begin.

A program interrupt has occurred at hex location 110620 as a result of a data exception.

```
OSO3I PROGRAM CHECK INTERRUPTION - HEX LOCATION 110620 - CONDITION CODE 2 - DATA EXCEPTION
```

We must now find the erroneous instruction. Referring to the linkage editor map, we find the load or starting point of the program has a symbolic name **DEBUG** (defined in the **START** statement) and an actual address of **110520**.

```
PHASE
      DEBUG              110520  110881   000000 000361        362        866
```

By subtracting the load point from the address of the interrupt, we are able to ascertain the displacement in the program where the error occurred:

$$
\begin{array}{rl}
110620 & \text{Address of error} \\
-\ 110520 & \text{Load point} \\
\hline
000100 & \text{Displacement}
\end{array}
$$

We find the instruction at **LOC 100** to be the **MP** instruction;

LOC	SOURCE STATEMENT	
100	MP	SHIFT2LT,HUNDRED

In analyzing the field sizes, we find the first operand does *not* contain a sufficient number of high-order zeros. Remember, **SUM** was 3 bytes in length and **HUNDRED** is also 3 bytes. The product field should therefore be 6 bytes. To correct this problem, we simply enlarge the field size:

SHIFT2LT	DS	CL6

Computer Run Number 3 See Figure 10-9. Success at last. Our program has finally generated output, but we cannot assume that all of our problems are over.

We must compare the computer produced results with our own manual calculations of what the results should be. Suppose our input test data consisted of 4 cards:

	FLDA	FLDB
Card 1:	200	400
Card 2:	100	200
Card 3:	50	100
Card 4:	50	100

Based on our calculations, **AOUT**, the total of **FLDA**'s, should be 400; **BOUT**, the total of **FLDB**'s should be 800; and average should equal (400 + 800)/8 (number of fields) = 150.00.

Note that the correct average prints but **AOUT** and **BOUT** print as 40 and 80, respectively, off by a factor of 10. Hence there is an error.

First, we must check the keypunching of the test data to be sure that no errors occurred during the keypunching process. Our check of the data verifies that the input cards were properly prepared. Therefore, our problem lies within the program. We must examine instructions that use **TOTALA**, **TOTALB**, **AOUT**, and **BOUT** as receiving fields. The instructions referencing these fields can be found in the Symbol Reference Table:

```
LOC    OBJECT CODE   ADDR1  ADDR2   STMT   SOURCE STATEMENT              DOS/VS ASSEMBLER REL 34.0  17.24

000000                                1    DEBUG   PRINT NOGEN
                                      2            START 0
                                           DTFCD   BLKSIZE=80,RECFORM=FIXUNB,DEVADDR=SYSIPT,               X   HSKP
                                                   WORKA=YES,IOAREA1=BUFFRIN,EOFADDR=EOF
                                      3    INFILE
                                     24    OUTFILE DTFPR   BLKSIZE=132,DEVICE=1403,DEVADDR=SYSLST,IOAREA1=BUFFROUT,X  HSKP
                                                   CONTROL=YES,PRINTOV=YES,WORKA=YES                           HSKP
                                     45            CDMOD   WORKA=YES                                            HSKP
                                    137            PRMOD   WORKA=YES,CONTROL=YES,PRINTOV=YES                    HSKP
000068 05C0                   006A   257    BEGIN   BALR  12,0                                                  HSKP
                                    258            USING  *,12                                                 HSKP
                                    259            OPEN   INFILE,OUTFILE
```

```
LOC    OBJECT CODE        ADDR1  ADDR2   STMT   SOURCE STATEMENT              DOS/VS ASSEMBLER REL 34.0  17.24

00007E D283 COD3 COD2     013D   013C   269            MVC   LINEOUT,SPACES
000084 925C COD3          013D          271            MVI   LINEOUT+1(L'31),LINEOUT  CORRECTION 1
000088 COD4 COD3          013E   013D   272            MVI   LINEOUT+1(L'31),LINEOUT  CORRECTION 2
                                         278            PUT   OUTFILE,LINEOUT
0000AE FA10 C1B6 C2EE     0220   00358  284    READ    GET   INFILE,CARDIN
0000B4 F224 C157 C1D0     01C1   001D0  285            PACK  NOFLDS=P'2'
0000BA F224 C15A C1D1     01C4   0021B  286            PACK  PFLDB,FLDB
0000C0 FA22 C15D C157     01CA   001C1  287            PACK  PFLDA,FLDA
0000C6 FA22 C160 C15A     01CA   001C4  288            AP    TOTALA,PFLDA
0000CC 47F0 C034          013D   0009E  289            AP    TOTALB,PFLDB   CORRECTION 3
0000D0 D283 COD3 COD2     01CD   0015D  291    EOF     B     READ
0000D6 FA22 C163 C15D     015B   001C7  292            MVC   LINEOUT,SPACES
0000DC DE04 C0F1 C1C0     01CD   001C7  293            AP    SUM,TOTALA
0000E2 DE04 C0F1 C163     01CA   0015B  294            MVC   AOUT,PATTERN
0000E8 FA22 C163 C160     01CD   001CA  295            ED    AOUT,TOTALA
0000EE DE04 C0F4 C16A     01CA   0016A  296            AP    SUM,TOTALB
0000F4 F842 C1BB C163     0225   001CD  297            MVC   BOUT,PATTERN
0000FA FD41 C1BB C0F2     0225   00220  298            ED    BOUT,TOTALB
000100 FC41 C1BB C1B6     0225   00359                 ZAP   SHIFT2LT,SUM
00010C D208 C10F C2EF     0179   00225  300            DP    SHIFT2LT,NOFLDS
000112 DE08 C10F C1BB     0179   00225  301            MVC   AVERAGE,=X'40202020202148202020'
                                         302            ED    AVERAGE,SHIFT2LT
                                                       PUT   OUTFILE,LINEOUT
                                         317            CLOSE INFILE,OUTFILE
                                                       EOJ
```

DOS/VS ASSEMBLER REL 34.0   17.24

```
LOC       OBJECT CODE       ADDR1 ADDR2   STMT   SOURCE STATEMENT

000013C   40                        320   SPACES    DC  CL1' '            CORRECTION 10  MUST PRECEDE LINEOUT
000013D                             321   LINEOUT   DS  OCL132            CORRECTION 4
00015B                              322             DS  CL30
00016A                              323   AOUT      DS  CL10
00016F                              324   BOUT      DS  CL5
000179                              325             DS  CL10
000182                              326             DS  CL9
                                    327   AVERAGE   DS  CL63              CORRECTION 9
0001C1                              328   *    **** PACKI NOT USED BY PROGRAM, THEREFORE REMOVED   CORR 5
0001C4    00000C                    330   PFLDA     DS  PL3
0001C7    00000C                    331   PFLDB     DS  PL3
0001CA    00000C                    332   TOTALA    DC  X'00000C'         CORRECTION 6
0001CD                              333   TOTALB    DC  PL3'0'
0001D0                              334   SUM       DC  PL3'0'            CORRECTION 7
                                    335   CARDIN    DS  OCL80             CORRECTION 8
0001D5                              336   FLDA      DS  CL5
                                    337             DS  CL70
00021B                              338   FLDB      DS  CL5
000220    000C                      339   NOFLDS    DC  PL2'0'
000222    00100C                    340   HUNDRED   DC  PL3'100'
                                    341   SHIFT2LT  DC  PL5
00022A    40202020202020            342   PATTERN   DC  X'40202020202020'


LOC       OBJECT CODE       ADDR1 ADDR2   STMT   SOURCE STATEMENT

000230                              344   BUFFRIN   DS  CL132
0002B4                  03068       345   BUFFROUT  DS  CL132
                                    346             END  BEGIN
000338    5B5BC2D6D7C5D540          347            =C'$$BOPEN '
000340    5B5BC2C3D3D6E2C5          348            =C'$$BCLOSE'
000348    00000038                  349            =A(OUTFILE)
00034C    0000013D                  350            =A(LINEOUT)
000350    00000000                  351            =A(INFILE)
000354    0000010D                  352            =A(CARDIN)
000358    2C                        353            =P'2'
000359    40202020214B2020          354            =X'40202020214B2020'
```

Figure 10-8   (Continued on next page.)

263

DIAGNOSTICS AND STATISTICS

NO ERRORS FOUND

THE FOLLOWING MACRO NAMES HAVE BEEN FOUND IN MACRO INSTRUCTIONS
DTFCD   CDMOD   PRMOD   OPEN   PUT   GET   CLOSE   EOJ
DTFPR

OPTIONS FOR THIS ASSEMBLY - ALIGN, LIST, XREF, LINK, NORLD, NODECK, NOEDECK

THE ASSEMBLER WAS RUN IN 65416 BYTES
END OF ASSEMBLY

EOP $3ASM
// EXEC LNKEDT

JOB INST   17.25.01 F-LE-E FAST-LINKAGE-EDITOR VM4.0   DOS/VS R34-0A G O A L   S Y S T E M S

ACTION TAKEN MAP CLEAR REL LINK
LIST PHASE MONITOR,ROOT
LIST INCLUDE ILFFEXIT
LIST AUTOLINK IJDFAPZZ
LIST PHASE STDPGM,*
LIST ENTRY

PHASE-CSECT-ENTRY LO-LNK HI-LNK LO-REL HI-REL LN-HEX LN-DEC XF-LNK XF-REL G O A L   S Y S T E M S

LINK PARTITION = F3 110000 169FFF 000000 059FFF 5A000 368,640 110076 000078

ROOT   MONITOR   110076 11051B 000000 0004A3 4A4 1,188 110078 000000 RELOCATABLE
       ILFFEXIT   110078 1103F9 000000 000381 382   898
       *EXIT   1101004   00000007C 11C   284
       IJDFAPZZ   110400 11051B 000388 0004A3
       * IJDFAZZZ 110400   000388

PHASE STDPGM   110520 1109A9 000000 000489 48A 1,162 110588 000068 RELOCATABLE
       DEBUG   110888 11088F 000000 000361 362   866
       IJCFZIWO   110888 11088F 000368 00030F   78   120
       IJDFCPZW   110900 1109A9 0003E0 000489   AA   170
       * IJDFZPZW 110900   0003E0
       * IJOFZZZW 110900   0003E0
       * IJDFCZZW 110900   0003E0

NORMAL COMPLETION, BLOCKS AVAIL = 334, USED IN EDIT = 4, PCIL=X'1C6', CYL=001, SERIAL=WORKO1.

// EXEC
****

OS031 PROGRAM CHECK INTERRUPTION - HEX LOCATION 11D620 - CONDITION CODE 2 - DATA EXCEPTION
OS001 JOB INST CANCELED

264

CROSS-REFERENCE

SYMBOL	LEN	ID	VALUE	DEFN	REFERENCES	
AOUT	00005	01	00015B	00323	0292	0293
AVERAGE	00009	01	000179	00327	0300	0301
BEGIN	00002	01	000068	00257	0345	
BOUT	00005	01	00016A	00325	0295	0296
BUFFRIN	00132	01	000231	00343	0017	0020
BUFFROUT	00132	01	0002B5	00344	0038	0043
CARDIN	00080	01	0001D0	00334	0351	
DEBUG	00001	01	000000	00002	0136	0256
EOF	00006	01	0000D0	00290	0019	
FLDA	00005	01	0001D0	00335	0285	
FLDB	00005	01	00021B	00337	0286	
HUNDRED	00003	01	000222	00339	0298	

As illustrated, the table is arranged in alphabetic sequence. AOUT will be the first field of our group to be checked.

Note that AOUT is referenced by instructions 292 and 293. At statement 292, the edit pattern is moved to AOUT.

In checking the field descriptions we find AOUT has a length of 5 bytes while PATTERN contains 6 bytes. The object code of the MVC instruction is now checked and we find a length of 5 bytes (04 + 1) specified by the move. This is our first problem. The failure to utilize an explicit MVC instruction has resulted in truncation of the edit pattern, as well as truncation of our results. We can correct this problem by redefining the areas AOUT and BOUT.

The program will now process the data correctly. Figure 10-10 is a correct listing of the program and its output.

Sometimes more elaborate test data will need to be prepared to further test:

a. Each and every branch of the program.

b. All possible combinations of data incorporating the extremes or limits with regard to the size of fields, records processed, etc.

As we have seen, there is a great deal of work involved in correctly debugging assembler language programs because of the machine-like level and detail of the instructions involved.

SELF-EVALUATING QUIZ

1. Examine the partial assembly listing in Figure 10-11. Explain each of the errors.

2. Examine the assembly listing in Figure 10-12. Explain each of the errors. Note that when there is an error within a macro instruction, the particular instruction that is part of the macro is listed with a plus (+) sign next to the statement number.

Solutions 1.

Statement Number	Explanation of Error
46	NEXT-10 is an invalid label because of the hyphen.
54	There is a space after the comma.
55	The immediate data should be defined with a C for character, not an X.
61	NEXT-10 is an invalid label because of the hyphen.
69	SALARY should be defined as a DS. With a DC operation code, the assembler expects to find a constant defined in the operand. CL5 is not a valid operand for a DC.

```
LOC    OBJECT CODE  ADDR1 ADDR2  STMT  SOURCE STATEMENT

000000                             1        PRINT NOGEN
                                   2 DEBUG  START 0
                                   3 INFILE DTFCD BLKSIZE=80,RECFORM=FIXUNB,DEVADDR=SYSIPT,         X
                                                  WORKA=YES,IOAREA1=BUFFRIN,EOFADDR=EOF          HSKP
                                  24 OUTFILE DTFPR BLKSIZE=132,DEVICE=1403,DEVADDR=SYSLST,IOAREA1=BUFFKOUT,X HSKP
                                                  CONTROL=YES,PRINTOV=YES,WORKA=YES             HSKP
                                  45        CDMOD WORKA=YES                                     HSKP
                                 137        PRMOD WORKA=YES,CONTROL=YES,PRINTOV=YES             HSKP
000068 05C0                      257 BEGIN  BALR  12,0                                          HSKP
                                 258        USING *,12                                          HSKP
             0006A               259        OPEN  INFILE,OUTFILE                                HSKP
```

```
LOC    OBJECT CODE       ADDR1 ADDR2  STMT  SOURCE STATEMENT

00007E D283 C0D3 C0D2    0013C 0013D  269        MVC   LINEOUT,SPACES
000084 925C C166               0013D  270        MVI   LINEOUT,C'*'
000088 D282 C0D4 C0D3    0013E 0013D  271        MVC   LINEOUT+1(131),LINEOUT
                                      272        PUT   OUTFILE,LINEOUT
0000AE FA10 C1B6 C2F6    00220 00360  278 READ   GET   INFILE,CARDIN
0000B4 F224 C157 C166    001C1 001D0  284        AP    NOFLDS,=P'2'
0000BA F224 C15A C15A    001C4 0021B  285        PACK  PFLDA,FLDA
0000C0 FA22 C15D C157    001C7 001C1  286        PACK  PFLDB,FLDB
0000C6 FA22 C160 C15A    001CA 001C4  287        AP    TOTALA,PFLDA
0000CC 47F0 C034         0009E        288        AP    TOTALB,PFLDB
0000D0 D283 C0D3 C0D2    0013D 0013C  289        B     READ
0000D6 FA22 C163 C15D    001CD 001C7  290 EOF    MVC   LINEOUT,SPACES
0000DC D204 C0F1 C15D    0015B 001C7  291        AP    SUM,TOTALA
0000E2 DE04 C0F1 C163    0015B 001CD  292        MVC   AOUT,TOTALA
0000E8 FA22 C160 C160    001CA 001CA  293        ED    AOUT,PATTERN
0000EE D204 C100 C16A    0016A 00228  294        AP    SUM,TOTALB
0000F4 DE04 C100 C16A    0016A 001CD  295        MVC   BOUT,PATTERN
0000FA F852 C1BB C163    00225 001CD  296        ED    BOUT,TOTALB
000100 FC52 C1BB C1BB    00225 00220  297        ZAP   SHIFT2LT,SUM
000106 D208 C1BB C1BB    00225 00361  298        MP    SHIFT2LT,HUNDRED
00010C D208 C10F C2F7    00179 00361  300        MVC   AVERAGE,=X'402020202021482020'
000112 DE08 C10F C1BB    00179 00225  301        MVC   AVERAGE,SHIFT2LT
                                      302        ED    AVERAGE,LINEOUT
                                      308        PUT   OUTFILE,LINEOUT
                                                 CLOSE INFILE,OUTFILE
```

```
       317  SPACES    EOJ
000013C 40
000013D 320  LINEOUT   DC   CL1' '
000013D      321            DS   OCL132
000015B      322            DS   CL30
0000160      323  AOUT      DS   CL5
000016A      325  BOUT      DS   CL10
000016F      326            DS   CL10
0000179      327  AVERAGE   DS   CL9
0000182      328  PFLDA     DS   CL63
00001C1      329  PFLDB     DS   PL3
00001C1      330            DS   PL3
00001C4 00000C  331  TOTALA    DC   X'00000C'
00001C7 00000C  332  TOTALB    DC   PL3'0'
00001CA 00000C  333  SUM       DC   PL3'0'
00001D0      334  CARDIN    DS   OCL80
00001D0      335  FLDA      DS   CL5
00001D5      336            DS   CL70
00021B      337  FLDB      DS   CL5
000220 000C  338  NOFLDS    DC   PL2'0'
000222 0100C  339  HUNDRED   DC   PL3'100'
           340  SHIFT2LT  DS   PL6
00022B 402020202020  341  PATTERN   DC   X'402020202020'
```

CORRECTION INCREASED FIELD SIZE

```
LOC     OBJECT CODE     ADDR1 ADDR2   STMT  SOURCE STATEMENT
000231                            343  BUFFKIN  DS   CL132
0002B5                            344  BUFFKOUT DS   CL132
              00068             345          END  BEGIN
                                  346  =C'$$BOPEN '
000340 5B5BC2D6D7C5D540           347  =C'$$BCLOSE'
000348 5B5BC2C3D3D6E2C5           348  =A(OUTFILE)
000350 00000038                   349  =A(LINEOUT)
000354 0000013D                   350  =A(INFILE)
000358 00000000                   351  =A(CARDIN)
00035C 000001D0                   352  =P'2'
000360 2C                         353  =X'40202020214B2020'
000361 40202020214B2020
```

DIAGNOSTICS AND STATISTICS

NO ERRORS FOUND

THE FOLLOWING MACRO NAMES HAVE BEEN FOUND IN MACRO INSTRUCTIONS
DTFCD   CDMOD   DTFPR   PRMOD   OPEN   PUT   GET   CLOSE   EOJ

OPTIONS FOR THIS ASSEMBLY - ALIGN, LIST, XREF, LINK, NORLD, NODECK, NOEDECK

THE ASSEMBLER WAS RUN IN 65416 BYTES
END OF ASSEMBLY

Figure 10-9

```
LOC    OBJECT CODE    ADDR1  ADDR2   STMT   SOURCE STATEMENT                    DOS/VS ASSEMBLER REL 34.0 17.29

000000                                  1   DEBUG  PRINT NOGEN
                                        2          START 0
                                        3   INFILE DTFCD BLKSIZE=80,RECFORM=FIXUNB,DEVADDR=SYSIPT,         X
                                                          WORKA=YES,IOAREAL=BUFFRIN,EOFADDR=EOF,            X    HSKP
                                       24   OUTFILE DTFPR BLKSIZE=132,DEVICE=1403,DEVADDR=SYSLST,IOAREAI=BUFFROUT,X
                                                          CONTROL=YES,PRINTOV=YES,WORKA=YES                HSKP
                                       45          CDMOD  WORKA=YES                                        HSKP
                                      137          PRMOD  WORKA=YES,CONTROL=YES,PRINTOV=YES                HSKP
000068 05C0           0006A           257   BEGIN  BALR  12,0                                              HSKP
                                      258          USING *,12                                              HSKP
                                      259          OPEN  INFILE,OUTFILE                                    HSKP
```

```
LOC    OBJECT CODE        ADDR1  ADDR2   STMT   SOURCE STATEMENT                DOS/VS ASSEMBLER REL 34.0 17.29

00007E D283 COD3 C2F6   0013D  0013C    269          MVC   LINEOUT,SPACES
000084 925C      C166          0013D    270          MVI   LINEOUT+[1],C'*'
000088 D282 COD4 COD3   0013E  0013D    271          MVC   LINEOUT+[113],LINEOUT
                                        278   READ   PUT   OUTFILE,LINEOUT
0000AE FA10 C1B6 C157   00220  001C1    284          GET   INFILE,CARDIN
0000B4 F224 C15A C1B1   001C4  0021B    285          AP    NOFLDS,=P'2'
0000BA F224 C150 C1B7   001C7  001C1    286          PACK  PFLDA,FLDA
0000C0 FA22 C160 C1CA   001CA  001C1    287          PACK  PFLDB,FLDB
0000C6 FA22 C15A        009E            288          AP    TOTALA,PFLDA
0000CC 47F0 C034                        289          AP    TOTALB,PFLDB
0000D0 D283 COD2 C15D   0013C  001CD    290          B     READ
0000D6 FA22 C163 C1C1   001CD  0015B    291   EOF    MVC   LINEOUT,SPACES
0000DC DE05 COF1 C1C7          0015D    292          AP    SUM,TOTALA
0000E2 DE05 C163 C1CD   0015B  001CA    293          MVC   AOUT,PATTERN
0000E8 FA22 C163 C160   001CD  0016B    294          ED    AOUT,TOTALA
0000EE DE05 C101 C1CA   001CD  001CA    295          AP    SUM,TOTALB
0000F4 DE05 C16B C160          001CD    296          MVC   BOUT,PATTERN
0000FA FC52 C1BB C163   00225  001CD    297          ED    BOUT,TOTALB
000100 FD51 C1BB C1B6   00225  00220    298          ZAP   SHIFT2LT,SUM
000106 D208 C1BB C2F7   00220  00361    299          MP    SHIFT2LT,HUNDRED
00010C DE08 C111 C1BB          0017B    301          DP    SHIFT2LT,NOFLDS
000112 DE08 C111 C1BB   0017B  00225    302          MVC   AVERAGE,=X'40202020202021482020'
                                        303          ED    AVERAGE,SHIFT2LT
                                        308          PUT   OUTFILE,LINEOUT
                                        317          CLOSE INFILE,OUTFILE
                                                     EOJ
```

```
LOC     OBJECT CODE       ADDR1 ADDR2   STMT  SOURCE STATEMENT

00013C  40                              320 SPACES   DC   CL1' '
00013D                                  321 LINEOUT  DS   OCL132
00015B                                  322          DS   CL30
000161                                  323 AOUT     DS   CL6
00017B                                  324          DS   CL10
000171                                  325 BOUT     DS   CL10
000184                                  326          DS   CL9
0001C1                                  327 AVERAGE  DS   CL61       CORRECTION INCREASED FIELD SIZE
0001C4                                  328 PFLDA    DS   PL3
0001C7  00000C                          329 PFLDB    DS   PL3
0001CA  00000C                          330 TOTALA   DC   X'00000C'
0001CD  00000C                          331 TOTALB   DC   PL3'0'
0001D0                                  332 SUM      DC   PL3'0'
0001D5                                  333 CARDIN   DS   OCL80
00021B                                  334 FLDA     DS   CL5
000220  000C                            335          DS   CL70       CORRECTION INCREASED FIELD SIZE
000222  00100C                          336 FLDB     DS   CL5
000225                                  337 NOFLDS   DS   PL5
00022B  4020202020                      338 HUNDRED  DC   PL2'0'
                                        339 SHIFT2LT DC   PL3'100'
                                        340          DS   PL6
                                        341 PATTERN  DC   X'4020202020'


LOC     OBJECT CODE       ADDR1 ADDR2   STMT  SOURCE STATEMENT

000231                                  343 BUFFRIN  DS   CL132
0002B5                                  344 BUFFROUT DS   CL132
                              00068     345 BEGIN    END
000340  5B5BC2D6D7C5D540                346          =C'$$BOPEN '
000348  5B5BC2C3D3D6E2C5                347          =C'$$BCLOSE'
000350  00000038                        348          =A(OUTFILE)
000354  0000013D                        349          =A(LINEOUT)
000358  000001D0                        350          =A(INFILE)
00035C  2C                              351          =A(CARDIN)
                                        352          =P'2'
000361  40202020214B2020                353          =X'40202020214B2020'
```

DOS/VS ASSEMBLER REL 34.0 17.29

Figure 10-10 (Continued on next page.)

DIAGNOSTICS AND STATISTICS

NO ERRORS FOUND

THE FOLLOWING MACRO NAMES HAVE BEEN FOUND IN MACRO INSTRUCTIONS
DTFCD   CDMOD   PRMOD   OPEN   PUT   GET   CLOSE   EOJ
DTFPR   CDMOD

OPTIONS FOR THIS ASSEMBLY - ALIGN, LIST, XREF, LINK, NORLD, NODECK, NOEDECK

THE ASSEMBLER WAS RUN IN 65416 BYTES
END OF ASSEMBLY

EOP $3ASM
// EXEC LNKEDT

JOB INST   17.30.02 F-LE-E FAST-LINKAGE-EDITOR VM4.0   DOS/VS R34-0A G O A L S Y S T E M S

ACTION TAKEN   MAP CLEAR REL   LINK
LIST   PHASE MONITOR,ROOT
LIST   INCLUDE ILFFEXIT
LIST   AUTOLINK IJDFAPZZ
LIST   PHASE STDPGM,*
LIST   ENTRY

PHASE-CSECT-ENTRY	LO-LNK	HI-LNK	LO-REL	HI-REL	LN-HEX	LN-DEC	XF-LNK	XF-REL	G O A L S Y S T E M S
LINK PARTITION = F3	110000	169FFF	000000	059FFF	5A000	368,640	110078	000078	
ROOT MONITOR	110078	11051B	000000	0004A3	4A4	1,188	110078	000000	RELOCATABLE
ILFFEXIT	110078	1103F9	000000	000381	382	898			
	1100F4			00007C					
*EXIT									
IJDFAPZZ	110400	11051B	000388	0004A3	11C	284			
* IJDFAZZZ	110400		000388						
PHASE STDPGM	110520	1109B1	000000	000491	492	1,170	110588	000068	RELOCATABLE
DEBUG	110520	110889	000000	000369	36A	874			
IJDFZIWD	110890	110907	000370	0003E7	78	120			
IJDFCPZW	110908	1109B1	0003E8	000491	AA	170			
** IJDFZPZW	110908		0003E8						
** IJDFZZW	110938		0003E8						
IJDFCZZW	110938		0003E8						

NORMAL COMPLETION, BLOCKS AVAIL =   334, USED IN EDIT =   4, PCIL=X'106', CYL=001, SERIAL=WORK01.

// EXEC
800   150.00
400

```
        LOC   OBJECT CODE        ADDR1 ADDR2  STMT   SOURCE STATEMENT

      000080  D283 C102 C101    00108 00107    46 NEXT-10   MVC  OUTAREA,SPACES        SAM00230
              *** ERROR ***
      000086                                   47           GET  INFILE,RECORD         SAM00240
      000094  D20E C107 C0B6    0010D 000BC    52           MVC  LNAME,LAST            SAM00250
      00009A  D209 C12A C0C5    00130 000CB    53           MVC  FNAME,FIRST           SAM00260
      0000A0  0000 0000 0000    00000 00000    54           MVC  SALOUT, SALARY        SAM00270
              *** ERROR ***
      0000A6  0000 0000               00000    55           MVI  SALOUT-1,X'$'         SAM00280
              *** ERROR ***
      0000AA  0000 0000                        56           PUT  OUTFILE,OUTAREA       SAM00290
      0000B8  0000 0000               00000    61           B    NEXT-10               SAM00300
              *** ERROR ***

      0000BC                                   66 RECORD    DS   OCL80          CARD FORMAT    SAM00350
      0000BC                                   67 LAST      DS   CL15                  *        SAM00360
      0000CB                                   68 FIRST     DS   CL10                  *        SAM00370
                                               69 SALARY    DC   CL5                   *        SAM00380
              *** ERROR ***
      0000D5                                   70 SPACES    DS   CL50                  *        SAM00390
      000107  40                               71 SPACES    DC   CL1' '                         SAM00400
      000108                                   72 OUTAREA   DS   OCL132         PRINT FORMAT    SAM00410
      000108                                   73           DS   CL5                   *        SAM00420
      00010D                                   74 LNAME     DS   CL15                  *        SAM00430
      00011C                                   75 FNAME     DS   CL20                  *        SAM00440
      000130                                   76 FNAME     DS   CL10                  *        SAM00450
      00013A                                   77           DS   CL20                  *        SAM00460
      00014E                                   78 SALOUT    DS   CL5                   *        SAM00470
      000153                                   79 BLANK     DS   CL57                  *        SAM00480
```

Figure 10-11

```
LOC    OBJECT CODE      ADDR1 ADDR2  STMT   SOURCE STATEMENT

                                       8 *                                                      SAM00080
                                       9 *       HOUSEKEEPING INSTRUCTIONS GO HERE          **  SAM00090
                                      10 *                                                  **  SAM00100
000000E 000000                        11    OPEN (INFILE,INPUT,OUTFILE,OUTPUT)                  SAM00110
000019                                17+   DC   AL3(OUTFILE)          DCB ADDRESS
        *** ERROR ***
00001E D2B3 C057 C056 0005D 0005C     19 READ MVC  OUTAREA,SPACES                               SAM00120
000024 0000 0000        00000         20    GET  CARDFILE,RECORD                                SAM00130
                                      21+   LA   1,CARDFILE            LOAD PARAMETER REG 1
        *** ERROR ***
000032 0000 0000 0000   00000 00000   25    MVC  LNAME,LAST                                     SAM00140
        *** ERROR ***
000038 0000 0000 0000   00000 00000   26    MVC  FNAME,FIRST                                    SAM00150
        *** ERROR ***
00003E 0000 0000 0000   00000 00000   27    MVC  SALOUT,SALARY                                  SAM00160
        *** ERROR ***
000044 0000 0000                      28    PUT  OUTFILE,OUTAREA                                SAM00170
000044                                29+   LA   1,OUTFILE             LOAD PARAMETER REG 1
        *** ERROR ***
000052 0000 0000        00000         33    B    READRTN                                        SAM00180
        *** ERROR ***
000056                  00000         34 EOF CLOSE (INFILE,OUTFILE)                             SAM00190
        *** MNOTE ***
                                      37+12,*** IHB002 INVALID OPTION OPERAND SPECIFIED-OUTFILE
                                      38 *
00005C                                39 RECORD   DS  0CL80                                     SAM00200
00005D 40                             40 SPACES   DC  CL1' '                                    SAM00210
00005D                                41 OUTAREA  DS  0CL132                                    SAM00220
000062                                42          DS  CL15                                      SAM00230
000071                                43 LNAME    DS  CL20                                      SAM00240
000085                                44          DS  CL10                                      SAM00250
00008F                                45 FNAME    DS  CL20                                      SAM00260
0000A3                                46          DS  CL5                                       SAM00270
0000A8                                47 SALOUT   DS  CL50                                      SAM00280
0000DC                                48 BLANK    DS  18F                                       SAM00290
                                      49 SAVEAREA DS                                            SAM00310
                                      50 INFILE   DCB DDNAME=INFILE,MACRF=GM,BLKSIZE=80,        SAM00320
        *** MNOTE ***
                                      51+12,*** IHB052 DSORG OMITTED
        *** MNOTE ***
                                      52+12,*** IHB066 INCONSISTENT OPERAND
000124                                54          LRECL=80,DSORG=PS,EODAD=EOF
        *** ERROR ***
000124                                55 PRTFILE  DCB DDNAME=OUTFILE,MACRF=PM,BLKSIZE=132,LRECL=132,DSORG=PS  SAM00330
000124                                109         END                                          SAM00340
```

Figure 10-12

272

2.   Statement Number   Explanation of Error

17	The error is in the OPEN macro (+ sign next to statement number). There is no DCB defined for OUTFILE. (Note that a DCB labeled PRTFILE appears in the program, but it is not referenced.)
21	The error is in the GET macro (+ sign next to statement number.) CARDFILE is not described by a DCB. (Note that a DCB labeled INFILE appears in the program, but it is not referenced.)
25	LAST is not defined. Notice that RECORD is defined by DS 0CL80. The first 0 indicates that RECORD will be subdivided into fields. However, this was not done.
26	FIRST is not defined. (Same explanation as for statement 25.)
27	SALARY is not defined. (Same explanation as for statement 25.)
29	The error is in the PUT macro (+ sign next to statement number.) There is no DCB for OUTFILE.
33	READRTN is not defined as a label or name of any instruction to which a branch can be made. (Notice that there is a label READ at the beginning of the loop.)
37	The error is in the CLOSE macro (+ sign next to statement number.) There is no DCB for OUTFILE.
51, 52, and 54	The errors are in the DCB macro. The continuation character was omitted on the first line of the DCB. The assembler thus interpreted the second line to be an independent instruction with an invalid operation code. It therefore indicated that the required operand DSORG was omitted from the first line of the DCB, since it did not treat the second line as a continuation.

KEY TERMS
Addressable location
Assembler
Assembly

Base
Base register
Bit
Byte

CSECT

Displacement

Effective address
END statement

Instruction formats

Location counter

Memory
Mnemonics
Multiprogramming

Object module
Object program

PRINT NOGEN

Relocatability

Source program
Symbol cross-reference table
Symbolic address

UNIT IV

Registers and Binary Operations

Chapter 11

Binary Operations Using RX Format Instructions

In this section we will discuss operations that maximize the efficient use of the computer.

Instructions operating on *binary* data are among the most efficient operations that a computer can perform. If a number is stored in decimal or hexadecimal form, it takes longer to execute an arithmetic operation using that number, than if the data was stored in binary form.

In short, to maximize the efficient use of computers, we operate on data in binary form. The use of the *general purpose registers* in arithmetic operations also maximizes the efficiency of the computer. General registers can be used in arithmetic operations only if data is entered in *binary form*.

General Purpose Registers

You will recall that there are 16 general purpose registers, numbered 0–15. As a general rule only registers 2–12 should be used, since the other registers are used for special purposes by the computer.

1. General registers may be used as *accumulators* in add, subtract, multiply, and divide operations.

2. General registers may also be used as index registers.

An *index register* is frequently employed in processing tables and arrays and in performing matrix operations. The index register contains an address that is modified during execution of the program. Therefore, data such as a tax table may be stored in consecutive locations of primary storage. By modifying the contents (or address) of the index register, the programmer can "look up" any desired tax schedule contained in the table. The use of index registers will be discussed in depth in Chapter 16.

3. General registers may be used for looping.

Looping, as we have seen, is essential for handling repetitive data processing operations. Scientific and mathematical problems involve repetitive (iterative) computational techniques. Looping can be performed most efficiently through the use of registers.

In summary, the general purpose register functions as an accumulator with regard to arithmetic operations, as an address modifier in indexing and for looping as well. The efficient programmer uses registers whenever possible in order to avoid the more time-consuming operations needed to manipulate data in primary storage.

Representing Data in Binary Form in Registers: A Review

Registers are each 4-bytes or *one fullword* in length. Data is represented in registers in *binary* form. This is referred to as *fixed-point* data. The high-order bit of a 32-bit register (8 bits/byte × 4 bytes) is used for a sign bit: 0 for + and 1 for −. There are thus 31 bits that can be used to represent a number. The 32 bits of a general register are assigned values as illustrated below, where S denotes the sign bit.

Positional value	S 2^{30} ...... 2^2 2^1 2^0
Bits	0 1 31

The number represented by the rightmost three bits on, for example, is +7 (4 + 2 + 1), or $2^3 - 1$. Similarly, the largest number that can be represented in a general register is $2^{31} - 1 = 2,147,483,647$. The smallest number that can be stored is $-(2^{31} - 1)$.

Examples

a. +5 in a general register would be represented as follows:

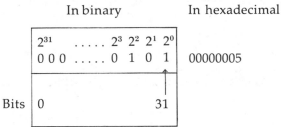

b. −5 in a general register would be represented as follows:

        In binary   In hexadecimal

2^{31} .... 2^2 2^1 2^0	FFFFFFFB
1 1 1 ..... 1 1 1 0 1 1	

Bits 0   31

Recall that a negative number in binary is represented in *complement* form. To represent −5 in binary, we do the following.

1. Represent the number as a positive value

    0000 0101

       32 bits

2. Complement the number. A 1 in the high-order bit position designates the field as negative. (A 0 designates the field as positive.)

    1111 1010

       32 bits

3. Add 1 to the result.

    1111 1011

       32 bits

To represent the number in hexadecimal, we group 4 bits at a time:

    1111   ....   1111 1011

     F FFFFF F   B

Review of Registers
1. Registers can function as accumulators.
2. A general purpose register may be used as an index register.
3. There are 16 general purpose registers, each 4 bytes (one fullword) in length.
4. Registers are numbered 0–15. Note, however, that the programmer is usually restricted to the use of registers 2–12.
5. Data is represented in registers in *binary* form. This is referred to as fixed-point data. The leftmost (high-order) bit is interpreted as an algebraic sign. For positive numbers, the sign bit is off (contains the digit 0).
6. Negative numbers are identified by the sign bit being on (containing the digit 1), and negative numbers are stored in *complement* form.
7. Arithmetic is performed 2–4 times faster in registers than in storage locations, depending upon the 360/370 model.
8. The largest positive and negative numbers that can be stored in a fullword are +2,147,483,647 (decimal) and −2,147,483,648.

SELF-EVALUATING QUIZ

1. Data is represented in registers in _____ form.
2. The general purpose registers are numbered _____ through _____ .
3. The number of binary digits, including the sign, which can be used for storing a number in a register is _____ .
4. A 1 in the high-order position of a register identifies the number as _____ .
5. A 0 in the high-order position of a register identifies the number as _____ .
6. (True or False) The number 2 is a valid high-order digit in a register.
7. (True or False) Arithmetic operations can be performed more efficiently using general purpose registers.
8. (True or False) A general purpose register can be used as an index for table look-up operations.
9. Each register is ___(number)___ bytes in length.
10. (True or False) 32 bits are equal to one fullword.

Questions 11–17 are designed to review binary and hexadecimal numbers that were discussed in Chapter 2. If you are confident that you understand the nature of numbers in base 2 and base 16, then you may skip these exercises.

11. $(1011001)_2 = (?)_{10}$
12. $(10A7)_{16} = (?)_{10}$
13. $(121)_{10} = (?)_2$
14. $(121)_{10} = (?)_{16}$
15. How is −6 represented in 2 bytes in binary?
16. How is +7 represented in 2 bytes in binary?
17. The following binary number is located in 2 bytes.

    00000000   11111001
    First byte   Second byte

    a. What is the number in base 10?
    b. What is the number in hexadecimal notation?

Solutions
1. Binary
2. 0–15
3. 32
4. Negative
5. Positive
6. False. 0 or 1 only.
7. True
8. True
9. 4
10. True
11. 89 (1 + 8 + 16 + 64)
12. 4263 (1 × 7 + 10 × 16 + 1 × 4096)
13. 1111001
14. 79. (Four binary digits are grouped to form 1 hexadecimal digit: $[0111\ 1001]_2 = [79]_{16}$. Notice that a high-order zero was added to make a group of 4 digits.
15.
11111111	11111010
First byte	Second byte

    Two bytes consist of 16 bits (binary digits). Negative numbers are represented in binary in two's complement form. The following three steps illustrate the conversion process:

    1. Represent the number as a positive value:

00000000	00000110
First byte	Second byte

    2. Complement the number. Recall that a 1 in the high-order bit position designates the field as negative.

11111111	11111001
First byte	Second byte

    3. Add 1 to the result.

11111111	11111010
First byte	Second byte

16.
00000000	00000111
First byte	Second byte

    Recall that a 0 in the high-order bit position designates the field as positive.

17. a. +249 (High-order bit position is 0; therefore the number is positive.)
    b. +00F9

There are two classes of instructions that utilize registers.

Instructions That Use Registers

Type	Meaning	Type of Operands
RX	Register and indexed storage	One operand = register One operand = storage (+indexing,[1] only if applicable)
RR	Register-to-register	Both operands are registers

[1] Indexing will be discussed in Chapter 16.

In this chapter, we will discuss the basic RX instructions. The RR instructions will be presented in the next chapter.

Register and Indexed Storage Instructions

Instructions classified as RX instructions perform operations using both registers and storage locations. Initially, we will assume that indexing is not performed.

The operands used with RX format instructions must be fixed length, either a halfword or a fullword. The data in storage, as well as the data in the registers, must be in *binary* form.

F, H, and D Formats for Data in Storage

You will recall that by assigning F for fullword, H for halfword, or D for doubleword to a DC or Define Constant statement, data will be entered into the field in binary form. A constant assigned as follows:

LABEL	OPERATION	
1	10	16
A,M,T	D,C	F,'.∅.'

assures that the result, which appears in AMT, is in binary form.

Using RX instructions in the S/360, the address of the storage locations used as operands must begin on fullword, halfword, or sometimes doubleword boundaries. This *boundary alignment* is automatically assured when the F, H or D formats, respectively, are used in define constant (DC) and Define Storage (DS) statements. Note that this boundary requirement is only necessary when running programs on the S/360. The S/370 does *not* have this limitation.

In short, we use the F, H, or D as field specifications for constants or work areas to be employed with RX instructions where possible. If data to be operated on is entered as input and is in zoned-decimal or packed form, it must *first* be converted to binary form before an RX instruction can be executed.

Summary
1. RX operations use operands of fixed length, either:
   a. Fullword
   b. Halfword
   or
   c. Doubleword
2. The data in storage must be in the binary format.
3. In the S/360, fullword, halfword, or doubleword boundary alignment is necessary.
4. No boundary alignment is required in the S/370. DS CL4 and DS F both establish 4-byte areas; the latter provides the necessary boundary alignment for RX format instructions on the S/360. We will use the F format throughout.

Examples of RX Instructions

1. Load Instruction The general format for the Load instruction is:

Operation 10	Operand 16
L	REG,OPERAND

Instruction:	Load
Op code:	L
Operand 1:	Register (2–12)
Operand 2:	Four-byte storage area or self-defining operand containing binary data
Purpose:	Data transmitted from storage to register
Limitations:	S/360: Operand 2 must be on a fullword boundary
	S/370: no boundary requirement

The movement of data from a storage location to a register is called *loading*. The purpose of the load instruction is to provide the register with an initial value where necessary. The load instruction is similar to the MVC instruction. The MVC instruction moves zoned decimal data between storage locations; the load instruction moves 4 bytes of binary data from storage to a register.

The receiving field is the general purpose register identified in the first operand. Its contents change as a result of this instruction. The sending field is a fullword in storage and its contents do not change. An example of this instruction is as follows:

```
        L       8,NUMBER
        •
        •
        •
NUMBER  DC      F'121'
```

Before

Register 8 | 01 | 23 | 45 | 67 |

NUMBER | 00 | 00 | 01 | 21 |

After

Register 8 | 00 | 00 | 00 | 79 | →This is the hexadecimal

NUMBER | 00 | 00 | 01 | 21 | equivalent of 121.

In actuality, the number in register 8 is in a *binary* format. Internally, register 8 has the following bit configuration that represents the number 121:

$$\underbrace{00 \ldots 001111001}_{32 \text{ bits}}$$

Note that in storage dumps, the contents of a register are displayed as *8 hexadecimal digits*, since 4 binary digits are grouped together to form 1 hexadecimal digit. We will use 8 digits to represent the contents of registers, but these 8 digits from now on will be shown in *decimal* form rather than hexadecimal form. This approach is intended to simplify the illustrations and to make the results of the various operations easier to understand. Note, however, that when you debug an actual program and locate the contents of general registers, the contents will be displayed hexadecimally.[2] Register 8 would therefore contain $\boxed{00 \mid 00 \mid 00 \mid 79}$ (hexadecimal), which simply is another means of representing decimal 121.

The load instruction can also be used with a self-defining operand (literal) as follows:

LABEL	OPERATION 10	OPERAND 16
	L	8,=F'121'

This instruction will produce the same results as the previous example.

The examples below illustrate what happens when the following instruction is used:

LABEL	OPERATION 10	OPERAND 16
	L	8,FULLWORD

Register 8 Before Execution	Contents of FULLWORD	Register 8 After Execution	
	(decimal)	(decimal)	(binary)
+12 34 56 78	+00 00 01 51	+00 00 01 51	$\boxed{0\ldots010010111}$
+12 34 56 78	−00 00 00 25	−00 00 00 25	$\boxed{1\ldots\ldots100111}$
+12 34 56 78	+00 00 00 50	+00 00 00 50	$\boxed{0\ldots\ldots0110010}$

2. Store Instruction   The general format for a Store Instruction is:

Operation 10		Operand 16
ST		REG,OPERAND

Instruction:	Store
Op code:	ST
Operand 1:	Register 2–12
Operand 2:	Storage area
Explanation:	Four bytes of binary data transmitted from register to storage
	NOTE: Movement is from *first* operand to second operand.
Limitations:	S/360: Operand 2 on a fullword boundary
	S/370: no restriction

[2] The illustrations in this chapter demonstrate how instructions operate on data. To simplify these demonstrations for ease of reading, we have represented all numbers in decimal form. Some students, however, may be having difficulty with the actual hexadecimal and/or binary representation of numbers. We have, therefore, included in the self-evaluating questions at the end of each unit problems that illustrate and test the student's ability to understand instructions that operate on data in the actual hexadecimal or binary form.

The store instruction produces the opposite results of the load instruction. The purpose of the store instruction is to *move* data *from* a general purpose register to main storage. The entire contents of a register are moved into 4 bytes (fullword) of main storage. The store instruction is different from most instructions in that the *first* operand is the *sending field*, while the second operand is the *receiving field*.

The first operand is a register, and the second operand is an area in storage. In the S/360, the receiving field in main storage must be specified on a fullword boundary with specification F. However, this restriction does not apply to S/370 where CL4 would be OK.

The register is the sending field and its contents *remain the same*. The storage location is the receiving field and its contents change. The operation of this instruction is shown in the following illustration.

```
          ST      8,NUMBER
                  .
                  .
                  .
NUMBER    DS      F
```

Before Execution[3]		After Execution		
Register 8	+00 00 01 21	Register 8		+00 00 01 21
NUMBER	+12 34 56 78	NUMBER	decimal	+00 00 01 21
			binary	00 ... 01111001

Here are other examples using the same store instruction.

INSTRUCTION	Contents of Register 8	Contents of NUMBER Before Execution	Contents of NUMBER After Execution
ST 8,NUMBER	+00 00 00 03	+12 34 56 78	+00 00 00 03
	−00 00 04 00	+12 34 56 78	−00 00 04 00
	+05 00 00 00	+12 34 56 78	+05 00 00 00

SELF-EVALUATING QUIZ

1. In an RX instruction, the first operand refers to a _____ and the second operand refers to a _____ .
2. The data in both operands of an RX instruction must be in _____ form.
3. The instruction **TOTAL DC F'0'** establishes a field that is ___(number)___ bytes long and that contains ___(type)___ data.
4. (True or False) It is necessary on some computers, such as the S/360, to consider boundary requirements when using an RX instruction.
5. (True or False) The use of an F or H format in Define Constant statements automatically assures proper boundary alignment.
6. The purpose of a load (L) instruction is to _____ .
7. The load (L) instruction moves ___(number)___ bytes from storage to a register.
8. In a load instruction, the first operand is the *(sending/receiving)* field while the second operand is the *(sending/receiving)* field.
9. The purpose of a store (ST) instruction is to _____ .
10. In a store instruction, the first operand is the *(sending/receiving)* field, while the second operand is the *(sending/receiving)* field.

[3] NOTE: These contents are given in decimal form for purposes of clarification only.

11. (True or False) The contents of the first operand in a load instruction remain unchanged after execution.
12. (True or False) The contents of the first operand in a store instruction remain unchanged after execution.
13. Write an instruction to move the value 1234 into register 3.
14. Write an instruction to move the contents of register 8 into a field called STORE.

Solutions

1. Register
   Storage location
2. Binary
3. 4
   Binary
4. True. (There are no boundary requirements on the S/370.)
5. True
6. Provide a register with an initial value
7. 4
8. Receiving
   Sending
9. Move data from a register to storage
10. Sending
    Receiving
11. False. (The first operand, a register, is the *receiving* field.)
12. True. (The first operand, a register, is the *sending* field.)
13. L 3,=F'1234'
14. ST 8,STORE

3. Add Instruction: RX Format   The general format for the RX add instruction is:

Operation 10		Operand 16
A		REG,OPERAND

Instruction:	Add
Op code:	A
Operand 1:	General register 2–12
Operand 2:	Four-byte storage area or self-defining operand containing binary data.
Explanation:	Binary contents of second operand added to contents of general register.
Limitations:	S/360: Operand 2 must be aligned on a fullword boundary. S/370: no boundary requirement.

The purpose of this add instruction is to add the contents of a four-byte field in storage to the contents of a general purpose register (2–12). As usual, the contents of the first operand are destroyed, while the contents of the second operand remain the same. A sample instruction would appear as follows:

```
        A       8,TEN
          ·
          ·
          ·
TEN     DC      F'10'
```

Before Execution[4]   *After Execution*

	Decimal			*Decimal*	*Binary*
Register 8	+00 00 01 21		Register 8	+00 00 01 31	0...10000011
TEN	+00 00 00 10		TEN	+00 00 00 10	

The above could also be accomplished using a self-defining operand in the instruction:

```
   LABEL       OPERATION
1              10          16
   |   |   |   |  A   |   |   8,=F'10'
```

Other examples of how the instruction operates include:

Instruction	Register 8 Before Execution	Contents of NO	Register 8 After Execution
A 8,NO	+00 00 56 78	+00 00 00 78	+00 00 57 56
	+00 00 00 75	+00 00 01 00	+00 00 01 75
	−00 00 01 25	+00 00 01 25	+00 00 00 00
	−00 00 02 50	−00 00 03 00	−00 00 05 50
	+00 00 07 85	−00 00 00 15	+00 00 07 70

4. Subtract Instruction: RX Format

The general format of the RX subtract instruction appears as follows:

General Format

Operation	Operand
10	16
S	Register,Operand 2

where

S denotes the arithmetic subtraction operation.

Register is a number that refers to a general register (2–12).

Operand 2 is either the name of a 4-byte storage location containing binary data or a self-defining binary operand.

---

[4] NOTE: The contents are given in decimal form for purposes of clarification only.

> Instruction: Subtract
> Op code: S
> Operand 1: General register 2–12
> Operand 2: Four-byte storage area or self-defining operand containing binary data.
> Explanation: Contents of second operand are subtracted from first operand.
> Limitations: S/360: Second operand must be aligned on a fullword boundary.
> S/370: no boundary requirement.

The subtract instruction functions in a manner similar to the add instruction. However, it subtracts the contents of a 4-byte (fullword) field in storage from the contents of a register.

This instruction might thus appears as follows:

```
        S       8,NO
        *
        *
        *
NO      DC      F'20'
```

Before Execution[5]   *After Execution*

	Decimal		*Decimal*	*Binary*
Register 8	+00 00 02 70	Register 8	+00 00 02 50	0...011111010
NO	+00 00 00 20	NO	+00 00 00 20	

The above instruction could also be written with a self-defining operand as

LABEL	OPERATION	
1	10	16
	S	8,=F'20'

Other examples of subtraction include:

Instruction	Register 8 Before Execution	Contents of NO	Register 8 After Execution
S 8,NO	+00 00 56 78	+00 00 00 78	+00 00 56 00
	+00 00 00 75	+00 00 01 00	−00 00 00 25
	−00 00 01 25	+00 00 01 25	−00 00 02 50
	−00 00 02 50	−00 00 03 00	+00 00 00 50
	+00 00 07 85	−00 00 00 15	+00 00 08 00

SELF-EVALUATING QUIZ

1. Write a series of instructions to clear register 4, add AMT1 and AMT2 in register 4, and place the answer in a field called TOTAL. Assume all fields have been defined properly and that AMT1 and AMT2 are in binary form.
2. Write a series of instructions to subtract AMT3 from AMT4 and place the answer in DIFF. Use registers and assume all fields have been established properly and that AMT3 and AMT4 are in binary form.

[5] NOTE: The contents are given in decimal form for purposes of clarification only.

3. Write a routine, using registers, to add AMT1 and AMT2 and to subtract AMT3; where AMT1, AMT2, and AMT3 have been defined as follows:

    ```
    AMT1    DC    F'1234'
    AMT2    DC    F'2680'
    AMT3    DC    F'2222'
    ```

4. Using the above, add an instruction that will place the results in a field called HOLD.

5. In place of

    L   4,AMT1

    in Question 3, would the following serve just as well?

    A   4,AMT1

6. Write another statement or series of statements to accomplish

    L   4,AMT1

7. Most instructions place results in the *(first/second)* operand. An exception to this is the _____ instruction.

8. After the following instructions are executed, what are the contents of registers 5 and 6? Show the results in binary as well as hexadecimal form.

    ```
    L       6,=F'10'
    L       5,=F'0'
    A       5,=F'125'
    S       6,=F'16'
    ```

Solutions

1.  ```
    L     4,=F'0'
    A     4,AMT1
    A     4,AMT2
    ST    4,TOTAL
    ```
2.  ```
    L     4,AMT4
    S     4,AMT3
    ST    4,DIFF
    ```
3.  ```
    L     4,AMT1
    A     4,AMT2
    S     4,AMT3
    ```
4.  ```
            ST      4,HOLD
    HOLD    DC      F
    ```
5. No.   The add will not clear out the original contents of the register.
6.  ```
    L     4,=F'0'
    A     4,AMT1
    ```
7. First
    Store (ST)
8. Register 5: $\underbrace{0000 \ldots 01111101}_{\text{32 bits}}$ $(0000007D)_{16}$ (125_{10})

    Register 6: $\underbrace{1111 \ldots 11111010}_{\text{32 bits}}$ $(FFFFFFFA)_{16}$ $(-6)_{10}$

5. Converting Input Data to Binary

Here is the general format for this instruction.

Operation 10	Operand 16
CVB	REG,OPERAND
    ```

Instruction:	Convert to binary
Op code:	CVB
Operand 1:	Register 2–12 (receiving field)
Operand 2:	Storage location (sending field) 8 bytes long (doubleword)
Explanation:	Contents of doubleword packed data converted to binary form and placed in general register.
Limitation:	For S/360, Operand 2 must be on a doubleword boundary.

As we have seen, to use registers for calculations, the data must be in a binary format. Input data entered in the conventional zoned-decimal format must be converted to binary in two steps:

Steps for Converting Data to Binary Form for Use with Registers
1. Pack the data in a doubleword.
2. Convert the packed-decimal data to binary and load in a register.

You are already familiar with the **PACK** instruction. The ConVert to Binary (CVB) is used to convert a *doubleword* of packed-decimal data to binary form and store the results in a register.

A doubleword of packed-decimal data in the second operand is converted into a 32-bit binary number in the register specified as the first operand. If the contents of the packed field are positive, the sign of the binary result will be positive (high-order bit = 0). When the contents of the packed field are negative, the binary result will be negative (high-order bit = 1).

An example follows in which a zoned-decimal **AMT** field is packed and then converted to binary.

```
              PACK    AMTIN,AMT
              CVB     9,AMTIN
                .
                .
                .
RECORD        DS      OCL80
AMT           DS      CL4
              DS      CL76
*
AMTIN         DS      D
```

Before Execution (PACK)

AMTIN   00 00 00 00 00 00 00 00
AMT   F0 F0 F9 C8

After Execution (PACK)

AMTIN   00 00 00 00 00 00 09 8C
AMT   F0 F0 F9 C8

Before Execution[6] (CVB)

Register 9   +12 34 56 78
AMTIN 00 00 00 00 00 00 09 8C

After Execution (CVB)

	Decimal	*Binary*
Register 9	+00 00 00 98	0...01100010
AMTIN 00 00 00 00 00 00 09 8C		

Note the actual contents of register 9 are represented in binary, which in turn are displayed in hexadecimal when a storage dump occurs. Therefore, the 98 in decimal would appear as 62 in hexadecimal. In the following examples, assume AMTIN is already in packed form.

[6] NOTE: The contents are given in decimal form for purposes of clarification only.

Instruction	Register 9 After Execution	AMTIN (Packed Decimal)
CVB 9,AMTIN	00 00 98 76	00 00 00 00 00 09 87 6C
	−00 00 01 51	00 00 00 00 00 00 15 1D
	00 00 00 00	00 00 00 00 00 00 00 0C
	01 23 45 67	00 00 00 00 12 34 56 7C

The largest number that can be converted is the maximum number that a register may hold (2,147,483,647). With the S/360, the storage location used with the CVB instruction must begin on a doubleword boundary. You will recall that we can define a doubleword with a D. If no doubleword boundary alignment is required we could define the field as CL8.

> **Summarizing the CVB Instruction**
> 1. The CVB instruction converts a doubleword of packed-decimal data into binary and stores it in a register.
> 2. The second operand must contain packed-decimal data and be aligned on a doubleword boundary (for the S/360).
> 3. Invalid data in the second operand causes a data exception.
> 4. The first operand must be a register, and receives the converted data in binary form.
> 5. The magnitude of the numbers that may be converted is restricted to that of a 32-bit register: ±2,147,483,647.

6. Convert to Decimal   The general format of the CVD instruction is

Operation 10	Operand 16
CVD	Register,Operand 2

where

CVD instructs the computer to convert to decimal
Operand 1 is a register (sending field) containing binary data.
Operand 2 is an 8-byte storage location (on a doubleword boundary for the S/360).

> Instruction: Convert to decimal
> Op code: CVD
> Operand 1:   Register 2–12 (sending field)
> Operand 2:   Storage location (receiving field 8 bytes long)
> Explanation: Binary contents of register converted to decimal form and placed in storage location.
> Limitation: For S/360, Operand 2 must be on a doubleword boundary.
>
> NOTE: Operand 1 (register) is the sending field and operand 2 (storage) is the receiving field.

The purpose of this instruction is to convert the binary contents of a register to packed-decimal format and place the result in a storage location.

This instruction is necessary because binary data must first be converted to packed decimal and then either unpacked or edited (ED) before the result can be printed. Like the *store instruction,* the first operand of the convert to decimal (CVD) instruction is the *sending field* (register) and the second operand is the *receiving field* (storage location). For the S/360, the storage location must be a *doubleword* boundary or else a specification exception error will cause a program interrupt. This limitation is for the S/360 only, not the S/370. If the contents of the register are positive, the sign bits of the packed resultant field will contain a hex C. If the contents of the register are negative, the sign bits will contain a hex D.

Example

LABEL	OPERATION	
1	10	16
	C V D	8 , A N S

Before Execution[7]

	Decimal	*Binary*
Register 8	00 00 07 89	0...01100010101
ANS	12 34 56 78 12 34 56 78	

After Execution

Register 8	00 00 07 89
ANS	00 00 00 00 00 00 78 9C

(ANS in packed-decimal format)

After execution, register 8 will remain unchanged and **ANS** will contain the packed-decimal equivalent. The sign supplied to the packed field is a hex C. If the high-order bit of the register is 0, then C is the sign generated; if the high-order bit of the register is 1, then D is the sign generated. A few additional examples will clarify this concept.

Instruction	Register 8 (Binary)	ANS after Execution (Packed Decimal)
CVD 8,ANS	+00 00 98 76	00 00 00 00 00 09 87 6C
	−00 00 01 51	00 00 00 00 00 00 15 1D
	+00 00 00 00	00 00 00 00 00 00 00 0C
	−01 23 45 67	00 00 00 00 12 34 56 7D

ANS can be defined as a doubleword with the following instruction:

LABEL	OPERATION	
1	10	16
A N S	D S	D

This will define **ANS** as an 8-byte area in storage and will align it on a doubleword boundary.

Printed Results   The following program excerpt allows us to print the results instead of simply storing the data in **ANS**. Note that **ANS** contains 15 decimal digits, and we are assuming that it is signed positive.

[7] NOTE: The contents are given in decimal form for purposes of clarification only.

```
            CVD     9,ANS
            MVC     LINEOUT,SPACES
            MVC     LINEOUT(16),=X'402020202020202020202020202020'
            ED      LINEOUT(16),ANS
            PUT     OUTFILE,LINEOUT
                .
                .
                .
ANS         DS      D
SPACES      DC      C' '
LINEOUT     DS      CL132
```

There are many times when we use RX format instructions to operate on data in registers and we know that the high-order bytes of the doubleword will be zero. If, for example, registers are used to perform arithmetic operations on 4-, 5-, or even 6-digit positive numbers, we can be reasonably certain that the result in **ANS**, when converted back to decimal, has zeros in the 4 high-order bytes. In such cases, the following coding may be used to edit the results;

```
            CVD     9,ANS
            MVC     LINEOUT,SPACES
            MVC     LINEOUT(8),=X'4020202020202020'
            ED      LINEOUT(8),RESULT
            PUT     OUTFILE,LINEOUT
                .
                .
                .
ANS         DS      0D
            DS      CL4
RESULT      DS      CL4
SPACES      DC      C' '
LINEOUT     DS      CL132
```

We can normally assume for the purpose of this type of illustration that the result in **ANS** will contain at most *seven* significant digits plus a sign, (4 bytes rather than 8), with the remaining high-order positions filled with zeros. Notice that the edit pattern contains a blank (**40**) as a fill character for zero suppression and *seven* digit select characters (**20**). Note that while **ANS** is 8 bytes long, the edit (**ED**) instruction edits only the low-order 4 bytes labelled **RESULT**, (ANS+4 through ANS+7), which contain the seven significant digits plus a sign.

An alternative solution would have been to unpack **ANS**, as shown below. Remember, the **UNPK** instruction operates from right to left. The high-order zeros would simply be truncated.

```
            CVD     9,ANS
            MVC     LINEOUT,SPACES
            UNPK    LINEOUT(7),ANS
            OI      LINEOUT+6,X'F0'
            PUT     OUTFILE,LINEOUT
                .
                .
                .
ANS         DS      D
SPACES      DC      C' '
LINEOUT     DS      CL132
```

Review   When performing arithmetic operations with the use of registers, the following sequence of instructions is required for fields entered in zoned-decimal format:

PACK   (Zoned-decimal fields must be packed.)

CVB   (Packed fields must be converted to binary.)

$$
\begin{bmatrix}
\text{OPERATIONS} \\
\text{ARITHMETIC}
\end{bmatrix}
\quad \text{RR or RX Format}
$$

CVD   (Binary results must be converted to decimal.)

UNPK or ED   (Results must then be unpacked or edited for readability.)

SELF-EVALUATING QUIZ

1. The CVB instruction converts a *(fullword/doubleword)* of *(packed/binary)* data into *(packed/binary)* form.
2. The first operand in a CVB instruction is _____ .
3. (True or False) The following is a valid instruction.

         CVB   FLDA,FLDB

4. What, if anything, is wrong with the following:

         CVB   FLDA,1

             .

             .

             .

         FLDA   DS   F

5. (True or False) The first operand in a CVD instruction is the sending field.
6. (True or False) The following is a valid instruction.

         CVD   2,HOLD

             .

             .

             .

         HOLD   DS   D

7. After using a CVD instruction to convert the binary contents of a register to packed-decimal format, we generally _____ or _____ the result before it is printed.

Solutions

1. Doubleword
   Packed
   Binary
2. A general register
3. False. The first operand must be a register.
4. In a CVB instruction, the first operand is a register (2–12) and the second operand is a doubleword in storage containing packed-decimal data.
5. True
6. True
7. Unpack (UNPK)
   Edit (ED)

KEY TERMS
Binary numbers
Binary operations
Binary representation
Bit
Boundary alignment (S/360)

Doubleword

Fixed-Point data
Fullword

General purpose registers

Halfword

Index register

Loading

Review Questions

1. Why are registers used?
2. How would the decimal number −127 be represented in a register in hexadecimal?
3. How would the decimal number +127 be represented in a register in hexadecimal?
4. Discuss what is meant by boundary requirements on the S/360.
5. Discuss how data in registers can be printed out.
6. Write a program to count the number of cards in a deck and print the result out with the message 'THE NUMBER OF CARDS IS.' Use a register for the addition.
7. Write a program to read in cards with the following format and print out each employee's name and salary with a $500 bonus added on. HINT: Use a CVB to move the salary (after it is packed) to a register. Use an A instruction to add the bonus to that register.

NAME	SALARY	
1 20	21 26	

8. Write a program to read in cards with the following format and print out for each card the amount fields, each reduced by 5. HINT: Use a CVB to move each amount (after it is packed) to a different register. Use an S instruction to subtract 5 from each register.

NAME	AMT1	AMT2	
1–20	21–23	24–26	

9. Write a routine, using registers, to compute the following:
$$C = D + E + 50 - F - 200$$
Assume D, E and F are packed-decimal fields, 4 bytes in length. Print C, using the UNPK and OI instructions.
10. Write a routine, using registers, to compute the following: (Note that 4W = W added to itself three times.)
$$X = 4W - 275 + Y$$
Assume W and Y are zoned-decimal fields containing 3 digits. Print X with editing.

11. (True or False) The first operand of a load instruction must be a register.
12. (True or False) The contents of the first operand of a load instruction are replaced by the contents of the second operand.
13. (True or False) The second operand of an L instruction must begin on a halfword boundary.
14. (True or False) The load instruction moves data from main storage to a register.
15. (True or False) The first operand of a store instruction is always a register.

Practice Problems 1. Write a program to print a report from the following transaction card records:

    1–5   Employee number
    6–20 Employee name
    21–25 Pay xxx.xx
    26–80 Not used

Each line of the report contains the following fields:

    1–15 Employee name
    36–40 Employee number
    61–67 Gross pay $xxx.xx
    76–82 Net pay $xxx.xx
    91–95 Date (month and year: xx/xx)

NOTES:
a. Gross pay = Pay + Bonus
b. Net pay = Gross pay − Bond deduction
c. Every employee gets the same Bonus and has the same Bond deduction taken out. The following constants are to be defined in binary and used for these amounts:
     Bonus amount   200.00
     Bond deduction   56.25
d. If Net pay is negative, stop the run.
e. Place today's date in the Date field.
f. Use registers for performing the arithmetic operations.

2. Consider transaction cards with the following data:

     1–20 Customer name
     21 Type of transaction (1 = Master that contains previous balance)
                            (2 = Deposit)
                            (3 = Withdrawal)
    22–26 Amount
    27–31 Account number
    32–80 Not used

All cards are in sequence by Account Number and by Type within Account Number. Write a program that will print the name of each depositor and the corresponding *number* of deposits and withdrawals. At the end of the report, print the number of customers processed. Keep in mind that there is only one Type 1 (previous balance) card per account number, but there may be numerous deposit and withdrawal cards. Use RX format instructions for all arithmetic operations.

3.   Consider the following insurance cards:
   1–20 Name
      21 Sex (M-male, F-female)
   22–25 Birth date (month and year)
      26 Number of traffic violations in last 18 months
   27–28 Number of accidents in last 18 months

Write a program to print:
a.   Total number of drivers under 25.
b.   Total number of female drivers.
c.   Total number of drivers who have had more than 2 traffic violations in last 18 months.
d.   Total number of drivers who have had one or more accidents in last 18 months.
e.   Total number of drivers in the sample.

Use RX format instructions for arithmetic operations.

Chapter 12

Register-to-Register Instructions (RR) And Additional RX Instructions

I. RR Format

Register-to Register instructions (RR type) are used to move data from one register to another and to perform arithmetic operations using only registers. These instructions function in a manner similar to the RX type, except that there are no storage locations used, only registers. The general format for these RR instructions is given below.

General Format for RR Instructions

Operation	Operand
10	16
OP	REG1,REG2

The operations to be discussed initially will be the following:

LR Load Register
AR Add Register
SR Subtract Register

REG1 is the receiving field and its contents change.
REG2 is the sending field and its contents remain unchanged.

Load Register

Instruction: LR
Meaning: Load Register
Operands: Both must be general registers.
               Both contain binary data.
Result: Operand 1: Receiving field
               Operand 2: Sending field, remains unchanged.
               Contents of Operand 2 are loaded or moved to Operand 1.

Example

LABEL	OPERATION	
1	10	16
	L R	8 , 5

Before Execution[1]

| Register 5 | 00 | 00 | 12 | 34 |
| Register 8 | 56 | 78 | 90 | 12 |

After Execution

| Register 5 | 00 | 00 | 12 | 34 |
| Register 8 | 00 | 00 | 12 | 34 |

Test your understanding of the LR instruction by carefully following the series of instructions below. Assume they are executed in sequence.

Examples of Load Register (LR)

| Instruction | Contents of Registers | | | |
	Register 5	Register 6	Register 7	Register 8
Before Execution	+00 00 01 23	+00 00 04 56	−00 00 01 00	+00 00 00 19
LR 8,5				+00 00 01 23
LR 5,7	−00 00 01 00			
LR 7,6			+00 00 04 56	
LR 6,8		+00 00 01 23		
After Execution	−00 00 01 00	+00 00 01 23	+00 00 04 56	+00 00 01 23

Add Register (AR)   The general format of the AR instruction is:

Operation 10	Operand 16
AR	REG1,REG2

Instruction:	AR
Meaning:	Add Register
Operands:	Both must be registers.
	Both contain binary data.
Result:	Contents of Operands 1 and 2 are added together—
	Result replaces contents of Operand 1
	Operand 2 remains unchanged.

Example

LABEL	OPERATION 10	16
1		
	AR	8,5

Before Execution[2]

| Register 5 | +00 00 01 50 |
| Register 8 | +00 00 02 00 |

After Execution

| Register 5 | +00 00 01 50 |
| Register 8 | +00 00 03 50 |

Review the following sequence of AR instructions:

[1] NOTE: The contents are given in decimal form for purposes of clarification only.
[2] NOTE: The contents are given in decimal form for purposes of clarification only.

Examples of Add Register (AR)

Instructions	Contents of Register			
	Register 5	Register 6	Register 7	Register 8
Before Execution	+00 00 01 23	+00 00 04 56	−00 00 01 00	+00 00 00 19
AR 8,5 AR 5,7 AR 7,6 AR 6,8 AR 5,5	+00 00 00 23 +00 00 00 46	 +00 00 05 98	 +00 00 03 56	+00 00 01 42
After Execution	+00 00 00 46	+00 00 05 98	+00 00 03 56	+00 00 01 42

Notice in the last example that AR 5,5 has the effect of doubling or multiplying register 5 by two. This is a simple method to accomplish multiplication, which we will see later becomes quite involved.

The following program excerpt illustrates how the AR instruction can be used in a program.

Consider the following card layout:

AMT1	AMT2	
1 5	6 10	

Problem
Add these two amount fields using registers.

Solution

```
        PACK    DWORD1,AMT1
        PACK    DWORD2,AMT2
        CVB     4,DWORD1
        CVB     3,DWORD2
        AR      4,3
          .
          .
          .
CARDIN  DS      0CL80
AMT1    DS      CL5
AMT2    DS      CL5
        DS      CL70
DWORD1  DS      D
DWORD2  DS      D
```

Subtract Register (SR) Here is the general format.

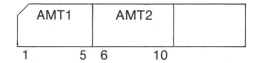

Operation 10		Operand 16
SR		REG1,REG2

Instruction:	SR
Meaning:	Subtract Register
Operands:	Both must be registers.
	Both contain binary data.
Result:	Contents of Operand 2 subtracted from Operand 1.
	Result replaces Operand 1.
	Operand 2 remains unchanged.

Example

```
      LABEL        OPERATION
 1                 10        16
 |  |  |  |  |  |  | S R |  |  | 8 , 5 |  |
```

Before Execution[3]

Register 5   +00 00 01 50
Register 8   +00 00 02 00

After Execution

Register 5   +00 00 01 50
Register 8   +00 00 00 50

The following sequence of SR instructions clarifies its use in programming.

Examples of Subtract Register (SR)

Instruction	Contents of Register			
	Register 5	Register 6	Register 7	Register 8
Before Execution	+00 00 01 23	+00 00 04 56	−00 00 01 00	+00 00 00 19
SR 8,5				−00 00 01 04
SR 5,7	+00 00 02 23			
SR 7,6			−00 00 05 56	
SR 6,8		+00 00 05 60		
SR 5,5	+00 00 00 00			
After Execution	+00 00 00 00	+00 00 05 60	−00 00 05 56	−00 00 01 04

In the last example, register 5 was set to zero by subtracting the contents of the register from itself. Whenever it is necessary to clear a register to zero, this method can be utilized.

[3] NOTE: These contents are given in decimal form for purposes of clarification only.

The following review of the subtraction process will aid in your understanding of the results obtained above.

Review of Subtraction Rules
1. Change sign of the number to be subtracted (contents of second operand or register).
2. Proceed as in addition.

Examples
a. $+12 - (+13) = +12 + (-13) = -1$
b. $-5 - (-2)\ \ \ = -5 + (+2)\ \ \ = -3$
c. $-4 - (+2)\ \ \ = -4 + (-2)\ \ \ = -6$
d. $+12 - (-15) = +12 + (+15) =\ \ 27$

SELF-EVALUATING QUIZ

Exercises 1–7 are basically designed to review the way RR instructions operate. In addition, they are designed to review your ability to add and subtract in hexadecimal. Indicate the result in hex in each case. Treat each example independently *not* sequentially. (NOTE: Each hex digit $= 4$ binary digits.)

Instruction	Contents of Registers (in Hex)			
	Register 4	Register 5	Register 6	Register 7
	00 00 00 11 (17_{10})	00 00 00 7E (126_{10})	00 00 00 11 (17_{10})	FFFFFF7A (-134_{10})
1. AR 6,5				
2. SR 5,4				
3. SR 4,6				
4. SR 4,7				
5. LR 4,6				
6. L 4,=F'123'				
7. AR 4,6 SR 4,7				

8. Write a routine to add the numbers 456 and 223 using registers.
9. Write an RX-type instruction to subtract 100 from the contents of register 5.
10. Code the above instruction using an RR-type instruction for the subtraction.

Solutions

1. Register 5: 00 00 00 7E   Register 6: 00 00 00 8F (143_{10})
2. Register 4: 00 00 00 11   Reg. 5: 00 00 00 6D (109_{10})
3. Register 6: 00 00 00 11   Register 4: 00 00 00 00 (0_{10})
4. Register 7: FFFFFF7A   Register 4: 00 00 00 97 (151_{10})
5. Register 6: 00 00 00 11   Register 4: 00 00 00 11 (17_{10})
6. Register 4: 00 00 00 7B   (This is an RX instruction that can have a self-defining operand.) (123_{10})

7. Register 6: 00 00 00 11   Register 7: FFFFFF7A
   Register 4: 00 00 00 A8   (00 00 00 11 + 00 00 00 11 − [FFFFFF7A]
8. L   4,=F'223'
    L   5,=F'456'
    AR   4,5
9. S   5,=F'100'
10. L   4,=F'100'
    SR   5,4

II. RR and RX Format Instructions

Now that you understand the general format of RX and RR-type instructions, we will consider the remaining instructions in pairs:

A. *Comparison:*

C	is an RX instruction
CR	is an RR instruction

B. *Multiplication:*

M	is an RX instruction
MR	is an RR instruction

C. *Division:*

D	is an RX instruction
DR	is an RR instruction

A. Binary or Fixed-Point Compare Instructions (C and CR)

As we already know, compare instructions are used to set the condition code in order that conditional branching may take place. Many other instructions affect the condition code setting, as we will see in the next section. Thus, it is advisable to follow immediately a compare instruction with a branch instruction to ensure that another instruction does not alter the condition code setting.

The *Compare Register* (CR) and *Compare* (C) instructions perform an *algebraic* compare between the two operands. You will recall that the Compare Pack (CP) is also an algebraic comparison. The CR instruction is used to compare the contents of two registers and follows the general format.

Compare Registers (CR)

Instruction:	Compare Registers
Op Code:	CR
Operand 1:	Register
Operand 2:	Register
Result:	Condition code will be set to low, equal, or high depending upon whether operand 1 is <, =, or > operand 2, respectively.
	Contents of registers are not affected by the comparison.

Operation 10	Operand 16
CR	REG1,REG2

CR indicates a register-to-register comparison.
REG1 is the first operand and tests high, low or equal with respect to REG2.
REG2 is the second operand and is a general register.

Neither operand is affected by the compare. Note that since we are dealing with an algebraic comparison, a negative value is considered lower than a positive value. (High-order 1 compares *low* to high-order zero.)

For a review of how condition codes are affected by operations discussed is this section, consider this table.

Instruction		Condition Code			
		0	1	2	3
CR	Compare Register	=	First < second	First > second	Not set by compare
C	Compare (RX)	=	First < second	First > second	Not set by compare
AR	Add Register	= 0	<0	>0	Overflow
A	Add (RX)	= 0	<0	>0	Overflow
SR	Subtract Register	= 0	<0	>0	Overflow
S	Subtract (RX)	= 0	<0	>0	Overflow

A few examples will illustrate how the instruction operates.[4]

Instruction	Contents of Register 5	Contents of Register 6	Condition Code Setting
CR 5,6	+00 00 01 25	+00 00 01 08	HIGH
	+00 00 02 58	+00 00 02 58	EQUAL
	−00 00 00 17	+00 00 00 00	LOW
	−00 00 00 15	−00 00 00 21	HIGH
	+00 00 00 07	+00 00 00 08	LOW

The following illustration shows how the **CR** instruction can be coded in a program.

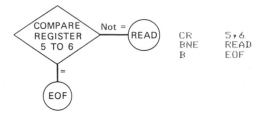

[4] NOTE: The contents are shown in decimal form for purposes of clarification only.

Compare Fullword (C)

Instruction:	Compare
Op Code:	C
Operand 1:	Register
Operand 2:	Four-byte storage area or self-defining operand containing binary data.
Result:	Condition code will be set to low, equal, or high depending upon whether operand 1 is $<$, $=$, or $>$ operand 2, respectively.
	Registers are not affected by the comparison.
Limitations:	For S/360, the storage area must be on a fullword boundary.

The compare fullword (C) instruction is used to compare the contents of a storage location with the contents of a general register. Here is the general format.

Operation 10	Operand 16
C	REG,FULLWD

C indicates a register-to-(indexed) storage comparison.
REG is the first operand and tests high, low, or equal with respect to FULLWD.
FULLWD is the second operand and either a storage location or a self-defining operand of 4 bytes (fullword). With the S/360, the FULLWD operand must be on a fullword boundary.

Neither operand is affected by the execution of this instruction. As with the CR instruction, a negative value is considered less than a positive value. The following examples clearly illustrate this point.[5]

Instruction	Contents of Register 7	Contents of FULLWORD	Condition Code Setting
C 7,FULLWORD	+00 00 01 25	+00 00 01 18	HIGH
	+00 00 02 58	+00 00 02 58	EQUAL
	−00 00 00 17	+00 00 00 00	LOW
	−00 00 00 15	−00 00 00 21	HIGH
	+00 00 00 07	+00 00 00 08	LOW

The following illustration shows how the C instruction might be coded in a payroll program.

[5] NOTE: The contents are given in decimal form for clarification purposes only.

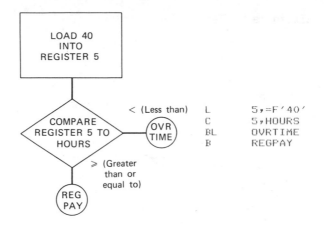

```
                                   < (Less than)    L     5,=F'40'
  COMPARE                 OVR                        C     5,HOURS
REGISTER 5 TO            TIME                        BL    OVRTIME
  HOURS                                              B     REGPAY
                                  ≥ (Greater
                                     than or
                                     equal to)
```

If the HOURS an employee has worked are greater than 40, (Register 5 < HOURS) then we want to go to the OVRTIME routine; otherwise, we go to the REGPAY routine. If register 5 (contents 40) compares low to HOURS, that means that the employee has worked over 40 hours and is entitled to overtime pay.

Summarizing C and CR Instructions

1. The first operand of a Compare (C) or Compare Register (CR) instruction is always a register.
2. The condition code always refers to the status of the first operand (register) relative to the second operand and is set EQUAL, LOW, or HIGH.
3. The comparison is *algebraic*, meaning that positive numbers have a higher value than negative numbers.
4. The length of the comparison is 4 bytes.

Condition Code Tested After Arithmetic Operations

The condition code is set as a result of all arithmetic as well as comparison operations. After an arithmetic or compare instruction, a conditional branch can be coded that will alter the sequence of instructions to be executed if a given condition is met. This *conditional branch* tests the value of the condition code. The results of the *arithmetic* operations may be zero, negative (minus), positive, or overflow. After an arithmetic operation is performed, the conditional branch instructions may be coded as in the following table.

Conditional Branch Operation	Arithmetic Condition Tested	Actual Condition Code Setting (for Programmer's Information)
BZ	Zero result	0
BNZ	Not zero result	1, 2, or 3
BM	Minus (negative) result	1
BNM	Not minus	0, 2 or 3
BP	Positive result	2
BNP	Not positive result	0, 1 or 3
BO	Overflow	3

A few examples follow.

Example 1 Testing for Overflow

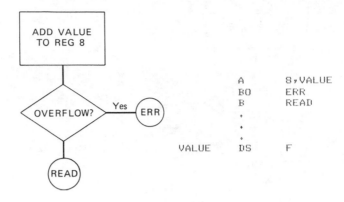

A	8,VALUE
BO	ERR
B	READ
.	
.	
.	
VALUE DS	F

Register 8 is being used as an accumulator and a test is made for an overflow condition. You will recall that overflow occurs in a register when the result is larger than the largest number that can be stored in a register. In a general register, the largest number that can be stored is 2,147,483,647. If this number were exceeded, overflow would occur and the program would branch to the error routine labeled **ERR**. Similarly a negative number less than −2,147,483,648 could not be stored in a register.

Example 2 Testing a Counter for Zero

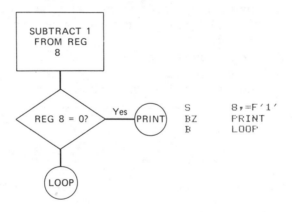

S	8,=F'1'
BZ	PRINT
B	LOOP

The register serves as a counter. With each pass through the loop, the counter is reduced by 1 until it reaches zero. When this condition occurs, the program will branch to the routine called **PRINT**.

SELF-EVALUATING QUIZ

Indicate the condition code setting after each instruction is executed.

	Contents in Hex
Register 2:	00 00 26 E3
Register 3:	FF A2 2D 80
AMT1:	02 68 75 AC
AMT2:	FE 30 26 E3

1. CR   2,3
2. CR   3,2
3. C   2,AMT1
4. C   3,AMT2
5. C   2,AMT2
6. AR   3,2

7.	S	2,AMT1
8.	SR	3,3
9.	AR	3,3
10.	A	2,AMT2

Solutions

	Condition Code	*Explanation*
1.	High	Register 3 contains a negative amount
2.	Low	
3.	Low	
4.	High	AMT2 is considered < register 3 because AMT2 has a larger negative amount.
5.	High	Positive number > negative number.
6.	Condition Code 1: Less than zero result	
7.	Condition Code 1: Less than zero result	
8.	Condition Code 0: Zero result	
9.	Condition Code 3: Overflow	
10.	Condition Code 1: Less than zero result	

**Branch on Condition

What you have learned thus far is called *extended mnemonics*; it enables the programmer to utilize an operation code that itself tests a specific condition. Below is the generalized format for a branch condition, one which may be used for *all* types of branches.

BC ⎣___Mask Value___⎦ , ⎣___Label to be Branched to___⎦

			Previous Result	
Mask Value	Mask	Condition Code Settings	of Comparison	of Arithmetic
8	1000	0	OP1=OP2	=0 no overflow
4	0100	1	OP1 < OP2	<0 no overflow
2	0010	2	OP1 > OP2	>0 no overflow
12	1100	0,1	OP1 ≤ OP2	≤0 no overflow
10	1010	0,2	OP1 ≥ OP2	≥0 no overflow
6	0110	1,2	OP1≠OP2	≠0 no overflow
14	1110	0,1,2	All	no overflow
1	0001	3	None	overflow

**This is an optional topic.

9	1001	0,3	OP1=OP2	0 or overflow
5	0101	1,3	OP1<OP2	<0 or overflow
3	0011	2,3	OP1>OP2	>0 or overflow
13	1101	0,1,3	OP1≤OP2	≤0 or overflow
11	1011	0,2,3	OP1≥OP2	≥0 or overflow
7	0111	1,2,3	OP1≠OP2	≠0 or overflow

Examples

Coding   *Meaning*

1. C   6,FLD1   Branch to RTN1 if Reg 6 = FLD1
   BC   8,RTN1

2. CR   6,9   Branch to STEP1 if Reg 6 ≤ Reg 9
   BC   12,STEP1

3. S   5,=F'1'   Subtract 1 from contents of register 5. Branch to LOOP1 if
   BC   7,LOOP1   register 5 ≠ 0. Note that BC 6,LOOP1 is also OK.

The BC instruction is simply another method of coding the extended form of the branch.

BC and Extended Mnemonics

Extended Form		Ordinary Form		Meaning
BM	label	BC	4,label	Branch on minus
BZ	label	BC	8,label	Branch on zero
BNP	label	BC	13,label	Branch on not plus
BNM	label	BC	11,label	Branch on not minus
BNZ	label	BC	7,label	Branch on not zero
BO	label	BC	1,label	Branch on overflow

The following instructions, then, are equivalent

1. BM   STEP1   BC   4,STEP1
2. BNZ   STEP4   BC   7,STEP4

B. Binary or Fixed-Point Multiplication: Multiply (M) and Multiply Register (MR) Review

Recalling the principles of multiplication, we find

```
    123   multiplicand
×    45   multiplier
   ----
   615
   492
   ----
  5535   product
```

where the total number of digits in the final product cannot exceed the sum of the digits of the multiplicand and multiplier. This is an important consideration as we shall see. The M and MR instructions use 4-byte or 32-bit operands. That is, both the first and second operands are 4 bytes long. When two 32-bit operands are multiplied, the product requires 64 bits. Obviously, the result is too long to be stored in a single register. Therefore, *two consecutive even-odd registers* are used to store the product. The registers must be *adjacent* and the odd-numbered register must be one greater than the even-numbered register. That is, registers 4 and 5 would be suitable, but register 5 and 6 would not (odd-numbered register not greater than even-numbered register.) The steps necessary to multiply 123 by 45 are shown below.

See Figure 12-1 for a more detailed explanation.

```
L       5,=F'123'
M       4,=F'45'
```

Figure 12-1 Finding the product of 123 × 45.

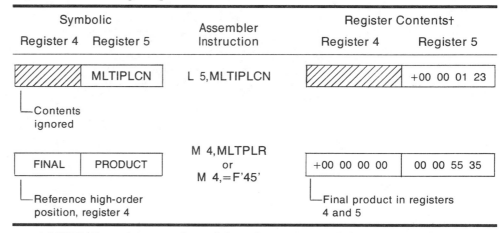

† NOTE: Data shown in decimal form for purposes of clarification only. MLTIPLCN will be set equal to 123. MLTPLR will be set equal to 45.

Registers 4 and 5 will be used to store the final product. In principle, registers 4 and 5 serve as an 8-byte accumulator. The multiplicand is placed in the *rightmost* 4 bytes of the even-odd register pair; that is, in the odd register. (See L instruction above.) The multiply instruction must reference the *even* register of the even-odd pair.

The general formats of the M and MR instructions are as follows:

Operation	Operand
M	EVEN REG, FULLWD
MR	EVEN REG, REG

where

M and MR indicate fullword multiplication.

EVEN REG is the even register of an even-odd pair and before execution its contents are ignored. After execution, the product is stored in the even-odd pair of registers.

REG is a general register containing the multiplier.

FULLWD is a fullword in storage containing the multiplier. With S/360, FULLWD must be aligned on a fullword boundary.

The only *valid* register pairs that may be used for multiplication are illustrated below. (See also Figure 12-2.)

Register Pair		Load Multipli-cand in Register	First Operand in Multiply Instruction	Product Contained in Registers
Even Register	Odd Register			
2	3	3	2	2–3
4	5	5	4	4–5
6	7	7	6	6–7
8	9	9	8	8–9
10	11	11	10	10–11

Figure 12-2   Schematic of MR Instruction.

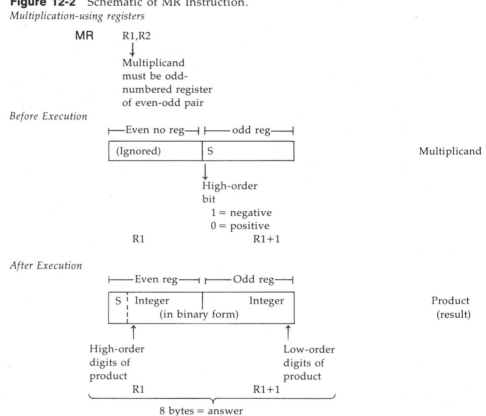

Multiplication-using registers

A specification exception resulting in a program interrupt will occur if the even-odd pair is incorrectly referenced.

The multiply instruction is best illustrated with a few examples. For reasons of clarification, only 4 decimal digits will be used in the examples.

Multiply Instruction (M)

Instruction	Multiplicand Register 7	Fullword (MLTPLR)	Final Product Registers 6 and 7
M 6,MLTPLR	+00 78	+00 02	+01 56
	−02 50	+00 06	−15 00 (− × + = −)
	+07 12	−00 04	−28 48
	−03 00	−00 12	+36 00 (− × − = +)

Depending upon the values of the multiplier and multiplicand, the product may extend beyond register 7 and into register 6. However, if you are certain that the result or product can be stored in 4 bytes, you need only reference register 7 when using a CVD or ST instruction in preparation for printing the results.

Multiply Register (MR) Instruction

Instruction	Multiplicand Register 7 (Contents)	Register 9	Final Product Registers 6 and 7
MR 6,9	+12 34	+00 02	+24 68
	−00 17	+00 05	−00 85
	+07 50	−00 03	−22 50
	−06 12	−00 04	+24 48

Notice that the multiplicand must first be placed in register 7, the low-order register of an even-odd (6–7) pair.

Summary M and MR: Binary or Fixed-Point Multiplication

1. With binary multiplication, an even-odd pair of registers are linked together to form an 8-byte accumulator.
2. The even-odd register pair serves as the first operand of the multiply instruction.
3. The multiplicand is placed in the odd register.
4. Ignore contents of the even register before multiplication takes place.
5. The second operand contains the multiplier and is either
    a. a general register (MR), or
    b. a fullword in storage (M) (on a fullword boundary for the S/360).
6. The multiply instruction always references the even register of the even-odd pair in the first operand.
7. The product is right justified in the even-odd register pair after execution.
8. Overflow cannot occur.
9. A specification exception will occur if the even-odd register pair is incorrectly referenced.

Suppose registers 6 and 7 contain the product of a multiplication. How do we access these 8 bytes for purposes of printing? The following represents a method of preparing the data for future printing.

```
        CVD     6,DWORD
        CVD     7,DWORD+4
        .
        .
        .
DWORD   DS      D
```

The contents of 8 bytes beginning at DWORD can now be unpacked or edited as necessary.

C. Binary or Fixed-Point Division: Divide (D) and Divide Register (DR)

Let us review the principles of division:

```
                              126    Quotient
          Quotient     121 | 15268   Dividend
Divisor | Dividend     Divisor 121
                              316
                              242
                              748
                              726
                               22    Remainder
```

As with multiplication, binary division requires the use of an even-odd register pair.

The dividend is loaded in the rightmost positions of the even-odd register pair. The divide instruction must reference the *even* register. The divisor is referenced by the second operand and is either:

a.   A fullword in storage using D as the op code or
b.   A general register using DR as the op code

However, division results in two answers, the quotient and the remainder. Both must be accommodated and accessible to the programmer. After division, the quotient and the remainder are stored in the even-odd register pair, as follows.

> 1.   Even contains the remainder.
> 2.   Odd contains the quotient.

See Figure 12-3.

Since the dividend is loaded in the odd register of the even-odd pair, the *even* register must be set to *zero*. Remember, the divide instruction treats the even-odd pair as one large 8-byte accumulator that contains the dividend. The steps necessary to divide 15,268 by 121 are shown in Figure 12.4.

> **Errors**
> An error called a *fixed-point divide* occurs in these two cases.
> a.   The quotient is too large to be stored in a register.
> b.   The divisor is zero.

Under these circumstances, *no* division takes place and the even-odd registers remain unchanged.

The general format for binary division, then, is

Operation	Operand
D	EVEN REG, FULLWD
DR	EVEN REG, REG

where   D and DR indicate fullword binary division.
          EVEN REG is the even register of an even-odd pair.
          REG is a general register containing the divisor.
          FULLWD is a fullword in storage containing the divisor.
                As before, with the S/360, FULLWD must be aligned on a fullword boundary.

Since the D and DR are so similar, only examples of the D will be presented. The data is shown in decimal form only for purposes of clarification.

Figure 12-3 Schematic of divide instruction

Division—Using Registers

DR   REG,REG

Dividend → Divisor   Operation to
(Odd-numbered   be
register of   performed
even-odd pair)
_____

                                      Quotient
                          Divisor │ Dividend
                                    _____

                                    Remainder

Before Execution

Bits	0	1	31	0	31	
	S			Dividend		(First Operand)

2 Registers
Even-odd pair

0	1	31	
S	Divisor		(Second operand)

Register

Result: First operand (even-odd pair)

0	1		0	1	31
S	Remainder		S	Quotient	

Example   DR   **2,4**

Machine instruction:

1 D	2 4

Registers 2–3:   −1443   Register 4:   −12 (decimal)
(decimal)

Result

−3	+120	Decimal
FFFFFFFD	00000078	

Remainder   Quotient

Figure 12-4 Binary division: 15,268 ÷ 121.

Symbolic		Instruction	Contents†	
Register 4	Register 5		Register 4	Register 5
0 0	/////	SR 4,4	+00000000	+00099999
	DIVIDEND	L 5,DIVIDEND	+00000000	+00015268
Remainder	Quotient	D 4,DIVISOR	+00000022	+00000126

† NOTE: Data shown in decimal form for purposes of clarification only.

Instruction	Dividend: Register 6 and Register 7	Fullword in Storage (Divisor)	Remainder Register 6	Quotient Register 7
D 6,DIVISOR	+00 00 01 51	+00 00 00 12	+00 07	+00 12
	−00 00 01 09	+00 00 00 09	−00 01	−00 12
	−00 00 02 48	−00 00 00 06	−00 02	+00 41
	+00 00 24 68	−00 00 00 08	+00 04	−03 08

Note that the sign of the quotient depends upon the signs of the divisor and dividend. Like signs produce positive results, while unlike signs produce a negative quotient. The remainder receives the sign of the dividend.

Summary—Binary Division
1. Binary division requires the use of an even-odd register pair that serves as the first operand. Usually, the even register is set to zero, and the dividend is loaded into the odd register.
2. When the dividend is less than 4 bytes (2,147,483,647 in decimal), the even register is set to zero. The dividend is then loaded into the odd or low-order register.
3. The second operand contains the divisor, and is either
    a. A fullword in storage (D), or
    b. A general register (DR)
4. The divide binary instructions always reference the *even* register in the first operand.
5. After division takes place, the even register contains the remainder, and the sign is the same as the dividend.
6. The odd register contains the quotient. The sign is negative only when the signs of the dividend and divisor are not alike.
7. A specification error will result if the even-odd register pair is incorrectly referenced.
8. A fixed-point divide error occurs when the divisor is zero, or the quotient is too large to be stored in a register.
9. When a fixed-point divide error occurs, division does not take place.

Halfword Binary Instructions   Halfword (16-bit) operands may be used in many instances in place of the fullword operands. The primary advantage of halfword instructions is the more efficient use of storage and faster performance. However, to preserve precision, the fullword instruction is recommended.

The largest decimal number that can be stored in a halfword is +32,767, while the smallest is −32,768. If the data falls within this range, the halfword instructions may be used. Operationally, halfword instructions function in a manner similar to the fullword instructions. For example, when a halfword is loaded into a register, the halfword is *automatically* expanded to a fullword. This is accomplished by propagating the sign bit through the leftmost 16 bits in the register. The following examples illustrate how this operates.

Examples

Decimal Number	Halfword Representation (in Hex)	Fullword Representation (in Hex)
+10	00 0A	00 00 00 0A
−10	FF F6	FF FF FF F6

In effect, the results are the same as if a fullword were used. The only limitation is that the numbers must range approximately between ±32,767. In the S/360, halfword data must be located on halfword integral boundaries.

The general format for halfword (RX) instructions is:

Operation 10	Operand 16
OP	REG,HLFWD

where

OP is any of the operations LH, AH, SH, MH, STH, CH:
These instructions are halfword equivalents of all the instructions discussed in this chapter.

Halfword Instructions	
LH:	Load Halfword
AH:	Add Halfword
SH:	Subtract Halfword
MH:	Multiply Halfword
STH:	Store Halfword
CH:	Compare Halfword

(Because of the limitations placed on the size of the operands, Divide Halfword is *not* an available option.)
REG denotes the first operand is a general register.
HLFWD is a location in storage, 2 bytes in length (and located on a halfword boundary for the S/360).

Comparison of Fullword and Halfword Instructions

	Fullword Instruction	Corresponding Halfword Instruction	Differences
1.	L 8,FULLWD	LH 8,HLFWD	None
2.	A 8,FULLWD	AH 8,HLFWD	None
3.	S 8,FULLWD	SH 8,HLFWD	None
4.	M 8,FULLWD	MH 5,HLFWD	Product is stored in a *single* register. There is no need for even-odd pairs. Product cannot exceed ±2,147,483,647 (decimal). If an arithmetic overflow occurs, it is ignored. Thus an arithmetic overflow will produce incorrect results.
5.	C 5,FULLWD	CH 5,HLFWD	Halfword operand is expanded to fullword for the comparison. Again, negative numbers have a lesser value than positive numbers.
6.	D 8,FULLWD	No halfword instruction exists.	
7.	ST 8,FULLWD	STH 8,HLFWD	The low-order 2 bytes of register 8 (16 bits) are placed in the storage location HLFWD.

Figure 12-5 illustrates a program to solve an equation using RX instructions. Figure 12-6 illustrates a program to solve the same equation using RR instructions.

```
*
*                 HOUSEKEEPING INSTRUCTIONS GO HERE
*
*         SOLVE THE EQUATION R = 8A - 4B + C + 3D + 15 USING RX TYPES
*
          LH      9,AA
          MH      9,=H'8'          8*A IN REG 9
          LH      3,BB
          MH      3,=H'4'          4*B IN REG3
          SR      9,3              8A - 4B
          AH      9,CC
          LH      3,DD
          MH      3,=H'3'
          AR      9,3              8A-4B+C+3D
          AH      9,=H'15'
          CVD     9,DBLE
          MVC     LINEOUT,SPACES
          MVC     LINEOUT+2(6),=X'402020202020'
          ED      LINEOUT+2(6),DATA+1
          PUT     OUTFILE,LINEOUT
*
*                 HOUSEKEEPING INSTRUCTIONS GO HERE
*                 ALONG WITH DTF OR DCB FOR OUTFILE
*
DBLE      DS      0D
          DS      CL4
DATA      DS      CL4
SPACES    DC      C' '
LINEOUT   DS      CL132
AA        DC      H'16'
BB        DC      H'12'
CC        DC      H'125'
DD        DC      H'250'
          END
```

Figure 12-5

```
*
*                 HOUSEKEEPING INSTRUCTIONS GO HERE
*
*         SOLVE THE EQUATION R = 8A - 4B + C + 3D + 15 USING RR TYPES
*
          L       4,A
          AR      4,4              REG4 CONTAINS 2*A
          AR      4,4                   CONTAINS 4*A
          AR      4,4                   CONTAINS 8*A
          L       5,B
          A       5,B              REG5 CONTAINS 2*B
          AR      5,5                           4*B
          SR      4,5              REG4 CONTAINS 8A-4B
          A       4,C                           8A-4B+C
          L       5,D              REG5 CONTAINS D
          A       5,D                           2D
          A       5,D                           3D
          AR      4,5              REG4      8A-4B+C+3D
          L       5,=F'15'
          AR      4,5              REG4      8A-4B+C+3D+15
          CVD     4,DBLE
          MVC     LINEOUT,SPACES
          MVC     LINEOUT+2(6),=X'402020202020'
          ED      LINEOUT+2(6),DATA+1
          PUT     OUTFILE,LINEOUT
*
*                 HOUSEKEEPING INSTRUCTIONS GO HERE
*                 ALONG WITH DCB FOR OUTFILE
*
DBLE      DS      0D
          DS      CL4
DATA      DS      CL4
SPACES    DC      C' '
LINEOUT   DS      CL132
A         DC      F'16'
B         DC      F'12'
C         DC      F'125'
D         DC      F'250'
          END
```

Figure 12-6

SELF-
EVALUATING
QUIZ
For Questions 1–5, indicate the result of each instruction and specify the field description of the operand.

1. CVD   4,TOTAL
2. LH   8,AMT
3. ST   6,ANS
4. M   8,CONST1
5. D   6,CONST2
6. Indicate two types of errors that can occur when a divide operation is executed.

Using binary operations, perform the calculations in Questions 7 and 8.

7. $A = \dfrac{(B - C)}{D}$

8. $E = F^2$

9. RX format instructions are instructions in which _____ .

10. RR format instructions are instructions in which _____ .

Solutions

1. The contents of register 4 are placed in **TOTAL** in *packed-decimal* format. That is, the contents are converted from binary to packed decimal. **TOTAL** must be a doubleword:

   TOTAL   DS   D

2. The contents of **AMT** are loaded into register 8. **AMT** is a halfword:

   AMT   DS   H

3. The contents of register 6 are stored in the field called **ANS**. For S/360, **ANS** must be on a fullword boundary.

4. **CONST1** and the contents of register 9 are multiplied together. Registers 8 and 9 contain the results. **CONST1** must be a fullword field, aligned on a fullword boundary for S/360.

5. **CONST2** is the divisor. The contents of register 7 is divided by **CONST2**. The quotient is contained in register 7 and the remainder is in register 6.

6. Overflow
   Attempt to divide by 0

7.
```
L     5,B
S     5,C
D     4,D
ST    4,A
ST    5,A+4
```

   Notice that the remainder is stored in the fullword at **A** and the quotient is stored in the fullword at **A+4**.

8.
```
L     5,F
M     4,F
ST    4,E
ST    5,E+4
```

9. The first operand is a register and the second operand is a storage location.
10. Both operands are registers.

KEY TERMS

Condition code

Dividend
Divisor

Fullword

Halfword

Multiplicand
Multiplier

Product

Quotient

Remainder

Review Questions

1. Using registers, write a routine to find the product of A and B where A is a number in register 3 and B is a number in register 6.

2. Using registers, write a routine to branch to OUT1 if AMT is between 100.3 and 207.5 inclusive.

3. Using registers, write a program to add all the even numbers from 2 to 100.

4. Using registers, write a routine to find the largest of each set of 3 fields A, B, and C read in on a card. Each field is 5 positions long.

5. Given the following fields:

BALANCE	DS	F
WITHDRWL	DS	F
DEPOSITS	DS	F

Write a routine, using registers, to compute the following:

NEWBAL = BALANCE + DEPOSITS − WITHDRWL

If NEWBAL is zero branch to ALERTRTN

If NEWBAL is negative branch to OVERDRWN

If NEWBAL is positive branch to PRINT

6. Write a routine using registers to compute the following:

$$\text{RESULT} = A \times B - \frac{C + D}{F}$$

where A, B, C, D, and F are defined as fullwords and RESULT is to be a packed-decimal field.

7. Using registers, write a routine to convert Celsius temperatures into Fahrenheit using the formula:

$$F = \frac{9}{5} C + 32$$

F and C are zoned-decimal fields.

8. Given three 5-digit amount fields in cc1-15 (cc1-5, cc6-10, cc11-15) of a card, write a routine to add these quantities using registers and to place the answer in a packed-decimal field called TOTAL. Branch to ERROR if TOTAL is negative.

9. Using registers, write a routine to compute:

$$C = A^2 + B^2$$

Assume A and B are fullwords. C is a zoned-decimal field.

10. Using registers, compute WAGES where:

WAGES = RATE × REGHRS + (1.5 × RATE × OVTHRS).

Two fields are supplied in zoned-decimal form as input: RATE (3 digits) and HRS (2 digits). OVTHRS is equal to the number of hours worked (HRS) in excess of 40, if the employee worked more than 40 hours. REGHRS = 40, if hours worked (HRS) is in excess of 40; otherwise REGHRS = HRS. Note: RATE is to be interpreted as a dollars and cents figure.

Practice Problems

1. Write a program using registers to print out each student's class average. The input records are student class cards with the following format:

  1–20 Student name
21–23 Exam 1 score
24–26 Exam 2 score
27–29 Exam 3 score
30–32 Exam 4 score
33–80 Not used

Each output line should contain student name and class average, spaced anywhere on the line.

NOTE: First line should include heading: CLASS GRADES

2. Write a program to compute compound interest from the following formula using the RR or RX format instructions.

$$P_n = P_0(1 + r)^n$$

P_n = amount of principal after n periods of investment of P_0 at rate r/period

The input is a card file with the following format:

1–6   Principal P_0
7–8   Rate .xx r
9–80 Not used

Output is a printed report with compound interest calculated from periods 1 year to 10 years ($n = 1, 2, \ldots, 10$):

```
                              PRINCIPAL—xxxxxx
                                   RATE—.xx
               PERIODS            AMOUNT
                  1               xxxxxx.xx
                  2               xxxxxx.xx
                  .
                  .
                 10               xxxxxx.xx
```

All amount fields must be edited.

3. Write a program using RR or RX format instructions to compute the arithmetic mean for an input file with the following format:

Card 1 for group: 1–5   Account number
                                 6–7   Number of cards in group
Remainder of cards for group: 1–5   Account number
                                 6–10 Amount

Print. Account number and arithmetic mean for each group.

Chapter 13

Branching and Looping with Registers

Introduction

Assembler language statements are executed in the order in which they appear, unless the computer is instructed to do otherwise with a *branch* instruction.

Thus far, we have learned the method used for unconditional branching:

B   LABEL

We have learned, as well, the method used for conditional branching:

$$\begin{bmatrix} BE \\ BNE \\ BH \\ BL \\ BNH \\ BNL \end{bmatrix} \quad LABEL$$

In this chapter, we will consider additional operation codes that may be used for altering the path of a program. These op codes are used for performing loops.

You will recall that a *loop* is a series of operations performed until a specific condition occurs. Every high-level programming language contains special looping instructions for sequence control, as shown in the following table.

Language	Instruction
BASIC	FOR/NEXT
FORTRAN	DO
COBOL	PERFORM . . . VARYING
PL/1	DO

Branch on Count (BCT) Instruction

Instruction:	BCT
Meaning:	Branch on Count
Operand 1:	Register: Contains number of times loop is to be performed.
Operand 2:	Name or label of an instruction that is the beginning of a loop.

The Branch on Count (BCT) instruction provides the assembly language programmer with loop control. Here is the general format of this instruction.

Operation 10	Operand 16
BCT	REG,LABEL

where

BCT signifies the branch on count loop routine.

REG is a register and contains the number of times the loop is to be repeated.

LABEL references a label appearing in the name field of an instruction. It is usually the first instruction of the loop.

The flowchart in Figure 13-1 indicates the logic inherent in the BCT instructions.

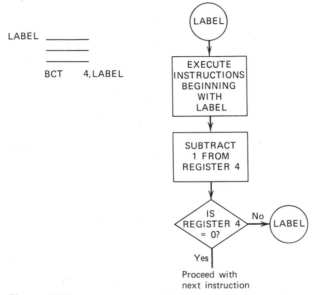

Figure 13-1

Initially, the number of times the loop is to be repeated is placed in the register (REG). The CPU *automatically* subtracts one from the contents of the register (REG) each time the BCT instruction is executed. If, after subtraction, the contents of the register *are not zero,* the program branches to the routine named in the second operand. When the contents of the register reach zero, *no* branch occurs and the instruction *following* the Branch On Count instruction is then executed.

Note that if the register in the above had contents of 0 initially, the logic would be incorrect. One is subtracted from the register *before* it is compared to zero. Hence an initial value of zero would be decreased by 1, making the contents −1, which is not equal to 0. Each additional pass through the routine decreases the register by another 1. The value of the register, then, becomes −1, −2, −3, . . . never reaching zero again. This condition would cause a program interrupt. To avoid it, you must make certain that the initial value of the register used in a BCT is not zero or a negative value.

We will now analyze a series of instructions using the BCT for loop control.

Example 1

Calculate the product: 5 × AVALUE using repeated addition rather than multiplication (Figure 13-2).

The Add instruction will be executed five times. As a result, register 8 will contain the answer, 5 × AVALUE. Note in the example that the BCT instruction references the label DO5X, which is the first instruction of the loop. When the loop is completed, register 2 will contain a zero since one was subtracted each time the BCT instruction was executed.

```
         L      8,=F'0'
         L      2,=F'5'
DO5X     A      8,AVALUE
         BCT    2,DO5X
         ST     8,ANSWER
           .
           .
           .
AVALUE   DC     F'100'
ANSWER   DS     F
```

Figure 13-2

Example 2

Write a routine to add all even numbers from 2 to 100 (Figure 13-3).

```
         L      3,FIFTY        DO 50 TIMES
         L      5,ZEROS        ANSWER REGISTER
         L      2,TWO          EVEN NO.
LOOP     AR     5,2
         A      2,TWO
         BCT    3,LOOP
         ST     5,ANSWER
*
FIFTY    DC     F'50'
ZEROS    DC     F'0'
TWO      DC     F'2'
ANSWER   DS     F
```

Figure 13-3

Example 3

Write a routine to find A^N, where A and N are binary input fields. Assume $N \geq 1$ (Figure 13-4).

```
         L      3,N
         L      5,ONE
LOOP     M      4,A
         BCT    3,LOOP
           .
           .
           .
*
ONE      DC     F'1'
```

Figure 13-4

The programmer must make sure that the loop is always entered from the top so that the control register is initialized. If, for some reason, this instruction is bypassed and we enter in the middle of the loop, we would have a serious problem.

Load and Test Register (LTR)   We noted above that the register used in a BCT instruction should not have an initial value which is zero or negative. This would cause the register to be decreased by one each time (-1, -2, -3, . . .), which would result in an infinite loop.

The programmer can avoid this problem by using a Load and Test Register instruction. A Load and Test Register (LTR) instruction sets the condition code. It may be followed by any of the following conditional branches.

Conditional Branches That Can Be Used After Arithmetic or LTR Instructions

Op Code	Meaning
BZ	Branch if Zero
BM	Branch if Minus
BP	Branch if Positive
BNZ	Branch if Not Zero
BNM	Branch if Not Minus
BNP	Branch if Not Positive

Instruction:	LTR
Meaning:	Load and Test Register
Operand 1:	General register
Operand 2:	General register (same)
Purpose:	Used for testing the contents of a register for −, +, 0 value; usually followed by BM, BP, BZ.
Application:	1. To avoid the possibility of BCT causing an infinite loop.
	2. To avoid the possibility of dividing by zero.
	3. In general, to test the sign of a register.

The LTR instruction is used in a manner similar to that described for the ZAP instruction. To determine if the control register (register 9, for example) contains a negative value, we simply add the following instructions to the loop (Figure 13-5).

```
LTR    9,9
BM     ERROR
```

Figure 13-5

If register 9 inadvertently contained a negative number, the condition code would be set and the program would branch to a routine named ERROR and the infinite loop would be avoided.

An infinite loop may also occur if the register inadvertently contained zero. We therefore include the following within the loop (Figure 13-6).

```
LOOP       .
           .
           .
           LTR    9,9
           BNP    ERROR
           BCT    9,LOOP
```

Figure 13-6

The above insures that register 9 remains positive throughout the loop.

The LTR instruction may be used in a similar manner to prevent the computer from inadvertently dividing by zero. You will recall that a divisor of zero will cause a program interrupt when a divide instruction is executed. If the divisor is in a register, then the LTR instruction can be used prior to the divide (Figure 13-7).

```
LTR    5,5
BZ     ERROR
DR     2,5
```

Figure 13-7

In summary, whenever the sign of the contents of a register must be known, the LTR instruction can be used.

The Branch Register (BR)
and Load Address (LA)
Instructions

The Branch Register (BR) instruction causes a branch to the *address* stored in the referenced register.

Instruction:	BR
Meaning:	Branch to Address Specified in Register.
Operands:	Operand 1 only—Register that contains address to be branched to.

Here is the general format.

Operation 10	Operand 16
BR	REG

It functions identically to the Branch (B) instruction; however the general register contains the *address of the instruction* to which we want to branch. For example, if register 9 contained the address of the instruction named LOOP, the program would branch to LOOP using either of the following.

Unconditional Branch to LOOP

LABEL	OPERATION 10	16
	B	L,O,O,P

or

LABEL	OPERATION 10	16
	B,R	9

The BR instruction provides the programmer with still another means of unconditional branching. To use the BR instruction correctly, we place the address of an instruction (LOOP) in the register. The actual loading of an address into the register is performed with the Load Address (LA) instruction that follows.

Load Address (LA)

The purpose of the Load Address (LA) instruction is to place an *address* of a reference point (label) in a program into a register. This address then becomes the branch point for branching operations. Here is the general format.

Operation	Operand
LA	REG,LABEL

where

LA   indicates the RX instruction Load Address.

REG   is a general register that receives the address of the instruction named in the second operand.

LABEL   identifies a labeled instruction or an entry point in the program.

For example, the two sets of instructions illustrated below would both cause an unconditional branch to the instruction named LOOP.

LABEL	OPERATION 10	16
	B	L,O,O,P

LABEL	OPERATION 10	16
	L,A	9,,L,O,O,P
	B,R	9

The Load Address instruction places the actual or effective address of LOOP in register 9. The BR instruction creates an unconditional branch to the effective *address* stored in register 9, which is the instruction identified as LOOP. If the instruction identified as LOOP were stored in the actual location 8C910, then the address 8C910 would be placed in register 9 when the LA instruction was executed.

Branch On Count
Register (BCTR)

Instruction:	BCTR
Meaning:	Branch on Count Register
Operand 1:	Register that contains the number of times a loop is to be repeated.
Operand 2:	Register that contains the address of first instruction of the loop.

NOTE: Address must be loaded into operand 2 *before* BCTR is executed.

The BCTR like BCT instruction is used to control the looping process. The difference, however, is that the second operand is a *register* in the BCTR instruction instead of a label. This register points to the entry point in the program where the loop begins. The address of the entry point (the beginning of the loop) must first be placed in a register using a Load Address (LA) instruction.

The general format for the BCTR is as follows:

Operation 10	Operand 16
BCTR	REG1,REG2

where
BCTR   denotes a *B*ranch on *Count* *R*egister operation.
REG1   contains the number of times the loop is to be repeated.
REG2   contains the address of the beginning (first instruction) of the loop.

The number of times the loop is to be repeated is placed in the first operand (REG1). The *address of the first instruction* (the beginning of the loop) is loaded into the second operand (REG2). As with the BCT instruction, the contents of REG1 are reduced by one *automatically* with each pass through the loop. As long as the contents of REG1 are not zero, the program branches to the *address* stored in the second operand (REG2). When REG1 reaches zero, no branch occurs and the instruction following the BCTR instruction is executed next. A sample program will tie these ideas together.

In the following example, multiplication will be performed by repeated addition. See Figure 13-8. Compare this example with that presented for the BCT instruction and note that the only differences are:

1.   The Load Address (LA) instruction is used.

2.   The BCT instruction is replaced by a BCTR.

```
              LA      5,DO5X
              L       2,=F'5'
   DO5X       A       8,AVALUE
              BCTR    2,5
              ST      8,ANSWER
              .
              .
              .
   AVALUE     DC      F'100'
   ANSWER     DS      F
```

Figure 13-8

Another use of the BCTR instruction is to subtract one from any register at any time in the program. This occurs when the second operand is identified as *register zero*. For example, the instructions

LABEL	OPERATION		
1	10	16	
	BCTR	8,0	

LABEL	OPERATION		
1	10	16	
	S	8,=F'1'	

will both cause the contents of register 8 to be reduced by one.

Again, a word of caution is advised in using both the BCT and BCTR instructions. If the initial count is zero, the first execution of the instruction (BCT or BCTR) will result in a minus one being stored in the first operand. This will cause a branch to occur since the count is not zero and we will find ourselves in an endless loop. It is most important that the programmer realize that the CPU does not check the contents of the count register until *after* it has subtracted one. An understanding of these concepts provides the programmer with a powerful tool: automatic loop control.

Summary
1. The BCT and BCTR instructions are used for loop control.
2. The first operand is always a register and contains the number of times the loop is to be repeated.
3. Each time the loop is repeated, one is automatically subtracted from the contents of the first operand.
4. If the contents of the first operand are not zero, a branch to the beginning of the loop occurs.
5. When the first operand reaches zero, no branch occurs and the instruction following the BCT/BCTR is then executed.
6. The Load and Test Register (LTR) instruction may be used to test the control register and insure that its contents are not negative.
7. The Load Address (LA) instruction is used to store the address of the first instruction of a loop in a register so that the BCTR may be used.

KEY TERMS
Control register

Infinite loop
Initialization

Loop

SELF-
EVALUATING
QUIZ

**SELF-
EVALUATING
QUIZ**

1. Write a routine to perform a loop function 5 times.
2. Indicate the error in the following:

```
              L              5,=F'0'
LOOP

              ____
              ____
              ____
              ____
              BCT            5,LOOP
```

3. What sequence of steps may be used to insure that an infinite loop will not inadvertently be executed?

Indicate what, if anything, is wrong with the following two instructions.

4. RTN1   BCT   9,RTN1
5. LOOP   L   9,=F'1'
             AR   6,5
             BCT   9,LOOP

6. Consider the following:

```
EAST          ____
              ____
              ____
              BCT            5,EAST
```

After proceeding through **EAST** the first time, register 5 is _____ .
Then a _____ is performed. If register 5 is _____ , a branch to **EAST** occurs. If not, then _____ .

7. Code a single instruction that can be used in place of the following:

```
LA        7,LOOP1
BR        7
```

8. Using a BR instruction, code a branch to RTN5.
9. When is a BCTR instruction used in place of a BCT instruction?
10. Write a routine to sum all the odd integers from 1 to 101.

Solutions

1.
```
              L              5,=F'5'
LOOP          ____
              ____
              ____
              BCT            5,LOOP
```

2. The result will be an infinite loop. Since register 5 has an initial value of 0, BCT will decrease the register by 1 and then compare it to 0. Register 5 will become $-1, -2, -3, \ldots$, never reaching zero again.

3.
```
LTR       5,5
BNP       ERROR
```
These instructions should directly precede the BCT instruction.

4. The label RTN1 should be on the first instruction of the *loop*.

5. The load instruction that initializes the control register should not be inside the loop. In addition, since a value of 1 is placed in the control register there is no need to set up a loop at all! These instructions are not intended to be repeated.

6. Decreased by 1
   Test or comparison
   Not equal to 0
   The next sequential instruction is executed.

7. B   LOOP1

8.
```
LA        6,RTN5
BR        6
```

9. When the address of an instruction to be branched to is in a register.

```
BCT          5,LOOP1
        or
LA           9,LOOP1
        .
        .
        .
BCTR         5,9
```

10. One solution follows in Figure 13-9.

```
          L     5,=F'50'
          L     3,=F'0'
          L     2,=F'1'
LOOP      AR    3,2
          A     2,=F'2'
          BCT   5,LOOP
```

Figure 13-9

Review Questions

1. Write a routine to determine $N!$, where $N! = N \times N - 1 \times N - 2 \times \ldots 1$
   For example, $5! = 5 \times 4 \times 3 \times 2 \times 1$.

2. Given P_0, r, n, compute
   $$P_N = P_0(1 + r)^N$$

   where

   P_0 = principal
   r = rate .xx
   N = Number of periods of investment of P_0 at rate r/period
   P_N = principal after N periods of investment of P_0 at rate r/period

3. Write a program to read in 20 cards each with a student name in CC 1–20 and a final exam grade in CC 21–23. Print the class average.

4. There are 15 salesmen in company **ABC**. For each salesman, there are 5 input cards, one for each day of the week.
   1–2 Salesman number
     3 Day number (1–5)
   4–8 Amount of sales
   Prepare a report that prints for each salesman the salesman number and the weekly sales amount.

UNIT V

Debugging
Assembler Programs

Chapter 14

Using Instruction Formats and Interrupt Codes for Debugging Programs

I. Instruction Formats

The following table provides an overview of the five instruction types in assembler language and their actual length when translated into machine language.

Instruction Types

Description	Format	Instruction Length in Bytes
Register to Register (Both operands are registers.)	RR	2
Register and Indexed Storage (Operand 1—register Operand 2—storage)	RX	4
Register and Storage (Operand 1—register Operand 2—storage)	RS	4
Storage Immediate (Operand 1—storage Operand 2—one byte constant defined within instruction)	SI	4
Storage to Storage (both operands are storage locations)	SS	6

To read storage dumps and to understand how instructions actually appear in machine language, it is necessary to be able to determine the format of each instruction and the number of bytes it utilizes.

From the above, we see that instruction formats can be specified in three lengths: one, two or three halfwords (2, 4, or 6 bytes) depending upon the general category and the specific operation code or mnemonic. Before discussing each instruction format, these general rules apply:

General Rules

1. Operation Codes = 1 byte
   Every operation code, regardless of the format of the instruction, is *one* byte long (two hexadecimal digits).

2. The first *two bits* of each operation code specify the type of instruction, as in the following table.

Two High-Order Bits of Op Code
Indicate Instruction Type

High-Order Bits	Instruction Type
00	RR
01	RX
10	RS ⎱ Note these are
10	SI ⎰ the same.
11	SS

A. One Halfword Instructions: RR   Note that an instruction in which both operands are general registers is 2 bytes, or one halfword, in length.

RR Format

OP CODE	FIRST OPERAND	SECOND OPERAND
OP	R1	R2

Machine language equivalent   8 bits   4 bits   4 bits   = 2 bytes

For RR-type instructions, as with most assembly language instructions, the first operand is the receiving field. The 4 bits used to represent R1 and the 4 bits used to represent R2 can contain 0000–1111 in binary, or 0–15 in decimal. Since general registers can be numbered from 0–15, the 4-bit representation suffices.

Example

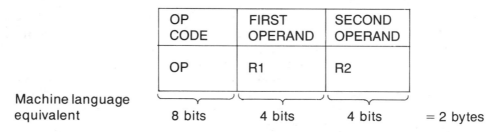

Assembly Instruction	Machine Language Equivalent
AR 4,5	OP R1 R2

Binary | 0001   1010 | 0100   0101 |

Hex | 1 | A | 4 | 5 |

On the inside of the back cover is a listing of the machine language equivalent for each RR instruction discussed in this text. Figure 14-1 illustrates sample RR instructions.

Figure 14-1   Sample RR instructions.

Instruction	Op Code	Machine Language Equivalent
Add Registers	AR	1A
Branch and Link Registers	BALR	05
Branch on Condition	BCR	07
Branch on Count	BCTR	06
Compare Registers	CR	19
Divide Registers	DR	1D
Load Registers	LR	18
Multiply Registers	MR	1C
Subtract Registers	SR	1B

High-Order Bits

Note that the first two bits of each operation code that utilizes two registers as its operands are *00*.

If the AR instruction is stored beginning in address 3001, for example, then bytes 3001–3002 when printed as part of a dump will appear as

1   A   4   5

B. Two Halfword Instructions

{ RX
  RS
  SI

All instructions of this type have one operand that is defined as a storage location and another operand that is not. These instructions are two halfwords or 4 bytes in length.

1. RX Instructions (see Figure 14-2)

Figure 14-2 Sample RX instructions.

Instruction	Op Code	Machine Language Equivalent
Add	A	5A
Add Halfword	AH	4A
Branch and Link	BAL	45
Branch on Condition	BC	47
Branch on Count	BCT	46
Compare	C	59
Compare Halfword	CH	49
Convert to Binary	CVB	4F
Convert to Decimal	CVD	4E
Divide	D	5D
Load	L	58
Load Address	LA	41
Load Halfword	LH	48
Multiply	M	5C
Multiply Halfword	MH	4C
Store	ST	50
Store Halfword	STH	40
Subtract	S	5B
Subtract Halfword	SH	4B

RX Format

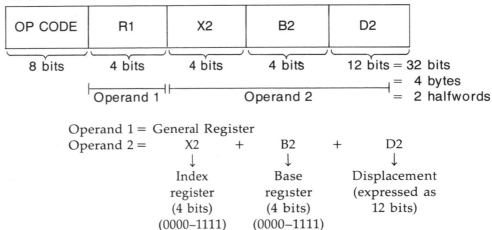

Operand 1 = General Register
Operand 2 = $X2$ + $B2$ + $D2$

B2 and D2   All effective addresses of storage areas are obtained by adding:

    a. A 12-bit displacement (D2)
        this is the absolute storage address from 000–4095 in value

    b. The 24 lower-order bits of the base register (B2)
        (3 low-order bytes)

      As we will see, all storage areas must be defined using this 36-bit representation—12 bits for the displacement and 24 bits for the base register.

X2   For RX-type instructions *only*, an additional specification is necessary for determining the effective address of the storage area, in this case the second operand. X2 refers to a general register that may be used for indexing, which is a form of address modification discussed in Chapter 16. If, however, an RX format instruction is required and no indexing is utilized, then X2 will contain 0000.

Example
The Add instruction:

LABEL	OPERATION 10	16
	A	2,TOTAL

is an RX instruction. TOTAL is a storage area, which when converted to machine language, is specified with an index register X2, a base register, B2, and a displacement, D2. Hence this Add may be represented as follows (the actual representation will depend on the address assigned to TOTAL):

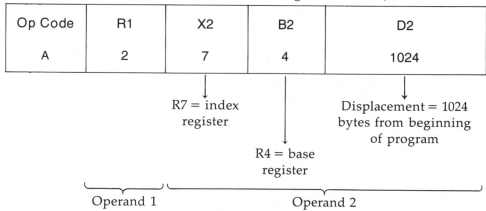

Op Code	R1	X2	B2	D2
A	2	7	4	1024

R7 = index register

R4 = base register

Displacement = 1024 bytes from beginning of program

Operand 1   Operand 2

|Operation—Add|
Operand 1 = Contents of general register 2
Operand 2 = the effective address of TOTAL
           = contents of register 7 + contents of register 4 + 1024

Machine Language Equivalent

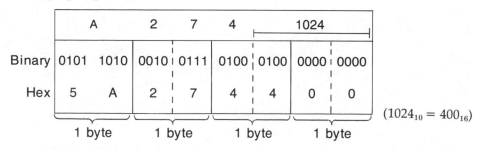

	A	2	7	4		1024	
Binary	0101 1010	0010	0111	0100	0100	0000	0000
Hex	5	A	2	7	4	4	0	0

    1 byte   1 byte   1 byte   1 byte

$(1024_{10} = 400_{16})$

Note that all dumps will print the hex notation. Hence the above would be expressed in a storage dump as:

5A 27 44 00

High-Order Bits The actual machine language equivalent of the A instruction had 01 in its first two high-order bits. In fact, *all* RX instructions have a 01 in the two high-order bits of the operation code.

2. RS Instructions (see Figure 14-3)

Figure 14-3 Sample RS instructions.†

Instruction	Op Code	Machine Language Equivalent
Branch on Index High	BXH	86
Branch on Index Low or Equal	BXLE	87
Load Multiple	LM	98

† (These will be discussed in later chapters.)

The RS instructions, like the preceding RX type, are register and storage instructions. The RS type, however, does *not* have an indexing factor but may include a third specification as part of the operands.

RS Format

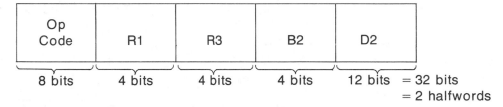

Op Code	R1	R3	B2	D2
8 bits	4 bits	4 bits	4 bits	12 bits

= 32 bits
= 2 halfwords

Example
The Load Multiple Instruction:

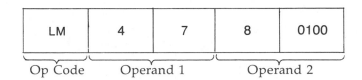

LABEL	OPERATION	OPERAND
	LM	4,7,TOTAL LOADS TOTAL INTO R4-R7

will require **TOTAL** to be translated into some address that specifies a base register and a displacement as in the following:

LM	4	7	8	0100

Op Code — Operand 1 — Operand 2

Purpose of the Instruction
Contents of registers 4–7 are replaced by the contents of the storage locations beginning at Operand 2.

In the above, **TOTAL**, which is Operand 2, has an effective address of B2 + D2. That is, the contents of register 8 are added to the displacement of 100 to obtain the effective address.

Machine Language Equivalent

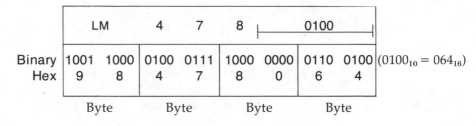

A dump would list this instruction as

9 8 4 7 8 0 6 4

High-Order Bits   RS instructions all have 10 in the first 2 bits of the operation code.

3. SI Instructions (see Figure 14-4)

Figure 14-4   Sample SI instructions.

Instruction	Op Code	Machine Language Equivalent
Compare Logical Immediate	CLI	95
Move Immediate	MVI	92

This format is employed when the first operand is in main storage and the second operand is contained within the instruction itself.

SI Format

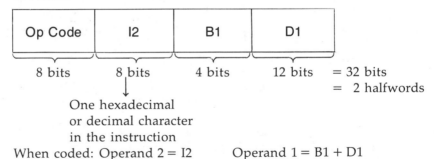

Note that the machine language equivalent of SI instructions places the second operand coded, I2, in bits 8–15 and the first operand coded which is B1 + D1 in bits 16–31. The order of the operands, then, is reversed during the conversion.

Example
The Move Immediate instruction:

LABEL	OPERATION 10 16	OPERAND
	M V I	H O L D , C ' 5 '

may convert to the following, depending upon the actual address of HOLD.

MVI	5	4	1000

Machine Language Equivalent

MVI		5	4	1000	
1001 0010	1111 0101	0100 0011	1110 1000		
9 2	F 5	4 3	E 8		

NOTE: This is actually *coded* as the second operand but is assembled as indicated.

High-Order Bits   Like the RS format, SI instructions always have a 10 in the high-order bits of the op code.

C. 3 Halfword Instructions: SS   See Figure 14-5.

Figure 14-5 Sample SS instructions.

Instruction	Op Code	Machine Language Equivalent
Add Packed Decimal	AP	FA
Compare Packed Decimal	CP	F9
Divide Packed Decimal	DP	FD
Multiply Packed Decimal	MP	FC
Edit	ED	DE
Subtract Packed Decimal	SP	FB
Zero and Add Packed	ZAP	F8
Compare Logical	CLC	D5
Move Characters	MVC	D2
Pack	PACK	F2
Unpack	UNPK	F3

These instructions are sometimes called variable length formats since the actual number of storage positions affected by the instruction is not fixed but depends on the specification of the specific operation itself. The length of the instruction itself, however, is fixed.

SS Format

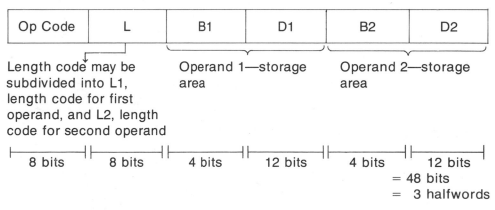

Length Code   The length code specifies the number of bytes (*in excess of one*) that are to be processed. Hence, if the length of an operand to be operated on is 4 bytes, the length code would contain 3 (3 bytes in excess of 1 are to be processed).

For some instructions, such as move operations, only one length code is required. That is, for these instructions one operand determines the length of the operation (only one explicit length may be indicated). For other instructions such as the Add operation, the length of *both* operands may be specified.

Example
The Add Packed instruction:

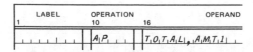

must convert **TOTAL** and **AMT1** to actual machine addresses. The following represents a partial conversion:

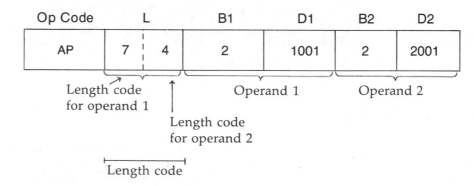

Suppose base register 2 contains 1000. Operand 1 would have an address of 2001 (1001 + 1000) while Operand 2 would have an address of 3001 (2001 + 1000).

The length code of 7 means that *8* bytes of the first operand are operated on. The length code of 4 means that *5* bytes of the second operand are operated on.

Result
The above operation would result in the addition of the contents of storage locations 3001–3005 to 2001–2008.

Machine Language Equivalent

AP	7	4	2	1001	2	2001
1111 1010	0111 0100	0010 0011	1110 1001	0010 0111	1101 0001
F A	7 4	2 3	E 9	2 7	D 1
⊢Op Code⊣⊢	L ⊣⊢B1⊣⊢	D1 ⊣	⊢B2⊣ ⊢	D2 ⊣	

High-Order Bits For SS instructions, the first two bits of the operation code will contain 11.

Summary
On the inside of the back cover there is a table that indicates:

> Every instruction discussed in this text.
> The format for that instruction.
> The machine language op code.

This information will prove exceedingly useful when debugging programs. Using this table you can determine the machine language equivalent of all instructions. Moreover, you can read a dump and determine the meaning of each machine instruction by translating it using this table.

1. When instructions are assembled they may be __(number)__ , __(number)__ , or __(number)__ bytes in length. Hence all instruction addresses are divisible by __(number)__ .
*****
2, 4, 6
2

2. The first part of every instruction is the _____, which is __(number)__ bits long.
*****
Operation code
8

3. A program can be relocated in storage by changing the contents of the _____ register.
*****
base

4. All storage addresses are obtained by adding the contents of the _____ to the _____. RX format instructions require a(n) _____ whose contents must also be added to obtain a storage address.
*****
base register
displacement
index register

5. Each register is converted to a __(number)__ bit representation.
*****
four

6. The displacement is specified as a __(number)__ bit field.
*****
12

7. For the following operation codes expressed hexadecimally, indicate the binary or bit configuration of the two high-order bits. From this configuration derive the length of the instruction in halfwords. Then "look up" the instruction in the table that appears on the inside of the back cover.
   a. 1A
   b. 95
   c. FD

   *****
   a. 1A

0001	1010

   RR
   one halfword
   1A = **AR** instruction (Add Register)
   b. 95

1001	0101

   (RS or SI)
   two halfwords
   95 = **CLI** instruction (Compare Logical Immediate). Therefore, we know it is **SI** format.

c. FD

SS

three halfwords

FD = **DP** instruction (Divide Packed Decimal)

8. The displacement has a range, in decimal, from 0 to ___(number)___ bytes.

*****

4095. This is the largest number that can be represented in 12 bits.

9. Only general registers ___(number)___ through ___(number)___ can be used as a base register.

*****

2–12

10. Label the fields in the following formats. Also indicate the number of bits for each field:

a. RR
b. RX
c. RS
d. SI
e. SS

*****

a. RR

b. RX

c. RS

d. SI

e. SS

11. For most assembler instructions, the results replace the _(first/second)_ operand.

*****

first

12. Only the _____ format uses an index register.

*****

RX

13. Only the _____ format requires a length code to indicate the number of bytes to be operated on.

*****

SS

14. In the SI format, the second operand (I2), is ___(number)___ bytes long.

*****

one

15. Given the following machine language instructions, give the assembler language equivalent. Assume the following storage definitions and base register 3.

```
1000    TOTAL    DS    PL4
1004    HOLD     DS    PL4
```

a.

1 9	5 3

b.

1 8	7 9

c.

F 9	3 3	3 3	E 8	3 3	E C

*****

```
a.    CR    5,3
b.    LR    7,9
c.    CP    TOTAL,HOLD
```

II. Program Interrupts and Program Status Words

Introduction

On first and second generation computers any unanticipated problem would cause the computer to "hang up," that is, stop processing. It was then the operator's job to determine the source of the problem, correct it if possible, or abort the job and move on to the next application. Such a procedure was exceedingly inefficient since the time required to resolve a problem while the computer was idle proved to be very costly.

Third and fourth generation computers are designed to operate with minimum manual intervention and maximum computer efficiency. The *supervisor* controls the operations of the computer in such a way that when unanticipated situations arise it can redirect the activities of the machine, resolve or bypass the source of the problem, or abort a job if necessary and read in the next job. The method used to handle problems is called an *automatic interrupt system* and is under the control of the supervisor.

If you have actually run any programs, you are probably familiar with the procedure used by the computer to handle programming errors. This procedure is part of the interrupt system. If a major error has occurred in your program, the supervisor prints an error message, aborts the run, and automatically begins to process the next program.

There are other types of interrupts in addition to those caused by program errors, as listed below.

Types of Interrupts
1. Conditions external to the system, (for example, the interrupt key is depressed and the system is turned off)
2. Input/output problem
3. Program error
4. Machine error
5. Supervisor call, (for example, the end of job results in an interrupt that returns control to the supervisor)

Note that every job ends with an interrupt. If the job has been processed with no execution errors, the interrupt that occurs is called a "Supervisor Call." In assembly language, when the END statement is executed, this "Supervisor

Call" interrupt returns control to the supervisor so that the next program may be processed.

When debugging a program, you may find that other interrupts have caused your job to be aborted. Most often, however, it is a program error that was responsible and we will focus our attention, for the most part, on program interrupts. Keep in mind, however, that a job that has been aborted can be the result of one of the other interrupts.

To determine the cause of an aborted run, the programmer must be able to read and decipher the Program Status Word (PSW), which provides valuable information on the status of a program at the time an interrupt has occurred. Learning how to interpret a PSW will not only enable you to find the actual type of interrupt and/or error that caused the problem, but will provide you with information on the contents of key fields when the interrupt occurred.

Program Status Words (PSW)
And Interrupts

Each time an instruction is executed a *Current PSW* is generated. This is a doubleword of information on the status of that instruction. If any interrupt occurs (machine, program, supervisor, external or I/O), the current PSW is placed in a field called the *Old PSW*. The address of a routine used to patch or resolve such an interrupt is automatically loaded into the current PSW by the supervisor. If the interrupt can be resolved by the interrupt handling routine, then the old PSW is loaded back into the current PSW and the program continues.

When an Interrupt Occurs

1.   Current PSW

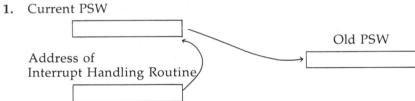

2.   Interrupt Handling Routine

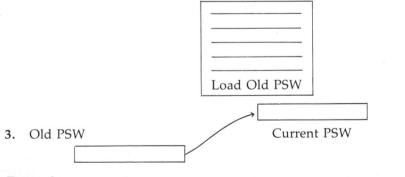

3.   Old PSW

Example

Suppose a PUT instruction is executed that attempts to write a line on the printer. If there is no paper in the printer, an interrupt will occur. The current PSW is loaded into the Old PSW. The supervisor calls in an interrupt handling routine that prints a message on the console to the computer operator. Once the printer is ready, the interrupt handling routine loads the Old PSW back into the current PSW and the program continues executing.

Most often the interrupt handling routine is part of the operating system. It is, however, possible for programmers to write their own interrupt handling routines. Such a procedure is considered beyond the scope of this text.

When an irresolvable program error or other interrupt has occurred, the machine simply prints the contents of the PSW, aborts the job, and reads in the next job. (If the interrupt that occurs is a result of a machine error, the computer shuts itself off completely.)

Contents of PSW

As an overview, note that the following elements are part of the doubleword PSW that provides the programmer with the status of a program at the time of an interrupt.

Elements of the PSW: An Overview
1. Type of interrupt
2. Address of next instruction to be executed
3. Length of the previous instruction
4. Condition Code at time of interrupt
5. The state of the CPU at time of interrupt
   stopped or operating
   problem or supervisory state
6. Status of system (to be discussed)

We will *not* discuss the entire PSW in depth but only those elements that are likely to be of value when debugging a program. The other elements will be discussed only briefly.

Interrupt Code   You will recall that the PSW is a 64-bit, or doubleword, field with bits numbered 0–63. The interrupt code is in bits 16–31:

PSW

	Interrupt code	

0   16   31   63

Bits 16–23 of the interrupt code provide information on the exact type of interrupt that occurred. Since we are focusing our attention on program interrupts, we will not concern ourselves with the contents of bits 16–23. Bits 24–31, however, provide the programmer with the type of program error that caused the interrupt, as given below.

Interrupt Codes (Bits 24–31 of PSW)

Hexadecimal	Binary	Error Condition
01	0000 0001	Operation
02	0000 0010	Privileged operation
03	0000 0011	Execute
04	0000 0100	Protection
05	0000 0101	Addressing
06	0000 0110	Specification
07	0000 0111	Data
08	0000 1000	Fixed-point overflow
09	0000 1001	Fixed-point divide
0A	0000 1010	Decimal overflow
0B	0000 1011	Decimal divide
†0C	0000 1100	Exponent overflow
†0D	0000 1101	Exponent underflow
0E	0000 1110	Significance
†0F	0000 1111	Floating-point divide

† Error conditions that are outside the scope of
this book.

Here are some examples of error conditions that cause interrupts.

Examples

1. **Specification Error (06)**

LABEL	OPERATION	OPERAND
1	10	16
	Z A P	T O T A L , A M T
	.	
	.	
	.	
T O T A L	D S	P L 6
A M T	D C	C L 5 ' 1 2 3 4 5 '

AMT is not a valid packed field. When the interrupt occurs and the PSW is printed, bits 24–31 will contain 00000110 (06) that denotes a specification error.

2. **Decimal Divide (0B)**

LABEL	OPERATION	OPERAND
1	10	16
	D P	S A L E S , Q T Y
	.	
	.	
	.	
S A L E S	D S	P L 5
Q T Y	D C	P L 3 ' ∅ ∅ ∅ '

Any attempt to divide by zero will produce a **0B** interrupt.

Similary, a quotient too large for the allotted field will produce this interrupt.

The following table represents a more extensive explanation of the kinds of interrupts you may encounter. (The interrupts that occur in the case of more complex instructions have been omitted):

Type of Interrupts

Interrupt Code	Definition	Meaning
1	Operation	Op code is illegal
2	Privileged operation	Attempt made to execute an instruction that can only be executed in supervisor state.
4	Protection	Attempt made to operate on data in storage protection area.
5	Addressing	Address used is outside limits of available storage.
6	Specification	Incorrect operand—(i.e. If first operand (register) is odd in D, DR, M, and MR instruction, this error will result; incorrect boundary alignment will also cause this error.)
7	Data	Operand does not contain valid digit and/or sign.

| 8 | Fixed-point overflow | Binary operations that produce results too large to be accommodated. |
| 9 | Fixed-point divide | Attempt to divide by zero or quotient too large for receiving field. |

PSW: Address of Next Instruction to Be Executed

PSW

	Interrupt Code		Address of Next Instruction to Be Executed
	16	31	40 63

The low-order 24 bits of the doubleword PSW contain the address of the next instruction to be executed. Consider the following:

Storage Location		*Instruction*
2060	DP	HOLD,AMT
2066	AP	TOTAL,AMT

If this program were aborted and bits 40–63 of the PSW contained the address 2066, then the instruction *prior* to the one at 2066, in this case the DP, would be in error.

In general, one would look at the instruction directly preceding the one specified in the PSW for an error. This cannot, however, be taken as a general rule. If an instruction that is branched to from several points in a program has its address indicated in the PSW, then the erroneous instruction could be any of the instructions prior to the branch. Consider the following instructions:

LABEL	OPERATION	OPERAND
STEP1	AP	TOTAL,AMT1
	B	STEP3
STEP2	CP	HOLD,AMT2
	BE	STEP3
	B	STEP1
STEP2A	MVI	LINEOUT+6,C'5'
STEP3	.	
	.	
	.	

If the address of STEP3 were listed in the PSW, *any* of the instructions prior to the branch to STEP3 (AP, CP, MVI) could be in error.

Instruction Length Code   The instruction length code (ILC) appears in bits 32–33 of the PSW.

PSW

	Interrupt Code	ILC		Instruction Address
	16 31	32 33		40 63

The ILC is interpreted as follows:

ILC			
Binary Value of ILC	Decimal Value	Length of Last Instruction	Format of Last Instruction
01	1	1 halfword	RR
10	2	2 halfwords	RX, RS, SI
11	3	3 halfwords	SS

As indicated above, it is not always possible to determine the source of an error simply by knowing the address of the next instruction to be executed (bits 40–63). If that next instruction can be reached from several points, the exact cause of the error may not be obvious.

By using the Instruction Length Code (ILC), however, we can determine the length of the last instruction executed. This information, combined with knowledge of the next instruction to be executed, may be enough to determine precisely the source of the error.

If, in our previous illustration, the ILC were 10, we would know that the instruction in error was the MVI, not the AP or CP. The MVI, an SI instruction, has a 4-byte length whereas AP and CP, as SS instructions, are each 6 bytes in length.

Condition Code Bits 34–35 of the PSW indicate the setting of the condition code at the time of the interrupt:

PSW

	Interrupt code	ILC	CC		Instruction address

0   16   31 32   33 34   35   40   63

Condition codes are affected by arithmetic and compare instructions as shown in the following table.

Review of Condition Codes

ARITHMETIC

Arithmetic Result	Condition Code	
	Binary	Hex
= 0	00	0
< 0	01	1
> 0	10	2
Overflow	11	3

COMPARISON

	Condition Code	
	Binary	Hexa-decimal
=	00	0
Low	01	1
High	10	2

Note that a condition code remains set until another arithmetic or compare instruction resets it. Hence, if an Add instruction, for example, results in an overflow, the condition code of 11 may remain part of the PSW even if the interrupt occurs several instructions after the Add.

Use of condition codes in debugging programs is helpful in determining the value of the last arithmetic or compare instruction executed.

State of CPU   There are four bits referred to as AMWP that are specified in bits 12–15 of the PSW.

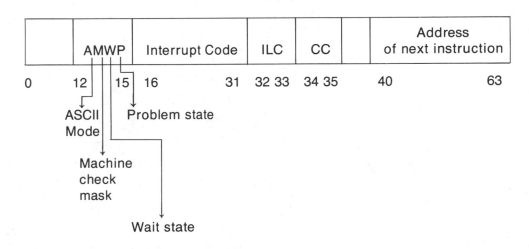

Each of these AMWP bits can contain a 0 or 1.

AMWP Bits (12–15)

Bit	Code	Meaning	Values		Standard Entry When Executing
			0	1	
12	A	Is mode ASCII or EBCDIC?	EBCDIC	ASCII	0
13	M	Should machine failure cause interrupt?	Mask or avoid interrupt	Machine check will cause interrupt	1
14	W	Is machine in wait or run state?	Run	Wait	0
15	P	Is machine in problem or supervisory state?	Supervisory state	Problem state	1

System Considerations   The remaining fields of the PSW usually are not of much significance to the student. We will list them here, but not provide an indepth analysis.

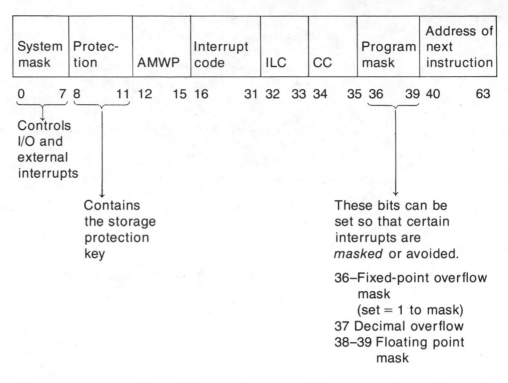

System mask	Protec- tion	AMWP	Interrupt code	ILC	CC	Program mask	Address of next instruction

0   7 8   11 12   15 16   31 32 33 34   35 36   39 40   63

Controls
I/O and
external
interrupts

Contains
the storage
protection
key

These bits can be
set so that certain
interrupts are
masked or avoided.

36–Fixed-point overflow
    mask
    (set = 1 to mask)
37 Decimal overflow
38–39 Floating point
      mask

The program can use special instructions to mask interrupts. These change the contents of the Program Mask field of the PSW.

SELF-EVALUATING QUIZ

1. PSW is an abbreviation for _____.
2. The number of bits in a PSW is __(number)__.
3. When an interrupt occurs, the current PSW is moved to _____ PSW and an _____ is moved to current PSW.
4. Indicate the types of interrupts that can occur.
5. When a program is finished, it signals the supervisor via an _____.
6. The location and type of the last instruction executed prior to the interrupt can be determined by examining the _____ PSW.
7. Provide a schematic of the PSW.
8. Which part of the PSW can actually be programmed?
9. A 1 in bit 14 of the PSW signals _____.
10. A 11 in bits 34–35 signals that _____.
11. (True or False) Knowing the instruction address of the next instruction to be executed will always provide you with the instruction which caused the interrupt.
12. If ILC contained a 11, the format of the instruction that caused the error is _____.

Solutions

1. Program status word
2. 64
3. OLD; interrupt-handling routine address
4. Machine
   Program
   I/O
   External
   Supervisor

5. Interrupt (supervisor call)
6. OLD
7.

System mask	Protection key	AMWP	Inter-rupt code	ILC	CC	Program mask	Instruc-tion address
0 7	8 11	12 15	16 31	32 33	34 35	36 39	40 63

8. Program mask
9. That the program is in the wait state
10. An overflow condition has occurred
11. False. If it were branched to from several points, we may not know.
12. SS format

KEY TERMS
Debug

Execution phase
External interrupts

Input/Output interrupts
Instruction Length Code (ILC)
Interrupt
Interrupt code

Machine check interrupt
Masking

Problem state
Program interrupt
Program Status Word (PSW)

Supervisor call interrupt
System mask

Test data
Translation phase

Wait state

Review Questions   Given the fact that the base register is 3, convert the following instructions to machine language:

Assume the following storage assignments have been made by the computer.

Location			
006	AMT	DS	PL4
00A	HOLD	DS	PL6
010	ONE	DS	CL1
011	TWO	DS	CL2

	Location	Instruction	
1.	024	CLI	ONE,C'6'
2.	040	AP	HOLD,AMT
3.	060	AR	5,6
4.	080	MVC	ONE,TWO
5.	090	CP	HOLD,AMT

Indicate the assembler language equivalent of the following instructions:

```
LOC   OBJECT CODE
```

```
 6. 000652 D283 B822 B821
 7. 000666 9240 B821
 8. 00066A D283 B822 B821
 9. 000670 D208 B841 B74C
10. 000676 D500 B75B B92B
11. 00067C 4780 B68C
12. 000680 D500 B75B B92C
13. 000686 4780 B6B4
14. 000698 47F0 B648
15. 00069C D205 B863 B755
16. 0006B0 F275 B9B8 B755
17. 0006B6 4F80 B9B8
```

18.   Indicate the meaning of the following:

```
*
* ---  PSW AT INTERRUPT   071D0007   8F3F06BE
*
```

Chapter 15

Debugging Using the PDUMP and SNAP

Introduction

During the testing of a program, errors frequently occur that are difficult to pinpoint. Sometimes programs "bomb out," which means that execution is aborted because of some error that the computer cannot resolve. Sometimes, the execution of a program produces erroneous output.

To make debugging easier, a tool is used that enables the programmer to display data fields or intermediate work areas at various checkpoints. Thus, after a major calculation or during some phase of it, we might wish to examine fields not normally printed as output to ascertain if the calculations are being performed properly.

Displaying Fields

This debugging technique of displaying fields requires the programmer to determine the routines or instructions that require special attention. Sometimes this is done *after* an error has actually occurred, in which case the program is then modified to display the required fields. Sometimes programmers routinely incorporate display instructions during the debugging phase just to facilitate the checking of specified segments of the programs.

To test a program adequately, the programmer manually performs the operations required and compares the results obtained with those produced by the computer. If a discrepancy exists, a logic error in the program is usually the cause. Displaying fields during the test phase enables the programmer to test the logic at various points in the program as needed. Once debugging has been completed, the instructions used for display purposes are no longer needed and are removed from the source deck.

The methods used to display key fields are:

```
PDUMP—DOS
SNAP  —OS
```

We will discuss these two methods separately.

Depending upon your system's specifications and your job control, you may or may not get a dump of storage whenever the program bombs. This system dump provides you with a hexadecimal representation of *all* storage. Because such a listing is very long, it is cumbersome to read, making it difficult to pinpoint the fields you actually want to examine. The advantages of a SNAP or PDUMP are:

1. Only specified areas are displayed.
2. A dump can be obtained during normal execution of a program, not just when it bombs.

A Note on the Organization of this Chapter

The PDUMP is coded for DOS systems and the SNAP is coded for OS systems. The procedures for reading storage dumps, whether generated by a PDUMP or a SNAP, are *exactly* the same. Hence, it is highly recommended that both DOS and OS users read this *entire* chapter, focusing on the problems provided and the ways in which one can interpret storage dumps. For DOS users, the rules specified for the SNAP macro may be viewed as fundamentally analogous to those for the PDUMP. Similarly, for OS users, the rules for the PDUMP macro may be viewed as fundamentally analogous to those for the SNAP.

PDUMP

The PDUMP instruction that is available under DOS enables the programmer to obtain storage dumps of specified fields during the normal execution of the program. The format of the PDUMP instruction is as follows:

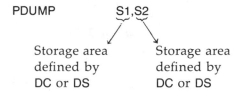

PDUMP   S1,S2

Storage area   Storage area
defined by   defined by
DC or DS   DC or DS

Operation

The computer will print all storage areas defined in the program, in sequence, beginning with S1 and ending with S2, but *not including* S2.

Example

```
          .
          .
          .
          PDUMP   CONST1,CONST5
          .
          .
          .
CONST1    DS      CL5
CONST2    DS      PL3
CONST3    DS      CL6
CONST4    DS      PL2
CONST5    DS      F
```

Result:

Storage dumps of CONST1–CONST4 will be provided when PDUMP instruction is encountered.

> IMPORTANT NOTE: S1, the first operand in the PDUMP instruction (CONST1 in example) must be defined by a DS or DC that *precedes* the definition of S2, the second operand in the PDUMP instruction (CONST2 in example).

The PDUMP differs from dumps initiated by the operating system, such as ABEND (*ab*normal *end*) dumps, in that control is returned to the *next instruction* in your program after the PDUMP has been executed.

The programmer will find the PDUMP a most valuable asset in finding and correcting programming errors. Here is an example of using the PDUMP to display storage after a card is read.

```
           •
           •
           •
           GET    INFILE,CARDIN
           PDUMP  A,Z+4
           •
           •
           •
A          DS     CL3
CARDIN     DS     CL80
           •
           •
Z          DS     F
           END
```

Note that a displacement of 4 is necessary if the contents of the storage area Z are to be exhibited.

HELPFUL HINTS

It is sometimes useful to establish blank areas between fields that will be dumped to make the dump more readable.

Example

```
           •
           •
           •
           PDUMP  CONST1,CONST5
           •
           •
           •
CONST1     DS     CL5
           DC     CL4'    '
CONST2     DS     PL3
           DC     CL4'    '
CONST3     DS     CL6
           DC     CL4'    '
CONST4     DS     PL2
           DC     CL4'    '
CONST5     DS     F
```

The Storage Dump The contents of the 16 general registers and main storage are displayed on the computer listing as a result of the PDUMP.

Consider a line that is dumped as in Figure 15-1. The format for storage dumps is fairly standard. In its most common form, the contents of storage are displayed in hex. Eight words of storage are printed on each line. Each word is separated from the next by several blanks to improve readability.

To the right we find the EBCDIC representation of the data contained on

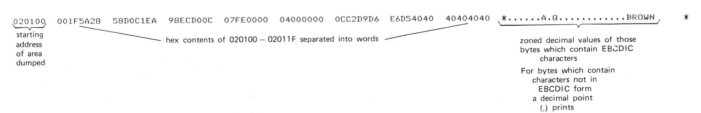

Figure 15-1 One line of a dump.

	WORD 1	WORD 2	WORD 3	WORD 4	WORD 5	WORD 6	WORD 7	WORD 8	
020120	40404040	D3C5D9D6	E8404040	40404040	40404040	40404040	40404040	40404040	∗ LEROY

0 2 0 1 2 0	0 2 0 1 2 3	0 2 0 1 2 4	0 2 0 1 2 7	0 2 0 1 2 8	0 2 0 1 2 B	0 2 0 1 2 C	0 2 0 1 2 F
0 2 0 1 3 0	0 2 0 1 3 3	0 2 0 1 3 4	0 2 0 1 3 7	0 2 0 1 3 8	0 2 0 1 3 B	0 2 0 1 3 C	0 2 0 1 3 F

Note: Each byte is displayed in a dump as two hex digits.

Figure 15-2 Schematic of one line of a dump and its actual contents.

each line of the printout. Because data is often stored in binary or packed-decimal form, a great deal of the data is not in valid **EBCDIC** form and cannot print as a recognizable character. Note that periods (.) are printed for these characters.

To the extreme left of each line is the address of the first byte of storage. See Figure 15-2.

Recall that 2 hex digits comprise a byte of storage. Therefore, a 4-byte word consists of 8 hex digits. Each line of the listing contains 20_{16} bytes or 32_{10} bytes (8 words). A brief look at the storage dump of 020120–2013F reveals that spaces (40) occupy bytes 020120–20123 and bytes 020129–2013F. The hex digits D3 C5 D9 D6 E8 occupy bytes 020124–020128. If you consult a conversion table you will find that these digits represent the word **LEROY**. Note that on the right-hand side of the listing the word **LEROY** prints.

Suppose it were necessary to inspect the contents of a 2-byte field beginning at location 020150. Since addresses are printed 20 hex bytes at a time, we would need to find 020140 (020160 would be too late). We would then check the addresses printed to the left until we found 020140. By counting 16 bytes from the *zero position*, we arrive at 020150 (020150 − 020140 = 10_{16} = 16_{10}). Remember, the first byte of each line always contains a low-order zero. Therefore, 020150 would be the first byte of word 5. See Figure 15-3.

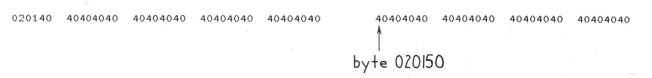

Figure 15-3 Finding a byte in a storage dump.

The contents of this location are **40** or a space. Again, 2 hex digits make up a byte.

Now that we are able to examine the contents of storage, let us see how this can assist us in debugging a sample program.

Example: Sample Program 1[1]

Consider the program in Figure 15-4. Figure 15-5 indicates the results of the first run. Note that there were no diagnostics when the program was assembled

---

[1] Note that this is a **DOS** listing. Assume all of the I/O is correct. The rest of the program would be the same for **DOS** or **OS** runs. Thus, the program can be studied by both types of users.

and that no output was obtained except a dump. A PROGRAM CHECK INTER-RUPTION occurred, however, at hex location 1105D6.

Finding Error Point
Subtract load point (entry point) address from interrupt address.

LO-LINK for the program entitled DUMP contains the entry point, which is 110520.

1105D6	Interrupt point
−110520	Load point
B6	Relative address (LOC) of instruction that caused the interrupt.

Looking back at the source listing to find address B6, we see that the error occurred when the CP instruction was executed. If the error is not easily ascertained by desk checking, it is useful to dump fields to examine their contents prior to the interrupt. Sometimes it is useful to include PDUMP at strategic points in a program even before any execution has been attempted. In this way, careful checking of program steps can be achieved.

Examine the PDUMP illustrated in Figure 15-5 that accompanies the program.

Interpreting the Dump Locations

Note that a PDUMP instruction precedes the instruction in question. The contents of CSUM, the first operand at hex location 142, through PATTRN3 (but exclusive of PATTRN3), at location 26D, print just prior to the interrupt. Adding the actual load or entry point, of 110520, the PDUMP will provide a storage dump of 110662–11078D. (Note that such additions are *hex* additions.)

If you examine the storage dump in Figure 15-5, again, you will note that storage positions 110660–11078F are dumped. Since 8 words per line are provided, lines of a dump always begin on a doubleword boundary.

Determining the Contents of Fields Using Dumps

Note that the CP instruction that resulted in the interrupt has two operands:

SALES
P'500'

Examining the ADDR1 field of the CP instruction we find that SALES is located at relative address 1E4, which is within the limits of our PDUMP (142–26D). Adding the starting point 110520, we can locate the contents of SALES just prior to the CP when PDUMP was executed, at hex 110704.

Located between 110700 and 110720 is the following:

40404040 F3F0F040 40404040 40404040 40404040 40404040 40404040 40404040
           SALES

Counting bytes, we find that F3F0F0 is contained within the field called SALES. You should realize that this is *not* a packed field and, hence, when used with a CP instruction will cause an interrupt. Reading up several lines in the program, we find that SALES was packed into COMM and hence COMM should have been the first operand in the CP instruction. Note that COMM at relative address 1D1 and effective address 1106F1 does indeed contain 300 in packed form:

40404040 40404040 40404040 40404040 40000030 0FC8C1D9 D9C9D5C7 E3D6D540
                                            COMM

```
LOC    OBJECT CODE   ADDR1 ADDR2  STMT  SOURCE STATEMENT

                                    1    DUMP    PRINT NOGEN
000000                              2            START 0
                                    3    INFILE  DTFCD BLKSIZE=80,RECFORM=FIXUNB,DEVADDR=SYSIPT,        X   HSKP
                                                       WORKA=YES,IOAREA1=BUFFRIN,EOFADDR=EOF                HSKP
                                   24    OUTFILE DTFPR BLKSIZE=132,DEVICE=1403,DEVADDR=SYSLST,IOAREA1=BUFFROUT,X   HSKP
                                                       CONTROL=YES,PRINTOV=YES,WORKA=YES                    HSKP
                                   45    CDMOD
                                  137    PRMOD   WORKA=YES,CONTROL=YES,PRINTOV=YES
000068 05C0                       257    BEGIN   BALR  12,0
                      0006A       258            USING *,12
                                  259            OPEN  INFILE,OUTFILE
```

```
LOC    OBJECT CODE        ADDR1 ADDR2  STMT  SOURCE STATEMENT

00007E D283 C0E3 C0E2     0140  0014C  269   READ  MVC  LINEOUT,SPACES
                                       270         GET  INFILE,CARDIN
000094 D20E C1CB C16B     001D5 001D1  276         MVC  NAMEO,NAME
00009A F232 C167 C17A     001D1 001E4  277         MVC  COMM,SALES
0000A0 FA33 C1BB C1E0     00225 001D1  278         PACK TOTAL,COMM
0000A6 D202 C1E0 C17A     0024A 001E4  279         MVC  DOLLARS,SALES
                                       280         PDUMP CSUM,PATTRN3
0000B6 F921 C17A C08C     001E4 003A8  285         CP   SALES,=P'500'
0000C0 FC31 C167 C340     001D1 003AA  286         BNL  PREM
0000C6 FA33 C0D8 C167     00142 001D1  287   REG   MP   COMM,=P'12'
0000CC D206 C1ED C1F4     00257 0025E  288   EDIT  AP   CSUM,COMM
0000D2 DE06 C1ED C168     00257 001D2  289         MVC  COMMOUT,PATTRN
0000D8 9258 C1ED          0014D        290         ED   COMMOUT,COMM+1
0000DC D232 C0E3 C1C1     0014D 0022B  291         MVI  COMMOUT,C'$'
                                       292         MVC  LINEOUT(51),DETAIL
                                       293         PUT  OUTFILE,LINEOUT
0000F2 47F0 C014          0007E        299         B    READ
0000FC FC31 C167 C342     001D1 003AE  301   PREM  MP   COMM,=P'18'
000102 47F0 C05C          030C6        302         MVC  LINEOUT+54(3),=C'***'
000106 D207 C0F6 C1FB     00160 00265  303         B    EDIT
00010C DE07 C0F6 C1BB     00160 00225  304   EOF   ED   LINEOUT+19(8),PATTRN2
000112 F853 C0DC C1E3     00168 0024D  305         MVC  LINEOUT+19(8),TOTAL
000118 F051 C0DC C0D8     00146 00229  306         ZAP  LINEOUT+27(3),CENTS
00011E FD51 C0DC C1BF     00146 00260  307         DP   DIVIDE,CSUM
000124 DE07 C206 C0DD     0016D 00260  308         MVC  DIVIDE,NO
00012A      C103 C0DD     0016D 00147  309         MVC  LINEOUT+32(7),PATTRN3
                                       310         ED   LINEOUT+32(8),AVERAGE+1
                                       316         PUT  OUTFILE,LINEOUT
                                                   EOJ
```

358

```
000142  0000000C            319  CSUM      DC   PL4'0'
000146                      321  DIVIDE    DS   OPL6
00014A                      322  AVERAGE   DS   PL4
00014C                      323  RMDR      DS   PL2.
00014D  40                  324  SPACES    DC   CL.' '
0001D1                      325  LINEOUT   DS   CL132
0001D5                      326  COMM      DS   OCL80
0001E4                      327  CARDIN    DS   CL4
0001E7                      328  NAME      DS   CL15
                            329  SALES     DS   CL3
                                                CL62
000225  0000000C            330  *         DC   PL4'0'
000229  000C                331  TOTAL     DC   PL2'0'
00022B                      332  NO        DS   OCL51
000235                      333  DETAIL    DS   CL10
                            334            DS   CL15
                            335  NAMEO     DS   CL4.'
000244  40404040            336            DC   CL2'$'
000248  5B40                337  DULLARS   DS   CL3'.00'
00024A  4BF0F0404040404040  338  CENTS     DS
000257  402020214B2020      339            DC   X'40202142B2020'
00025E  40202020202021      340  COMMOUT   DS
000265  402020214B2020      341  PATTKN    DC   X'4020202020202021'
00026D  40202020214B2020    342  PATTRN2
                            343  PATTRN3        X'40202142B2020'
0002F8                      344  BUFFRIN   DC   CL132
                            345  BUFFROUT  DS   CL132
                            346            BEGIN
                            347            END
00068                       348            =CL8'$$BOPEN '
                            349            =CL8'$$BPDUMP'
000380  5B5BC2D6D7C5D540    350            =A(CSUM,PATTRN3)
000388  5B5BC2D7C4E4D4D7    351            =A(INFILE)
000390  00000142 0000026D   352            =A(CARDIN)
00039C  000001D5            353            =A(OUTFILE)
0003A0  00000038            354            =A(LINEOUT)
0003A4  0000014D            355            =P'500'
0003A8  500C                356            =P'12'
0003AA  012C                357            =P'18'
0003AC  018C                                =C'***'
0003AE  5C5C5C
```

Figure 15-4

DIAGNOSTICS AND STATISTICS

NO ERRORS FOUND

THE FOLLOWING MACRO NAMES HAVE BEEN FOUND IN MACRO INSTRUCTIONS
DTFCD   DTFPR   CDMOD   PRMOD   OPEN   GET   LINK   PUT   EOJ

OPTIONS FOR THIS ASSEMBLY - ALIGN, LIST, XREF, LINK, NORLD, NODECK, NODECK

THE ASSEMBLER WAS RUN IN 65416 BYTES
END OF ASSEMBLY
EOJ $3ASM
// EXEC LNKEDT

JOB   INST   09.10.31   F-LE-E   FAST-LINKAGE-EDITOR   VM4.0   DOS/VS R34-0A G O A L   S Y S T E M S

ACTION TAKEN   MAP CLEAR   REL   LINK
LIST   PHASE MONITOR,ROOT
LIST   INCLUDE ILFFEXIT
LIST   AUTOLINK IJDFAPZZ
LIST   PHASE STDPGM,*
LIST   ENTRY

	PHASE-CSECT-ENTRY	LO-LNK	HI-LNK	LO-REL	HI-REL	LN-HEX	LN-DEC	XF-LNK	XF-REL	G O A L S Y S T E M S
	LINK PARTITION = F3	110000	169FFF	000000	059FFF	5A000	368,640	110078	000078	
ROOT	MONITOR	110078	11051B	000000	0004A3	4A4	1,188	110078	000000	RELOCATABLE
	ILFFEXIT	110078	1103F9	000000	000381	382	898			
	*EXIT		1100F4		00007C					
	IJDFAPZZ	110400	11051B	000388	0004A3	11C	284			
	*IJDFAZZZ		110400		000388					
PHASE	STDPGM	110520	1109F9	000000	0004D9	4DA	1,242	110588	000068	RELOCATABLE
	DUMP	1108D8	11094F	0003B8	00042F	3B1	945			
	IJCFZIWO									
	IJDFCPZW	110950	1109F9	000430	0004D9	AA	170			
	*IJDFZPZW	110950		000430						
	*IJDFZZZW	110950		000430						
	*IJDFCZZW	110950								

NORMAL COMPLETION, BLOCKS AVAIL =   334, USED IN EDIT =   4, PCIL=X'1C6', CYL=001, SERIAL=WORK01.
// EXEC   INST

GR 0-7	001108B0	001108A8	00169FFF	0000F416	80000035	80000035	00169FFF
GR 8-F	80112880	0A16180C	4011007A	182F07F1	40110588	D406D5C9	80110584	00110808
FP REG	42540000	00000000	41100000	00000000	00000000	00000000	00000000
CR 0-7	80400JE0	0200FA80	FFFF0000	00000000	00000000	00000000	00000000
CR 8-F	00000000	00000000	00000000	00000000	00000000	EF000000	00000000

110660	0A0E0000	000C0000	00000000	40404040	40404040	0FC8C1D9	D9C9D5C7	E3D6D540
110680	40404040	--SAME--		40404040	40404040	40404040	40404040	40404040
1106E0	40404040	40404040	40404040	40000030	0FC8C1D9	D9C9D5C7	E3D6D540
110700	40404040	F3F0F040	40404040	40404040	40404040	40404040
110720	40404040	--SAME--		40000030	0C000C00	00000000	00000000
110740	40404040	40000030	5840F3F0	F04BF0F0	00C8C1D9	D9C9D5C7	E3D6D540
110780	20214B20	20402020	21402020	40404000	00000000	00000000	00004020

OS03I PROGRAM CHECK INTERRUPTION - HEX LOCATION 1105D6 - CONDITION CODE 2 - DATA EXCEPTION
OS00I JOB INST CANCELED

Figure 15-5

Inserting the following in place of the erroneous CP will produce the correct results:

CP   COMM,=P'500'

Note that once the program is error-free, we remove the PDUMP since it is a debugging tool and not normally a part of desired output.

Example: Sample Program 2

Consider the sample program in Figure 15-6. The results of the assembly and execution of this program are indicated in Figure 15-7.

Note that this program has produced some output before it bombed. An error occurred when executing the instruction at hex location 11063E. By subtracting the entry point 110520 for this program, we can determine the LOC of the instruction as 11E, which is the DP instruction. This should come as no surprise since the interrupt was caused by a DECIMAL DIVIDE EXCEPTION.

To find the error, we need to examine the contents of the two fields, DIVIDE and NO, which are operated on in the DP instruction.

Field	Displacement	Load Point	Effective Address
DIVIDE	146	110520	110666
NO	229	110520	110749

The PDUMP inserted prior to the divide lists all storage areas from CSUM, 142, to PATTRN3, 26D. That is, all areas from the effective address 110662 (110520 + 142)–11078D (110520 + 26D) will print.

Checking this dump we note that:

DIVIDE   contains 00 00 00 52 72 2C
NO   contains 00 0C

The error, then, is obvious. An attempt has been made to divide by zero. NO was never updated to contain a nonnegative value.

The student can now begin to appreciate the advantages of using dumps in the debugging process. Nothing need be left to "interpretation" since the machine language instructions and the contents of storage can be analyzed on a microscopic level.

PDUMP's, then are debugging tools that are used to find errors by examining actual storage locations. All areas to be studied are simply specified as parameters.

With the use of the appropriate job control cards, the computer can be instructed to provide an automatic dump of all storage used by the program in case of an interrupt. Note, however, that this form of dump (1) only occurs in case of an interrupt whereas a PDUMP will allow continuous execution of the program, and (2) it dumps *all* storage associated with the program, not just selected areas, such as those obtainable with the PDUMP.

PDUMP's and Fixed-Point Arithmetic

Another advantage of using the PDUMP is the display of the 16 general purpose registers. Since these registers are used in fixed point arithmetic, their contents are usually a clue to pinpointing a program error. To illustrate this point a sample program has been constructed. We will analyze it, focusing our attention primarily on registers. The program is shown in Figure 15-8. Recall that each register contains 4 bytes, or a fullword. In addition, negative

DOS/VS ASSEMBLER REL 34.0 09.12

LOC   OBJECT CODE   ADDR1 ADDR2   STMT   SOURCE STATEMENT

```
000000                                 1          PRINT NOGEN
                                       2  DUMP    START 0
                                       3  INFILE  DTFCD BLKSIZE=80,RECFORM=FIXUNB,DEVADDR=SYSIPT,          X  HSKP
                                                        WORKA=YES,IOAREA1=BUFFRIN,EOFADDR=EOF
                                      24  OUTFILE DTFPR BLKSIZE=132,DEVICE=1403,DEVADDR=SYSLST,IOAREA1=BUFFROUT,X  HSKP
                                                        CONTROL=YES,PRINTOV=YES,WORKA=YES                        HSKP
                                      45          CDMOD WORKA=YES
                                     137          PRMOD WORKA=YES,CONTROL=YES,PRINTOV=YES
000068 05C0                          257  BEGIN   BALR  12,0
       0006A                         258          USING *,12                                                     HSKP
                                     259          OPEN  INFILE,OUTFILE
```

```
LOC     OBJECT CODE       ADDR1  ADDR2   STMT       SOURCE STATEMENT

00007E  D283 C0E3 C0E2    0014D  0014C   269  READ  MVC   LINEOUT,SPACES
000094  D20E C1CB C16B    00235  001D5   270        GET   INFILE,CARDIN
00009A  F232 C167 C17A    001D1  001E4   276        MVC   NAMEO,NAME
0000A0  FA33 C1BB C167    00225  001D1   277        PACK  COMM,SALES
0000A6  F433 C1E0 C167    0024A  001E4   278        AP    TOTAL,COMM
0000AC  F931 C167 C33E    001D1  003A8   279        CP    DOLLARS,SALES
0000B2  47B0 C082         000EC          280        BNL   COMM,=P'500'    CORRECTION 1
0000B6  FC31 C167 C082    001D1  000EC   282  REG   MP    COMM,=P'12'
0000BC  FA33 C0D8 C167    00142  001D1   283        AP    CSUM,COMM
0000C2  D206 C1ED C1F4    00257  001D1   284        MVC   COMMOUT,PATTRN
0000C8  DE06 C1ED C168    00257  001D2   285        ED    COMMOUT,COMM+1
0000D2  925B C1ED         00257          286        MVI   COMMOUT,C'$'
0000D2  D232 C0E3 C1C1    0014D  0022B   287        MVC   LINEOUT(51),DETAIL
                                         288        PUT   OUTFILE,LINEOUT

0000E8  47F0 C014         0007E          294  PREM  B     READ
0000EC  FC31 C167 C119    001D1  00183   295        MP    COMM,=P'18'
0000F2  47F0 C052         000BC          296        B     EDIT
0000FC  D207 C0F6 C1FB    00160  00265   297  EOF   MVC   LINEOUT+54(3),=C'***'
000102  DE07 C0F6 C1BB    00160  00225   298  EDIT  ED    LINEOUT+19(8),PATTRN2
000108  D202 C0FE C1E3    00168  0024D   300        MVC   LINEOUT+19(8),TOTAL
          F853 C0DC C0D8  00146  00142   301        ZAP   LINEOUT+27(3),CENTS
00011E  FD51 C0DC C1BF    00146  00148   307        DP    DIVIDE,CSUM
000124  D206 C103 C203    0016D  0026D   308        MVC   DIVIDE,NO
00012A  DE07 C103 C0DD    0016D  00147   309        ED    LINEOUT+32(7),PATTRN3
                                         310        PUT   LINEOUT+32(8),AVERAGE+1
                                                    EOJ   OUTFILE,LINEOUT

000142  0000000C                         316  CSUM     DC    PL4'0'
000146                                   319  DIVIDE   DS    0PL6
000146                                   320  AVERAGE  DS    PL4
00014A                                   321  RMDR     DS    PL2
00014C  40                               322  SPACES   DC    CL2' '
00014D                                   323  LINEOUT  DS    CL132
0001D1                                   324  COMM     DS    PL4
0001D5                                   325  CARDIN   DS    0CL80
0001D5                                   326  NAME     DS    CL15
0001E4                                   327  SALES    DS    CL3
0001E7                                   328           DS    CL62

000225  0000000C                         330  *TOTAL
000229  000C                             331  TOTAL    DC    PL4'0'
00022B                                   332  NU       DC    PL2'0'
00022B                                   333  DETAIL   DS    0CL51
000235                                   334  NAMEO    DS    CL15
000244  40404040                         335  NAMEO    DS    CL10
000248  5B40                             336  DOLLARS  DC    CL15' '
00024A  4BF0F0404040                     337           DC    CL2'.'
000257                                   338  CENTS    DC    CL2'.00'
00025E  402002148 2020                   339  COMMOUT  DS    CL7
000266  402002020J2021                   340  PATTRN   DC    X'402002148 2020'
00026D  402002148 2020                   341  PATTRN2  DC    X'402002020J2021'
000274                                   342  PATTRN3  DC    X'402002148 2020'
0002F8                                   343  BUFFRIN  DS    CL132
                         00068           344  BUFFROUT DS    CL132
                                         346  BEGIN    END

000380  5B5BC2D6D7C5D540                 348           =C'$$BOPEN '
000388  5B5BC2D7C4E4D4D7                 349           =CL8'$$BPDUMP'
000390  000000142000026D                 350           =A(CSUM,PATTRN3)
00039C  00001D5                          351           =A(INFILE)
0003A0  00000038                         352           =A(CARDIN)
0003A4  0000014D                         353           =A(OUTFILE)
                                         354           =A(LINEOUT)
0003A8  500C                             355           =P'500'
0003AA  012C                             356           =P'12'
0003AC  018C                             357           =P'18'
0003AE  5C5C5C                                         =C'***'
```

Figure 15-6

DIAGNOSTICS AND STATISTICS

NO ERRORS FOUND

THE FOLLOWING MACRO NAMES HAVE BEEN FOUND IN MACRO INSTRUCTIONS
DTFCD   CDMOD   PRMOD   OPEN   GET   PUT   PDUMP   EOJ

OPTIONS FOR THIS ASSEMBLY - ALIGN, LIST, XREF, LINK, NORLD, NODECK, NOEDECK

THE ASSEMBLER WAS RUN IN 65416 BYTES
END OF ASSEMBLY

EOP $3ASM
// EXEC LNKEDT

JOB INST   09.12.45 F-LE-E FAST-LINKAGE-EDITOR VM4.0   DOS/VS R34-0A G O A L   S Y S T E M S

ACTION TAKEN MAP CLEAR REL LINK
LIST PHASE MONITOR,ROOT
LIST INCLUDE ILFFEXIT
LIST AUTOLINK IJDFAPZZ
LIST PHASE STDPGM,*
LIST ENTRY

PHASE-CSECT-ENTRY	LO-LNK	HI-LNK	LO-REL	HI-REL	LN-HEX	LN-DEC	XF-LNK	XF-REL	G O A L S Y S T E M S
LINK PARTITION = F3	110000	169FFF	000000	059FFF	5A000	368,640	110078	000078	
ROOT MONITOR	110078	11051B	000000	0004A3	4A4	1,188	110078	000000	RELOCATABLE
ILFFEXIT	110078	1103F9	000000	000381	382	898			
*EXIT	1100F4		00007C		11C	284			
IJDFAPZZ	110400	11051B	000388	0004A3					
*IJDFAZZZ	110400		000388						
PHASE STDPGM	110520	1109F9	000000	0004D9	4DA	1,242	110588	000068	RELOCATABLE
DUMP	110520	1108D0	0003B0	00042F	3B1	945			
IJCFZIW0	1108D8	11094F			78	120			
IJDFCPZW	110950	1109F9	000430	0004D9	AA	170			
*IJDFZPZW	110950		000430						
*IJDFZZZW	110950		000430						
*IJDFCZZW	110950		000430						

NORMAL COMPLETION, BLOCKS AVAIL = 334, USED IN EDIT = 4, PCIL=X'1C6', CYL=001, SERIAL=WORK01.

// EXEC
HARRINGTON	$ 300.00	$ 36.00	***
MCNAMARA	$ 654.00	$117.72	***
SAGER	$ 889.00	$160.02	
THOMAS	$ 123.00	$ 14.76	
WHITE	$ 456.00	$ 54.72	
VOSS	$ 800.00	$144.00	***

```
      INST                                                                                              PAGE    1

GR 0-7   00110880 001108A8 00169FFF 00001BB0   0000F416 80000035 80000035 00169FFF
GR 8-F   80112880 0A16180C 4011007A 182F07F1   4011058A D4D6D5C9 0011061C 001108D8
FP REG   42540000 00000000 41100000 00000000   00000000 00000000 00000000 00000000
CR 0-7   804000E0 0200FA80 FFFF0000 00000000   00000000 00000000 00000000 00000000
CR 8-F   00000000 00000000 00000000 00000000   00000000 00000000 EF000000 00000000

110660   0A0E0052 722C0000 0052722C 40404040   40404040 40404040 40404040 40404040      ............
110680   40404040 F3F2F2F2 4BF0F040 40404040   40404040 40404040 40404040 40404040         3222.00
1106A0   40404040 --SAME--
1106E0   40404040 40404040 40404040 40404040   40001440 0CE5D6E2 E2404040 40404040                          .. .VOSS
110700   40404040 F8F0F040 40404040 40404040   40404040 40404040 40404040 40404040        800
110720   40404040 --SAME--
110740   40404040 40000322 2C000C00 00000000   00000000 00E5D6E2 E2404040 40404040          ..........  .....VOSS
110760   40404040 40404040 5B40F8F0 F04BF0F0   40404040 4040405B F1F4F44B F0F04020             $ 800.00          $144.00 .
110780   20214B20 20402020 20202020 21402020                                              ..... ....... ..

0S03I PROGRAM CHECK INTERRUPTION - HEX LOCATION 11063E - CONDITION CODE 2 - DECIMAL DIVIDE EXCEPTION
0S00I JOB INST      CANCELED
```

Figure 15-7

```
     LOC   OBJECT CODE     ADDR1 ADDR2  STMT    SOURCE STATEMENT

                                        144 *
                                        145 *         SOLVE  SUM = 5 * A  +  3 * B
                                        146 *
  000030  05C0                          147 BEGIN     BALR  12,0
                              00032     148           USING *,12
  000032  5670 C042           00074     149 FIRST     O     7,MASK              USED TO ALLOW FIXED-POINT OVERFLOW
  000036  0470                          150           SPM   7                   SINCE IT IS NORMALLY MASKED
  000038  4170 0005           00005     151           LA    7,5
  00003C  4180 0000           00000     152           LA    8,0
  000040  F872 C046 C04E 00078 00080    153           ZAP   DBLE,A(3)
  000046  4FA0 C046           00078     154           CVB   10,DBLE
  00004A  1A8A                          155 LOOP1     AR    8,10
  00004C  4670 C018           0004A     156           BCT   7,LOOP1
  000050  F872 C046 C051 00078 00083    157           ZAP   DBLE,B(3)
  000056  4F90 C046           00078     158           CVB   9,DBLE
  00005A  1A89                          159 LOOP2     AR    8,9
  00005C  4670 C028           0005A     160           BCT   7,LOOP2
  000060  5080 C03E           00070     161           ST    8,ANSWER
                                        162           PDUMP BEGIN,BUFFROUT
                                        167           EOJ
                                        170 *
                                        171 *
                                        172 *
                                        173 *
  000070                                174 ANSWER    DS    F
  000074  08000000                      175 MASK      DC    X'08000000'
  000078                                176 DBLE      DS    D
  000080  01000C                        177 A         DC    P'1000'
  000083  01050C                        178 B         DC    P'1050'
  000086                                179 BUFFRIN   DS    CL132
  00010A                                180 BUFFROUT  DS    CL132
                              00030     181           END   BEGIN
```

Figure 15-8

numbers are stored as complements. Therefore any register containing any digit 8 through F in the high-order hex position (1000_2–1111_2) contains a negative number in complement form.

In our sample problem, we are using register 12 as the base register. Let us examine its contents. See Figure 15-9. We find register 12 contains a base address of 0960AA, which is, as we would expect, different from the load or entry point. In fact, the base address references the instruction labeled FIRST in our program. By subtracting the displacement of the instruction FIRST from the base address, we can calculate the loadpoint or entry address.

$$
\begin{array}{ll}
0960AA & \text{Base address} \\
-0000 3 2 & \text{Address of FIRST} \\
\hline
0960 7 8 & \text{Load point}
\end{array}
$$

This exercise is useful in that the programmer can always double-check the load point in this manner. However, a more serious problem is apparent since an interrupt has occurred in our program. The interrupt message indicates that a fixed-point overflow at location 0960D2 has caused the termination of the program. We are again able to find the instruction causing the interrupt by subtracting the load or entry point (096078) from the location of the interrupt. This will provide us with the displacement in our program of the error-causing instruction. The instruction at fault is located at 00005A (0960D2 − 096078) and is coded:

```
LOOP2            AR            8,9
```

Both operands are registers and we find general register 9 correctly contains the hex equivalent of 1050_{10} or $41A_{16}$. See Figure 15-9. However, general register 8 indicates a very large binary number, which leads us to believe that

Register 8   Register 9   Register 12   Register 7   PAGE   1

```
GR 0-F   00096078 000960A8 000E6FFF 0000EA40   C000E882 80000035 80000035 FFE0CADF
         800000FC 0000041A 000003E8 182F07F1   400960AA D7C8C1E2 C55C5C5C 000E6FFF
```

Figure 15-9

fixed point overflow has occurred. When correctly programmed, the LOOP1 procedure would be performed five times while the LOOP2 procedure should be executed three times. Apparently LOOP1 was executed without any detectable problems and, thus, we will now turn our attention to LOOP2. The BCT instruction controls the loop by the value contained in register 7. Let's examine register 7. First, register 7 contains a negative value. How can this be?

Register 7 was given an initial value of 5 prior to entering the LOOP1 procedure. When the program entered LOOP2, however, register 7 contained the value zero. Therefore, from this point on, the BCT instruction continued to subtract 1 with each pass. Our correction is simple. To initialize register 7 to 3 prior to entering the LOOP2 procedure:

```
LA          7,3              CORRECTION
```

Note that on the next run, a PDUMP (STMT 162 in Figure 15-8) is used to display the contents of the general registers (see Figure 15-10). The answer found in register 8 is correct. Register 8 contains 1FD6 in hex or 8150 in decimal. As expected, the loop counter has been decreased to zero as evidenced by the contents of register 7. When using fixed-point binary instructions, the contents of registers play an important role in debugging.

SNAP Macro

The SNAP macro enables the OS programmer to obtain storage dumps of specified fields during the normal execution of the program.

The general format of a SNAP instruction and the required additions to the program are as follows:

```
SNAP          DCB=XX,PDATA=(PSW,REGS),STORAGE=(S1,S2)
```

An explanation follows:

1. DCB=XX

    The SNAP instruction requires an additional DCB within the program, since we want to create a separate file for writing the dump out. The DCB appears as follows.

Register 8   Register 7   PAGE   1

```
GR 0-7   00084218 00084210 00095FFF 0000F9F8   C000EA3E 80000025 80000025 00000000
GR 8-F   00001FD6 0000041A 000003E8 182F07F1   40C840AA D7C8C1E2 C55C5C5C 00095FFF
```

Figure 15-10

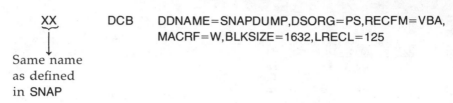

```
     XX              DCB     DDNAME=SNAPDUMP,DSORG=PS,RECFM=VBA,    *
                             MACRF=W,BLKSIZE=1632,LRECL=125
```

Same name
as defined
in **SNAP**

The **DDNAME** has been arbitrarily chosen as **SNAPDUMP**. Since an additional **DCB** macro is required with the **SNAP** to indicate that another form of output is to be produced, an additional **DD** card is required as part of job control. (See Appendix B for details or job control.)

```
//GO.SNAPDUMP          DD          SYSOUT=A
```

The **RECFM** operand indicates that the records will be variable in length (V) and blocked (B). The "A" indicates that **ASA** control characters are being used.

The "W" in the **MACRF** operand indicates that we are using the **SNAP** macro to write (W) out a file.

2. PDATA=(PSW,REGS)

Execution of the **SNAP** instruction with this operand will display:

Program Status Word (PSW)
general registers (REGS)

3. STORAGE=(S1,S2)

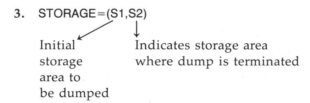

Initial   Indicates storage area
storage   where dump is terminated
area to
be dumped

Since we have added a **DCB** to the program for writing out the dump, we must remember to **OPEN** and **CLOSE** this output file as with any other file.

The following program excerpt illustrates the *four* instructions that must be added to an **OS** program when we want to use the **SNAP**.

```
* ILLUSTRATION OF SNAP
           .
           .
           .
           OPEN    (SNAP,OUTPUT)
           .
           .
           .
           SNAP    DCB=SNAP,PDATA=(PSW,REGS),STORAGE=TOTAL1,TOTAL5
           .
           .
           .
           CLOSE   (SNAP)
           .
           .
SNAP       DCB     DDNAME=SNAP,DSORG=PS,MACRF=(W),BLKSIZE=1632,    *
                   LRECL=125,RECFM=VBA
           .
           .
TOTAL1     DC      PL4'0'
TOTAL2     DC      PL4'0'
TOTAL3     DC      PL4'0'
TOTAL4     DC      PL4'0'
TOTAL5     DC      PL4'0'
```

Result

The PSW and the general registers will be displayed when the SNAP macro is executed.

Storage dumps of TOTAL1—TOTAL4 will also be provided.

Note that TOTAL5, the second delimiter of the storage areas to be printed, does *not* itself print. The dump is provided up to, but not including, TOTAL5.

> IMPORTANT NOTE: S1, the first operand in the SNAP instruction (TOTAL1 in example), must be defined by a DS or DC that precedes the definition of S2, the second operand in the SNAP instruction (TOTAL5 in the example).

Example 1

Figure 15-11 shows a program designed to add up the salary fields from each input card and print a total. The program was assembled with *no* diagnostics or errors. Upon execution, however, an interrupt message appeared indicating that a DECIMAL DATA EXCEPTION OCCURRED AT 020032.

On the computer on which the program was executed, all programs start at hexadecimal address 020000. We know, therefore, that the interrupt occurred at relative address 000032 (020032 − 020000). By examining Figure 15-12, we see that the instruction at 000032 is AP TOTAL,PKDSAL.

To find the error, we must examine the contents of storage at the time of the interrupt. This is done by including the SNAP macro before the AP instruction, along with its associated DCB, OPEN, and CLOSE macros, as shown in Figure 15-13. We then execute the program again. Figure 15-14 shows the dump that is obtained.

In order to find why the AP instruction caused the interrupt, we need to examine the contents of the fields operated on in this instruction, TOTAL and PKDSAL.

The address of TOTAL, a 4-byte field, is indicated in the AP instruction under ADDR1 (Figure 15-13), which refers to operand 1 of the corresponding instruction. From this instruction, we find that the address of TOTAL is 000111. The address of TOTAL may also be found by examining the LOC (Location) field of the DC labeled TOTAL. It, too, has an address of 000111.

The address of PKDSAL, the 3-byte sending field in the AP instruction, is listed under ADDR2 (operand 2) of that instruction.

The address, 0010E, may also be found under ADDR1, or operand 1, of the PACK instruction, or in the LOC field of the DC labeled PKDSAL.

By examining the dump in Figure 15-14, we discover that the contents of PKDSAL at the time of the interrupt is 000004. This is *not* a valid packed number, since the digit 4 is *not* a valid sign. We therefore look at the field that was packed into PKDSAL by the PACK instruction. That field is SALARY, which is a 5-byte field in the input record, starting at address 00012E. By looking at the contents of these 5 bytes, we find that SALARY contains 4040404040, or five blanks. We have just located the cause of the interrupt. Since the SALARY field contains all *blanks*, this resulted in an invalid sign when the field was packed, as illustrated below.

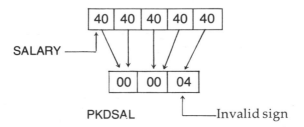

```
LOC      OBJECT CODE      ADDR1  ADDR2   STMT  SOURCE STATEMENT

                                            8  *                                            * SAM00080
                                            9  *          HOUSEKEEPING INSTRUCTIONS GO HERE  * SAM00090
                                           10  *                                            * SAM00100
000000E                                     11         OPEN  (INFILE,INPUT,OUTFILE,OUTPUT)     SAM00110
00001E                                      19  READ   GET   INFILE,RECORD                     SAM00120
00002C   F224 C072 C092   00078  00098      24         PACK  PKDSAL,SALARY                      SAM00130
000032   FA32 C075 C072   0007B  00078      25         AP    TOTAL,PKDSAL                       SAM00140
000038   47F0 C018        0001E             26         B     READ                               SAM00150
00003C   D283 COCA COC9   000D0  000CF      27  EOF    MVC   OUTAREA,SPACES                     SAM00160
000042   D218 COCA C25A   000D0  00260      28         MVC   OUTAREA+25(25),=C'TOTAL ANNUAL SALARIES IS '  SAM00170
000048   F363 C0E3 C075   000E9  0007B      29         UNPK  OUTAREA+31,TOTAL                   SAM00180
00004E   96F0 C0E9        000EF             30         OI    OUTAREA+31,X'F0'                   SAM00190
000052                                      31         PUT   OUTFILE,OUTAREA                    SAM00200
000060                                      36         CLOSE (INFILE,OUTFILE)                   SAM00210
                                            44  *                                            * SAM00220
                                            45  *          HOUSEKEEPING INSTRUCTIONS GO HERE  * SAM00230
                                            46  *          ALONG WITH DCB MACROS              * SAM00240
                                            47  *                                            * SAM00250
000078                                      51  PKDSAL  DS   PL3                                SAM00290
00007B   0000000C                           52  TOTAL   DC   PL4'0'                             SAM00300
00007F                                      53  RECORD  DS   OCL80         CARD FORMAT          SAM00310
00007F                                      54  LAST    DS   CL15                             * SAM00320
00008E                                      55  FIRST   DS   CL10                             * SAM00330
000098                                      56  SALARY  DS   CL5                              * SAM00340
00009D                                      57          DS   CL50                             * SAM00350
0000CF   40                                 58  SPACES  DC   CL1' '                             SAM00360
0000D0                                      59  OUTAREA DS   OCL132        PRINT FORMAT         SAM00370
0000D0                                      60          DS   CL5                              * SAM00380
0000D5                                      61  LNAME   DS   CL15                             * SAM00390
0000E4                                      62  FNAME   DS   CL20                             * SAM00400
0000F8                                      63          DS   CL10                             * SAM00410
000102                                      64          DS   CL20                             * SAM00420
000116                                      65  SALOUT  DS   CL5                              * SAM00430
00011B                                      66  BLANK   DS   CL57                             * SAM00440
                                           176          END                                     SAM00490
```

Figure 15-11

370

```
LOC    OBJECT CODE      ADDR1 ADDR2  STMT  SOURCE STATEMENT

                                        8  *
                                        9  *
                                       10  *                HOUSEKEEPING INSTRUCTIONS GO HERE                * SAM00080
                                                                                                             * SAM00090
                                                                                                             * SAM00100
00000E                                 11      OPEN  (INFILE,INPUT,OUTFILE,OUTPUT)                              SAM00120
00001E                                 19 READ GET   INFILE,RECORD                                             SAM00130
00002C F224 C072 C092  00078 00098     24      PACK  PKDSAL,SALARY                                             SAM00140
000032 FA32 C075 C072  0007B 00078     25      AP    TOTAL,PKDSAL                                              SAM00150
000038 47F0 C018        0001E          26      B     READ                                                     SAM00160
00003C D283 C0CA C0C9  000D0 000CF     27 EOF  MVC   OUTAREA,SPACES                                            SAM00170
000042 D218 C0CA C25A  000D0 00260     28      MVC   OUTAREA(25),=C'TOTAL ANNUAL SALARIES IS '                SAM00180
000048 F363 C0E3 C075  000E9 0007B     29      UNPK  OUTAREA+25(7),TOTAL                                       SAM00190
00004E 96F0 C0E9        000EF          30      OI    OUTAREA+31,X'F0'                                          SAM00200
000052                                 31      PUT   OUTFILE,OUTAREA                                           SAM00210
000060                                 36      CLOSE (INFILE,OUTFILE)                                          SAM00220
                                       44  *                                                                 * SAM00230
                                       45  *                HOUSEKEEPING INSTRUCTIONS GO HERE                * SAM00240
                                       46  *                ALONG WITH DCB MACROS                            * SAM00250
                                       47  *                                                                   SAM00290
000078                                 51 PKDSAL  DS   PL3                                                     SAM00300
00007B 0000000C                        52 TOTAL   DC   PL4'0'                                                  SAM00310
00007F                                 53 RECORD  DS   OCL80      CARD FORMAT                                  SAM00320
00007F                                 54 LAST    DS   CL15                *                                  SAM00330
00008E                                 55 FIRST   DS   CL10                 *                                 SAM00340
000098                                 56 SALARY  DS   CL5                   *                                SAM00350
00009D                                 57         DS   CL50                                                   SAM00360
0000CF 40                              58 SPACES  DC   CL1' '                                                 SAM00370
0000D0                                 59 OUTAREA DS   OCL132     PRINT FORMAT                                SAM00380
0000D0                                 60         DS   CL5                 *                                  SAM00390
0000D5                                 61 LNAME   DS   CL15                *                                  SAM00400
0000E4                                 62         DS   CL20                 *                                 SAM00410
0000F8                                 63 FNAME   DS   CL10                  *                                SAM00420
000102                                 64         DS   CL20                   *                               SAM00430
000116                                 65 SALOUT  DS   CL5                     *                              SAM00440
00011B                                 66 BLANK   DS   CL57                                                   SAM00490
                                      176         END
```

Figure 15-12

371

```
LOC     OBJECT CODE       ADDR1  ADDR2   STMT   SOURCE STATEMENT

                                            8    *                                                        * SAM00080
                                            9    *          HOUSEKEEPING INSTRUCTIONS GO HERE             * SAM00090
                                           10    *                                                        * SAM00100
00000E                                      11    OPEN  (INFILE,INPUT,OUTFILE,OUTPUT)                        SAM00110
00001E                                      19    OPEN  (SNAP,OUTPUT)                                        SAM00120
00002A                                      25 READ  GET   INFILE,RECORD                                     SAM00130
000038  F224 C108 C128   0010E  0012E       30    PACK  PKDSAL,SALARY                                        SAM00140
00003E                                      31    SNAP  DCB=SNAP,PDATA=(PSW),STORAGE=(PKDSAL,BLANK)          SAM00150
000062  FA32 C10B C108   00111  0010E       46    AP    TOTAL,PKDSAL                                         SAM00160
000068  47F0 C024               0002A       47    B     READ                                                SAM00170
00006C  D283 C160 C15F   00166  00165       48 EOF   MVC   OUTAREA,SPACES                                    SAM00180
000072  D218 C160 C2F2   00166  002F8       49    MVC   OUTAREA(25),=C'TOTAL ANNUAL SALARIES IS '           SAM00190
000078  F363 C179 C10B   0017F  00111       50    UNPK  OUTAREA+25(7),TOTAL                                 SAM00200
000082  96F0 C17F               00185       51    OI    OUTAREA+31,X'F0'                                    SAM00210
000090                                      52    PUT   OUTFILE,OUTAREA                                      SAM00220
00009E                                      57    CLOSE (INFILE,OUTFILE)                                     SAM00230
                                            65    CLOSE (SNAP)                                              SAM00240
0000AA                                      71 SNAP  DCB   DDNAME=SNAP,DSORG=PS,MACRF=(W),BLKSIZE=1632    *  SAM00250
                                                         LRECL=125,RECFM=VBA                                 SAM00260
                                           122    *                                                        * SAM00270
                                           123    *          HOUSEKEEPING INSTRUCTIONS GO HERE             * SAM00280
                                           124    *              ALONG WITH DCB MACROS                     * SAM00290
                                           125    *                                                        * SAM00300
00010E                                     129 PKDSAL DS    PL3                                              SAM00340
000111  0000000C                           130 TOTAL  DC    PL4'0'                                           SAM00350
000115                                     131 RECORD DS    0CL80        CARD FORMAT                         SAM00360
000115                                     132 LAST   DS    CL15                          *                  SAM00370
000124                                     133 FIRST  DS    CL10                          *                  SAM00380
00012E                                     134 SALARY DS    CL5                           *                  SAM00390
000133                                     135 SPACES DS    CL50                                             SAM00400
000165  40                                 136        DC    CL1' '                                           SAM00410
000166                                     137 OUTAREA DS   0CL132       PRINT FORMAT                        SAM00420
00016B                                     138        DS    CL5                           *                  SAM00430
00017A                                     139 LNAME  DS    CL15                          *                  SAM00440
00018E                                     140        DS    CL20                          *                  SAM00450
000198                                     141 FNAME  DS    CL10                          *                  SAM00460
0001AC                                     142        DS    CL20                          *                  SAM00470
0001B1                                     143 SALOUT DS    CL5                           *                  SAM00480
                                           144 BLANK  DS    CL57                          *                  SAM00490
                                           254        END                                                    SAM00540
```

Figure 15-13

372

```
                                                  PKDSAL      TOTAL
GR 0-7   00020115  A0020044  00000000  80019D3E      0001261A  00000006  0000B8A0  00000868
GR 8-F   00018E90  00019E90  40404040  001F8000      40020006  000201EC  40020038  101F5378
         PSW=  FFE4003360020062
020100   001F5A28  58D0C1EA  98ECD00C  07FE0000      04000000  00C2D9D6  E6D54040  40404040   *......A.Q............BROWN      *
020120   40404040  D3C5D9D6  E8404040  40404040      40404040  40404040  40404040  40404040   *     LEROY                      *
020140   40404040  40404040  40404040  40404040      40404040  40404040  40404040  40404040   *                                *
020160   40404040  40400000  00000000  00000000      00000000  00000000  00000000  00000000   *     .........................*
020180   00000000  00000000  00000000  00000000      00000000  00000000  00000000  00000000   *..............................*
                   *** DUPLICATE CORE LOCATIONS ***
                                                  SALARY
```

Figure 15-14

```
LOC     OBJECT CODE          ADDR1 ADDR2  STMT       SOURCE STATEMENT

                                             8  *                                                             * SAM00080
                                             9  *                                                             * SAM00090
                                            10  *          HOUSEKEEPING INSTRUCTIONS GO HERE                  * SAM00100
00000E                                      11         OPEN  (INFILE,INPUT,OUTFILE,OUTPUT)                      SAM00110
00001E                                      19 READ    GET   INFILE,RECORD                                     SAM00120
00002C  F224 COFC C11C  00102 00122         24         PACK  PKDSAL,SALARY                                     SAM00130
000032                                      25         SNAP  DCB=SNAP,PDATA=(PSW),STORAGE=(PKDSAL,BLANK)       SAM00140
000056  FA32 COFF COFC  00105 00102         40         AP    TOTAL,PKDSAL                                      SAM00150
00005C  47F0 C018       0001E               41         B     READ                                             SAM00160
000060  D283 C154 C153  0015A 00159         42 EOF     MVC   OUTAREA,SPACES                                    SAM00170
000066  D218 C154 C2E8  0015A 002E8         43         MVC   OUTAREA(25),=C'TOTAL ANNUAL SALARIES IS '        SAM00180
00006C  F363 C16D COFF  00173 00105         44         UNPK  OUTAREA+25(7),TOTAL                              SAM00190
000072  96F0 C173       00179               45         OI    OUTAREA+31,X'F0'                                 SAM00200
000076                                      46         PUT   OUTFILE,OUTAREA                                   SAM00210
000084                                      51         CLOSE (INFILE,,OUTFILE)                                 SAM00220
000092                                      59         CLOSE (SNAP)                                            SAM00230
                                                                                                             *SAM00240
00009E                                      65 SNAP    DCB   DDNAME=SNAP,DSORG=PS,MACRF=(W),BLKSIZE=1632       SAM00250
                                                               LRECL=125,RECFM=VBA                            SAM00260
                                           116  *                                                             * SAM00270
                                           117  *          HOUSEKEEPING INSTRUCTIONS GO HERE                  * SAM00280
                                           118  *          ALONG WITH DCB MACROS                              * SAM00290
                                           119  *                                                               SAM00330
000102                                     123 PKDSAL  DS    PL3                                               SAM00340
000105  0000000C                           124 TOTAL   DC    PL4'0'                                            SAM00350
000109                                     125 RECORD  DS    0CL80          CARD FORMAT                        SAM00360
000109                                     126 LAST    DS    CL15                                            * SAM00370
000118                                     127 FIRST   DS    CL10                                            * SAM00380
000122                                     128 SALARY  DS    CL5                                             * SAM00390
000127                                     129         DS    CL50                                              SAM00400
000159  40                                 130 SPACES  DC    CL1' '                                            SAM00410
00015A                                     131 OUTAREA DS    0CL132         PRINT FORMAT                       SAM00420
00015A                                     132         DS    CL5                                             * SAM00430
00015F                                     133 LNAME   DS    CL15                                            * SAM00440
00016E                                     134         DS    CL20                                            * SAM00450
000182                                     135 FNAME   DS    CL10                                              SAM00460
00018C                                     136         DS    CL20                                            * SAM00470
0001A0                                     137 SALOUT  DS    CL5                                             * SAM00480
0001A5                                     138 BLANK   DS    CL57                                              SAM00530
                                           248         END
```

Figure 15-15

374

```
GR 0-7   0002016D   A002009C   00000000   80019D3E       0001261A   00000006   0000B8A0   00000868
GR 8-F   00018E90   00019E90   40404040   001F8000       40020006   00020244   40020090   101F5378
         PSW=  FFE40033600200BA
020160   98ECD00C   07FE1345   0F000000   0CC1C4C1       D4E24040   40404040   40404040   D1D6E8C3
020180   C5404040   4040F1F3   F4F5F040   40404040       40404040   40404040   40404040   40404040
0201A0   40404040   40404040   40404040   40404040       40404040   40404040   40404040   40404040
              *** DUPLICATE CORE LOCATIONS ***
```

Figure 15-16

SELF-
EVALUATING
QUIZ

1. Explain the meaning of the following SNAP macro:
   SNAP   DCB=SNAPDCB,PDATA=(PSW),STORAGE=(COUNT,BLANK)
2. What other instructions must be included in the program when the SNAP macro is utilized?
3. (True or False) The SNAP macro can be used to pinpoint syntax errors; that is, errors that violate the rules of the language.
4. Examine the program listing in Figure 15.15 and explain why no dump was obtained, even though a SNAP macro is included.
   For Questions 5–7, examine the dump in Figure 15-16.
5. What data is located in the 15 bytes starting at $02016D_{16}$? Show the data in hexadecimal and zoned-decimal forms.
6. What data is located in the 10 bytes starting at 02017C? Show the data in hexadecimal and zoned-decimal forms.
7. What data is located in the 5 bytes starting at 020186_{16}? Show the data in hexadecimal and zoned-decimal forms.

Solutions

1. The SNAP instruction requires a DCB macro, arbitrarily named SNAPDCB, to describe the file to be used for writing out the dump. The data to be displayed includes:
   a. The Program Status Word (PSW).
   b. The contents of the storage areas starting with COUNT up to, but not including BLANK.
2.
```
          OPEN     (SNAPDCB,OUTPUT)
SNAPDCB   DCB      DDNAME=SNAPDUMP,DSORG=PS,MACRF=(W),   *
                   BLKSIZE=1632,LRECL=125,RECFM=VBA
          CLOSE    (SNAPDCB)
```
3. False. The SNAP is used to debug errors in *logic*.
4. The file for the SNAP was not opened.
5. C1 C4 C1 D4 E2 40 40 40 40 40 40 40 40 40 40
   A D A M S
6. D1 D6 E8 C3 C5 40 40 40 40 40
   J O Y C E
7. F1 F3 F4 F5 F0
   1 3 4 5 0

UNIT VI

Advanced Concepts

Chapter 16 {style="display:inline"} Indexing

Introduction

You will recall that a loop is a sequence of instructions executed a fixed number of times. An example of a loop is a routine that reads in five input cards and adds an **AMT** field from each card, to produce one **TOTAL**. In general, the sequence of steps necessary for looping includes the following:

Steps in a Loop	Example
1. Initialize all fields (including a counter (CTR) field.)	

```
                      ZAP    TOTAL,=P'0'
                      ZAP    CTR,=P'0'
              LOOP    GET    INFILE,RECORD
                      PACK   PAMT,AMT
                      AP     TOTAL,PAMT
                      AP     CTR,P'1'
                      CP     CTR,=P'5'
                      BE     OUT
                      BNE    LOOP
```

1. Initialize all fields (including a counter (CTR) field.)

2. Perform the necessary operations.

3. Add 1 to **CTR**.

4. Does **CTR** = desired number?

5. If yes, branch out.

6. If no, repeat from Step 2.

Such a routine saves us the trouble of having to code the three instructions beginning at **LOOP** five times, one for each card. Imagine the savings if we had 100 cards to process in this way! Suppose, however, we wish to add five, 4-byte amount fields that are in storage defined either as:

```
ITEM1    DS    F
ITEM2    DS    F
ITEM3    DS    F
ITEM4    DS    F
ITEM5    DS    F
```

or more simply as:

```
ITEM     DS    5F
```

A simple loop will not suffice to add these fields since we are not operating on the *same* field repeatedly as in the previous looping example.

Indexing is a method that enables the programmer to increment the *address* of the fields to be operated on. Using indexing, we can code one looping routine that contains an add instruction and that also increments the *address* of the field to be added.

In the above example, we could perform the add operation and then increment the address of the field to be operated on, by four:

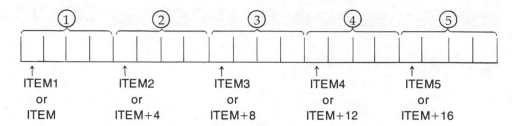

From the illustration, we see that relative addressing, as well as looping, is an integral part of indexing:

Indexing
1. Performs a looping procedure.
2. Utilizes relative addressing. (Field to be operated on is changed within the loop.)

Note that to utilize an index for incrementing the fields to be operated on, these fields must meet certain requirements:

Requirements for Fields when Indexing
1. Fields must be located adjacent to one another in storage, that is, defined sequentially in the program. Or, the fields may be separated by some fixed number of bytes.
2. Fields must all be the same length.

The ITEM fields described above meet these requirements and can, therefore, be indexed.

Additional Applications of Indexing

Fields arranged in the manner described above are sometimes referred to, collectively, as a table, list, matrix, or array. A table, to use the most common term, consists of a series of items called *elements*. Indexing is the method used to process tables.

The specification:

                    ITEM   DS   5F

for example, defines a 20-byte table of 5 elements, each 4 bytes long.

A table can be created in storage for the purpose of summing the elements, or producing a series of totals. A table can also be created for *look-up* purposes. That is, a tax table, for example, may be read into storage with a STATE and COUNTY code and a corresponding SALESTAX rate for each state and county. Indexing, in this instance, is *not* used for totaling, but for "looking-up" a SALESTAX rate from the table. If input cards have a STATE and COUNTY code, we can find the appropriate SALESTAX rate by a look-up procedure that utilizes the *indexing* technique.

Steps Involved in Indexing

Let us return to our example where we have five ITEM fields, which we want to add together using indexing to produce a TOTAL. Here are the steps involved.

> **Steps Involved in Indexing**
> 1. Initialize TOTAL.
> 2. Establish a counter (CTR).
> 3. Establish an index register that will contain the address of ITEM.
> 4. Add ITEM, indexed, to TOTAL.
> 5. Add 4 to index to obtain the next ITEM (each ITEM is 4 bytes long).
> 6. Add 1 to CTR.
> 7. Test CTR for five.
> 8. If =, branch out.
> 9. If not equal, branch to Step 4.

We can generalize these steps to apply to any indexing problem, as illustrated in Figure 16-1.

Indexing can be performed using RX or SS type instructions. We will examine RX instructions first.

Indexing Using RX Instructions

RX (Register and Indexed Storage) format instructions utilize a register in conjunction with storage areas. To perform indexing, we may use RX instructions for obtaining a TOTAL of the 5 ITEM fields. Steps 3–5, which include the indexing procedures, will of course be discussed in detail. Before discussing them, however, we must review and expand our understanding of RX instructions.

```
1.              L       3,=F'0'         REG3=TOTAL
2.              L       2,=F'0'         REG2=CTR
3. *****                                                *****
4. *****    INDEXING PROCEDURES STEPS 3-5               *****
5. *****    (STEP4 IS LABELED LOOP)                     *****
6.              A       2,=F'1'
7.              C       2,=F'5'
8.              BE      OUT
9.              B       LOOP
                .
                .
                .
    ITEM1       DS      F
    ITEM2       DS      F
    ITEM3       DS      F
    ITEM4       DS      F
    ITEM5       DS      F
```

Expanded Version of RX Instructions   You will recall that the actual or effective address of all storage locations is obtained by adding a displacement to a base address, where the base address is stored in a base register. This base address *cannot* be altered during the execution of the program.

When using the RX format, the programmer has the option of including another element for calculating the effective address. This third element is an additional displacement that is stored in an *index register*.

Let us review the format of RX instructions:

Op code	R	X2	B2	D2

An index register is a general purpose register that may be used to store an adjustment or displacement in a manner similar to the base register. However, the index register, unlike the base register, *may be altered* during the program's

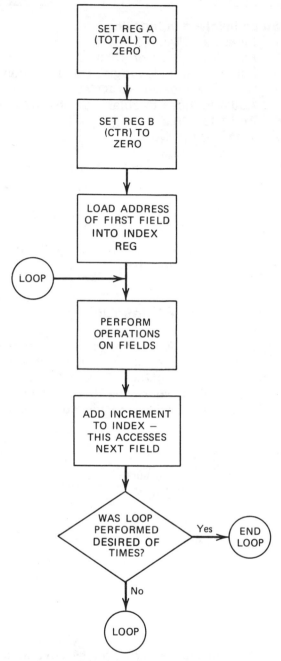

Figure 16-1   General format for RX indexing.

execution. When indexing is to be performed, the programmer must specify which general purpose register is to be used as the index register.

RX Format: Without Indexing

Consider the following RX instruction:

$$A \qquad 5,AMT$$

AMT is a symbolic name that is converted, during the assembly process, to an actual address expressed as X2+B2+D2. Since indexing is *not* being performed in the above, X2 will be given a value of 0. Hence the effective address of AMT may, for example, have the following value:

BASE ADDRESS   8040
DISPLACEMENT   1024
INDEX VALUE   0
EFFECTIVE ADDRESS OF AMT   9064
(no indexing)

Note that an index of 0 does *not* mean register 0, but means that no indexing is being performed.

When an RX instruction contains an operand such as ITEM above, which will be incremented, then the operand must be coded using a different format, one that includes the index register.

Expanded Format(s) for RX Instructions

1.

Operation	Operand
OP	REG,D(X,B)

D = displacement

X = index register

B = base register

or

2.

Operation	Operand
OP	REG,D(X)

where the computer keeps track of the value of the base register

In our example, let us use general register 4 as an index register. Suppose that the index register already contains the address of ITEM. The following instructions (steps 4 and 5 on page 381) allow us to add each ITEM to TOTAL (register 3) and then to increment the index register by four so that the next ITEM is added:

4.	A	3,0(4)	Add ITEM (no displacement) to Register 3 (total).
5.	A	4,=F'4'	Increment address (of ITEM) by four.

The entire indexing procedure then is complete except for the instruction that loads the address of ITEM into index register 4. Figure 16-2 shows the entire program. The LA or Load Address instruction (Step 3) will be explained below.

Summary
1. All RX-type instructions may include an index register if one is desired.
2. For RX-type instructions that are not processed for indexing, the machine language equivalent includes a 0, denoting that *no* indexing is to be performed.

```
* INDEXING PROCEDURE
                L      3,=F'0'
                L      2,=F'0'
                LA     4,ITEM1
LOOP            A      3,0(4)
                A      4,=F'4'
                A      2,=F'1'
                C      2,=F'5'
                BE     OUT
                B      LOOP
                .
                .
                .
ITEM1     DS    F
ITEM2     DS    F
ITEM3     DS    F
ITEM4     DS    F
ITEM5     DS    F
```

Figure 16-2

**The LA Instruction and
Explicit Addressing**

Instruction:	LA
Meaning:	Load Address
Operand 1:	Register
Operand 2:	Symbolic address or displacement with index and/or base register indicated in parentheses.
Result:	The effective address obtained by adding the displacement, index register contents, and base register contents is loaded into the first operand.

The primary function of the Load Address (**LA**) instruction is to place an actual or effective address specified in the second operand into the register specified as the first operand. The address, when contained in a register, can then be modified for indexing purposes. It is important to realize that the **LA** instruction does not load the *contents* of the location, just the address itself. Here is the general format for the **LA** instruction when used for explicit addressing.

Operation	Operand
LA or LA	REG,D(X,B) REG,OP2

where

LA   denotes the operation Load Address.
REG is a register and the first operand.
D   is a displacement
X   specifies an index register. } Second operand
B   specifies the base register.

The contents of the base register (B) and the contents of the index register (X) are added together. This sum is then added to the displacement to determine the actual or effective address.

An example will clarify the operation of this instruction.

LA   3,ITEM

This instruction loads the address of ITEM into register 3, the index register in this example.

We may now refer to register 3 to obtain the address of ITEM:

0(3) refers to ITEM1
4(3) refers to ITEM1 + 4 (ITEM2)
8(3) refers to ITEM1 + 8 (ITEM3)
12(3) refers to ITEM1 + 12 (ITEM4)
16(3) refers to ITEM1 + 16 (ITEM5)

Examine Figure 16-2 again to be sure you understand how indexing is performed using the LA instruction.

SELF-EVALUATING QUIZ

1. (True or False) Assembler language instructions may produce indexed results by using a base + displacement + index format or by using a symbolic name + index.
2. Indicate the results of the following:
   a. LA   7,CARDIN
   b. LA   7,CARDIN(7)
   c. LA   6,200(5,4)
   d. LA   5,3(5)
3. Write a routine to add 30, 4-position numbers at TABLE into register 5. Assume that each 4-position number is in binary form.

Solutions

1. True
2. a. Address of CARDIN loaded into register 7.
   b. Register 7 = address of CARDIN + previous contents of register 7.
   c. Register 6 = 200 + contents of register 5 + contents of register 4.
   d. Register 5 = 3 + previous contents of register 5.
3.

```
            L       5,=F'0'     SET REG5 (TOTAL) TO ZERO
            L       6,=F'0'     SET REG6 (COUNTER) TO ZERO
            LA      3,TABLE     ADDRESS OF FIRST NUMBER
LOOP        A       5,0(3)      ADD NUMBER TO TOTAL
            A       6,=F'1'     ADD 1 TO COUNTER
            A       3,=F'4'     ADD 4 TO ADDRESS TO ACCESS NEXT NUMBER
            C       6,=F'30'    WAS ROUTINE PERFORMED 30 TIMES?
            BNE     LOOP        IF NOT,REPEAT
            .
            .
            .
TABLE       DS      30F
```

An Indepth Look at the Load Address Instruction

The LA instruction may be used in the following ways:

1. Using Symbolic Names
   LA   5,CARDIN—This instruction loads the *address* of CARDIN into register 5.

2. Using the base-displacement format

Operation	Operand
LA	5,200(3,4)

This instruction loads into register 5, 200 + the contents of index register 3 + the contents of base register 4.

Example

Before Execution   *After Execution*

Register 3   00 00 20 00   Register 3   00 00 20 00
Register 4   00 00 10 00   Register 4   00 00 10 00
Register 5   00 12 34 56   Register 5   00 00 32 00

Register 5 now contains the address, or storage location, 3200. The contents of register 3 and register 4 are added to a displacement of 200. Note that the displacement is coded in decimal and may range in value from 0 to 4095.

When either the base or index register is specified as 0, it means that these elements of the instruction are to be omitted. It does *not* mean that register 0 is to be used as an index register or base register. In addition, the 0 specification may be omitted from the instruction entirely. For example, the following three **LA** instructions all produce the same results:

Instruction		Register 3 Before Execution	Register 5 After Execution
LA	5,350(3,0)	2000	2350
LA	5,350(3)	2000	2350
LA	5,2350	2000	2350

The last example is interesting in that the decimal displacement (2350) is loaded into register 5. Since the base and index registers have been omitted, only the displacement value (2350) has been stored in register 5. The register makes *no* distinction between an address and constants used in a program. The decimal value 2350 is converted to binary and stored in the register. The **LA** instruction, then, provides us with an additional means of giving a register a starting value.

In order to zero out register 5, we simply code **LA** 5,0. The value zero would then be placed in register 5.

Loading Constants with the **LA** Instruction

The following illustrations of the **LA** instruction will improve your understanding of explicit addressing and increase your efficiency as a programmer.

The effect of the instructions below is to add 4 to the contents of register 5.

| LA   5,4(5) | or | A   5,=F'4' |

(Register 5 = 4 + Register 5)
= Displacement of 4 + contents of register 5

The **LA** instruction, however, is more efficient, since a fullword containing a 4 was not required. The advantage of this approach is that it saves 4 bytes of storage each time a constant is added to a register. Whenever a register is to be initialized, the same approach may be taken. For example, to set a register to zero, any of the following instructions could be used:

Load Address   *Load Halfword*   *Load Fullword*
LA   8,0   LH   8,=H'0'   L   8,=F'0'

The most efficient method is to use the Load Address since the other instructions require either a halfword or fullword with value of zero. Consequently, 2 or 4 bytes of storage are wasted if the other instructions are used.

Indexed Addressing and Symbolic Names

When an RX (Register—Indexed Storage) instruction refers to a storage location by name, the assembler converts the actual address of that storage location to the base-displacement format. When the index register is specified, it is used by the CPU to calculate the effective address. If storage areas were defined as follows:

```
ITEM1    DC      F'15'
ITEM2    DC      F'7'
ITEM3    DC      F'91'
ITEM4    DC      F'11'
ITEM5    DC      F'82'
```

we would reference the data in these areas in several ways.

First, we could code the instruction

Operation	Operand
LA	3,ITEM1

to store the actual address of ITEM1 in register 3. If it were necessary to reference the other items we could now use any of the following alternatives in referencing ITEM1–ITEM5.

Using Symbolic Name	Relative Addressing	Explicit Addressing
		Displacement
ITEM1	ITEM1	0(3) Index register
ITEM2	ITEM1+4	4(3) [Contents of index register 3 (ITEM1) + 4]
ITEM3	ITEM1+8	8(3) [Contents of index register 3 (ITEM1) + 8]
ITEM4	ITEM1+12	12(3) [Contents of index register 3 (ITEM1) + 12]
ITEM5	ITEM1+16	16(3) [Contents of index register 3 (ITEM1) + 16]

Remember that register 3 contains the effective address of ITEM1. The displacement values are added to this address to arrive at the actual address. The following instructions would, then, all be equivalent.

A	9,ITEM5

A	9,ITEM1+16

LA	3,ITEM1
A	9,16(3)

In addition, a fourth format may be used as follows, first loading into register 5 the decimal value 16:

Operation	Operand
LA	5,16
A	9,ITEM1(5)

The base-displacement address of ITEM1 and the contents of register 5 are added to produce the effective address. If register 5 contained the decimal value 16, the second operand would reference ITEM5. However, if register 5 contained a zero, then the Add instruction would be referencing ITEM1.

Therefore, there are 2 formats for explicitly referencing **RX** instructions as illustrated in the table below.

Summary

Symbolic Address	Explicit Type 1 (may be coded this way)	Explicit Type 2 (may be coded this way)	Register 5 (in Decimal)	Register 3
ITEM1	0(3)	ITEM1(5)	000	[Contains the
ITEM2	4(3)	ITEM1(5)	004	address of
ITEM3	8(3)	ITEM1(5)	008	ITEM1]
ITEM4	12(3)	ITEM1(5)	012	
ITEM5	16(3)	ITEM1(5)	016	

Indexing Example 2

Write a routine to sum the contents of 20 consecutive fullwords, the first of which is located at **AMTS**. We will use the **LA** instruction in place of less efficient instructions. We will count the number of times the routine is being performed. When the count is equal to 20, we have added all 20 numbers:

```
* SOLUTION TO INDEXING EXAMPLE 2
         LA      6,0     SET REGISTER 6 (TOTAL) TO ZERO
         LA      7,0     SET REGISTER 7 (CTR) TO ZERO
         LA      5,AMTS    REGISTER 5 IS INDEX REGISTER
LOOP     A       6,0(5)    ADD AMT TO TOTAL
         LA      7,1(7)    ADD 1 TO CTR
         LA      5,4(5)    ADD 4 TO ADDRESS
         C       7,=F'20'  WAS ROUTINE PERFORMED 20 TIMES?
         BNE     LOOP    IF NOT,REPEAT
         .
         .
         .
AMTS     DS      20F
```

SELF-EVALUATING QUIZ

1. Question 3 in the previous section stated the following:
    Write a routine to add 30, 4-position numbers at **TABLE** into register 5. Assume that each 4-position number is in binary form.
    Code this same procedure using **LA** instructions:

```
******
         LA      5,0       SET REG 5(TOTAL) TO ZERO
         LA      6,0       SET REG 6(CTR) TO ZERO
         LA      3,TABLE   ADDRESS OF FIRST NUMBER
LOOP     A       5,0(3)    ADD NUMBER TO TOTAL
         LA      6,1(6)    ADD 1 TO CTR
         LA      3,4(3)    ADD 4 TO ADDRESS TO GET NEXT NUMBER
         C       6,=F'0'   WAS ROUTINE PERFORMED 30 TIMES?
         BNE     LOOP    IF NOT, REPEAT
```

2. Why is the **LA** instruction more efficient than the **A** or **L** instruction used in the previous section?
    *****
    The **A** and **L** instructions require self-defining constants that utilize a fullword of storage. The instruction **L** 3,=F'0', for example, sets up a 4-byte constant of zero. This is unnecessary when using an **LA** instruction.

3. (True or False) The **LA** instruction loads into Operand 1 the contents of Operand 2, if Operand 2 is defined as a symbolic name.
    *****
    False. It loads in the *address* of Operand 2, not the contents, if Operand 2 is defined as a symbolic name.

Address Constants In our routines so far, we have tested for the end of a loop by *counting* the number of times the loop has been performed. The logic has been basically as follows:

```
             LA        3,0      SET REGISTER 3 (COUNTER) TO ZERO
             .
             .
LOOP         .
             .
             .
             LA        3,1(3)   ADD 1 TO COUNTER
             C         3,LIMIT  WAS ROUTINE PERFORMED LIMIT TIMES?
             BNE       LOOP     IF NOT, REPEAT
```

This test includes the following items.

---

1. Initialize a register as a counter.
2. Add 1 to the register every time we process LOOP.
3. Compare the register or counter to the desired number.
4. Branch back to LOOP if the desired number has not been reached.

Another method for testing for the end of a loop is to use an ADCON, which is an abbreviation for *add*ress *con*stant. If, for example, we want to operate on CARDIN until the appropriate register used for address modification is equal to CARDIN+80, we can program it as follows:

```
             LA        5,CARDIN
             .
             .
             .
LOOP         .
             .
             .
             C         5,=A(CARDIN+80)
             BNE       LOOP
```

The operand =A(CARDIN+80) indicates the *address of* CARDIN+80. The compare instruction thus compares the contents of register 5 (an address) with the address of CARDIN+80.

By using an address constant, we need not establish a separate register as a counter. Similarly, we need not add 1 to the counter every time we pass through the loop. Figure 16-3 is an alternative method for coding the ITEM problem using an ADCON in place of a register as a counter.

Note, too, that if items are added to the table, the use of the address constant eliminates the need to alter the program.

```
* INDEXING PROCEDURE USING ADDRESS CONSTANT IN PLACE OF COUNTER
             LA        3,0
             LA        2,0
             LA        4,ITEM1
LOOP         A         3,0(4)
             LA        4,4(4)
             C         4,=A(ITEM1+20)
             BE        OUT
             B         LOOP
             .
             .
             .
ITEM1        DS        F
ITEM2        DS        F
ITEM3        DS        F
ITEM4        DS        F
ITEM5        DS        F
```

Figure 16-3

Indexing Using SS Instructions

Thus far, we have illustrated how indexing can be performed using RX instructions. Indexing is not, however, limited to RX instructions; it can be performed on SS (storage-to-storage) instructions as well.

Advantage of SS Indexing A main advantage of using SS instructions for indexing is that the length of each element of a stored table is not limited. Since RX instructions place results in a register, indexing is limited to 4 bytes. With SS indexing, each element of a table may contain from 1 to 256 bytes. This, of course, provides a good deal more flexibility.

Requirements of SS Indexing Indexing of main storage requires that *explicit* addresses be used. An index register is referenced as part of the explicit address. It must *not* be the program's base register; that is, the register used for indexing may *not* be specified in the USING instruction.[1]

Expanded Format for SS Instructions The symbolic format for explicit operands when using storage-to-storage (SS) operations is somewhat different from that discussed for RX operations:

Operand
DISP(LENGTH,REG)

where

DISP specifies a displacement. This displacement will be added to the contents of the register to arrive at an actual address. With indexing, this displacement is usually specified as 0.

LENGTH refers to the length of the field to be operated on, in bytes. With indexing, it will usually be the length of each element of the table.

REG indicates a general register that contains the address of the first item to be indexed. This register will serve as an index register.

An LA or Load Address instruction is usually needed for loading the required address into the index register.

Example

```
LA       7,CARDIN              ┌──→ Length of move
MVC      LINEOUT+10(80),0(80,7)    └──→ Register containing address
                                         of data to be moved
         └→Displacement
         (usually 0 for indexing)
```

Result

Eighty positions at CARDIN are moved to LINEOUT. The following will also produce the same results:

```
MVC      LINEOUT+10(80),CARDIN
```

---

[1] See Appendix F for a discussion of how a base register is assigned.

If the programmer were also required to test card columns 79–80 for a state code such as NY, the following CLC instruction could be coded:

Operation	Operand
CLC	78(2,7),=C'NY'

The second operand is self-defining and contains the EBCDIC configuration for NY. The first operand is referencing CARDIN+78, or position 79 of the input area. Recall that register 7 contains the *address* of CARDIN while a displacement of 78 bytes from that point of reference has been prescribed. We are therefore referencing the 79th position of CARDIN or column 79 of the input data card. The number of bytes to be compared has been specified as 2. Therefore, positions 79 and 80 of CARDIN will be compared to the EBCDIC configuration of NY. When an equal condition occurs, we want to branch to a routine called BIGAPPLE where further processing will take place. This instruction would be coded as follows:

```
BE        BIGAPPLE
```

As we will see in the following examples, explicit addressing is a powerful tool for the programmer and is essential for storage-to-storage indexing.

Example 1

Suppose a population table consisting of 50 state population figures has been read into an area called STATE:

```
STATE        DS        50PL4
```

The above entry defines the storage area for the table. Data must be read from an input device and moved into this area. Later in this chapter we will discuss the routines necessary for reading and accumulating the table data. For now, let us assume that STATE contains all the data; that is the 50 packed figures have been accumulated in this table and are now available for processing.

We want to write a routine to find the total population of 50 states and place the answer in register 3. Examine the following program excerpt.

```
      * FIND TOTAL USA POPULATION USING INDEXING
1.          LA     3,0               REG 3 = TOTAL
2.          LA     5,STATE           REG 5 = INDEX REGISTER
3.  LOOP    ZAP    DWORD,0(4,5)      STATE POPS ARE ADDED
4.          CVB    2,DWORD               USING
5.          AR     3,2               RR FORMAT ADDITIONS
6.          LA     5,4(5)            INDEX REGISTER INCREMENTED BY 4
7.          C      5,=A(STATE+200)   ARE WE FINISHED?
8.          BNE    LOOP              IF NOT, REPEAT
                 .
                 .
                 .
      DWORD   DS     D
      STATE   DS     50PL4
```

Explanation

1. The first instruction initializes register 3 at 0.
2. The second instruction loads the address of STATE into register 5.
3. Instruction 3 places the field specified in a doubleword, (DWORD DS D), initially STATE, then STATE+4, and so on.
4. Instruction 4 converts the field specified into binary and places the result in register 2.
5. Instruction 5 adds the binary field to register 3.
6. Instruction 6 increments register 5 by 4.
7. Instruction 7 tests to see if all fields have been added; if the address in register 5 is equal to STATE+200, we have completed the table.

The following illustration will clarify this:

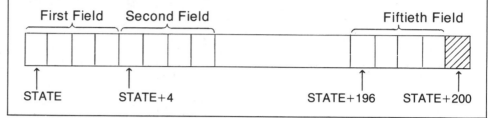

If the table has not been completely processed, a branch to **LOOP** occurs at instruction 8.

Example 2

Using the Population Table (**STATE**) referred to in Example 1, find the number of states with population figures in excess of 1,000,000.

```
* FIND THE NUMBER OF STATES WITH POPULATIONS IN EXCESS OF 1,000,000
*
         L      2,=F'1000000'
         LA     5,STATE
LOOP     ZAP    DWORD,0(4,5)
         CVB    4,DWORD
         CR     2,4
         BNL    NOCOUNT
         AP     TOTAL,=P'1'
NOCOUNT  LA     5,4(5)
         C      5,=A(STATE+200)
         BNE    LOOP
*
* TOTAL NOW EQUALS THE NUMBER OF STATES WITH
* POPULATION GREATER THAN 1,000,000
             .
             .
             .
DWORD    DS     D
STATE    DS     50PL4
TOTAL    DC     PL2'0'
```

Let us use our population table again:

STATE	DS	50PL4

Note that if we are using SS-type instructions, each **STATE** field need not be restricted to 4 bytes. That is, the following table would be valid, if used with SS-type instructions:

STATE   DS   50PL6

To be consistent, however, we will use the original description of **STATE** (50PL4) for the following problems.

Example 3

Assuming that the state figures are in alphabetic sequence, write the instructions necessary to move the population of Alabama (1st state) and Wyoming (50th state) to output areas called POP1 and POP50, respectively.

```
        UNPK        POP1,STATE(4)
        UNPK        POP50,STATE+196(4)
```

Example 4

Write a routine to find the largest state population figure. Place this figure in an area called HOLD:

```
* FIND THE LARGEST STATE POPULATION FIGURE
        LA        7,STATE
        ZAP       HOLD,STATE(4)
LOOP    CP        HOLD,0(4,7)
        BNL       NEXT
        ZAP       HOLD,0(4,7)
NEXT    A         7,4(7)
        C         7,=A(STATE+200)
        BNE       LOOP
*
* HOLD NOW CONTAINS LARGEST STATE POPULATION FIGURE
*
            .
            .
            .
HOLD    DS        PL4
STATE   DS        50PL4
```

Instruction 1 indicates that register 7 will be the index register. The address of STATE is loaded into register 7. Instruction 2 moves the first state field into HOLD. The LOOP compares HOLD to the first field. If HOLD is equal to or greater than the STATE figure, no operation is performed. If HOLD is less than the state figure, the new state figure is moved into HOLD.

Register 7 is compared to the address of STATE+200 to determine if all fields in the table have been compared. If not, a branch to LOOP occurs. When the routine has been performed 50 times, HOLD will contain the largest state population figure.

In the example thus far presented in this section, we have assumed that our population table (STATE) has been previously read in and accumulated in storage. Let us now consider the routine that will actually read in and accumulate the data into the table.

Suppose there are 50 table cards, each with a 7-position population figure. We wish to accumulate these 50 figures in STATE for future processing. Note that the table data is *not* simply read and immediately processed, as is the convention with other forms of input. Rather, the table data is read and *stored* for future processing.

The card format is as follows:

```
RECORD    DS        0CL80
POP       DS        CL7
          DS        CL73
```

We will read 50 such cards and accumulate the data in the following area:

```
STATE     DS        50PL4
```

The following loop may be used:

```
         LA     7,STATE
LOOP     GET    INFILE,RECORD
         PACK   0(4,7),POP
         LA     7,4(7)
         C      7,=A(STATE+200)
         BNE    LOOP
          .
          .
          .
STATE    DS     50PL4
RECORD   DS     0CL80
POP      DS     CL7
         DS     CL73
```

SELF-EVALUATING QUIZ

1. Explain the meaning of the following instruction:

    ```
    C      7,=A(INDATA+50)
    ```
2. What is a main advantage of storage-to-storage indexing as compared to indexing used with RX instructions.
3. (True or False) Indexing of main storage requires that explicit addresses be used.
4. Write the instructions necessary to move bytes 1–50 from **INDATA** to positions 11–60 of **LINEOUT**. Use explicit addressing.
5. Explain the meaning of the following instructions:

    ```
    LA     5,STATE
    ZAP    DWORD,0(4,5)
    ```
6. Write an **LA** instruction to add 4 to the contents of register 7.
7. If there are twenty 4-byte figures stored in **TABLE**, write an instruction to unpack into **TDATA** the fifth entry in the table.
8. (True or False) The instruction **LA 9,ITEM** usually indicates that register 9 will be an index register.
9. Using the state population table defined in this section, write a routine to find the total number of states with population figures less than 250,000.
10. Using the state population table defined in this section, write a routine to find the smallest state population figure and the *number* of that state.

Solutions

1. The instruction compares the contents of register 7 (an address) with the address of **INDATA+50**.
2. With SS instructions, each element of a stored table is not limited to 4 bytes as it is with RX instructions. With SS indexing, each element of a table may contain from 1 to 256 bytes.
3. True
4.  ```
    LA     8,INDATA
    MVC    LINEOUT+10(50),0(50,8)
    ```
5. The address of **STATE** is loaded in register 5. Next, we **ZAP** a field 4 bytes in length, starting at the address found in register 5.
6. `LA     7,4(7)`
7. `UNPK   TDATA,TABLE+16(4)`
8. True. The address of **ITEM** is loaded into register 9.
9.
    ```
    * SOLUTION  TO SELF-EVALUATING QUIZ Q. 9
             L      2,=F'250000'
             LA     5,STATE
    LOOP     ZAP    DWORD,0(4,5)
             CVB    4,DWORD
             CR     2,4
             BNH    NOCOUNT
             AP     TOTAL,=F'1'
    NOCOUNT  LA     5,4(5)
             C      5,=A(STATE+200)
    ```
    ```

```
                    BNE    LOOP
* TOTAL CONTAINS THE NUMBER OF STATES
*    WITH POPULATION FIGURES LESS THAN 250,000
                      .
                      .
                      .
DWORD    DS     D
TOTAL    DC     PL2'0'
STATE    DS     50PL4
```

10.
```
* SOLUTION TO SELF-EVALUATING QUIZ Q.10
         LA     7,STATE
         ZAP    CTR,=P'0'
         ZAP    HOLD,0(4,7)
LOOP     CP     HOLD,0(4,7)
         BNH    NEXT
         ZAP    HOLD,0(4,7)
         ZAP    HOLDNO,CTR
NEXT     A      7,4(7)
         AP     CTR,=P'1'
         C      7,=A(STATE+200)
         BNE    LOOP
* HOLD CONTAINS SMALLEST STATE POPULATION FIGURE
* HOLDNO CONTAINS STATE NUMBER WITH SMALLEST STATE POPULATION
                      .
                      .
                      .
HOLD     DS     PL4
HOLDNO   DS     PL2
STATE    DS     50PL4
```

The Branch Index Low or Equal (BXLE) Instruction

With the RX instruction, a field length of 4 bytes is specified in order to increment or step from one storage location of a table to the next. However, with storage-to-storage (SS) instructions, the fields may vary from 1 to 256 bytes. As we have already learned, the indexing increment must match the length of each element of the table. For example, if each element were 6 bytes in length, it would be necessary to add a value of 6 to the index register with each pass through the loop. The BXLE instruction allows us to combine many of the steps presented in the previous indexing problem into one instruction. The symbolic form of the BXLE instruction is:

Operation	Operand
BXLE	REG1,REG2,LABEL

where

BXLE indicates Branch on Index, Low or Equal.

REG1 specifies the index register.

REG2 is an *even-numbered register* (of an even-odd pair) and contains the field length in bytes of each element

REG3 (not coded) is an *implied odd register* numbered REG2+1 and contains the limit value to be used to end the loop.

LABEL identifies the first instruction of the loop as in the BCT instruction.

The index register (REG1) is used to identify the element of the table to be processed. The register specified as REG2 contains the field length of each element and is the *even* register of an *even-odd* pair. The *odd* register contains the limit value used to end the loop. Let us again review what operations this one instruction performs.

REG1	REG2	REG2+1
Index value	Field length	Limit

Index value points to a different element in the table with each pass through the loop.

Field length is the increment added to the index register with each pass through the loop.

Limit controls the number of passes through the loop.

Each time the BXLE instruction is executed, the following steps occur in the sequence shown:

Steps in BXLE

a. The field length specified in REG2 is added to the contents of REG1. This allows us to reference the next element in the table.

b. The contents of REG1 (the current index value) are then compared to the contents of REG2+1 (the limit value).

c. If the index register is *low or equal*, the program branches to the label (first instruction of the loop) specified in the second operand.

In the previous examples, involving a population table called STATE, we have used the following instructions to determine if the loop should be repeated. The loop is now performed 50 times, since there are fifty 4-byte fields to be processed. The address of the last field to be processed is STATE+196.

```
        LA      5,STATE             LOAD ADDRESS OF 1ST NO. INTO REG 5
                .
                .
                .
LOOP            .
                .
                .
        LA      5,4(5)              INCREMENT REG 5 BY 4
        C       5,=A(STATE+200)     WAS LOOP PERFORMED REQUIRED NO. TIMES?
        BNE     LOOP                IF NOT, REPEAT
```

By using the BXLE, we can replace these instructions with the following:

```
*   ILLUSTRATION OF BXLE IN INDEXING
        LA      5,STATE     LOAD ADDRESS OF 1ST NO. INTO REG5
        L       6,=F'4'     LOAD FIELD LENGTH OF 4 INTO REG 6
        L       7,=A(STATE+196)    LOAD LIMIT INTO REG 7
LOOP            .
                .
                .
        BXLE    5,6,LOOP
```

The limit value may be specified in two different ways.

Specifying Limit Value

1. By specifying the address of the *last element* of the table. (The method used above.)

2. By specifying the *length of the table* in bytes *and* then *subtracting one.*

When the table length is specified, we are required to subtract 1. The reason for the subtraction is as follows: You will recall that the field length is *first* added to the index register and then a comparison of the index register to the limit value is made. An example illustrates this point.

Assume that a table consists of 5 elements, each 4 bytes in length, and that the limit value is set up as 20. Let us examine what will happen when the last element is processed.

When the entire table has been processed, the index value and the limit value will both have a value of 20. At this point in the program the loop should end. However, the program will incorrectly branch back to the first instruction of the loop, since the BXLE is designed to branch on a low or *equal* condition. To prevent this from occurring, 1 is always subtracted from the length of the table. In this way the BXLE will branch out when the table has been completely processed, that is, when the limit value of 19 is exceeded.

If the programmer establishes the limit by specifying the address of the last element of the table, a load address (LA) instruction is used. We will apply both these techniques again in finding the sum of 5 items, ITEM1–ITEM5, in the following examples.

Example 1:

Specifying the limit as the length of the table minus 1.

```
* SPECIFYING THE LIMIT AS THE LENGTH OF THE TABLE MINUS ONE
         LH      6,=H'0'          SET TOTAL TO ZERO
         LH      7,=H'0'          SET INDEX REGISTER TO ZERO
         LH      8,=H'4'          FIELD LENGTH OF 4 BYTES PLACED IN EVEN REG
         LH      9,=H'19'         TABLE LENGTH MINUS ONE PLACED IN ODD REG
DO5X     A       6,ITEM1(7)
         BXLE    7,8,DO5X         IF REG7+REG8 > REG 9 END LOOP
         CVD     6,RESULT
         .
         .
```

Example 2:

Specifying the limit as the address of the last element of the table.

```
* SPECIFYING THE LIMIT AS THE ADDRESS OF THE LAST ELEMENT OF THE TABLE
         LA      6,0             SET TOTAL TO ZERO
         LA      7,ITEM1         STORE ADDRESS OF 1ST ELEMENT IN INDEX REG
         LA      8,4             FIELD LENGTH OF 4 PLACED IN REG 8
         LA      9,ITEM5         STORE ADDRESS OF LAST ELEMENT IN TABLE
DO5X     A       6,0(7)
         BXLE    7,8,DO5X
         CVD     6,RESULT
         .
         .
```

The field specifications for both examples appear as follows:

```
ITEM1    DC      F'15'
ITEM2    DC      F'7'
ITEM3    DC      F'91'
ITEM4    DC      F'11'
ITEM5    DC      F'82'
RESULT   DS      D
```

It is important to recognize that there are many ways to assign initial values to the registers. In Example 1, we used the LH (Load Halfword) instruction and in Example 2 the LA (Load Address) instruction. Remember, the LA instruction is more efficient since a 2-byte halfword constant is unnecessary, and only wastes storage.

We also note that explicit (RX) addressing is used in Example 2. Notice that in this example, register 7 initially contained the address of ITEM1. The BXLE adds the field length contained in register 8 to the address stored in register 7 with each pass through the loop.

The values of the registers at the *completion* of each pass through the loop in Example 1 are as follows. These values are shown in decimal for the purpose of clarification.

Example 1:		BXLE 7,8,DO5X		
After Pass	(Total) Register 6	Index Register 7	(Field Length) Register 8	(Limit Value) Register 9
1	15	4	4	19
2	22	8	4	19
3	113	12	4	19
4	124	16	4	19
5	206	20	4	19

When the contents of register 7 are greater than the contents of register 9, the looping process is terminated and the instruction following the BXLE is executed.

SELF EVALUATING QUIZ

1. BXLE is the mnemonic for _____ .
2. Consider the following instruction with the contents of registers 4, 6, and 7 as shown before execution:

$$\text{BXLE} \quad 4,6,\text{LOOP}$$
$$\text{Register } 4 = +8$$
$$\text{Register } 6 = +1$$
$$\text{Register } 7 = +16$$

When the BXLE instruction is executed, a branch to LOOP (*will, will not*) occur.

3. With the BXLE instruction, a branch only occurs when the sum of the first and second operands is _____ or _____ compared to the third operand.

For Questions 4–6, assume the following hexadecimal values in the registers 2–7:

```
R2:    00 00 00 0A
R3:    00 00 00 2A
R4:    00 00 00 0A
R5:    00 00 00 08
R6:    00 00 00 02
R7:    00 00 00 0C
```

Indicate whether or not a branch occurs:

4. BXLE   4,6,LOOP1
5. BXLE   4,2,LOOP2
6. BXLE   3,6,LOOP3

Solutions

1. Branch on index, low or equal
2. Will: the sum is less than contents of register 7.
3. Low or equal
4. A branch occurs. The limit is in register 7.

$$A+2 = C = Reg7 \qquad \text{Branch occurs on } =.$$

5. A branch occurs. The limit is in register 3.

$$A+A < 2A \quad (A_{16}+A_{16}=20_{10}; \ 2A_{16}=42_{10})$$

6. A branch does not occur. The limit is in register 7.

$$2A+2 > C \quad (2A_{16}+2_{16}=44_{10}; \ C_{16}=12_{10})$$

A Full Illustration of Storage-to-Storage Indexing

You will recall that storage-to-storage indexing permits a series of consecutive storage positions to be processed efficiently by a looping procedure that addresses the fields one at a time, in sequence. For example, let us assume that an input data card contains 30 fields, each 2 positions in length. These 30 fields represent the temperatures for each day of the month of April: that is, CC 1–2 has the temperature for April 1, CC 3–4 the temperature for April 2, and so on. To calculate the average temperature for the month, it is necessary to develop one sum of the 30 temperatures and then divide this sum by 30. Without indexing, 30 different symbolic names would be assigned to the 30 fields; moreover, 30 PACK and add (AP) instructions would be required.

Indexing simplifies the solution to this problem. Figure 16-4 contains the coded program. The 30 temperatures will occupy adjacent storage positions in the input area called RECORD. Therefore, the *address* of RECORD becomes a starting point and is placed in Register 7 by the LA instruction, LA 7,RECORD. Effectively, register 7 now points to the area called RECORD and will serve as an index register. Each temperature is then processed one at a time simply by incrementing the contents of the index register.

Explicit addressing is used to reference each data field. Note that the first temperature can be referenced as 0(2,7), where, you will recall:

> 0 refers to a zero displacement.
> 2 denotes a field length of 2 bytes.
> 7 is the general register serving as an index register.

Initially, the explicit address 0(2,7) points to RECORD and specifies the first field to be processed that consists of RECORD and RECORD+1. With each pass through the loop, the temperature will be packed and added to a field called TOTAL. The concept of indexing is illustrated in the schematic in Figure 16-5. Note that indexing is really a form of relative addressing. By adding 2 to the contents of the index register with each pass through the loop, the register will then point to the next temperature to be processed.

Clearly the advantages of indexing are (1) the reduction in the number of instructions required to perform a particular task and (2) the resulting efficiency.

```
*                                                                      *
*                                      HOUSEKEEPING INSTRUCTIONS GO HERE  *
*                                                                      *
          MVC    OUTAREA,SPACES
READ      GET    INFILE,RECORD
          ZAP    TOTAL,=P'0'
          LA     7,RECORD
          LA     5,RECORD+58
          LA     4,2
DO30X     PACK   0(2,7),0(2,7)
          AP     TOTAL,0(2,7)
          BXLE   7,4,DO30X
          ZAP    PROD,TOTAL
          MP     PROD,=P'100'
          ZAP    ANSWER,PROD+1(4)
          DP     ANSWER,=P'30'
          MVC    OUTAREA+10(9),=X'4020202020214B2020'
          ED     OUTAREA+10(9),QUOTNT
          PUT    OUTFILE,OUTAREA
*                                                                      *
*                                      HOUSEKEEPING INSTRUCTIONS GO HERE  *
*                                      ALONG WITH DTF OR DCB MACROS       *
*                                                                      *
RECORD    DS     CL80
SPACES    DC     CL1' '
OUTAREA   DS     CL132
ANSWER    DS     0CL6
QUOTNT    DS     CL4
REMDR     DS     CL2
TOTAL     DS     CL3
PROD      DS     CL5
          END
```

Figure 16-4

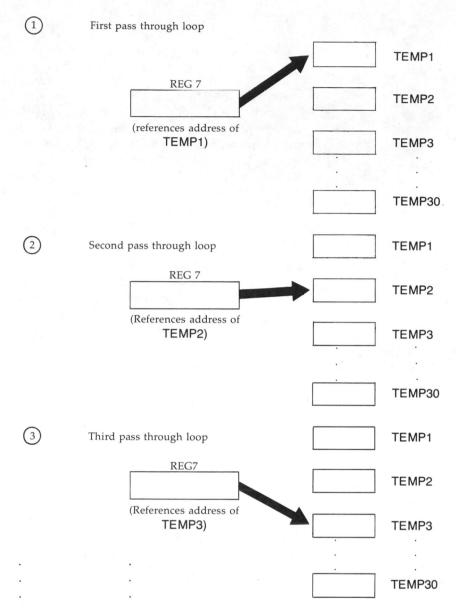

Figure 16-5 Schematic of Storage-to-Storage Indexing.

Summary

With storage-to-storage indexing the programmer must always be aware of the following facts:

1. The address of the first field to be indexed is placed in an index register with an LA instruction.
2. The number of times the loop is to be executed is placed in a register that serves as a counter.
3. Explicit addressing must be used: it specifies
   a. The index register
   b. The length of the data field
4. The index register is incremented by the length of the data field with each pass through the loop.
5. Execution of the loop will cease when all fields have been processed.

**SELF-
EVALUATING
QUIZ**

1. With storage-to-storage indexing, the data fields to be indexed may be in consecutive positions or they may be randomly located.
2. The address of the starting point of the area to be indexed is placed in a(n) _____ .
3. The type of instruction used to place the starting point in the index register is a(n) _____ .
4. To perform indexing, *(implicit/explicit)* addressing must be used.
5. With explicit addressing, the instruction **AP SUM,0(5,9)** uses_____ as the index register. The length of the field to be added is ___(number)___ bytes.
6. In order to perform indexing, addressing is performed within a _____ .
7. With each pass through the loop, the index register is incremented by the _____ .
8. The number of times the loop is to be executed is controlled by a _____ .
9. The count register is initialized *(before/after)* the loop is executed.
10. (True or False) A single general register may be used as both an index register and a base register.

Solutions

1. False. They must be in consecutive positions.
2. Index register
3. LA (Load Address)
4. Explicit
5. Register 9
   5
6. Loop
7. Length of the element or data field
8. Register
9. Before
10. False. Two separate registers must be used.

Table Look-Up Using Indexing

As we have seen, a *table* is simply a list of data, systematically organized to permit sequential reference to storage locations. Another feature of a table is to look up information. This function of table handling is commonly called a *table look-up* or *search*. Each item of data within the table is called an *element*. The elements of a table to be searched consist of two components: the *argument* and the *function*.

Consider the following table:

Argument	Function
Wage Category	Percent Federal Tax
750.00	0.35
615.00	0.32
500.00	0.29
385.00	0.26
307.00	0.24
230.00	0.22
154.00	0.20
77.00	0.17
20.00	0.14
00.00	0.00

The table consists of *ten* elements. The *argument* represents a weekly salary level while the *function* indicates the corresponding tax percentage to be used in calculating the federal tax deduction. The figure to be compared or "looked-up" in the table—in this case, weekly salary—is called the *argument*. The *function* is the figure sought from the table—in this case, the percent tax.

In summary, each element of the table contains a weekly wage, which will be defined as 3 packed bytes and the corresponding tax percentage, which will be defined as 2 packed bytes.

We will begin by assuming that the table has been defined within the program in the packed-decimal format:

```
***** TAX TABLE SPECIFICATIONS *****
TAXTBL     DS      0PL50
ARG1       DC      X'75000C'
FCN1       DC      X'035C'
ARG2       DC      X'61500C'
FCN2       DC      X'032C'
             .
             .
             .
ARG9       DC      X'02000C'
FCN9       DC      X'014C'
ARG10      DC      X'00000C'
FCN10      DC      X'000C'


***** TAX TABLE SPECIFICATIONS: A SHORT-CUT *****
TAXTBL     DS      0PL50
           DC      X'75000C035C'
           DC      X'61500C032C'
             .
             .
             .
           DC      X'02000C014C'
           DC      X'00000C000C'
```

The table consists of 10 elements, each 5 bytes in length, or a total of 50 bytes. Note that the placement of the decimal point is the programmer's responsibility and will be considered when the federal tax is edited. Hence, decimal points are not part of the arithmetic operations to be performed.

After a **PAY** field has been read from a card, the table will be searched to determine the correct tax percentage that applies to the **PAY** field. Starting at the first element of the table and proceeding through it sequentially, **PAY** is compared to each wage category (table argument). When **PAY** is greater than or equal to the wage category, then the appropriate entry in the table has been found (See Figure 16-6.) When **PAY** is greater than or equal to wage, the corresponding tax will be moved to an area called **TAXPCT** where it will be used in calculating the tax deduction. If, for example, **PAY** were equal to 400.00, the corresponding tax percentage of 0.26 would be moved to **TAXPCT** since 400.00 is greater than 385.00, but less than 500.00.

Figure 16-6   Schematic of table look-up.

PAY 400ᴧ00		Table	
		Argument	Function
1. **PAY** greater than or = ?	→	750ᴧ00	ᴧ35
2. If not, **PAY** greater than or = ?	→	615ᴧ00	ᴧ32
3. If not, **PAY** greater than or = ?	→	500ᴧ00	ᴧ29
4. If not, **PAY** greater than or = ?	→	385ᴧ00	ᴧ26
yes			
then tax percent = ᴧ26		307ᴧ00	ᴧ24

The Alternative to the Table Look-Up: Inefficiency

An alternative method of finding the percentage would be to code separate instructions to compare **PAY** to each wage category. The flowchart in Figure 16-7 illustrates this point.

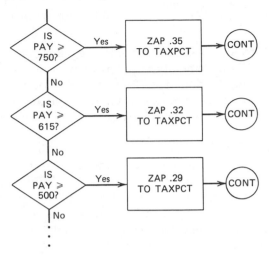

Figure 16-7   Flowchart excerpt of table look-up: Without indexing.

Using this method, ten compare and **ZAP** instructions would need to be coded. This method however is very inefficient and time-consuming. It also becomes increasingly impractical when the number of entries is greater than 10.

Programming a Table Look-up

The flowchart in Figure 16-8 illustrates the logic we will use in our program.

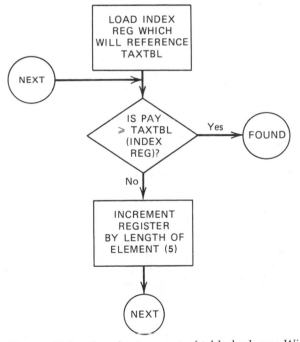

Figure 16.8   Flowchart excerpt of table look-up: With indexing.

PAY is input from a data card (CC 1–5) and must be converted to the packed-decimal format. The following instructions can be used for this purpose:

READ	GET	INFILE,CARDIN
	PACK	PAY,PAY

The coding necessary for the table look-up or search is as follows:

```
        LA      7,TAXTBL
NEXT    CP      PAY,0(3,7)      THREE BYTES OF ELEMENT
        BNL     FOUND
        LA      7,5(7)          ADD FIVE TO REG 7
        B       NEXT
```

The address of **TAXTBL** is placed in register 7. Register 7 then points to the area called **TAXTBL**. Remember each element consists of a 3-byte argument followed by a 2-byte function. The **CP** instruction compares the data field **PAY** with the table argument (wage category). An explicit length of 3 bytes has been specified as well as the use of index register 7. Consequently, the operand contains 0(3,7).

When the search condition is satisfied, the program branches to the routine called **FOUND**. If the condition is not met, the index register is incremented and the next table argument is compared. The process continues until the search condition is satisfied or until the end of the table is reached. If the end of the table has been reached and no match has been found, we might want to print some error message. Our table has 000 as its last entry. Assuming **PAY** is positive, it will compare high (or equal) to this argument.

Referencing the Table Function at the Routine Labeled FOUND

Recall that each element of the table consists of a 3-byte argument followed by a 2-byte function. When the appropriate entry in the table has been found, the program branches to the routine called **FOUND**. At this point, register 7 contains the address of the desired element. However, we are interested in moving *only* the tax percentage of the element, not the entire element. We must again utilize explicit addressing. We want to skip the first 3 bytes of the element in order to reference the table function only (percent federal tax).

The following instruction serves this purpose.

```
FOUND           ZAP             TAXPCT,3(2,7)
```

Note that for the first time, the *displacement* portion of explicit addressing is put to use. That is, the displacement in this case is *not* 0, but 3. Figure 16-9 is a program that prints **NAME** and **PAY** from each card and **TAXPCT** as looked up in the table. Note that we edit **PAY** beginning at **PAY+2**. When we packed **PAY** we only needed 3 bytes. However, by packing **PAY** into itself, 5 bytes were used. Two high-order bytes of zeros resulted.

Creating a Table from Input

In the previous example, the **TAXTBL** was defined internally through the use of the Define Constant (**DC**). Tables that are subject to frequent change are often placed on data cards and read into the program as variable data so that frequent changes to the programs are not required. The table data read into the input area would be in the following format:

CC			
	1–5	Wage category 1	(Argument 1)
	6–7	Percent tax 1	(Function 1)
	8–12	Wage category 2	(Argument 2)
	13–14	Percent tax 2	(Function 2)

Notice that a 5-byte wage field is followed by a 2-byte percent field. The resulting table consists of elements each containing a 3-byte packed wage field followed by a 2-byte packed percent field.

```
* ILLUSTRATION OF A TABLE LOOK-UP USING INDEXING
*
*
READ      GET     INFILE,CARDIN
          PACK    PAY,PAY
          LA      7,TAXTBL
NEXT      CP      PAY,0(3,7)
          BNL     FOUND
          LA      7,5(7)
          B       NEXT
FOUND     ZAP     TAXPCT,3(2,7)
          MVC     LINEOUT+5(20),NAME
          MVC     LINEOUT+30(7),=X'402020214B2020'
          ED      LINEOUT+30(7),PAY+2
          MVI     LINEOUT+30,C'$'
          MVC     LINEOUT+50(5),=X'40214B2020'
          ED      LINEOUT+50(5),TAXPCT
          PUT     OUTFILE,LINEOUT
          B       READ
                  .
                  .
                  .
LINEOUT   DS      CL132
TAXPCT    DS      PL2
CARDIN    DS      OCL80
PAY       DS      CL5
NAME      DS      CL20
          DS      CL55
TAXTBL    DS      OPL50
          DC      X'75000C035C'
          DC      X'61500C032C'
                  .
                  .
                  .
          DC      X'02000C014C'
          DC      X'00000C000C'
```

Figure 16-9

It is therefore necessary to use 2 index registers, one for accessing the input data and one for loading data into the table.

The following set of instructions would be coded immediately after the data card containing the table data was read. We begin by moving Percent Tax 1 into a 2-byte area in TAXTBL next to Wage Category 1.

```
          LA      6,10         SET COUNT REGISTER TO 10
          LA      7,CARDIN     INITIALIZE INPUT INDEX REGISTER
          LA      8,TAXTBL     INITIALIZE TABLE INDEX REGISTER
*
SETUP     PACK    0(3,8),0(5,7)   PACK WAGE CATEGORY
          PACK    3(2,8),5(2,7)   PACK TAX PERCENT
          LA      7,7(7)          ADD 7 TO INPUT INDEX
          LA      8,5(8)          ADD 5 TO TABLE INDEX
          BCT     6,SETUP
```

The first pack instruction packs 5 bytes of data beginning with wage category 1 into a 3-byte area starting with TAXTBL.

The next instruction packs 2 bytes of data.

SELF-EVALUATING QUIZ

1. A table occupies storage positions that are *(consecutive/randomly placed)*.
2. Each element of a table consists of two components, the _____ followed by the _____.
3. A table look-up or search begins with the _____ element of the table.
4. The elements of the table are searched *(randomly/sequentially)*.
5. A table look-up requires *(implicit/explicit)* addressing as well as a procedure known as _____ in order that the next element of the table will be processed when the tested condition is not satisfied.
6. When the search condition is satisfied, the loop is *(terminated/continued)*.

7. The index register is initialized with a(n) _____ instruction.
8. With each pass through the loop, the index register is incremented by the length of the *(table/argument/function/element)*.
9. Once the search condition is satisfied, the next step is to reference the *(table/argument/function/element)*.
10. In referencing the function, a displacement must be used equal to the _____ .
11. Assume an element consisted of 10 bytes, with an argument of 4 bytes and a function of 6 bytes. Register 9 is serving as the index register. Write the instruction to move the function (indexed) to an area called STATED.

Solutions

1. Consecutive or adjacent
2. Argument
   Function
3. First
4. Sequentially
5. Explicit
   Looping
6. Terminated
7. LA (Load Address)
8. Element
9. Function
10. Argument
11. MVC   STATED(6),4(6,9)

KEY TERMS
Address
Address constant
Argument

Base address
Base register

Displacement

Explicit addressing

Function

Index register
Indexing

Relative addressing

Table
Table look-up

Review Questions

1. Write a program using indexing to sum all of the odd numbers from 1 to 99.
2. Write a program using indexing to read in cards with the following format. Print a report that lists for each student his/her name and average grade.

NAME	EXAM1	EXAM2	EXAM3	EXAM4	EXAM5	
1 20	21 23	24 26	27 29	30 32	33 35	

3. Write a program using indexing to read in cards for each sales person with sales figures (in dollars) for each day of the week. Print a report that lists for each salesperson his/her I.D. number and the average sales for the week.

SALESMAN ID	SALES MON	SALES TUES	SALES WED	SALES THURS	SALES FRI	SALES SAT	SALES SUN	
1 5	6 10	11 15	16 20	21 25	26 30	31 35	36 40	

4. Write the instructions necessary to create a table with the following format:

Argument (Number of Years Employed)	*Function* (Number of Weeks Vacation)
8	7
7	6
6	5
5	4
4	3
3	2
2	1

5. Using the table created in Question 4, write a program to do the following. Read in cards with the format shown below and print, for each employee, his/her employee number and the number of weeks vacation he/she is entitled to.

Employee Number	*Number of Years Employed*
1–7	8

Practice Problems

1. Input table entries have the following format:

    1–3   Warehouse number
    4–6   Product number
    7–11 Unit price xxx.xx
    12–80 Not used

The above input is entered on cards.
There are 250 of these table entries.
The detail card file that follows the table cards has the following format:

    1–3   Product number
    4–7   Quantity
    8–20 Customer name
    21–80 Not used

Create an output report containing product number, unit price, quantity, total amount, and customer name for each detail card. Total amount is equal to unit price multiplied by quantity.

Note that, for each detail card, the product number must be found on the table file to obtain the corresponding unit price.

2. There are 20 salesmen in Company XYZ. Each sale that they have made is punched into a card with the following format:

    1–2   Salesman number (from 1 to 20)
    3–17 Salesman name
    18–22 Amount of sale xxx.xx
    23–80 Not used

The number of input cards is unknown. Salesman X may have 10 sales, Salesman Y may have 5 sales, etc. The cards are *not* in sequence.

Write a program to print the total amount of sales for each salesman. Note that x number of input cards will be read and that 20 total amounts are to be printed, one for each salesman. All figures must be edited.

Print:

Salesman	Total Amount
1	xxxxx.xx
.	.
.	.
20	xxxxx.xx

3. Write a program to print 12 transaction amounts, one for each month of the year and, in addition, a grand yearly total. The input is as follows:

1–5 Transaction amount xxx.xx
6–30 Not used
31–32 Month number
33–80 Not used

Note that an undetermined number of cards will serve as input, but only 12 totals are to be printed. All figures must be edited. NOTE: The cards are *not* in sequence.

** The Branch on Index High (BXH) Instruction

This instruction is similar in format to the BXLE:

Operation	Operand
10	16
BXH	REG1,REG2,LABEL

The index register is REG1.

The increment is in REG2, which must be an even-numbered register (2,4,6, etc.).

The register following REG2, called here REG2 + 1, is an odd-numbered register (3,5,7, etc.) containing the limit value to be used to end the loop.

LABEL refers to the branch point.

Function of the BXH
1. The contents of REG2 are added to REG1.
2. If REG1 is greater than REG2 + 1, a branch is taken to the branch point.
3. If REG1 is less than or equal to REG2 + 1, the next sequential step is executed.

Examples
1. BXH   7,4,BRANCH

** Two asterisks identify an optional topic.

	Before		*After*
REG 7:	00 00 00 02	REG 7:	00 00 00 06
REG 4:	00 00 00 04	REG 4:	00 00 00 04
REG 5:	00 00 00 20	REG 5:	00 00 00 20

NOTE: Branch does not occur (6 < 20).

Regardless of whether or not the branch occurs, however, the contents of register 4 are added to register 7 and the result placed in register 7.

2.   BXH   7,4,LOOP

	Before
REG 7:	00 00 00 06
REG 4:	FF FF FF FF (−1)
REG 5:	00 00 00 00

The BXH will be executed 5 times with a branch to LOOP occurring. The 6th time the BXH is executed, REG 7 will contain zero. (Remember that −1 will be added to REG 7 *before* the compare.) Thus, the 6th time the BXH is executed, REG 7 will equal REG 5. Thus, a branch to LOOP will not occur, since REG 7 is no longer greater than REG 5. In short, the 6th time BXH is executed, the next sequential instruction will be executed.

Comparing the BXH to the BXLE

You will note that the BXH is used in exactly the same manner as the BXLE, only instead of a branch if the index register is less than or equal to a quantity, we branch if the index register is greater than a specific quantity.

Let us examine the BXLE as used previously and adapt the problem using the BXH:

Previous Illustration Using BXLE:
Specifying the Limits as the Length of the Table − 1

```
          LH     6,=H'0'      SET TOTAL TO ZERO
          LH     7,=H'0'      SET INDEX REGISTER TO ZERO
          LH     8,=H'4'      FIELD LENGTH OF FOUR BYTES IN EVEN REG
          LH     9,=H'19'     TABLE LENGTH MINUS ONE IN ODD REGISTER
DO5X      A      6,ITEM1(7)
          BXLE   7,8,DO5X     IF REG 7 > REG 9 THEN END LOOP
          CVD    6,RESULT
            .
            .
            .
```

Same Problem, Using BXH.

```
*  THE USE OF BXH WITH INDEXING
          LH     6,=H'0'      SET TOTAL TO ZERO
          LH     7,=H'16'     SET INDEX REGISTER TO LAST ELEMENT IN TABLE
          LH     8,=H'-4'     INDEX REGISTER WILL BE INCREMENTED BY -4
          LH     9,=H'-4'       WHEN INDEX REGISTER = -4, TIME TO STOP
LOOP      A      6,ITEM1(7)
          BXH    7,8,LOOP     WILL BRANCH TO LOOP UNTIL XREG = -4
          CVD    6,RESULT
            .
            .
            .
```

** Assigning Registers: The Equate (EQU) Statement

The EQU statement allows the programmer to assign or equate a symbolic name to a register. It also serves to document the program. The general format of the EQU instruction is:

** This is an optional topic.

Name	Operation	Operand
SYMNAME	EQU	REG

where

SYMNAME is a name by which a register may be identified.
EQU identifies the operation Equate.
REG is the register to be referenced by the name.

Example 1

```
* PROGRAM EXCERPT USING EQU
           •
           •
           •
           LA      INDEX,0
           A       TOTAL,=F'5'
           •
           •
           •
TOTAL      EQU     9
INDEX      EQU     8
```

Example 2

```
           USING   BEGIN,12
BEGIN      MVI     FLDA,C'A'
```

The symbolic names **TOTAL** and **INDEX** replace the numeric specifications of the registers, making the program easier to read and understand. There is, however, another advantage to utilizing the **EQU** instruction.

It sometimes happens, with very long or complex programs, that a programmer inadvertently uses the *same* register for more than one function. Correcting such an error can be quite cumbersome since it requires the programmer to examine carefully every source statement. If, instead, all registers used were equated to symbolic names, as in the following program, correcting the duplicate use of a register would be simplified:

```
TOTAL1     EQU     9
TOTAL2     EQU     8
X1         EQU     6
FINTOT     EQU     4
PROD       EQU     3
TOTAL3     EQU     6       (ERROR: DUPLICATE ASSIGNMENT)
```

Since instructions would use the symbolic name rather than the register number, all duplicate assignments could be corrected by simply revising the **EQU** statement. In the above, for example, it would *not* be necessary to alter all instructions that use **TOTAL3** the way it would if we had referenced register 6 throughout. Rather, we would simply write another **EQU** statement to correct the duplication:

```
           TOTAL3      EQU        7
```

Another use of the **EQU** statement is to establish meaningful labels or reference points in a program. The purpose of doing this is to improve program documentation. An asterisk is placed in the operand field of the **EQU** statement as follows:

```
           BL      ERRMSG1
           •
           •
           •
ERRMSG1    EQU     *
           MVC     LINEOUT+10(20),MSSG1
           •
           •
           •
```

In this example, we are assigning the symbolic name ERRMSG1 to the next instruction, the MVC instruction. This serves not only to document the program, but permits the program to be written in segments, each with a specific purpose. This facilitates program segmentation and structured programming, which will be discussed in depth in Chapter 18.

Chapter 17

Additional Considerations for Packed-Decimal Fields

I. The Need for Shifting

A. Shifting Packed-Decimal Fields to the Right

Purpose: Deleting Low-Order Digits

Typical Application: In Multiplication

You will recall that a multiplication operation results in a product that contains the same number of digits as the sum of the digits in the multiplier and multiplicand. To multiply, then, 12.50 by 10.25, for example, we would need to provide for an *eight*-digit product, one with four integers and four decimal digits. If, however, only *two* decimal digits are required in the answer, we could *shift* the product *right, as soon as* the multiplication is completed, to eliminate two excess decimal places. This is discussed on the next page.

B. Shifting Packed-Decimal Fields to the Left: Adding Zeros

Purpose: To Add Low-Order Zeros

Applications: (1) Addition and Subtraction
(2) Division

You will recall that decimal points are not part of arithmetic operations and that the computer does not automatically decimally align data. It is the programmer's responsibility to make certain that data is aligned decimally prior to any arithmetic operation.

Example 1: Add operation performed on data with the same number of decimal places

If 2.37 is to be used in an arithmetic operation, it will be entered as 237. If 1.16 is to be added to this field, then 116 would be entered, added, and 353 would represent the sum. The edit operation may then be used for printing the result decimally aligned as 3.53. Hence, when operating on data with the same number of decimal positions, no special programming is required.

Example 2: Arithmetic Operations Performed on Data with a Different Number of Decimal Places

Suppose that 1.2 is to be added to 2.37. In this case, a problem could arise. Since 2.37 and 1.2 do not, as in the above, have the same number of decimal places, adding them without attention to decimal alignment will produce erroneous results:

$$237 + 12 = 249$$

whereas 2.37 + 1.2 = 3.57

Aligning Data by Shifting Left or Multiplying

It is the programmer's responsibility to align fields *before* addition or subtraction, where necessary, by shifting left or multiplying by a factor of 10. That is, by adding 237 to *120*, instead of 12, in the above, 357 would represent the sum that, when edited, is the correct result.

Note that multiplying 12, in the above, by 10 would also produce decimal alignment. In general, one could shift left *or* multiply by a factor of 10 to achieve the same results.

Rules for Decimal Alignment

When the number of decimal positions in a field to be added or subtracted differs from the number of decimal positions in the other field(s) of the operation, shifting left will provide decimal alignment.

Example 3:   Shifting to Obtain Decimal Quotients After Division

Suppose we wish to divide 15 by 30. Using normal rules for division .50 would result. Using a computer and the divide operations (DP, D, DR) we have learned, however, the quotient would be 00 and the remainder 15. Division operations result in a quotient that contains the same number of digits as in the dividend. To produce the correct decimal (rather than integer) results in the above, we would need to divide *1500* by 30 to obtain a result of 50 which, when edited, would print· as .50. Here, again, we would need to *shift* the dividend *to the left* two positions. We could multiply the dividend by 100 or use a move instruction that shifts digits to the left.

Review

Shifting may be required

A.   SHIFT RIGHT: Delete digits
1.   MULTIPLICATION
Purpose: To eliminate excess decimal positions.
Example: $1.25 \times 1.35 = 1.6875$
(decimal points not part of operation)
If only 1.68 is required, *shifting right* two decimal places must be achieved
B.   SHIFT LEFT: Add zeros
1.   ADDITION or SUBTRACTION
Purpose: To align decimal places.
Example: To add 1.65 + 1.3, 1.3 must be converted to 1.30. This is accomplished by shifting left a single position.
2.   DIVISION
Purpose: To obtain decimal or fractional quotients.
Example: 25/100 would equal 0 unless 25 were shifted left the desired number of decimal places.

**A. Shifting Right
Deleting Digits**

Using the Move Numeric (MVN) Instruction

The Move Numeric (MVN) instruction may be used after a decimal multiplication or other arithmetic operation, to truncate low-order decimal positions.

Example

Suppose we want to multiply a tax percent by a purchase amount to obtain SALESTAX. Consider the following

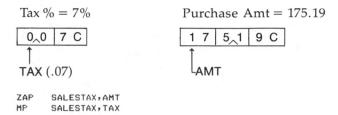

Tax % = 7%   Purchase Amt = 175.19

TAX (.07)   AMT

```
ZAP    SALESTAX,AMT
MP     SALESTAX,TAX
```

where **SALESTAX** is 5 bytes long.

(Number of bytes in product = number of bytes in multiplier
+ number of bytes in multiplicand)

0	0	0 1	2ᴧ2	6 3	3 C

SALESTAX   (12.2633)

Since **SALESTAX** represents a field that is to be printed as a dollars and cents figure, the two low-order decimal digits are unnecessary.

The **MVN** instruction is used to move data in the *low-order* 4 bits of a byte in the sending field to the low-order 4 bits of a byte in the receiving field:

MVN   FLD1(1),FLD2

Before Execution

F 3		F 6
FLD1		FLD2

After Execution

F 6		F 6
FLD1		FLD2

The **MVN** functions as a typical Move instruction. It operates, however, only on the low-order 4 bits of each byte. The **MVN**, then, is the converse of the **MVZ** instruction that is used to move the *high-order* 4 bits of each byte. The **MVN** may include an explicit length specifier or it may be implicit.

To truncate the 2 low-order digits of **SALESTAX** so that it is reduced to 2 decimal positions instead of 4, we use the **MVN** as follows:

MVN   SALESTAX+3(1),SALESTAX+4

Before Execution

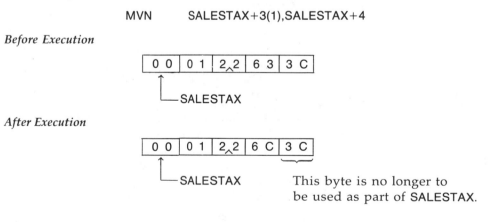

0 0	0 1	2ᴧ2	6 3	3 C

SALESTAX

After Execution

0 0	0 1	2ᴧ2	6 C	3 C

SALESTAX   This byte is no longer to
be used as part of **SALESTAX**.

Using a Truncated field
After an MVN

By accessing **SALESTAX(4)**, which contains 0001226C, we may:

1. Perform additional calculations:

that is,   AP   TOTAL,SALESTAX(4)

2. Use the Edit instruction to print the results with only 2 decimal places:

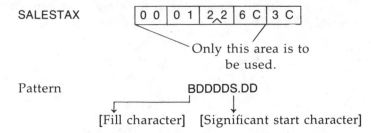

SALESTAX

| 0 0 | 0 1 | 2̭2 | 6 C | 3 C |

Only this area is to
be used.

Pattern   BDDDDS.DD

[Fill character]   [Significant start character]

Since the Edit instruction operates from left to right, we may shorten the edit pattern or mask to accept 7 digits instead of 9. In this way, truncation of rightmost digits will occur.

```
MVC    LINEOUT+25(9),=X'4020202020214B2020'
ED     LINEOUT+25(9),SALESTAX
```

This edit method is used only when further calculations are not required.

3. The above two methods require the programmer to use the truncated field **SALESTAX** cautiously so that the truncated byte does not enter into subsequent operations. We can, instead, reinitialize **SALESTAX** so that the low-order byte is *actually* truncated entirely. For this we use the **ZAP** instruction:

ZAP   SALESTAX,SALESTAX(4)

Before Execution

| 0 0 | 0 1 | 2̭2 | 6 C | 3 C |

After Execution

| 0 0 | 0 0 | 0 1 | 2̭2 | 6 C |

Note again that shifting any field to the right may be accomplished by dividing by a multiple of 10.

Shifting Right (or Deleting) an Odd Number of Digits

Note that using the MVN operation to truncate low-order digits is effective only if an *even* number of digits must be eliminated.

Example

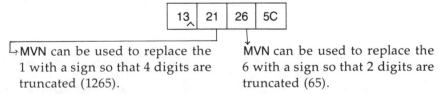

| 13̭ | 21 | 26 | 5C |

↳MVN can be used to replace the   MVN can be used to replace the
1 with a sign so that 4 digits are   6 with a sign so that 2 digits are
truncated (1265).   truncated (65).

To truncate an *odd* number of digits, however, the replacement character (or digit to be replaced) would be in the *high-order* 4 bits of the byte. MVN cannot be used to achieve this result. Moreover, changing the high-order bits to a sign (using for example, the MVZ) will not enable the field to be used as a packed-decimal field.

In short, additional programming is required if an *odd* number of digits is to be truncated.

The Move with Offset (MVO)   Assume that the following is a TAX field resulting from an arithmetic operation. It has 5 decimal positions and is in packed-decimal form.

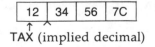

| 12 | 34 | 56 | 7C |

TAX (implied decimal)

We want to access this field as a dollars and cents figure, that is, with only two decimal places. Thus, we want to truncate, or shift right, 3 digits. This can be accomplished by dividing by 1000 or by using the Move with Offset (MVO) instruction.

Note that we cannot simply move TAX(2) to a storage area with an MVC since TAX(2) does not contain a sign that is required of all packed-decimal fields. The MVO:

1. Retains the contents of the low-order 4 bits of the receiving field.
2. Then moves the sending field to the receiving field, the latter being filled with high-order zeros as required.

Example

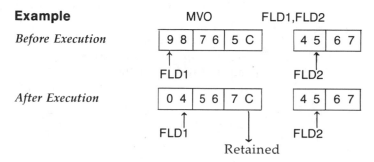

Since the low-order 4 bits of the receiving field contain a sign if the field is in packed-decimal form, the MVO may be used for truncating digits while retaining the sign. To do this, we must MVO a field into itself with the use of explicit addressing:

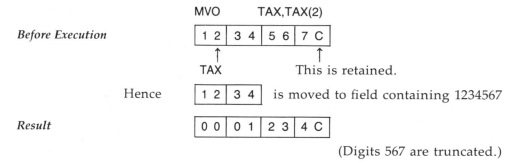

> **Review of Rules for Truncating Low-Order Digits**
> 1. Even number of digits to be deleted or truncated: Use MVN.
> 2. Odd number of digits to be deleted or truncated: Use MVO.

SELF-EVALUATING QUIZ

1. The shifting of packed-decimal fields is usually performed to align _____.
2. Excess decimal positions resulting from multiplication can be truncated by shifting the field to the *(right/left)*.
3. The instruction required to shift a field an *even* number of positions to the *right* is the _____.
4. The purpose of the MVN instruction is to move the *(low-order/high-order)* bits of a byte.
5. Data fields used strictly for printed output employ the _____ instruction to truncate the excess low-order digits after an MVN has been executed.

6. To shift a field an *odd* number of positions to the right, the _____ instruction is used.
7. The MVO instruction processes the data from *(right/left)* to *(right/left)*.
8. The first operand of the MVO and MVN is the *(sending/receiving)* field.
9. The contents of the first operand change in the MVO with the exception of the _____ bits in the _____ byte.
10. With packed-decimal data the low-order 4 bits always contain the _____ .
11. The MVO instruction is used to shift data an *(odd/even)* number of positions to the *(right/left)*.
12. If the first operand is shorter than the second operand in an MVO instruction, truncation of *(high-order digits/high-order zeros)* results.
13. (True or False) Only packed-decimal data may be processed with the MVO instruction.
14. High-order zeros are inserted when an MVO instruction is executed if the *(first/second)* operand is the longer.
15. Indicate the results in the first operand after execution of the following instructions. Treat the instructions independently.

FLDA	1 2	3 4	5 6	7 C

FLDB	9 8	7 6	5 4	3 2	1 C

   a. MVO   FLDB,FLDA
   b. MVO   FLDA,FLDA(3)
   c. MVO   FLDA,FLDB+1(3)
   d. MVO   FLDB(3),FLDA+2(2)
   e. MVN   FLDA+2(1),FLDA+3
   f. MVN   FLDB(4),FLDA

16. In each case indicate whether you would need to use the MVO or MVN to obtain the required results.

   a.
1 2	3ˬ4	5 6	0C

   Truncated to 2 decimal places

   b.
0 9	1 2	3 4	5 6	7 C

   Truncated to 1 decimal place

Solutions
1. Decimal points
2. Right
3. MVN
4. Low-order
5. Edit
6. MVO (Move with Offset)
7. Right to left
   (low-order to high-order)
8. Receiving
9. Low-order or rightmost 4
   Low-order or rightmost
10. Sign
11. Odd, right
12. High-order digits
13. False. No check is made on the data but usually the packed decimal form is used.
14. First

15. a. FLDB | 0 0 | 1 2 | 3 4 | 5 6 | 7 C |

  b. FLDA | 0 1 | 2 3 | 4 5 | 6 C |

  c. FLDA | 0 7 | 6 5 | 4 3 | 2 C |

  d. FLDB | 0 5 | 6 7 | C 4 | 3 2 | 1 C |

  e. FLDA | 1 2 | 3 4 | 5C | 7 C |

Presumably this byte will
no longer be used.

  f. FLDB | 9 2 | 7 4 | 5 6 | 3 C | 1 C |

16. MVN. Even number of digits to be truncated (60).
  MVN. Even number of digits to be truncated (4567).

**B. Shifting Packed-Decimal
Fields to the Left:
Adding Zeros**

You will recall that shifting to the left is necessary in order to add low-order zeros to packed decimal fields. Addition and subtraction operations require this for decimal alignment.

Example 1
Adding 10.4 to 12.68 requires 10.4 to be shifted left. Thus 10.40 can be added decimally to 12.68.

Shifting left is also required for greater precision in divide operations.

Example 2
Dividing 120 by 240 will produce a quotient of 0 and a remainder of 120. To obtain 5 or 50, which can then be edited to print as .5 or .50, respectively, 120 must be shifted left one or two positions.
  Moreover, shifting left can increase the decimal precision required.

Example 3
If the sum of the temperature for a month totaled 2630 and we were to divide by 30, a result of 87 would be obtained. However, if further accuracy were required, the dividend could be shifted 2 places to the left (263000) in order to obtain a more accurate result.
  Hence,

$$
\begin{array}{r}
87.66 \\
30\overline{)263000} \\
240 \\ \hline
230 \\
210 \\ \hline
200 \\
180 \\ \hline
200 \\
180 \\ \hline
20 \quad \text{remainder}
\end{array}
$$

The net result of shifting to the left 2 positions is the same as multiplying the dividend by 100. Again with shifting left, 2 different methods are used to accomplish a shift to the left: (1) one for an even shift and (2) one for an odd number of positions.

Shifting Left An Even Number of Places
(Adding An Even Number of Digits)

Suppose we have a field called SUM that we want to shift left 2 places and move to DVDND, to serve as a dividend, for a subsequent divide operation:

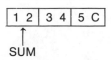

We want DVDND to contain:

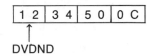

This can be accomplished in 3 stages:

1. MVC   DVDND(3),SUM
    Since DVDND is a 4-byte field, this operation will retain the original contents of the low-order byte.

Example

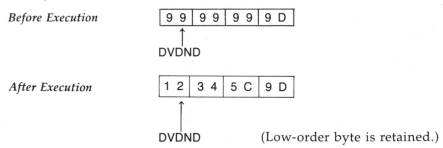

2. '5C' in DVDND+2 must be changed to '50'. (In general DS must be changed to DØ, where D = digit, S = sign.)
    We can establish a storage area with a 0 in the low-order 4 bits and use the MVN to move it to DVDND+2.
    Or, we can use an *immediate* instruction, called AND IMMEDIATE (NI) to change the low-order 4 bits to that specified in the self-defining constant:

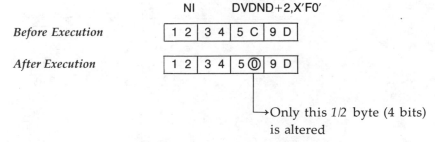

3. To alter DVDND+3 from '9D' to '0C' use a simple MVC:
                    MVC   DVDND+3(1),=X'0C'

Result | 1 2 | 3 4 | 5 0 | 0 C |

Effect   Shift left two places.

The following illustration summarizes the above steps.

	DVDND	SUM	Comments
	9 9 · 9 9 · 9 9 · 9 D	1 2 · 3 4 · 5 C	Initial contents.
MVC DVDND(3),SUM	1 2 · 3 4 · 5 C · 9 D	1 2 · 3 4 · 5 C	Shift field to left.
NI DVDND+2,X'F0'	1 2 · 3 4 · 5 0 · 9 D	1 2 · 3 4 · 5 C	Change C to zero.
MVC DVDND+3(1),=X'0C'	1 2 · 3 4 · 5 0 · 0 C	1 2 · 3 4 · 5 C	Add zero and sign.
	1 2 · 3 4 · 5 0 · 0 C	1 2 · 3 4 · 5 C	Result.

Shifting Left an Odd Number of Places
(Adding an Odd Number of Zeros)

Assume it is necessary to perform a 3-position shift to the left. The first step taken would be to shift left 4 places. Once this is accomplished an MVO instruction would adjust the field one position to the right. The result, as desired, is a 3-position shift to the left. See the table below for an example.

Instruction		DVDND	SUM
Before:		9 9 · 9 9 · 9 9 · 9 9 · 9 D	1 2 · 3 4 · 5 C
MVC	DVDND(3),SUM	1 2 · 3 4 · 5 C · 9 9 · 9 D	
NI	DVDND+2,X'F0'	1 2 · 3 4 · 5 0 · 9 9 · 9 D	
MVC	DVDND+3(2),=X'000C'	1 2 · 3 4 · 5 0 · 0 0 · 0 C	
MVO	DVDND,DVDND(4)	0 1 · 2 3 · 4 5 · 0 0 · 0 C	
After:		0 1 · 2 3 · 4 5 · 0 0 · 0 C	1 2 · 3 4 · 5 C

Requirements for Shifting Digits

A. Shifting to the right—deleting digits.
Commonly used after multiplication on packed decimal fields
PURPOSE: To eliminate excess decimal places resulting from multiplication.
METHODS: 1. Divide by 10 for each decimal place to be eliminated.
2. Shift with:
MVN: To eliminate an *even* number of digits.
MVO: To eliminate an *odd* number of digits.

B. Shifting to the left: Adding zeros
Commonly used before addition, subtraction, or division of packed-decimal field.
METHODS: 1. Multiply result by 10 for each shift required.
2. Shift with:
MVC, NI. This adds an *even* number of digits.
MVC, NI, MVO. This adds an *odd* number of digits.

SELF-EVALUATING QUIZ

Indicate the results for questions 1–3. Treat each question independently.

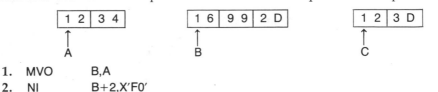

1. MVO   B,A
2. NI   B+2,X'F0'
3. MVC   C+1,=X'0C'

4. Write a sequence of steps to add three zeros to the following field:

TEST

5. Write a sequence of steps to add two zeros to the following field:

TEST

Solutions **1.**

Ø 1 | 2 3 | 4 D

B⌐

2. 1 6 | 9 9 | 2 Ø

B⌐

3. 1 2 | Ø C

C⌐

4.
```
          MVC     HOLD(2),TEST
          NI      HOLD+1,X'F0'
          MVC     HOLD+2(2),=X'000C'
          MVO     HOLD,HOLD(3)
            .
            .
            .
HOLD      DS      PL4
```

5.
```
          MVC     HOLD(2),TEST
          NI      HOLD+1,X'F0'
          MVC     HOLD+2,=X'0C'
            .
            .
            .
HOLD      DS      PL3
```

II. Rounding

Consider the following example, where a caret (∧) denotes an implied decimal point.

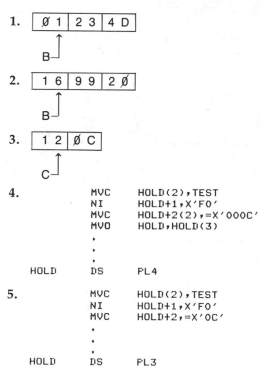

AP   TOTAL,AMT

Before Execution   TOTAL   AMT

1 2 | 8 5 | 7 C   2 5 | 1 4 | 2 C

After Execution   TOTAL   AMT

3 7 | 9 9 | 9 C   2 5 | 1 4 | 2 C

If we intend to print this result as a dollars and cents field, 37.99 would result.

This procedure is not uncommon in programming. Two fields, each with 3 decimal positions, are added together and the answer desired is valid to 2 decimal places.

It should be clear that a more desirable result in this case would be 38.00. Results are more accurate if answers are *rounded* to the nearest decimal position.

Rule for Rounding
Add 5 to the leftmost or high-order digit to be truncated.

If the digit were originally equal to or greater than 5, rounding will add 1 to the result:

Example

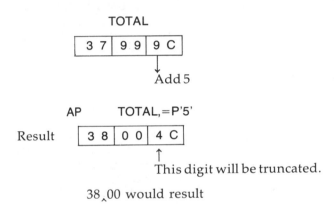

38ˏ00 would result

If the leftmost digit to be truncated were less than 5, adding 5 and then truncating would not affect the results:

Example

HOLD has 4 decimal positions. We wish to truncate to 2 decimal positions:

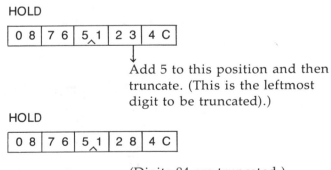

(Digits 84 are truncated.)

8765ˏ12 results

Adding 5 in the above is accomplished by:

AP   HOLD,=P'50'

See Figures 17-1 and 17-2 for additional illustrations.

Figure 17-1   Illustration of rounding.

Rounding and truncation

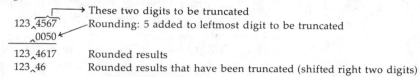

123.4617   Rounded results
123.46   Rounded results that have been truncated (shifted right two digits)

Rounding and truncation (rounding where results are unchanged)

765.4321
     .0050
765.4371   Rounded
765.43   Rounded and truncated

Rule for Rounding Negative Fields
Instead of *adding* 5 to the leftmost or high-order digit to be truncated, we must *subtract* 5.

Examples

1.

| 1 5 | 3 0 | 2 2 | 4 5 | 3 D |
FLDA

Note that **FLDA** is negative. To round to 2 decimal places in this case, we wish to subtract 5, or add −5, to the high-order bits of **FLDA+3** The digit 4).

Result

| 1 5 | 3 0 | 2 2 | 9 5 | 3 D |

(Digits 953 are truncated.)

1530.22 results

If we added 5 in the above case, subtraction would have occurred, which would not have provided the correct answer. See Figure 17-3.

Figure 17-2   Rounding illustration: Correct and incorrect methods.

Correct method: Rounding to 2 decimal places

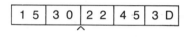

Before

| 1 2 | 3 4 | 5 6 | 7 C |

TOTAL

After

| 1 2 | 3 4 | 6 1 | 7 C |

TOTAL

Actual rounding calculations

```
    123ˌ4567
       ˌ0050
  ─────────
    123ˌ46ˌ17
            ˌ
            └─── later truncated
```

NOTE: 123.46 will be the correctly rounded result.

Incorrect method: Rounding to 2 decimal places

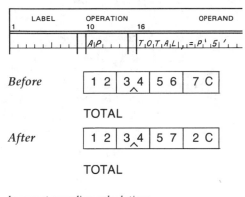

LABEL	OPERATION 10	16	OPERAND
	AP		TOTAL,=P'5'

Before

1	2	3ˌ4	5 6	7 C

TOTAL

After

1	2	3ˌ4	5 7	2 C

TOTAL

Incorrect rounding calculations

```
    123ˌ4567
       ˌ0005
  ─────────
    123ˌ45ˌ72
            ˌ
            └─── later truncated
```

NOTE: 123.45 will be the *incorrectly* rounded result.

If there is a *possibility* that a field contains a negative amount, rounding must be performed as follows:

---

1. Move sign of field to the sign of a constant containing a '5'.

```
              MVN    CON,TOTAL+2    ←  Sign of TOTAL moved to CON.
               •
               •
               •
       CON     DC     P'5'          ←  5C is generated.
       TOTAL   DS     PL3           ←  Field to be rounded to 2 decimal
                                       places.
```

---

2. Add and truncate. See Figure 17-4.

```
AP       TOTAL+2(1),CON
MVO      TOTAL,TOTAL(2)                          Eliminate low-order byte.
```

NOTE: This need only be performed if there is a possibility that the field to be rounded is negative.

Figure 17-3 Rounding negative fields: Incorrect method + correct method.

Incorrect method: Adding 5 to negative number

```
      1978ˏ876  −
          ˏ005  +
  ─────────────
  −   1978ˏ871        Rounded incorrectly
  −   1978ˏ87         Later truncated
```

Correct method: Addding −5 to negative number

```
      1978ˏ876  −
          ˏ005  −
  ─────────────
  −   1978ˏ881        Rounded correctly
  −   1978ˏ88         Later truncated
```

Figure 17-4 Rounding and truncating (shifting right) one digit.

```
                                      FLD                    CONST

                              | 1 9 | 7 8 | 8 7 | 6 D |     | 5 C |   Before
MVN     CONST,FLD+3           | 1 9 | 7 8 | 8 7 | 6 D |     | 5 D |
AP      FLD,CONST
MVO     FLD,FLD(3)            | 1 9 | 7 8 | 8 8 | 1 D |     | 5 D |

                              | 0 1 | 9 7 | 8 8 | 8 D |     | 5 D |   After
```

Rounding and truncating (shifting right) two digits.

```
                                      FLD                      CONST

                          | 0 1 | 2 3 | 4 5 | 6 C |     | 0 5 | 0 C |   Before
MVN     CONST+1(1),FLD+3  | 0 1 | 2 3 | 4 5 | 6 C |     | 0 5 | 0 C |
AP      FLD,CONST
MVN     FLD+2(1),FLD+3    | 0 1 | 2 3 | 5 0 | 6 C |     | 0 5 | 0 C |
ZAP     FLD,FLD(3)
                          | 0 1 | 2 3 | 5 C | 6 C |     | 0 5 | 0 C |

                          | 0 0 | 0 1 | 2 3 | 5 C |     | 0 5 | 0 C |   After
```

Recall that to truncate or shift right an even number of places we can divide by 10^n where n is the number of places to be truncated. Or we can use an MVN and ZAP.

If, for example, FLD contained 12̬3456 and we wanted to round and truncate the results to print as a dollars and cents field, the following coding could be used:

		FLD	CON
Before Execution			

FLD: | 0 1 | 2 3 | 4 5 | 6 C | CON: | 0 5 | 0 C |

Instruction

MVN	CON+1(1),FLD+3		0 1	2 3	4 5	6 C		0 5	0 C	

AP   FLD,CON | 0 1 | 2 3 | 5 0 | 6 C |

MVN FLD+2(1),FLD+3 | 0 1 | 2 3 | 5 C | 6 C |

ZAP FLD,FLD(3) | 0 0 | 0 1 | 2 3 | 5 C |

After Execution | 0 0 | 0 1 | 2 3 | 5 C | | 0 5 | 0 C |

Summary of Rounding
1. Add 5 to the high-order or leftmost digit to be truncated.
2. If field may be negative move the sign of the field to the constant (5). Adding this constant then achieves normal addition for positive fields and subtraction for negative ones.

SELF-EVALUATING QUIZ

Round the following fields as indicated:
1. 99̬987   to 2 decimal places.
2. 123̬5863   to 1 decimal place.
3. 67̬1925   to 2 decimal places.
4. −23̬6835   to 2 decimal places.
5. | 9 8 | 7 6 | 4 C |
        ↑
      TOTAL
   Write the instructions to round to *two* decimal places.
6. | 9 8 | 7 6 | 4 C |
        ↑
      TOTAL
   Write the instructions to round to *one* decimal place.

Solutions

1.   99̬987
    _____5_
      99̬992

2.   123̬5863
    _____5_
      123̬6363

3.   67̬1925
    _____5_
      67̬1975

4.   −23̬6835
    _____−5_
      −23̬6885

5.	AP	TOTAL,=P'5'
	MVO	TOTAL,TOTAL(2)
6.	AP	TOTAL=P'50'
	NI	TOTAL+1,X'F0'
	MVC	TOTAL+2,=X'0C'

† Combining the Shift and Rounding Operations Using a Single Instruction on the S/370

The method(s) presented in this chapter for rounding and truncating are somewhat cumbersome. A new instruction has been added to the instruction set of the S/370 to facilitate this process. Because it is a new instruction, its format differs somewhat from instructions thus far encountered:

Instruction:	SRP
Meaning:	Shift and Round Packed
Operation:	1. *Can shift left:* multiplies by factors of 10—no rounding necessary.
	2. *Can shift right:* divides by factors of 10 thereby truncating low-order digits—with or without rounding.

Format: SRP Field,n_1,n_2

Field: Field to be operated on.

n_1: A number that indicates both the direction and number of digits to be shifted.

n_2: Rounding factor (usually 5) (used with *right shift only*).

n_1 can be any of the values given in the following table.

n_1	Meaning
	Left Shift
0	0
1	.
2	.
3	.
.	.
31	31
	Right Shift
32	32
33	31
34	30
.	.
61	3
62	2
63	1
64	0

† This section may be omitted by S/360 users.

Examples
$n_1 = 5$ left shift 5
$n_1 = 61$ right shift 3

1.   SRP   HOLD,61,5

     HOLD

                         Before   *After*

Packed digits in HOLD are shifted 3 digits to the right. The '6' has a 5 added to it before the low-order 3 digits are truncated

2.   SRP   AMT,3,0

             Before   *After*

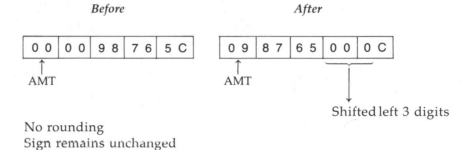

                                                Shifted left 3 digits

No rounding
Sign remains unchanged

III.   Testing For Valid Numeric Data

If input fields are to be used in arithmetic operations, it is frequently necessary, as a precautionary measure, to test them for validity. Suppose, for example, that AMT is an input field that is to be packed and then added to TOTAL. If AMT were incorrectly coded, or contained blanks instead of valid numeric characters, the instruction to PACK AMT would cause the following:

Invalid numeric data (3 blanks)

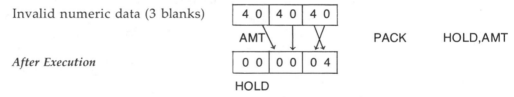

                              AMT   PACK   HOLD,AMT

After Execution

                              HOLD

Since 4, which should represent the sign of a packed field is invalid (a sign can only be C, D, or F), a data exception would result and the job terminated when an arithmetic operation would be performed on HOLD.

     To avoid the abnormal termination of a program because of errors in numeric data fields, we can test these fields *prior* to performing any arithmetic operations on them.

Test for Valid Unpacked Numeric Data
Make certain that the high-order bits of each byte contain a valid zone portion (usually F).

     Let us restrict our discussion to unsigned numeric fields that are entered as input. The zone portion of each character, then, must be 'F'.

We use the MVN instruction in conjunction with the CLC to test numeric data for validity:

Test
1. Use MVN to change the digit portion of each byte to 0.
2. Use CLC to perform a bit-by-bit comparison of changed field to zeros in zoned-decimal form (F0F0...)

Our valid numeric field will contain:

NUM | F D | F D | F D |

F = 1111 in zone portion.
D = any digit

Change each D to 0000 using the MVN.

If field is valid, the following will result:

Hex

| F 0 | F 0 | F 0 |

Binary

| 11110000 | 11110000 | 11110000 |

Compare this, bit by bit, to C'000':

C'000' converts to F0F0F0 in zoned-decimal format.

NUM after MVN (Valid Field)

| 11110000 | 11110000 | 11110000 |

Self-defining constant used in compare.

| 11110000 | 11110000 | 11110000 |

The two fields will be equal if the original numeric field were valid. If the zone portion were *not* 1111 for each digit, then this would signal an error—the numeric input was not valid.

Since the original numeric field should not be cleared to zeros with an MVN, it must first be moved to a storage area of the same length before it is operated on:

```
         MVC     HOLD,NUM
         MVN     HOLD,=C'000'
         CLC     HOLD,=C'000'
         BNE     ERROR
          .
          .
          .
HOLD     DS      CL3
```

Example 1

Valid Data in QTY

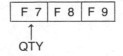

| F 7 | F 8 | F 9 |

QTY

QTY refers to a 3-position zoned decimal field.

	TEST	Second Operand
MVC TEST,QTY	F 7 | F 8 | F 9	F 7 | F 8 | F 9
MVN TEST,=C'000'	F 0 | F 0 | F 0	F 0 | F 0 | F 0
CLC TEST,=C'000'		
BL ERROR1	F 0 | F 0 | F 0	F 0 | F 0 | F 0

Equal condition indicates valid data; no branch to ERROR1.

Example 2

Invalid Data in QTY

4 0 \| F 2 \| F 3

↑
QTY

Note the blank in the high-order byte.

	TEST	Second Operand
MVC TEST,QTY	4 0 | F 2 | F 3	4 0 | F 2 | F 3
MVN TEST,=C'000'	4 0 | F 0 | F 0	F 0 | F 0 | F 0
CLC TEST,=C'000'		
BL ERROR1	4 0 | F 0 | F 0	F 0 | F 0 | F 0

Low condition indicates invalid data; branch to ERROR1 occurs.

If, in addition, the possibility exists that the numeric field were entered signed positive or signed negative, the low-order byte would need to be compared to +0 (C0) and −0 (D0) since these, too, would be valid characters.

SELF-EVALUATING QUIZ

Indicate which of the following represent valid numeric data in zoned-decimal format. Also indicate the value of each valid field.

1. | F 0 | F 1 | C 3 |
2. | C 0 | C 3 | C 5 |
3. | F 0 | F 2 | D 6 |
4. | F 3 | F 4 | F 5 |
5. | F 0 | F 0 | 4 0 |
6. | E 6 | E 3 | E 2 |
7. Write a routine to test TAX to assure that it contains valid numeric data. TAX is a zoned-decimal 4-byte field.)

Solutions

1. Valid +013
2. Invalid. Sign C would appear only in a low-order byte.
3. Valid −026
4. Valid 345

5. Invalid. 40 (blank) is *not* a valid numeric character.
6. Invalid. E in zone portion is invalid.
7.
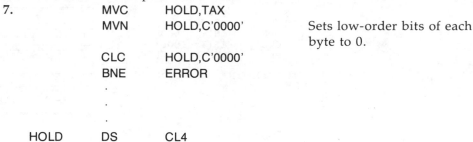

```
            MVC        HOLD,TAX
            MVN        HOLD,C'0000'        Sets low-order bits of each
                                          byte to 0.

            CLC        HOLD,C'0000'
            BNE        ERROR
                .
                .
                .

HOLD        DS         CL4
```

IV. Sign Control When Editing Numeric Fields

You will recall that in Chapter 9 we discussed the edit symbol used to print a minus sign for negative fields (see Figure 17-6).

```
MVC     LINEOUT(5),=X'4020202060'
ED      LINEOUT(5),FLD
```

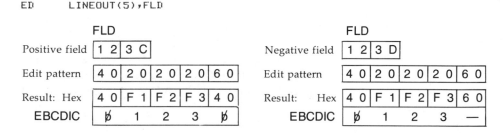

Figure 17-6   Examples of editing using sign control in **ED** instruction.

It is possible to use sign indicators, instead of the minus sign, to indicate that a field is signed negative. These indicators include **CR** and **DB**. In accounting applications specifically, but in other applications as well, **CR**, which means credit, or **DB**, which means debit, may be the manner in which we wish to represent a negative amount.

In the following, for example, the **AMT** field associated with **ITEM3** is negative. All other fields are positive. See below.

STATUS REPORT	
ITEM	AMT
ITEM1	$ 110.43
ITEM2	$ 25.68
ITEM3	$ 5,875.26 CR

Similarly, in the following report, **TOTAL** is negative for **CUST3**. In this report, **DB**, or debit, means a negative balance.

```
┌─────────────────────────────────────────┐
│               REPORT 586                 │
│                                          │
│     CUSTOMER                TOTAL         │
│      CUST1               $ 387.25         │
│      CUST2               $ 682.25         │
│      CUST3               $  25.36  DB     │
│                                          │
└─────────────────────────────────────────┘
```

How CR and DB are Printed as Edit Symbols

The actual characters, either C R or D B are included in the edit pattern. When the field to be printed is positive, the CR or DB is suppressed and replaced by the fill character (the first character of the edit pattern). See Figure 17-7.

Note that the letters CR (or DB) are transmitted only when the field to be edited contains a negative amount. When the field is positive, in Example 1, the fill character (hex **40** or ∅) replaces the *three* extra positions to the right.

In Examples 3 and 4 when the field is positive, the low-order characters in the edit pattern are replaced by the fill character (5C). Also recognize that a negative field transmits the characters precisely as they appear in the pattern.

Figure 17-7 Use of CR and DB symbols.

Example 1

Positive field	1 2	3 C						

Edit Pattern: 4 0 | 2 0 | 2 0 | 2 0 | 4 0 | C 3 | D 9 (C R)

Result — Hex: 4 0 | F 1 | F 2 | F 3 | 4 0 | 4 0 | 4 0

Result — EBCDIC: ∅ 1 2 3 ∅ ∅ ∅

Example 2

Negative field	1 2	3 D

Edit Pattern: 4 0 | 2 0 | 2 0 | 2 0 | 4 0 | C 3 | D 9

Result — Hex: 4 0 | F 1 | F 2 | F 3 | 4 0 | C 3 | D 9

Result — EBCDIC: ∅ 1 2 3 ∅ C R

Example 3

Positive field	1 2	5 7	5 C

Edit Pattern: 5 C | 2 0 | 2 0 | 2 0 | 4 B | 2 0 | 2 0 | 4 0 | C 4 | C 2 (D B)

Result — Hex: 5 C | F 1 | F 2 | F 5 | 4 B | F 7 | F 5 | 5 C | 5 C | 5 C

Result — EBCDIC: * 1 2 5 . 7 5 * * *

Example 4

Negative field	1 2	5 7	5 D

Edit Pattern: 5 C | 2 0 | 2 0 | 2 0 | 4 B | 2 0 | 2 0 | 4 0 | C 4 | C 2

Result — Hex: 5 C | F 1 | F 2 | F 5 | 4 B | F 7 | F 5 | 4 0 | C 4 | C 2

Result — EBCDIC: * 1 2 5 . 7 5 ∅ D B

A final example of sign control appears in Figure 17-8.
The use of sign control is summarized below.

Summary
1. The editing of negative fields transmits the extra pattern characters to the receiving field unchanged; that is, they will appear in the receiving field precisely as they appear in the pattern.
2. The editing of positive fields will cause these characters to be replaced by the fill character of the pattern.

SELF-EVALUATING QUIZ

Edit the following fields as indicated.
1. AMT—3 bytes
   Zero-suppress (with blanks)
   Decimal point for dollars and cents figure
   $ In high-order position
   CR if negative directly after last digit
2. TOTAL—4 bytes
   Zero-suppress (with *)
   Decimal point and comma for dollars and cents figure
   $ In high-order position
   DB if negative (leave two blanks between low-order digit and DB)

Indicate the results in each of the following:

```
MVC        LINEOUT+10(10),=X'402020214B202040C3D9'
ED         LINEOUT+10(10),HOLD
```
3. HOLD

| 0 1 | 9 9 | 3 D |

4. HOLD

| 0 0 | 9 6 | 2 C |

```
MVC     OUTFLD(13),=C'4020206B2020214B202040C3D9'
ED      OUTFLD(13),PFLD
```

Before Edit	After Edit
PFLD	OUTFLD
0 1 2 3 4 5 6 C	⌀ ⌀ 1 , 2 3 4 . 5 6 ⌀ ⌀ ⌀
0 0 7 8 9 0 1 D	⌀ ⌀ ⌀ ⌀ 7 8 9 . 0 1 ⌀ C R
0 0 0 4 5 6 7 C	⌀ ⌀ ⌀ ⌀ ⌀ 4 5 . 6 7 ⌀ ⌀ ⌀
0 0 0 0 2 3 4 D	⌀ ⌀ ⌀ ⌀ ⌀ ⌀ 2 . 3 4 ⌀ C R
0 0 0 0 0 9 9 C	⌀ ⌀ ⌀ ⌀ ⌀ ⌀ ⌀ . 9 9 ⌀ ⌀ ⌀
0 0 0 0 0 0 8 D	⌀ ⌀ ⌀ ⌀ ⌀ ⌀ ⌀ . 0 8 ⌀ C R

Figure 17-8

Solutions	1. MVC	LINEOUT+10,=X'402020214B202040C3D9'
	ED	LINEOUT+10(10),AMT
	MVI	LINEOUT+10,X'5B'
	2. MVC	LINEOUT+10,=X'5C20206B2020214B20204040C4C2'
	ED	LINEOUT+10(14),HOLD
	MVI	LINEOUT+10,X'5B'

3. ᵇᵇ19.93ᵇCR
4. ᵇᵇᵇ9.62ᵇᵇᵇ

V. Edit and Mark Instruction and Floating Dollar Signs

Examine the following sample output:

CUSTOMER NAME	QTY SOLD	AMT
J. JONES	5,000	$38,725.67
A. SMITH	2	$ 3.00

Although the fields are edited properly, the format is striking and inadvisable to use in one respect. The dollar sign of **AMT** on the second detail line appears several spaces from the first numeric character. This result is a necessary consequence of the editing thus far discussed in which the fill character (in this case a blank) has been used to replace 0's.

The pattern must contain enough characters (20) to accommodate the entire sending field. If, however, the sending field has many nonsignificant zeros (for example, 0000300C), an appreciable number of blanks will appear between the dollar sign and the first significant digit.

A dollar sign may be made to appear in the position *directly preceding* the first significant digit with the use of a *floating* dollar sign. That is, the $ may be made to "float" with the field; that is, it will cause suppression of leading zeros and, at the same time, force the $ to appear in the position directly to the left of the first significant digit.

For example:

Examples of the Floating Dollar Sign
$12,345.67
$8,901.23
$456.78
$90.12
$3.45
$.67
$.09

Note that the dollar sign appears in different positions depending on the length of the edited field.

The Edit and Mark instruction (EDMK) is used in place of the Edit (ED) instruction to allow dollar signs to float.

There are two essential parts to this process:

1. Establishing the address where the dollar sign is to be placed.

2. Editing the data.

Example

(See Figure 17-9.)

Thus the illustrated **EDMK** achieves the exact editing as previously discussed. How, then, do we get the dollar sign to float?

It is essential to note a special feature of the **EDMK** instruction. The **EDMK** operation *automatically* places the *address* of the first significant digit in general register 1. Register 1, then, contains the address of the leftmost nonzero digit in the resulting area. In the above illustration, register 1 would contain the address of **LINEOUT+2**, since this position contains the first significant digit.

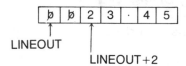

We need to print a $ in the position that is *one less than* the contents of general register 1, that is, in **LINEOUT+1** in this example. The necessary coding is given below.

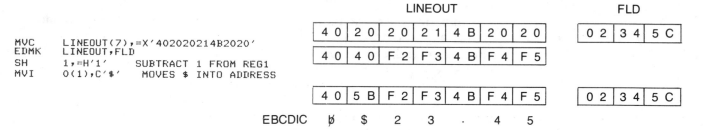

```
MVC    LINEOUT(7),=X'402020214B2020'
EDMK   LINEOUT,FLD
SH     1,=H'1'    SUBTRACT 1 FROM REG1
MVI    0(1),C'$'   MOVES $ INTO ADDRESS
```

The **EDMK** (Edit and Mark) instruction and floating dollar signs.

Figure 17-9 Illustration of EDMK (Edit and Mark) in preparation for printing a floating dollar sign.

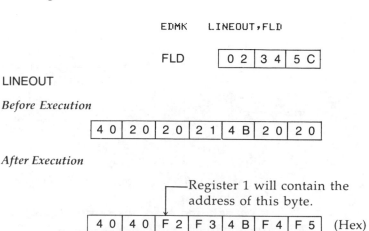

The address of the first significant digit is placed in register 1 *automatically* by the CPU. To determine the address of the position immediately to the left (where the dollar sign is to be located), we subtract 1 from register 1 with the Subtract Halfword instruction (or we could use the S instruction). Now, register 1 points to the precise location where the dollar sign is to be inserted.

Using explicit addressing, with the Move Immediate (MVI), we insert the dollar sign into the edited result. Recall that the operand 0(1) references the address contained in register 1, with a zero displacement.

Additional Coding

There is however one potential problem. When the significant start digit (hex 21) is used to force the editing of the pattern characters (to the right of the decimal) *nothing* will be placed in register 1. That is, when there are no nonzero digits before the significant start character which forces printing, register 1 will *not* contain the results intended. Therefore, before the EDMK is executed, the address of the *decimal point* must be placed in register 1 by the programmer with an LA instruction. If nothing happens to register 1 because significance is forced, the dollar sign will correctly appear immediately to the left of the decimal point, since we loaded the address of the decimal point into register 1.

The Load Address instruction is added to our coding sequence to store the address of the decimal point in the output field LINEOUT:

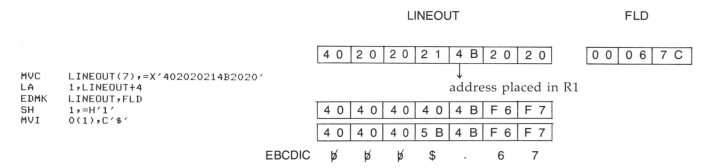

```
MVC    LINEOUT(7),=X'402020214B2020'
LA     1,LINEOUT+4
EDMK   LINEOUT,FLD
SH     1,=H'1'
MVI    0(1),C'$'
```

This represents the full routine using the EDMK (Edit and Mark) instruction to float the dollar sign.

The decimal point is located at LINEOUT+4, and this address is placed in register 1 as a form of protection. Remember, when significance is forced, nothing is placed by the computer in register 1. However, we are also aware that when significance is forced, the output field (LINEOUT) will only contain digits in the cents portion of the field. When this situation exists, the dollar sign will be correctly positioned to the left of the decimal point as a result of the LA or Load Address instruction.

SELF-EVALUATING QUIZ

Indicate the results in each of the cases (Questions 1–8) if the following instructions were executed:

```
MVC    OUT(13),PATTRN
LA     1,OUT+7
EDMK   OUT,FLD
SH     1,=H'1'
MVI    0(1),C'$'
  .
  .
  .
PATTRN  DC    X'4020206B2020214B202040C3D9'
* PATTRN = BDD,DDS.DDBCR
```

FLD

1. | 12 | 34 | 56 | 7C |
2. | 01 | 23 | 45 | 6D |
3. | 00 | 12 | 34 | 5C |
4. | 00 | 01 | 23 | 4D |
5. | 00 | 00 | 12 | 3C |
6. | 00 | 00 | 01 | 2D |
7. | 00 | 00 | 00 | 1C |
8. | 00 | 00 | 00 | 0C |

9. (True or False) There is nothing the ED instruction can do that the EDMK instruction cannot do.
10. What is the difference between the ED and EDMK?

Solutions

1. $12,345.67
2. $1,234.56 CR
3. $123.45
4. $12.34 CR
5. $1.23
6. $.12 CR
7. $.01
8. $.00
9. True
10. The EDMK instruction causes the address of the first significant digit of the result to be placed in general register 1.

KEY TERMS

Editing

Floating dollar sign

High-order

Low-order

Multiplicand
Multiplier

Packed data

Rounding

Shifting
Sign control

Truncation

Zoned-decimal data

Review Questions

1. Write the appropriate edit instruction and pattern that will result in the following type of editing:
   a. Zero suppression—replaced by blanks.
      $
      ,
      . (2 decimal digits)
      CR, if negative, two positions after last digit.
      Field to be edited is | D D | D D | D D | D S | .
   b. Zero suppression—replaced by *.
      DB, if negative, two positions after last digit.
      Field to be edited | D D | D S | .

2. Use an Edit and Mark sequence to achieve floating dollar signs in the above editing processes.
3. Shift the following fields left or right as indicated:
   a. D D   D S   Shift left two digits.
   b. D D   D D   D S   Shift right two digits.
   c. D D   D D   D S   Shift left three digits.
   d. D D   D D   D S   Shift right three digits.

   NOTE: You may use **SRP** if you are operating with a S/370.
4. Given the following, what is the result in **QUOTIENT** after the instructions are executed?

   FLD1 | D 1 | D 2 | D 3 | D 4 |

   QUOTIENT (before) | F 0 | F 0 | F 0 | F 0 |

   MVN   QUOTIENT,FLD1
5. The following is executed:

              MP   TOTAL,AMT

              .

              .

              .

   TOTAL   DS   PL4
   AMT   DS   PL2
   a. Write a routine to shift **TOTAL** right two places.
   b. Write a routine to shift **TOTAL** right one place.
6. Round the results in the previous examples before truncating.
7. Consider the following field:

                     DVDND   DS   PL8

   a. Write a routine to add two zeros in preparation for dividing.
   b. Write a routine to add three zeros in preparation for dividing.
8. Indicate the pattern in each of the following cases:

DS	Contents	Edited Results	
a. PL3	0 0 1 2 3 C	$ 1.23	
b. PL3	0 0 1 2 3 D	$ 1.23	
c. PL3	0 0 1 2 3 D	$ 1.23	CR
d. PL3	0 0 1 2 3 D	$ 1.23–	

Practice Problems 1. **Input:** Card

   1–5   Customer number
   6–7   Number of items bought (in 100's)
   8–10 Cost of each item x.xx
   11–80 Not used

   Output: Printed Report (edited) with floating dollar sign

   1–5   Customer number
   16–25 Total charge xx,xxx.xx

   NOTES:

   1. Total charge = number of items (total) × cost/item
   2. If customer number is a multiple of 10 (i.e., 00010, 00150), then customer has credit rating of A—allow 2% discount on total charge.

   2. **Input:** Cards

   1–20 Name of employee
      21 Code 1—wages, 2—salary, 3—commission
   22–26 Amt1   xxx.xx

27–31 Amt2   xxx.xx

32–80 Not used

Output: Print name and earned amount edited with a floating dollar sign.

NOTES:

1. If wages (code = 1) multiply Amt1 by Amt2 to obtain earned amount.
2. If salary (code = 2) earned amount is equal to Amt1.
3. If Commission (Code = 3) multiply Amt1 by Amt2 and add on an additional 8%.
4. Round all results.

Chapter **18**   Structured Programming in Assembler Language

Introduction

Structured programming is a coding technique that involves designing programs with a limited number of control structures or branching functions. It is a technique that results in a more efficient program regardless of the language utilized. Structured programming is an effort to modularize or segment programs into independent sections or modules. Here is a list of some of the objectives of this technique.

Objectives of Structured Programming
1. Simplify debugging.
2. Facilitate the coding of long and complex problems.
3. Make programs more efficient.
4. Make programs easier to read and understand.

Structured Programming Techniques

Since most nonstructured programs include numerous branch points, it often becomes difficult to follow the logic and to debug a program when an error occurs. A major purpose of structured programming is to reduce the number of entry and exit points in a program. For that reason, structured programming is sometimes referred to as "GO TO-LESS" programming, where a "GO TO" statement is the high-level equivalent of a branch. Using the techniques of structured programming, the GO TO or branch statement becomes unnecessary. In COBOL, this means writing programs where sequences are controlled by PERFORM statements. In FORTRAN, this means writing programs where sequences are controlled by DO statements and subroutines. In assembler language, this means writing programs where sequences are controlled by BALR and BAL statements.

By using this technique, we can handle each section of a program independently without too much concern for where it enters the logic flow and what must be coded after that section has been completed. With such a modularized concept, it is possible for different programmers to code different sections of a large and complex program with only minimal concern for the interrelationships among the sections.

Top-Down Approach

A more recent term used to describe a structured program is "top-down" programming. The term implies that efficient programs can be read from the first instruction in the program and read down the page in sequence to the last instruction. In this way, one can test the logic of each segment of a program regardless of any other segment. To use this approach effectively we must consider subroutines.

The Subroutine and Modular Concepts

The subroutine is a sequence of instructions, or block, that performs a particular function. It is called into the main program as needed but is coded as a separate entity. Sometimes the same series of instructions is required at different places in a program or in different programs. It is possible to code these series of instructions *only once* as a subroutine and call it into a single program at several points as needed or call it into different programs as needed. An error printout routine, for example, may be required at different points of a program depending upon the type of error that has occurred. A single subroutine may be written and called into the program at the various error points.

Types of Subroutines

1. External Subroutines

Subroutines may be totally independent of a program and written for a wide variety of applications. External subroutines are stored in a library and called into a program as needed. These subroutines have their own base register, are relocatable, and have a "stand alone" capability. An edit routine, for example, that performs limit tests, validity checks and so on, may be written as a subroutine and called into individual programs as required. We will *not* discuss external subroutines in depth but will consider them briefly in Appendix D.

2. Internal Subroutines

Internal subroutines are written, in modular fashion, by a programmer and called into the main body of the program as required. When a subroutine is to be executed, a call from the main program is issued.

The subroutine's first instruction, called the *entry point*, is then executed as are all instructions in sequence. Upon completing the last instruction in the subroutine, we return to the main program, which continues executing in sequence, from the *return address*—the next instruction in the main program after the subroutine is called.

An illustration of this process is presented in Figure 18-1. The routine HDGRTN identifies a block of code that is separate from the main program. The main program branches to the subroutine, and the subroutine is then executed. When the subroutine is completed, a branch to the *return address* in the main program occurs. In this example the return address references the instruction CLEAR LINEOUT.

The subroutine may be referenced at any time and from any point in the main program. See Figure 18-2 for an illustration.

Again, when the subroutine is completed, it will return to the instruction that follows the CALL. In this instance, the return address will be the instruction ADD 1 to LINES.

Advantage of Subroutines

The major advantage of subroutines is that they are coded only once, but may be referenced frequently from different points in the program. In addition, subroutines allow the programmer the flexibility of segmenting the program into modules. Even though a subroutine may be executed only once by the pro-

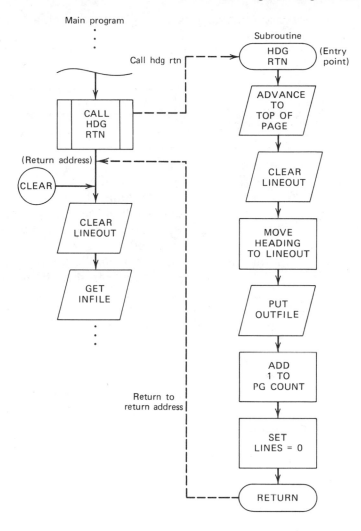

Figure 18-1 A subroutine interfacing with a main program.

gram, the sectioning of the program into modules is advantageous since it lends itself to top-down structured programming. It also assists in debugging, since each section or module can be debugged independently.

An additional advantage of segmentation is the ease of incorporating program changes when the program requirements of the job are subsequently modified. As students, you rarely encounter this maintenance problem in the classroom environment. In industry, however, changes become a normal part of program maintenance.

Linkage to Subroutines

In order to utilize subroutines, a *linkage* must be established:

1. The address of the *entry point* in the subroutine must be stored so that a branch to it may be executed.

2. The *return address* in the main program must be stored so that the subroutine may branch back to the main program.

This linkage is performed with a Branch and Link (BAL) instruction.

Format

Operation	Operand
BAL	REG, SUBRTN

Operation Code: BAL
Meaning: Branch and Link
Operand 1:   General register
                As a result of the BAL, it will contain the address of the next sequential instruction (in main program) to be executed.
Operand 2:   Label or symbolic address:
                Entry point (of subroutine)—address to be branched to

---

As its name implies, the Branch and Link performs two separate functions:

1. It stores the address of the next instruction in the main program to be executed.

2. It branches to a routine.

Example

```
* MAIN PROGRAM
        .
        .
        .
        BAL     5,HDGRTN
        AP      LINES,=P'1'
        .
        .
        .
```

These instructions illustrate how the second CALL in Figure 18-2 can be coded.

The address of the AP instruction is stored in register 5. The program branches to HDGRTN. Linkage to the subroutine has been accomplished.

As we will see next, an additional instruction is required in the subroutine HDGRTN to branch back to the return address in the main program after the subroutine has been executed.

The Branch Register (BR) Instruction

Format

Operation	Operand
BR	REG

Operation code: BR
Meaning: Branch Register
Operand 1:   General Register
Result: A branch to the address contained in the register will occur.

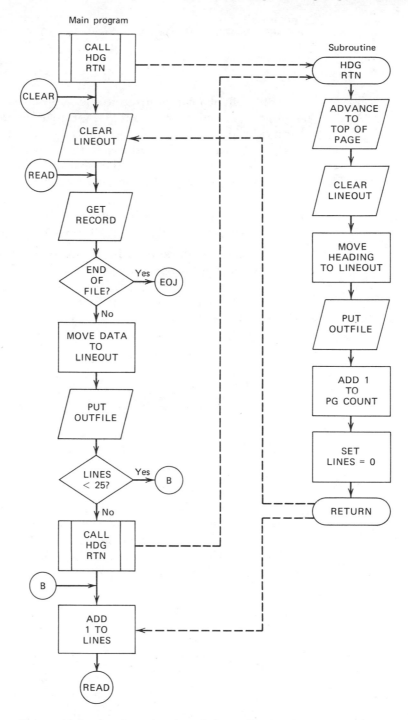

Figure 18-2 A subroutine interfacing with a main program from two points.

To complete the linkage with our subroutine we have the following:

```
* MAIN PROGRAM
        •
        •
        •
        BAL     5,HDGRTN
        AP      LINES,=P'1'
        •
        •
        •
```

```
* SUBROUTINE
HDGRTN    CNTRL    OUTFILE,SK,1    ADVANCE TO TOP OF PAGE
            .
            .
            .
          BR       5
```

Thus, when a call is made to the subroutine HDGRTN, the address of the next instruction in the main program, the AP, is stored in register 5. At the end of the subroutine, the BR instruction causes a branch to the address contained in register 5, which is the address of the AP instruction. The main program thus continues with the next sequential instruction *after* the CALL.

To review, linkage is accomplished by the following:

1. By storing in a register the address of the next instruction of the main program when branching to the subroutine (BAL).

2. After executing the subroutine, branching to the address of the next sequential instruction in the main program (BR).

Note that a Load Address instruction followed by an unconditional branch may be coded instead.

```
* MAIN PROGRAM
            .
            .
            .
          LA       5,ADD
          B        HDGRTN
ADD       AP       LINES,=P'1'
            .
            .
            .
* SUBROUTINE
HDGRTN    CNTRL    OUTFILE,SK,1    ADVANCE TO TOP OF PAGE
            .
            .
            .
          BR       5
```

The LA instruction loads the address of the AP instruction into register 5. Notice that a label, ADD, was put on the AP instruction so that it could be referenced in the LA instruction. If we wish to branch to the subroutine HDGRTN again at some later point, we may include another BAL instruction as shown below:

```
* MAIN PROGRAM
            .
            .
            .
          BAL      5,HDGRTN
          AP       LINES,=P'1'
            .
            .
            .
          BAL      5,HDGRTN
          AP       TOTAL,AMT
* SUBROUTINE
HDGRTN    CNTRL    OUTFILE,SK,1    ADVANCE TO TOP OF PAGE
            .
            .
            .
          BR       5
```

Linking Subroutines to Subroutines

It is a common practice in programming to have subroutines call other subroutines. In Figure 18-3, we see that the subroutine DETLINE (DETail LINE) calls, or links to, the subroutine HDGRTN.

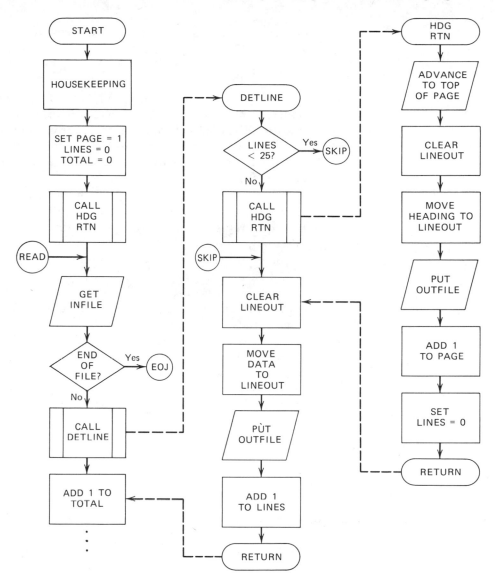

Figure 18-3 Illustration of subroutines that call in subroutines.

It is important to note that when subroutine one calls subroutine two, the former acts as the *calling program,* just as the main program did in the previous example. A different register must be used for proper linkage. The following will thus produce the correct results:

```
* MAIN PROGRAM
        .
        .
        .
        BAL     5,DETLINE
        AP      TOTAL,=P'1'
        .
        .
        .
* SUBROUTINE ONE
DETLINE CP      LINES,=P'25'
        BL      SKIP
        BAL     4,HDGRTN
SKIP    MVC     LINEOUT,SPACES
        .
        .
        .
        BR      5
```

```
* SUBROUTINE TWO
HDGRTN   CNTRL  OUTFILE,SK,1    ADVANCE TO TOP OF PAGE
         .
         .
         .
         BR    4
```

In the main program, a call is made to the subroutine DETLINE, with register 5 being used to store the return address to the main program. The subroutine DETLINE, in turn, calls the subroutine HDGRTN, with register 4 being used to store the return address to the subroutine DETLINE.

If the *same* register were used in the program, an error would occur. See Figure 18-4.

Register 5 would initially contain the return address in the main program. However, when executing the routine DETLINE, a new return address would be placed in register 5, destroying its original contents. When BR 5 in DETLINE is executed, an error will occur. That is, an infinite loop in the DETLINE routine would result since register 5 still points to the entry point within DETLINE, the MVC instruction.

We can avoid this problem by using different registers. But this may become problematic if registers are required for normal processing within these subroutines.

To avoid this problem, we save the contents of register 5 in a storage area for later reference. When we are ready to return to the calling program, the register is reloaded with its original contents and the linkage is then completed. The Store Register (ST) and Load (L) instructions are utilized for the purpose of saving and restoring the register.

Review of Store Register (ST) Instruction

Operation	Operand
ST	REG,FULLWD

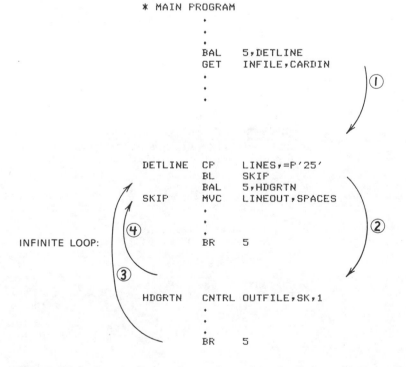

Figure 18-4 Incorrect use of a single register for linkage in two subroutines.

where

ST denotes storing data from a register.
REG is a general purpose register and the sending field.
FULLWD is a storage location, 4 bytes in length (and located on a fullword boundary for S360). Usually, it is defined by a DS instruction and an operand of F.

Result

Contents of REG are moved to FULLWD.

Examples

```
          ST      3,SAVE
          ST      4,HOLD1
          ST      5,HOLD2
                  .
                  .
                  .
SAVE      DS      F
HOLD1     DS      F
HOLD2     DS      F
```

Before Execution

Registers		Storage	
Register	Contents	Name	Contents
3	00 00 56 78	SAVE	?
4	00 12 34 56	HOLD1	?
5	00 00 03 45	HOLD2	?

After Execution

Registers		Storage	
Register	Contents	Name	Contents
3	00 00 56 78	SAVE	00 00 56 78
4	00 12 34 56	HOLD1	00 12 34 56
5	00 00 03 45	HOLD2	00 00 03 45

The contents of registers 3, 4, and 5 are stored in the storage locations named SAVE, HOLD1, and HOLD2, respectively. Remember the register is the sending field and the storage location is the receiving field.

We will see that for subroutine linkage, the contents of the register holding the return address will be stored in a fullword storage area.

Review of Load (L) Instruction

Operation	Operand
L	REG,FWD

where

L denotes a load operation.
REG is a general register and the receiving field.
FWD is a 4-byte storage location (aligned on a fullword boundary for S360).
The second operand is the sending field.

Result:
The contents of the fullword storage area are loaded into a register. See the following example.

```
        L       6,SAVE    CONTENTS OF SAVE MOVED TO REGISTER 6
        L       7,TEMP1   CONTENTS OF TEMP1 MOVED TO REGISTER 7
        L       8,TEMP2   CONTENTS OF TEMP2 MOVED TO REGISTER 8
                .
                .
                .
SAVE    DS      F
TEMP1   DS      F
TEMP2   DS      F
```

The contents of the storage locations SAVE, TEMP1, and TEMP2 are placed in the general registers 6, 7, and 8, respectively.

Linkage of Internal Subroutines

In order to use the *same* register for storing a return address for two or more subroutines:

1. The original contents of the register (which holds the return address for subroutine 1) must be stored (ST) in a fullword storage area.

2. After subroutine 2 (or more) is executed, the contents of this storage area are loaded (L) back into the register.

We will utilize the Load (L) and Store (ST) instructions in completing the subroutine linkages. Figure 18-5 shows the logic of a subroutine calling in a subroutine with the necessary linkage. Figure 18-6 illustrates the correct coding of this linkage.

1. Main Program
The BAL instruction in the main program stores the return address (AP instruction) in register 5. Then a branch to DETLINE takes place.

2. DETLINE
Upon entering the routine DETLINE, the return address to the main program is stored in a save area (SAVE1) by the Store instruction. This frees register 5 for other programming tasks.

3. DETLINE
The BAL instruction then saves the address of the MVC instruction in register 5 and the program branches to HDGRTN.

4. HDGRTN
Upon entering HDGRTN, the return address to the calling program (DETLINE) is immediately stored in a save area (SAVE2) by the Store instruction. It is best to follow a consistent set of rules. Even though we are not using registers, we still free register 5 by saving its contents in the save area.

5. HDGRTN
The Load (L) instruction restores register 5 with its original contents, the return address to DETLINE.

6. HDGRTN
The Branch Register (BR) returns control to the MVC instruction in DETLINE.

7. DETLINE
The Load (L) instruction restores register 5 with the return address to the AP instruction in the MAIN program. The main program is again ready to continue processing.

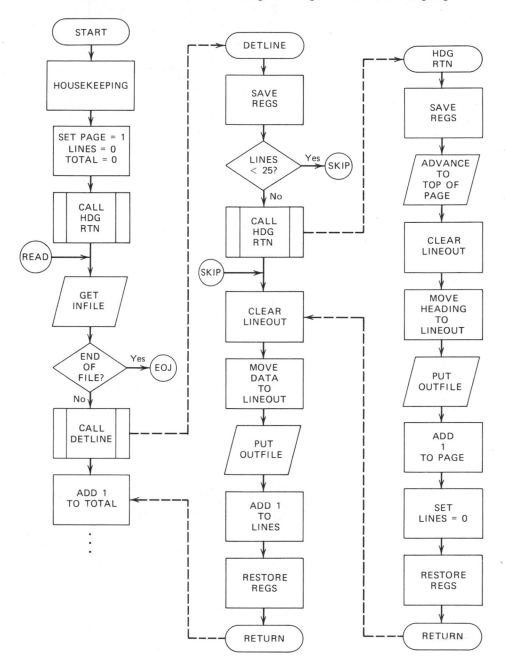

Figure 18-5 Illustration of subroutines that call in subroutines.

The example in Figure 18-7 illustrates a full program that uses structured programming modules or subroutines.

Explanation of Changes

1. Note that DETLINE begins by processing the first record. When the first record has been completely processed, we insert in DETLINE a GET that reads another record. Hence DETLINE is an independent routine that if executed indefinitely would be a complete routine for processing all records.

2. To execute DETLINE indefinitely we want the

       BAL   5,DETLINE

in the main routine executed indefinitely. Under normal circumstances, the BR 5 in the DETLINE subroutine will take us back to the main routine, to the step *after* the BAL. To execute the BAL again, we subtract 4 (the length of the

```
* MAIN PROGRAM
          .
          .
          .
          BAL     5,DETLINE
          AP      TOTAL,=P'1'
          .
          .
          .
* SUBROUTINE ONE
DETLINE   ST      5,SAVE1
          .
          .
          .
          BAL     5,HDGRTN
          MVC     LINEOUT,SPACES
          .
          .
          .
          L       5,SAVE1
          BR      5
* SUBROUTINE TWO
HDGRTN    ST      5,SAVE2
          .
          .
          .
          L       5,SAVE2
          BR      5
```

Figure 18-6 Correct use of a single register for linkage in two subroutines.

BAL instruction) prior to BR 5 in DETLINE subroutine. The BR 5 then would take us back to the main routine to the BAL 5,DETLINE that executes the subroutine again. This process will continue until EOF is executed. In this way we can write our main routine so that it contains *no* branches.

Alternative Method of Linking to a Subroutine: The Branch and Link Register Instruction (BALR)

The Branch and Link Register (BALR) instruction is the Register-to-Register version of the Branch and Link (BAL). It serves the same purpose as the BAL instruction but is of the RR type.

Operation	Operand
BALR	REG1,REG2

where
>   BALR indicates the Branch and Link Register instruction.
>   REG1 is a general register and contains the address of the next sequential instruction.
>   REG2 is a general register that contains the *address* of a routine that is branched to.

Result

The address of the next sequential instruction of the calling program is loaded into REG1 and a branch to the address in REG2 is executed.

For example,

```
          LA      5,RTN1
          BALR    4,5
NEXT      MVC     FIELDA,FIELDB
```

```
*                                                                          *
*                                 HOUSEKEEPING INSTRUCTIONS GO HERE        *
*                                                                          *
          BAL    5,HDGRTN
READ      GET    INFILE,CARDIN
          BAL    5,DETLINE
HDGRTN    ST     5,SAVE1
          CNTRL  OUTFILE,SK,1
          MVC    LINEOUT,SPACES
          MVC    LINEOUT+45(27),=C'MY-T-FINE AUTO SUPPLY CORP.'
          MVC    LINEOUT+95(5),=C'PAGE '
          UNPK   LINEOUT+100(3),PAGE
          OI     LINEOUT+102,X'F0'
          CNTRL  OUTFILE,SP,,3
          PUT    OUTFILE,LINEOUT
          AP     PAGE,=P'1'
          ZAP    LINES,=P'0'
          L      5,SAVE1
          BR     5
DETLINE   ST     5,SAVE2
          CP     LINES,=P'25'
          BL     SKIP
          BAL    5,HDGRTN
SKIP      MVC    LINEOUT,SPACES
          MVC    PARTO,PART
          MVC    DESCO,DESC
          PUT    OUTFILE,LINEOUT
          AP     LINES,=P'1'
          GET    INFILE,CARDIN
          L      5,SAVE2
          S      5,=F'4'
          BR     5
*                                                                          *
*                                 HOUSEKEEPING INSTRUCTIONS GO HERE        *
*                                 ALONG WITH DTF OR DCB MACROS             *
*                                                                          *
SAVE1     DS     F
SAVE2     DS     F
PAGE      DC     PL2'1'
LINES     DC     PL2'0'
SPACES    DC     CL1' '
LINEOUT   DS     0CL132
          DS     CL46
PARTO     DS     CL4
          DS     CL6
DESCO     DS     CL20
          DS     CL56
CARDIN    DS     0CL80
PART      DS     CL4
DESC      DS     CL20
          DS     CL56
          END
```

Figure 18-7

---

is the same as

```
          BAL    4,RTN1
NEXT      MVC    FIELDA,FIELDB
```

Initially, the address of RTN1 is placed in register 5 with an LA instruction. The BALR instruction thus has the following results:

1. It places the address of the MVC instruction in register 4.

2. It causes a branch to RTN1 to take place.

KEY TERMS

Calling program

Entry point
External subroutines

Internal subroutines

Linkage

Modular programming

Return address

Structured programming
Subroutines

Top-down programming

**SELF-
EVALUATING
QUIZ**

1. A major purpose of structured programming is to reduce the number of _____ in a program.
2. A subroutine is a _____.
3. There are two types of subroutines: _____ and _____.
4. An entry point is the _____ in a subroutine.
5. When the last instruction in a subroutine is completed, a _____ is made to the main program, where execution continues with _____.
6. Explain what is meant by the following instruction:
   BAL   6,BONUS
7. Write the necessary linkage instructions using the **BAL** and **BR** instructions in order to call in a subroutine **PREMIUM** and then return to the main program when the subroutine is executed. The first instruction in **PREMIUM** clears **OUTAREA**.
8. (True or False) Only one register has to be used for linkage when a main program calls a subroutine that in turn calls another subroutine.
9. Write the linkage instruction(s) for Question 7 using the **BALR** instruction.
10. Are the following instructions a correct solution for Question 9?
   L   6,PREMIUM
   BALR   5,6

Solutions

1. Entry and exit points (branches)
2. Sequence of instructions that performs a particular function
3. External
   Internal
4. First instruction
5. Return
   The next instruction after the subroutine is called
6. The address of the next instruction is stored in register 6. Then, a branch is made to the routine whose first instruction has a label or name of **BONUS**.
7.   BAL   6,PREMIUM
             .
             .
             .

   PREMIUM   MVC   OUTAREA,SPACES
             .
             .
             .
             BR   6
8. True. (The **ST** and **L** instructions can be used to save return addresses.)
9. LA   6,PREMIUM
   BALR   5,6
10. No. The first instruction loads the contents of **PREMIUM**, not the *address* of the subroutine to be branched to. An **LA** instruction must be used:
   LA   6,PREMIUM

Review Questions

1. Explain the major objectives of structured programming.

2. What are the differences between internal and external subroutines?

3. Explain how the necessary linkage between the main program and a subroutine is accomplished with the BAL and BR instructions.

4. Explain what instructions can be used for linkage when a subroutine calls another subroutine.

Practice Problems   Rewrite the programs at the end of Chapter 16 using the structured program approach.

Appendix A

Glossary

A

Addressable Location. Storage position that can be accessed or referred to by a specific address.

Algebraic Comparison. A comparison in which negative numbers are considered to have less value than positive numbers despite the bit configuration.

Argument. The item in a table that is compared to a variable data field for "lookup" or search purposes.

Assembler (Assembly). The translator (process) that produces an absolute or actual machine language equivalent of an assembler language program.

B

Base. See *Base Register*.

Base Register. This is a general register from 2–12 assigned by the programmer to contain the actual starting point of the program. When the contents of the base register are added to the displacement, an effective, or actual, machine address is obtained.

Binary Coded Decimal (BCD). A computer code used to represent characters; most frequently used on second-generation computers and on 7-track tapes; contrast with EBCDIC.

Binary Numbers. See *Binary Representation*.

Binary Operations. Computer instructions that operate on data in binary form.

Binary Representation. The representation of data or numbers by a combination of 0's and 1's. This is ideally suited for use in computers where 0 represents the "off" state and 1 represents the "on" state.

Bit. A contraction for *binary digit*. The term refers to the representation of data in binary form, as a series of on-off or 1-0 digits.

Block Size (BLKSIZE). The number of characters in a physical record. Since tape and disk records are frequently blocked where several logical records are used to represent one physical record, BLKSIZE on tape and disk will vary. BLKSIZE for cards is 80 and for print records is 132 (or 133).

Boundary Alignment. Fixed point or binary instructions of the RX format are required to have storage operands aligned on storage addresses that are evenly divisible by 2, 4, or 8 depending upon the instruction. This is a S360 limitation only.

Branching. Changing the sequence of instructions to be executed; see *Conditional and Unconditional Branches*.

Conditional branches require *two* assembler instructions, one that compares one field to another and the second that branches depending on the condition code.

Buffer. A second input or output area reserved for overlapped I/O processing.

Burst. Separating a continuous form into single sheets of paper.

Byte. A single storage position; consists of 8 bits.

C

Calling Program. The program that calls in a subroutine.

Carriage Control Tape. Used for skipping to a specific print line or testing for a specific line, such as the last print line.

Check bit. See *Parity Bit.*

Check Protection Symbol (*). An asterisk (*), or check protection symbol, is frequently used to replace leading zeros. This symbol is used to ensure that checks are not tampered with.

Compiler (Compilation). The translator (process) that produces an actual machine language equivalent of a high-level symbolic program such as one written in COBOL, BASIC, FORTRAN, etc.

Complementation. The method used to represent negative numbers in binary form. All zeros are replaced by ones and all ones are replaced by zeros. Then one is added to the result to obtain a complement.

Complementation and End Around Carry. This is a method of performing subtraction on binary numbers.

Condition Code. A special code that is set as a result of arithmetic and compare operations. Conditional branches may be coded by testing the results of the condition code.

Conditional Branch. An instruction that will cause a change in the sequence of instructions to be executed, *only* if a specific condition is met; contrast with unconditional branch.

Conditional Statement. Any statement that tests for the existence of some condition. A conditional statement is usually followed by a conditional branch.

Constant. A fixed value used in the program.

Continuous Forms. Computer-produced output forms that are connected with perforated paper where each perforation indicates the end of an individual page. After all continuous forms in a report have been generated, the individual pages must be burst, or separated, into single sheets.

Control Section. See CSECT.

CSECT. An absolute address from 000–FFF that identifies a block or module consisting of 4096 bytes.

D

Data Exception. An error condition that occurs if field specifications are invalid. An add operation performed on a zoned-decimal or unpacked field, for example, would result in such an error.

Debug. To eliminate errors from a program.

Detail Line. A print line that contains the data from an individual input record.

Disk Operating System. See DOS.

Displacement. A relative address from 000–FFF that indicates how far from the starting point of the program a particular instruction is located. Relocatable programs have a base and displacement assigned to them.

Dividend. The field to be divided. For example in A/B=C, A is the dividend.

Divisor. The field one divides by. For example, in A/B=C, B is the divisor.

DOS. An abbreviation for disk operating system. Refers to an intermediate-level operating system where programs are accessed from a disk. Contrast with OS.

Doubleword. Eight bytes in length. Some instructions must begin on a doubleword boundary. This means that the instruction address must be divisible by eight.

E

EBCDIC (pronounced eb-ce-dick). An abbreviation for Extended Binary Coded Decimal Interchange Code.

Editing. The insertion of special characters such as $, ., and , in fields of data to make them clearer and neater for their specific purpose.

Effective Address. The contents of the base register added to the displacement provides the *effective address* of any instruction.

END Statement. The statement that indicates the first instruction to be executed once the assembly process has been completed.

Entry Point. The first instruction to be executed in a subroutine.

Even Parity. The use of an internal check bit to ensure that an even number of bits are on in any given storage position.

Exclusive Comparison. A test that does not include endpoints.

Execution Phase. The actual running of a program that has been translated into machine language.

Explicit Operation. An operation that contains a length specifier that allows the programmer to indicate the precise number of bytes involved.

Extended Binary Coded Decimal Interchange Code (EBCDIC). A computer code used to represent characters; most frequently used on third-generation computers and 9-track tapes.

External Interrupt. Caused by an operator depressing the interrupt key on the console; also caused by the external timer going from a positive to negative state—normally indicates that the system is to be shut down.

External Subroutine. A subroutine that is *not* part of the program but that is called in from a library as needed.

F

Field. A group of consecutive positions used to represent an item of data.

File. A collection of individual records that are treated as one unit. A Payroll File, for example, refers to a company's complete collection of employee records.

Fixed Point Data. Data for which the programmer must establish or fix where the decimal point falls; typically refers to binary data.

Floating Dollar Sign. A dollar sign that prints directly to the left of the first significant digit rather than printing in a fixed position that could be several spaces away from the first significant digit.

Form Overflow Condition. When the number of lines to be printed on a single page has been reached, a form overflow condition has occurred. We test for a form overflow in a program so that an appropriate margin is left at the bottom of a page and so that we can skip to the top of a new form.

Fullword. Four bytes in length. Some instructions such as the RX instruction in S/360, must begin on a *fullword boundary*. This means that the instruction address must be divisible by four.

Function. The item in a table that is actually "looked up" or searched.

G

General Register. See *Registers*.

H

Halfword. Two bytes in length. Some instructions must begin on a *halfword boundary*. This means that the instruction address must be divisible by two.

Header Information. The identifying data on reports that generally indicate report name, date, page number, and field designations. Headers, or headings, are essential for clear presentation when printing output.

Hexadecimal Numbering System. Base 16 positional numbering system.

High-Level Language. A symbolic programming language that is relatively easy for the programmer to code, is least like the machine's own code, and requires a complex translation process.

High-Order Position. The leftmost position of a field; the position that contains the most significant character.

Housekeeping Instructions. Those entries (mostly I/O macros) that are required in all programs for efficient assembly and execution. They have been precoded in this text.

I

Identification Sequence. The field specified as columns 73–80 of the assembler coding sheet; used to code a value that identifies the program and provides some sort of numbering. An edit program, for example, may have a source deck with cards containing EDIT0010, EDIT0020, EDIT0030, etc. in the identification-sequence field.

ILC. See *Instruction Length Code*.

Immediate Instructions. Those instructions that operate on *one* byte of data only.

Implicit Operations. Instructions in which the length of operation is strictly determined by the length of the first operand.

Inclusive Comparison. The test or comparison includes endpoints.

Index Register. When a register is modified systematically during the execution of a program, it is used as an index register. This feature is frequently employed in processing tables or performing repetitive operations on consecutive fields.

Infinite Loop. A sequence of instructions executed repeatedly with no programmed branch point. This is usually the result of an incorrectly coded procedure.

Input/Output Interrupt. Commonly caused when channels communicate error status or completion of I/O operations to supervisor.

Instruction Formats. Instructions in assembler language are classified by instruction formats. Each format differs in length as well as in type.

Instruction Length Code (ILC). That part of the PSW that indicates the length of the last program instruction executed.

Internal Subroutine. A subroutine that is part of the program but that is executed as a module.

Interrupt. Automatic interruption of program execution; the 5 classes include: (1) external; (2) I/O; (3) program; (4) machine; (5) supervisor call.

Interrupt Code. The part of the PSW that indicates the type of interrupt.

IOCS. An abbreviation for input-output control system; the part of the operating system that contains a series of routines, options, and macros available to the programmer for facilitating I/O processing.

J

Job. The program or application that constitutes a single unit for computer processing.

Job Control Language (JCL). The language used by the programmer or user to communicate job requirements to the supervisor. JCL specifications include the type of translation desired, input/output equipment and macros to be used, start of data and end of data indicators, and so on.

L

Label. A name or symbolic address associated with a specific instruction, usually assigned so that the program can branch to that instruction.

Linkage. The process of linking a program with subroutines and/or with the computer.

Linkage Editor (LNKEDT). The name of the program that is loaded in from the operating system to test and execute the programmer-supplied job.

Loading. This is a term used to describe the transfer of data from storage to a general register.

Location Counter. A counter that keeps track of the relative addresses of instructions to be assembled.

Logical Record. The actual size of the record that is created as an independent unit for processing.

Loop. A sequence of steps in a program that is to be executed a fixed number of times.

Low-Level Language. A programming language that most closely resembles actual machine language; it is somewhat more difficult for the programmer to code and requires a relatively simple translation process. Assembler language is a low-level language.

Low-Order Position. This is the rightmost position of any field.

M

Machine Check Interrupt. Indicates a malfunction of the computer system.

Macro. An instruction that, when assembled, requires the assembler to generate many machine-language statements. Most I/O instructions in assembler language are coded as macros.

Masking. The ability to override interrupts. Some masking can only be performed by the supervisor; others can be programmed.

Memory. The storage capacity of a computer system.

Mnemonics. Operation codes coded in assembler language.

Modular Programming. See *Structured Programming*.

Multiplicand. One of the numbers used in a multiplication operation. In assembler language, it must be the *larger* of the two numbers. In A×B=C, for example, A is the multiplicand if it is larger than B.

Multiplier. One of the numbers used in a multiplication operation. In assembler language, it must be the *smaller* of the two numbers. In A×B=C, for example, B is the multiplier if it is smaller than A.

Multiprogramming. Ability of a computer system to execute two or more programs simultaneously; this is a common feature of time-sharing and data communications systems.

O

Object Module. See *Object Program*.

Object Program. A machine language equivalent of a source program; output from an assembly process.

Octal Numbering System. Base 8 positional numbering system.

Odd Parity. The use of an internal check bit to ensure an odd number of on-bits in a given storage position.

Operands. The fields or storage areas to be operated on or branched to in each assembler language instruction. In the instruction A 4,TOTAL, for example, which adds the contents of TOTAL to register 4, TOTAL and 4 are operands.

Operating System. A series of control programs that enables a computer to handle automatically tasks that would otherwise require manual intervention. These tasks include compilation, scheduling input/output control and so on. See OS and DOS. Assembler language programs will vary slightly depending on whether they are OS or DOS.

Operation Code. The item or verb that instructs the computer as to the operation to be performed. In the instruction A 4,TOTAL, for example, which adds the contents of TOTAL to register 4, A is the operation code.

OS. An abbreviation for operating system or full operating system. Refers to the most elaborate or most sophisticated form of operating system.

Overflow. This occurs when an arithmetic operation produces a result that is too large for the receiving field. Such a condition may be tested within the program.

Overlapped Fields. The term used to describe two or more adjacent fields in storage that, usually inadvertently, acquire overlapped results because of an operation that did not explicitly indicate the length of the fields to be operated on. Sometimes, however, this is a useful method of processing, particularly in clearing the print area.

P

Packed-Decimal Format. When numeric data is represented in storage in such a way that each byte of a field contains two digits, except for the low-order byte that contains a digit and a sign. To perform storage to storage arithmetic, numeric data must be packed.

Packing (Pack). The operation of converting zoned-decimal data to packed format so that arithmetic or compare instructions can be executed.

Parity. A system used to check that bits have not been lost or added within the computer during transmission; see *Odd Parity* and *Even Parity*.

Physical Record. The size of the block of logical records. If 10 records of 50 characters each are blocked, for example, then the size of the physical record or block is 500 characters.

Positional Numbering System. A numbering system in which the place value of each digit has significance.

Print Layout Sheet. See *Printer Spacing Chart*.

Print Nogen. The statement responsible for the suppression of macro-generated instructions. The use of this statement makes the program listing easier to read and decipher.

Printer Spacing Chart. A tool used by the programmer to assist in the preparation of reports. The chart is used for aligning data in a report.

Problem State. When the computer is executing a specific program, as opposed to waiting for something or being in the supervisory state.

Product. The result of a multiplication operation. In A×B=C, for example, C is the product.

Program. A set of instructions that reads input data, processes it, and produces output information.

Program Interrupt. A result of a programming error.

Program Status Word (PSW). Contains status information about the program at the time of interrupt.

Propagation. The repeated movement of data through storage usually as a result of an implicit move.

PSW. See *Program Status Word*.

Q

Quotient. The result in a divide operation. In A/B=C, for example, C is the quotient.

R

Receiving Field. The first operand in a move instruction; the field that will receive the results. Data is transmitted from the sending field to the receiving field in a move.

Record. A unit of information representing, for example, an employee's time card, payroll information, and so on. Records consist of fields of data.

Register. A register serves as an accumulator or temporary storage area. The use of registers greatly facilitates the processing of data by the computer. There are 16 general registers, numbered 0–15.

Register and Indexed Storage (RX) Instruction. An assembler language instruction in which the first operand is a register and the second operand is a storage area that may or may not be indexed.

Register to Register (RR) Instruction. An assembler language instruction in which both operands are registers.

Relative Addressing. A method for referencing data in storage that does not contain a symbolic name. The nearest symbolic name is used; we count from that point the number of bytes needed to reach the desired storage location.

Relocatability. The concept that enables several programs to be executed at the same time. Relocatable programs are assembled independent of actual storage locations and then assigned such locations at execution time.

Remainder. In a divide operation, after an integer value is obtained for the quotient, the remaining integers are referred to as the *remainder*.

Remainder Method. This is a technique used for converting a decimal number to a number in any other numbering system.

Return Address. The address of the next sequential instruction in the main program to be executed *after* the subroutine.

Rounding. To adjust the decimal value of a field either by truncating or by adding one (1) depending upon whether the least significant digit was less than five, or greater than or equal to five.

Routine. A series of instructions that perform, in total, a specified sequence or task.

S

Search. See *Table Look-Up*.

Self-Defining Operand. A constant that is part of an executable instruction. The use of a self-defining operand eliminates the need to establish a DC.

Sending Field. The second operand in a move instruction. The field whose data will be transmitted to the receiving field.

Shifting. This is a technique used for decimal alignment of packed-decimal fields; shifting may be to the right or left depending upon the application.

Sign Control. An editing feature that enables the programmer to print a minus sign for negative quantities or a plus sign for positive quantities.

Simple Conditional. A condition test that tests a *single* condition only.

Skipping. Refers to the spacing of a form in such a manner that the paper advances to a specific line.

Source Program. A program written in a symbolic programming language; source programs must be translated before they can be executed.

Spacing of Forms. Forms, unlike other types of output, must be properly spaced for ease of reading. Certain entries must be single spaced, double spaced, or triple spaced.

Storage Immediate (SI) Instruction. An assembler language instruction in which the first operand is a storage area and the second operand is an immediate, one-byte constant.

Storage-to-Storage (SS) Instruction. These are assembler language instructions in which both operands are data fields in storage.

Structured Programming. A technique for coding programs in modules or separate blocks, each treated as an independent entity, for ease of reading and debugging.

Subroutine. An independent sequence of instructions that may be coded as part of a program or that may be called in from a library as needed.

Supervisor. A program that is part of the operating system but that resides in the CPU for the purpose of controlling the operations of the entire system.

Supervisor Call Interrupt. Caused when the program returns control to the supervisor.

Symbol Cross-Reference Table. A cross-reference of all symbols used in the program along with the statements in which they are used.

Symbolic Address. A programmer-supplied name used to denote an address in the source program. This is converted to an actual machine language address during the assembler process.

System Mask. A mask that can be used to override I/O or external interrupts. Part of PSW.

T

Table Look-Up. The process of systematically searching through a table to find a specific entry or entries. This process requires indexing and the use of a loop.

Test Data. Sample data used to test or debug a program.

Top-Down Programming. See *Structured Programming*.

Translation Phase. Converting a source program to an object program; an assembly or compilation process.

Truncation. When high-order positions of a field are lost or eliminated because the resulting operand is not large enough.

U

Unconditional Branch. An instruction that, when executed, always causes a change in the sequence of instructions; contrast with conditional branch.

Unpacking. The conversion of packed data to an unpacked or zoned decimal format so that it can be printed.

V

Variable Data. Data that changes during the execution of the program. Input and output areas, for example, consist of variable data.

Virtual Storage. The dynamic interaction between primary storage and auxiliary storage in such a way that the CPU appears to have more storage than it actually has. This involves breaking a program up into segments or pages, and bringing each part into the CPU, one at a time.

W

Wait State. When a computer is not executing a problem but waiting for further instructions. The PSW indicates if the computer is in a wait state.

Z

Zoned-Decimal Format. The standard way for representing character data using the EBCDIC code. Each byte contains a zone and digit portion.

Appendix B

Communicating with the Operating System Using Job Control Language

What Is an Operating System?

Since computers can operate on data far more quickly than people can, computer systems have been designed to minimize the degree of human intervention. A major development in computer technology that has decreased the need for operator intervention in computer processing is called the *operating system*. An operating system is a sophisticated control system that enables a computer to handle automatically many tasks that have previously required time-consuming manual intervention by a computer operator. Examples of such tasks are listed below.

Sample Functions of an Operating System

1. Automatic logging in of date, time, cost, and other details relating to each program:
   Savings:

   Operator not needed to maintain this information for each program.

2. Automatic maintenance and easy access of compilers, assemblers, and other special programs usually supplied by the manufacturer.
   Savings:

   Less operation time needed to load programs from off-line devices.

3. Automatic procedures for terminating jobs even if errors have occurred; automatic restart procedures that can read new jobs so that they can be batched.
   Savings:

   Operator not needed to watch for programming errors or input errors that may cause the computer to halt; operator not needed to clear out malfunctioning program or to load in each program as needed.

4. Automatic communication of requirements from computer to operator and from operator to computer via a console.
   Savings:

   Operator can determine the status and requirements of each program easily and efficiently.

5. Automatic operations permitting terminal, real-time and time-sharing functions that would otherwise be impossible.

How Operating System Interfaces with Computer

A major program providing the operating system with much of its capability and flexibility is the *supervisor*. The supervisor, sometimes called a *monitor*, controls the functions of the operating system, which is typically stored on a high-speed, direct-access medium such as magnetic disk. The supervisor must be *loaded* into storage each day prior to any processing, unless the computer operates on a 24-hour basis in which case it permanently resides in storage. This control program calls in each user program for execution and extracts items, routines, or programs, as needed, from the system.

Sample Control Functions Performed by Supervisor
1. Calls in assembler, input/output macros, etc. as required by the program.
2. Calls in special interrupt routines in case of error.

Example of Supervisory Functions Called for by Programmer

A programmer who writes a program in assembler language must, for example, instruct the supervisor to:

1. Call in the assembly program from the operating system.

2. Release control to the assembler for translation.

3. Call in the appropriate subroutines that will supply a source listing, diagnostic messages, storage maps, and any other features deemed appropriate.

4. Abort the run if major errors have occurred.

5. Load the object program into main storage for execution.

6. Release control to the object program for execution.

7. At the end of the job, read in a new program.

Programmers communicate their job requirements to the supervisor in a special instruction format called *job control language*. Job control languages are dependent upon the type of operating system on which one is running.

Types of Operating Systems

The type of operating system employed with a computer depends upon its size and processing requirements. The two most common types of operating systems are:

Types of IBM Operating Systems
DOS—Disk Operating System
OS—(Full) Operating System

Both DOS and OS utilize operating systems that reside on direct-access devices such as disk and that are called in, as needed, by the supervisor. A

DOS system is somewhat less comprehensive and sophisticated than an OS system.[1] The job control language, that is, the method of communicating with the supervisor, differs somewhat depending upon whether one is using OS or DOS.

Job Control Language (JCL)

Main Purpose of Job Control Language
1. To communicate the programmer's needs to the supervisor.
2. To access features of the operating system required by the programmer.

Every programmer must become familiar with job control specifications. We would like to supply them in their entirety as part of this text but, unfortunately, there are numerous options and entries to be coded that are dependent upon the requirements of each computer installation. Hence the JCL utilized at one data processing center will differ, if only slightly, from that used at another center. We will consider JCL for the following systems:

> IBM S/360 DOS
> IBM S/360 OS
> IBM S/370 DOS
> IBM S/370 OS
> UNIVAC 9000 OS

Before providing specific rules for each of these systems, let us consider some generalizations. The actual sequence of cards discussed is considered in the next section.

Coding Rules   Coding rules must be followed *precisely*.

If a card requires // JOB in columns 1–6, for example, with a blank in column 3, then *no* variations are permitted.

1. JOB Card—IBM
LOGON Card—UNIVAC

A JOB or LOGON card indicates to the supervisor that a new job is being entered. Such a card normally specifies identifying information such as programmer name, job name, and date. Sometimes JOB cards are also required to have codes or passwords that are only known to authorized users.

> JOB name—usually 1 to 8 alphanumeric characters,
> with the first being alphabetic.

2. OPTION or PARAM Card

This is a JCL card that specifies the options or parameters required for the specific run. There are numerous options that may be called for in a program. See Figures B-1 and B-5 for a listing of the more common ones.

Each computer system sets up its operating system to supply some of these options automatically, without even the need to call for them with a JCL card. In such cases, the JCL OPTION or PARAM card can be used to *suppress* the option.

---

[1] It should be noted that with a virtual storage computer, it is possible to have a DOS/VS system or an OS/VS system. See Appendix H for additional information on virtual storage.

Summary of OPTION or PARAM Card
1. Determine which options are provided as a standard.
2. Use the OPTION or PARAM card to call for additional options not automatically provided.
3. Use the OPTION or PARAM card to suppress options not needed.

3. EXEC Card

This JCL card specifies the program or routine to be executed. Since assembler language programs require translation, linkage, and execution, usually three EXEC cards are included in a run.

a. Translation of Assembler Program

The first EXEC card calls for execution of the assembler—using your program as input and creating an object program as output. This object program may then be executed.

b. EXEC LNKEDT

Prior to the execution of an object program, that program must be loaded into an appropriate area of main storage and prepared for the run. These processes are placed under control of the linkage editor and must be executed *before* the object program can be run.

c. Execution of Assembler Program

The third EXEC card calls for execution of the object program.

4. Data Definition Cards (ASSGN or DD)

For every device utilized in a program, a device specification card is required, indicating the device classification, unit number, features of the file type, and so on. Since a card reader is usually designated as the system's input device and a printer as the system's output device, these devices sometimes do not require data definition cards. For all other file types, however, such as tape, disk, and punched card output, data definition cards are required.

5. /* CARD

This JCL card is used to denote the end of a file. It is the *last* card of a *source program,* signaling the assembler that there are no more instructions to be assembled. It is also used as the last data card when cards are used as input to a program. A /* card is automatically interpreted to mean there are no more cards to be processed.

6. // (IBM)
/LOGOFF (UNIVAC)

This JCL card indicates the end of the run. It returns control to the supervisor which automatically loads in the next job.

JOB CONTROL —IBM DOS

Figure B-2 illustrates JCL coding for assembler language programs run on IBM S/360 DOS or IBM S/370 DOS.

NOTE: Uppercase letters—required entries.
Lowercase letters—programmer supplied.
Phrases in parentheses are optional or system dependent.
Required entries must be coded in the precise positions indicated.

Figure B-1 Sample options.

PARAM or OPTION Coded	MEANING
LOG	Log control statements on SYSLST (printer) are desired.
NOLOG	Suppress LOG option.
DUMP	DUMP registers and storage if an interrupt occurs.
NODUMP	Suppress DUMP option.
LINK	Write the output of the language translator.
NOLINK	Suppress LINK.
DECK	Punch an object deck.
NODECK	No object deck is required.
LIST	Produce output listing of source statements on SYSLST.
NOLIST	Suppress LIST.
LISTX	Produce output listing of object program on SYSLST (usually printer).
NOLISTX	Suppress LISTX.
SYM	Punch symbol deck on cards.
NOSYM	Suppress SYM option.
XREF	Produce symbolic cross-reference list on SYSLST.
NOXREF	Suppress XREF.
ERRS	Produce listing of errors in source program on SYSLST.
NOERRS	Suppress ERRS.

NOTE: The order indicated above is usually the one required. Hence if **SYM**, **XREF**, and **ERRS** are required, they must be coded in that sequence.

NOTE: Remember to check the defaults of your system to see which options are automatically provided.

Review of Functions of JCL for IBM 360 and 370/DOS

1. JOB card
   JOB name—Programmer supplied.
   —Name by which computer will refer to program.
   —1 to 8 alphanumeric characters.
   Other identifying information such as programmer name, password, etc. may be required at specific installations.

2. OPTION
   See Figure B-1 for an illustration of all the possible entries.
   Each system establishes its own defaults—options that are automatically supplied.
   The programmer, then, need only include options that are different from defaults.

3. ASSGN
   SYSnnn is the symbolic name for the devices(s) used in the program.
   SYSnnn may be any number SYS000–244. Sometimes SYS001–SYS004 are reserved.
   SYSIPT—system input device—usually reader.
   SYSRDR—system's input device for reading control messages—usually reader. (SYSIPT and SYSRDR are the same.)
   SYSLST—system's main output device —usually printer.

	LABEL	OPERATION		OPERAND	COMMENTS
	1	10	16		
1.	// JOB job name				
2.	// OPTION	option1,option2,.....			
3.	// ASSGN	SYSnnn,x'cuu'(optional specifications may also be included.)			
4.	// EXEC	ASSEMBLY			
	(source program inserted at this point.)				
5.	/*				
6.	// EXEC	LNKEDT			
7.	// EXEC				
	(test data, if on cards, is entered here.)				
8.	/*				
9.	/&				

Figure B-2

SYSPCH—card punch.
SYSLOG—console typewriter.
SYSRES—system resident disk unit.
SYSLNK—disk unit used by linkage editor.

The symbolic device assignment is made by each individual computer installation.

NOTE: An assign card is *only* required for each device used by the program.

X'cuu'—address of physical unit used only for tapes or disk
    c—channel number
    uu—device number
Check installation for exact specification.

4. // EXEC ASSEMBLY
    assembly program called in—must be followed by source program.

5. /*
    signals the end of source deck.

6. // EXEC LNKEDT
    links object module in preparation for execution.

7. // EXEC
    executes the object program—followed by test data.

8. /*
    Signals the end of test data (only included if test data is on cards).

9. /&
    signals the end of the run.

Job Control—IBM OS or OS/VS
S/360 or S/370

The following illustration includes the job control used with assembler language programs on IBM OS systems.

NOTE: Uppercase letters—required entries.
Lowercase letters—programmer-supplied.
Phrases in parentheses are optional or system dependent.
Required entries must be coded in the precise positions indicated or directly following programmer-supplied entry.

---

1. JOB card
   JOB name—1 to 8 characters—placed directly after //.
   Other identifying data following JOB may be required by your specific system.

2. // EXEC ASMFCLG. This is followed by the source program if it is on cards. ASMFCLG is the name of the assembler procedure for assembling, linkage editing, and executing the program. If an assembly process—but *no* execution—is desired, then ASMFC is the name used.

3. // ASM.SYSIN DD *
   notifies the assembler that the source program is on punched cards.

4. /*
   signals the end of the source program.

5. // GO.SYSPRINT DD SYSOUT = A
   indicates that all output from execution of program will be on printer.

6. // GO.SYSIN DD *—followed by test data—
   indicates that test data for execution of the program is on cards.

	LABEL	OPERATION		OPERAND
	1	10	16	
1.	//jobname	JOB	(password),programmer name	
2.	//	EXEC	ASMFCLG	
3.	//	ASM.SYSIN	DD *	
	(source program follows)			
4.	/*			
5.	//GO.SYSPRINT	DD	SYSOUT=A	
6.	//GO.SYSIN	DD	*	
	(test data entered here)			
7.	/*			
8.	//			

Figure B-3

7. /*
   indicates the end of test data.

8. //
   indicates end of run.

To change an option, we use the PARM parameter with the EXEC card in OS.

// EXEC ASMFCLG, PARM.ASM = 'option 1, option 2, . . .'

Job Control—UNIVAC 9000 OS

See Figure B-4.

> NOTE: Uppercase letters—required entries.
> Lowercase letters—programmer supplied (phrases in paren-
> theses are optional).
> Required entries must be coded in the precise positions indi-
> cated.

Review of UNIVAC 9000 JCL

1. /LOGON
   identifies the program to the system.

2. /OPTION
   If a dump is required when a program is aborted, then /OPTION DUMP = YES
   must be coded.

3. /PARAM
   specifies the options that may be included.
   Figure B-5 specifies some UNIVAC 9000 options.

	LABEL	OPERATION	OPERAND
	1	10	16
1.	/LOGON user id.		,,A (account no.),
2.	/OPTION	DUMP=YES	
3.	/PARAM option1=	YES NO,	option2= YES NO, ...
4.	/EXEC ASSEMB		
	(source	program entered here,)	
5.	/*		
6.	/EXEC LNKEDT		
7.	/EXEC		
	(test data entered here,)		
8.	/*		
9.	/LOGOFF		

Figure B-4

Figure B-5 Some PARAM statement parameters for UNIVAC†

Parameter	Meaning
LIST $\begin{cases} = \text{YES} \\ = \text{NO}* \end{cases}$	indicates whether a source program listing is to be included.
MAP $\begin{cases} = \text{YES}* \\ = \text{NO} \end{cases}$	indicates whether the program's object summary and storage maps are to be printed.
DISC $\begin{cases} = \text{YES}* \\ = \text{NO} \end{cases}$	indicates whether an object module is to be generated.
DEBUG $\begin{cases} = \text{YES} \\ = \text{NO}* \end{cases}$	indicates that object time diagnostics from the debug routine contain source statement line numbers generated by the compiler.

† An asterisk denotes the default that is automatically included.

4. /EXEC ASSEMB is followed by the source program.
   This statement calls in the assembler program, which will translate the source program into an object program.

5. /*
   indicates the end of the source program.

6. /EXEC LNKEDT
   indicates that the object module is to be linked in preparation for execution.

7. /EXEC—followed by test data—
   executes the object program.

8. /*
   indicates the end of the test data.

9. /LOGOFF
   indicates the end of the run.

SELF-EVALUATING QUIZ

1. The _____ is another name for the control program that controls the operations of the computer system.
2. The typical operating system is usually stored on a _____.
3. The programmer communicates with the supervisor in _____ language.
4. (True or False) The control program within the computer system can minimize programmer and operator effort, if utilized properly.
5. (True or False) When a source program requires translation prior to execution, the control program must call in the appropriate compiler or assembler.
6. (True or False) The supervisor is called into the computer system by each user program.
7. (True or False) The Job Control Language is the same for all computers produced by any manufacturer.
8. (True or False) The OS system is more sophisticated and comprehensive than the DOS system.
9. (True or False) During the execution of any program, the supervisor is always maintained in the CPU.
10. The JCL card that usually signals the end of a file is called the _____ card.

Solutions

1. Supervisor
2. Direct-access device such as a disk

3. Job control (JCL)
4. True
5. True
6. False. The supervisor calls in the user programs.
7. False
8. True
9. True
10. /*

KEY TERMS

Default

DOS (Disk Operating System)

Full Operating System (OS)

Job

Job control language

Linkage editor (LNKEDT)

Monitor

Operating system

Real time

Supervisor

Time-sharing

User program

Review questions

1. If a program needs to be assembled, the _____ program calls in the required assembler.
2. The entire control system that is typically stored on a direct-access device is referred to as a(n) _____ system.
3. State the major functions of a supervisor.
4. State the major functions of Job Control Language.
5. Indicate the major function of each of the following:
   a. JOB card
   b. OPTION card
   c. EXEC LNKEDT
   d. /*
   e. //

Appendix **C**

Instruction Formats and Other Specifications

Instruction Formats

Type	Length	Contents of Two High Order Bits of Op Code	Format
A. One halfword			
RR	2 bytes	00	

			First operand	Second operand
		Op Code	R1	R2
Number of bits		8	4	4

B. Two halfwords			

			First operand		Second operand	
RX / 4 bytes / 01	Op Code	R1	X2	B2	D2
Number of bits	8	4	4	4	12

			First operand		Second operand	
RS / 4 bytes / 10	Op Code	R1	R3	B2	D2
Number of bits	8	4	4	4	12

			Second operand	First operand	
SI / 4 bytes / 10	Op Code	I2	B1	D1
Number of bits	8	8	4	12

C. Three halfwords			

	Length		First operand		Second operand	
SS / 6 bytes / 11	Op Code	Length L1 ¦ L2	B1	D1	B2	D2
Number of bits	8	8	4	12	4	12

Assembler and Macro Instructions

	Chapter
CLOSE	4
CNTRL	9
DC	3
DC (Address Constants)	16
DCB	4
DS	3
DTF	4
END	4
EOJ	4
GET	4
PRTOV	9
PUT	4
START	4
USING	4

Extended Mnemonics

Extended Code		Machine Instruction		Meaning
Unconditional Branches				
B	D2(X2,B2)	BC	15,D2(X2,B2)	Unconditional branch
BR	R2	BCR	15,R2	Unconditional branch
After Compare (Operand 1 to Operand 2)				
BH	D2(X2,B2)	BC	2,D2(X2,B2)	Branch if operand 1 is high.
BL	D2(X2,B2)	BC	4,D2(X2,B2)	Branch if operand 1 is low.
BE	D2(X2,B2)	BC	8,D2(X2,B2)	Branch if operands are equal.
BNH	D2(X2,B2)	BC	13,D2(X2,B2)	Branch if operand 1 is not high.
BNL	D2(X2,B2)	BC	11,D2(X2,B2)	Branch if operand 1 is not low.
BNE	D2(X2,B2)	BC	7,D2(X2,B2)	Branch if operands are not equal.
After Arithmetic Instructions				
BO	D2(X2,B2)	BC	1,D2(X2,B2)	Branch on overflow.
BP	D2(X2,B2)	BC	2,D2(X2,B2)	Branch if plus.
BM	D2(X2,B2)	BC	4,D2(X2,B2)	Branch if minus.
BZ	D2(X2,B2)	BC	8,D2(X2,B2)	Branch on zero.
BNP	D2(X2,B2)	BC	13,D2(X2,B2)	Branch if not plus.
BNM	D2(X2,B2)	BC	11,D2(X2,B2)	Branch if not minus.
BNZ	D2(X2,B2)	BC	7,D2(X2,B2)	Branch if not zero.

Condition Codes

Instructions Not Affecting Condition Codes

Op Code	Meaning
BALR	Branch and Link Register
BR	Branch to Register
CVB	Convert to Binary
CVD	Convert to Decimal
D	Divide
DR	Divide Register
L	Load
LA	Load Address
LH	Load Halfword
LR	Load Register
M	Multiply
MH	Multiply Halfword
MR	Multiply Register
MVC	Move Character
PACK	Pack
ST	Store
STH	Store Halfword
UNPK	Unpack

Condition Codes Set

	Instruction	Condition Code			
		0	1	2	3
A	Add	= 0	<0	>0	Overflow
AP	Add Packed	= 0	<0	>0	Overflow
AR	Add Register	= 0	<0	>0	Overflow
C	Compare	=	First < second	First > second	
CP	Compare Packed	=	First < second	First > second	
CR	Compare Register	=	First < second	First > second	
S	Subtract	0	<0	>0	Overflow
SP	Subtract Packed	0	<0	>0	Overflow
SR	Subtract Register	0	<0	>0	Overflow

Edit and Mark Symbols

Symbol	Meaning
Hex 40	Blank
Hex 21	Significant start character
Hex 22	Field separator character
Hex 20	Digit select character

Specifications for Constants

Code	Type	Meaning	Example		

				Coding	Representation
					F 1
C	Character or Zoned Decimal	Eight-bit code for each specification		C'1'	1111 | 0001
				C'A'	1100 | 0001
					C 1

				Coding	Representation
X	Hexadecimal	Four-bit code for each specification		X'F1'	1111 | 0001
				X'C1'	1100 | 0001

				Coding	Representation
B	Binary	Binary digits represented as 0's and 1's		B'11110001'	1111 | 0001
				B'11000001'	1100 | 0001

				Coding	Representation
P	Packed Decimal	Four bits per digit + sign		P'1'	0001 | 1111
					1 F

				Coding	Representation
F	Fixed-Point Fullword	Signed, fixed-point binary format, fullword		F'1'	0 0001
					32 bits– 4 bytes

				Coding	Representation
H	Fixed-Point Halfword	Signed, fixed-point binary format, halfword		H'1'	0 . . . 0001
					16 bits 2 bytes

				Coding	Representation
D	Fixed-Point Doubleword	Signed, fixed-point binary format, doubleword		D'1'	00 0001
					64 bits 8 bytes

Program Status Word (PSW)

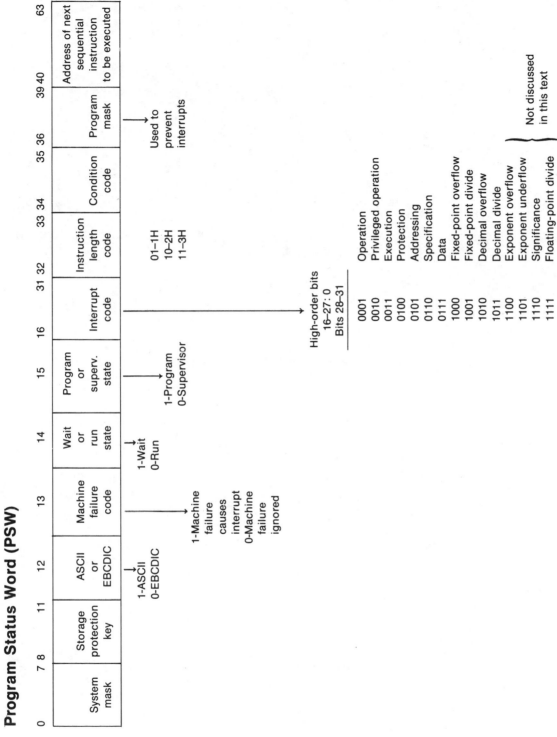

Appendix D

External Subroutines and Linkage Considerations

An external subroutine is stored as an independent set of procedures in a library. It is then called into the main program as needed. In this way, external subroutines may be shared by many different users. The linkage procedure, that of linking the external subroutine to the main program, is the most difficult aspect of this process. Efforts have been made by IBM and other manufacturers to standardize linkage procedures. A fixed set of rules may be used, which

1. simplifies the coding of subroutines, and

2. reduces the possibility of errors.

These rules, when adapted to your system's requirements, will facilitate linkage. It is possible to deviate from standard conventions. However, the programmer then runs the risk of writing programs that may not correctly interface with the operating system. To avoid this problem, it is strongly recommended that the consistent set of rules developed in this section be followed.

You will recall that the linking of internal subroutines to a main program required the following steps.

Review
Main Program
1. Using a BAL instruction, place the address of the next instruction (to be branched to after execution of the subroutine) in a register. This is called the return address.
2. Branch to the entry point in the subroutine.
Subroutine
1. Store the contents of the register containing the return address in a save area.
2. Restore (Load) the register with the return address immediately prior to branching back to the main program.
3. Branch to the return address in the main program.

Along with these elements, there are several additional requirements that must be used for linking *external* subroutines.

Linkage

1. The main program and subroutine are *completely independent* blocks of code that are *relocatable.* Therefore, each module must establish addressability through a base register.

2. A subroutine *must* restore the registers to their original status prior to returning to the calling program (the main program in this instance). This requires us to temporarily store the contents of the registers in a save area and then to later restore them. This is similar to the procedure used with internal subroutines; however, *all* of the registers will be saved, not just the one used for linking.

The Save Area   The standard size for the register save area is 18 fullwords. In our main program, we can define the register save area as follows.

LABEL	OPERATION 10	16
SAVMAIN	DS	18F

Using the standard established, registers are saved in the following order:

$$14,15,0,1,2,\ldots 12$$

starting with the fourth word of the save area.

SAVE AREA

SAVMAIN

Contents Reg 14
Contents Reg 15 Contents Reg 0
Contents Reg 12

The first 3 words will be discussed later as they are needed.

The save area is not filled with the registers' contents until the subroutine is entered. That is, the first instruction executed in the subroutine will save the contents of the registers in a save area in the main program. This means that the address of the save area in the main program (SAVMAIN) must be passed to the subroutine or the subroutine will be unable to restore the registers. Standard linkage procedures use register 13 for this purpose. We will now examine the steps necessary in the main program (MAIN) to establish linkage to the subroutine (SUB1).

The Main Program   The registers in the main program are programmed to contain the following data immediately before the subroutine is called.

Register	Use
13	Address of save area (SAVMAIN)
14	Return address in MAIN
15	Entry address in called subroutine (SUB1)

The instructions needed to properly load registers 13, 14, and 15 are shown in Figure D-1.

```
         LA      13,SAVMAIN
         L       15,=V(SUB1)
         .
         .
         .
         BALR    14,15
GO       MVC
         .
         .
         .
SAVMAIN  DS      18F
```

Figure D-1

The circled numbers in Figure D-2 are used to illustrate the effect of each of the above instructions on general registers 13–15.

Summary
1. The save area (SAVMAIN) is defined with a DS statement, and consists of 18 fullwords, each aligned on fullword boundaries.
2. The address of the save area (SAVMAIN) is loaded into register 13.
3. The V-type address is used to reference an external routine. This will be discussed later in this appendix. For now, this instruction sets up the entry point in the subroutine (SUB1).
4. The BALR instruction saves the address of the next instruction (labeled GO) in register 14. This address is the return address. The program then branches to the address contained in register 15, the routine SUB1.

The Subroutine (SUB1) Upon entering the subroutine (SUB1), the present status of the program is as illustrated in Figure D-2. As the instructions in the subroutine are executed, the changes that take place are described below. Figure D-3 shows the instructions in the subroutine.

The following explanations will clarify the purpose of each of the above instructions.

⑤ The subroutine is assigned the symbolic name SUB1 with the START instruction.

⑥ The STM instruction saves the status of the registers in the save area of the MAIN program. The contents of registers 14, 15, 0, ..., 12 are transmitted to the storage area beginning with storage location 12(13). Recall that a displacement of 12 is added to the address stored in register 13. This address therefore references the *fourth* word in the area called SAVMAIN.

⑦ Establishes the base register.

⑧ The address of the main save area (SAVMAIN) is placed in the *second word* of the subroutine save area (SAVSUB1). (SAVSUB1 is defined as DS 18F in the subroutine.) This is the *key* to later accessing of the save area of the main program and restoring the registers to their original status.

⑨ In case another subroutine is called, the address of the save area in SUB1 is loaded into register 13 in accordance with the linkage conventions set forth by IBM.

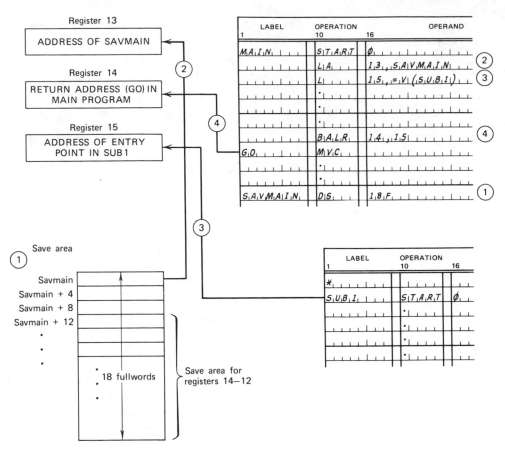

Figure D-2 The effect of each instruction in the main program on general registers 13–15.

(10) Once the subroutine is completed, the address of the main save area (**SAVMAIN**), the key to returning the registers to their original status, is loaded into register 13.

(11) Starting with the fourth word in **SAVMAIN**, all of the general registers are restored to their original status, with the exception of register 13, by the LM instruction.

(12) The BR instruction returns control to the entry point in MAIN. Remember, register 14 originally contained the return address, and it was restored to this status.

In summary, here are the steps taken thus far in both the main program and subroutine.

```
 5.  SUB1      START  0
 6.            STM    14,12,12(13)
              BALR   12,0
 7.            USING  *,12
 8.            ST     13,SAVSUB1+4
 9.            LA     13,SAVSUB1
                .
                .
                .
10.            L      13,SAVSUB1+4
11.            LM     14,12,12(13)
12.            BR     14
              END
```

Figure D-3

MAIN

1. Establish an 18-word save area.
2. Load the address of the save area (SAVMAIN) into register 13.
3. Load the entry point of the subroutine into register 15.
4. Load the return address into register 14 and branch to the subroutine.

Subroutine

1. Store the contents of the registers in the save area of the calling program.

2. Save the address of the main (or calling program) in the second word of the subroutine's save area (SAVSUB1).

3. Load the subroutine's save area address in register 13 in case another subroutine is called from SUB1.

4. Upon completing the subroutine, restore register 13 with the address of the main save area (SAVMAIN).

5. Restore registers 14, 15, 0, 1, 2, . . ., 12.

6. Return to the entry point contained in register 14.

OS Linkage Conventions With an (OS) Operating System and VS (Virtual Storage), the main program is treated as if it were a subroutine of the supervisor. All of the steps outlined in the preceding section for subroutines are utilized in the *main program.* Notice that the housekeeping routines prescribed in Chapter 4 for OS are *identical* to those developed in this appendix.

DOS Standard Linkage Conventions In Disk Operating Systems (DOS), the main program is not treated as a subroutine, but is handled differently. Actually, the DOS linkage conventions are simpler than those of OS and require the *removal* of a few instructions. The STM and LM instructions at the beginning of the program, for example, are unnecessary and *must* be omitted. The BR 14 instruction is replaced with the EOJ macro instruction. It is to be noted that the housekeeping routines specified in Chapter 4 incorporate all of the instructions necessary to set up a main program in DOS.

Figure D-4 illustrates the instructions to be added to a DOS main program to call a subroutine. Figure D-5 illustrates the instructions to be added to the DOS *subroutine.* Notice that the instructions in Figure D-5 are the same as the ones we have used in an OS *main* program.

LABEL	OPERATION	OPERAND		COMMENTS
1	10	16		
*	DOS MAIN PROGRAM SHELL FOR CALLING A SUBROUTINE			
MAIN	START	Ø		
	BALR	12,Ø		
	USING	*,12		
*				CALLING PROGRAM SUBROUTINE LINKAGE
	LA	13,SAVMAIN		POINT REG 13 TO SAVE AREA
	L	15,=V(HDGRTN)		LOAD EXTERNAL ENTRY POINTS
	LA	14,RETRNPT		SET UP RETURN ADDRESS
	BAL	14,15		CALL HDGRTN
*				
RETRNPT	·			
	·			
	EOJ			
*				
SAVMAIN	DS	18F		

Figure D-4

LABEL	OPERATION	OPERAND	COMMENTS
* OS AND	DOS	SUBROUTINE SHELL	
*			
HDGRTN	START	0	
	STM	14,12,12(13)	SAVE REGISTERS IN SAVMAIN
	BALR	12,0	
	USING	*,12	
	ST	13,SAVSUB1+4	SAVE KEY TO SAVMAIN
	.		
	.		
	.		
	L	13,SAVSUB1+4	FETCH KEY
	LM	14,12,12(13)	RESTORE REGISTERS
	BR	14	RETURN
SAVSUB1	DS	18F	
	.		
	.		
	.		
	END		

Figure D-5

External References In our program, we coded L 15,=V(SUB1) to store the entry address of SUB1 in register 15. There are several other possibilities, such as:

LA	15,SUB1	or	LA	15,SUB	
				.	
				.	
			SUB DC	A(SUB1)	

The second example you will recall is an A-type of address or ADCON. In both of these examples, the address of SUB1 must be available within the program. By definition, external subroutines are not part of the main program, but are separate entities. The entry address of a subroutine represents an external symbol since it is not addressable within our main program. The linkage editor resolves the addresses of the object modules at execution time. This means that V-type addresses signal the linkage editor that an external address (SUB1) is to be located and made available to the main program.

Figure D-6 illustrates an entire DOS main program that calls in an external subroutine (Figure D-7).

```
*                                                       *
*                          HOUSEKEEPING INSTRUCTIONS GO HERE  *
*                                                       *
           BALR  12,0
           USING *,12
           OPEN  INFILE,OUTFILE
           LA    13,SAVMAIN      POINT REG 13 TO SAVE AREA
           LA    14,READ         SET UP RETURN ADDRESS
           L     15,=V(HDGRTN)   LOAD EXTERNAL ENTRY
           BALR  14,15                CALL HEADING ROUTINE
READ       GET   INFILE,CARDIN
           BAL   5,DETLINE
           B     READ
DETLINE    ST    5,SAVE2
           CP    LINES,=P'25'
           BL    SKIP
           LA    13,SAVMAIN      POINT REG 13 TO SAVE AREA
           LA    14,ZERO         SET UP RETURN ADDRESS
           L     15,=V(HDGRTN)        LOAD EXTERNAL ENTRY
           BALR  14,15                CALL HEADING ROUTINE
ZERO       ZAP   LINES,=P'0'
SKIP       MVC   LINEOUT,SPACES
           MVC   PARTO,PART
           MVC   DESCO,DESC
           PUT   OUTFILE,LINEOUT
           AP    LINES,=P'1'
           L     5,SAVE2
           BR    5
EOF        CLOSE INFILE,OUTFILE
           EOJ
*                                                       *
*                          DTF MACROS & IOAREA DS'S GO HERE  *
*                                                       *
SAVMAIN    DS    18F
SAVE2      DS    F
LINES      DC    PL2'0'
SPACES     DC    CL1' '
LINEOUT    DS    0CL132
           DS    CL46
PARTO      DS    CL4
           DS    CL6
DESCO      DS    CL20
           DS    CL56
CARDIN     DS    0CL80
PART       DS    CL4
DESC       DS    CL20
           DS    CL56
           END
```

Figure D-6

```
HDGRTN     START 0
           PRINT NOGEN
           STM   14,12,12(13)    SAVE REGISTERS IN MAIN PROGRAM
           BALR  12,0
           USING *,12
           ST    13,SAVSUB1+4    SAVE KEY TO SAVMAIN
           OPEN  OUTFILE
           CNTRL OUTFILE,SK,1
           MVC   LINEOUT,SPACES
           MVC   LINEOUT+45(27),=C'MY-T-FINE AUTO SUPPLY CORP.'
           CNTRL OUTFILE,SP,,3
           PUT   OUTFILE,LINEOUT
           CLOSE OUTFILE
           L     13,SAVSUB1+4    FETCH KEY
           LM    14,12,12(13)    RESTORE REGISTERS
           BR    14              RETURN TO MAIN
SPACES     DC    C' '
LINEOUT    DS    CL132
SAVSUB1    DS    18F
*                                                       *
*                          OUTFILE DTF & IOAREA1 DS GO HERE  *
*                                                       *
           END
```

Figure D-7

Appendix E

Generating IOCS Modules for DOS Systems

In a DOS system, there are several hundred IOCS (Input/Output Control System) routines and options available to the programmer. Each installation in setting up its own system will catalog in its relocatable library those routines frequently used by its programming personnel. These input-output routines are therefore available and automatically incorporated in the module being assembled and executed.

However, if a routine is not commonly used and is therefore not available in the relocatable library, an error message will be issued by the "link edit" program, indicating an unresolved external reference.

If you find your system does not include any desired IOCS routine, it can be generated by including an XXMOD macro in your program, where XX = CD or PR. The macros CDMOD (card module) and PRMOD (print module) will generate the appropriate IOCS routines for the corresponding DTF. The modules are described below, and the default option is underlined. When the entry is omitted, this is the option automatically assumed by the system.

PRMOD

The operands are:

$$RECFORM = \begin{bmatrix} FIXUNB \\ VARUNB \\ UNDEF \end{bmatrix}$$

$$CTLCHR = \begin{bmatrix} YES \\ ASA \end{bmatrix}$$

CONTROL = YES
PRINTOV = YES
IOAREA2 = YES
WORKA = YES

The options selected cause the generation of a module that will correctly support the specified DTFPR. The print module is referenced by a code, IJDabcde and listed in the External Symbol Dictionary where the following are substituted for abcde.

a = F, V, or U, depending upon RECFORM.
b = Y if CTLCHR=YES; A if CTLCHR=ASA; C if CONTROL=YES; and Z if neither is specified.
c = P for PRINTOV; Z without PRINTOV
d = I for IOAREA2; Z without it.
e = W for WORKA; Z without it.

Thus, a module listed in the External Symbol Dictionary as IJDFCPZW, for example, supports a DTFPR specifying fixed-length records, use of the control (CNTRL) and print overflow (PRINTOV) macros, and a work area.

The print module would be specified in the program as:

LABEL	OPERATION 10	16	OPERAND
	PRMOD		CONTROL=YES, PRINTOV=YES, WORKA=YES

In a similar manner, the card module is defined:

$$RECFORM = \begin{bmatrix} \underline{FIXUNB} \\ VARUNB \\ UNDEF \end{bmatrix}$$

$$CTLCHR = \begin{bmatrix} YES \\ ASA \end{bmatrix}$$

$$CONTROL = YES$$

$$TYPEFLE = \begin{bmatrix} \underline{INPUT} \\ OUTPUT \\ CMBND \end{bmatrix}$$

$$WORKA = YES$$
$$IOAREA2 = YES$$

$$DEVICE = \begin{bmatrix} 2540 \\ 1442 \\ 2501 \\ 2520 \end{bmatrix}$$

$$CRDERR = RETRY$$

The card module is referenced by a code IJCabcde where the following are substituted for abcde.

a = F, V, or U depending upon RECFORM
b = Y if CTLCHR=YES; A if CTLCHR=ASA; C if CONTROL=YES; and Z if neither is specified
c = I, O, or C, depending upon TYPEFLE
d = W for WORKA; I for IOAREA2; B for both; and Z for neither
e = 0 for 2540; 1 for 1442; 2 for 2520; 3 for 2501; 4 for 2540 and CRDERR; 5 for 2520 and CRDERR.

A module listed in the External Symbol Dictionary as IJCFZIW0, for example, supports a DTFCD specifying fixed-length records, an input type of file, a 2540 card reader, and a work area.

The card module would be specified as:

LABEL	OPERATION 10		OPERAND
1		16	
	CDMOD		WORKA=YES

An alternate solution is to generate the desired IOCS routine separately. The object module can then be punched out and loaded into the relocatable library for future use. This task is usually assigned to the systems personnel responsible for the operation of the installation.

Appendix F

Additional Explanations of Housekeeping Routines

The BALR Instruction This instruction is frequently used to load the base register. When establishing a base register, the branch to the address contained in the second operand is to be eliminated. This is done by specifying zero as the second operand. For example, the instruction,

LABEL	OPERATION	
1	10 16	
	BALR	12,0

causes the address of the next instruction to be placed in register 12. However, *no* branch will occur since the second operand contains a zero. We are still able to continue with the next sequential instruction. When establishing a base register, the **USING** instruction immediately follows the **BALR**.

The USING Instruction The USING instruction is used to indicate the base register to the assembler. It is a nonexecutable instruction. This means that it does not appear in the object program, *but only provides information to the assembler*. The USING instruction:

1. Identifies the register to be used as a base register (the second operand).

2. Specifies a storage location that is to be the starting point (the first operand).

The general format of the USING instruction is as follows:

Operation	Operand
USING	LOC,REG

where

USING is a nonexecutable instruction necessary to set up a base register.
LOC denotes a storage location to be used as the base address or starting point of the program.
REG is a general register (2–12) identified as the base register.

For example, the following USING instruction

```
         USING BEGIN,12
BEGIN    MVI   FLDA,C'A'
```

specifies register 12 as the base register, and the instruction labeled BEGIN as the first executable instruction in the program.

Recall that a block or module of 4096 bytes is serviced by one register. When a program is longer than 4096 bytes, more than one base register must be specified.

The instruction USING *, 12 simply points to the next sequential instruction, as well as establishing 12 as the base register. To establish two base registers, each for one module of 4096 bytes, we may use the following:

LABEL	OPERATION	OPERAND
1	10 16	
	USING	BEGIN,12,11

Note that register 11 must be set up to contain BEGIN+4096. This is accomplished with the code in Figure F-2.

```
        USING BEGIN,12,11
BEGIN   LR    11,12
        A     11,=F'4096'
```
Figure F-2

We simply add 4096 to the base address contained in register 12. If the program exceeded 8192 bytes, then another register would be specified as in Figure F-3.

```
        USING BEGIN,12,11,10
BEGIN   LR    11,12
        A     11,=F'4096'
        LR    10,12
        A     10,=F'8192'
```
Figure F-3

The address stored in register 10 is BEGIN+8192. Remember, the USING instruction merely informs the assembler of the base address or starting point. The programmer must load the value of BEGIN, the first instruction in our example, into the base register.

Setting Up the Base Register

To load the base register and identify it to the assembler, two instructions are necessary at the beginning of the program, as in Figure F-4.

The BALR instruction stores the address of the next instruction in register 12. A branch does not occur because of the zero specified in the second operand. Since the USING instruction does *not* occupy space in the object program, the address of the BEGIN instruction is stored in register 12 at the time when the program is ready to be executed.

From this point on, all addresses assigned by the assembler will utilize the base address as well as the displacements resulting from the instructions. At execution time, the BALR instruction takes the actual address of the store instruction in the above example and places that address in the base register. The actual address depends on where the program was loaded by the system.

Remember, programs in the S/360/370 are relocatable. The system may decide to locate the program at location 4000 one time and at 8000 another. This does not present a problem, since the BALR instruction will store the *actual address* of the next instruction in the base register.

The BALR instruction has an RR format and is thus two bytes long. Consequently, in the above example, the address that is placed in register 12 will be the starting address plus 2.

```
        BALR  12,0
        USING BEGIN,12
BEGIN   ST    13,SAVEAREA+4
```
Figure F-4

Example 1

Starting address: 4000   Base register: 4002

Example 2

Starting address: 8000   Base register: 8002

Clearly, our starting address and base address are not the same. This sometimes causes confusion in reading core dumps, since students tend to confuse the two. It is the starting point (load-point) that is most frequently utilized in reading core dumps.

Summarizing, the designation and assignment of base registers are housekeeping operations that must be carried out in order that a program can be relocated and addressed by the S/360/370.

Load Multiple (LM)   The LM instruction is an extension of the load (L) instruction. However, with the load multiple, up to 16 fullwords of consecutive storage may be loaded into all 16 registers.

Operation	Operand
LM	REG1,REG2,LOC

where

LM indicates a load multiple operation.
REG1 is the first register to be loaded.
REG2 is the last register to be loaded.
LOC identifies the storage area where loading is to start.

The storage areas must be consecutive fields, each being a fullword in length. For example, the instruction in Figure F-5 produces the following results:

```
          LM      5,8,FLD1
                  .
                  .
                  .
FLD1      DC      F'1'
FLD2      DC      F'2'
FLD3      DC      F'3'
FLD4      DC      F'4'
```

Figure F-5

Before Execution		After Execution	
Register	Contents	Register	Contents
5	?	5	00 00 00 01
6	?	6	00 00 00 02
7	?	7	00 00 00 03
8	?	8	00 00 00 04

Note that all registers from 5 through 8 (inclusive) are loaded from consecutive locations with this single instruction.

An important consideration of this instruction is the wrap-around feature.

This means that the registers are arranged in ascending sequence (0,1,2, . . ., 15), with register 0 following register 15. Therefore, the instruction

LABEL	OPERATION 10	16	OPERAND
	L M	1 4 , 2 , F L W D	

would load the five registers 14, 15, 0, 1, 2.

Most important,

LABEL	OPERATION 10	16	OPERAND
	L M	1 4 , 1 2 , S A V E	

would load 15 registers, beginning with register 14. A block of 15 fullwords would be loaded starting from the storage location called **SAVE**. All of the general registers would be loaded with this instruction, with the exception of register 13.

Store Multiple Instruction (STM)

The Store Multiple instruction reverses the process of the Load Multiple (LM) instruction. The contents of the sending registers are transmitted to consecutive locations in main storage. As with the Store (ST) instruction the first operand is the *sending* field, and the second operand is the receiving field.

We may store the contents of as many as 16 registers in consecutive fullwords in main storage with one **STM** instruction.

Example

LABEL	OPERATION 10	16
	S T M	5 , 8 , S A V E

Register	Contents	Storage Before Execution		Storage After Execution	
5	00 00 00 01	SAVE	01 23 34 56	SAVE	00 00 00 01
6	00 00 00 02	SAVE+4	06 54 32 10	SAVE+4	00 00 00 02
7	00 00 00 03	SAVE+8	01 35 78 98	SAVE+8	00 00 00 03
8	00 00 00 04	SAVE+12	08 34 56 75	SAVE+12	00 00 00 04

The wrap-around feature described in the LM instruction is an available option when using the STM. For external subroutine linkages, the STM and LM are used extensively. The STM is used to place the contents of registers in a storage area. Later, the registers are restored to their original status with the LM instruction.

Appendix G

Shell for DOS Program

LABEL	OPERATION	OPERAND / COMMENTS	72	80
	PRINT	NOGEN		
	START	[PLACE NAME OF PROGRAM IN COLS 1-8]		
	BALR	12,0		
	USING	*,12		
	OPEN	INFILE,OUTFILE		
CLEAR	MVC	OUTAREA,SPACES		
	GET	INFILE,RECORD		
** LOGIC	GOES	HERE		
**	:			
	PUT	OUTFILE,OUTAREA		
	B	CLEAR		
** INCLUDE	END	OF JOB ROUTINES HERE, THEN CLOSE-IF NO EOJ ROUTINE INCL:		
EOF	CLOSE	INFILE,OUTFILE		
	EOJ			
INFILE	DTFCD	DEVADDR=SYSIPT,BLKSIZE=80,IOAREA1=BUFFRIN,WORKA=YES,	*	
		DEVICE=2540,TYPEFILE=INPUT,EOFADDR=EOF		
OUTFILE	DTFPR	DEVADDR=SYSLST,BLKSIZE=132,IOAREA1=BUFFROUT,WORKA=YES,	*	
		DEVICE=1403		
BUFFRIN	DS	CL80		
BUFFROUT	DS	CL132		
RECORD	DS	0CL80		
** PLACE	DS'S	FOR FIELDS IN INPUT RECORD HERE		
SPACES	DC	CL' '		
OUTAREA	DS	0CL132		
** PLACE	DS'S	FOR FIELDS IN OUTPUT RECORD HERE-INCLUDING BLANK AREAS,		
** ALL OTHER	DS'S	AND DC'S NECESSARY FOR PROCESSING GO HERE		
	END			

Shell for OS Program

LABEL	OPERATION	OPERAND	COMMENTS		
1	10	16		72	80
	PRINT	NOGEN			
	START		[PLACE NAME OF PROGRAM IN COLS 1-8]		
	STM	14,12,12(13)			
	BALR	12,0			
	USING	*,12			
	ST	13,SAVEAREA+4			
	LA	13,SAVEAREA			
	OPEN	(INFILE,INPUT,OUTFILE,OUTPUT)			
CLEAR	MVC	OUTAREA,SPACES			
	GET	INFILE,RECORD			
** LOGIC	GOES	HERE			
**	:				
	PUT	OUTFILE,OUTAREA			
	B	CLEAR			
** INCLUDE	END-OF-JOB ROUTINES HERE THEN CLOSE; IF NO EOJ ROUTINE INCL:				
EOF	CLOSE	(INFILE,,OUTFILE)			
	L	13,SAVEAREA+4			
	LM	14,12,12(13)			
	BR	14			
SAVEAREA	DS	18F			
RECORD	DS	0CL80			
**PLACE	DS'S	FOR FIELDS IN INPUT RECORD HERE			
SPACES	DC	CL1' '			
OUTAREA	DS	0CL132			
**PLACE	DS'S	FOR FIELDS IN OUTPUT RECORD HERE - INCLUDING BLANK AREAS			
INFILE	DCB	DDNAME=INFILE,MACRF=GM,BLKSIZE=80,LRECL=80,DSORG=PS,		*	
		EODAD=EOF			
OUTFILE	DCB	DDNAME=OUTFILE,MACRF=PM,BLKSIZE=132,LRECL=132,DSORG=PS			
	END				

Appendix H

Features of Operating Systems

Various distinctions between OS and DOS have been presented throughout the text. It should be noted, however, that because of the development of Virtual Storage (VS) systems, a particular computer may actually be running under DOS/VS or OS/VS. The following discussion serves to introduce the concept of virtual storage and suggests ways to write more efficient assembler language programs when VS is available.

Virtual storage involves the dynamic interaction between primary storage of the CPU and auxiliary storage on a direct-access device such as magnetic disk. As a consequence of this interaction, it is possible to treat the computer as if it has more primary storage than it actually does. Thus, for example, a computer with a CPU capacity of 256,000 bytes can be made to appear as if it has, instead, several million bytes.

The basic idea of a virtual storage system is that when a program is written, it is broken into various segments. Each segment, sometimes referred to as a *page*, is then transferred from auxiliary storage into the CPU, one at a time. After a page has been executed, the next page to be executed is transferred into the CPU, thereby overlaying the previous page, which is no longer needed. It is this efficient management of the allocation and use of storage within the CPU that allows a virtual storage system to appear larger than it really is.

Here are some of the advantages of virtual storage.

1. Very large programs can be run more easily. On systems that do not utilize virtual storage, it is sometimes difficult to fit a large program in its entirety into a relatively small CPU. You will recall that part of the CPU always has a supervisor program in it to control the operations of the system. In addition, there may be other programs in the CPU if the system has multiprogramming capability. Thus, without virtual storage, it is sometimes necessary to expend much effort in trying to reduce the size of a program so that it is manageable.

2. Online systems can handle many more terminals, since more efficient management of primary storage is possible with virtual storage.

3. It is possible, in general, for a high-priority job to be started without causing serious disruption to any jobs that are currently running.

The question arises as to whether or not a virtual storage system affects programming logic when writing a program in assembler language. The answer is yes and no. It is possible to program in assembler language without paying any attention at all to the virtual storage feature of most computers. What is sacrificed by this approach is efficiency.

If an assembler language programmer wishes to maximize the efficiency of the program and have it better fit the virtual storage capability of the computer, then certain techniques may be employed when writing the program.

One suggestion is to segment your program so that fields in storage operated on by particular instructions are defined near those instructions. In this way, accessing data will be made easier, since these instructions and the corresponding data being referenced will be contained within the same page in the CPU.

Similarly, if your program requires an external subroutine that is relatively short and that is used only a few times during execution, it should be coded within the main program. In this manner, it is possible to have contained within one page all the necessary logic for processing a particular phase of the program.

It is recommended that you check the reference manual for the particular operating system on your computer for further details on how you can take full advantage of the virtual storage concept.

The following chart illustrates selected characteristics for assembler language programs run under various operating systems. It should be noted that some non-IBM assemblers have comparable characteristics. The Amdahl 470, for example, is completely designed for the same operating environment as the System 360 and 370. The Amdahl assemblers are identical to the IBM assemblers. The same is essentially true for UNIVAC's assemblers.

Characteristics	360/DOS	360/OS	370/DOS	370/OS
1. Maximum number of lines per stmt	2	3	3	3
2. Input character code	EBCDIC	EBCDIC	EBCDIC	EBCDIC
3. Alignment of constants when no align is specified	Align/Not Align option NA	Constants aligned	Constants not aligned	Constants not aligned
4. Extended mnemonics	Y	Y	Y	Y
5. Maximum addressable byte				
(a) Decimal	16,777,216	16,777,216	16,777,216	16,777,216
(b) Hex	FFFFFF	FFFFFF	FFFFFF	FFFFFF
6. Largest value stored in register	2,147,483,647	2,147,483,647	2,147,483,647	2,147,483,647
7. Multiple control sections (base registers)	Y	Y	Y	Y
8. Maximum bytes per CSECT				
Length (a) Decimal	4096	4096	4096	4096
(b) Hex	1000	1000	1000	1000
Range	0–FFF	0–FFF	0–FFF	0–FFF
9. Control sections initiated by a CSECT start at zero	N	N	Y	N
10. Main program linkage same as subroutine	N	Y	N	Y

ASSEMBLER INSTRUCTIONS

Characteristics	360/DOS	360/OS	370/DOS	370/OS
11. Copy				
Nesting depth permitted	None	None	3	5
Macro definition copied	N	N	Y	Y
12. Drop with blank operand	NA	NA	Drops all current base reg	Drops all current base reg
13. END Sequence symbol as				
name entry	Y	Y	Y	Y
generated or copied	N	N	N	Y
14. EQU				
Second operand as length spec	N	N	N	Y
Third operand as type attribute	N	N	N	Y
15. PRINT: Inside macro definition	N	N	Y	Y

ADVANCED INSTRUCTIONS

	360/DOS	360/OS	370/DOS	370/OS
Compare Logical Character Long (CLCL)	N	N	Y	Y
Compare Logical under Mask (CLM)	N	N	Y	Y
Edit and Mark (EDMK)	Y	Y	Y	Y
Insert Character under Mask (ICM)	N	N	Y	Y
Move Character Long (MVCL)	N	N	Y	Y
Multiply Extended Double (MXD)	N	N	Y	Y
Set Program Mask (SPM)	Y	Y	Y	Y
Shift and Round Packed (SRP)	N	N	Y	Y
Store Character (STC)	Y	Y	Y	Y
Store Character under Mask (STCM)	N	N	Y	Y
Store Multiple (STM)	Y	Y	Y	Y
Translate (TR)	Y	Y	Y	Y
Translate and Test (TRT)	Y	Y	Y	Y

Appendix I

System/370 Reference Summary[1]

[1] Reprinted by permission of International Business Machines Corporation.

System/370 Reference Summary

GX20-1850-3

Fourth Edition (November 1976)

This reference summary is a minor revision and does not obsolete the previous edition. Changes include the addition of some new DASD and 3203 printer commands, the EBCDIC control characters GE and RLF, and minor editorial revisions.

The card is intended primarily for use by S/370 assembler language application programmers. It contains basic machine information on Models 115 through 168 summarized from the *System/370 Principles of Operation* (GA22-7000-4), frequently used information from the VS and VM assembler language manual (GC33-4010), command codes for various I/O devices, and a multi-code translation table. The card will be updated from time to time. However, the above manuals and others cited on the card are the authoritative reference sources and will be first to reflect changes.

To distinguish them from instructions carried over from S/360, the names of instructions essentially new with S/370 are shown in italics. Some machine instructions are optional or not available for some models. For those that are available on a particular model, the user is referred to the appropriate systems reference manual. For a particular installation, one must ascertain which optional hardware features and programming system(s) have been installed. The floating-point and extended floating-point instructions, as well as the instructions listed below, are not standard on every model. Monitoring (the MC instruction) is not available on the Model 165, except by field installation on purchased models.

Conditional swapping	CDS, CS
CPU timer and clock comparator	SCKC, SPT, STCKC, STPT
Direct control	RDD, WRD
Dynamic address translation	LRA, PTLB, RRB, STNSM, STOSM
Input/output	CLRIO, SIOF
Multiprocessing	SIGP, SPX, STAP, STPX
PSW key handling	IPK, SPKA

Comments about this publication may be sent to the address below. All comments and suggestions become the property of IBM.

IBM Corporation, Technical Publications/Systems, Dept. 824, 1133 Westchester Avenue, White Plains, N.Y. 10604.

MACHINE INSTRUCTIONS

NAME	MNEMONIC	OP CODE	FORMAT	OPERANDS
Add (c)	AR	1A	RR	R1,R2
Add (c)	A	5A	RX	R1,D2(X2,B2)
Add Decimal (c)	AP	FA	SS	D1(L1,B1),D2(L2,B2)
Add Halfword (c)	AH	4A	RX	R1,D2(X2,B2)
Add Logical (c)	ALR	1E	RR	R1,R2
Add Logical (c)	AL	5E	RX	R1,D2(X2,B2)
AND (c)	NR	14	RR	R1,R2
AND (c)	N	54	RX	R1,D2(X2,B2)
AND (c)	NI	94	SI	D1(B1),I2
AND (c)	NC	D4	SS	D1(L,B1),D2(B2)
Branch and Link	BALR	05	RR	R1,R2
Branch and Link	BAL	45	RX	R1,D2(X2,B2)
Branch on Condition	BCR	07	RR	M1,R2
Branch on Condition	BC	47	RX	M1,D2(X2,B2)
Branch on Count	BCTR	06	RR	R1,R2
Branch on Count	BCT	46	RX	R1,D2(X2,B2)
Branch on Index High	BXH	86	RS	R1,R3,D2(B2)
Branch on Index Low or Equal	BXLE	87	RS	R1,R3,D2(B2)
Clear I/O (c,p)	CLRIO	9D01	S	D2(B2)
Compare (c)	CR	19	RR	R1,R2
Compare (c)	C	59	RX	R1,D2(X2,B2)
Compare and Swap (c)	CS	BA	RS	R1,R3,D2(B2)
Compare Decimal (c)	CP	F9	SS	D1(L1,B1),D2(L2,B2)
Compare Double and Swap (c)	CDS	BB	RS	R1,R3,D2(B2)
Compare Halfword (c)	CH	49	RX	R1,D2(X2,B2)
Compare Logical (c)	CLR	15	RR	R1,R2
Compare Logical (c)	CL	55	RX	R1,D2(X2,B2)
Compare Logical (c)	CLC	D5	SS	D1(L,B1),D2(B2)
Compare Logical (c)	CLI	95	SI	D1(B1),I2
Compare Logical Characters under Mask (c)	CLM	BD	RS	R1,M3,D2(B2)
Compare Logical Long (c)	CLCL	0F	RR	R1,R2
Convert to Binary	CVB	4F	RX	R1,D2(X2,B2)
Convert to Decimal	CVD	4E	RX	R1,D2(X2,B2)
Diagnose (p)		83		Model-dependent
Divide	DR	1D	RR	R1,R2
Divide	D	5D	RX	R1,D2(X2,B2)
Divide Decimal	DP	FD	SS	D1(L1,B1),D2(L2,B2)
Edit (c)	ED	DE	SS	D1(L,B1),D2(B2)
Edit and Mark (c)	EDMK	DF	SS	D1(L,B1),D2(B2)
Exclusive OR (c)	XR	17	RR	R1,R2
Exclusive OR (c)	X	57	RX	R1,D2(X2,B2)
Exclusive OR (c)	XI	97	SI	D1(B1),I2
Exclusive OR (c)	XC	D7	SS	D1(L,B1),D2(B2)
Execute	EX	44	RX	R1,D2(X2,B2)
Halt I/O (c,p)	HIO	9E00	S	D2(B2)
Halt Device (c,p)	HDV	9E01	S	D2(B2)
Insert Character	IC	43	RX	R1,D2(X2,B2)
Insert Characters under Mask (c)	ICM	BF	RS	R1,M3,D2(B2)
Insert PSW Key (p)	IPK	B20B	S	
Insert Storage Key (p)	ISK	09	RR	R1,R2
Load	LR	18	RR	R1,R2
Load	L	58	RX	R1,D2(X2,B2)
Load Address	LA	41	RX	R1,D2(X2,B2)
Load and Test (c)	LTR	12	RR	R1,R2
Load Complement (c)	LCR	13	RR	R1,R2
Load Control (p)	LCTL	B7	RS	R1,R3,D2(B2)
Load Halfword	LH	48	RX	R1,D2(X2,B2)
Load Multiple	LM	98	RS	R1,R3,D2(B2)
Load Negative (c)	LNR	11	RR	R1,R2
Load Positive (c)	LPR	10	RR	R1,R2
Load PSW (n,p)	LPSW	82	S	D2(B2)
Load Real Address (c,p)	LRA	B1	RX	R1,D2(X2,B2)
Monitor Call	MC	AF	SI	D1(B1),I2
Move	MVI	92	SI	D1(B1),I2
Move	MVC	D2	SS	D1(L,B1),D2(B2)
Move Long (c)	MVCL	0E	RR	R1,R2
Move Numerics	MVN	D1	SS	D1(L,B1),D2(B2)
Move with Offset	MVO	F1	SS	D1(L1,B1),D2(L2,B2)
Move Zones	MVZ	D3	SS	D1(L,B1),D2(B2)
Multiply	MR	1C	RR	R1,R2
Multiply	M	5C	RX	R1,D2(X2,B2)
Multiply Decimal	MP	FC	SS	D1(L1,B1),D2(L2,B2)
Multiply Halfword	MH	4C	RX	R1,D2(X2,B2)
OR (c)	OR	16	RR	R1,R2

MACHINE INSTRUCTIONS (Contd) ③

NAME	MNEMONIC	OP CODE	FOR- MAT	OPERANDS
OR (c)	O	56	RX	R1,D2(X2,B2)
OR (c)	OI	96	SI	D1(B1),I2
OR (c)	OC	D6	SS	D1(L,B1),D2(B2)
Pack	PACK	F2	SS	D1(L1,B1),D2(L2,B2)
Purge TLB (p)	PTLB	B20D	S	
Read Direct (p)	RDD	85	SI	D1(B1),I2
Reset Reference Bit (c,p)	RRB	B213	S	D2(B2)
Set Clock (c,p)	SCK	B204	S	D2(B2)
Set Clock Comparator (p)	SCKC	B206	S	D2(B2)
Set CPU Timer (p)	SPT	B208	S	D2(B2)
Set Prefix (p)	SPX	B210	S	D2(B2)
Set Program Mask (n)	SPM	04	RR	R1
Set PSW Key from Address (p)	SPKA	B20A	S	D2(B2)
Set Storage Key (p)	SSK	08	RR	R1,R2
Set System Mask (p)	SSM	80	S	D2(B2)
Shift and Round Decimal (c)	SRP	F0	SS	D1(L1,B1),D2(B2),I3
Shift Left Double (c)	SLDA	8F	RS	R1,D2(B2)
Shift Left Double Logical	SLDL	8D	RS	R1,D2(B2)
Shift Left Single (c)	SLA	8B	RS	R1,D2(B2)
Shift Left Single Logical	SLL	89	RS	R1,D2(B2)
Shift Right Double (c)	SRDA	8E	RS	R1,D2(B2)
Shift Right Double Logical	SRDL	8C	RS	R1,D2(B2)
Shift Right Single (c)	SRA	8A	RS	R1,D2(B2)
Shift Right Single Logical	SRL	88	RS	R1,D2(B2)
Signal Processor (c,p)	SIGP	AE	RS	R1,R3,D2(B2)
Start I/O (c,p)	SIO	9C00	S	D2(B2)
Start I/O Fast Release (c,p)	SIOF	9C01	S	D2(B2)
Store	ST	50	RX	R1,D2(X2,B2)
Store Channel ID (c,p)	STIDC	B203	S	D2(B2)
Store Character	STC	42	RX	R1,D2(X2,B2)
Store Characters under Mask	STCM	BE	RS	R1,M3,D2(B2)
Store Clock (c)	STCK	B205	S	D2(B2)
Store Clock Comparator (p)	STCKC	B207	S	D2(B2)
Store Control (p)	STCTL	B6	RS	R1,R3,D2(B2)
Store CPU Address (p)	STAP	B212	S	D2(B2)
Store CPU ID (p)	STIDP	B202	S	D2(B2)
Store CPU Timer (p)	STPT	B209	S	D2(B2)
Store Halfword	STH	40	RX	R1,D2(X2,B2)
Store Multiple	STM	90	RS	R1,R3,D2(B2)
Store Prefix (p)	STPX	B211	S	D2(B2)
Store Then AND System Mask (p)	STNSM	AC	SI	D1(B1),I2
Store Then OR System Mask (p)	STOSM	AD	SI	D1(B1),I2
Subtract (c)	SR	1B	RR	R1,R2
Subtract (c)	S	5B	RX	R1,D2(X2,B2)
Subtract Decimal (c)	SP	FB	SS	D1(L1,B1),D2(L2,B2)
Subtract Halfword (c)	SH	4B	RX	R1,D2(X2,B2)
Subtract Logical (c)	SLR	1F	RR	R1,R2
Subtract Logical (c)	SL	5F	RX	R1,D2(X2,B2)
Supervisor Call	SVC	0A	RR	I
Test and Set (c)	TS	93	S	D2(B2)
Test Channel (c,p)	TCH	9F00	S	D2(B2)
Test I/O (c,p)	TIO	9D00	S	D2(B2)
Test under Mask (c)	TM	91	SI	D1(B1),I2
Translate	TR	DC	SS	D1(L,B1),D2(B2)
Translate and Test (c)	TRT	DD	SS	D1(L,B1),D2(B2)
Unpack	UNPK	F3	SS	D1(L1,B1),D2(L2,B2)
Write Direct (p)	WRD	84	SI	D1(B1),I2
Zero and Add Decimal (c)	ZAP	F8	SS	D1(L1,B1),D2(L2,B2)

Floating-Point Instructions

NAME	MNEMONIC	OP CODE	FOR- MAT	OPERANDS
Add Normalized, Extended (c,x)	AXR	36	RR	R1,R2
Add Normalized, Long (c)	ADR	2A	RR	R1,R2
Add Normalized, Long (c)	AD	6A	RX	R1,D2(X2,B2)
Add Normalized, Short (c)	AER	3A	RR	R1,R2
Add Normalized, Short (c)	AE	7A	RX	R1,D2(X2,B2)
Add Unnormalized, Long (c)	AWR	2E	RR	R1,R2
Add Unnormalized, Long (c)	AW	6E	RX	R1,D2(X2,B2)
Add Unnormalized, Short (c)	AUR	3E	RR	R1,R2
Add Unnormalized, Short (c)	AU	7E	RX	R1,D2(X2,B2)

c. Condition code is set.
n. New condition code is loaded.

p. Privileged instruction.
x. Extended precision floating-point.

Floating-Point Instructions (Contd) ④

NAME	MNEMONIC	OP CODE	FOR- MAT	OPERANDS
Compare, Long (c)	CDR	29	RR	R1,R2
Compare, Long (c)	CD	69	RX	R1,D2(X2,B2)
Compare, Short (c)	CER	39	RR	R1,R2
Compare, Short (c)	CE	79	RX	R1,D2(X2,B2)
Divide, Long	DDR	2D	RR	R1,R2
Divide, Long	DD	6D	RX	R1,D2(X2,B2)
Divide, Short	DER	3D	RR	R1,R2
Divide, Short	DE	7D	RX	R1,D2(X2,B2)
Halve, Long	HDR	24	RR	R1,R2
Halve, Short	HER	34	RR	R1,R2
Load and Test, Long (c)	LTDR	22	RR	R1,R2
Load and Test, Short (c)	LTER	32	RR	R1,R2
Load Complement, Long (c)	LCDR	23	RR	R1,R2
Load Complement, Short (c)	LCER	33	RR	R1,R2
Load, Long	LDR	28	RR	R1,R2
Load, Long	LD	68	RX	R1,D2(X2,B2)
Load Negative, Long (c)	LNDR	21	RR	R1,R2
Load Negative, Short (c)	LNER	31	RR	R1,R2
Load Positive, Long (c)	LPDR	20	RR	R1,R2
Load Positive, Short (c)	LPER	30	RR	R1,R2
Load Rounded, Extended to Long (x)	LRDR	25	RR	R1,R2
Load Rounded, Long to Short (x)	LRER	35	RR	R1,R2
Load, Short	LER	38	RR	R1,R2
Load, Short	LE	78	RX	R1,D2(X2,B2)
Multiply, Extended (x)	MXR	26	RR	R1,R2
Multiply, Long	MDR	2C	RR	R1,R2
Multiply, Long	MD	6C	RX	R1,D2(X2,B2)
Multiply, Long/Extended (x)	MXDR	27	RR	R1,R2
Multiply, Long/Extended (x)	MXD	67	RX	R1,D2(X2,B2)
Multiply, Short	MER	3C	RR	R1,R2
Multiply, Short	ME	7C	RX	R1,D2(X2,B2)
Store, Long	STD	60	RX	R1,D2(X2,B2)
Store, Short	STE	70	RX	R1,D2(X2,B2)
Subtract Normalized, Extended (c,x)	SXR	37	RR	R1,R2
Subtract Normalized, Long (c)	SDR	2B	RR	R1,R2
Subtract Normalized, Long (c)	SD	6B	RX	R1,D2(X2,B2)
Subtract Normalized, Short (c)	SER	3B	RR	R1,R2
Subtract Normalized, Short (c)	SE	7B	RX	R1,D2(X2,B2)
Subtract Unnormalized, Long (c)	SWR	2F	RR	R1,R2
Subtract Unnormalized, Long (c)	SW	6F	RX	R1,D2(X2,B2)
Subtract Unnormalized, Short (c)	SUR	3F	RR	R1,R2
Subtract Unnormalized, Short (c)	SU	7F	RX	R1,D2(X2,B2)

EXTENDED MNEMONIC INSTRUCTIONS†

Use	Extended Code* (RX or RR)	Meaning	Machine Instr.* (RX or RR)
General	B or BR	Unconditional Branch	BC or BCR 15,
	NOP or NOPR	No Operation	BC or BCR 0,
After Compare Instructions (A:B)	BH or BHR	Branch on A High	BC or BCR 2,
	BL or BLR	Branch on A Low	BC or BCR 4,
	BE or BER	Branch on A Equal B	BC or BCR 8,
	BNH or BNHR	Branch on A Not High	BC or BCR 13,
	BNL or BNLR	Branch on A Not Low	BC or BCR 11,
	BNE or BNER	Branch on A Not Equal B	BC or BCR 7,
After Arithmetic Instructions	BO or BOR	Branch on Overflow	BC or BCR 1,
	BP or BPR	Branch on Plus	BC or BCR 2,
	BM or BMR	Branch on Minus	BC or BCR 4,
	BNP or BNPR	Branch on Not Plus	BC or BCR 13,
	BNM or BNMR	Branch on Not Minus	BC or BCR 11,
	BNZ or BNZR	Branch on Not Zero	BC or BCR 7,
	BZ or BZR	Branch on Zero	BC or BCR 8,
After Test under Mask Instruction	BO or BOR	Branch if Ones	BC or BCR 1,
	BM or BMR	Branch if Mixed	BC or BCR 4,
	BZ or BZR	Branch if Zeros	BC or BCR 8,
	BNO or BNOR	Branch if Not Ones	BC or BCR 14,

†Source: GC33-4010; for OS/VS,VM/370 and DOS/VS.

*Second operand, not shown, is D2(X2,B2) for RX format and R2 for RR format.

SOME EDIT AND EDMK PATTERN CHARACTERS (in hex)

20—digit selector	40—blank	5C—asterisk
21—start of significance	4B—period	6B—comma
22—field separator	5B—dollar sign	C3D9—CR

CONDITION CODES ⑤

Condition Code Setting	0	1	2	3
Mask Bit Value	8	4	2	1

General Instructions

Add, Add Halfword	zero	<zero	>zero	overflow
Add Logical	zero, no carry	not zero, no carry	zero, carry	not zero, carry
AND	zero	not zero	—	—
Compare, Compare Halfword	equal	1st op low	1st op high	—
Compare and Swap/Double	equal	not equal	—	—
Compare Logical	equal	1st op low	1st op high	—
Exclusive OR	zero	not zero	—	—
Insert Characters under Mask	all zero	1st bit one	1st bit zero	—
Load and Test	zero	<zero	>zero	—
Load Complement	zero	<zero	>zero	overflow
Load Negative	zero	<zero	—	—
Load Positive	zero	—	>zero	overflow
Move Long	count equal	count low	count high	overlap
OR	zero	not zero	—	—
Shift Left Double/Single	zero	<zero	>zero	overflow
Shift Right Double/Single	zero	<zero	>zero	—
Store Clock	set	not set	error	not oper
Subtract, Subtract Halfword	zero	<zero	>zero	overflow
Subtract Logical	—	not zero, no carry	zero, carry	not zero, carry
Test and Set	zero	one	—	—
Test under Mask	zero	mixed	—	ones
Translate and Test	zero	incomplete	complete	—

Decimal Instructions

Add Decimal	zero	<zero	>zero	overflow
Compare Decimal	equal	1st op low	1st op high	—
Edit, Edit and Mark	zero	<zero	>zero	—
Shift and Round Decimal	zero	<zero	>zero	overflow
Subtract Decimal	zero	<zero	>zero	overflow
Zero and Add	zero	<zero	>zero	overflow

Floating-Point Instructions

Add Normalized	zero	<zero	>zero	—
Add Unnormalized	zero	<zero	>zero	—
Compare	equal	1st op low	1st op high	—
Load and Test	zero	<zero	>zero	—
Load Complement	zero	<zero	>zero	—
Load Negative	zero	<zero	—	—
Load Positive	zero	—	>zero	—
Subtract Normalized	zero	<zero	>zero	—
Subtract Unnormalized	zero	<zero	>zero	—

Input/Output Instructions

Clear I/O	no oper in progress	CSW stored	chan busy	not oper
Halt Device	interruption pending	CSW stored	channel working	not oper
Halt I/O	interruption pending	CSW stored	burst op stopped	not oper
Start I/O, SIOF	successful	CSW stored	busy	not oper
Store Channel ID	ID stored	CSW stored	busy	not oper
Test Channel	available	interruption pending	burst mode	not oper
Test I/O	available	CSW stored	busy	not oper

System Control Instructions

Load Real Address	translation available	ST entry invalid	PT entry invalid	length violation
Reset Reference Bit	R=0, C=0	R=0, C=1	R=1, C=0	R=1, C=1
Set Clock	set	secure	—	not oper
Signal Processor	accepted	stat stored	busy	not oper

CNOP ALIGNMENT

DOUBLEWORD							
WORD				WORD			
HALFWORD		HALFWORD		HALFWORD		HALFWORD	
BYTE	BYTE	BYTE	BYTE	BYTE	BYTE	BYTE	BYTE
↗0,4 0,8		↗2,4 2,8		↗0,4 4,8		↗2,4 6,8	

ASSEMBLER INSTRUCTIONS† ⑥

Function	Mnemonic	Meaning
Data definition	DC	Define constant
	DS	Define storage
	CCW	Define channel command word
Program sectioning and linking	START	Start assembly
	CSECT	Identify control section
	DSECT	Identify dummy section
	DXD*	Define external dummy section
	CXD*	Cumulative length of external dummy section
	COM	Identify blank common control section
	ENTRY	Identify entry-point symbol
	EXTRN	Identify external symbol
	WXTRN	Identify weak external symbol
Base register assignment	USING	Use base address register
	DROP	Drop base address register
Control of listings	TITLE	Identify assembly output
	EJECT	Start new page
	SPACE	Space listing
	PRINT	Print optional data
Program Control	ICTL	Input format control
	ISEQ	Input sequence checking
	PUNCH	Punch a card
	REPRO	Reproduce following card
	ORG	Set location counter
	EQU	Equate symbol
	OPSYN*	Equate operation code
	*PUSH**	Save current PRINT or USING status
	POP*	Restore PRINT or USING status
	LTORG	Begin literal pool
	CNOP	Conditional no operation
	COPY	Copy predefined source coding
	END	End assembly
Macro definition	MACRO	Macro definition header
	MNOTE	Request for error message
	MEXIT	Macro definition exit
	MEND	Macro definition trailer
Conditional assembly	ACTR	Conditional assembly loop counter
	AGO	Unconditional branch
	AIF	Conditional branch
	ANOP	Assembly no operation
	GBLA	Define global SETA symbol
	GBLB	Define global SETB symbol
	GBLC	Define global SETC symbol
	LCLA	Define local SETA symbol
	LCLB	Define local SETB symbol
	LCLC	Define local SETC symbol
	SETA	Set arithmetic variable symbol
	SETB	Set binary variable symbol
	SETC	Set character variable symbol

SUMMARY OF CONSTANTS†

TYPE	IMPLIED LENGTH, BYTES	ALIGNMENT	FORMAT	TRUNCATION/ PADDING
C	—	byte	characters	right
X	—	byte	hexadecimal digits	left
B	—	byte	binary digits	left
F	4	word	fixed-point binary	left
H	2	halfword	fixed-point binary	left
E	4	word	short floating-point	right
D	8	doubleword	long floating-point	right
L	16	doubleword	extended floating-point	right
P	—	byte	packed decimal	left
Z	—	byte	zoned decimal	left
A	4	word	value of address	left
Y	2	halfword	value of address	left
S	2	halfword	address in base-displacement form	—
V	4	word	externally defined address value	left
Q*	4	word	symbol naming a DXD or DSECT	left

†Source: GC33-4010; for OS/VS, VM/370, and DOS/VS.
*OS/VS and VM/370 only.

I/O COMMAND CODES ⑦

Standard Command Code Assignments (CCW bits 0-7)

xxxx 0000	Invalid		†††† ††01	Write
†††† 0100	Sense		†††† ††10	Read
xxxx 1000	Transfer in Channel		†††† ††11	Control
†††† 1100	Read Backward		0000 0011	Control No Operation

x—Bit ignored.　　†Modifier bit for specific type of I/O device

CONSOLE PRINTERS

Write, No Carrier Return	01	Sense	04
Write, Auto Carrier Return	09	Audible Alarm	0B
Read Inquiry	0A		

3504, 3505 CARD READERS/3525 CARD PUNCH

Source: GA21-9124

Command	Binary	Hex	Bit Meanings
Sense	0000 0100	04	SS　Stacker
Feed, Select Stacker	SS10 F011		00　　1
Read Only*	11D0 F010		01/10　2
Diagnostic Read (invalid for 3504)	1101 0010	D2	F　Format Mode
Read, Feed, Select Stacker*	SSD0 F010		0　Unformatted
Write RCE Format*	0001 0001	11	1　Formatted
3504, 3505 only			D　Data Mode
Write OMR Format†	0011 0001	31	0　1—EBCDIC
			1　2—Card image
3525 only			L　Line Position
Write, Feed, Select Stacker	SSD0 0001		5-bit binary value
Print Line*	LLLL L101		

*Special feature on 3525.　　†Special feature.

PRINTERS: 3211/3811 (GA24-3543), 3203/IPA, 1403*/2821 (GA24-3312)

	After Write	Immed		
Space 1 Line	09	0B	Write without spacing	01
Space 2 Lines	11	13	Sense	04
Space 3 Lines	19	1B	Load UCSB without folding	FB
Skip to Channel 0†	—	83	Fold†	43
Skip to Channel 1	89	8B	Unfold†	23
Skip to Channel 2	91	93	Load UCSB and Fold (exc. 3211)	F3
Skip to Channel 3	99	9B	UCS Gate Load (1403 only)	EB
Skip to Channel 4	A1	A3	Load FCB (exc. 1403)	63
Skip to Channel 5	A9	AB	Block Data Check	73
Skip to Channel 6	B1	B3	Allow Data Check	7B
Skip to Channel 7	B9	BB	Read PLB†	02
Skip to Channel 8	C1	C3	Read UCSB†	0A
Skip to Channel 9	C9	CB	Read FCB†	12
Skip to Channel 10	D1	D3	Diag. Check Read (exc. 3203)	06
Skip to Channel 11	D9	DB	Diagnostic Write†	05
Skip to Channel 12	E1	E3	Raise Cover†	6B
Adv. to End of Sheet (3203 only)		5B	Diagnostic Gate†	07
			Diagnostic Read (1403 only)	02

*UCS special feature; IPA diagnostics are model-dependent.　　†3211 only.

3420/3803, 3410/3411 MAGNETIC TAPE

(**Indicates 3420 only)

See GA32-0020, -0021, -0022 for special features and functions of specific models.

		Density	Parity	DC	Trans	Cmd
Write	01					
Read Forward	02			on	off	13
Read Backward	0C	200	odd	off	off	33
Sense	04				on	3B
Sense Reserve**	F4		even	off	off	23
Sense Release**	D4				on	2B
Request Track-in-Error	1B			on	off	53
Loop Write-to-Read**	8B	556	odd	oif	off	73
Set Diagnose**	4B				on	7B
Rewind	07		even	off	off	63
Rewind Unload	0F				on	6B
Erase Gap	17			on	off	93
Write Tape Mark	1F	800	odd	off	off	B3
Backspace Block	27				on	BB
Backspace File	2F		even	off	off	A3
Forward Space Block	37				on	AB
Forward Space File	3F	Mode Set 2 (9-track), 800 bpi				CB
Data Security Erase**	97	Mode Set 2 (9-track), 1600 bpi				C3
Diagnostic Mode Set**	0B	Mode Set 2 (9-track), 6250 bpi**				D3

Mode Set 1 (7-track)

DIRECT ACCESS STORAGE DEVICES ⑧

3330-3340-3350 SERIES (GA26-1592, -1617, -1619, -1620, -1638); **2305/2835** (GA26-1589); **2314, 2319** (GA26-3599, -1606)

See systems reference manuals for restrictions.

Command		MT Off	MT On*	Count
Control	Orient (c)	2B		Nonzero
	Recalibrate	13		Nonzero
	Seek	07		6
	Seek Cylinder	0B		6
	Seek Head	1B		6
	Space Count	0F		3 (a); nonzero (d)
	Set File Mask	1F		1
	Set Sector (a,f)	23		1
	Restore (executes as a no-op)	17		Nonzero
	Vary Sensing (c)	27		1
	Diagnostic Load (a)	53		1
	Diagnostic Write (a)	73		512
Search	Home Address Equal	39	B9	4
	Identifier Equal	31	B1	5
	Identifier High	51	D1	5
	Identifier Equal or High	71	F1	5
	Key Equal	29	A9	KL
	Key High	49	C9	KL
	Key Equal or High	69	E9	KL
	Key and Data Equal (d)	2D	AD	
	Key and Data High (d)	4D	CD	Number
	Key and Data Eq. or Hi (d)	6D	ED	of bytes
Continue	Search Equal (d)	25	A5	(including
Scan	Search High (d)	45	C5	mask bytes)
	Search High or Equal (d)	65	E5	in search
	Set Compare (d)	35	B5	argument
	Set Compare (d)	75	F5	
	No Compare (d)	55	D5	
Read	Home Address	1A	9A	5
	Count	12	92	8
	Record 0	16	96	
	Data	06	86	Number
	Key and Data	0E	8E	of bytes
	Count, Key and Data	1E	9E	to be
	IPL	02		transferred
	Multiple Count, Key, Data (b)	5E		> Max. track len.
	Sector (a,f)	22		1
Sense	Sense I/O	04		24 (a); 6 (d)
	Sense I/O Type (b)	E4		7
	Read, Reset Buffered Log (b)	A4		24
	Read Buffered Log (c)	24		128
	Device Release (e)	94		24 (a); 6 (d)
	Device Reserve (e)	B4		24 (a); 6 (d)
	Read Diagnostic Status 1 (a)	44		16 or 512
Write	Home Address	19		5, 7, or 11
	Record 0	15		8+KL+DL of R0
	Erase	11		8+KL+DL
	Count, Key and Data	1D		8+KL+DL
	Special Count, Key and Data	01		8+KL+DL
	Data	05		DL
	Key and Data	0D		KL+DL

* Code same as MT Off except as listed.　d. 2314, 2319 only.
a. Except 2314, 2319.　　e. String switch or 2-channel switch
b. 3330-3340-3350 series only.　　required.
c. 2305/2835 only.　　f. Special feature required on 3340.

IBM

GX20-1850-3

International Business Machines Corporation
Data Processing Division
1133 Westchester Avenue, White Plains, New York 10604
(U.S.A. only)

IBM World Trade Corporation
360 Hamilton Avenue, White Plains, New York 10601
(International)

CODE TRANSLATION TABLE (9)

Dec.	Hex	Instruction (RR)	BCDIC	EBCDIC(1)	ASCII	7-Track Tape BCDIC(2)	Card Code EBCDIC	Binary
0	00			NUL	NUL		12-0-1-8-9	0000 0000
1	01			SOH	SOH		12-1-9	0000 0001
2	02			STX	STX		12-2-9	0000 0010
3	03			ETX	ETX		12-3-9	0000 0011
4	04	SPM		PF	EOT		12-4-9	0000 0100
5	05	BALR		HT	ENQ		12-5-9	0000 0101
6	06	BCTR		LC	ACK		12-6-9	0000 0110
7	07	BCR		DEL	BEL		12-7-9	0000 0111
8	08	SSK		GE	BS		12-8-9	0000 1000
9	09	ISK		RLF	HT		12-1-8-9	0000 1001
10	0A	SVC		SMM	LF		12-2-8-9	0000 1010
11	0B			VT	VT		12-3-8-9	0000 1011
12	0C			FF	FF		12-4-8-9	0000 1100
13	0D			CR	CR		12-5-8-9	0000 1101
14	0E	MVCL		SO	SO		12-6-8-9	0000 1110
15	0F	CLCL		SI	SI		12-7-8-9	0000 1111
16	10	LPR		DLE	DLE		12-11-1-8-9	0001 0000
17	11	LNR		DC1	DC1		11-1-9	0001 0001
18	12	LTR		DC2	DC2		11-2-9	0001 0010
19	13	LCR		TM	DC3		11-3-9	0001 0011
20	14	NR		RES	DC4		11-4-9	0001 0100
21	15	CLR		NL	NAK		11-5-9	0001 0101
22	16	OR		BS	SYN		11-6-9	0001 0110
23	17	XR		IL	ETB		11-7-9	0001 0111
24	18	LR		CAN	CAN		11-8-9	0001 1000
25	19	CR		EM	EM		11-1-8-9	0001 1001
26	1A	AR		CC	SUB		11-2-8-9	0001 1010
27	1B	SR		CU1	ESC		11-3-8-9	0001 1011
28	1C	MR		IFS	FS		11-4-8-9	0001 1100
29	1D	DR		IGS	GS		11-5-8-9	0001 1101
30	1E	ALR		IRS	RS		11-6-8-9	0001 1110
31	1F	SLR		IUS	US		11-7-8-9	0001 1111
32	20	LPDR		DS	SP		11-0-1-8-9	0010 0000
33	21	LNDR		SOS	!		0-1-9	0010 0001
34	22	LTDR		FS	"		0-2-9	0010 0010
35	23	LCDR			#		0-3-9	0010 0011
36	24	HDR		BYP	$		0-4-9	0010 0100
37	25	LRDR		LF	%		0-5-9	0010 0101
38	26	MXR		ETB	&		0-6-9	0010 0110
39	27	MXDR		ESC	'		0-7-9	0010 0111
40	28	LDR			(		0-8-9	0010 1000
41	29	CDR			)		0-1-8-9	0010 1001
42	2A	ADR		SM	*		0-2-8-9	0010 1010
43	2B	SDR		CU2	+		0-3-8-9	0010 1011
44	2C	MDR			,		0-4-8-9	0010 1100
45	2D	DDR		ENQ	-		0-5-8-9	0010 1101
46	2E	AWR		ACK	.		0-6-8-9	0010 1110
47	2F	SWR		BEL	/		0-7-8-9	0010 1111
48	30	LPER			0		12-11-0-1-8-9	0011 0000
49	31	LNER			1		1-9	0011 0001
50	32	LTER		SYN	2		2-9	0011 0010
51	33	LCER			3		3-9	0011 0011
52	34	HER		PN	4		4-9	0011 0100
53	35	LRER		RS	5		5-9	0011 0101
54	36	AXR		UC	6		6-9	0011 0110
55	37	SXR		EOT	7		7-9	0011 0111
56	38	LER			8		8-9	0011 1000
57	39	CER			9		1-8-9	0011 1001
58	3A	AER			:		2-8-9	0011 1010
59	3B	SER		CU3	;		3-8-9	0011 1011
60	3C	MER		DC4	<		4-8-9	0011 1100
61	3D	DER		NAK	=		5-8-9	0011 1101
62	3E	AUR			>		6-8-9	0011 1110
63	3F	SUR		SUB	?		7-8-9	0011 1111

CODE TRANSLATION TABLE (Contd) (10)

Dec.	Hex	Instruction (RX)	BCDIC	EBCDIC(1)	ASCII	7-Track Tape BCDIC(2)	Card Code EBCDIC	Binary
64	40	STH		Sp Sp	@		no punches	0100 0000
65	41	LA			A	(3)	12-0-1-9	0100 0001
66	42	STC			B		12-0-2-9	0100 0010
67	43	IC			C		12-0-3-9	0100 0011
68	44	EX			D		12-0-4-9	0100 0100
69	45	BAL			E		12-0-5-9	0100 0101
70	46	BCT			F		12-0-6-9	0100 0110
71	47	BC			G		12-0-7-9	0100 0111
72	48	LH			H		12-0-8-9	0100 1000
73	49	CH			I		12-1-8	0100 1001
74	4A	AH		¢ ¢	J		12-2-8	0100 1010
75	4B	SH	.	. .	K	BA8 21	12-3-8	0100 1011
76	4C	MH	⌑)	< <	L	BA8 4	12-4-8	0100 1100
77	4D		[	((	M	BA8 4 1	12-5-8	0100 1101
78	4E	CVD	<	+ +	N	BA842	12-6-8	0100 1110
79	4F	CVB	‡	| |	O	BA8421	12-7-8	0100 1111
80	50	ST	& +	& &	P	BA	12	0101 0000
81	51				Q		12-11-1-9	0101 0001
82	52				R		12-11-2-9	0101 0010
83	53				S		12-11-3-9	0101 0011
84	54	N			T		12-11-4-9	0101 0100
85	55	CL			U		12-11-5-9	0101 0101
86	56	O			V		12-11-6-9	0101 0110
87	57	X			W		12-11-7-9	0101 0111
88	58	L			X		12-11-8-9	0101 1000
89	59	C			Y		11-1-8	0101 1001
90	5A	A		! !	Z		11-2-8	0101 1010
91	5B	S	$	$ $	[	B 8 21	11-3-8	0101 1011
92	5C	M	*	* *	\	B 84	11-4-8	0101 1100
93	5D	D	]	))	]	B 84 1	11-5-8	0101 1101
94	5E	AL	;	: ;	¬ ^	B 842	11-6-8	0101 1110
95	5F	SL	△	¬ ¬	_	B 8421	11-7-8	0101 1111
96	60	STD	-	- -	`	B	11	0110 0000
97	61		/	/ /	a	A 1	0-1	0110 0001
98	62				b		11-0-2-9	0110 0010
99	63				c		11-0-3-9	0110 0011
100	64				d		11-0-4-9	0110 0100
101	65				e		11-0-5-9	0110 0101
102	66				f		11-0-6-9	0110 0110
103	67	MXD			g		11-0-7-9	0110 0111
104	68	LD			h		11-0-8-9	0110 1000
105	69	CD			i		0-1-8	0110 1001
106	6A	AD		! !	j		12-11	0110 1010
107	6B	SD	,	, ,	k	A8 21	0-3-8	0110 1011
108	6C	MD	% (	% %	l	A 84	0-4-8	0110 1100
109	6D	DD	Y		m	A 84 1	0-5-8	0110 1101
110	6E	AW	\	> >	n	A 842	0-6-8	0110 1110
111	6F	SW	⧺	? ?	o	A 8421	0-7-8	0110 1111
112	70	STE			p		12-11-0	0111 0000
113	71				q		12-11-0-1-9	0111 0001
114	72				r		12-11-0-2-9	0111 0010
115	73				s		12-11-0-3-9	0111 0011
116	74				t		12-11-0-4-9	0111 0100
117	75				u		12-11-0-5-9	0111 0101
118	76				v		12-11-0-6-9	0111 0110
119	77				w		12-11-0-7-9	0111 0111
120	78	LE			x		12-11-0-8-9	0111 1000
121	79	CE		`	y		1-8	0111 1001
122	7A	AE	đ	: :	z	A	2-8	0111 1010
123	7B	SE	# =	#	{	8 21	3-8	0111 1011
124	7C	ME	@ '	@ @	|	84	4-8	0111 1100
125	7D	DE	:	' '	}	84 1	5-8	0111 1101
126	7E	AU	>	" "	~	842	6-8	0111 1110
127	7F	SU	√	" "	DEL	8421	7-8	0111 1111

1. Two columns of EBCDIC graphics are shown. The first gives IBM standard U.S. bit pattern assignments. The second shows the T-11 and TN text printing chains (120 graphics).
2. Add C (check bit) for odd or even parity as needed, except as noted.
3. For even parity use CA.

TWO-CHARACTER BSC DATA LINK CONTROLS

Function	EBCDIC	ASCII
ACK-0	DLE,X'70'	DLE,0
ACK-1	DLE,X'61'	DLE,1
WACK	DLE,X'6B'	DLE,;
RVI	DLE,X'7C'	DLE,<

CODE TRANSLATION TABLE (Contd)   ⑪

Dec.	Hex	Instruction and Format	BCDIC	EBCDIC(1)	ASCII	7-Track Tape BCDIC(2)	Card Code EBCDIC	Binary
128	80	SSM -S					12-0-1-8	1000 0000
129	81			a	a		12-0-1	1000 0001
130	82	LPSW -S		b	b		12-0-2	1000 0010
131	83	Diagnose		c	c		12-0-3	1000 0011
132	84	WRD SI		d	d		12-0-4	1000 0100
133	85	RDD		e	e		12-0-5	1000 0101
134	86	BXH		f	f		12-0-6	1000 0110
135	87	BXLE		g	g		12-0-7	1000 0111
136	88	SRL		h	h		12-0-8	1000 1000
137	89	SLL		i	i		12-0-9	1000 1001
138	8A	SRA					12-0-2-8	1000 1010
139	8B	SLA RS		{			12-0-3-8	1000 1011
140	8C	SRDL		≤			12-0-4-8	1000 1100
141	8D	SLDL		(			12-0-5-8	1000 1101
142	8E	SRDA		+			12-0-6-8	1000 1110
143	8F	SLDA		+			12-0-7-8	1000 1111
144	90	STM					12-11-1-8	1001 0000
145	91	TM SI		j	j		12-11-1	1001 0001
146	92	MVI		k	k		12-11-2	1001 0010
147	93	TS -S		l	l		12-11-3	1001 0011
148	94	NI		m	m		12-11-4	1001 0100
149	95	CLI		n	n		12-11-5	1001 0101
150	96	OI SI		o	o		12-11-6	1001 0110
151	97	XI		p	p		12-11-7	1001 0111
152	98	LM -RS		q	q		12-11-8	1001 1000
153	99			r	r		12-11-9	1001 1001
154	9A						12-11-2-8	1001 1010
155	9B			}			12-11-3-8	1001 1011
156	9C	SIO, SIOF		⊔			12-11-4-8	1001 1100
157	9D	TIO, CLRIO S		)			12-11-5-8	1001 1101
158	9E	HIO, HDV		±			12-11-6-8	1001 1110
159	9F	TCH		■			12-11-7-8	1001 1111
160	A0			-			11-0-1-8	1010 0000
161	A1			~	°		11-0-1	1010 0001
162	A2			s	s		11-0-2	1010 0010
163	A3			t	t		11-0-3	1010 0011
164	A4			u	u		11-0-4	1010 0100
165	A5			v	v		11-0-5	1010 0101
166	A6			w	w		11-0-6	1010 0110
167	A7			x	x		11-0-7	1010 0111
168	A8			y	y		11-0-8	1010 1000
169	A9			z	z		11-0-9	1010 1001
170	AA						11-0-2-8	1010 1010
171	AB			⌐			11-0-3-8	1010 1011
172	AC	STNSM		⌐			11-0-4-8	1010 1100
173	AD	STOSM SI		[			11-0-5-8	1010 1101
174	AE	SIGP -RS		≥			11-0-6-8	1010 1110
175	AF	MC -SI		●			11-0-7-8	1010 1111
176	B0			0			12-11-0-1-8	1011 0000
177	B1	LRA -RX		1			12-11-0-1	1011 0001
178	B2	See below		2			12-11-0-2	1011 0010
179	B3			3			12-11-0-3	1011 0011
180	B4			4			12-11-0-4	1011 0100
181	B5			5			12-11-0-5	1011 0101
182	B6	STCTL RS		6			12-11-0-6	1011 0110
183	B7	LCTL		7			12-11-0-7	1011 0111
184	B8			8			12-11-0-8	1011 1000
185	B9			9			12-11-0-9	1011 1001
186	BA	CS RS					12-11-0-2-8	1011 1010
187	BB	CDS		⌐			12-11-0-3-8	1011 1011
188	BC			⌐			12-11-0-4-8	1011 1100
189	BD	CLM		]			12-11-0-5-8	1011 1101
190	BE	STCM RS		+			12-11-0-6-8	1011 1110
191	BF	ICM		—			12-11-0-7-8	1011 1111

Op code (S format)

B202 - STIDP	B207 - STCKC	B20D - PTLB
B203 - STIDC	B208 - SPT	B210 - SPX
B204 - SCK	B209 - STPT	B211 - STPX
B205 - STCK	B20A - SPKA	B212 - STAP
B206 - SCKC	B20B - IPK	B213 - RRB

CODE TRANSLATION TABLE (Contd)   ⑫

Dec.	Hex	Instruction (SS)	BCDIC	EBCDIC(1)	ASCII	7-Track Tape BCDIC(2)	Card Code EBCDIC	Binary
192	C0		?	{		B A 8 2	12-0	1100 0000
193	C1		A	A	A	B A 1	12-1	1100 0001
194	C2		B	B	B	B A 2	12-2	1100 0010
195	C3		C	C	C	B A 2 1	12-3	1100 0011
196	C4		D	D	D	B A 4	12-4	1100 0100
197	C5		E	E	E	B A 4 1	12-5	1100 0101
198	C6		F	F	F	B A 4 2	12-6	1100 0110
199	C7		G	G	G	B A 4 2 1	12-7	1100 0111
200	C8		H	H	H	B A 8	12-8	1100 1000
201	C9		I	I	I	B A 8 1	12-9	1100 1001
202	CA						12-0-2-8-9	1100 1010
203	CB						12-0-3-8-9	1100 1011
204	CC		ʃ				12-0-4-8-9	1100 1100
205	CD						12-0-5-8-9	1100 1101
206	CE		Ч				12-0-6-8-9	1100 1110
207	CF						12-0-7-8-9	1100 1111
208	D0		!	}		B 8 2	11-0	1101 0000
209	D1	MVN	J	J	J	B 1	11-1	1101 0001
210	D2	MVC	K	K	K	B 2	11-2	1101 0010
211	D3	MVZ	L	L	L	B 2 1	11-3	1101 0011
212	D4	NC	M	M	M	B 4	11-4	1101 0100
213	D5	CLC	N	N	N	B 4 1	11-5	1101 0101
214	D6	OC	O	O	O	B 4 2	11-6	1101 0110
215	D7	XC	P	P	P	B 4 2 1	11-7	1101 0111
216	D8		Q	Q	Q	B 8	11-8	1101 1000
217	D9		R	R	R	B 8 1	11-9	1101 1001
218	DA						12-11-2-8-9	1101 1010
219	DB						12-11-3-8-9	1101 1011
220	DC	TR					12-11-4-8-9	1101 1100
221	DD	TRT					12-11-5-8-9	1101 1101
222	DE	ED					12-11-6-8-9	1101 1110
223	DF	EDMK					12-11-7-8-9	1101 1111
224	E0		ǂ	\		A 8 2	0-2-8	1110 0000
225	E1						11-0-1-9	1110 0001
226	E2		S	S	S	A 2	0-2	1110 0010
227	E3		T	T	T	A 2 1	0-3	1110 0011
228	E4		U	U	U	A 4	0-4	1110 0100
229	E5		V	V	V	A 4 1	0-5	1110 0101
230	E6		W	W	W	A 4 2	0-6	1110 0110
231	E7		X	X	X	A 4 2 1	0-7	1110 0111
232	E8		Y	Y	Y	A 8	0-8	1110 1000
233	E9		Z	Z	Z	A 8 1	0-9	1110 1001
234	EA						11-0-2-8-9	1110 1010
235	EB						11-0-3-8-9	1110 1011
236	EC		⊣				11-0-4-8-9	1110 1100
237	ED						11-0-5-8-9	1110 1101
238	EE						11-0-6-8-9	1110 1110
239	EF						11-0-7-8-9	1110 1111
240	F0	SRP	0	0	0	8 2	0	1111 0000
241	F1	MVO	1	1	1	1	1	1111 0001
242	F2	PACK	2	2	2	2	2	1111 0010
243	F3	UNPK	3	3	3	2 1	3	1111 0011
244	F4		4	4	4	4	4	1111 0100
245	F5		5	5	5	4 1	5	1111 0101
246	F6		6	6	6	4 2	6	1111 0110
247	F7		7	7	7	4 2 1	7	1111 0111
248	F8	ZAP	8	8	8	8	8	1111 1000
249	F9	CP	9	9	9	8 1	9	1111 1001
250	FA	AP		|			12-11-0-2-8-9	1111 1010
251	FB	SP					12-11-0-3-8-9	1111 1011
252	FC	MP					12-11-0-4-8-9	1111 1100
253	FD	DP					12-11-0-5-8-9	1111 1101
254	FE						12-11-0-6-8-9	1111 1110
255	FF			EO			12-11-0-7-8-9	1111 1111

ANSI-DEFINED PRINTER CONTROL CHARACTERS
(A in RECFM field of DCB)

Code	Action before printing record
blank	Space 1 line
0	Space 2 lines
-	Space 3 lines
+	Suppress space
1	Skip to line 1 on new page

MACHINE INSTRUCTION FORMATS

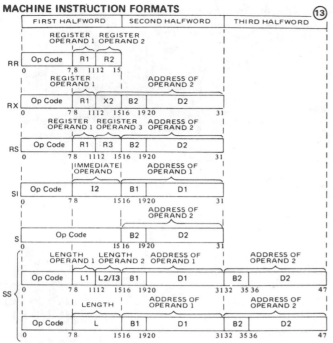

	FIRST HALFWORD	SECOND HALFWORD	THIRD HALFWORD

RR — Op Code | R1 | R2 — (REGISTER OPERAND 1, REGISTER OPERAND 2)

RX — Op Code | R1 | X2 | B2 | D2 — (REGISTER OPERAND 1, ADDRESS OF OPERAND 2)

RS — Op Code | R1 | R3 | B2 | D2 — (REGISTER OPERAND 1, REGISTER OPERAND 3, ADDRESS OF OPERAND 2)

SI — Op Code | I2 | B1 | D1 — (IMMEDIATE OPERAND, ADDRESS OF OPERAND 1)

S — Op Code | B2 | D2 — (ADDRESS OF OPERAND 2)

SS — Op Code | L1 | L2/I3 | B1 | D1 | B2 | D2 — (LENGTH OPERAND 1, LENGTH OPERAND 2, ADDRESS OF OPERAND 1, ADDRESS OF OPERAND 2)

SS — Op Code | L | B1 | D1 | B2 | D2 — (LENGTH, ADDRESS OF OPERAND 1, ADDRESS OF OPERAND 2)

CONTROL REGISTERS

CR	Bits	Name of field	Associated with	Init.
0	0	Block-multiplex'g control	Block-multiplex'g	0
	1	SSM suppression control	SSM instruction	0
	2	TOD clock sync control	Multiprocessing	0
	8-9	Page size control	Dynamic addr. transl.	0
	10	Unassigned (must be zero)		0
	11-12	Segment size control		0
	16	Malfunction alert mask		0
	17	Emergency signal mask	Multiprocessing	0
	18	External call mask		0
	19	TOD clock sync check mask		0
	20	Clock comparator mask	Clock comparator	0
	21	CPU timer mask	CPU timer	0
	24	Interval timer mask	Interval timer	1
	25	Interrupt key mask	Interrupt key	1
	26	External signal mask	External signal	1
1	0-7	Segment table length	Dynamic addr. transl.	0
	8-25	Segment table address		0
2	0-31	Channel masks	Channels	1
8	16-31	Monitor masks	Monitoring	0
9	0	Successful branching event mask		0
	1	Instruction fetching event mask		0
	2	Storage alteration event mask	Program-event record'g	0
	3	GR alteration event mask		0
	16-31	PER general register masks		0
10	8-31	PER starting address	Program-event record'g	0
11	8-31	PER ending address	Program-event record'g	0
14	0	Check-stop control	Machine-check handling	1
	1	Synch. MCEL control		1
	2	I/O extended logout control	I/O extended logout	0
	4	Recovery report mask		0
	5	Degradation report mask		0
	6	Ext. damage report mask	Machine-check handling	1
	7	Warning mask		0
	8	Asynch. MCEL control		0
	9	Asynch. fixed log control		0
15	8-28	MCEL address	Machine-check handling	512

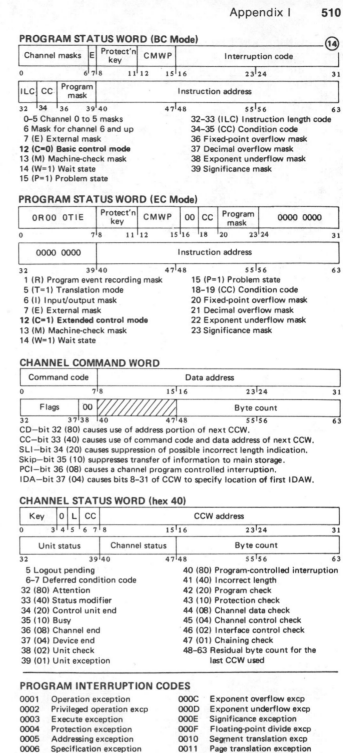

PROGRAM STATUS WORD (BC Mode)

Channel masks	E	Protect'n key	CMWP	Interruption code
0 6	7	8 11	12 15	16 23 24 31

ILC	CC	Program mask	Instruction address
32 34	36	39 40	47 48 55 56 63

0–5 Channel 0 to 5 masks
6 Mask for channel 6 and up
7 (E) External mask
12 (C=0) Basic control mode
13 (M) Machine-check mask
14 (W=1) Wait state
15 (P=1) Problem state

32–33 (ILC) Instruction length code
34–35 (CC) Condition code
36 Fixed-point overflow mask
37 Decimal overflow mask
38 Exponent underflow mask
39 Significance mask

PROGRAM STATUS WORD (EC Mode)

0R00 0TIE	Protect'n key	CMWP	00	CC	Program mask	0000 0000
0 7	8 11	12 15	16 18	20	23 24	31

0000 0000	Instruction address
32 39 40	47 48 55 56 63

1 (R) Program event recording mask
5 (T=1) Translation mode
6 (I) Input/output mask
7 (E) External mask
12 (C=1) Extended control mode
13 (M) Machine-check mask
14 (W=1) Wait state

15 (P=1) Problem state
18-19 (CC) Condition code
20 Fixed-point overflow mask
21 Decimal overflow mask
22 Exponent underflow mask
23 Significance mask

CHANNEL COMMAND WORD

Command code	Data address
0 7	8 15 16 23 24 31

Flags	00	/////	Byte count
32 37	38 40	47 48	55 56 63

CD—bit 32 (80) causes use of address portion of next CCW.
CC—bit 33 (40) causes use of command code and data address of next CCW.
SLI—bit 34 (20) causes suppression of possible incorrect length indication.
Skip—bit 35 (10) suppresses transfer of information to main storage.
PCI—bit 36 (08) causes a channel program controlled interruption.
IDA—bit 37 (04) causes bits 8-31 of CCW to specify location of first IDAW.

CHANNEL STATUS WORD (hex 40)

Key	0	L	CC	CCW address
0 3	4	5	6 7	8 15 16 23 24 31

Unit status	Channel status	Byte count
32 39 40	47 48 55 56 63

5 Logout pending
6-7 Deferred condition code
32 (80) Attention
33 (40) Status modifier
34 (20) Control unit end
35 (10) Busy
36 (08) Channel end
37 (04) Device end
38 (02) Unit check
39 (01) Unit exception

40 (80) Program-controlled interruption
41 (40) Incorrect length
42 (20) Program check
43 (10) Protection check
44 (08) Channel data check
45 (04) Channel control check
46 (02) Interface control check
47 (01) Chaining check
48-63 Residual byte count for the last CCW used

PROGRAM INTERRUPTION CODES

0001	Operation exception	000C	Exponent overflow excp
0002	Privileged operation excp	000D	Exponent underflow excp
0003	Execute exception	000E	Significance exception
0004	Protection exception	000F	Floating-point divide excp
0005	Addressing exception	0010	Segment translation excp
0006	Specification exception	0011	Page translation exception
0007	Data exception	0012	Translation specification excp
0008	Fixed-point overflow excp	0013	Special operation exception
0009	Fixed-point divide excp	0040	Monitor event
000A	Decimal overflow exception	0080	Program event (code may be
000B	Decimal divide exception		combined with another code)

FIXED STORAGE LOCATIONS ⑮

Area, dec.	Hex addr	EC only	Function
0- 7	0		Initial program loading PSW, restart new PSW
8- 15	8		Initial program loading CCW1, restart old PSW
16- 23	10		Initial program loading CCW2
24- 31	18		External old PSW
32- 39	20		Supervisor Call old PSW
40- 47	28		Program old PSW
48- 55	30		Machine-check old PSW
56- 63	38		Input/output old PSW
64- 71	40		Channel status word (see diagram)
72- 75	48		Channel address word [0-3 key, 4-7 zeros, 8-31 CCW address]
80- 83	50		Interval timer
88- 95	58		External new PSW
96-103	60		Supervisor Call new PSW
104-111	68		Program new PSW
112-119	70		Machine-check new PSW
120-127	78		Input/output new PSW
132-133	84		CPU address assoc'd with external interruption, or unchanged
132-133	84	X	CPU address assoc'd with external interruption, or zeros
134-135	86	X	External interruption code
136-139	88	X	SVC interruption [0-12 zeros, 13-14 ILC, 15:0, 16-31 code]
140-143	8C	X	Program interrupt. [0-12 zeros, 13-14 ILC, 15:0, 16-31 code]
144-147	90	X	Translation exception address [0-7 zeros, 8-31 address]
148-149	94		Monitor class [0-7 zeros, 8-15 class number]
150-151	96	X	PER interruption code [0-3 code, 4-15 zeros]
152-155	98	X	PER address [0-7 zeros, 8-31 address]
156-159	9C		Monitor code [0-7 zeros, 8-31 monitor code]
168-171	A8		Channel ID [0-3 type, 4-15 model, 16-31 max. IOEL length]
172-175	AC		I/O extended logout address [0-7 unused, 8-31 address]
176-179	B0		Limited channel logout (see diagram)
185-187	B9	X	I/O address [0-7 zeros, 8-23 address]
216-223	D8		CPU timer save area
224-231	E0		Clock comparator save area
232-239	E8		Machine-check interruption code (see diagram)
248-251	F8		Failing processor storage address [0-7 zeros, 8-31 address]
252-255	FC		Region code*
256-351	100		Fixed logout area*
352-383	160		Floating-point register save area
384-447	180		General register save area
448-511	1C0		Control register save area
512†	200		CPU extended logout area (size varies)

*May vary among models; see system library manuals for specific model.
†Location may be changed by programming (bits 8-28 of CR 15 specify address).

LIMITED CHANNEL LOGOUT (hex B0)

0	SCU id	Detect	Source	000	Field validity flags	TT	00	A	Seq.
0	1 3	4 7	8 12	13 15	16 23	24 26	28	29	31

4 CPU	12 Control unit	24-25 Type of termination
5 Channel	16 Interface address	00 Interface disconnect
6 Main storage control	17-18 Reserved (00)	01 Stop, stack or normal
7 Main storage	19 Sequence code	10 Selective reset
8 CPU	20 Unit status	11 System reset
9 Channel	21 Cmd. addr. and key	28(A) I/O error alert
10 Main storage control	22 Channel address	29-31 Sequence code
11 Main storage	23 Device address	

MACHINE-CHECK INTERRUPTION CODE (hex E8)

MC conditions	000	00	Time	Stg. error	0	Validity indicators
0	8	9	13	14 16	18 19	20 31

0000	0000	0000	00	Val.	MCEL length
32	39 40	45	46	48	55 56 63

0 System damage	14 Backed-up	24 Failing stg. address
1 Instr. proc'g damage	15 Delayed	25 Region code
2 System recovery	16 Uncorrected	27 Floating-pt registers
3 Timer damage	17 Corrected	28 General registers
4 Timing facil. damage	18 Key uncorrected	29 Control registers
5 External damage	20 PSW bits 12-15	30 CPU ext'd logout
6 Not assigned (0)	21 PSW masks and key	31 Storage logical
7 Degradation	22 Prog. mask and CC	46 CPU timer
8 Warning	23 Instruction address	47 Clock comparator

DYNAMIC ADDRESS TRANSLATION ⑯
VIRTUAL (LOGICAL) ADDRESS FORMAT

Segment Size	Page Size		Segment Index	Page Index	Byte Index
64K	4K	Bits 0 - 7 are ignored	8 - 15	16 - 19	20 - 31
64K	2K		8 - 15	16 - 20	21 - 31
1M	4K		8 - 11	12 - 19	20 - 31
1M	2K		8 - 11	12 - 20	21 - 31

SEGMENT TABLE ENTRY

PT length	0000*	Page table address	00*	I
0 3	4 7	8 28	29	31

*Normally zeros; ignored on some models.   31 (I) Segment-invalid bit.

PAGE TABLE ENTRY (4K)

Page address	I	00	
0 11	12	13	15

12 (I) Page-invalid bit.

PAGE TABLE ENTRY (2K)

Page address	I	0	
0 12	13	14	15

13 (I) Page-invalid bit.

HEXADECIMAL AND DECIMAL CONVERSION

From hex: locate each hex digit in its corresponding column position and note the decimal equivalents. Add these to obtain the decimal value.

From decimal: (1) locate the largest decimal value in the table that will fit into the decimal number to be converted, and (2) note its hex equivalent and hex column position. (3) Find the decimal remainder. Repeat the process on this and subsequent remainders.

Note: Decimal, hexadecimal, (and binary) equivalents of all numbers from 0 to 255 are listed on panels 9 – 12.

HEXADECIMAL COLUMNS

	6		5		4		3		2		1
HEX	= DEC	HEX	= DEC	HEX	= DEC	HEX	= DEC	HEX	= DEC	HEX	= DEC
0	0	0	0	0	0	0	0	0	0	0	0
1	1,048,576	1	65,536	1	4,096	1	256	1	16	1	1
2	2,097,152	2	131,072	2	8,192	2	512	2	32	2	2
3	3,145,728	3	196,608	3	12,288	3	768	3	48	3	3
4	4,194,304	4	262,144	4	16,384	4	1,024	4	64	4	4
5	5,242,880	5	327,680	5	20,480	5	1,280	5	80	5	5
6	6,291,456	6	393,216	6	24,576	6	1,536	6	96	6	6
7	7,340,032	7	458,752	7	28,672	7	1,792	7	112	7	7
8	8,388,608	8	524,288	8	32,768	8	2,048	8	128	8	8
9	9,437,184	9	589,824	9	36,864	9	2,304	9	144	9	9
A	10,485,760	A	655,360	A	40,960	A	2,560	A	160	A	10
B	11,534,336	B	720,896	B	45,056	B	2,816	B	176	B	11
C	12,582,912	C	786,432	C	49,152	C	3,072	C	192	C	12
D	13,631,488	D	851,968	D	53,248	D	3,328	D	208	D	13
E	14,680,064	E	917,504	E	57,344	E	3,584	E	224	E	14
F	15,728,640	F	983,040	F	61,440	F	3,840	F	240	F	15
	0 1 2 3		4 5 6 7		0 1 2 3		4 5 6 7		0 1 2 3		4 5 6 7
	BYTE				BYTE				BYTE		

POWERS OF 2

2^n	n
256	8
512	9
1 024	10
2 048	11
4 096	12
8 192	13
16 384	14
32 768	15
65 536	16
131 072	17
262 144	18
524 288	19
1 048 576	20
2 097 152	21
4 194 304	22
8 388 608	23
16 777 216	24

$2^0 = 16^0$
$2^4 = 16^1$
$2^8 = 16^2$
$2^{12} = 16^3$
$2^{16} = 16^4$
$2^{20} = 16^5$
$2^{24} = 16^6$
$2^{28} = 16^7$
$2^{32} = 16^8$
$2^{36} = 16^9$
$2^{40} = 16^{10}$
$2^{44} = 16^{11}$
$2^{48} = 16^{12}$
$2^{52} = 16^{13}$
$2^{56} = 16^{14}$
$2^{60} = 16^{15}$

POWERS OF 16

16^n	n
1	0
16	1
256	2
4 096	3
65 536	4
1 048 576	5
16 777 216	6
268 435 456	7
4 294 967 296	8
68 719 476 736	9
1 099 511 627 776	10
17 592 186 044 416	11
281 474 976 710 656	12
4 503 599 627 370 496	13
72 057 594 037 927 936	14
1 152 921 504 606 846 976	15

INDEX